C++26 for Lazy Programmers

Quick, Easy, and Fun C++ for Beginners

Third Edition

Will Briggs

Apress®

C++26 for Lazy Programmers: Quick, Easy, and Fun C++ for Beginners, Third Edition

Will Briggs
Lynchburg, VA, USA

ISBN-13 (pbk): 979-8-8688-1858-5
ISBN-13 (electronic): 979-8-8688-1859-2
https://doi.org/10.1007/979-8-8688-1859-2

Managing Director, Apress Media LLC: Welmoed Spahr
Acquisitions Editor: Melissa Duffy
Coordinating Editor: Gryffin Winkler

Cover designed by eStudioCalamar

Cover image by Freepik.com

Distributed to the book trade worldwide by Springer Science+Business Media New York, 1 New York Plaza, New York, NY 10004. Phone 1-800-SPRINGER, fax (201) 348-4505, e-mail orders-ny@springer-sbm.com, or visit www.springeronline.com. Apress Media, LLC is a Delaware LLC and the sole member (owner) is Springer Science + Business Media Finance Inc (SSBM Finance Inc). SSBM Finance Inc is a **Delaware** corporation.

For information on translations, please e-mail booktranslations@springernature.com; for reprint, paperback, or audio rights, please e-mail bookpermissions@springernature.com.

Apress titles may be purchased in bulk for academic, corporate, or promotional use. eBook versions and licenses are also available for most titles. For more information, reference our Print and eBook Bulk Sales web page at http://www.apress.com/bulk-sales.

Any source code or other supplementary material referenced by the author in this book is available to readers on GitHub (https://github.com/Apress). For more detailed information, please visit https://www.apress.com/gp/services/source-code.

If disposing of this product, please recycle the paper

To Addie: spinner of tales, both great and small.

Table of Contents

About the Author

Will Briggs, PhD, is a professor of computer science at the University of Lynchburg in Virginia. He has 30 years' experience teaching C++, 18 of them using earlier drafts of this book, and about as many years teaching other languages including C, JavaScript, LISP, Pascal, PHP, PROLOG, and Python. His primary focus is teaching of late while also being active in research in artificial intelligence.

About the Technical Reviewer

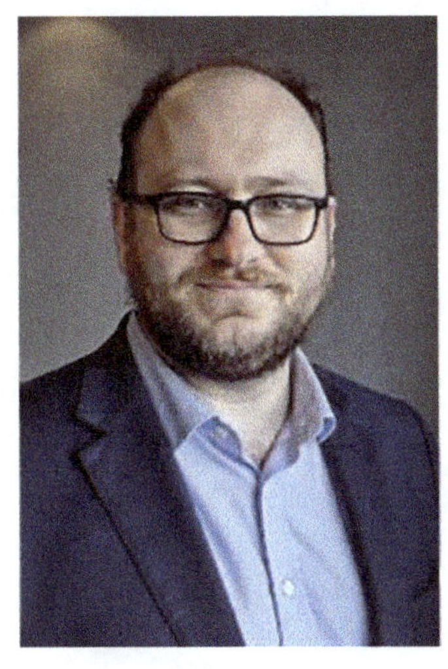

Marius Iulian Mihailescu is an associate professor at the Faculty of Engineering and Computer Science, specializing in cybersecurity, artificial intelligence, machine learning, cloud computing, Internet of Things (IoT), and blockchain technologies. With a strong multidisciplinary background, he teaches a wide range of undergraduate and postgraduate courses, including functional programming with Haskell and F#, web development applications, information security systems, cloud fundamentals, blockchain technologies, Internet of Things engineering, information security management, software security, software development languages (C#, Python, Java), databases (Microsoft SQL Server, Oracle, and PostgreSQL), and software development methods.

He has authored and co-authored numerous books, book chapters, research papers, and conference presentations in the fields of cybersecurity, cryptography, AI-driven cyber threat detection, quantum computing, and secure software development methodologies. His research spans both theoretical foundations and practical applications, with a particular interest in quantum cryptography, cyber threat intelligence, ethical hacking, secure cloud architectures, digital forensics, and AI-powered process optimization.

He is actively involved in European research projects under *Horizon Europe* and *European Defence Fund (EDF)* frameworks, contributing as both researcher and project coordinator. He collaborates with academia, industry, and governmental institutions to design advanced cybersecurity architectures, AI models for predictive analytics, and innovative IoT solutions for smart cities and critical infrastructures.

His current research interests include post-quantum cryptography, AI-driven anomaly detection, blockchain-based identity management, secure IoT frameworks, and digital twin technologies. He also mentors graduate and doctoral students in multidisciplinary projects that combine engineering, artificial intelligence, and applied information security.

Through his teaching, research, and innovation projects, he continues to contribute to the advancement of secure, intelligent, and resilient digital ecosystems at both national and international levels.

Acknowledgments

Special thanks to

- Apress
- Microsoft
- Google, for Google Fonts
- Pixabay.com and contributors, especially 3D Animation Production Company/QuinceCreative (Chapter 1, bullseye), David Mark/12019 (Chapter 2, beach), Free-Photos (Chapter 2, pug), Andi Caswell/andicaz (Chapter 6, scones), joakant (Chapter 11, tropical fish), Gerhard Janson/Janson_G (Chapter 12, UFO), 13smok (Chapter 12, alien sign), Prawny (Chapter 12, splat), Elliekha (Chapter 12, haunted house), pencil parker (Chapter 12, candy), Robert Davis/rescueram3 (Chapter 12, pumpkin photos), HolgersFotografie (Chapter 12, rubber duck)
- Wikipedia Commons, including ASpiegler (Chapter 24, normal distribution)[1]
- OpenClipArt.org and contributors, especially Firkin (Chapter 2, flamingo), GDJ (Chapter 3, camel)
- Flickr, especially Speedy McZoom (Chapter 12, jack-o-lantern art)
- FreeSound.org and contributors, especially Razor5 (Chapter 2, techno music), robbo799 (Chapter 2, churChapter bells), alqutis (Chapter 12, hovercar), Berviceps (Chapter 12, splat), mistersherlock (Chapter 12, Halloween graveyard), matypresidente (Chapter 12, water drop), Osiruswaltz (Chapter 12, bump), mrose6 (Chapter 12, echoed scream), robcro6010 (Chapter 12, circus theme)
- Chad Savage of Sinister Fonts for Werewolf Moon (Chapter 12)

[1] License: creativecommons.org/licenses/by-sa/4.0/deed.en. No changes made.

- Lazy Foo' Productions
- StackOverflow.com
- Hjörvar Hermannsson and Einar Egilsson of cardgames.io for images of card games and Nicu Buculei (`http://nicubunu.ro/cards`) for card images
- Alumni, colleagues, and students who gave me reviews – you're the best!

Introduction

Surely there's no shortage of C++ intro texts. Why write yet another?

I'm glad you asked.

Ever since moving from Pascal to C++ (back when dinosaurs roamed the earth), I've been underwhelmed by available resources. I wanted something quirky and fun to read, with sufficient coverage and fun examples, like the old *Oh! Pascal!* text by Cooper and Clancy. Even a perfectly accurate text with broad coverage gives you nothing if you fall asleep when you read it. Well, nothing but a sore neck.

But the other reason, of course, is to promote laziness.

We all want our projects to be done more quickly, with less wailing and gnashing of teeth. Sometimes, it's said, you have to put your nose to the grindstone. Maybe, but I like my nose too well for that. I'd rather do things the easy way.

But the easy way isn't procrastinating and dragging my feet: it's to find something I love doing and do it well enough that it feels relatively effortless. It's producing something robust enough that when it does break down, it tells me exactly what the problem is, so I don't have to spend a week pleading with it to explain itself. It's writing code that I can use again and again, adapting it to a new use in hours instead of days.

Here's what you can expect in this book:

- A pleasant reading experience.
- Adequate coverage.
- Games, that is, use of the SDL (Simple DirectMedia Layer) graphics library, which makes it easy to get graphics programs working quickly. It isn't fair that Python and Visual Basic should get all the eye candy.[1] The SDL library is used through Chapter 12. After that we'll mostly use standard I/O, so we can get practice with the more common console programs.

---

[1] "Eye candy": Things that look good on the screen. See *The New Hacker's Dictionary*, available at time of writing at `www.catb.org/jargon/`.

- An easy introduction to SDL's graphical magic, using the SSDL library (see below).
- Sufficient examples, and they won't all be about actuarial tables or how to organize an address book. (See "a pleasant reading experience" above.)
- Antibugging sections throughout the text to point out common or difficult-to-trace errors - and how to prevent them.
- For g++ programmers, instructions on using g++, the ddd/gdb debugger system, and Makefiles; for Visual Studio, use of the debugger and project files.
- Compliance with C++26, the latest standard, and some of the goodies it provides.
- Hands-on experience with advanced data types like strings, queues, vectors, and lists - not by reading about them, but by building them yourself.
- An appreciation of laziness.
- A cool title. Maybe I could have tried to write a *For Dummies* book, but after seeing *Bioinformatics for Dummies,* I'm not sure I have what it takes.

Why SDL?

It's surely more enjoyable to make programs with graphics and WIMP[2]-style interaction than to merely type things in and print them out. There's a variety of graphical libraries out there. SDL,[3] or Simple DirectMedia Layer, is popular, relatively easy to learn, portable between platforms, and fast enough for real-world work, as evidenced by its use in actual released games like the one in Figure 1.

[2] WIMP: window, icon, mouse, pointer. What we're all used to.

[3] Specifically, SDL2. The new SDL3 and its helper libraries exist at time of writing, but Unix installation is still somewhere between "not easy" and "minefield for beginners." The differences are minimal anyway.

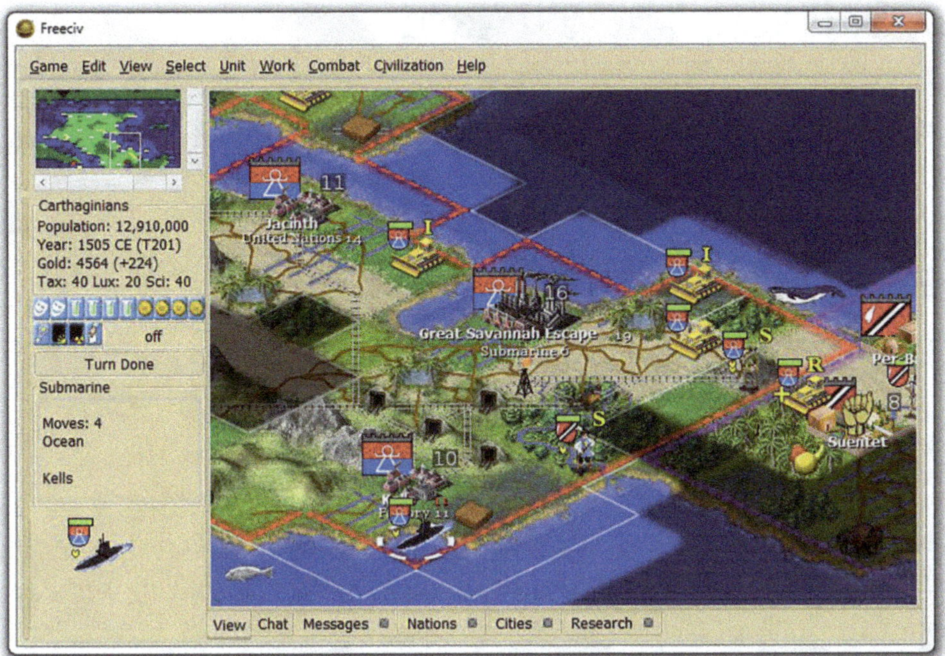

Figure 1. *A game of Freeciv, which uses the SDL library*

Why SSDL?

...but although SDL is *relatively* easy, it's not simple enough to start on day 1 of programming with C++. SSDL - *Simple* SDL - saves you from needing to know things we don't get to until Chapter 14[4] before doing basic things like displaying images (Chapter 2) or even printing a greeting (Chapter 1). It also hides the initialization and cleanup code that's pretty much the same every time you write a program and makes error handling less cumbersome.

You may want to keep using SSDL as is after you're done with this book, but if you decide to go on with SDL, you'll find you know a lot of it already, with almost nothing to unlearn: most SSDL function names are names from SDL with another "S" stuck on the front. We'll go into greater depth on moving forward with SDL in Chapter 29.

[4] Pointers.

(Free) Software You Will Need

At time of writing Microsoft Visual Studio (Community Edition) for Windows is absolutely free, and g++ always is. So are SSDL and the SDL2 libraries. See Chapter 1 and Appendix A for help installing these essentials.

Programming with sound may not be practical over remote connections because of the difficulty of streaming sound. If using Unix emulation, you might check the emulator's sound capabilities - say, by playing a video - and be aware: emulation slows things down. This includes WSL.

If This Is for a Course ...

C++26 for Lazy Programmers covers through pointers, operator overloading, virtual functions, templates, exceptions, STL - everything you might reasonably expect in two semesters of C++ - plus extras at the end.

The SSDL library does take a small amount of time, but the focus is firmly on writing good C++ programs, with SSDL there just to make the programs more enjoyable. How many labs or projects do you have in which it's hard to stop working because it's so much fun? It may not happen with *all* these problems, but I do see it happen.

SSDL also gives a gentle introduction to event-driven programming.

In the first 12 chapters, there is emphasis on algorithm development and programming style, including early introduction of constants.

After Chapter 12, the examples are mostly in standard I/O, though SSDL is still an option for a few exercises and is used in Chapter 21 and parts of Chapters 24–27.

A normal two-semester sequence should cover approximately the following:

- **Semester 1**: The first 12 chapters, using SSDL; Chapter 13, introducing standard I/O. With some exceptions (& parameters, stream I/O, `constexpr`), this looks a lot like C and includes variables, expressions, functions, control structures, arrays, and stream I/O.
- **Semester 2**: Chapters 14–23, using standard I/O, covering pointers, dynamic memory, character arrays, classes, operator overloading, templates, exceptions, virtual functions, multiple inheritance (briefly), and a taste of the Standard Template Library (STL) using vectors and linked lists.

Subsequent chapters cover material that wouldn't easily fit in two semesters, including more of the Standard Template Library, C programming, and advanced topics including the use of command-line arguments, format strings, and functional-style programming.

Online Help

For a reference for SDL functions, go to `wiki.libsdl.org/SDL2/` (URL correct at time of writing). If the URL has changed, a web search for the feature you want should get you there. You want SDL2, not SDL3.

Legal Stuff

Visual Basic, Visual Studio, Visual Studio Code, Microsoft Excel, Microsoft Windows, Microsoft Word, and Microsoft are trademarks of the Microsoft Corporation. All other trademarks referenced herein are property of their respective owners.

This book and its author are neither affiliated with nor authorized, sponsored, or approved by the Microsoft Corporation.

Screenshots of Microsoft products are used with permission from Microsoft.

CHAPTER 1

Getting Started

Most programs in the first half of this book use the SDL and SSDL graphics-and-games libraries,[1] on the theory that watching colorful shapes move across the screen and shoot each other is more interesting than printing text. Don't worry; when you're done you'll be able to write programs both with and without this library – and if I have anything to say about it, you'll have fun doing it.

If you've already chosen your platform, great. If not, here's my recommendation:

- If you just want to learn C++ on an easy and easily managed platform, Microsoft Visual Studio is the best choice.
- If you are a Unix system administrator or have good access to one and want to use that popular and powerful platform, go for it. And MSys2 (at `www.msys2.org`) is an option for Unix-savvy users who want to use their Microsoft Windows machines.

The programming won't differ much between platforms. But system setup can be an issue.

Initial Setup

First, you'll need the source code for the textbook. Download it from the book's web page at [`github.com/Apress/C-Plus-Plus-26-for-Lazy-Programmers-3rd-ed`].

Then unzip it. In Unix, the `unzip` command should work; in Windows, you can usually double-click it, or right-click and choose Extract or Extract All.

[1] SDL provides graphics, sound, and friendly interaction including mouse input. SSDL, standing for *Simple* SDL, is a "wrapper" library that wraps SDL's functions in easier-to-use versions. Both libraries are described in more detail in the Introduction.

W. Briggs, *C++26 for Lazy Programmers*, https://doi.org/10.1007/979-8-8688-1859-2_1

...in Microsoft Visual Studio

At the moment Visual Studio is absolutely free: go to Microsoft's download page (currently `https://visualstudio.microsoft.com/downloads/`) and download the Community Edition.

It'll take a long time to install. Be sure to put a check by Desktop development with C++ (Figure 1-1) – else, you'll have Visual Studio, all right, but it won't know C++.

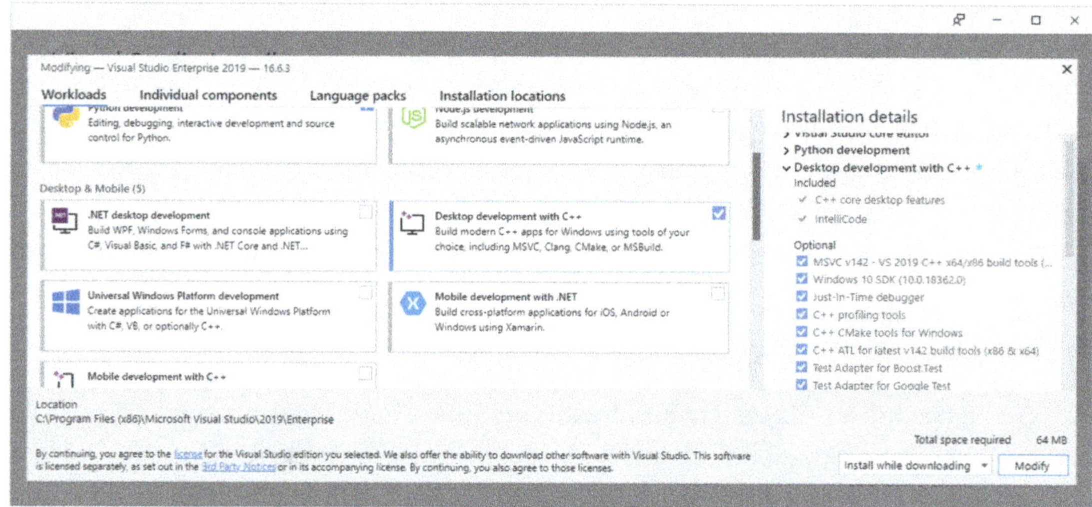

Figure 1-1. *Installing the C++ part of Visual Studio*

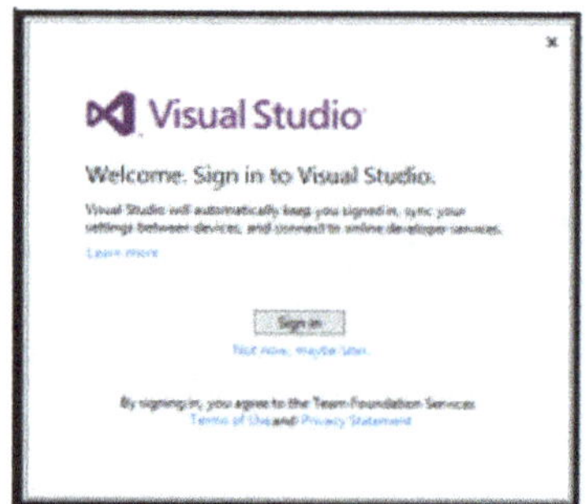

When it's installed, go to the book's source code folder, into the `ch1` subfolder; double-click the solution file, `ch1.sln` or `ch1`. (If it asks you to sign in and you're not ready to do that now ...notice the line "Not now, maybe later.")

Now, in the Solution Explorer window (see Figure 1-2), you should see at the bottom a project named **test-setup**. Right-click it, and select Debug ➤ Start New Instance.

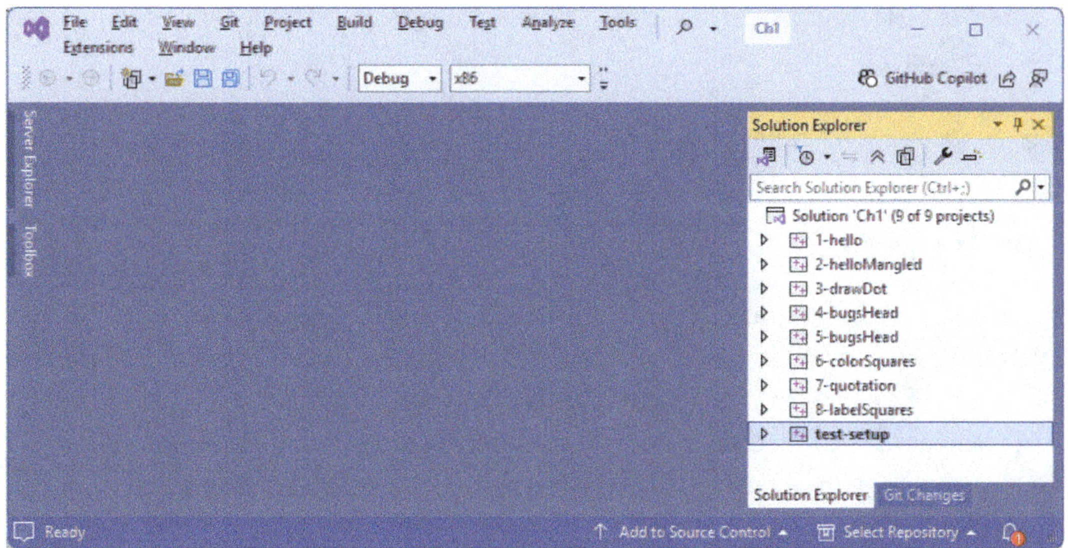

Figure 1-2. *The* `ch1` *solution in Visual Studio, with the* `test-setup` *project highlighted*

You should see and hear the program in Figure 1-3. (If not, see Appendix A.)

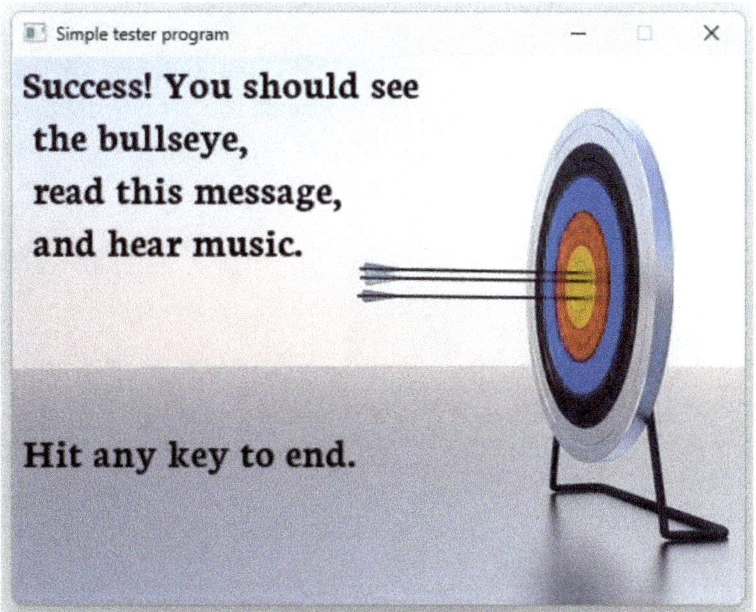

Figure 1-3. *Output of* `test-setup`

There is no installation of SDL or SSDL. Everything's in the folder you unzipped, and you just proved it.

You might take a moment now to try another program from `ch1`, like `1-hello`. Run it the same way you did `test-setup`.

...with MSys2

First, should you? If you're a raw beginner with a Microsoft Windows machine, use Microsoft Visual Studio – it's easy. But if you want Unix-style interaction with Windows ...you *could* use WSL, but I find it too slow for the game loops of Chapters 11 and 12.

You can get MSys2, at time of writing, at `msys2.org`.

Once you do, start up MSYS2 MINGW64 (not MSYS2 MSYS) and do these commands:

```
pacman -Sy      #gets things up to date
pacman -S mingw-w64-x86_64-gcc
pacman -S make # pacman -S mingw-w64-x86_64-make doesn't work for me
pacman -S mingw-w64-x86_64-SDL2        mingw-w64-x86_64-SDL2_image \
          mingw-w64-x86_64-SDL2_mixer mingw-w64-x86_64-SDL2_ttf
```

Next, navigate to the source code's `ch1/test-setup` folder, and enter `make` to build the file and `./runx` to run it. You should see (and hear) the program illustrated in Figure 1-3. (If not, see Appendix A.) You might take a moment to try another program from `ch1`, like `1-hello`. Run it the same way you did `test-setup`.

...in Unix

Getting around in Unix isn't in the scope of this book, but no worries: the basics of copying files, moving files, etc. are easy to pick up.[2]

[2] I recommend UNIX Tutorial for Beginners, at `www.ee.surrey.ac.uk/Teaching/Unix/`. Up through Tutorial 4 should be fine for now. Or search for your own.

System administration is *way* beyond the scope of this book.[3] But installing SSDL is easy. In that folder you just unzipped ...

- Go into `external/SSDL/unix`, and type `make`. This builds SSDL in a place where programs in the source code will know where to find it
- Go into `ch1/test-setup`
- `make`
- `./runx`

You should see (and hear) the program illustrated in Figure 1-3. (If not, something must be missing – please see Appendix A.) You might take a moment to try another program from `ch1`, like `1-hello`. Run it the same way you did `test-setup`.

A Simple Program

It's wise to start small. Fewer things can go wrong.

So we'll begin with a simple program that writes "Hello, world!" on the screen. We'll take it line by line to see what's in it. (In the next section we'll compile and run it. For now, sit tight.)

Example 1-1. "Hello, world!" is a classic program to start a new language with. (I think it's a law somewhere.) This program is in the source code, in the `ch1` folder, as `1-hello`

```
// Hello, world! program, for _C++26 for Lazy Programmers_
//   Your name goes here
//   Then the date[4]

// It prints "Hello, world!" on the screen.
//    Quite an accomplishment, huh?
```

[3] OK, I can't just let it go at that. Appendix A has suggestions on how to install the other tools you need (g++, SDL, etc.). But distributions of Unix vary, so it'll help to know what you're doing.

[4] From here on I'll put the title of the text, rather than name and date, because that's more useful for textbook examples. Ordinarily name of programmer and date are better for keeping track of what was done and who to track down if it doesn't work.

```
#include "SSDL.h"

int main(int argc, char** argv)
{
    sout << "Hello, world!  (Press any key to quit.)\n";

    SSDL_WaitKey(); // Wait for user to hit any key

    return 0;
}
```

The first set of lines are **comments**. They look like this – `//Something on a line after two slashes` – and are there just for you or for someone who later tries to understand your program. It's best to be kind to yourself and your maintainers – help them easily know what the program's doing, without having to search and figure it out.

Next, we have an `include` file. Some language features are built into the C++ compiler itself, like the comment markers `//` and `#include`. Others are only loaded if needed. In this case, we need to know how to print things on the screen using the SSDL library, so we include the file `SSDL.h`.

After that we have the `main` function. `main` is special: it's what tells the compiler, "This is what we're doing in the program; start here." I'll defer explaining the weird top line for now – we'll get to it in Chapter 25's section on command-line arguments – and just say: for now, we always write this the same way. If not, the C++ gods will punish us with incomprehensible error messages.

In this case, `main` only does two things.

First, it prints the `"Hello, world!"` message using the `sout` object, pronounced "S-out." The `\n` means "go on to the next line."

Second, it calls `SSDL_WaitKey`, which waits for you to hit a key before it ends the program. Otherwise, the program closes before you have a chance to see its message.

We `return 0` because `main` has to `return` something, largely for historical reasons. In practice we almost never care what `main` returns.

The curly braces `{}` tell `main` where to start taking action and where to end: whatever you want the program to do goes between the curly braces.

The compiler is very picky about what you type. Leave off a ; and the program won't compile. Change capitalization on something and C++ won't recognize it.

If you're curious what a simple program like this would look like without SSDL, see Chapter 30. It's not for the beginner, but later it should make sense.

Extra "Hello, world!" is often the first program a beginner writes in a new language. Although it was originally a simple example in C – from which the language C++ is descended – the practice of writing this as the first program has spread. Here's "Hello, world!" in BASIC:

```
10 PRINT "Hello, world!"
```

Not bad, huh?

This is what it looks like in APL. APL (*A Programming Language*) has been described as a "write-only" language because it's said you can't read the programs you wrote yourself. APL requires symbols such as ⎕, ∇, and ρ:

```
⎕←'Hello, world!'
```

Although those look easier than C++'s version, C++'s is neither the longest nor the toughest. I'll spare you the long ones to save trees (an example for the language Redcode took 158 lines, which may be why you've never heard of Redcode), but here's one of the tough ones, from a purposefully difficult language sometimes called BF:

```
++++++++++++++++[>++++>++++++>+++++++>+++>++<<<<<-
]>++++++++.>+++++.+++++++..+++.>>----.>.<<+++++++.<.>-----.
<---.--------.>>>+.
```

More "Hello, world!" examples, at time of writing, can be found at `helloworldcollection.de`.

Spacing

The compiler *doesn't* care about spacing. As long as you don't put a space inside a word, you can put it wherever you like. You can break lines or not as you choose; it won't care, as long as you don't break a `//comment` or a `"quotation"`.

Example 1-2. A blatant instance of evil and rude[5] in programming

```
// Hello, world! program, for _C++26 for Lazy Programmers_
//    It prints "Hello, world!" on the screen.
//    Quite an accomplishment, huh?

        #include "SSDL.h"

            int main(int argc, char** argv) {
    sout <<
"Hello, world!  (Press any key to quit.)\n";

            SSDL_WaitKey();     // Wait for user to hit any key

return 0;
    }
```

The compiler won't care about spacing – but the poor soul that has to understand your 500-page program will! Example 1-2's spacing would be a cruel thing to do to the people who later maintain your code.

Readability is a Good Thing.[6] The programmer struggling to figure what you meant may very well be you a few days after writing it. Most of the expense in software development is programmer time; you won't want to waste yours trying to decipher your own code. *Make it clear.*

---

[5] "Evil and rude" is a technical term meaning "maliciously awful." See *The New Hacker's Dictionary*, currently online at `hackersdictionary.com/html`, for other terms in programmers' slang.

[6] Good Thing: hacker slang for something that's completely wonderful and everybody knows it (or should).

Tip To be lazy, make your code clear *as you write it*, not later. Readable code helps with development, not just future maintenance.

To help further with clarity, I have things in Example 1-1, like initial comments, `#include`, and `main`, separated by **blank lines**. It's sort of like writing paragraphs in an English paper: each section is its own "paragraph." Blank lines increase readability.

I also indent in a way that makes the program easy to read. The default **indentation** is the left margin. But if something is contained in something else - as the `sout` statement is contained in the main function - it gets indented a few spaces.

This is like outline format for a paper or like the layout of a table of contents (Figure 1-4). What's contained in something else is indented slightly.

```
int main(int argc, char** argv)
{
        sout << "Hello, world!\n";

        SSDL_WaitKey();

        return 0;
}
```

```
My wonderful paper

     Part One

     Part Two
          Reasons Part One is wrong
               a. Why those reasons fail
               b. Reassurance it's right anyway
          Reasons Part Two is way better

     Conclusion
```

Figure 1-4. *Like an English paper outline, a C++ program is indented, with subparts indented relative to what they're parts of*

You'll have plenty of examples of clear indenting as you read on.

Golden Rule of Indenting

When something is part of what comes previously,

    it should be indented (like this).

When it's independent, it maintains the same indentation level.

Creating an SSDL Project

...with g++ (Unix and MSys2)

To create your own project, go into the `newWork` directory and copy `basicSSDLProject` to a new directory with some appropriate name – something like `cp -R basicSSDLProject myNewProject`.

To edit your program, on Unix, you might use vi/vim (I find it difficult, but maybe you don't), emacs,[7] or some other editor. On Windows, Notepad++ is a fine option. Familiarize yourself as needed, and open `main.cpp` for editing.

The program is valid, but it doesn't do anything interesting yet, so you'll want to give it some content. For now, you might type in the Hello, world! program from Example 1-1. To compile, type `make` at the command prompt to make the program.

Maybe you'll make some typos. If so, `make` will give you a list of error messages. Sometimes it's clear what the messages mean, sometimes not. Here's a typical one – I forgot a `;`:

```
main.cpp:11:53: error: expected ';' before 'SSDL_WaitKey'
```

Over time you'll understand more of what obscure error messages mean. For now, compare the program you typed to Example 1-1 and resolve any differences until you get the successful result in Figure 1-5. (The program actually prints white on black, unlike what's shown. Books, big black squares of ink, not a good mix.)

[7] For a quick start with emacs, you might try the Very Basic Emacs Tutorial at ocean. `http://ocean.stanford.edu/research/quick_emacs.html`.

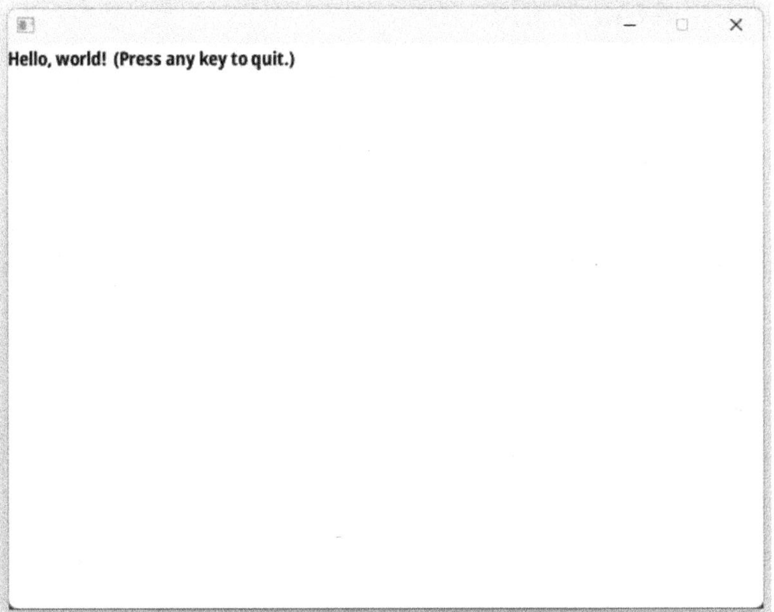

Figure 1-5. *Hello, world! running*

The Files You Created

In your new folder, type `ls` at the prompt. You'll see some files, possibly:

```
a.out main.cpp main.cpp~ main.o #and a bunch of other stuff
```

`a.out` is the executable program. `main.cpp` is the code you wrote to make it. `main.cpp~` is a backup file your editor may make of your `.cpp` file. `main.o` is an "object" file g++ may build on the way to creating your program. If you see it - you may not - it's perfectly safe to delete it:

```
rm main.o
```

To delete things listed here that you don't need, type `make clean`.

Cool Command-Line Tricks

- **Repeating a command:** Often at the command prompt, you can hit the up arrow to repeat the last command or several times to repeat an earlier command. If that doesn't work, ! followed by the first few letters of the command may repeat the last instance of it.
- **Using a wildcard in a directory name:** `cd partialname*` often saves time. `cd partialname` followed by the Tab key also may work.

Antibugging

In the "Antibugging" sections we consider things that can go wrong and how to repair or prevent them.

- **(MSys2) It complains there are no input files, but there are:**

  ```
  Makefile:73: target 'main' doesn't match the target pattern
  Makefile:73: target '-' doesn't match the target pattern
  g++ -std=c++2b -c -g `sdl2-config --cflags` -I../../external/SSDL/
  include  -o main
  g++: fatal error: no input files
  ```

  Microsoft Windows copies files like this: `main.cpp`'s copy is "`main - Copy.cpp`". Since this ends in .cpp, make tries to compile it and gets confused by the spaces in the filename.

  The solution is to make backup copies with `cp`: `cp main.cpp main.cpp.1`.

- **You run the program, and it never stops.** It might be waiting for some input (like hitting a key to continue), or it might have gone into la-la land forever. You can kill it with Ctrl-C (hold Ctrl down and hit C).
- **It stops with the message** `Segmentation fault: core dumped`. This means, more or less, "Something bad happened." For now, just remove the core file (`rm core`) and look in the program for the problem.

- **`^M`s show up in your text files; you didn't put them there.** Unix and Windows disagree on how to end a line. Move a file from one system to the other and read it, and you may see everything apparently jammed on one line or sporting a `^M` at the end of each line.

  Editors are often savvy about this. But if in Unix you see those `^M`s, you can find an online converter, or (if it's installed) use this command:

  ```
  dos2unix < windowsfile.txt > unixfile
  ```

  To go the other way, use `unix2dos`.

...in Microsoft Visual Studio

Here's the easiest way to start:

1. In the source code's `newWork` folder, make a copy of the `basicSSDLProject` subfolder, keeping your copy in the same location so it can find SDL and SSDL.
2. Rename it appropriately (`hello`, perhaps?).
3. Open its solution file `SSDL_Project.sln`. You should see something like Figure 1-6.[8]

[8] If you get a dialog box asking if you want to "Retarget Projects," accept the defaults and click OK. This happens if your machine and my machine have slightly different versions of a Windows library.

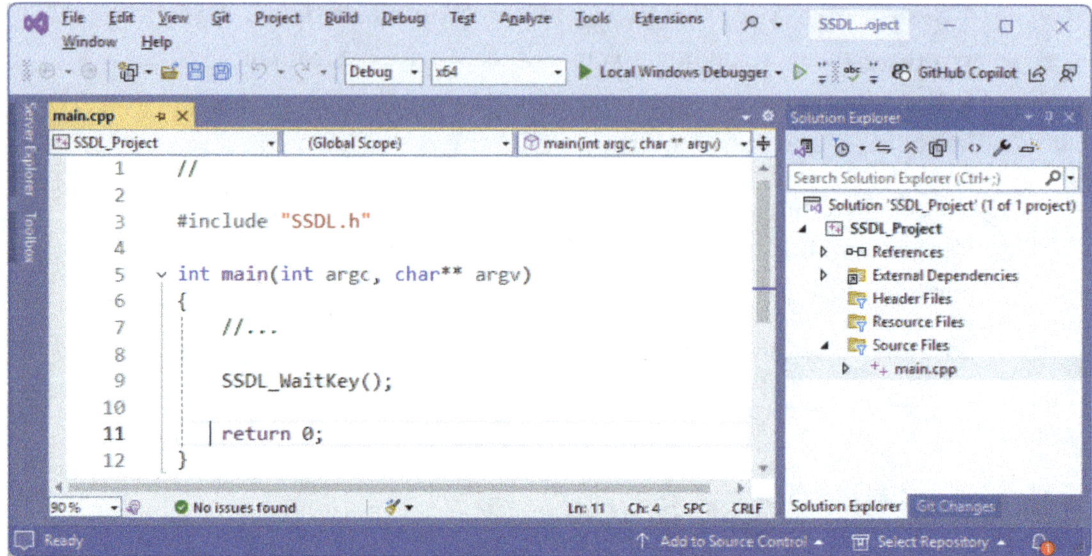

Figure 1-6. *An SSDL project. In the Solution Explorer window, click the triangles/arrowheads next to SSDL Project and then Source Files, and then double-click `main.cpp` to see the main program's (incomplete) contents*

Compiling Your Program

Your program doesn't do anything yet, so you'll want to give it some content. For now, you might type in the Hello, world! program from Example 1-1.

Maybe you'll make some typos.

If so, the editor may warn you by putting a squiggly red line under what it objects to (Figure 1-7). Wave your mouse pointer over the offending portion, and it'll give a hint as to what went wrong (though that hint may not always be clear).

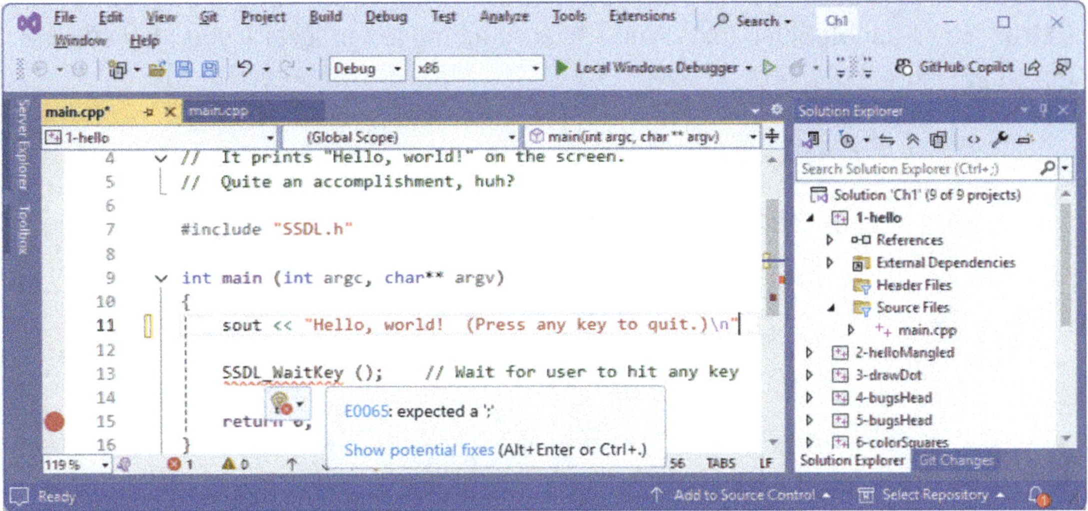

Figure 1-7. *Visual Studio highlights – and correctly identifies – an error*

Helpful as this can be, you can't be certain the editor is correct. You won't know for sure till you try to compile and run.

To compile your program, go to Build ➤ Build Solution. To run it, go to Debug ➤ Start without debugging. Alternately, click the green arrowhead or triangle near the top of the window with the label "Local Windows Debugger."

If your program doesn't compile, it will give a list of errors. Sometimes it's clear what the messages mean, sometimes not. Here's a typical one, using "..." to make it briefer – I forgot a `;`:

```
c:\...\main.cpp(13): error C2146: syntax error: missing ';' before
identifier 'SSDL_WaitKey'
```

Over time you'll understand more of what obscure error messages mean. For now, compare the program you typed to Example 1-1, and resolve any differences until you get this successful result: a window that displays the message `Hello, world! (Press any key to quit)`. When it runs, hit any key to end it.

Extra In Visual Studio, if you try to run an uncompiled program, you may see the dialog in Figure 1-8.

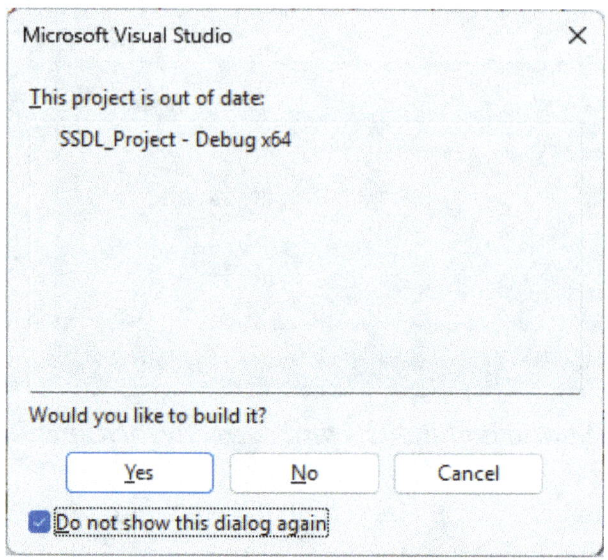

Figure 1-8. *"Would you like to build it?" window. Answering every time would be a pain*

If so, click "Do not show this dialog again" as shown, and click "Yes." This means that it will always try to recompile before running if needed.

If there are errors, you'll likely see the box in Figure 1-9.

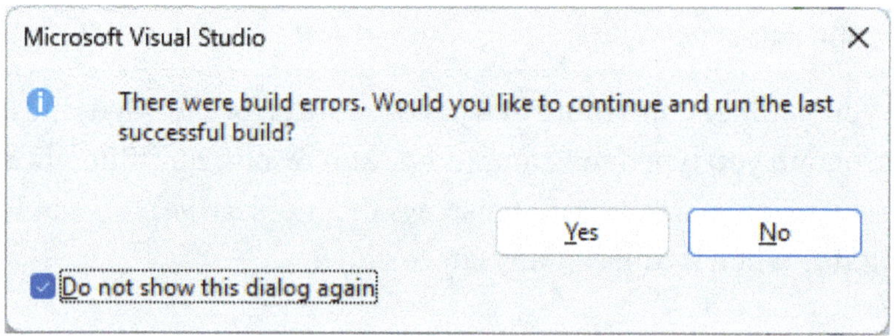

Figure 1-9. *Run the last successful build? Never*

Click "Do not show this dialog again" and say no. (Otherwise, when you make changes, it will go back to previous versions to find one that works, rather than your latest copy. Confusing!)

If you want to see the dialog boxes again – say, if you hit "Yes" when you meant "No" – you can fix it through the menus Tools ➤ Options ➤ Projects and Solutions ➤ Build And Run and reset the "On Run …" blanks to what you want (Figure 1-10).

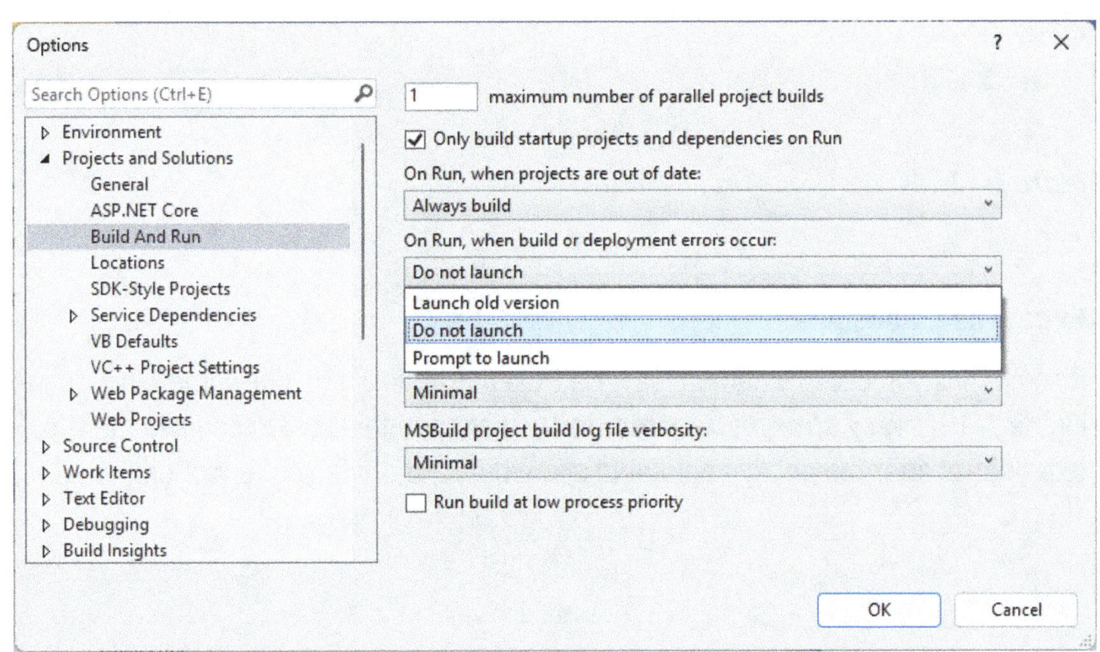

Figure 1-10. *How to reset the preferences set in Figures 1-8 and 1-9*

The Files You Created

Look through your folder now. (Access it through Windows Explorer or by opening its folder in Windows, whichever you like.) You should see something like Figure 1-11. (Details may differ, and some files are not shown, to keep it simple.)

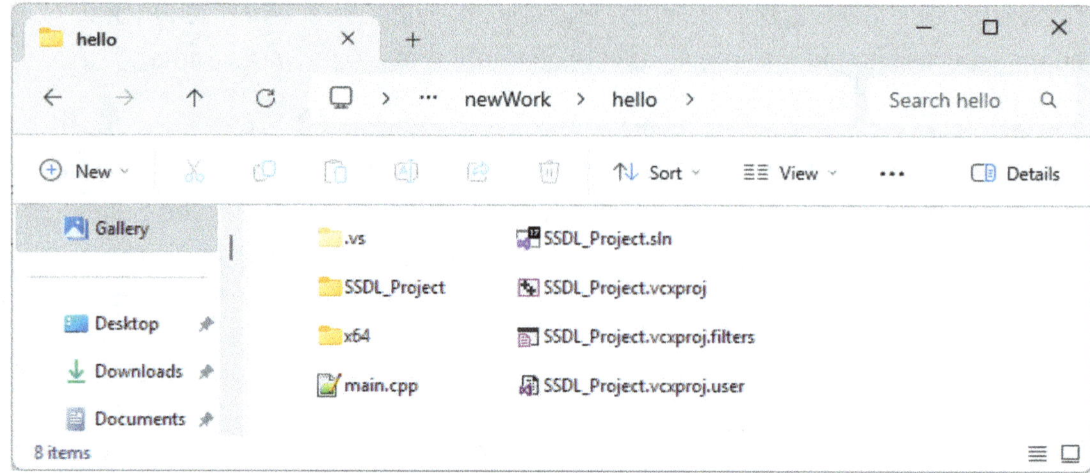

Figure 1-11. *Files in your project folder*

Extra: File Extensions

If some files you see are named (say) `main` rather than `main`-dot-something, as in Figure 1-12, I ***very strongly recommend*** you change this so you can see the **file extensions** after the dot. It's helpful to see what kind of file you're working with!

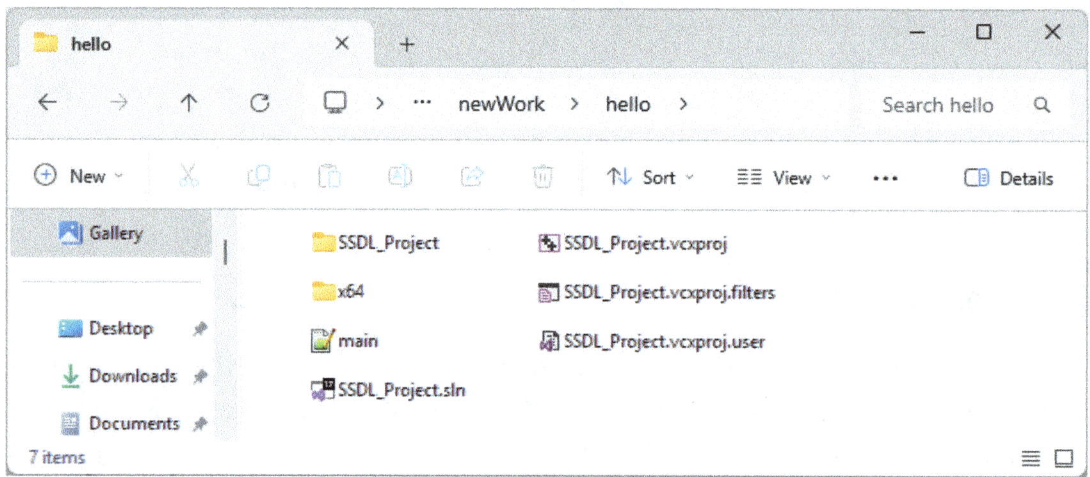

Figure 1-12. *A folder in which the .vs folder and the .cpp extension on main are not visible*

To do that, in the View tab of a folder (Figure 1-13), select View ➤ Show, and check File name extensions and Hidden items.

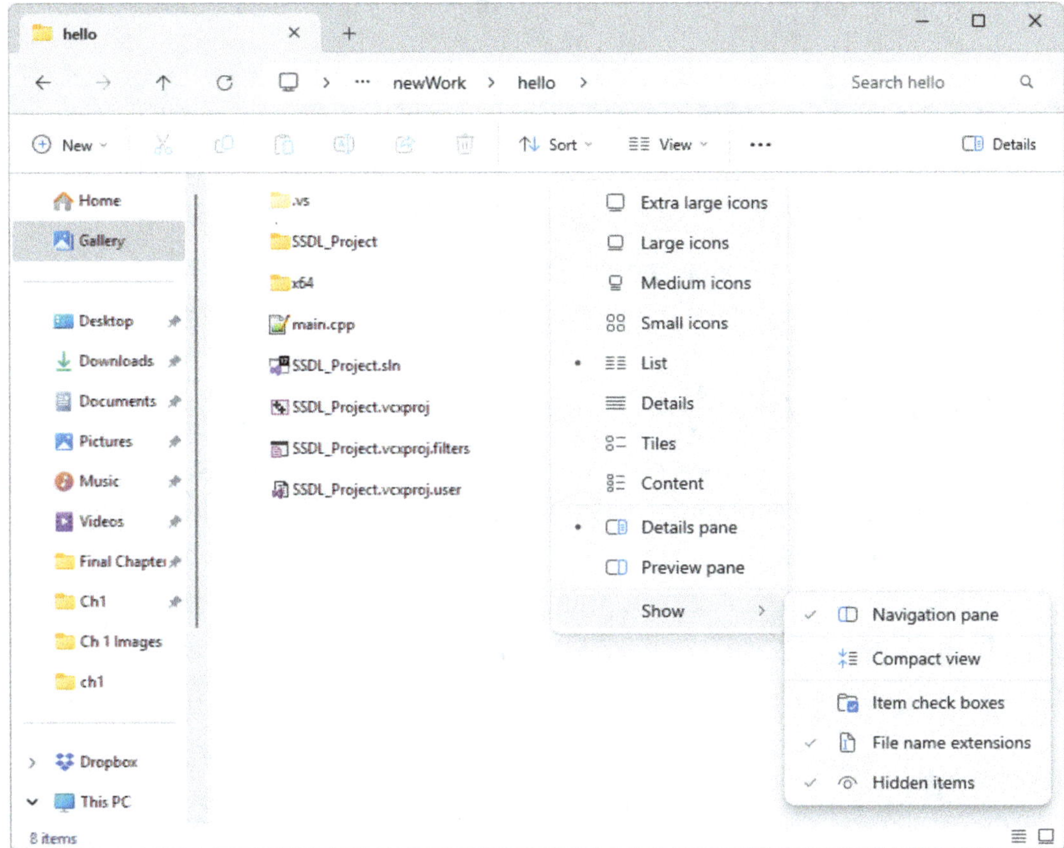

***Figure 1-13.** The folder options window in Microsoft Windows*

If that doesn't work, select Options (if you don't see it, check under the "..." symbol) and then the View tab; select Show hidden files, folders, or drives; and uncheck Hide extensions for known file types.

Important files in your folder include

- `SSDL_Project.sln`**, the "solution" file**: The main file that knows where the other files are.
- `SSDL_Project.vcxproj`**, the "project" file**: It knows that the program is stored in `main.cpp` and a few other things. You can't compile without it.

- `main.cpp`, your program.
- The `Debug`, or `Release` or `x64`, folder, which contains your executable. An `SSDL_Project` subfolder contains intermediate files.

Tip You can erase any Debug, `Release`, `.vs`, and `x64` folders and the folder with intermediate files. Visual Studio will recreate them as needed. This is important if space is crucial – say, if you plan to send the folder by email.

If you can't see the `.vs` folder, see the Extra above.

Reopening Your Project

If your computer is set up properly, you can double-click `hello.sln` to start Visual Studio and reopen what you were working on. (Double-clicking other things might not open all the files you need.)

Tip Reopen the `.sln` file, not the `.vcxproj` or `.cpp` files.

Antibugging

In the "Antibugging" sections we'll consider things that can go wrong and how to repair or prevent them.

Here are some common problems you'll find using Microsoft Visual Studio:

- **You open a solution (.sln) file, but it says none of the projects will load.** Maybe you moved things around in the source code folder; they have to stay where they are.

  Or maybe you're not in a folder at all, but in the zip file! The listing of a zip file looks like a folder, but it's not. Be sure you unzip the source code (see the section "Initial Setup" at the start of this chapter) and use the new folder, not the zip file.

- **It can't open an include file or a .lib file.** The error messages may say something like

  ```
  fatal error C1083: Cannot open include file: 'SSDL.h':
  No such file or directory
  ```

  or

  ```
  1>LINK : fatal error LNK1104: cannot open file 'sdl2_
  ttf.lib'
  ```

  The likeliest explanation at this point is that your project folder isn't in the right place in the source code repository. Make sure it's in the same place as the `basicSSDLProject` folder.

- **It's happy to accept edits, but doesn't offer an option to compile; or if it does, the edits have no effect.** It's likely that you didn't open the `.sln` file, but instead opened `main.cpp` or some other file. Close the file you're working on (saving it someplace so you can use those edits!) and reopen by double-clicking the `.sln` file.

- **You type something it should recognize, but the editor doesn't color it the way you'd expect or puts a squiggly red line under it.** Usually it will recognize `return` and `void` and color them to show it knows they're keywords. You may have a typo. Or the editor may be confused. Recompile to be sure.

- **It says the .exe file cannot be opened for writing.** You're probably still running the program; it can't overwrite the program because it's in use. Kill the program and try again.

- **It gives some other error message and won't finish building.** Often, trying again is enough to make it work.

- **It's taking forever to finish running the program**. You can be patient or kill it through Windows Task Manager. If it keeps happening, it's a good bet there's a problem with your program. (Or is it waiting for you to type something?)

- **It complains about Windows SDK**

  ```
  C:\...\Microsoft.Cpp.WindowsSDK.targets(46,5): error
  MSB8036: The Windows SDK version <some number or other>
  was not found. <More details.>
  ```

  or else just fails before attempting to compile.

  Solution: Right-click the project (not the solution or `main.cpp`), select Retarget Projects, and agree to what it says.

- **You try to open a source code solution, and it warns you "You should only open projects from a trustworthy source."** The good news: I'm trustworthy, so you can hit OK. Uncheck the box that says "Ask me for every project in this solution" to make it annoy you a little less.

Extra: `zip` Files

You may want to email someone your project; or you may want to store it compactly.

The usual way is to right-click the folder and select Add to Zip (or Add to `<folder name>.zip`) or Send to ... ➤ Compressed Folder. Then you can attach it to an email, if that's your plan.

Be sure you first erase any `Debug`, `Release`, or `.vs` folders and the Visual Studio–created subfolder with intermediate files. It saves space, and if you don't, some mail programs won't send the attachment.

How Not to Be Miserable (Whatever Your Platform)

These are problems you may encounter no matter what compiler you're using.

- **You get about a zillion errors.** This doesn't mean you did a zillion things wrong. Sometimes one error confuses the compiler so much it thinks everything that came later is wrong. For this reason, **fix the first error first.** It may eliminate a hundred subsequent error messages.

- **The line the error's on looks fine.** Maybe the problem is on the previous line. The compiler couldn't tell what was wrong until the next line, so it reported the error later than you'd have expected. This often happens with missing `;`'s.
- **You get warnings, but the program's still ready to run. Should you?** There are errors, and there are warnings. The compiler can still generate the program if it only gave a warning, but an error prevents compilation. You can ignore warnings, but they're often good hints as to something that really does need fixing.
- **Every program you write, it seems, starts out full of errors. You wonder if you're stupid.** If so, well, so are the rest of us. I might be able to get a Hello, world! program working the first time. Anything longer, forget it.

And here's the big one:

- **You made a mistake and the program, which had been doing mostly OK, now won't work at all.** Whenever you make a significant change (significant meaning "enough you're scared you might not be able to undo it") ...
    - **Windows:** Copy the folder that has your project in it (`.sln` file, `.vcxproj`, `.cpp`, all of it), and paste it (skipping any file it won't let you copy – it'll be something you don't care about anyway), thus creating a backup.
    - **Unix:** Copy your `.cpp` file, by saying something like `cp main.cpp main.cpp.copy1`. You could also copy the entire directory with `cp -R`.

    A trail of backup copies is absolutely essential for big projects. I urge you to get into the habit *now*. If not ... You've worked six months on your project. You did something that made it crash or refuse to compile or give the wrong output; worse yet, you did it yesterday and you've done several updates since. Wouldn't it be nice to go back to yesterday's code and get the almost-working version, rather than recreating six months of work? Backup copies are what every programmer, lazy or not, needs.

Golden Rule of Not Pulling Your Hair Out

Make backup copies as you edit your program. *Lots* of them.

EXERCISES

1. Using your compiler, type in the Hello, world! program, and get it working.
2. Write another program to print the lyrics of a song on the screen.
3. Take the Hello, world! program and deliberately introduce errors: take out semicolons or curly braces, break a quote in the middle, or try several different things. What kind of error messages do you get?
4. Clean up your folder (i.e., remove those extra, bulky files) and compress it.

Shapes and the Functions That Draw Them

Of course, we'll want to do more than say hello to the world. To get started with graphics, let's have a look again at that blank window you created the first time you ran an SSDL program (Figure 1-14).

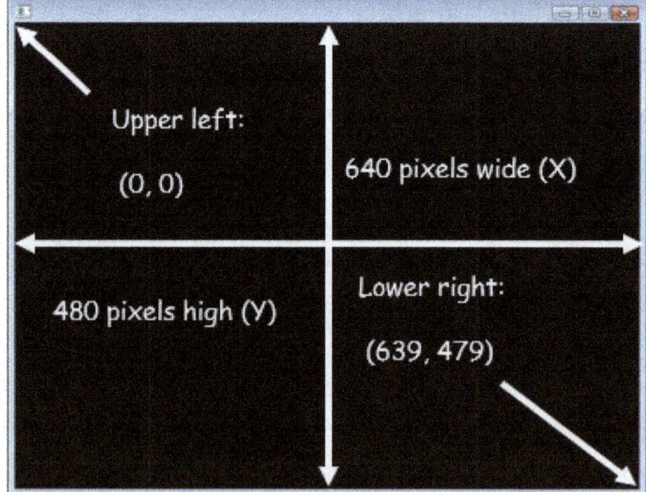

Figure 1-14. *Dimensions of the basic SSDL window*

Locations of shapes we put into this window are in (X, Y) coordinates. The upper-left corner is (0, 0); the lower right is (639, 479) – so the Y coordinates go *down* the page, not up. There are 640 locations going across (0 through 639 inclusive) and 480 going down. Each (X, Y) location is called a "pixel" (picture element).

This section shows some things we can do. The first, Example 1-3, draws a dot at location (320, 240). (It won't be as big as in my picture, but I wanted it to show up, so I enhanced it.)

Finding and Compiling Source Code All numbered examples are found in the book's source code, in the folder for the example's chapter (in this case, `ch1`), with some descriptive name starting with the example number. Example 1-3's is named, unimaginatively, `3-drawDot`.

Compile it the same way you did `test-setup` in the first section of this chapter. In the source code repository's `ch1` folder:

If using g++, go into the example's directory (`3-drawDot`), and enter `make`.

For Visual Studio, go into the `ch1` folder and open the `ch1` solution; right-click `3-drawDot` and select Debug ➤ Start New Instance.

Example 1-3. Program to draw a dot at the center of the screen. It's in the source code under `ch1`, as `3-drawDot`. Output is in Figure 1-15

```
// Draw a dot at the center of the screen
//        -- from _C++26 for Lazy Programmers_

#include "SSDL.h"

int main(int argc, char** argv)
{
    // draws a dot at the center position (320, 240)
    SSDL_RenderDrawPoint(320, 240);

    SSDL_WaitKey();

    return 0;
}
```

Figure 1-15. *Drawing a dot at the center of the screen*

Functions for drawing basic shapes are listed in Table 1-1. `int` means integer, that is, whole number. The function declarations, of form `void <function-name> (<bunch of stuff>);`, are precise descriptions of how to call the functions – their names and what kind of values they expect between the `()`'s. `SSDL_RenderDrawPoint` takes two integers for its two arguments `x` and `y`. `SSDL_RenderDrawLine` takes four: `x1`, `y1`, `x2`, `y2`. And so on.

Table 1-1. *Common SSDL drawing functions. For more SSDL functions, see Appendix G*

`void SSDL_RenderDrawPoint(int x, int y);`	Draw a dot at (x, y).
`void SSDL_RenderDrawLine (int x1, int y1, int x2, int y2);`	Draw a line from (x1, y1) to (x2, y2).
`void SSDL_RenderDrawCircle(int x, int y, int radius);`	Draw a circle with this radius, centered at (x, y).
`void SSDL_RenderFillCircle(int x, int y, int radius);`	Draw a filled circle with this radius, centered at (x, y).
`void SSDL_RenderDrawRect (int x1, int y1, int w, int h);`	Draw a box with (x1, y1) as its top-left corner and with width w and height h.
`void SSDL_RenderFillRect (int x1, int y1, int w, int h);`	Draw a filled box with (x1, y1) as its top-left corner, with width w and height h.

As an example of their use, this line of code makes a circle near the top left (see Figure 1-16, left): `SSDL_RenderDrawCircle (100, 100, 100);`.

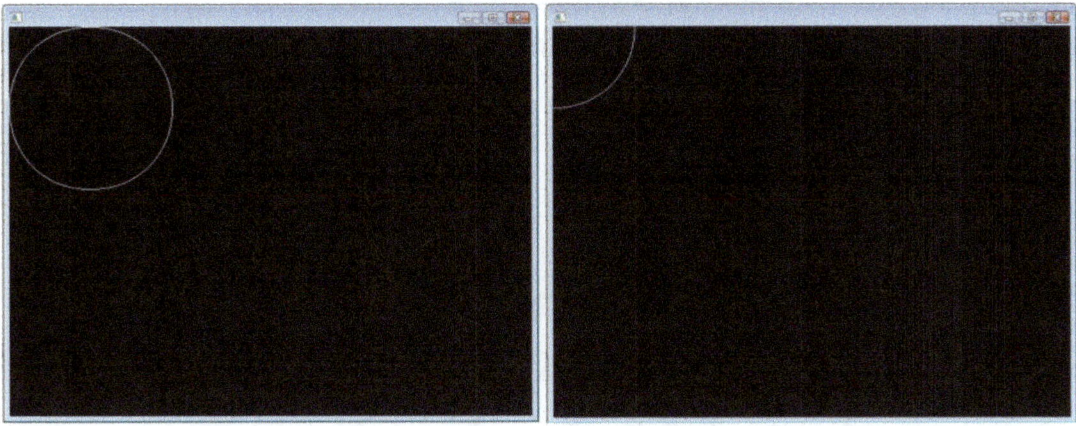

Figure 1-16. *On the left, a program with `SSDL_RenderDrawCircle (100, 100, 100);`. On the right, a program with `SSDL_RenderDrawCircle (0, 0, 100);`*

And this one gives you one *centered* on the top left, so you can only see a quarter of it (Figure 1-16, right): `SSDL_RenderDrawCircle (0, 0, 100);`. Not showing what would be outside the viewing area is called "clipping."

Now let's use these functions to make an interesting design. We'll need to plan ahead. There'll be a section on planning ahead more generally soon, but for now, you might make a storyboard, like movie producers or comic makers, for whatever design you want to make.

We may want graph paper (Figure 1-17, and there's a printable page in the source code folder).

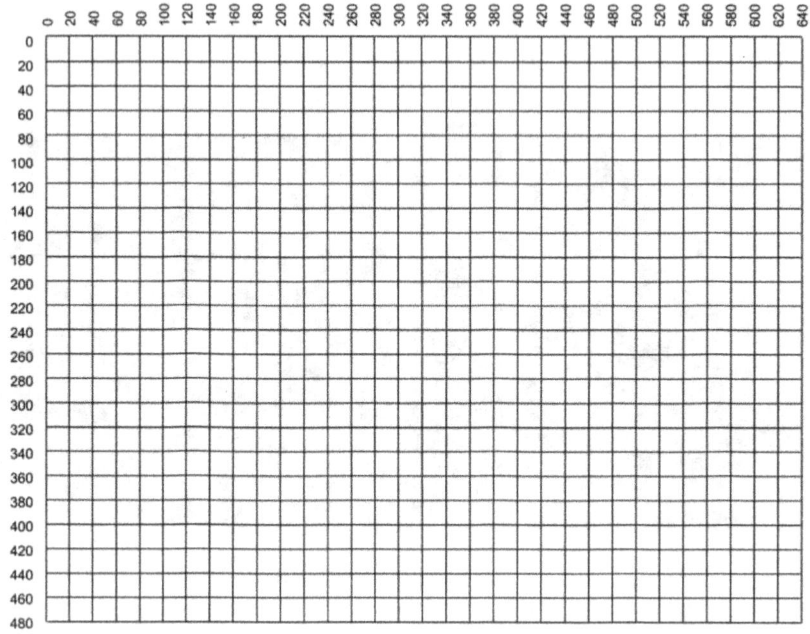

***Figure 1-17.** A graph of the viewing area, for designing what you want to display*

I decided to make a bug face: big eyes, big head, antennas. So I drew what I wanted (Figure 1-18).

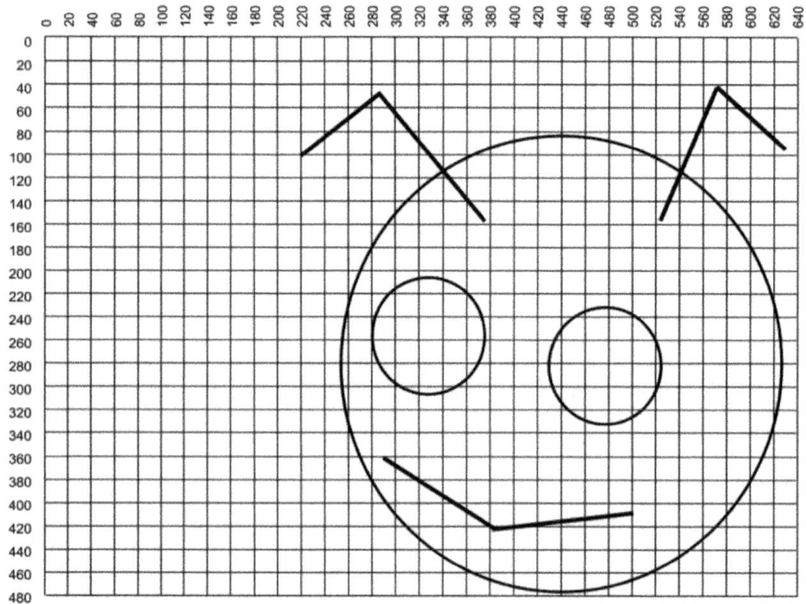

***Figure 1-18.** Drawing for the bug-head program*

I can now eyeball the locations. The center of the left eye is around (320, 250), and its radius is roughly 45. The big circle's center is around (430, 250), and its radius is about 150. And so on.

Here is my program (Example 1-4). I made several mistakes initially as I wrote it - confusing diameter with radius, reading the graph lines wrong. You will too. If not, well, that's true resume fodder.

Example 1-4. A bug's head. Found in the source code's `ch1` folder as `4-bugsHead`. The resulting output is shown in Figure 1-19

```
// Program to draw a cartoonish bug's head on the screen
//      -- from _C++26 for Lazy Programmers_

#include "SSDL.h"

int main(int argc, char** argv)
{
    SSDL_RenderDrawCircle(430, 250, 200);     // draw the bug's head

    SSDL_RenderDrawCircle(320, 250,  45);     // the left eye
    SSDL_RenderDrawCircle(470, 270,  45);     // the right eye

    SSDL_RenderDrawLine  (360, 140, 280,  40);// left antenna
    SSDL_RenderDrawLine  (280,  40, 210,  90);

    SSDL_RenderDrawLine  (520, 140, 560,  40);// right antenna
    SSDL_RenderDrawLine  (560,  40, 620,  80);

    SSDL_RenderDrawLine  (290, 350, 372, 410);// the smile
    SSDL_RenderDrawLine  (372, 410, 490, 400);

    SSDL_WaitKey();                           // Wait for user to hit a key

    return 0;
}
```

Figure 1-19. *A bug's head*

Notice how I rigorously documented in comments the purpose of everything I was doing. Suppose I hadn't put those comments in:

```
// Program to draw a cartoonish bug's head on the screen
//        -- from _C++26 for Lazy Programmers_

#include "SSDL.h"

int main(int argc, char** argv)
{
    SSDL_RenderDrawCircle(430, 250, 200);

    SSDL_RenderDrawCircle(320, 250,  45);
    SSDL_RenderDrawCircle(470, 270,  45);

    SSDL_RenderDrawLine  (360, 140, 280,  40);
    SSDL_RenderDrawLine  (280,  40, 210,  90);

    SSDL_RenderDrawLine  (520, 140, 560,  40);
    SSDL_RenderDrawLine  (560,  40, 620,  80);

    SSDL_RenderDrawLine  (290, 350, 372, 410);
    SSDL_RenderDrawLine  (372, 410, 490, 400);
```

```
    SSDL_WaitKey();

    return 0;
}
```

What a nightmare! You come back in a few months to reuse or upgrade this program, see the code, and think, *What the heck was I doing? Which line does what?*

Then you try to run it, and ...your system administrator has upgraded compilers or libraries, and the program no longer works. (Software rots: at least, *something* makes your programs stop working over time.) You have a nonworking program, and it will take detective work to identify even what the parts are meant to do.

Better to comment, so you can understand, maintain, and update your program as needed. In Example 1-5, I decide to add pupils to the eyes. It's easy to figure where they go, given the commenting.

Example 1-5. A bug's head, with pupils in the eyes. Found in the source code's `ch1` folder as `5-bugsHead`. Output is in Figure 1-20

```
// Program to draw a cartoonish bug's head on the screen
//       -- from _C++26 for Lazy Programmers_

#include "SSDL.h"

int main(int argc, char** argv)
{
    SSDL_RenderDrawCircle(430, 250, 200);      // draw the bug's head

    SSDL_RenderDrawCircle(320, 250,  45);      // the left eye
    SSDL_RenderFillCircle(300, 250,   5);      //  ... and its pupil
    SSDL_RenderDrawCircle(470, 270,  45);      // the right eye
    SSDL_RenderFillCircle(450, 270,   5);      //  ... and its pupil
    ...
}
```

Figure 1-20. *A bug's head, with pupils added*

Antibugging

- **You call an SSDL function, but it has no effect**. At this point the most likely guess is that it's drawing things outside the viewing area, so you can't see them. The best way to determine what's wrong is to examine the arguments you gave and be sure they're reasonable.
- **(For Visual Studio) You can't remember exactly how to call a function, and you don't want to look it up**. That's no bug, but it is a reality, and it shows admirable laziness, so let's roll with it. You can sometimes get a hint as you type (Figure 1-21). When you open the parentheses, it may give you a description of the function or what it expects; if you see an arrowhead or triangle on the description, click that to see multiple options.

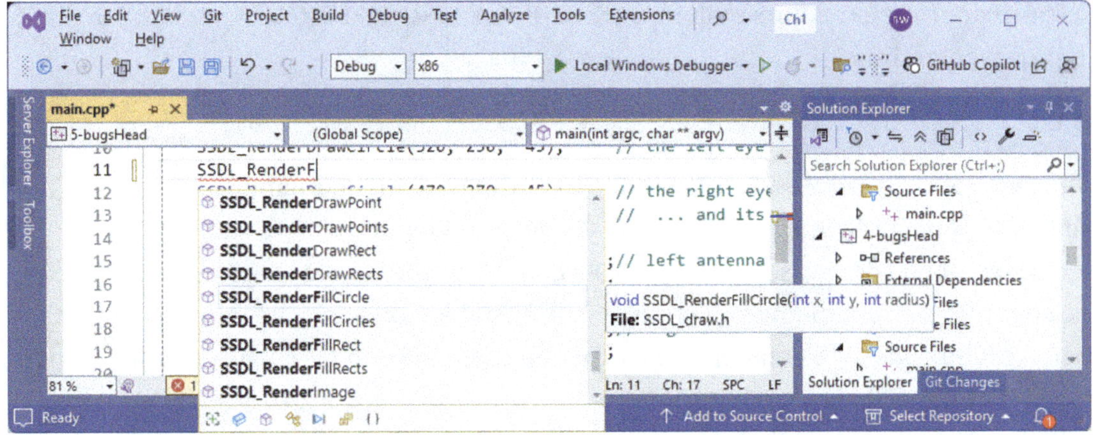

Figure 1-21. *Microsoft Visual Studio "IntelliSense" autocompletes of a function name*

...and sometimes nothing happens. Or it puts the red squiggly lines on things that are perfectly OK. Try retyping the line or compiling the code – one of those will usually do it.

EXERCISES

1. Design something of your own, and write a program to show it on the screen.
2. Draw a cube as seen not quite straight on, like the one shown here.

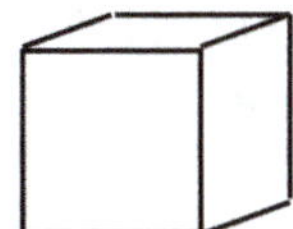

consts and Colors

Naturally we'll want to color our shapes too.

Colors on computers come in three parts: red, green, and blue. In our library they range from 0 (lowest) to 255 (highest). Black is 0, 0, 0; white is 255, 255, 255; red is 255, 0, 0 (red at max, the others at zero). Other combinations make other colors. You can use a website like `www.colorpicker.com` to find the red, green, and blue components of a color you want.

You can use a few colors built into SSDL (BLACK, WHITE, RED, GREEN, or BLUE) or create your own color thus:

```
const SSDL_Color MAHOGANY = SSDL_CreateColor(192,  64,   0);
```

Here, SSDL_Color MAHOGANY says we're creating a color and naming it MAHOGANY. SSDL_CreateColor(192, 64, 0) gives it the numbers we want.

Colors don't change, so we'll use C++'s const keyword to emphasize this and make the compiler prevent them from changing by mistake. Constants are written in ALL CAPS to make it obvious to the reader of the program that they don't change. (You get used to it, and it's unmistakable.)

To start using a color, do this:

```
SSDL_SetRenderDrawColor(RED);     // draw things in RED, from now
                                  // till the next call to this function
```

To clear the screen, do this:

```
SSDL_RenderClear(BLACK);         // erase the screen and make it BLACK
```

Here is a program that uses built-in and new colors to draw boxes on the screen.

Example 1-6. Use of colors to paint some rectangles. Found in the source code's ch1 folder as 6-colorSquares. Output is in Figure 1-6.

```
// Displays boxes of colors
//      -- from _C++26 for Lazy Programmers_

#include "SSDL.h"

int main(int argc, char** argv)
{
    SSDL_SetWindowTitle("Four squares in different colors");

    // We'll use 2 new colors, plus GREEN and WHITE...
    const SSDL_Color MAHOGANY   = SSDL_CreateColor (192,  64,   0);
    const SSDL_Color DARK_GREY  = SSDL_CreateColor (100, 100, 100);
```

```
    // Make a dark grey background
    SSDL_RenderClear            (DARK_GREY);

    // We'll have two squares across
    SSDL_SetRenderDrawColor     (GREEN);     // First square
    SSDL_RenderFillRect         (  0,    0, 100, 100);
    SSDL_SetRenderDrawColor     (MAHOGANY); // Second
    SSDL_RenderFillRect         (100,    0, 100, 100);

    // Program's end.
    // Must restore color to white, or we'll get mahogany text!
    SSDL_SetRenderDrawColor    (WHITE);
    sout << "Hit any key to end.\n";

    SSDL_WaitKey();

    return 0;
}
```

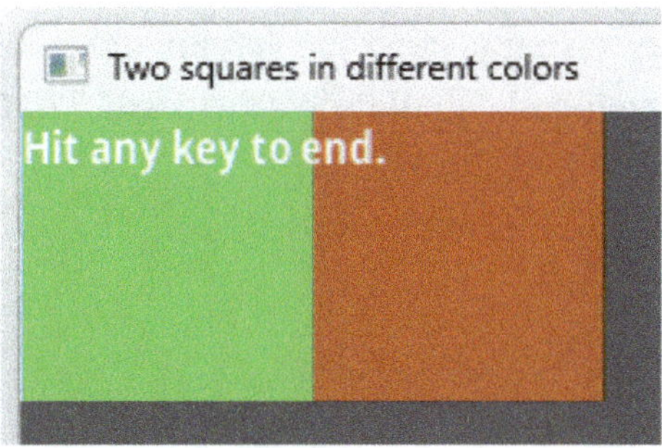

Figure 1-22. *Output of Example 1-6*

Table 1-2 contains functions relevant to colors and clearing the screen. Some declarations here don't precisely match those in the appendixes: they're simplified, but close enough.

Table 1-2. SSDL functions related to color

`SSDL_Color SSDL_CreateColor (int r, int g, int b);`[9]	Create and return a color. Max values for (r)ed, (g)reen, and (b)lue are 255.
`void SSDL_SetRenderDrawColor (SSDL_Color c);`	Set subsequent drawing, including text, to use color c.
`void SSDL_SetRenderEraseColor (SSDL_Color c);`	Set erasing, including clearing of the screen, to use color c.
`SSDL_Color SSDL_GetRenderDrawColor ();`	Get current drawing color, for example: `const SSDL_Color FOREGROUND = SSDL_GetRenderDrawColor();`
`SSDL_Color SSDL_GetRenderEraseColor ();`	Get current erasing color.
`void SSDL_RenderClear ();`	Clear the screen to current erasing color.
`void SSDL_RenderClear (SSDL_Color c);`	Clear screen to color c.

Some functions (the ones starting with `void`) don't calculate a value for you; they just do something (like draw a shape, clear the screen, or set a color). Others, like `SSDL_CreateColor`, have the job of calculating an answer. That one creates a color, so its "return type" is not `void`, but `SSDL_Color`.

We will cover functions and return types further in Chapter 7.

[9] You can give an optional fourth argument, "alpha," that can make the color transparent:

```
SSDL_Color SSDL_CreateColor(int r, int g, int b, int alpha);
```

Alpha ranges from 0 (completely transparent) to 255 (completely opaque). For example

```
const SSDL_Color GHOSTLY_GREY = SSDL_CreateColor(100, 100, 100, 128);
```

gives us a color that is about halfway transparent.

We won't use this, since we rarely want transparent geometric shapes, and the PNG format we'll use for images allows transparency without any special handling. But it's there if you want to experiment.

EXERCISES

1. Add color to a program you wrote to draw figures on the screen or to another program from this book's source code.
2. Make a scene for your favorite holiday: an orange scary face for Halloween or a green Christmas tree. Or get wild with Holi, the Festival of Colors.
3. Make the screen flash a variety of colors by alternating calls to `SSDL_RenderClear` with calls to `SSDL_WaitKey`.
4. Write the names of several colors, each written in that color ("RED" written in red and so on).

Text

sout, Escape Sequences, and Fonts

You can print multiple things with the SSDL library's `sout` - not just text, but also numbers.

```
sout << "The number pi is " << 3.14159 << ".\n";
sout << "...and the number e is "
     << 2.71828
     << ".\n";
```

How you space the lines in your program doesn't change what's printed; the line ends when you reach the `\n` character, the "end-of-line" character. The only reason for spacing the lines of code one way rather than another is for clarity. (The code above looks fine to me.)

But the spacing inside the quotes *does* matter. Note the space I put after the word "is": if you don't put it, your first line of output will look like this:

```
The number pi is3.14159.
```

There are other **escape sequences**, a.k.a "escape codes" – special characters that start with \:

- `\t`, the tab character, which takes you to the next tab stop. The tab stops are arranged at 0, 8 spaces, 16 spaces, etc. (Since most of our fonts are variable-width, we can't expect 8 Is or 8 Ms to be the same width as 8 spaces; it will be approximate.)
- `\"`, the " character. If we just put " in the text, like so – `"Quoth the raven, "Nevermore""` – C++ would be confused by the extra "'s. So we write it like this:

  ```
  "Quoth the raven, \"Nevermore.\""
  ```
- `\\`, the \ character. Because a single \ character has C++ trying to figure out what escape sequence you're starting.

For all available escape sequences, see Appendix D.

You may also decide where on the screen you want the text to appear. Here's how to **set the cursor** to X position 100, Y position 50:

```
SSDL_SetCursor(100, 50);
```

And you can change the **font and font size**. Font files must be in TTF (TrueType Font) format. C++ expects them to be in the same folder as your project:

```
const SSDL_Font FONT = SSDL_OpenFont("myFont.ttf", 16);
                                        // my font; 16 point
SSDL_SetFont(FONT);
```

If you want a font that comes with the system, one in the standard fonts folder, you can use this call instead:

```
const SSDL_Font FONT = SSDL_OpenSystemFont("verdana.ttf", 16);
                                        // Verdana font, 18 point, on Windows
```

or

```
const SSDL_Font FONT
   = SSDL_OpenSystemFont(""truetype/dejavu/DejaVuSans.ttf", 16", 16);
                                        // DejaVu, 16 point, on Ubuntu
```

The functions' descriptions are shown in Table 1-3.

Table 1-3. *SSDL functions for font and text position*

`void SSDL_SetCursor(int x, int y);`	Position the cursor at x, y for the next use of `sout` or `ssin` (described later).
`SSDL_Font SSDL_OpenFont (const char* filename,[11] int point);`	Creates a font from `filename` for a TrueType font, and `point`.
`SSDL_Font SSDL_OpenSystemFont (const char* filename, int point);`	Same, but loads from the system fonts folder.
`void SSDL_SetFont (SSDL_Font f);`	Use `f` as the font for text.

You can see what's on Windows by looking in `C:\Windows\Fonts`. Filenames aren't always obvious: for example, what shows up as "Bookman Old Style" in Microsoft Word is actually four files - `bookos.ttf`, `bookosb.ttf`, `bookosbi.ttf`, and `bookosi.ttf` - corresponding to normal, bold, bold italic, and italic.

In Unix, you can likely get a list of installed fonts with this command: `fc-list`. They'll probably be in `/usr/share/fonts` or a subfolder thereof.

The SDL2_ttf library is happy to make a font you give it italic, bold, whatever, but it can't compete with human artists. Where possible, use the enhanced version that comes in the font, as with `Times_New_Roman_Bold.ttf` or `timesbd.ttf` for Times New Roman Bold.[10]

Example 1-7. Using escape sequences, cursor, and fonts to print a poem. Found in the source code's `ch1` folder as `7-quotation`. Output is in Figure 1-23

```
//Prints a haiku
//      -- from _C++26 for Lazy Programmers_

#include "SSDL.h"
```

[10] If you can't, there's a function `TTF_SetFontStyle`, which can generate the new style, and is called thus:

```
TTF_SetFontStyle (myFont, TTF_STYLE_BOLD); //bold
```

or

```
TTF_SetFontStyle (myFont, TTF_STYLE_BOLD | TTF_STYLE_ITALIC); //bold italic
```

The available styles are `TTF_STYLE_BOLD`, `TTF_STYLE_ITALIC`, `TTF_STYLE_UNDERLINE`, `TTF_STYLE_STRIKETHROUGH`, and the default, `TTF_STYLE_NORMAL`.

```
int main(int argc, char** argv)
{
    // Window setup
    SSDL_SetWindowTitle("Hit any key to end");
    // Always tell user what's expected...

    // Load a font and start using it: Neuton, bold, 24 point
    const SSDL_Font NEUTON = SSDL_OpenFont("Neuton-Bold.ttf", 24);
    SSDL_SetFont(NEUTON);

    SSDL_SetCursor(0, 50);     // Start 50 pixels down

    // And now the poem
    sout << "\"The Sound of Water\"\n";
    sout << "\tby Matsuo Bashou\n\n";
    // Tab over for author's name, then
    //  double new line at the end of the line

    sout << "Down at the old pond\n";
    sout << "A frog is jumping into it...\n";
    sout << "The sound of water.\n\n";

    // End when user hits a key
    SSDL_WaitKey();

    return 0;
}
```

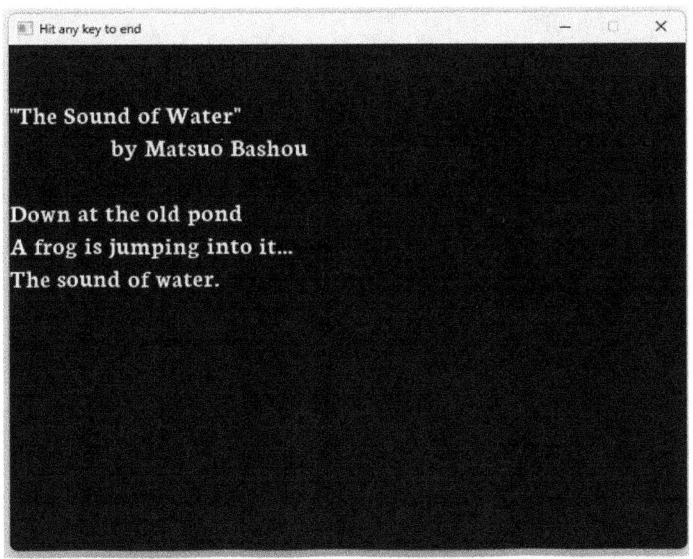

Figure 1-23. *Output of Example 1-7*

Extra: International Scripts

What if you want international scripts? That's now supported by SSDL! You'll need to do two things:

- Get a font that can handle the script you want. fonts.google.com is a great resource.
- Tell the compiler your text is international (specifically, "UTF-8") by putting u8 right before the quotation mark: u8"नमस्ते".

So if we add these lines to Example 1-7 (having downloaded the font, of course)

```
const SSDL_Font NOTO
          = SSDL_OpenFont ("NotoSansJP-ExtraBold.ttf", 24);
sout << "Original:\n";
SSDL_SetFont (NOTO);
sout << u8"古池や\n" << u8"蛙飛びこむ\n" << u8"水の音";
                                                   //Three verses
```

[11] We'll cover `const char*` later. For now, interpret it as text, like "`verdana.ttf`".

we get the display in Figure 1-24.

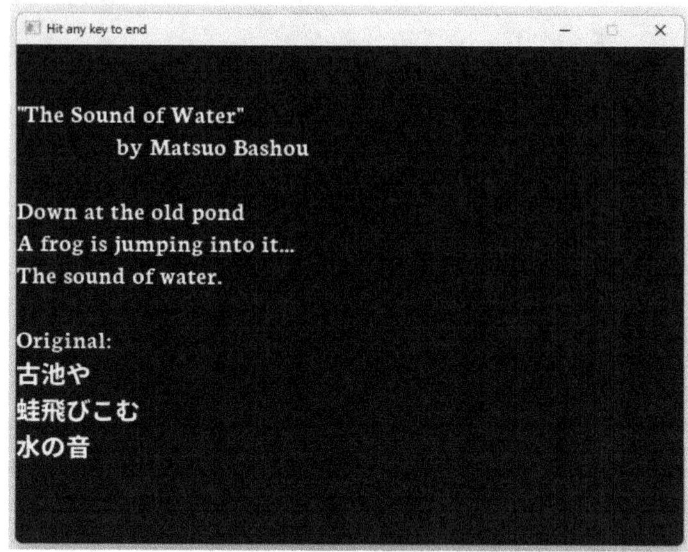

Figure 1-24. *The same poem displayed, but now with the Japanese original*

SSDL_RenderText, SSDL_RenderTextCentered

We can combine the setting of the cursor and font and the printing into one statement (and center text as well) with the two function calls below. If you don't specify the font, it'll use whatever font you were already using:

```
const SSDL_Font FONT_FOR_YEAR = SSDL_OpenSystemFont ("verdana.ttf", 14);
SSDL_RenderText("When did King Sejong publish the Korean alphabet?", 0, 0);
            // didn't specify font; use whatever we were using before...

SSDL_RenderText(1446, 500, 0, FONT_FOR_YEAR); //...use new font here
            // Year was 1446. Print at location 500, 0.
```

If you say `SSDL_RenderTextCentered`, the location you give will be the center of the text, not its left side.

These functions are described in Table 1-4.

Table 1-4. *Some SSDL functions for printing*

`void SSDL_RenderText (T thing, int x, int y, SSDL_Font font = currentFont);`	Print thing (which may be any printable type) at position x, y, using font if specified or otherwise using current font.
`void SSDL_RenderTextCentered (T thing, int x, int y, SSDL_Font font = currentFont);`	Print thing, as above, centered on x, y.

As with `sout`, the end-of-line character will take you to the next line – still centered if it's `SSDL_RenderTextCentered`, still indented to the position you specified if not – but the tab character is not supported.

To illustrate this, let's adapt Example 1-6 to display some labels using these new functions.

Example 1-8. An adaptation of Example 1-6 to include labels. Found in the source code's `ch1` folder as `8-labelSquares`

```
// Displays boxes of colors, labeled
//        -- from _C++ for Lazy Programmers_

#include "SSDL.h"

int main(int argc, char** argv)
{
    SSDL_SetWindowTitle("Two colored squares, with labels");

    // New colors
    const SSDL_Color MAHOGANY  = SSDL_CreateColor(192,  64,   0);
    const SSDL_Color DARK_GREY = SSDL_CreateColor(100, 100, 100);

    // Make a dark grey background
    SSDL_RenderClear(DARK_GREY);
    const SSDL_Color DARK_GREY = SSDL_CreateColor(100, 100, 100);

    // First square:
    SSDL_SetRenderDrawColor(GREEN);
    SSDL_RenderFillRect    (0, 0, 100, 100);
    SSDL_SetRenderDrawColor(WHITE);
```

```
    SSDL_RenderTextCentered("GREEN", 50, 50);      // dead center of
                                                   //    green square

    // Second square:
    SSDL_SetRenderDrawColor(MAHOGANY);
    SSDL_RenderFillRect    (100, 0, 100, 100);
    SSDL_SetRenderDrawColor(WHITE);
    SSDL_RenderTextCentered("MAHOGANY", 150, 50); // dead center of
                                                  //   mahogany square

    // Report number of colors, thus demonstrating non-centered text
    SSDL_RenderText        ("Number of colors:  ", 0, 100);
    SSDL_RenderText        (2, 150, 100);          // two colors

    sout << "Hit any key to end.\n";

    SSDL_WaitKey();

    return 0;
}
```

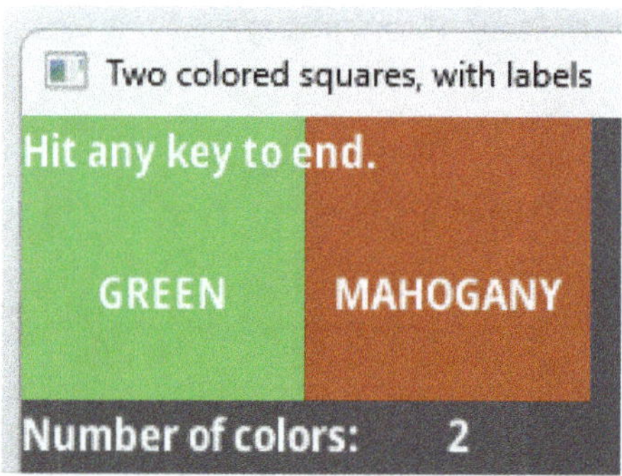

Figure 1-25. *Output of Example 1-8*

Figure 1-25 shows the output. Please note:

- `SSDL_RenderText` and `SSDL_RenderTextCentered` don't affect `sout`'s cursor. So `sout` still starts at the top of the page.
- `SSDL_RenderTextCentered` only centers left to right; it doesn't pay attention to Y values. To make the labels truly centered in the box, we'd have to calculate the Y position or just guess. SSDL's default

font is 14 point; half of 14 is 7, so we could subtract that from the true center of the box in the Y direction, 50, and pass 50 - 7 for the y argument into SSDL_RenderTextCentered. If we care.

EXERCISES

1. Put some appropriate text into a program you wrote earlier or found in the source code. For example, you could give the bug's head something to say.
2. Print a long poem or text, page by page, using SSDL_WaitKey and SSDL_RenderClear. Use an appropriate font and size.
3. Make up some statistics – isn't that how it's usually done? – and use the \t character to line up a table, like so:

```
Character        Coolness
=========         ===============
Greta Garbo       83%
Humphrey Bogart   87%
Marilyn Monroe    98%
me, if I were     99%
in the movies
```

4. Draw a stop sign: an octagon with STOP written in the middle.
5. Draw a yield sign: an inverted triangle with YIELD in the middle.

CHAPTER 2

Images and Sound

Enough of these line drawings: let's have something pretty.

Images and Changing Window Characteristics

Let's start by displaying an image using the code in Example 2-1. Run this and subsequent examples the same way as in the previous chapter: go to the source code and then the relevant subfolder (in this case, `ch2`). For g++, go into the folder for the example, and enter `make`. For Visual Studio, open `ch2.sln`, right-click the appropriate project, and select Debug ➤ Start New Instance.

Example 2-1. Displaying an image. Found in the source code, `ch2` folder, as `1-beach`. Other numbered examples are found similarly by chapter and example number.

```
// Program to show an image on the screen
// -- from _C++26 for Lazy Programmers_

#include "SSDL.h"

int main(int argc, char **argv)
{
    // Show image
    const SSDL_Image BEACH = SSDL_LoadImage ("beach.jpg");
    SSDL_RenderImage(BEACH, 0, 0);

    SSDL_WaitKey();

    return 0;
}
```


W. Briggs, *C++26 for Lazy Programmers*, https://doi.org/10.1007/979-8-8688-1859-2_2

This program loads an image called `beach.jpg` and shows it at location 0, 0 on the screen. That's it.

C++ will look for the picture in the same folder as `a.out` (g++) or as the `.vcxproj` file (Visual Studio). If we have more than one image, the folder may get messy. Let's put those images in a subfolder named `media` and load an image thus:

```
const SSDL_Image BEACH = SSDL_LoadImage ("media/beach.jpg");
```

...where `media/` means "inside the folder named `media`."[1]

You can at present load an image in GIF ("jiff"), JPG ("J-peg"), BMP ("bitmap"), or PNG ("ping") format or in LBM, PCX, PNM, SVG, TGA ("targa"), TIFF, WEBP, XCF, XPM, or XV format.

If you have another format, try loading it in GIMP or some other graphics editor and saving/exporting as JPG or PNG. I recommend PNG because it supports transparency.

You may be wondering as you see the result in Figure 2-1: can we scale the image? Yes, `SSDL_RenderImage(BEACH, 0, 0, 640, 480);` would make it a 640 × 480 image. But stretching it might make the image fuzzy, so let's resize the window to fit the image instead.

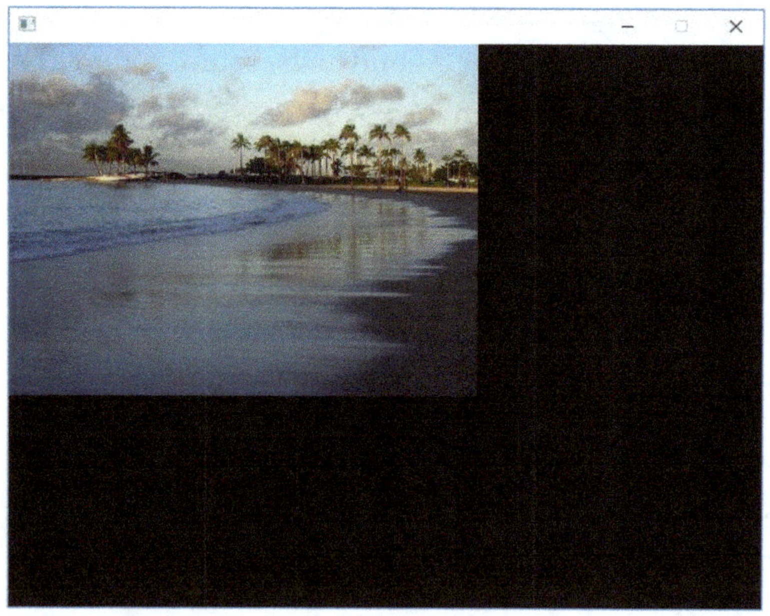

Figure 2-1. *Displaying an image*

[1] Yes, experienced Windows users, that's really a / not a \. This will work in Windows and Unix, and portability between operating systems is a Good Thing.

First, we'll find out how big it is.

Unix users can also say `exiv2 beach.jpg`. (If `exiv2` isn't installed, talk nice to your system administrator.)

Windows users can right-click the file in its folder (it's in `ch2/beach/media`) and select Properties and then the Details tab. You'll see the Width and Height listed as shown in Figure 2-2.

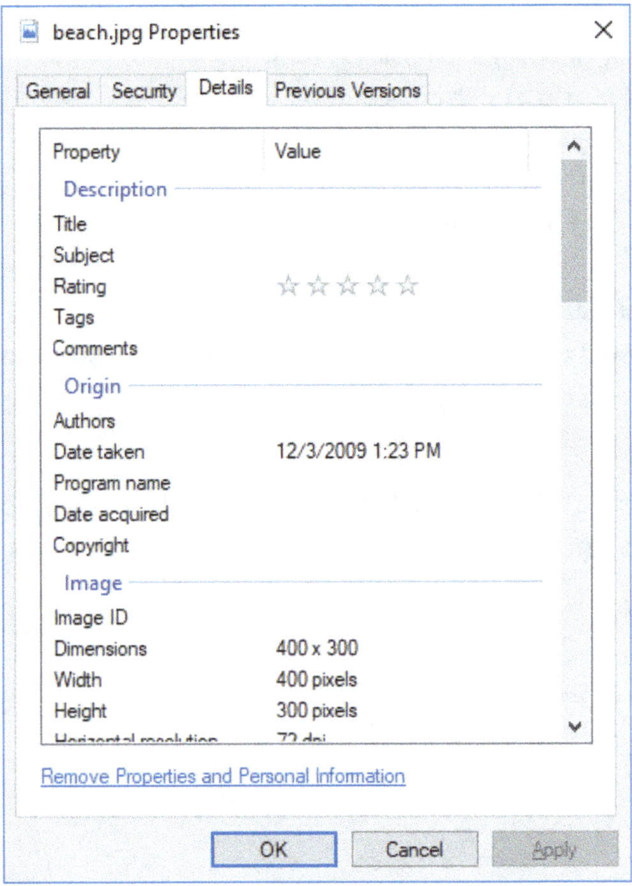

Figure 2-2. *Properties for an image in Microsoft Windows*

However we get the info, we'll tell the program to make the window the same size, giving it parameters of width and height in that order:

```
SSDL_SetWindowSize(400, 300); // make a 400x300 window
```

Since we're trying to make things cooler, let's also add a label to the window itself:

```
SSDL_SetWindowTitle("My trip to the beach ");
```

This puts `My trip to the beach` on the top bar of the display window (Example 2-2). The result is in Figure 2-3.

Example 2-2. Displaying an image, resized and titled

```
// Program to show an image on the screen
// -- from _C++26 for Lazy Programmers_

#include "SSDL.h"

int main(int argc, char **argv)
{
    // Set window parameters
    SSDL_SetWindowSize (400, 300);     // make a 400x300 window
    SSDL_SetWindowTitle("My trip to the beach");

    // Show image
    const SSDL_Image BEACH = SSDL_LoadImage("media/beach.jpg");
    SSDL_RenderImage(BEACH, 0, 0);

    SSDL_WaitKey();

    return 0;
}
```

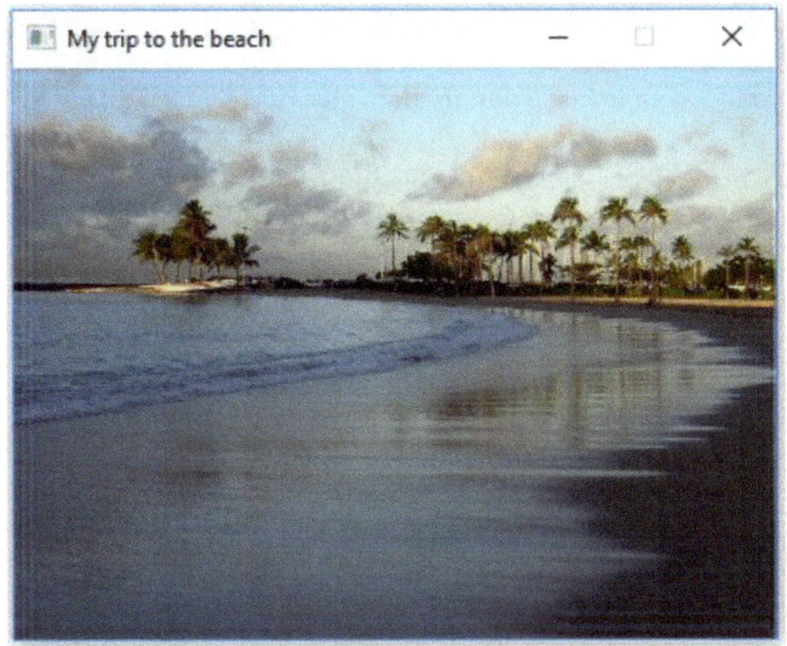

Figure 2-3. *A titled window resized to show an image with no extra space*

In Table 2-1 are declarations for our new functions related to images and window properties.

Table 2-1. *Some SSDL image and window functions*

`SSDL_Image SSDL_LoadImage (const char* filename);`	Load the image named filename, and provide an SSDL_image.
`void SSDL_RenderImage (SSDL_image img, int x, int y);`	Show the image img at position x, y, using img's width and height.
`void SSDL_RenderImage (SSDL_image img, int x, int y, int width, int height);`	Show the image img at position x, y, specifying width and height.
`void SSDL_SetWindowSize (int width, int height);`	Resize the window. (This erases the title on some platforms; do the resize first.)
`void SSDL_SetWindowTitle (const char* title);`	Give the window a title.
`int SSDL_GetWindowHeight ();`	Return window height.
`int SSDL_GetWindowWidth ();`	Return window width.

The last two functions return integers, just as SSDL_CreateColor returns an SSDL_Color, so we can use them wherever it makes sense to put an integer. Adding the line highlighted in Example 2-3 to our program gives us the result in Figure 2-4.

Example 2-3. Using SSDL_GetWindowHeight () and SSDL_GetWindowWidth () to center a message on the screen

```
int main(int argc, char **argv)
{
    // Set window parameters
    SSDL_SetWindowSize (400, 300);          // make a 400x300 window
    SSDL_SetWindowTitle("My trip to the beach");

    // Show image
    const SSDL_Image BEACH = SSDL_LoadImage("media/beach.jpg");
    SSDL_RenderImage(BEACH, 0, 0);

    // Make a label in the middle, centered
    SSDL_RenderTextCentered("BALI? BORA BORA? BEAUTIFUL, WHEREVER!",
                            SSDL_GetWindowWidth () / 2,
                            SSDL_GetWindowHeight() / 2);

    SSDL_WaitKey();

    return 0;
}
```

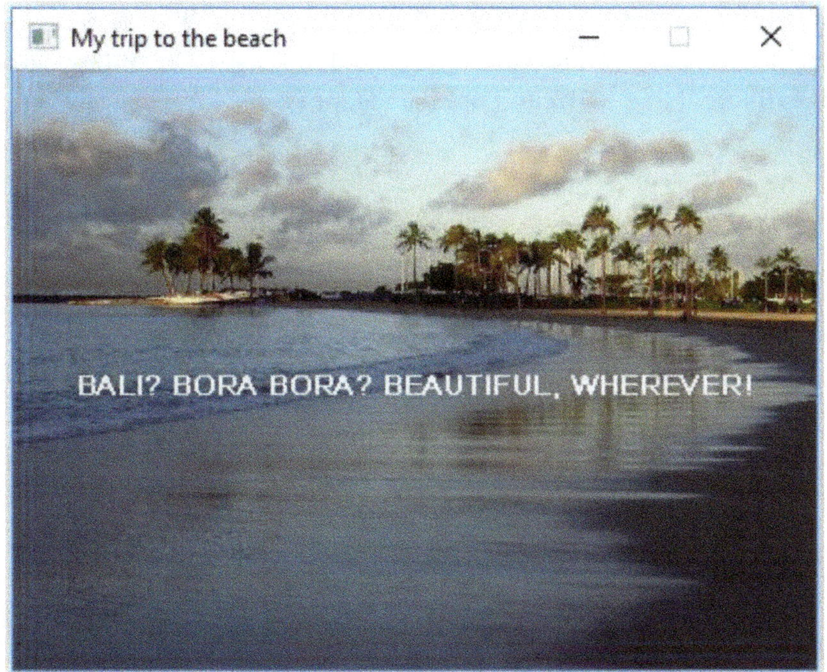

Figure 2-4. *Centered text using `SSDL_GetWindowWidth` and `SSDL_GetWindowHeight`*

Antibugging

The usual problem in this chapter, whether it's a crash or something not being visible, is

- An image didn't load.
- A font didn't load.

Here are possible culprits:

- **Folder location**: Files should be in the same folder as your `a.out` or `.vcxproj` file or in a subfolder as specified, like `media/`.
- **Spelling errors**: If you're like me, you *will* get names misspelled. When debugging the above program, I misspelled `beach.jpg` as `myImage.jpg`. Go figure.

- **(Microsoft Windows) You can't tell what kind of file it is**: You can't see the file extension, so you can't tell if it's .jpg, .png, or something very different that SDL can't use (see Figure 2-5).

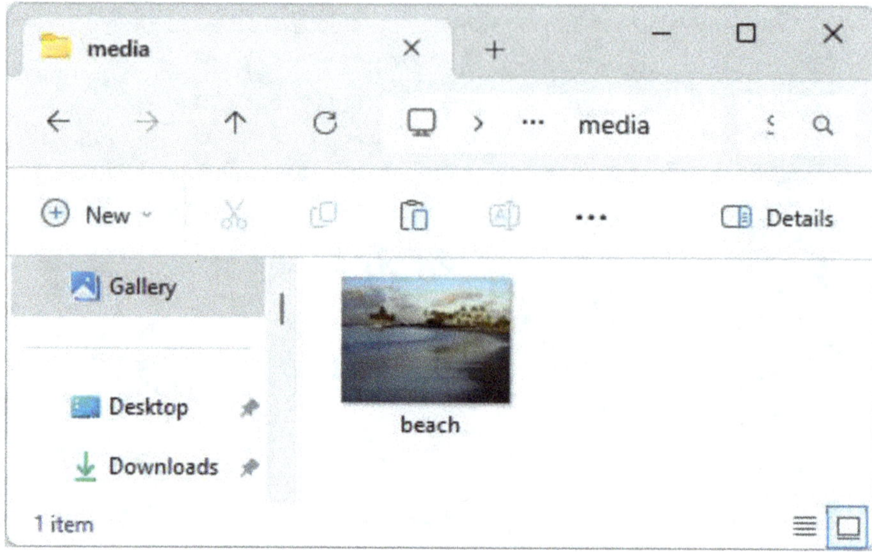

***Figure 2-5.** An unidentified file type in Microsoft Windows*

Solution: Un-hide extensions for known file types (see Chapter 1, section Creating an SSDL Project ➤ ...in Microsoft Visual Studio ➤ The Files You Created, Extra: File Extensions.)

- **The file is corrupted or has features your image loader can't handle:** One trick is to load up the file in a graphics editor. If it loads, export it in a different format or with different export options, and try the new file.
- **It's loading, but is being pasted off screen:** Try putting it at position 0, 0 and see if it becomes visible.
- **It's none of those things. What can you do?**

  If a new feature (say, images) is giving trouble, I can make, or copy from source code, a program that only does that one feature and make sure it works.

When it does, I add something else that makes it more like the final version I want. Once that works, I add another change and another, each time making a backup of the last working program, so if I mess up the new version, I can go back to what I just had.[2]

For me, this trail of backups is essential to getting new features working.

- **That feature you're struggling with just doesn't work, even in sample programs you trust:** Do you have the right project file or Makefile? Did you copy the folder from your source without alteration or rearrangement, and did it all copy correctly?

  It's unlikely, but compiler and library bugs *can* happen. For example, after calling `SSDL_SetWindowSize`, in some distributions of Unix `SDL_GetWindowSize` (needed by `SSDL_GetWindowWidth` and `SSDL_GetWindowHeight`) returns the *old* window dimensions. This problem's easy to circumvent: keep track of the dimensions yourself. I've always been able to work around compiler or library problems, even when I don't later discover it was my mistake all along.

Transparency

Pasting multiple images is easy with the SSDL library – you just put them on the screen in order from back to front, and you're there. And if they're partly transparent, all the better.

You can find images with transparency by doing an Internet image search, requiring the file type to be PNG. (Don't just right-click and download off the search page – you'll likely get a WebP file without transparency. You'll probably have to go to the site.)

If you can't find what you want already with a transparent background, you can easily use an AI tool to remove the background from a photo: at time of writing these include `www.remove.bg`, `bgeraser.com`, and `pixlr.com`.

[2] Remember the Golden Rule of Not Pulling Your Hair Out from Chapter 1: keep lots of backup copies as you make changes.

Online Extra: Removing Background with GIMP The AI tools work great for me, but if they don't get you what you want, see the code repository for a walkthrough of using GIMP to do this yourself.

Once you have your transparent image(s), paste them after the background, and they should show up with background showing through the transparent parts (Example 2-4).

Example 2-4. Multiple images, with transparency. Output is in Figure 2-6.

```
// Program that pastes two images onto a background
// -- from _C++26 for Lazy Programmers_

#include "SSDL.h"

int main(int argc, char **argv)
{
    // Set window parameters
    SSDL_SetWindowSize(400, 300);         // make a 400x300 window
    SSDL_SetWindowTitle("Pup dog and flamingo at the beach");

    // Load images
    const SSDL_Image BEACH      = SSDL_LoadImage("media/beach.jpg");
    const SSDL_Image FLAMINGO   = SSDL_LoadImage("media/flamingo.png");
    const SSDL_Image PUPDOG     = SSDL_LoadImage("media/pupdog.png");

    // Locations and dimensions for .png images
    const int FLAMINGO_X    =   0, FLAMINGO_Y    = 175;
                                   // Flamingo's on left, down screen
    const int PUPDOG_X      = 320, PUPDOG_Y      = 225;
                                   // Pupdog's on right down screen
    const int PUPDOG_WIDTH =  50, PUPDOG_HEIGHT =  75;
                                   // Pup dog is bigger than I want, so I
                                   //  make her 50x75. It's better to
                                   //  resize when making the image, but
                                   //  this works too

    // Paste in the background image, plus flamingo and pupdog
    SSDL_RenderImage(BEACH, 0, 0);
```

```
    SSDL_RenderImage(FLAMINGO, FLAMINGO_X, FLAMINGO_Y);
    SSDL_RenderImage(PUPDOG, PUPDOG_X, PUPDOG_Y,
                     PUPDOG_WIDTH, PUPDOG_HEIGHT); SSDL_WaitKey();

    return 0;
}
```

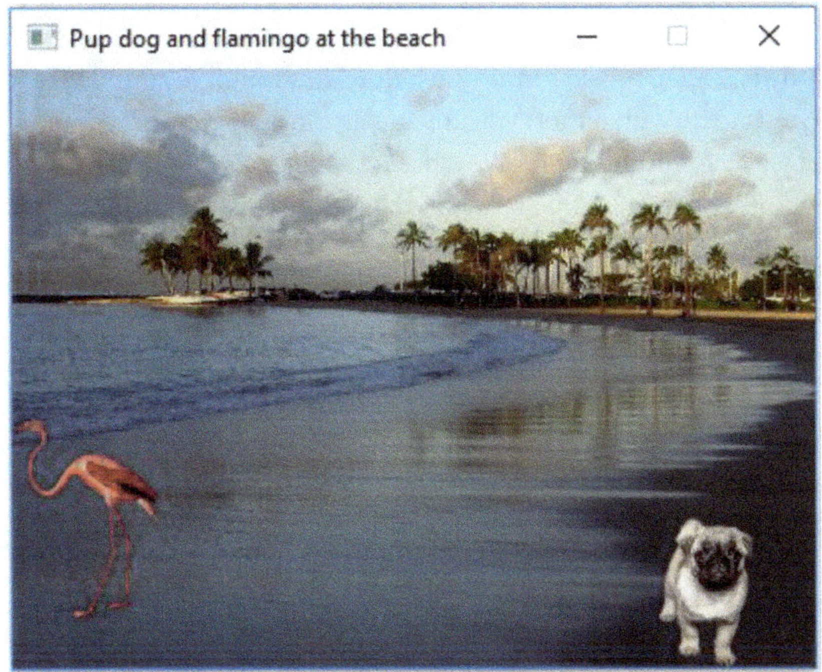

Figure 2-6. *Two transparent images pasted onto a background*

EXERCISES

1. Make a slide show of all the fabulous locations visited by pup dog and flamingo (or by your own dog or yard gnome). If you want to have the slides progress automatically, as opposed to waiting for the user to hit a key, you can use `SSDL_Delay`. When the program hits an `SSDL_Delay`, it stops for the given amount of time before continuing:

   ```
   SSDL_Delay (3000);
   // waits 3000 milliseconds, or 3 seconds
   ```

Sound

Sound is also easy in SSDL. I know what you're thinking: "I'll be the judge of that." But you'll agree. Unless your sound decides not to load and the program crashes.

There are two kinds of sounds: those that play continuously in the background and annoy the user to death, called "music," and those that occur with particular events such as collisions, called "sounds." Bottom line: Background sound is music; sound effects are sounds.

We can only have one music running at a time, but multiple sounds are fine. The main things you can do with either type are load it, play it, pause or resume it, and halt it. The format we'll commonly use is WAV, but music can also be in MP3. (If you have a sound file in another format and SSDL can't handle it, look for an online converter.)

The most common functions are in Table 2-2; a more complete listing is in Appendix G. When you see a parameter with a default value given, like `repeats` in `SSDL_PlaySound (SSDL_Sound s, int repeats=0)`, this means that if you leave out that argument, it uses the default:

```
SSDL_PlaySound (mySound, 2);  // repeat sound twice after you play it
SSDL_PlaySound (mySound);     // repeat sound 0 times after playing it --
                              // that's the default
```

Table 2-2. *Common SSDL sound and music functions*

`SSDL_Music SSDL_LoadMUS (const char* filename);`	Load music from `filename`.
`void SSDL_PlayMusic (SSDL_Music m, int numTimesToPlay=-1);`	Play music for a specified number of times; –1 means repeat forever.
`void SSDL_PauseMusic ();`	Pause music.
`void SSDL_ResumeMusic ();`	Resume music.
`int SSDL_VolumeMusic (int volume=-1);`	Set the volume, which should be 0 to MIX_MAX_VOLUME (which is 128), and return the new volume. If volume is –1, it only returns the volume.

(*continued*)

Table 2-2. *(continued)*

`void SSDL_HaltMusic ();`	Halt music.
`SSDL_Sound SSDL_LoadWAV (const char* file);`	Load sound from file. Despite the name, it can be in WAV format or other supported formats. See online documentation on the function `Mix_LoadWAV` for details.
`void SSDL_PlaySound (SSDL_Sound sound, int repeats=0);`	Play this sound, plus a specified number of repeats. If `repeats` is –1, it repeats forever.
`void SSDL_PauseSound (SSDL_Sound snd);`	Pause sound.
`void SSDL_ResumeSound (SSDL_Sound snd);`	Resume sound.
`int SSDL_VolumeSound (SSDL_Sound snd, int volume=MIX_MAX_VOLUME);`	Set the volume of sound, from 0 to MIX_MAX_VOLUME, which is 128; return the volume. If volume argument is –1, it only returns the volume.
`void SSDL_HaltSound (SSDL_Sound snd);`	Halt sound.

You can often find sounds online: do a web search for "free WAV" or some such. Copy what you need into your `media` folder.

Here's an example: a simple program that plays music and hits a gong when you hit a key (Example 2-5).

Example 2-5. A simple music and sound program

```
// Program to play sounds
// -- from _C++26 for Lazy Programmers_

#include "SSDL.h"

int main(int argc, char** argv)
{
    // Initial window setup
    SSDL_SetWindowTitle("Simple sound example");
```

```
    // Load our media
    SSDL_Music music
           = SSDL_LoadMUS("media/457729__razor5__boss-battle-2-0.wav");
    SSDL_Sound bell
           = SSDL_LoadWAV("media/321530__robbo799__church-bell.wav");

    SSDL_VolumeMusic(MIX_MAX_VOLUME/2);  // play music at half volume,
                                         // because...that was LOUD.
    SSDL_PlayMusic(music, SSDL_FOREVER); // ...looping continuously
                                         // SSDL_FOREVER means -1
    sout << "Hit a key to hear the bell.\n";
    SSDL_WaitKey();
    SSDL_PlaySound(bell);

    sout << "Hit another key to end.\n";
    SSDL_WaitKey();

    return 0;
}
```

Antibugging

Almost anything that goes wrong with a sound will make the program crash. Prime suspects are having the filename wrong or in the wrong folder or using an unsupported file type.

If there is a problem with sound quality, see Appendix A.

EXERCISES

1. Make your own music video, complete with lyrics, images, and sound, and play it. You'll need to time the delay between slides; see Exercise 1 in the previous section.
2. Play a song, adding a gong or some other annoying sound to every (say) fourth beat.

CHAPTER 3

Numbers

Numbers are what makes the computer's world go 'round, so let's examine ways to get the computer to handle those numbers for us.

Variables

Variables might seem like the letters we use in algebra – y = mx + b, that sort of thing – but in C++, they're just places to store values. Example 3-1 shows what it looks like when we create variables.

(Final reminder: As with all numbered examples, you can find Example 3-1 in the source code under the appropriate chapter – see Chapter 1's section "Shapes and the Functions That Draw Them" for how to find and run it.)

Example 3-1. Variable declarations for my American Idol obsession

```
int main(int argc, char** argv)
{
    int    seasonsOfAmericanIdol                = 18;
                     // after a while you lose track
    float  hoursIveWatchedAmericanIdol          = 432.5F;
                     // missed half an episode, dang it
    double howMuchIShouldCareAboutAmericanIdol = 1.0E-21;
                     // 1x10 to the -21 power
    double howMuchIDoCareAboutAmericanIdol     = 0.000000000000001;[1]
                     // So why'd I watch it if I don't care?
```

[1] I line up the ='s. Neatness makes for easier reading.

W. Briggs, *C++26 for Lazy Programmers*, https://doi.org/10.1007/979-8-8688-1859-2_3

```
    sout << "Through " << seasonsOfAmericanIdol
         << " seasons of American Idol...";

    // ...and some more output...

    // end program
    SSDL_WaitKey();
    return 0;
}
```

This gives us an integer variable; a float variable, which can take decimal places; and two double variables, which can take more decimal places. (How many more depends on the machine you're on.)

The trailing `F` on `432.5F` means it's a `float`, not a `double`, value. (If you don't specify, it's a `double`.) If you get these confused, you may get a warning from the compiler. To avoid the warning, I use `double` and forget the `F`.

`1.0E-21` is how C++ writes 1.0×10^{21}.

You can think of the main function as containing locations with these names, each of which can store a value of the appropriate type (see Figure 3-1).

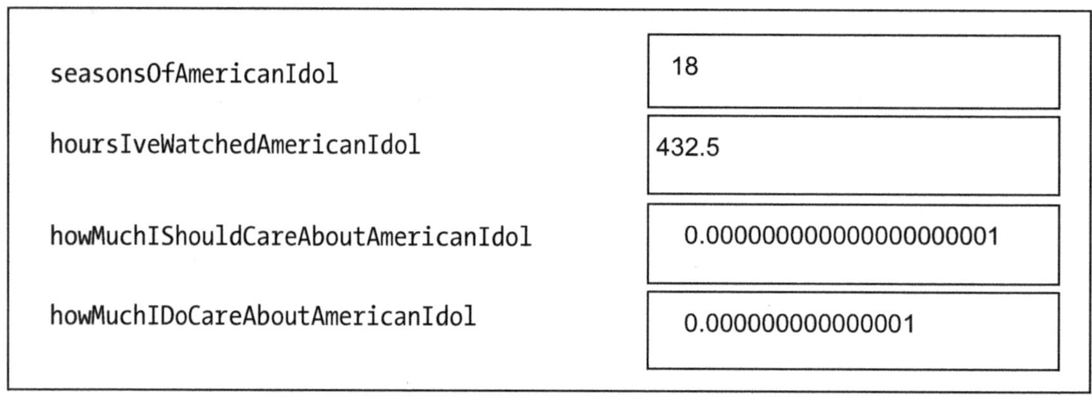

Figure 3-1. *Variables storing values in* `main`

We give these variables values soon as we made them, on the same line. We should: it's disappointing when you find that the number of dollars in your bank account is –68 million, because you didn't tell the computer what value to initialize it with and it just happened to start with a very inappropriate number.

For this reason as of C++26, your code must initialize its variables, or it won't compile. Your compiler doesn't know that at time of writing, but it'll catch up.

Golden Rule of Variables Initialize them.

It's also good to make descriptive names like the ones above. It's frustrating to search through code trying to find out what "`z`" or "`x`" means. But you know exactly what `seasonsOfAmericanIdol` means.

Variable names start with letters (possibly preceded with _'s), but after that they can have numerals in them. Capitalization matters: `temp` and `Temp` are different variables.

Extra Variable and constant names should be descriptive and shouldn't be the same as any of the built-in keywords in C++ (`const`, `int`, `void`, etc.).

By convention, C++ constants are written in ALL CAPS to SCREAM at the programmer that this is a CONSTANT, not a variable, value. To separate words jammed together, use _: `MAX_LENGTH`, for example.

Conventions for variable names are flexible. I use "camel case" variables: when you jam words together to make a variable, capitalize the first letter of all but the first: `firstEntry`, `minXValue`. I reserve initial capitals for created types like `SSDL_Image`. Initial _'s are for the compiler's own identifiers. There are other conventions; whatever convention you use, it's best to be clear as possible.

How do you think it got its name?

Constants

We've already made some constants:

```
const SSDL_Color MAHOGANY   = SSDL_CreateColor(192,  64,   0);
const SSDL_Font  FONT       = SSDL_OpenFont("Neuton-Bold.ttf", 24);
```

Now please consider these two simpler constant declarations:

```
constexpr double PI                     = 3.14159265359;
constexpr int    DAYS_PER_FORTNIGHT = 7+7; // A fortnight is two weeks, so...
```

What's the difference? `const` simply means "does not change." `constexpr` means "does not change *and* gets set at compile time, not when the program is running." The latter makes programs a little faster. We won't notice with the declarations above, but as programs get bigger and more complex, it should matter more. (I can't do it with, say, `SSDL_OpenFont` above, because it won't work till SDL is started at runtime.)

I use `constexpr` when the initial value is just numbers (like `3.14159265359` or `7+7`) and `const` when it's a function call (like `SSDL_OpenSystemFont("times", 18)`). Eventually we'll refine that (see Chapter 26), but it's good for now.

When to Use Constants, Not Literal Values

When should I use a literal value, like `100`, and when should I use a constant symbol, like `CENTURY`? The answer is almost always: use the constant rather than the bare literal value. There are two reasons.

One is **to be clear**, as shown above. You're going back through a program, and you see a reference to `7`. Seven what? Days in the week? The number of deadly sins? The age you were when you wrote your very first program? You'll have to do detective work to figure it out, especially if there's more than one 7 in your program. Detective work is not for the lazy. Better to document it with a clear name.

The other reason is **to easily change the value**. For example, there are by convention seven deadly sins, but using bare numeric literals like 7 is a pretty deadly sin in programmer terms. So maybe that `constexpr int NUMBER_OF_DEADLY_SINS = 7;` needs to be updated to 8. If you used this constant, you've got one line to change. If you put 7 all through your program, you'll have to go through figuring which 7's to change and which ones to leave alone. Detective work again.

The bottom line is clarity. We won't go back to the bug-face program in Chapter 1 and replace all those numbers with `constexprs`, because it would make the program *harder* to follow: each value is unique, and naming it doesn't make it clearer. (We have comments to show what it means anyway.) But the bug-face program is the exception. Generally, values should be named.

Golden Rule of Constants Any time it's not blindingly obvious what a numeric literal value is for, define it as a constant symbol, in ALL CAPS, and use that name whenever you refer to it.

Math Operators

Table 3-1 contains the arithmetic operators you can use in C++. They're used as you might expect: `2.6+0.4` or `alpha/beta` or `-2*(5+3)`.

Table 3-1. *The arithmetic operators*

Operator	Meaning
+	Addition
-	Subtraction, negation
*	Multiplication
/	Division
%	Modulus

Integer Division

Back before you learned fractions, when you only used whole numbers, the result was always a whole number: 5 divided by 2 was 2, with a remainder of 1. It's the same for C++'s integer division: `5/2` gives you another integer, `2`, not `2.5` – that's a floating-point value.

This can be confusing. `1/2` sure looks like it should be `0.5`, but since `1` and `2` are integers, `1/2` has to be an integer too: `0`.

In keeping with the way we divide integers, C++ also provides %, the modulus operator, which means "divide and take the remainder." 5%2 gives us 1, the remainder after dividing 5 by 2. We'll see more of % in Chapter 8, in the section on random numbers.

Assignment (=) Operators

We've been using = already:

```
const SSDL_Color MAHOGANY    = SSDL_CreateColor(192,  64,    0);
int   seasonsOfAmericanIdol = 18;
```

Constants can't be changed past that first line, or they wouldn't be constant, but variables can vary whenever you like:

```
x = 5; y = 10;
x = 10;          // I changed my mind: put a 10 in X, replacing the 5

seasonsOfAmericanIdol = seasonsOfAmericanIdol + 1; // Another year! Yay!
```

The latter means take whatever number is in that seasonsOfAmericanIdol memory location, add 1 to it, and put the resulting value back into that same place.

It can also be written this way:

```
seasonsOfAmericanIdol += 1;
```

They mean the same thing: add 1 to seasonsOfAmericanIdol.[2]

It works for other arithmetic operators: -=, *=, /=, and %= are all defined the same way.

A Diving Board Example

Now let's put this into practice with a program that uses math for sport (Example 3-2). Someone's going off the diving board. We'll make second-by-second images of the character as it plunges toward the water.

---

[2] If you want to add 1, rather than some other number, there's a special "increment" operator just for that:

```
++seasonsOfAmericanIdol;
```

We'll see that again in Chapter 5, along with "decrement" (--).

Example 3-2. A program to show a diver's path, using constexprs and math operators

```
// Program to draw the path of a diver
// -- from _C++26 for Lazy Programmers_

#include "SSDL.h"

int main(int argc, char** argv)
{
    SSDL_SetWindowTitle("Sploosh!  Hit a key to end");

    // Stuff about the board
    constexpr int BOARD_WIDTH       = 60,[3]
                  BOARD_THICKNESS   =  8,
                  BOARD_INIT_Y      = 20;

    SSDL_RenderDrawRect(0, BOARD_INIT_Y,
                        BOARD_WIDTH, BOARD_THICKNESS);

    // ...the water
    constexpr int SKY_HEIGHT        = 440;
    SSDL_SetRenderDrawColor(BLUE);
    SSDL_RenderFillRect(0, SKY_HEIGHT,
                        SSDL_GetWindowWidth(),
                        SSDL_GetWindowHeight() - SKY_HEIGHT);
                                 // height is window height - sky height

    // ...the diver
    constexpr int
        WIDTH              = 10, // Dimensions of "diver"
        HEIGHT             = 20,
        DISTANCE_TO_TRAVEL = 20, // How far to go right each time
        FACTOR_TO_INCREASE =  2; // Increase Y this much each time
```

[3] All these ='s lined up so precisely: is this overkill? Look how easy it is to find all my variables and their values! Another good habit to get into.

```
constexpr int INIT_X   = 50,
              INIT_Y   = 10;
int                x   = INIT_X; // Move diver to end of board
int                y   = INIT_Y; // and just on top of it

const SSDL_Color DIVER_COLOR = SSDL_CreateColor(200, 150, 90);
SSDL_SetRenderDrawColor(DIVER_COLOR);

// Now draw several images, going down as if falling, and right
// Remember x+=DISTANCE_TO_TRAVEL means x=x+DISTANCE_TO_TRAVEL
//    ...and so on

SSDL_RenderFillRect(x, y, WIDTH, HEIGHT);
x += DISTANCE_TO_TRAVEL;  // go right the same amount each time,
y *= FACTOR_TO_INCREASE;  //  down by an ever-increasing amount
SSDL_Delay(100);          // 100 ms -- 0.1 seconds

// Same thing repeated several times
SSDL_RenderFillRect(x, y, WIDTH, HEIGHT);
x += DISTANCE_TO_TRAVEL; y *= FACTOR_TO_INCREASE;
SSDL_Delay(100);          // 100 ms -- 0.1 seconds

SSDL_RenderFillRect(x, y, WIDTH, HEIGHT);
x += DISTANCE_TO_TRAVEL; y *= FACTOR_TO_INCREASE;
SSDL_Delay(100);          // 100 ms -- 0.1 seconds

SSDL_RenderFillRect(x, y, WIDTH, HEIGHT);
x += DISTANCE_TO_TRAVEL; y *= FACTOR_TO_INCREASE;
SSDL_Delay(100);          // 100 ms -- 0.1 seconds

SSDL_RenderFillRect(x, y, WIDTH, HEIGHT);
x += DISTANCE_TO_TRAVEL; y *= FACTOR_TO_INCREASE;
SSDL_Delay(100);          // 100 ms -- 0.1 seconds

SSDL_RenderFillRect(x, y, WIDTH, HEIGHT);
x += DISTANCE_TO_TRAVEL; y *= FACTOR_TO_INCREASE;
SSDL_Delay(100);          // 100 ms -- 0.1 seconds
```

```
    // end program
    SSDL_WaitKey();
    return 0;
}
```

Here are things to notice:

- I initialize all variables, as always.
- No bare numeric literals in any calculation or variable initialization: it's CONSTANT values all the way.
- I repeat the same pair of lines six times. Seriously? Is that lazy? We'll have a better way in Chapter 5.

Figure 3-2 is the result.

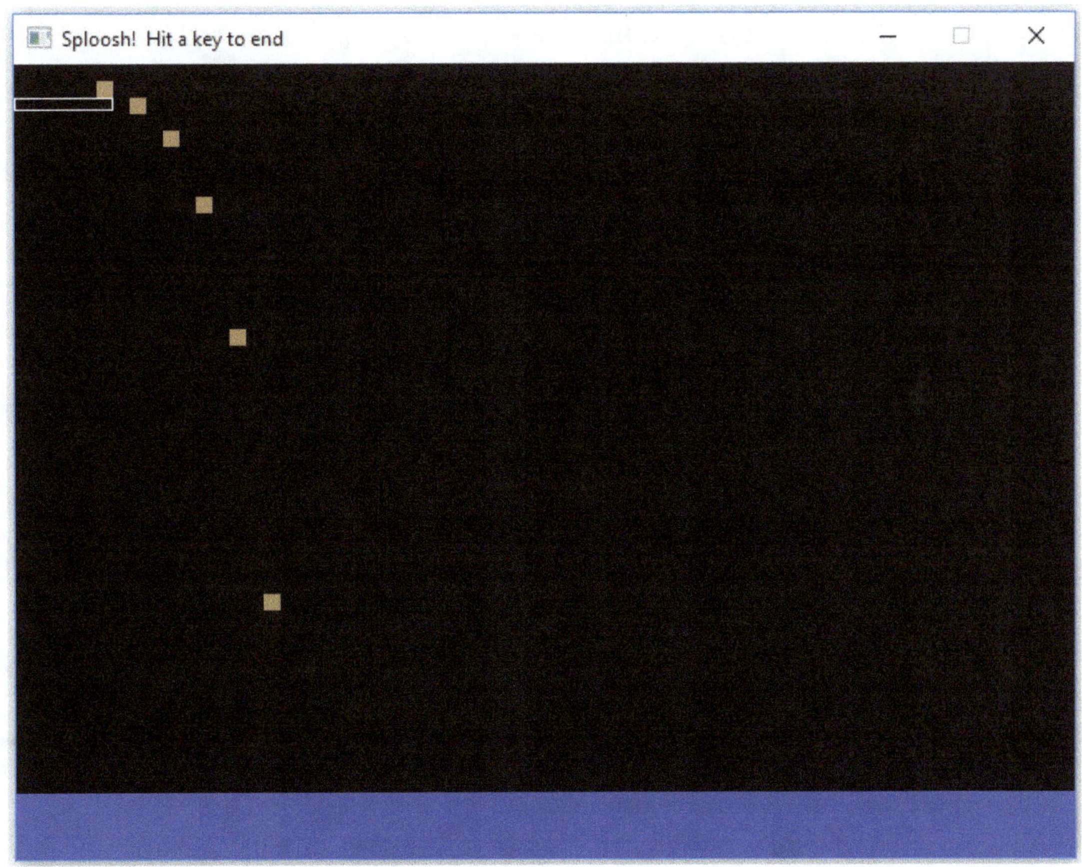

Figure 3-2. *A program that shows the path of a diver into the water*

That worked, and in some small sense evokes the terror I feel when I go off the high dive.

The No-Worries List for Math Operators

Here are some things C++ will handle naturally enough you won't need to memorize anything for them.

- **Precedence:** Consider a math expression, `2*5+3`. In C++, as in algebra class, we'd do the multiplying before the adding: this means `(2*5)+3` = `13`, not `2*(5+3)` = `16`. Similarly, in `8/2-1`, we divide before subtracting. In general, do it the way that makes sense to you and it'll be right. If not, use parentheses to force it to go your way: `8/(2-1)`.
- **Associativity:** In `27/3/3`, which division comes first? Is it done like `27/(3/3)` or `(27/3)/3`? Arithmetic operations are performed left to right. Assignment is done right to left: `x=5+2` requires you to evaluate the `5+2` before doing anything to the `x`.

  Precise details of precedence and associativity are in Appendix B.
- **Coercion:** If you want to cram a variable of one type into another, C++ will do it:

```
double Nothing = 0;   // Nothing becomes 0.0, not 0
int  Something = 2.7; // ints can't have decimal places, so
                      //  C++ throws away the .7;
                      //  Something becomes 2. No rounding, alas
```

If you mix integers and floating-point numbers in a calculation, the result will be the version with the most information, that is, floating-point. `10/2.0`, for example, gives you `5.0`.

EXERCISES

1. Using constants for centimeters per inch (2.54) and inches per foot (12), convert someone's height from feet and inches to centimeters, and report the result.
2. Now do the reverse: centimeters to feet and inches.

3. Accumulate this sum for as far as you're willing to take it: 1/2 + 1/4 + 1/8 + 1/16 + ..., using +=. Do you think if you did it forever you would reach a particular number? Or would it just keep getting bigger? The ancient philosopher Zeno of Elea would have an opinion on that (en.wikipedia.org/wiki/Zeno%27s_paradoxes, at time of writing). But he'd be wrong.

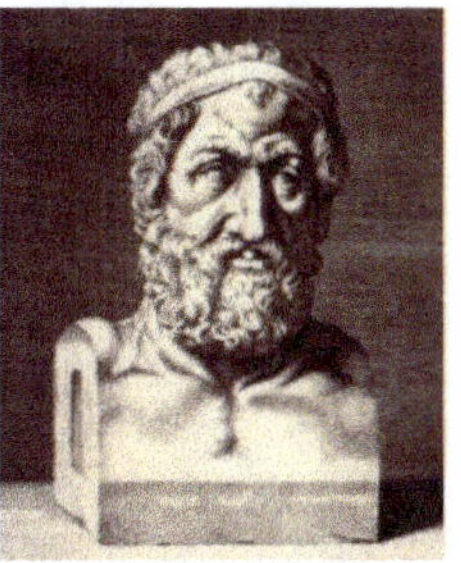

You can't get there from here.

—Zeno, sort of

4. Make a program to have a box move across the screen in 0.1-second jumps – like the diver moves, but clearing the screen at every jump so it looks like it's really moving. Maybe make the delay shorter for a better illusion of motion.

Built-In Functions and Casting

Now I want to make a geometric figure, a five-pointed star. But forget Chapter 1's graph paper: I want the computer to figure it out for me. Let it do its own (virtual) graph paper.

If I think of the star as inscribed in a circle ...I probably know the center, so what I need calculated is the points at the edges. Each point is 1/5 of the way further around the circle than the previous, so if a circle is 360 degrees, the angle between them is 360/5 degrees. If you use radians rather than degrees, like C++, that's $2\pi/5$ radians between the points.

SDL uses x, y coordinates, so we'll need a way to get that from the angle. We can do that using the picture in Figure 3-3. Since sine of the angle θ is the y distance divided by radius (if math isn't your thing, trust me), the y distance = RADIUS * sin (θ). Similarly the x distance is RADIUS * cos (θ).

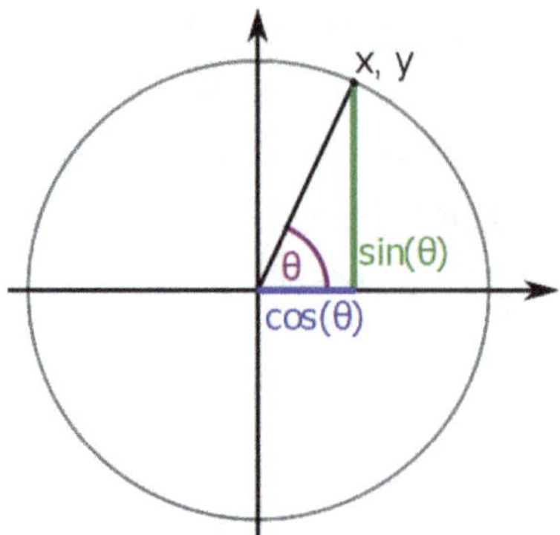

Figure 3-3. *Sine and cosine as they relate to x and y*

The `sin` and `cos` functions, like most C++ math functions, have their declarations in an include file called `cmath`,[4] added to our program thus:

```
#include <cmath> // System include files (those that come with the compiler)
                 // have <>'s not ""'s.
#include "SSDL.h"
```

This program is meant to draw a line from center to edge, turn 1/5 of the way around the circle, and do it again; keep going for a total of 5 lines.

Example 3-3. A star using `sin` and `cos` functions

```
// Program to make a 5-point star in center of screen
// -- from _C++26 for Lazy Programmers_

#include <cmath>
#include "SSDL.h"

int main(int argc, char** argv)
{
    constexpr double PI = 3.14159;
```

[4] Include files inherited from C++'s ancestor C start with "c": `cmath` and `cstdlib`, for example.

```
// Starting out with some generally useful numbers...

// center of screen
const     int CENTER_X         = SSDL_GetWindowWidth () / 2,
              CENTER_Y         = SSDL_GetWindowHeight() / 2;
constexpr int RADIUS           = 200,
              NUMBER_OF_POINTS =   5;

// angle information...
double    angle                  = 0;      // angle starts at 0
constexpr double ANGLE_INCREMENT = (2 / NUMBER_OF_POINTS) * PI;
                        // increases by whole circle/5 each time

// ...now we make the successive lines
int x, y;               // endpt of line (other endpt is center)

x = CENTER_X + int(RADIUS * cos(angle));       // calc endpoint
y = CENTER_Y + int(RADIUS * sin(angle));
SSDL_RenderDrawLine(CENTER_X, CENTER_Y, x, y); // draw line
angle += ANGLE_INCREMENT;                      // go on to next

x = CENTER_X + int(RADIUS * cos(angle));       // calc endpoint
y = CENTER_Y + int(RADIUS * sin(angle));
SSDL_RenderDrawLine(CENTER_X, CENTER_Y, x, y); // draw line
angle += ANGLE_INCREMENT;                      // go on to next

x = CENTER_X + int(RADIUS * cos(angle));       // calc endpoint
y = CENTER_Y + int(RADIUS * sin(angle));
SSDL_RenderDrawLine(CENTER_X, CENTER_Y, x, y); // draw line
angle += ANGLE_INCREMENT;                      // go on to next

x = CENTER_X + int(RADIUS * cos(angle));       // calc endpoint
y = CENTER_Y + int(RADIUS * sin(angle));
SSDL_RenderDrawLine(CENTER_X, CENTER_Y, x, y); // draw line
angle += ANGLE_INCREMENT;                      // go on to next

x = CENTER_X + int(RADIUS * cos(angle));       // calc endpoint
y = CENTER_Y + int(RADIUS * sin(angle));
```

```
    SSDL_RenderDrawLine(CENTER_X, CENTER_Y, x, y); // draw line
    angle += ANGLE_INCREMENT;                      // go on to next

    // end program
    SSDL_WaitKey();
    return 0;
}
```

Figure 3-4 shows the result. What—?

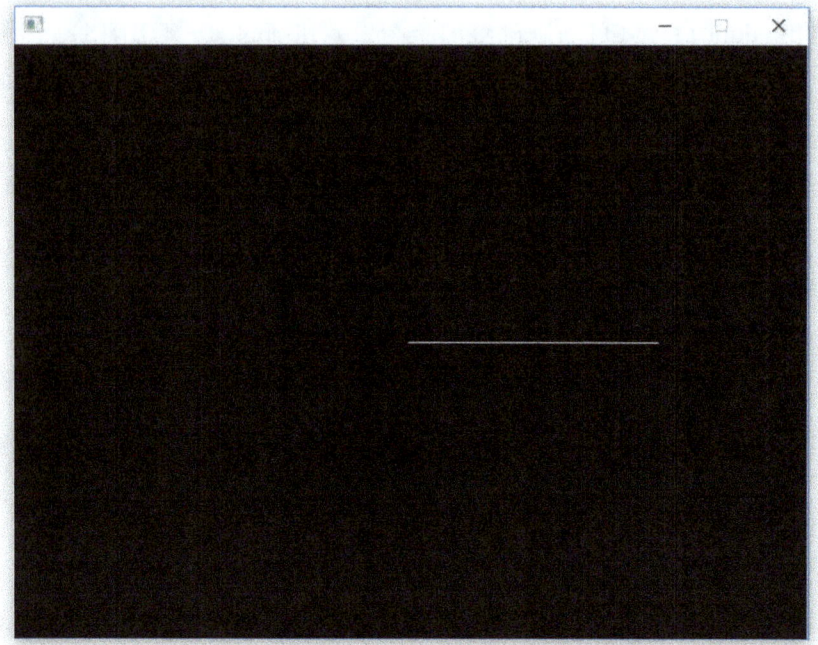

Figure 3-4. *A five-pointed star – at least, it was supposed to be*

This will be a breeze to debug once we've covered the debugger in Chapter 9, but for now, we'll just have to channel Sherlock Holmes. That line never changes. Which means `angle` never changes. Which must mean `ANGLE_INCREMENT` is 0. Why would it be 0?

Look at that calculation: `ANGLE_INCREMENT = (2/NUMBER_OF_POINTS)*PI`. The first thing to do is divide 2 by `NUMBER_OF_POINTS`, or 5. Since both are integers, we do integer division: 5 goes into 2 zero times (with a remainder of 2, for what it's worth), so `2/5` gives us zero. Zero times `PI` is zero. So `ANGLE_INCREMENT` is zero.

We needed floating-point division.

One way is to force 2 and 5 to be `float` or `double`. You can do this by saying

```
static_cast<double>(whatEverYouWantToBeDouble)
```

This is called **casting**.

This won't work

```
static_cast<double>(2/NUMBER_OF_POINTS)
```

because that divides 2 by 5, gets 0, and converts the 0 to 0.0. It's still doing integer division.

Any of the following will work. As long as one of the arguments of / is `double` or `float`, you'll get a result with decimal places:

```
static_cast<double>(2)/NUMBER_OF_POINTS
2/ static_cast<double>(NUMBER_OF_POINTS)
2.0 / NUMBER_OF_POINTS
```

So changing the beginning of `main` to what you see in Example 3-4 repairs the problem.

Example 3-4. A new beginning to `main`, to make Example 3-3 work

```
int main(int argc, char** argv)
{
    ...

    // angle information...
    double          angle              = 0;       // angle starts at 0
    constexpr double ANGLE_INCREMENT
      = (2 / static_cast<double>(NUMBER_OF_POINTS)) * PI; // right
                                // increases by whole circle/5 each time

    ...
```

Figure 3-5 shows the result.

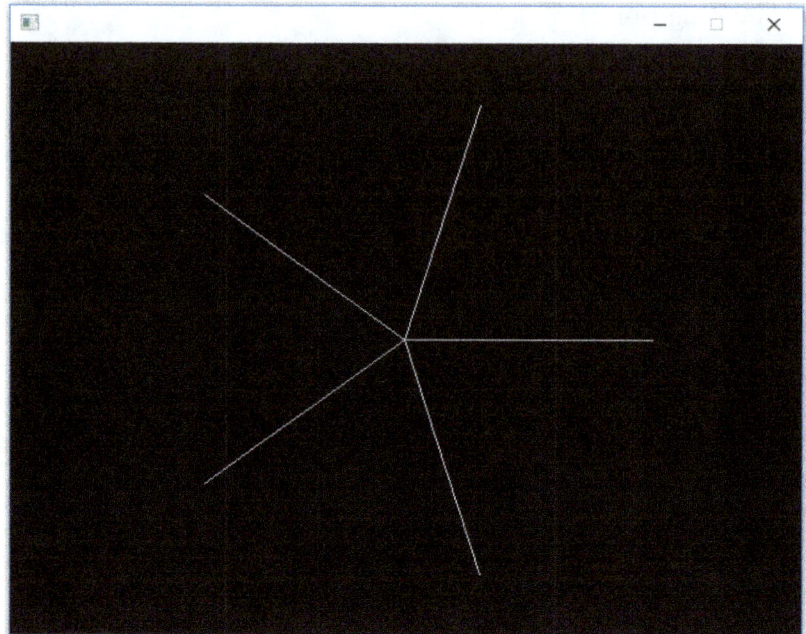

Figure 3-5. *A five-pointed star*

It's not vertical, it seems. Exercise 1 below is about turning it straight.

Other commonly useful mathematical functions include `asin` and `acos` (reverse sine and cosine), `pow` (raising a number to a power), `abs` (absolute value), and `sqrt` (square root). See Appendix E for more.

Antibugging

- **You call a value-returning function, but it has no effect.** Here's an example with a function we saw earlier:

  ```
  // Center "Blastoff!" on the screen
  SSDL_GetWindowWidth();
  SSDL_RenderTextCentered(320, 240, "Blastoff!");
  ```

  Sure, you called `SSDL_GetWindowWidth()` ...but you never did anything with the result! C++ is happy to let you waste time by calling functions and not using what they give you. (It's sort of a "let the programmer shoot self in the foot and laugh" language.) If you want to use the value, store it in a variable or constant:

```
const int SCREEN_WIDTH  = SSDL_ GetWindowWidth();
const int SCREEN_HEIGHT = SSDL_ GetWindowHeight();
SSDL_RenderTextCentered(SCREEN_WIDTH/2, SCREEN_HEIGHT/2,
                        "Blastoff!");
```

Or use it immediately:

```
SSDL_RenderTextCentered(SSDL_GetWindowWidth ()/2,
                        SSDL_GetWindowHeight()/2,
                        "Blastoff!");
```

- **You divided two integers to get a floating-point number between zero and one, but you got zero.** See Example 3-3 in this section. One of those operands of the / symbol should be cast to `float` or `double`.
- **You get a warning about conversion between types.** You can ignore it, but to make it go away, cast the offending item to what you wanted. Then the compiler will know it was intentional.

EXERCISES

1. Adjust the star in Example 3-4 so that the star's top point is straight up.
2. Make a clock face: a circle with numbers 1–12 in appropriate places.
3. (Harder) Here's how to get system time in seconds:

   ```
   #include <ctime>
   ...
   int timeInSeconds = static_cast<int>5(time(nullptr));
   ```

   Use % and / operators to find the current time in hours, minutes, and seconds. The hours may be off due to what time zone you're in; you can adjust appropriately.
4. ...and, having done Exercises 2 and 3, make a clock face that shows the current time.

[5] We cast to `int` to avoid that conversion warning mentioned in the "Antibugging" section above. The `time` function returns a `time_t` (whatever that is); we'll force it to be an `int`.

CHAPTER 4

Mouse and `if`

In this chapter we'll get mouse input and the art of making decisions, computer style.

Mouse Functions

Here's a program to detect where you clicked the mouse and report the result. Amazing, huh? Thus, we introduce three mouse functions: SSDL_GetMouseX, SSDL_GetMouseY, and SSDL_WaitMouse.

Example 4-1. A program to capture and show a mouse click. Excitement!

```
// Program to get a mouse click, and report its location
// -- from _C++26 for Lazy Programmers_

#include "SSDL.h"

int main(int argc, char** argv)
{
    sout << "Click the mouse and see where you clicked.\n";

    // Get the mouse click
    SSDL_WaitMouse();                 // wait for click...
    int xLocation = SSDL_GetMouseX(); // and get its location
    int yLocation = SSDL_GetMouseY();

    // Print the mouse click
    sout << "The X position of your click was "
         << xLocation << "\n";
    sout << "The Y position of your click was "
         << yLocation << "\n";
```


W. Briggs, *C++26 for Lazy Programmers*, https://doi.org/10.1007/979-8-8688-1859-2_4

```
    // End the program
    sout << "\nHit a key to end the program.\n";

    SSDL_WaitKey();

    return 0;
}
```

At this point

```
int xLocation = SSDL_GetMouseX();    // and get its location
int yLocation = SSDL_GetMouseY();
```

your program allocates space to store two integers, xLocation and yLocation, and puts a value in each.

And at this point the program prints them (Figure 4-1):

```
// Print the mouse click
sout << "The X position of your click was "
     << xLocation << "\n";
sout << "The Y position of your click was "
     << yLocation << "\n";
```

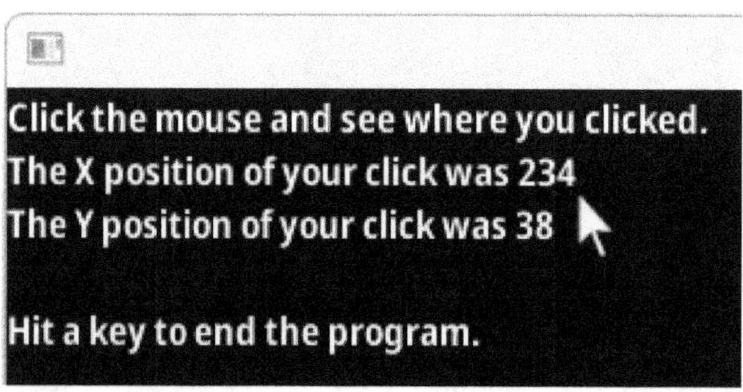

Figure 4-1. *Reporting a mouse click. Your click may vary*

In Table 4-1 are declarations for the new mouse functions.

Table 4-1. Basic mouse functions in SSDL

`int SSDL_GetMouseX();`	Return the X position of the mouse pointer.
`int SSDL_GetMouseY();`	Return the Y position of the mouse pointer.
`void SSDL_WaitMouse();`	Wait for any mouse button to be clicked.

Extra Where should you declare variables?

Putting them here

```
int main(int argc, char** argv)
{
  int xLocation=0;                // X and Y location
  int yLocation=0;                //   of mouse

  sout << "Click mouse & see where you clicked.\n";

  // Get the mouse click
  SSDL_WaitMouse ();              // wait for it...
  xLocation = SSDL_GetMouseX(); //   and get its
  yLocation = SSDL_GetMouseY(); //   location
   ...
```

instead of here

```
int main(int argc, char** argv)
{
  sout << "Click mouse & see where you clicked.\n";

  // Get the mouse click
  SSDL_WaitMouse ();                  // wait for it...
  int xLocation = SSDL_GetMouseX(); // and get its
  int yLocation = SSDL_GetMouseY(); // location
    ...
```

is an old-fashioned way of doing things, from when C++ was still just plain C. Some prefer it, because the variables are always easy to find: they're at the top! I don't, because

- I start looking for them where they're used, not at the top.
- I prefer to initialize them to useful values when possible (and in this case, that couldn't happen until after the `SSDL_WaitMouse` call).
- As this example shows, it leads to a need for more commenting.

The old way's not wrong, but "declare as late as possible" seems lazier.

Antibugging

- **The numbers reported for the mouse click don't have anything to do with where you actually clicked.** And your code looks like this:

  ```
  int xLocation = SSDL_GetMouseX(),
      yLocation = SSDL_GetMouseY(); // Get the location
  SSDL_WaitMouse();                 // wait for click...
  ```

  Thing is, `SSDL_GetMouseX` and `SSDL_GetMouseY` don't get a mouse *click* location; they just get a location. So here's what happens:

  ```
  1. The program gets the mouse X, Y location.
  2. You move the mouse where you want it while the program waits.
  3. You click.
  ```

  It gets the location *before* you move the mouse where it should go. No wonder it's wrong! Rearrange it thus:

  ```
  1. You move the mouse where you want it while the program waits.
  2. You click.
  3. The program gets the mouse X, Y location.
  ```

  ...as it was in Example 4-1.

EXERCISES

1. Write a program that lets you click twice to draw a line between your two mouse clicks.
2. Write a program that lets you click once to set the center of a circle and then again for a point on the edge of that circle; then it draws the circle.

`if`

So how can I determine if the mouse is in a particular area of the screen?

```
constexpr int HALF_SCREEN_WIDTH = 320;

if (xLocation < HALF_SCREEN_WIDTH)
    sout << It's on the left side of the screen.\n";
else
    sout << "It's on the right side of the screen.\n";
```

If `xLocation` is less than `HALF_SCREEN_WIDTH`, the program will tell us it's on the left; else, on the right.

The `else` part is optional. You can have the program report if `xLocation` is on the left and say nothing if it's on the right:

```
if (xLocation < HALF_SCREEN_WIDTH)
    sout << "It's on the left side of the screen.\n";
```

Note The general form of the `if` statement is

```
if (<condition>) <action 1> [else <action 2>]
```

where things in *<pointy brackets>* are blanks you'd fill in with something else and anything in *[square brackets]* can be omitted. This is called "Backus–Naur form" (BNF), and it's the conventional way to describe programming language structures.

The `if` statement does exactly what it looks like: if *condition* is true, it does *action 1*; else, it does *action 2*.

Naturally the `if` statement's condition must be something that can be true or false. It's often one of the true-or-false expressions in Table 4-2.

Table 4-2. *Using comparison operators in C++*

Condition	Meaning
X< Y	X is less than Y.
X <= Y	X is less than or equal to Y.
X> Y	X is greater than Y.
X >= Y	X is greater than or equal to Y.
X == Y	X is equal to Y. (X = Y, using a single =, means "store the value of Y in X.")
X != Y	X is not equal to Y.

You can also have the `if` part or the `else` part contain multiple actions:

```
if (xLocation < HALF_SCREEN_WIDTH)
{
    int howFarLeft = HALF_SCREEN_WIDTH - xLocation;
    sout << "It's this far left of the middle of the screen: "
         << howFarLeft << "\n.";
}
else
{
    int howFarRight = xLocation - HALF_SCREEN_WIDTH;
    sout << "It's this far right of the middle of the screen: "
         << howFarRight << "\n.";
}
```

The curly braces ({}) cause the compiler to bundle the actions within together and consider them one thing (the `if` action or the `else` action). If you declare a variable inside the {}'s - why not? - the variable only has definition within those {}'s; if you refer to it outside them, the compiler will tell you it's never heard of it: "`howFarLeft` not declared in this scope" or some such.

Note the indenting. Things contained in the if, whether in {}'s or not, are part of the if statement and are therefore indented relative to it – just as what's contained in main's {}'s is indented relative to it. Not indenting drives other programmers crazy:

```
if (xLocation < HALF_SCREEN_WIDTH)
{
int howFarLeft = HALF_SCREEN_WIDTH - xLocation; //Noooo!
sout << "It's this far left of the middle of the screen:";
sout << howFarLeft << ".\n";
}
```

Fortunately, your programmer-friendly editor will indent code for you: hit Enter at the end of a line and it'll take you where the next line should start. Unless (say) you forgot a semicolon and it got confused.

Extra There are different styles of layout for if. Here's a good way to string together if statements to handle exclusive options:

```
if      (x < 0) sign = -1; // it's positive
else if (x > 0) sign = +1; // it's negative
else            sign = 0;  // it's 0
```

Here's a common variation for if statements using {}'s:

```
if (xLocation < HALF_SCREEN_WIDTH) {
  // "Egyptian" brackets, so called because they
  //  look like where the Egyptian's hands are
  //  in Figure 4-2

  // I'd guess the Bangles' song "Walk Like an
  //  Egyptian" gave us this bit of silliness,
  //  but who knows

  int howFarLeft = HALF_SCREEN_WIDTH - xLocation;
  sout << "It's this far left of the middle "
       << "of the screen: ";
  sout << howFarLeft << ".\n";
}
```

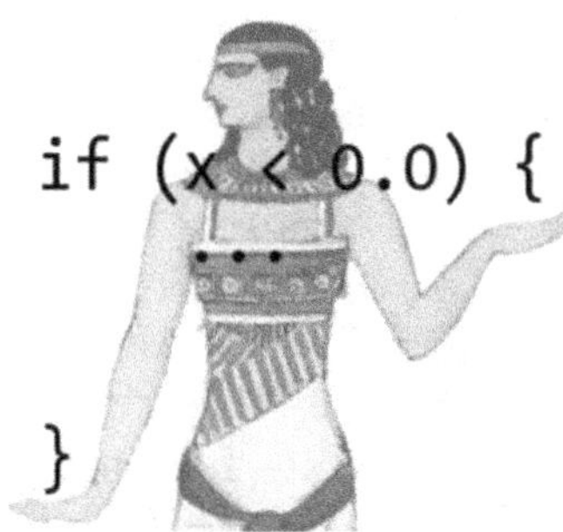

***Figure 4-2.** Where "Egyptian brackets" got the name*

The writer saved a line by putting the first { on the line with the condition. But it's harder to scan the left margin now and ensure that all the {}'s are matched. I won't say it's wrong, but I think you'll make fewer errors if you put each { and } on a line by itself.

Coercion and `if` Conditions (`if`'s Dirty Little Secret)

You probably won't *mean* to use something other than a true-or-false condition inside the `()`'s of an `if` statement ...but what if you did?

```
int x;
...
if (x) ...;
```

As it happens, C++ considers 0 to mean false and all other integers to mean true. So if `x` is 0, the `if` statement fails; otherwise, it executes.

If you meant to do that and it's clear, OK. But sometimes it sneaks up on us, as we see in the "Antibugging" section below.

Combining Conditions with &&, ||, and !

There's something else we can do with conditions: combine them. Consider these expressions:

- `X>0 && X<10`. The "&&" is read as "and." This means `X` is more than `0` *and* less than `10`.
- `X<=0 || X>=10`. The "||" is read as "or." This means `X` is either `0` or less, or it's `10` or more.
- `! (X<0)`. The "`!`" is read as "not." This means it isn't true that `X` is less than `0`. (You need the `()`'s. If you type `! X < 0`, C++'s precedence rules make it interpret this as `(! X) < 0`. Go figure.)

The odd look of these operators (why "&&" rather than "&" or "and"?) is a historical artifact. You get used to it.[1]

---

[1] We also have single & and single | as operators (see Chapter 25) – but that's another matter.

So, to adapt the earlier example, here's a way of seeing if the mouse click stored in `xLocation` and `yLocation` is in the upper left of the screen:

```
if ((xLocation < HALF_SCREEN_WIDTH) &&
    (yLocation < HALF_SCREEN_HEIGHT))
    sout << "That's in the upper left quadrant.";
```

Antibugging

- **The condition always fails or always succeeds, though you're sure it shouldn't,** like this:

  ```
  // Cinderella must leave the dance at midnight.
  //    Does she have time?
                                // 3 p.m. -- plenty of time!
  int minutesLeftTillMidnight = 32400;

                               // Warn her if time's up
  if (minutesLeftTillMidnight = 0)
     sout << "It's midnight! Cinderella, go home now!\n";

                               // Print time left
  sout << "You have " << minutesLeftTillMidnight
       << " minutes left.\n";
  ```

  This reports she has 0 minutes left - which is wrong! - and if she did, shouldn't it have warned her to go home?

  The problem is the condition. `minutesLeftTillMidnight = 0`, as we know, means store 0 in `minutesLeftTillMidnight`. So we alter the variable when we shouldn't.

  But we're not done yet! Now the `if` statement must decide whether the condition is true. No problem: 0 is false, and we just got a zero value between the parentheses, so the `if` doesn't fire and Cinderella, despite losing all her time, doesn't get her warning.

  We meant `minutesLeftTillMidnight == 0`. This is the infamous **double-equals error**. It has its own name because everybody does it.

Solution: Try not to, and don't hit yourself when you do. The compiler may warn you. It's a Good Thing to notice compiler warnings.

- **It does the action in the if, even if the condition is false.** Maybe you put a ; after the condition.

```
if (2+2==5);
   sout << "Orwell was right: "
        << the Party even controls math!\n";
```

; signals that the statement you're working on is over. C++ interprets the above code as if 2+2==5, do nothing (since nothing is what comes next, before the ;). After that, print that Orwell was right.

Solution: Remove the first ;.

- **It does the later actions in the if, even if the condition is false.**

```
if (2+2==5)
   sout << "Orwell was right: "
        << the Party even controls math!\n";
   sout << "2+2==5 if I say it does!\n";
```

This code will print

```
2+2==5 if I say it does!
```

Since there are no {}'s, C++ doesn't bundle those two sout statements together as the things to do if the condition succeeds. It interprets the statements as if the condition succeeds, print that Orwell was right. Then, whatever happens, print 2+2==5. Solution:

```
if (2+2==5)
{
   sout << "Orwell was right: "
        << the Party even controls math!\n";
   sout << "2+2==5 if I say it does!\n";
}
```

The last two problems were exacerbated by *correct* indenting, which made it look like everything was OK. The editor can help prevent that.

Tip When using a programmer-friendly editor, if you find yourself correcting the editor's indenting, it may have found a punctuation error. You can trace the weird indenting back to the problem.

- **You can't figure which if an else goes with.**

  ```
  if (TodayIsSaturday)
      if (IAmAtWork)
          sout << "I need a life.\n";
  else
         sout << "Life is good.\n";
  ```

  What do we do if today isn't Saturday? Print "Life is good."? Which `if` does the `else` go with? Indenting doesn't matter to the compiler. The compiler needs a clear rule, and here it is: *the* `else` *always goes with the most recent* `if`. In this case, "Life is good." is printed if `TodayIsSaturday` is `true` but `IAmAtWork` is false. If today isn't Saturday, the code prints nothing.

  This ambiguity is called the **dangling else problem**, and most languages solve it just as C++ does here.

- **It fails to accurately process whether something's in a range.**

  ```
  int x = 100;
  if (0 <= x < 10) sout << "Single digit number here!\n";
  ```

  $0 \leq x < 10$ works fine in math, but C++ thinks differently. Here's what it does:

  - Reading left to right, it first evaluates `0 <= x`. This is true, so the result is `true` (`1`).
  - Next, it compares that result to 10. `1 < 10` evaluates to `true`. So the whole thing results in `true`.

  This fixes the problem:

  ```
  if (0 <= x && x < 10) // if 0<=x *and* x < 10
  ```

EXERCISES

1. Write code to report whether the square root of some X is greater than 1.
2. Given two integers, report what order they're in (correct order, reverse order, or equal).
3. Given a numeric score for a grade, 0–100, print whether it's an A, B, C, D, or F.
4. Write an if statement that will print whether a mouse click is in the upper-left quarter of the screen, the upper right, the lower left, or the lower right.
5. Write code that will print "Out of range!" if X is less than 0 or greater than 8 – and will force it to be in range (by changing X to 0 if it's too small and to 8 if it's too big).

Boolean Values and Variables

If we can use true-or-false values in our `if` statements, can we also store them in a variable for later use? Sure. Here's one:

```
bool isRaining = true;
               // bool means "It's got to be true or false;
               // nothing else allowed"
```

And here is how you might use it:

```
if (isRaining) sout << "I need an umbrella.\n";
```

Tip I usually start `bool` variable names with `is`, so it's obvious the value should be true or false.

The possible values for a Boolean variable are – wait for it – `true` and `false`.

You can also calculate these values in expressions, as you can with `int` or `double` or `float` variables:

```
bool isTooHotForGolf = (temperature > 85);
```

But if you prefer to use an `if`, that also works:

```
bool isTooHotForGolf;
if (temperature > 85) isTooHotForGolf = true;
else                  isTooHotForGolf = false;
```

Why would you want Boolean variables? For convenience and clarity. Suppose you want to find out if it's a good day for golf, but you're really finicky. You can say

```
if (windSpeed<10 &&
    (cloudCover>50 && (temperature>75 && temperature<85) ||
    (cloudCover<50 && (temperature>60 && temperature<75)))
          // Aaaigh!  What does this mean?
```

or you can initialize some `bool` variables and say

```
if (isCalm && ((isCloudy && isWarm) || (isSunny && isCool)))
    // Cloudy & warm or sunny & cool -- as long as it's calm
```

I think I've proved my point.

Extra George Boole (1815–1864) is the founder of modern symbolic logic: that is, using symbols as variables that can be true or false.

Prior to Boole, there certainly was an understanding of logic, but people were unsure that you could express logical expressions without reference to the meaning and not run the risk of error. (Some may have a hard time trusting that, say, "p and q implies p," but have no trouble with "If it's raining and cold, it's raining.") Even Boole was cautious: in the introduction to his book *The Mathematical Analysis of Logic*, he anticipated arguments that what he was doing was a really bad idea, but suggested it might not be totally useless. He was right: it was a resounding success, and the computer in front of you as you program is evidence of it.

EXERCISES

1. Wait for a mouse click, and set a Boolean variable to true if the X is greater than the Y. Report whether it was by printing a message on the screen.
2. Get two mouse clicks, and set Boolean variables for whether the second is to the right of the first and whether it's below the first. Then report the second's relation to the first as north, northeast, east, southeast, or whatever's correct.

A Hidden-Object Game

Somewhere in a field of rocks (Figure 4-3) is a fossilized ammonite. We'll make a game to train budding paleontologists: click the screen, and if you get the fossil, you win.

Figure 4-3. *An image to search. The fossil's in there somewhere ...*

What we need is a sort of imaginary "bounding" box around it: if I click in the box, I win; elsewhere, I lose. It's too hard to guess the coordinates of the box. Maybe I can draw a box on the image, and if it looks wrong, adjust. My wrong guess is in Example 4-2.

Example 4-2. Drawing a box on the screen, to find the bounding box we want for part of the image. Output is in Figure 4-4.

```
// Program to draw a box around a fossil,
//     to find its coordinates
//          -- from _C++26 for Lazy Programmers_

#include "SSDL.h"

int main(int argc, char** argv)
{
    // Resize window to fit the background image
    SSDL_SetWindowSize(500, 375);          // image is 500x375
    SSDL_SetWindowTitle
        ("A box to enclose the fossil -- hit a key to end");

    // Load up the world to find fossil in
    const SSDL_Image BACKGROUND
                = SSDL_LoadImage ("media/ammonitePuzzle.jpg");
    SSDL_RenderImage(BACKGROUND, 0, 0);

    // arguments below mean: left x, top y, width, height
    SSDL_RenderDrawRect(375, 175, 80, 50); // first guess

    // End program
    SSDL_WaitKey ();

    return 0;
}
```

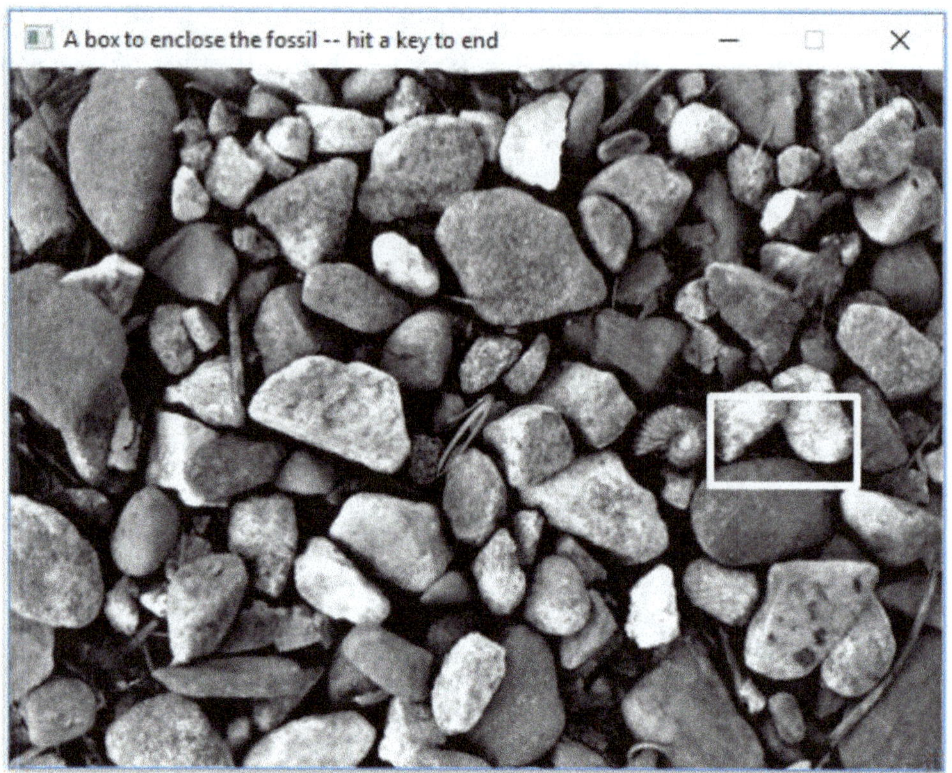

Figure 4-4. *Looks like the bounding box for the ammonite needs some changes (I adjusted the lines' thickness to make it easier to see)*

After some playing around I get a new bounding box, the one that results in Figure 4-5:

```
SSDL_RenderDrawRect(335, 180, 45, 35); // corrected numbers
```

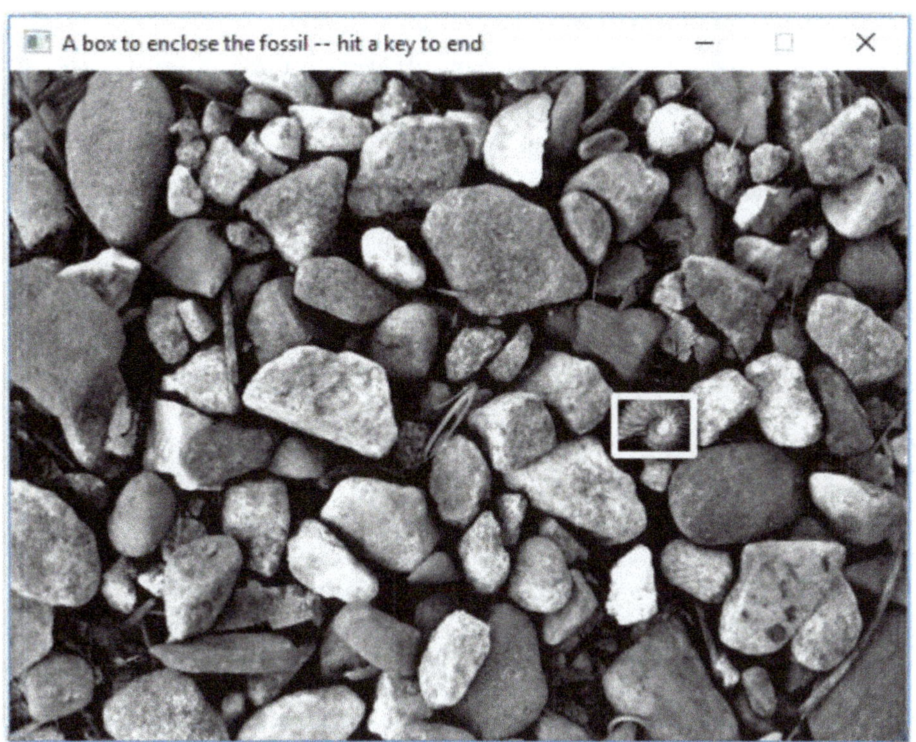

Figure 4-5. *The bounding box is correct*

So now we'll have a program that detects whether a mouse click is inside that box. It uses a couple of Boolean variables, and it flashes the bounding box in red and white if you win (Example 4-3).

Example 4-3. My fossil-hunt game: trying to find an object with a mouse. Figure 4-6 shows possible output.

```
// Program to find a fossil in a field of stones
//                -- from _C++26 for Lazy Programmers_

#include "SSDL.h"

int main(int argc, char** argv)
{
    // Set up window
    constexpr int PICTURE_WIDTH=500, PICTURE_HEIGHT=375;
                                 // size of the picture
```

```
constexpr int WINDOW_WIDTH =500, WINDOW_HEIGHT =450;
                        // size of entire window
                        // (has extra room for messages)
SSDL_SetWindowTitle("Fossil hunt: a hidden-object game");
SSDL_SetWindowSize (WINDOW_WIDTH, WINDOW_HEIGHT);

// Load up the world to find the fossil in
const SSDL_Image BACKGROUND
           = SSDL_LoadImage("media/ammonitePuzzle.jpg");
SSDL_RenderImage(BACKGROUND, 0, 0);

// Print instructions to the user
SSDL_SetCursor(0, PICTURE_HEIGHT);
sout << "Where's the ammonite?  Click it to win.\n";

// Get that mouse click
SSDL_WaitMouse();

// See where we clicked, and report if fossil was found
// I got these numbers by running the 2-searchBox program
constexpr int BOX_LEFT = 335, BOX_TOP    = 180;
constexpr int BOX_WIDTH=  45, BOX_HEIGHT=  35;

int x= SSDL_GetMouseX(), y = SSDL_GetMouseY();

// Is X between left side of box and right?
// Is Y also within bounds?
bool isXInRange = (BOX_LEFT< x && x< BOX_LEFT+BOX_WIDTH );
bool isYInRange = (BOX_TOP < y && y< BOX_TOP +BOX_HEIGHT);

if (isXInRange && isYInRange)
{
    sout << "You found the ammonite! Here's your Ph.D.\n";

    // Now we'll flash where the fossil was
    SSDL_SetRenderDrawColor(RED);
    SSDL_RenderDrawRect(BOX_LEFT, BOX_TOP,
                        BOX_WIDTH, BOX_HEIGHT);
    SSDL_Delay(250); // 250 msec, or 1/4 sec

    SSDL_SetRenderDrawColor(WHITE);
```

```
        SSDL_RenderDrawRect(BOX_LEFT, BOX_TOP,
                            BOX_WIDTH, BOX_HEIGHT);
        SSDL_Delay(250); // 250 msec, or 1/4 sec

        SSDL_SetRenderDrawColor(RED);
        SSDL_RenderDrawRect(BOX_LEFT, BOX_TOP,
                            BOX_WIDTH, BOX_HEIGHT);
        SSDL_Delay(250); // 250 msec, or 1/4 sec

        SSDL_SetRenderDrawColor(WHITE);
        SSDL_RenderDrawRect(BOX_LEFT, BOX_TOP,
                            BOX_WIDTH, BOX_HEIGHT);
        SSDL_Delay(250); // 250 msec, or 1/4 sec
    }
    else
        sout << "You lose.\n";

    // End program
    sout << "Hit a key to end.";

    SSDL_WaitKey ();

    return 0;
}
```

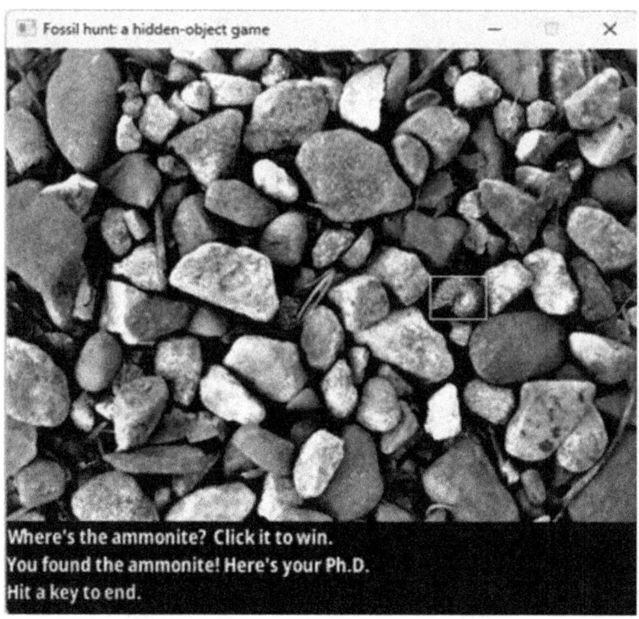

Figure 4-6. *The completed fossil-hunt game*

EXERCISES

1. Write a program that displays a box, waits for a mouse click, and tells you whether you clicked within the box.

   To make it more fun, put up a roughly square image of something interesting. I like Spam. Special thanks to the creative people who made "Find the Spam" (`www.smalltime.com/findthespam/`) for this surreal game.

2. Make a hidden-object game: the user must click the objects you provide (have two or more) in order to win. You can require the user to do it in order. A click on something that *isn't* one of the objects, or isn't the correct object in order, ends the game in a loss.

   You may consider each object to be a square area on the screen.

3. Write a program that draws a bubble wherever you clicked. Always the same-size bubble …but it won't let you put one *partly* on the screen. If you click too close to an edge, it moves the bubble away from the edge enough that it does not cross the edge. You might also add a sound effect when you create a bubble.

CHAPTER 5

Loops, Input, and char

In this chapter we'll look at repeated actions, input, and things to do with the character type.

Keyboard Input

Consider this code:

```
int ageInYears;
sout << "How old are you? "; ssin >> ageInYears;
```

This prints the query about age and then waits for keyboard input. If the user enters a number, that number is stored in ageInYears. (Anything else is likely to give ageInYears a 0 value.) ssin[1] waits for you to hit Enter before it processes input, so backspacing is allowed.

ssin uses the same font and cursor as sout; they are both part of SSDL.

You may note how the << arrows go: with sout, they go from the value to the output; with ssin, they go from the input to the variable.

This is as good a time as any to introduce a new basic type: char, or character. Examples of chars include 'A' and 'a' (which are distinct), '?', '1', ' ' (the space character), and '\n'. Here is some code that uses a char variable:

```
char answer;
sout << "Are you sure (Y/N)? "; ssin >> answer;
if (answer == 'y')
    sout << "Are you *really* sure?\n";
```

[1] I could have called it sin and waited for the puns to start, but sin already means something in C++: the sine function. "S-in" might be a good way to pronounce it.

W. Briggs, *C++26 for Lazy Programmers*, https://doi.org/10.1007/979-8-8688-1859-2_5

You can also chain things you're reading in with >> :

```
ssin >> firstThingReadIn >> secondThingReadIn;
```

Whether reading chars or numbers or whatever, ssin skips whitespace (spaces, tabs, and returns); so you can type what you want with spaces between, and it can handle it.

Here's a sample program that finds ways to insult you no matter what your response (Example 5-1). Figure 5-1 shows a sample session.

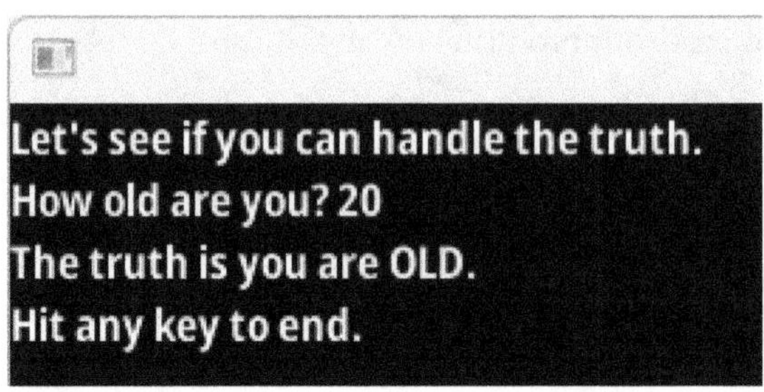

Figure 5-1. *Insulting the world, one person at a time*

Example 5-1. A program using ssin

```
// Program to insult the user
//     based on input
//        -- from _C++26 for Lazy Programmers_

#include "SSDL.h"

int main(int argc, char** argv)
{
    int ageInYears = 0;

    sout << "Let's see if you can handle the truth.\n";
    sout << "How old are you? "; ssin >> ageInYears;

    bool isOlder = (ageInYears >= 20);
    // Seriously? Well, 20 *is* old if you're a computer program

    if (isOlder) sout << "The truth is you are OLD.\n";
    else         sout << "You're not old enough. Sorry, kid.\n";
```

```
    sout << "Hit any key to end.\n";

    SSDL_WaitKey();

    return 0;
}
```

Antibugging

- **You get a string of error messages like this**[2]

```
main.cpp: In function 'int main(int, char**)':
main.cpp:11:39: error: no match for 'operator<<' (operand types
are 'std::istream' {aka 'std::basic_istream<char>'} and 'int')
     sout << "How old are you? "; ssin << ageInYears;
                                  ~~~~~^~~~~~~~~~~~~
main.cpp:11:39: note: candidate: 'operator<<(int, int)' <built-in>
main.cpp:11:39: note:   no known conversion for argument 1 from
'std::istream' {aka 'std::basic_istream<char>'} to 'int'
In file included from /usr/include/c++/8/string:52,
                 from /usr/include/c++/8/bits/locale_classes.h:40,
                 from /usr/include/c++/8/bits/ios_base.h:41,
                 from /usr/include/c++/8/ios:42,
                 from /usr/include/c++/8/istream:38,
                 from /usr/include/c++/8/sstream:38,
                 from ../../external/SSDL/include/SSDL_display.h:26,
                 from ../../external/SSDL/include/SSDL.h:27,
                 from main.cpp:4:
/usr/include/c++/8/bits/basic_string.h:6323:5: note: candidate:
'template<class _CharT, class _Traits, class _Alloc> std::basic_
ostream<_CharT, _Traits>& std::operator<<(std::basic_ostream<_
CharT, _Traits>&, const std::__cxx11::basic_string<_CharT, _
Traits, _Alloc>&)'
```

[2] This is from the g++ compiler. Visual Studio gave me three lines and clearly identified << as the problem. Nice!

```
operator<<(basic_ostream<_CharT, _Traits>& __os,
^~~~~~~~
```

and then literally pages more. Good luck decoding that.

It all came from one error: the `>>`'s went the wrong way on an `ssin` statement. It should have been `ssin << ageInYears`. Compilers sometimes get confused.

You may get another flood of errors if you try to `ssin >> "\n"` or something else that isn't a variable.

EXERCISES

1. Write a program for converting inches to centimeters, using the formula centimeters = 2.54*inches. Make it interactive, that is, ask the user for the value to convert.

2. Write a program that identifies what generation you're in (`Gen Z`, `millennial`, etc.), based on the age or year of birth the user inputs. You get to pick the ranges.

3. The Body Mass Index (BMI) tells you if you're heavy, thin, or in the middle. (It's imprecise, but if nothing else, maybe I could convince my grandmother I won't starve if I don't take seconds.)

   Per Wikipedia, these are the ranges:

Underweight	Less than 18.5
Normal weight	18.5–25
Overweight	25–30
Obese	30+

   So write a program to calculate the user's BMI. The formula is

   BMI = Weight in kg / (Height in meters)^2

If you're in a country that uses English units, you'll also need this information: 1 kg = 2.2 pounds; 1 meter = 39.37 inches.

4. Write a program that asks the user for two times (such as 1:06 or 12:19) and prints the difference neatly (11:03, e.g., or 0:40, but not 13:0 or –12:70). You provide the times with keyboard input – we're not asking the *computer* what time it is.

5. ...but now we are. Instead of asking the user for the times, *measure* the two times that the user hits the return key, getting the current system time like so:

   ```
   int myTime = time (nullptr);
   ```

   This gives you time in seconds since midnight, January 1, 1970 (on systems I know). You'll need to `#include <ctime>`.

while and do-while

The program can do something *if* a condition is true ...or it can do something *while* a condition is true.

Here's a way to determine how many times you can divide a number by 10 before you get 1. (This will be the same as the number of digits in the number if you print it.)

```
int digits = 0;
while (number > 1)          // while we haven't reached 1
{
    number /= 10;           // divide it by 10
    digits += 1;            // that's one more digit!
}
```

In Backus-Naur form (BNF), the `while` statement is

```
while (<condition>) <action>
```

As long as the condition is true, the while loop will execute the action. When it stops being true, the loop ends, and the program moves on to whatever comes after.

There's a variation on while, exactly the same except that it checks the condition *after* doing the action: do-while. Its BNF form is

```
do <action> while (<condition>)
```

and an example is

```
do
{
    sout << "Ready to rumble (Y/N)? "; ssin >> answer;
}
while (answer != 'n' && answer != 'y');
    // while answer isn't yes or no, ask again and again

if (answer == 'y')
    ... // rumble!
```

That wouldn't work as a while statement

```
while (answer != 'n' && answer != 'y') ...
```

because you don't know what answer is until you've asked at least once.

The bottom line is that do-while does the action at least once (before testing the condition), whereas while *might* quit before taking any action at all. We usually use while, but sometimes do-while is the very thing we need. Thus, we have the Golden Rule of Loops:

Golden Rule of Loops (Version 1)

If you want the loop to execute at least once, use do-while.

If it makes any sense for it to execute zero times, use while.

Loops with SSDL

There's something I didn't tell you about SSDL. It doesn't update the screen every time you draw or print. To save update time, it puts this off till it has a reason to wait on the user: an ssin statement or an SSDL_WaitKey or SSDL_WaitMouse. The loop below, which is intended to keep showing you "Move mouse to right half of screen to end." until you move the mouse to the right, will never display anything:

```
while (SSDL_GetMouseX() < WHERE_IT_IS)
{
    SSDL_RenderClear ();
    SSDL_SetCursor (0, 0);
    sout << "Move mouse to right half of screen to continue.";
}
```

SSDL also doesn't check for things that make it quit the program - hitting Escape or clicking the X to kill the window - until it's waiting on you. So the code above won't let you quit, either.

The fix is the same for both problems: the function `SSDL_IsQuitMessage`. It updates the screen, checks for input messages (mouse clicks, keystrokes), and returns whether there's been a command to quit:

```
while (! SSDL_IsQuitMessage() && SSDL_GetMouseX() < WHERE_IT_IS)
{
    SSDL_RenderClear();
    SSDL_SetCursor(0, 0);
    sout << "Move mouse to right half of screen to continue.";
}
```

Here's the ready-to-rumble do-while loop from earlier, adapted to allow the user to quit easily. Both it and the while loop above are in a source code example `ch3/loops-with-SSDL`:

```
do
{
    sout << "Ready to rumble (Y/N)? "; ssin >> answer;
}
while (!SSDL_IsQuitMessage() && (answer != 'n' && answer != 'y'));
```

Extra In that last do-while loop, we could ask the user to type 1 for yes and 2 for no, if we wanted to expose ourselves as user-hostile throwbacks to the 1970s and never get hired again. (What does 2 have to do with "no"?) It's much easier on the user to remember that `'n'` means no.

If there are more options to choose than yes and no – say, your program manipulates files, opening, saving, and renaming – it's still **user-friendly** to give options with letters (O, S, and R) rather than numbers.

How to make your programs easy to interact with is the subject of one sub-field of computer science: human–computer interaction.

---

break and continue

break means leave the loop immediately. Here's a version of the above while loop, now using break. You decide which way's clearer:

```
while (SSDL_GetMouseX() < WHERE_IT_IS)
{
    if (! isQuitMessage ()) break;
    SSDL_RenderClear ();
    SSDL_SetCursor (0, 0);
    sout << "Move mouse to right half of screen to end.";
}
```

continue means skip the rest of this iteration of the loop and go back to the top. I rarely use it.

Some programming-style mavens are horrified by break and continue. They think you should be able to look at the loop's continuation condition and see immediately under what circumstance the loop can end – essentially, that these keywords reduce clarity. I agree clarity is crucial, but I'm not sure break is the problem. Certainly if a loop is 50 lines long, it'll be tedious to examine it for breaks. But I think the solution is not to have loops 50 lines long. Simple is good.

Antibugging

- **The program won't end, and you can't even kill the program.** You're probably stuck in a loop, but how do you stop it? First try Ctrl-C (hold Ctrl down and hit C). If that doesn't work, try these actions:

- **Visual Studio**: Debug ➤ Stop Debugging, or hit the reddish square for stop near the top of the window.
- **MinGW**: Kill it with Task Manager.
- **Unix**: If you don't even have a command prompt, hit Ctrl-Z in the command window to get it.

There are two commands that can help us. ps lists active processes:

```
PID TTY          TIME CMD
14972 pts/0    00:00:00 bash
15046 pts/0    00:00:00 bash
15047 pts/0    00:00:01 a.out
15054 pts/0    00:00:00 ps
```

kill -9 <process-id> means something like "I tried, but I can't find a nice way to end this process, so just kill it." The -9 says "I really mean it."

a.out is what we're trying to kill, but if we ran it with a script like runx, we'll want that gone too. It's probably the most recent shell command, some command with "sh" in its name. (Get the wrong one and you may kill your terminal. Oops.) This command will kill it and its dependent process a.out:

```
kill -9 15046
```

- **The loop repeats forever, and you can't quit.** Maybe it isn't checking for quit messages. Make your loop condition look like this

```
while (! SSDL_IsQuitMessage () &&
                    ...whatever else you want to check... )
    ...;
```

or, if it's a do-while,

```
do
{
    ...
}
while (! isQuitMessage () && ...);
```

- **The loop repeats forever until you hit quit** or does something forever that you wanted done a few times.

  Consider under what condition you break the loop. It must be that it's never met:

  ```
  int rectanglesDrawn = 0;
  while (!SSDL_IsQuitMessage () &&
                rectanglesDrawn < MAX_RECTANGLES)
  {
      SSDL_RenderDrawRect (...);
  }
  ```

  The loop never incremented `rectanglesDrawn` ...so no matter how many you draw, the loop doesn't end. This line should do it:

  ```
      ...
      rectanglesDrawn += 1;
  }
  ```

- **The loop repeats forever or won't repeat when it should.** It's easy to get confused when the loop has a combination of conditions:

  ```
  do
  {
      sout << "Answer Y or N: "; ssin >> answer;
  }
  while (! isQuitMessage () && (answer != 'n' || answer != 'y'));
  ```

  This may look right, but it actually says: keep looping while nobody said quit, and the answer is not yes *or* not no. Well, it's always either not yes *or* not no! Suppose it's yes: then "not no" is true, so it keeps going. Suppose it's no: then "not yes" is true, so it keeps going.

  The solution is to keep going while it's not yes *and* it's also not no – while it's a nonsensical answer like `'7'` or `'X'`:

```
do
{
    sout << "Answer Y or N: "; ssin >> answer;
}
while (! isQuitMessage () && (answer != 'n' && answer != 'y'));
```

EXERCISES

1. Have the user to keep entering a number until successfully guessing some number you pick.
2. ...and have the program print how many guesses it took.
3. Write a program that asks for a (capital) letter and counts from 'A' till it finds it. Its output will be something like `'E' is the 5th letter of the alphabet!`
4. ...now adapt the program so it keeps repeating till you give it a '.' to end.
5. Write a program that draws a bubble wherever you click. The bubble's size should depend on how long since the last mouse click. Use the Internet to read up on the function `SDL_GetTicks()`.
6. Update Exercise 2 from the end of the previous chapter – the hidden-object game – so the user can click the hidden objects in any order.
7. Make your own music player: put boxes marked "Music on" and "Music off" near the bottom of the screen, and turn sound on or off appropriately when the user clicks the boxes.

For Loops

A for loop is a loop that counts through a range. Here's a simple one:

```
for (int count=0; count < 10; count += 1)
    sout << count << ' '; // print these numbers, separated by spaces
```

And here's its output:

```
0 1 2 3 4 5 6 7 8 9
```

In Backus–Naur form, a for loop is

```
for (<initialization section>; <continuing-condition>; <increment>)
    <action>
```

Let's look at that piece by piece.

The **initialization section** – int count=0, above – is done when the loop starts. As you can see, you can declare variables in it. The variables are only visible inside the loop.

As long as the **continuing condition** is true, the loop continues.

At the end of each time through the loop, each "iteration," C++ does the **increment** part. This could be anything, but it usually increments an index variable (i.e., the variable we're using to count with).

The order that the computer does the sections is

1. do <initialization section>
2. is <continuing-condition> true? If not, leave the loop
3. do <action>
4. do <increment-section>
5. go back to step 2

Increment Operators

We often find we need to add 1 to a variable. (Or subtract 1.) C++ provides operators for this. Here are two examples:

```
++y; //  adds 1 to y. This is called "increment."
--x; //  subtracts 1 from x. This is called "decrement."
```

Most computers have a built-in instruction to add 1 and another to subtract 1 – so we're telling the compiler to use them. It's efficient.

We often do this in for loops, like so:

```
for (int count=0; count < 10; ++count)
    sout << count << ' ';
```

We can also use decrement operators:

```
for (int count=10; count > 0; --count) // A countdown, 10 to 1...
    sout << count << ' ';
sout << "Liftoff!\n";
```

You can increment by other amounts, though it's unusual:

```
for (int count=2; count <= 8; count += 2) // 2 4 6 8...
    sout << count << ' ';
sout << "Who do we appreciate?\n";
```

There's another type of increment, called "post-increment," and a corresponding post-decrement. It looks like this: `count++`, not `++count`. Here's how they differ:

Pre-increment: `Y = ++X` means `X = X+1; Y = X`. That is, add 1 to X; Y gets X's new value, and then use the value of X (copy it to Y).

Post-increment: `Y = X++` means `Y = X; X = X+1`. That is, add 1 to X; Y gets X's *old* value.

You won't notice the difference unless you put the expression on the right side of an = or as an argument to a function.

An Example: Averaging Numbers

Suppose you want to average a list of ten numbers given by the user. I know: how exciting. But we can't play games *all* the time; people will start thinking programming is too much fun and pay us less. Here's my plan:

```
tell the user what we're doing

total = 0                                  // so far, nothing in the total...

for ten times
    get a number from the user
    add that to the total

average = total/10.0  // floating-point division, for a floating-point answer
                            // better not use int division -- remember
                   // Example 3-3 (drawing a star), in which our division
                              // answers kept showing up as zeroes...
print average
```

Here's my program.

Example 5-2. A program to average numbers, using a for loop

```
// Program to average numbers
//        -- from _C++26 for Lazy Programmers_

#include "SSDL.h"

int main(int argc, char** argv)
{
    constexpr int MAX_NUMBERS = 10;

    sout << "Enter " << MAX_NUMBERS
         << " numbers to get an average.\n";

    double total = 0.0;

    // Get the numbers
    for (int i = 0; i < MAX_NUMBERS; ++i)
    {
        double number;

        sout << "Enter the next number:  ";
        ssin >> number;

        total += number;
    }

    // Print the average
    double average = total / MAX_NUMBERS;
    sout << "The average is " << average << ".\n";

    sout << "Hit any key to end.\n";
    SSDL_WaitKey();

    return 0;
}
```

The keywords `break` and `continue` work in for loops just as they do in while and do-while loops. They're available, but not, in my experience, useful.

So we now have three kinds of loops. You know how to decide between while and do-while - the Golden Rule of Loops, earlier in this chapter. What about for loops?

By convention and by reason, we use for loops when we're counting through a range - when we know what we're counting from and to. Thus, we have the final Golden Rule of Loops:

Golden Rule of Loops (Final Version)

If you know in advance how many times you'll do it, use `for`. Otherwise:

If you want the loop to execute at least once, use `do-while`.

If it makes any sense for it to execute zero times, use `while`.

Antibugging

- **Later actions are done once, not many times**. A common problem. Here's an example:

  ```
  // Code to print several powers of 2
  int product = 1;
  sout << "Here are several successive powers of 2: ";
  for (int i = 0; i < 10; ++i)
      sout << product << ' ';
      product *= 2;
  ```

  I forgot the {}'s. I assumed the code would do this:

  ```
  for i goes from 0 through 9
      print product
      multiply product by 2
  ```

  But it actually does this:

  ```
  for i goes from 0 through 9
      print product
  multiply product by 2
  ```

To prevent this, let your editor indent for you as you go, thus catching the error.

- ***No* action gets repeated.**

```
for (int i = 0; i < N; ++i);     // This loop prints only one *
    sout << '*';
```

There's an extra `;` at the end of the first line.

- **Your loop goes one step too far.**

```
for (int i = 0; i <=4; ++i) ...
```

The last time through, `++i` makes `i` equal 4. But if you wanted 4 entries, you just got 5: 0, 1, 2, 3, 4. Solution: Use < for the condition.

To be sure you have the right range, trace through the code *before* compiling. Or always use the form

```
for (int i = 0; i < howManyTimes; ++i) ...
```

Tip For loops almost always start at 0 and use <, not <=, for the continuation condition: `i < howManyTimes`, not `i <= howManyTimes`.

EXERCISES

1. Print the numbers 1–10 ...and their squares (first 20 square integers: 1, 4, 9, 16, etc.).
2. Using characters now, use a for loop to print the letters A–Z.
3. ...backward.
4. Write a program like the average program in Example 5-2, but let it provide not average, but maximum.
5. Adapt Example 3-2, the one with the diving board, to use a for loop rather than repeating the code to draw the diver.

6. Adapt Example 3-3/Example 3-4 (drawing a star) so that it asks the user for the radius, center, and number of points – and uses a for loop to draw the lines.
7. Write a program that asks the user for an integer and a power to raise it to and prints the result. Calculate with for, of course.
8. Write a program to ask the user for N times (times as in 2:30), summing to get total hours and minutes.
9. Write a program that has the user guess a number (that number can be a `constexpr`) and keeps taking guesses until the user runs out of turns – you decide how many – or gets it right. Then it reports success or failure. You'll need a Boolean variable `isSuccess`.
10. (Hard) Draw a graph of some function (sine is a good one). Add X and Y axes and appropriate labels.
11. According to Archimedes, and he's right, you can approximate π by getting the perimeter of a polygon of many sides. So write a program that illustrates this, thus:

    Give it a radius and a number of sides, and have it draw a regular polygon with that many sides and that radius. (Hint: You can do this with the star-drawing function from earlier.)

    Since a circle's perimeter is 2πr, you can now approximate π as perimeter/2r. Is it close? Does it help to have more sides?

chars and cctype

Example 5-3 compares two input characters to see whether they're given in alphabetical order.

Example 5-3. A program to compare characters

```
// Program to tell if two letters are in alphabetical order
//        -- from _C++26 for Lazy Programmers_

#include "SSDL.h"
```

```
int main(int argc, char** argv)
{
    char char1, char2;

    sout << "Give me a letter: "; ssin >> char1;
    sout << "Give me another: ";  ssin >> char2;

    if      (char1 < char2)
        sout << "You gave me two characters in order.\n";
    else if (char1 > char2)
        sout << "They are in reverse order.\n";
    else
        sout << "It's the same letter.\n";

    SSDL_WaitKey();

    return 0;
}
```

It mostly works. It's a little strange that 'a' comes after 'Z.' But that's how the computer thinks of it: lowercase letters, a–z, come after the uppercase range. The precise ordering of the characters was decided in 1967 and is maintained by the American National Standards Institute (ANSI). You can surely find a complete listing of this American Standard Code for Information Interchange (ASCII) codes online.

I'd rather my comparison ignore capitalization. Here's one way – convert it to uppercase:

```
char myChar            = 'b';
char upperCaseVersion = myChar - 'a' + 'A';
```

It looks weird, but ...to get the uppercase version of `'b'`, we do this: subtract `'a'` first. This gives us a difference of `1`, of course. We then add this `1` to `'A'`, which gives us `'B'`. This will work for any lowercase letter.

What if we aren't sure it's lowercase? We can use an `if` statement to be sure:

```
if (myChar >= 'a' && myChar <= 'z') // if it's lower case -- fix it
    upperCaseVersion = myChar - 'a' + 'A';
else                                // if not -- leave it alone
    upperCaseVersion = myChar;
```

This is so useful we'll want to do it again and again. Fortunately, the makers of C and C++ agree. They've given us a suite of functions for handling capitalization and a few other qualities of characters; these are found in the include file `cctype`. Some are in Table 5-1; for more such functions see Appendix E.

Table 5-1. *Some useful functions regarding capitalization*

`int islower(int ch);`	Return whether `ch` is lowercase. (Non-letter characters are not lowercase.)
`int isupper(int ch);`	Return whether `ch` is uppercase. (Non-letter characters are not uppercase.)
`int tolower(int ch);`	Return the lowercase version of `ch`. If `ch` is not a letter, it returns `ch`.
`int toupper(int ch);`	Return the uppercase version of `ch`. If `ch` is not a letter, it returns `ch`.

These functions existed in C, the language C++ grew out of. This explains something that looks odd: we're dealing with characters, but the type is not `char` but `int`! Well, characters are like integers, in a way, so this is tolerable, if not absolutely clear.

The other odd thing about these functions is similar: `islower` and `isupper` return `int`. Shouldn't they return `true` or `false`? Yes, but since C++ interprets 0 as `false` and other integers all as `true`, `int` will serve, as in this code snippet:

```
if (isupper (myChar))
    sout << "You have an upper-case letter.\n";
```

Example 5-4 uses `toupper` to compare characters without regard to case.

Example 5-4. Using true alphabetical order rather than simple ASCII order

```
// Program to tell if two letters are in alphabetical order,
//   regardless of upper or lower case
//        -- from _C++26 for Lazy Programmers_

#include <cctype>
#include "SSDL.h"
```

```
int main(int argc, char** argv)
{
    char char1, char2;

    sout << "Give me a letter: "; ssin >> char1;
    sout << "Give me another: ";  ssin >> char2;

    if      (toupper(char1) < toupper(char2))
        sout << "You gave me two characters in order.\n";
    else if (toupper(char1) > toupper(char2))
        sout << "They are in reverse order.\n";
    else
        sout << "It's the same letter.\n";

    SSDL_WaitKey();

    return 0;
}
```

Antibugging

- **You try to print a char with a converted case and it prints a number instead.**

  ```
  sout << "The upper-case version of '" << char1
       << "' is '" << toupper(char1) << ".'\n";
  ```

  If we run this, the output will be something like

  ```
  The upper-case version of 'a' is '65.'
  ```

  The problem is that toupper returns not char but int – so sout prints that int. Here's the fix – casting:

  ```
  sout << "The upper-case version of '" << char1
       << "' is '" << static_cast<char>(toupper(char1)) << ".'\n";
  ```

- **You're assigning to a char and get something like "`Cannot convert from const char[2] to char`".**

  This code looks right, but is not: `char c = "x"; // wrong!`

  chars need single quotes, like so: `char c = 'x';`

  The way to remember: Single quotes are for single chars. Double quotes are for two (or more) chars, that is, "quoted text."

Extra So far we've seen these types:

`int double float bool char`

Some can have modifiers. For example, a `long double` has more decimal places than a regular `double`; how many is compiler-dependent. `int` can be preceded by the keywords `signed`, `unsigned`, `short`, `long`, or `long long` (I guess the word "humongous" was taken), as in `unsigned long int`. As you can imagine, `short` and `long` refer to how big the number can be. `int` may be omitted: `unsigned short x;` or `long y;`.

If not specified, an `int` is `signed`. If a `char` is not specified as `signed` or `unsigned`, it is up to the compiler to decide which it is. It shouldn't matter.

`wchar_t` ("wide character"), `char8_t`, `char16_t`, and `char32_t` are larger character types, used when `char` isn't big enough, that is, for international characters.

Suffixes on the literal values – as in `5.0f` or `42u` – are there to tell the compiler "this is a `(f)loat`, not a `double`"; "this is `(u)nsigned`"; etc. Suffixes can be uppercase.

If you want to know just how big an `int`, `long int`, etc. can be, you can find out using `#include <climits>`, which defines constants for maximum and minimum values for the various types. You can get the size of one of these in bytes[3] with `sizeof`: `sizeof (int)` or `sizeof (myInt)`, where `myInt` is an `int`.

---

[3] A "byte" is a single memory location, big enough on all systems I've heard of to store one `char`.

If you store values that are too big, they'll wrap around: with `signed`, instead of a too-large positive number, you'll have a negative number. This is almost never a problem. If it is, use a `long int` or a `long long int`.

For a complete list of basic types, see Appendix C.

EXERCISES

1. Write a program to determine whether the creature you just saw was a fairy, troll, elf, or some other magical creature, assuming you carried your computer into the Enchanted Forest. You pick the distinguishing features of each type of creature. A session might start like so:

   ```
   Welcome to the Enchanted Forest.
   This creature you have seen:
   Does it have wings (Y/N)? Y
   ...
   ```

   The user should be able to type either 'y' or 'Y' and either 'n' or 'N,' to answer. (If the user types something that doesn't make sense, you can assume that means "no.")

CHAPTER 6

Algorithms and the Development Process

Let's step back from the details of C++ and think about something in the big picture: specifically, the need for thinking about the big picture. In the rest of life, doesn't planning help? You wouldn't build a house, or cook a meal, without a plan. (Heating soup in the microwave doesn't count.)

In programming, the plan is called an *algorithm*: a sequence of steps, to be executed in order, that leads to a goal.

Adventures in Robotic Cooking

Imagine if we can get our computer to make biscuits (the fluffy kind – like scones, but not sweet). A computer can follow instructions, but they must be clear.

I get out a bowl, and ...what goes in biscuits, anyway? You got me. Flour should help. Don't they put eggs in biscuits? And milk? Tell the robot to dump some flour in a bowl, put in a couple of eggs and a glug of milk, mix it up hard as it can, roll them, and put them in the oven.

They'll come out hard as bricks, of course (Figure 6-1). Our robo-chef put eggs in – my grandmother would laugh at that – and mixed them way too much. I should have made a solid plan first.

W. Briggs, *C++26 for Lazy Programmers*, https://doi.org/10.1007/979-8-8688-1859-2_6

Figure 6-1. *(Left) Biscuits improperly made are often of use to the construction industry. At least you'll think so once you try to eat them. (Right) What I'm hoping to make instead*

Tip Write the algorithm before the program, even for simple tasks.

Exactly what should I have told it to do? Here's one option:

```
1 cup/250 mL all-purpose flour
1/2 tsp/3 mL salt
1/8 cup/30 mL cold shortening
1/3 cup/80 mL milk

Heat oven to 450° F/ 230° C
Mix dry ingredients
Mix in shortening just till it's distributed
Mix in milk
Form into balls
Bake in the oven
```

Oven heated? Check. The robot can mix the dry ingredients. Let it take a cup of flour and mix in the salt and baking soda. The cup will overflow as the robot mixes them. Why didn't it put the flour into a bowl? I didn't tell it to.

Next, it will mix in the shortening and then the milk. Of course, we'll get a wet mess. Then it will form the mess into balls – how many? I didn't say. Is two OK? Then it puts the seeping mess in the oven, at which point it falls through the rack onto the bottom ...I didn't tell it to use a tray, either. And I never told it to take the biscuits out! Got a fire extinguisher handy?

The steps weren't specific enough. For example, I told it to mix, but didn't tell it that one of the steps in that is to put things into a bowl. We need more detail. **Stepwise refinement** is how to solve that problem: write down what needs doing, then break that step into sub-steps, and then break *those* into sub-steps, until the steps so simple even a computer can handle them.

Tip Refine your algorithm till it's obvious how each line converts to C++.

Let's try again:

```
1 cup/250 mL all-purpose flour
1/2 tsp/3 mL salt
1/8 cup/30 mL cold shortening
1/3 cup/80 mL milk

Heat oven to 450° F/ 230° C
Mix dry ingredients:
    Put dry ingredients into a large bowl
    Mix them
Mix in shortening just till it's distributed:
    Cut shortening into small bits (half-centimeter sized)
    Put shortening into the large bowl
    Mix just till it's distributed
Mix in milk:
    Put milk into the large bowl
    Mix till it's distributed
Form into balls:
    Get a cookie sheet
    While there is dough left
        Put flour on your hands so the dough won't stick
        Take out dough the size of a baby's fist
        Put it on the cookie sheet, not touching any others
```

```
Bake in the oven:
    Put the cookie sheet in the oven
    Wait till the biscuits are golden brown on top
    Take the cookie sheet and biscuits out
```

Good. Now we're done. It's a tediously detailed algorithm, but if we're going to get a computer to understand, we have to break it down till it's obvious - to a computer! - what the steps mean.

Is it time-consuming to write all that detail? Not as time-consuming as puzzling out the same detail while writing code, getting it wrong, debugging, and starting again and again. Experts agree: time spent planning ahead *reduces* programming time spent overall. For that reason, lazy programmers use this rule:

Golden Rule of Algorithms Always write them.

Extra Lady Ada Lovelace (1815–1852) and Charles Babbage (1791–1871), shown in Figure 6-2, are credited with being the world's first computer scientists. Too bad computers hadn't been invented yet.

Figure 6-2. *Charles Babbage and Lady Ada Lovelace*

Babbage certainly tried. He got the British government to fund his Difference Engine, which was meant to be a mechanical calculator, and then his Analytical Engine, designed as a mechanical computer. (In those days, government funding of research was nearly unheard of. Maybe that's why it was called "the Age of Invention.") Machine parts weren't of sufficient refinement at the time, and the project failed.

Lovelace, daughter of the poet Lord Byron, took an interest in Babbage's machine and understood the nature of the programs it ran or, rather, would have run if it had existed. "The Analytical Engine has no pretensions whatever to originate anything," she said. "It can do whatever we know how to order it to perform." This is sometimes used as an objection to the concept of artificial intelligence.

Writing a Program, from Start to Finish

Let's apply this planning-ahead thing to a real, if small, programming task.

Here are the steps we might go through to create the program for some goal:

- Identify requirements, that is, make a precise statement of the goal.
- Write the algorithm.
- Trace the algorithm by hand.
- Convert the algorithm to valid C++ code.
- Compile.
- Test.

If there are errors along the way, we can go back to previous steps.

Requirements: What Do We Want to Do?

I want to make a series of concentric circles such that each circle is half the area of the one outside it. We'll keep going till they start to blur (maybe when the radius is around 1 pixel). The outer circle's radius is, oh, 200.

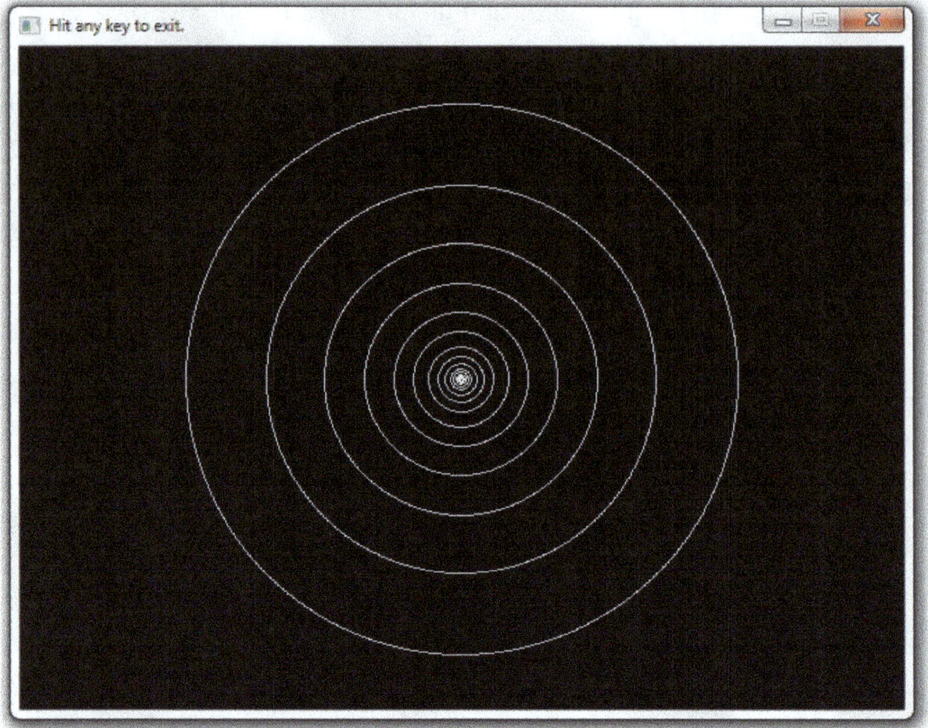

Figure 6-3. *A program that makes concentric circles, each half the area of the next bigger one*

Ready to start coding? Not yet. First, we'll make a plan, as discussed in the previous section.

Algorithm: How Do We Do It?

So what should happen at runtime?

```
draw the first circle
draw the second
keep going until the circle's too small to see -- radius 1, I'd suppose
```

Too obvious? I find that programming goes much more easily when I state the obvious, write it down, and try to refine it.

Tip State the obvious. Especially when just starting.

It's not specific enough yet. We don't know how to draw the circles because we don't know the radii.

The outermost circle's is 200. The next one in ...as previously stated, I want the area to be half that of the first. Remember the formula for the area of a circle: π radius^2. To get a halved area, we'll need next circle's area = first circle's area / 2. This works out to be that the next radius is the first radius / $\sqrt{2}$.

Here's the amended algorithm:

```
draw the first circle, with radius 200...
```

No – I didn't say where! Try again:

```
draw the first circle at center of screen, with radius 200
draw the second circle at center of screen, with radius 200/√2
draw the third circle at center of screen, with radius 200 / √2/√2...
```

Too complicated.

We *could* use variables. We'll start the value for radius at 200 and change it every time:

```
start radius at 200
draw a circle at center of screen, with this radius
divide radius by √2 to get a circle with half the area as before
keep going until the circle's too small to see -- radius 1, I'd suppose
```

That "keep going" sounds like we need a loop. We don't know how many times we'll do it, but it's at least once, so by the Golden Rule of Loops, it's a do-while:

```
start radius at 200
do
    draw a circle at center of screen, with this radius
    divide radius by√2
while radius > 1  (quit when circle's too small to see)
```

This is specific enough. Do you need to go to this trouble every time you write a program? Pretty much. As time goes by and your skills improve, you can specify less detail. But experts still write out steps for anything they're not certain of.

Trace the Algorithm: Will It Work?

Another thing I do is trace through the algorithm by hand, seeing what it does, and confirm that it does what I want.

First, radius is set to 200. The area is $\pi\, 200^2$. We draw a circle with that radius.

Next, radius is set to what it was divided by $\sqrt{2}$. The area is $\pi\, (200/\sqrt{2})^2 = \pi\, 200^2/2$, which is half the first area; that's what I wanted. We draw the new circle.

Next, radius is set to what it became divided by $\sqrt{2}$. The area is $\pi\, (200/\sqrt{2} / \sqrt{2})^2 = \pi\, 200^2/4$, which is 1/4 the first area. Good. We draw the new circle.

Seems OK.

As programs get more complex, reviewing your algorithms will be even more useful. Why spend time getting a program to compile, if it's not going to do what we want? I'm too lazy for that.

Coding: Putting It All Into C++ (Plus: Commenting the Lazy Way)

To create the program I start the usual way: I tell the reader exactly what I'm doing at the top of the file. Then I put the algorithm right into `main`, as comments, so I can refine it into a working program (below).

There's no point compiling until the code is written as, well, code. So I'll refine it over the next few pages until I get something that looks like it'll work:

```
// Program to draw 5 concentric circles
//    Each circle is twice the area of the one inside it
//         -- from _C++26 for Lazy Programmers_

#include "SSDL.h"

int main(int argc, char** argv)
{
    // start radius at 200
    // do
    //    draw a circle at center of screen, with this radius
    //    divide radius by sqrt (2)
```

```
    // while radius > 1 (quit when circle's too small to see)

    return 0;
}
```

The cops didn't arrest me for putting the algorithm right there into the editor, so I guess I'll keep going.

Tip Include the algorithm in the program, after //'s, and you've already written most of your comments.

The editor can turn text into comments quickly. (This is also useful for making troublesome bits of code stop generating errors: put 'em in comments – "comment them out" – till you're ready to deal with them.)

emacs Highlight the region; then select C++ > Comment out region to comment it; hit Tab to indent if needed. If you're in a nongraphical version of emacs, highlight the region by hitting Ctrl-space at one end of the region, and then move the cursor to the other end. Ctrl-C will turn it into comments, and Tab will indent.

(Note that final cool emacs tip too: highlight a region and hit Tab, and emacs indents the region all at once.)

Visual Studio Clicking the Comment out button will turn highlighted code into comments. (It looks like parallel horizontal lines and is highlighted at the top right of Figure 6-4.)

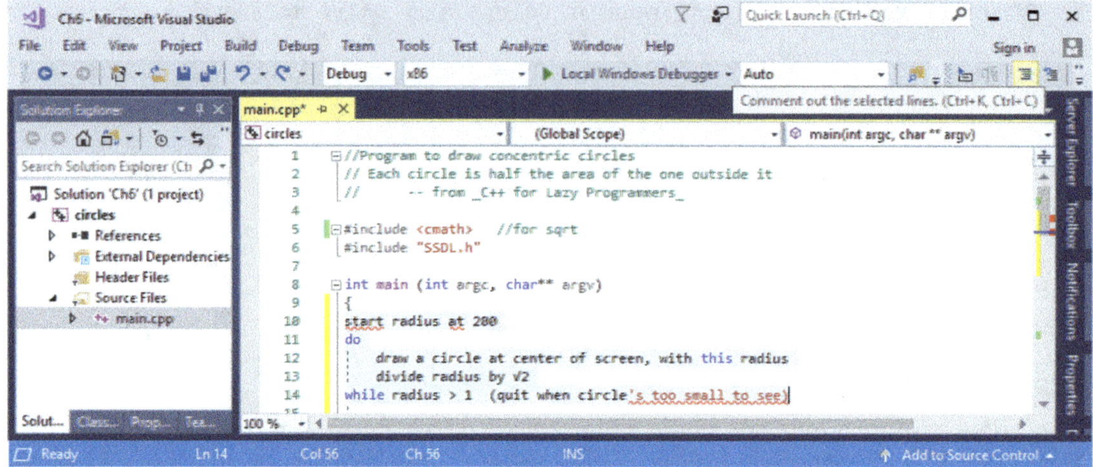

Figure 6-4. *The Visual Studio window, with the Comment out button highlighted (top right)*

Figure 6-5 shows the commenting.

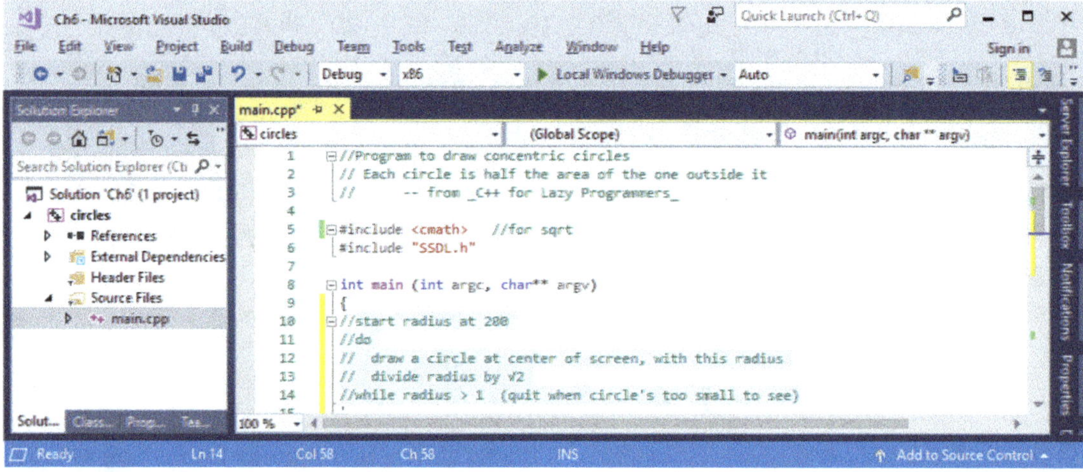

Figure 6-5. *The algorithm, in comments*

Now you can hit Tab to indent the region.

Sometimes, if an editor does the commenting for you, it will use a style of commenting we haven't covered yet: bracketing the comments in /* and */. That works too.

May as well code the easy parts first – the declaration of radius and the loop:

```
int main(int argc, char** argv)
{
    double radius = 200.0;//start radius at 200

    do
    {
        // draw a circle at center of screen, with this radius
        // divide radius by √2
    }
    while (radius > 1.0);//quit when circle's too small to see

    return 0;
}
```

Now put the middle steps in code, keeping the algorithm as comments:

```
int main(int argc, char** argv)
{
    double radius = 200.0;  //start radius at 200
    do
    {
        // draw a circle at center of screen, with this radius
        SSDL_RenderDrawCircle(CENTER_X / 2, CENTER_Y / 2,
                              static_cast<int>(radius));

        radius /= sqrt(2);     //divide radius by √2
    }
    while (radius > 1.0);//quit when circle's too small to see

    return 0;
}
```

Looks like we need the center point:

```
int main(int argc, char** argv)
{
    const int CENTER_X = SSDL_GetWindowWidth ();
    const int CENTER_Y = SSDL_GetWindowHeight();
```

```
    double radius = 200.0; //start radius at 200
    do
    {
      // draw a circle at center of screen, with this radius
        SSDL_RenderDrawCircle(CENTER_X / 2, CENTER_Y / 2,
                              static_cast<int>(radius));

        radius /= sqrt(2);//divide radius by √2
    }
    while (radius > 1.0);//quit when circle's too small to see

    return 0;
}
```

Put some friendliness at the program's start, and our usual wrap-up, and we have our program complete and already commented (Example 6-1).

Example 6-1. A program to draw concentric circles, each half the area of the one outside it. Output was in Figure 6-3.

```
// Program to draw concentric circles
//     Each circle is half the area of the one outside it
//        -- from _C++26 for Lazy Programmers_

#include <cmath>    // for sqrt
#include "SSDL.h"

int main(int argc, char** argv)
{
    SSDL_SetWindowTitle("Hit any key to exit.");

    const int CENTER_X = SSDL_GetWindowWidth();
    const int CENTER_Y = SSDL_GetWindowHeight();

    double radius = 200.0;  //start radius at 200
    do
    {
        // draw a circle at center of screen, with this radius
        SSDL_RenderDrawCircle(CENTER_X / 2, CENTER_Y / 2,
                              static_cast<int>(radius));
```

```
        radius /= sqrt(2); //divide radius by √2
    }
    while (radius > 1.0);//quit when circle's too small to see

    SSDL_WaitKey();

    return 0;
}
```

Note how the program is broken by blank lines into the major steps from the algorithm. This isn't a requirement, but it's not a bad idea.

Online Extra: "When You Just Can't Figure a Way to Get Started" Find it in the YouTube channel "Programming the Lazy Way," or www.youtube.com/watch?v=UJK4a623D2o.

EXERCISES

1. Write an algorithm to find the average of three numbers.
2. Write the corresponding program for Exercise 1.
3. Write an algorithm, then a program, to draw a *filled* circle, by drawing many circles with radii ranging from 0 to some radius R. It doesn't have to look completely filled.
4. Write the algorithm for a program to draw the Australian flag, the New Zealand flag, the Ethiopian flag, a Scandinavian flag, or some other flag using shapes you can draw with SSDL. Concentrate on what makes a coherent subtask or a repeated subtask. We'll be seeing more flag problems in subsequent chapters.

CHAPTER 7

Functions

In this chapter, we get the number one way to not get lost in pages of code till your eyes go blurry: functions.

Functions That Return Values

Consider how things are done in a candy factory. It has machines to make things we want. Each machine has things it needs piped in and the thing it produces piped out. Want a candy bar? Activate the machine, give it its inputs, and it'll provide the result (see Figure 7-1).

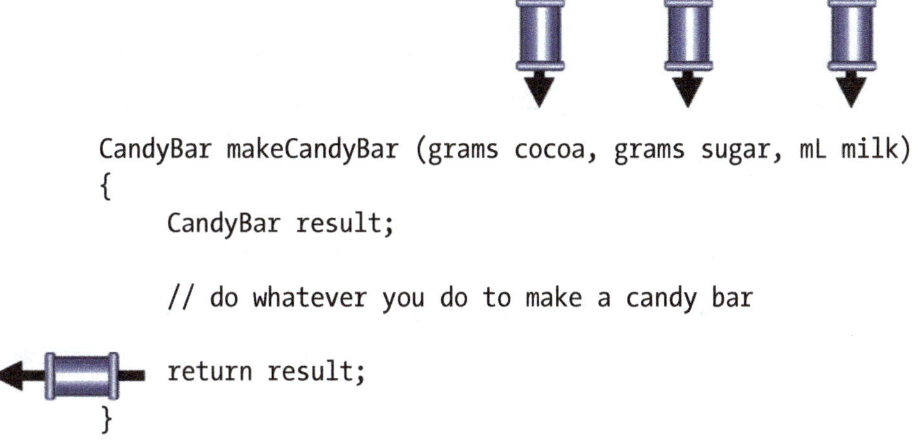

Figure 7-1. *Structure of a "makeCandyBar" machine*

C++ has "machines" too (called "functions"): for example, `SSDL_CreateColor`, `SSDL_WaitKey`, `sin` and `cos`. `SSDL_CreateColor`, for example (Figure 7-2), takes in three `ints` and returns an `SSDL_Color`.

W. Briggs, *C++26 for Lazy Programmers*, https://doi.org/10.1007/979-8-8688-1859-2_7

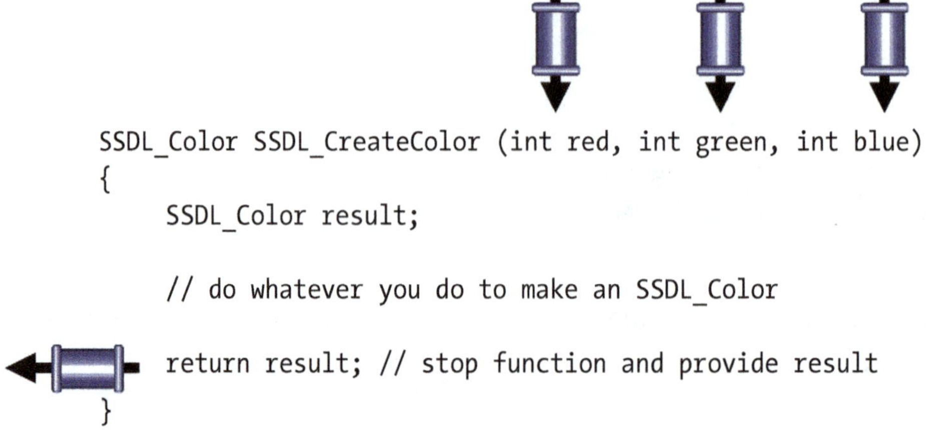

SSDL_Color SSDL_CreateColor (int red, int green, int blue)
{
SSDL_Color result;
// do whatever you do to make an SSDL_Color
return result; // stop function and provide result
}

Figure 7-2. *Structure of the* `SSDL_CreateColor` *function*

BNF for a function is

```
<return type> <name> (<parameters, separated by commas>) // "header"
{
       <thing to do -- variable declaration, action, whatever>*
}
```

where a *<parameter>* is a *<type>* plus a *<name>*: `int red`, for example.

The top line is the **function header**; the rest is the **function body**. We often copy the top line and put a ; at the end, for a precise description of how we interact with the function (its inputs and its outputs):

```
SSDL_Color SSDL_CreateColor (int red, int green, int blue);
```

This is a **function declaration** or **prototype** and was seen in previous chapters where library functions were described. It's useful not just for programmers learning but for the compiler (read on).

Now to make our own. Figure 7-3 shows a function to average three ints.

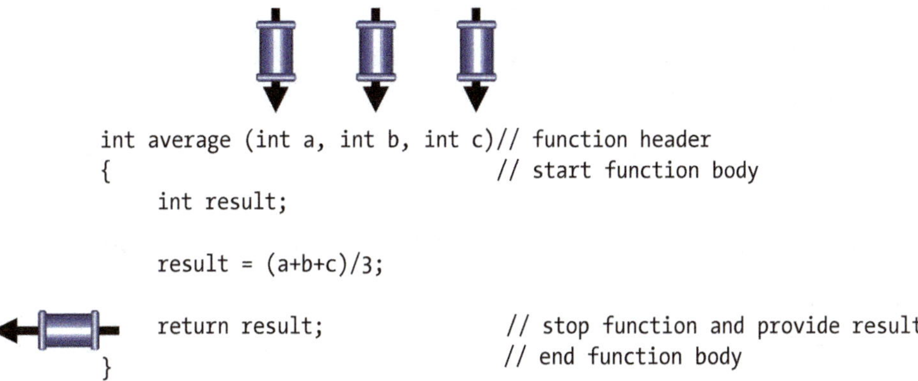
int average (int a, int b, int c)// function header
{ // start function body
int result;
result = (a+b+c)/3;
return result; // stop function and provide result
} // end function body

Figure 7-3. *The* `int average (int a, int b, int c)` *function*

The declaration is just the top line plus a `;`:

```
int average (int a, int b, int c);  // function declaration
```

We made the function, so let's use it. To use it means to store its value in a variable, print it, send it to another function (see the upcoming example) ...do *something* with the result; else, there was no point in calling the function:

```
int myAverage = average(1, 2, 12);// A "function call"
```

OK, that works. Instead of `int` literals we could give it variables

```
int i = 1, j = 2, k = 12;
int myAverage = average(i, j, k); //parameter a gets i's value,
                                   //   b gets j's...
```

...or constants, or expressions - anything with appropriate values:

```
int otherAverage = average(DAYS_PER_WEEK, 14/2, sqrt(144));
```

What we can't do is declare the variable between the parentheses like so:

```
int a = 1, b = 2, c = 12;
int myAverage = average(int a, int b, int c); // NO -- won't compile!
```

C++ reads something of form *<function name> (<parameter list, separated by commas>);* and thinks: *I know what that is - it's a declaration!* It may then get confused (like here) as to why you're setting an `int` equal to a function declaration. It may just say, "OK, I see the declaration," and go on. But one thing's for sure: it *won't* call the function.

Tip When calling a function, keep type information out of the ()'s. Type information is for declarations.

Extra Some programmers prefer only one return statement per function – not

```
if (condition)
    return this;
else
    return that;
```

but

```
if (condition)
    result = this;
else
    result = that;
return result;
```

This relates to easily tracing through the function and verifying correctness. As we go through examples in the coming chapters, you can see what you think.

Here's a function to make a grayscale equivalent of a given color, described as red, green, and blue components. It'll do this by averaging the red, green, and blue and applying the average to each component, to create and return an SSDL_Color:

```
   // Gets a greyscale color for a given r, g, b
SSDL_Color greyscale (int r, int g, int b)
{
   int rgbAverage = average(r, g, b);

   SSDL_Color result = SSDL_CreateColor(rgbAverage,
                                        rgbAverage,
                                        rgbAverage);

   return result;
}
```

I used the function `average` from earlier. *This is a Good Thing.* Code reuse is how to avoid doing the same work again and again, making fresh mistakes each time.

Golden Rule of Code Reuse

If you already wrote code to do something, don't write it again. Put it in a function and call that function.

The declaration, as always, is the top line and with `;` stuck on the end:

```
SSDL_Color greyscale (int r, int g, int b);
```

Example 7-1 shows a program that makes use of what we've done (output is in Figure 7-4). Note that the structure of the program got a little more complicated. Before it was

```
// initial comments
#include "SSDL.h"
main
```

but now it's

```
// initial comments
#include "SSDL.h"
function declarations[1]
main
function bodies
```

The compiler reads the function declarations before it gets to any code that might have a function call and thus can ensure the calls are correct (spelled right, right parameters, right use of return value).

[1] We could put function *bodies* up here too ...but people like to put `main` first so it's easy to see quickly what the program is `mainly` about.

Example 7-1. A program to make and use grayscale colors

```
// Program to change some colors to greyscale
//        -- from _C++26 for Lazy Programmers

#include "SSDL.h"

//Function declarations go here

// Averages 3 ints
int average(int, int, int);2

// Gets a greyscale color for a given r, g, b
SSDL_Color greyscale(int r, int g, int b);

int main(int argc, char** argv)
{
    sout     << "Some colors you know turned to black-and-white. "
             << "Hit any key to end.\n";

                    // By now the compiler knows that greyscale
                    //  takes 3 ints and returns an SSDL_Color, but doesn't
                    //  know how to do the greyscale...

    SSDL_SetRenderDrawColor(greyscale(255, 255, 255));
    sout << "WHITE\n";
    SSDL_SetRenderDrawColor(greyscale(255,   0,   0));
    sout << "RED\n";
    SSDL_SetRenderDrawColor(greyscale(  0, 255,   0));
    sout << "GREEN\n";
    SSDL_SetRenderDrawColor(greyscale(  0,   0, 255));
    sout << "BLUE\n";
    SSDL_SetRenderDrawColor(greyscale(181, 125,  41));
    sout << "MARIGOLD\n";
    SSDL_SetRenderDrawColor(greyscale( 50, 205,  50));
    sout << "LIME GREEN\n";
```

[2] As long as it doesn't hurt clarity, you can omit parameters' names in the declaration.

```
    SSDL_WaitKey();

    return 0;
}

// Function bodies come after main, by convention

// Averages 3 ints
int average(int a, int b, int c)
{
    return(a + b + c) / 3;
}

// Gets a greyscale color for a given r, g, b
SSDL_Color greyscale(int r, int g, int b)
{
    int rgbAverage = average(r, g, b);

    SSDL_Color result
        = SSDL_CreateColor(rgbAverage, rgbAverage, rgbAverage);

    return result;
}

                                  //...and now the compiler has all the information
                                  //   it needs about greyscale (and anything else)
```

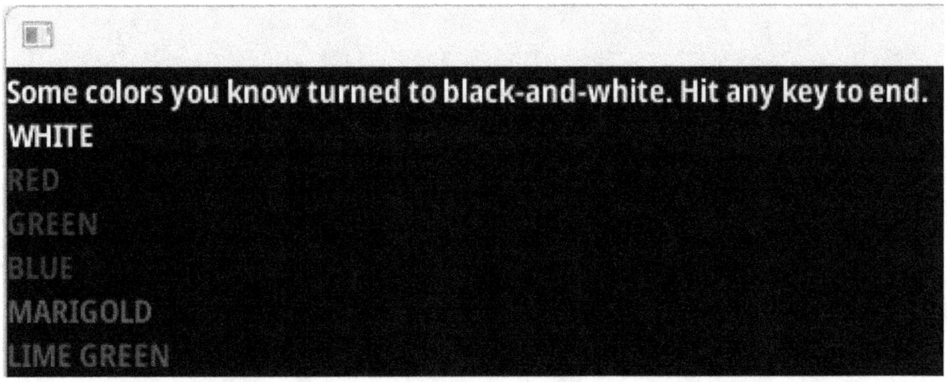

Some colors you know turned to black-and-white. Hit any key to end.
WHITE
RED
GREEN
BLUE
MARIGOLD
LIME GREEN

Figure 7-4. *Several bright colors, converted to monochrome by `SSDL_Color greyscale (int r, int g, int b);`*

EXERCISES

1. Write and test a function to get the screen's aspect ratio, that is, width divided by height.
2. Write and test a function to return the next letter: give it an 'A' and it'll return 'B,' for example. Yes, it really is that simple.
3. Write an algorithm for, then write and test, the distance formula, $\sqrt{(x2-x1)^2+(y2-y1)^2}$.

Functions That Return Nothing

Some functions don't return a value but do something else – draw a picture, print text, whatever.

Consider a function to draw not a rectangle or circle, like we already have, but a cross. With no points for originality, we'll name it `drawCross`.

What inputs will it need, so it can get started? It'll need to know *where* to draw the cross, so that's an x and a y. It'll also need to know size, the distance from center to ends. This will work:

```
void drawCross (int x, int y, int distanceToEnds)
{
    ...
}
```

The return type is `void`, meaning "I don't return anything." The meanings of the parameter names are blindingly obvious, which is a Good Thing.

Example 7-2 shows a sample program to use the `drawCross` function. Output is in Figure 7-5.

Example 7-2. A program that uses a function to draw a cross. The order of arguments sent in determines the order received: `crossX` is sent to `x`, `crossY` to `Y`, and `size` to `distToEnds`

```
// Program to draw a cross on the screen
//          -- from _C++26 for Lazy Programmers_

#include "SSDL.h"

void drawCross  (int x, int y, int distToEnds);

int main(int argc, char** argv)
{
    int crossX = 40, crossY = 25, size = 20;

    drawCross (crossX, crossY, size); //draw a cross

    SSDL_WaitKey();

    return 0;
}

// draw a cross centered at x, y, with a distance to ends as given
void drawCross (int x, int y, int distToEnds)
{
   SSDL_RenderDrawLine (x-distToEnds, y, x+distToEnds, y);
   // draw horizontal
   SSDL_RenderDrawLine (x, y-distToEnds, x, y+distToEnds);
   // draw vertical
}
```

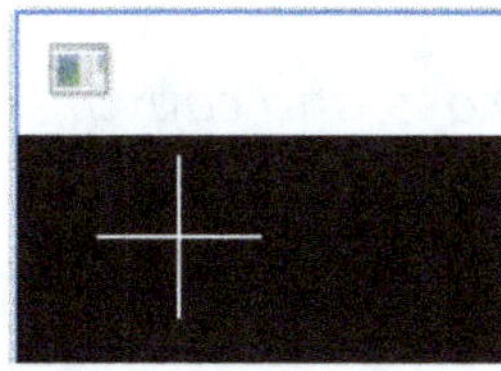

Figure 7-5. *Output from Example 7-2*

When using functions, I find it helpful to draw diagrams of what functions are active and what parameters and variables they have.

First, C++ creates an instance of the main function (Figure 7-6).

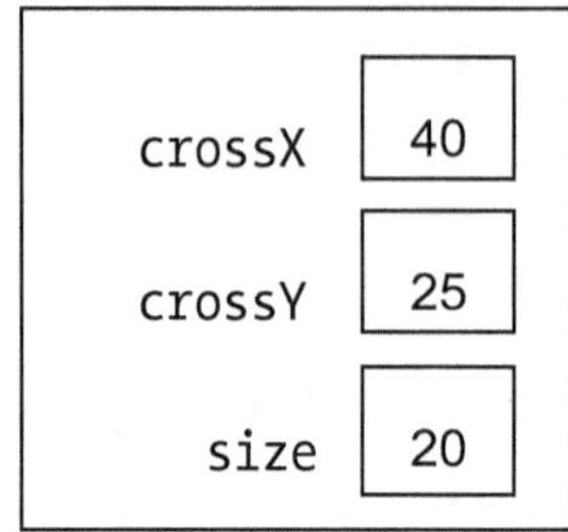

Figure 7-6. *main, in Example 7-2*

When main gets to this line

```
drawCross (crossX, crossY, size);
```

C++ creates a copy of drawCross, with its parameters (and any other variables it has), and copies the values in (Figure 7-7). This is why it doesn't matter whether main's arguments passed in and drawCross's parameters have the same names. Each function uses its own set of names.

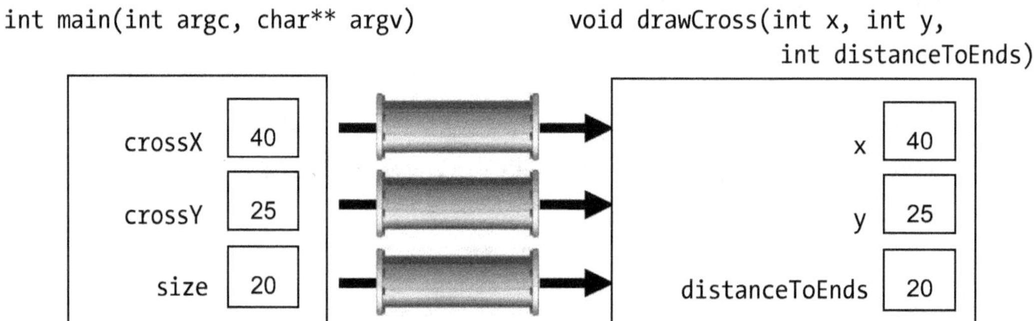

Figure 7-7. *main, calling drawCross and copying in values*

When our call to drawCross is finished, it's erased and we're back in main (Figure 7-8).

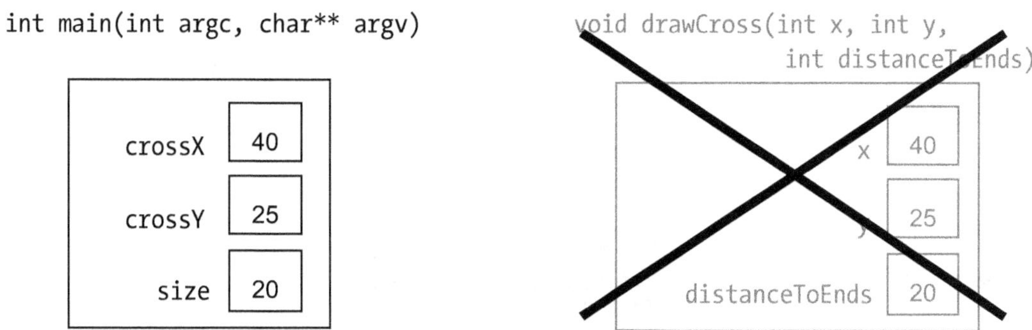

Figure 7-8. *Leaving drawCross and returning to main*

We can reuse drawCross as often as we like, just as we can SSDL_RenderDrawPoint, SSDL_RenderDrawCircle, etc.

Example 7-3. Calling function drawCross multiple times. Output is in Figure 7-9.

```
// Program to draw a cross on the screen
//          -- from _C++26 for Lazy Programmers_

#include "SSDL.h"

void drawCross(int x, int y, int distToEnds);

int main(int argc, char** argv)
{
    drawCross( 40, 40, 20); //draw three crosses
    drawCross( 80, 30, 15);
    drawCross(110, 50, 40);

    SSDL_WaitKey();

    return 0;
}

// draw a cross centered at x, y, with a distance to ends as given
void drawCross(int x, int y, int distToEnds)
{
    SSDL_RenderDrawLine(x - distToEnds, y, x + distToEnds, y);
                                                  // draw horizontal
```

```
    SSDL_RenderDrawLine(x, y - distToEnds, x, y + distToEnds);
                                                    // draw vertical
}
```

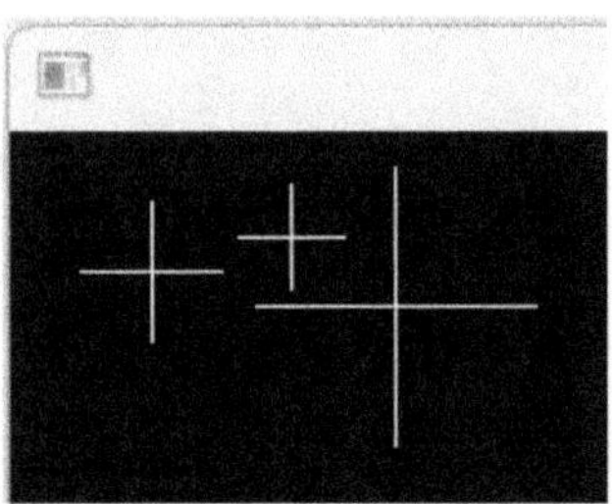

Figure 7-9. *Output from Example 7-3*

Global Variables

Some find this workaround: instead of passing in parameters, they'll make their variables *global* (meaning "not inside anybody's {}'s"), rather than *local* (inside main's {}'s or drawCross's or someone's) (Example 7-4).

Example 7-4. What not to do: use global variables

```
// Program to draw a cross on the screen
//          -- from _C++26 for Lazy Programmers_

#include "SSDL.h"

// GLOBAL VARIABLES: THE EIGHTH DEADLY SIN?
int         x = 40, y = 40;
int         distanceToEnds = 20;

// Function declarations
void drawCross  ();

int main(int argc, char** argv)
{
    // draw three crosses
    drawCross();
```

```
    x =  80; y = 30; distanceToEnds = 15; drawCross();
    x = 110; y = 50; distanceToEnds = 40; drawCross();

    SSDL_WaitKey();

    return 0;
}

// draw a cross centered at x, y, with distance to ends, all global
void drawCross ()
{
    SSDL_RenderDrawLine (x-distanceToEnds, y, x+distanceToEnds, y);
    SSDL_RenderDrawLine (x, y-distanceToEnds, x, y+distanceToEnds);
}
```

Easy, huh?

Not really. There are three drawbacks:

1. **It's hard to read and write:** `drawCross` will draw a cross, but where? You have to look inside the body to find out: it draws it at (x, y). What are `x` and `y`? Look at the top; they're (40, 40). Then look back in `main` to see how they've changed. And hope there's not some other function that *also* uses `x` and `y` for something else and changed their values. To be certain, you'll have to look through *all* the code. Try that with a 500-page program. Aaaigh!

2. **It's the devil to debug:** Looking all over the program to find what screwed up a variable is hard work. We try to break programs into relatively independent parts (functions), with parameter lists to specify clearly how those parts interact. This reduces the scope of where to look for an error. It also helps with group projects: different programmers can work on different functions, with minimal interference with each other's work. This is called **modularity**.

3. **Programmers who have to maintain your code will hate you:** Not as if you snubbed them, but as if you egged their cars and insulted their mothers. They don't want to inherit the debugging disaster.

4. For some offenses, I hear, Santa won't bring you any presents. For worse ones, **Santa actually takes your presents**. This is one of the latter kind.

Golden Rule of Global Variables

Just say no.

Antibugging

- **It's not calling the function.** You may have put type information in, so the compiler thinks it's a function declaration. Take the type info out.
- **You call a value-returning function, but it has no effect.** See Chapter 3, section "Built-In Functions and Casting," subsection "Antibugging" - same problem, same solution.
- **You get an error, something like "no local function definitions allowed."** If something's missing a closing }, the compiler may think you're still in one function when you start another. Be sure the {}'s are balanced. A good reason to avoid Egyptian brackets (see Chapter 4).

  To prevent this, when starting a function body, put both {}'s in place at the same time. If you do, the function will probably compile, even if it doesn't do anything yet. Such an empty function is called a **stub**. It's common to have them in unfinished programs.
- **It skips the latter part of the function**, as here:

```
int value (char letter) // score letters in a word game.
                        // Q, K are best
{
    return 1;           // default score is 1

    if (toupper (letter) == 'Q' || toupper (letter) == 'K')
        return 5;
}
```

This always returns 1. The reason is that first `return` didn't just establish a return value, but also stopped the function: it won't go on to run the `if`.

Solution: Recognize `return` as the last thing a function does.

- **No matter what parameters you give, the function always does the same thing**. Be sure they aren't being reset inside the function (see the next section "How to Write a Function in Four Easy Steps," subsection "Antibugging").
- **You repeat a function by having it call itself.** This is called recursion. It's fine, but you should know what you're doing, because it's not always appropriate.

  Suppose you want to play a game multiple times:

```
void playGame ()
{
    ...
    // now let's play again:
    playGame ();
}
```

  Thinking from the perspective of the diagrams in the previous section ...when you call a function, C++ creates a copy, which it keeps until the function is done. What happens when you're on your umpteenth game here? You get umpteen copies of the function, and each one requires memory (Figure 7-10). If "umpteen" becomes very large, it'll crash the program.

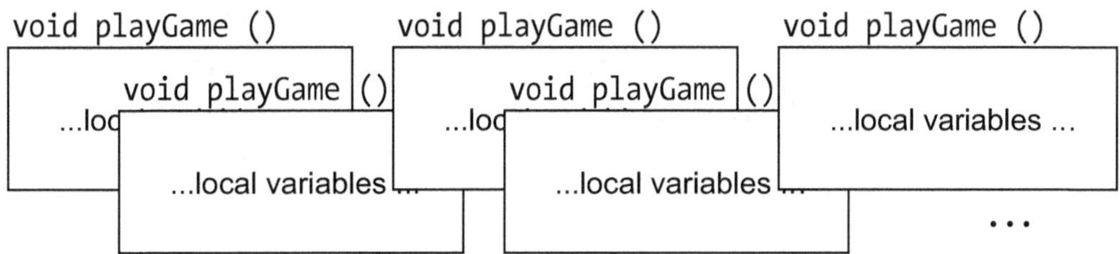

Figure 7-10. *Multiple "recursive" (self-calling) copies of a function. Keep adding new calls to a function without returning and eventually you're out of memory*

Better solution: Use a loop.

EXERCISES

Not many exercises yet: I really want you to see the next section before getting heavily into writing your own functions. But here are two:

1. Write an algorithm for, then write and test, a function to draw a triangle at some location specified by parameters.
2. Write a function to draw a circled number, like some speed limit signs. What parameters will it need?

How to Write a Function in Four Easy Steps (and Call It in One)

I urge using these steps for *every function you write* till you're certain you have functions nailed.

1. Put this after `main`, using your own function name and comment:

```
<return type> greaterNumber ()  // Returns the greater of two numbers
{
    <return type> result;
    return result;
}
```

2. What information will the function need to get started?
   Say you're the `greaterNumber` function and I'm `main`. I say to you: give me the greater number! You say: I can't – I need more information! Well, what information do you need?

You need the numbers. They go in the ()'s. You need to specify their types (int, double, char, etc.):

```
// Returns the greater of 2 numbers
double greaterNumber (double num1, double num2)
{
    double result;

    return result;
}
```

3. What kind of value does it return? Whatever it is, use that for the return type:

```
// Returns the greater of 2 numbers
double greaterNumber ()
{
    double result;

    return result;
}
```

If the function doesn't return anything, skip all the return stuff and make its type void:

```
void drawCross ()                    // Draws a cross
{
}
```

4. How does the function do its work?

   a. Put the problem description inside the function as comments. Then refine it to a sufficiently specified algorithm, as in Chapter 6. Skipping this step is a bad idea unless you really know what you're doing:

```
// Returns the greater of 2 numbers
double greaterNumber (double number1, double number2)
{
    double result;
```

```
        //if number1 is bigger, that's the result;
        //    else it's number2

        return result;
    }
```

b. Write valid C++ to do the task:

```
    // Returns the greater of 2 numbers
    double greaterNumber (double number1, double number2)
    {
        double result;

        // let result be the bigger of number1, number2
        if (number1 > number2)
            result = number1;
        else
            result = number2;

        return result;
    }
```

5. Use the function:

a. Copy the top line, put it above `main`, and end with a semicolon (below):

```
    // Returns the greater of 2 numbers
    double greaterNumber (double number1, double number2);
```

b. Call the function, and (if it isn't `void`) store the result or use it:

```
    int main(int argc, char** argv)
    {
        ...
     bigNum = greaterNumber (20, 30); or sout << bigNum; or such
```

Antibugging

In step 3, where do the values for the parameters come from? They're provided by `main` when we call the function, in Examples 7-1, 7-2, and 7-3. Since they're sent in from `main`, we would *not* do this

```
double greaterNumber (double number1, double number2)
                            // Returns the greater of two numbers
{
    double result;

    sout << "Enter two numbers: ";
    ssin >> number1;  // WRONG. It erases the numbers main gave us!
    ssin >> number2;

    ...

    return result;
}
```

or this:

```
double greaterNumber (double number1, double number2)
                  // Returns the greater of two numbers
{
    double result;

    number1 = 12;        // WRONG. It erases the numbers main gave us!
    number2 = 25;

    ...

    return result;
}
```

Another thing we won't need: printing. We almost never have a function print something (unless its named "printThis" or "outputSomething" or such). We return the value and let `main` decide what to do with it. (Think if, in the program for drawing a star in Example 3-3, `sin` and `cos` printed "The result of this function is ..." every time you called them, covering up your star with text. Aaaigh!)

```
double greaterNumber (double number1, double number2)
             // Returns the greater of two numbers
{
    double result;

    ...

    sout << "The bigger number is " << result;
             // WRONG. We're supposed to *return*, not *print*

    return result;
}
```

Tip Functions shouldn't print unless the name says something about output (as in `printDialog`) and shouldn't read anything unless the name includes something about input (as in `getUserResponse`). Keep separate tasks separate.

For now I urge you to **write out, for each function you write, each of the above steps**. Copy

```
<return type> greaterNumber () // Returns the greater of two numbers
{
    <return type> result;
    return result;
}
```

into your editor, replacing `greaterNumber` and the comment with your own stuff (that's step 1); replace the return type with your own (that's step 2); and so on.

There is a form for this process in the source code folder for Chapter 7. Please follow it in writing your own functions until you're confident!

EXERCISES

For all exercises, use the "four easy steps" above.

1. Write an algorithm for, then write and test, the power function. `myPow (a, b)` should return a^b. To make it easier, assume only integer values for the exponent: you can calculate `myPow (3, 2)`, but not `myPow (3, 2.1)`.
2. Write an algorithm for, then write and test, a function that, given a positive integer, returns the sum of all numbers up to that integer. For example, given a 5, it should return 1+2+3+4+5 = 15.
3. Write an algorithm for, then write and test, a function `log` that, given a positive integer number and an integer base, returns $\log_{base}$ (number). $\log_{base}$ (number) is defined as how many times you can divide number by base before getting to 1. For example, 8/2 gives 4, and 4/2 gives 2, and 2/2 gives 1; that's three divisions; so $\log_2 8$ is 3. We won't worry about fractional parts: $\log_2 15$ is also 3, because (using integer division) 15/2 is 7, 7/2 is 3, and 3/2 is 1.

Why Have Functions, Anyway?

Till now we've started with the function and then made use of it. Let's look now at writing a larger program and deducing what functions we need – the more usual approach.

Consider how we might write a program to show a comic, frame by frame. To make the drawing easy, we'll use stick figures that talk but don't move. We'll have four frames, showing one at a time.

We start our algorithm:

```
write the dialog for the left character
draw the line from the left character's head to the dialog
draw the left character's head
draw the left character's body
draw the left character's left arm
draw the left character's right arm
draw the left character's left leg
draw the left character's right leg
```

```
write the dialog for the right character
write the line from the right character's head to the dialog
...
```

Argh! That's a lot of writing. This isn't *C++26 for Programmers Who Want Carpal Tunnel Syndrome*! And when we start coding, we'll find that extra typing is the least of our worries. Twice as much code means five times as many opportunities for error. (This may not be mathematically sound, but based on experience, it's conservative.)

And if you do it that way ...as covered in the previous chapter, you write your algorithm, double-check it, write the program, and run it. Then you find an error – say, the dialog's in the wrong place – and fix it. In *one* of the frames. The other frames, you forget to fix. More errors.

Better to follow the Golden Rule of Code Reuse from earlier: put that dialog-drawing code in a function and call as needed.

We'll therefore bundle the algorithm (and, later, the code) into functions to enable code reuse.[3] Here's what `main` might look like:

```
main program:
    give the window a title
    draw frame 1; wait for user to hit a key
    draw frame 2; wait for user to hit a key
    draw frame 3; wait for user to hit a key
    draw frame 4; wait for user to hit a key
```

Did I cheat? I didn't actually say how to *do* anything. Well, that's not quite true: I said how to do *everything*! Just not in detail. That's no sin as long as I give that detail in another function – perhaps one named `draw frame`:

```
draw frame.
    clear the screen
    draw left character and its dialog
    draw right character and its dialog
```

[3] Taking a chunk of information and labeling it for reuse is *abstraction*: an essential way of keeping yourself sane in large programming projects.

Again, I put off most of the work! (What do you expect, from a lazy programmer?) But it's fine: `draw frame` is a coherent task. As long as `draw character` and `draw dialog` work, we'll be OK:

```
draw character:
    draw head as a circle
    draw body, a line
    draw arms, two lines
    draw legs, two lines
draw dialog:
    draw line
    draw the text
```

The process we went through – starting with the main program and writing its subtasks, then subtasks of subtasks, etc., until we get down to things we know how to write in C++ (drawing lines, circles, and text) – is called *top-down design,* and it's how we write programs. (Purists who point out other software engineering techniques exist are right, but you gotta start somewhere.)

We still need detail, but I'll leave that for now, because I want to talk about how we decide what pieces of code should be made into functions.

For one thing, I should make code into a function if the code is likely to be called repeatedly, like `draw character`. Making it into a function means it *can* be repeated (as we see in the `main program`).

The above examples (`draw character` and others) are also **coherent** tasks – like functions we've already seen, such as `sqrt`, `sin`, `SSDL_RenderText`, etc. Why not a function `SSDL_RenderPrintSin`, to "find the sine of an angle and print it on the screen"? It takes longer to describe, and that's a tipoff it'll be less generally useful. (How often do *you* want to print sines?) Better to break it into functions each of which does *one* thing.

Another criterion is that a function should be **short enough to understand**. If it's too big to see on the screen, it's too big to follow what it's doing as you write and debug it. Once it's more than a screenful, break it into subtasks.

Golden Rule of Functions

Make code into a function if it is likely to be called more than once, forms a coherent task, or is part of another function that's getting to be more than a screenful long.[4]

Extra Psychologists have measured the mind's ability to be aware of multiple things at once and determined that one can think of approximately seven items at a time.[5] For example, read these digits, then look away from the page, and see if you can repeat them.

5 7 16 19 28 29 32

Now try doing it with this sequence of numbers. Having a little trouble?

5 7 16 19 28 29 32 3 8 12 26 32 14 19 7 50 2 19 18 33 25 11 36 41 1

The point is: you can't keep arbitrarily long sets of data in your mind at one time. A version of the main program spanning hundreds of pages – or even one – is too long to understand.

We have the algorithm. Since it has functions, let's decide on each new function's parameters using the third question from the section "How to Write a Function in Four Easy Steps": what information will the function need to get started?

`draw dialog` requires the dialog (duh), so we'll pass that in. It'll also need to know where to put it (the left character's area or the right's):

---

[4] What's a screenful? Bjarne Stroustrup, creator of C++ and chief editor of the C++ Core Guidelines (`https://isocpp.github.io/CppCoreGuidelines/`), suggests, "Try 60 lines by 140 characters." But of course it's nothing so precise! Just use what works on your display; approximate is fine.

[5] George A. Miller, "The Magical Number Seven, Plus or Minus Two," *The Psychological Review*, 1956, vol. 63, pp. 81-97. The application of this to things that aren't sequences of digits - like I'm doing right now - has been condemned as urban legend material, on the grounds that the precise number of items one can keep in mind varies by type of cognitive task (`www.knosof.co.uk/cbook/misart.pdf`, at time of writing). True enough - but even if it does vary, there is a limit.

```
draw dialog (x, y, dialog) ...steps as before...
        draw character is always the same except for position, so that's
        all it needs.
draw character (x, y)
        ...steps as before...
```

`draw frame` draws a frame; it'll need the dialog. There are two parts to that: the left character's dialog and the right character's. Since the stick figures don't move, that should be all:

```
draw frame (left char's dialog, right char's dialog):
    draw character (left x, left y);
    draw dialog       (left x, left y, left char's dialog)
    draw character (right x, right y);
    draw dialog       (right x, right y, right char's dialog)
```

And here is `main`, showing arguments for the functions it calls:

```
main:
    give the window a title
    draw frame 1 (left char's dialog, right char's dialog);
    wait for user to hit a key
    draw frame 2 (left char's dialog, right char's dialog);
    wait for user to hit a key
    draw frame 3 (left char's dialog, right char's dialog);
    wait for user to hit a key
    draw frame 4 (left char's dialog, right char's dialog);
    wait for user to hit a key
```

The graph paper representation I used to help me draw is in Figure 7-11. Now, let's see that program (Example 7-5).

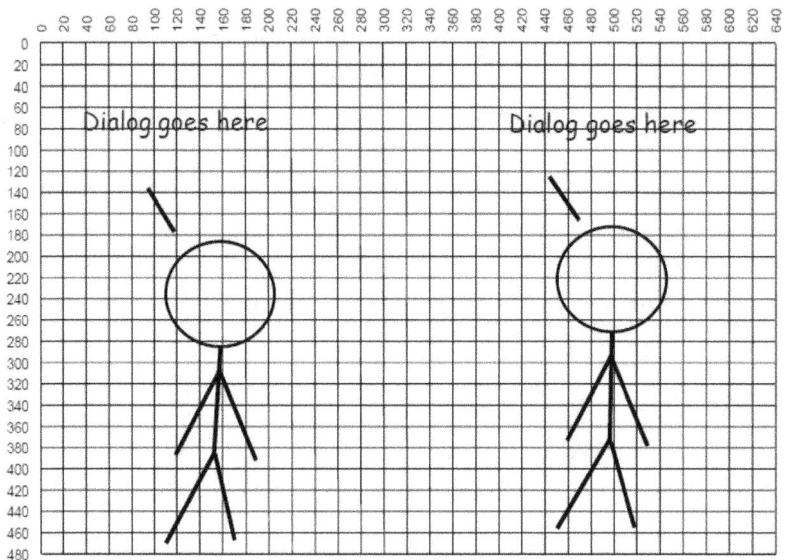

Figure 7-11. *Graph paper to plot out a cartoon frame*

It turned out that `wait for user to hit a key` was more than a bare call to `SSDL_WaitKey()`: for user-friendliness I wanted a prompt, and I wanted it nicely placed. The task is repeated and tedious to write, so following the Golden Rule of Code Reuse, it gets its own function.

Example 7-5. A program to do a four-panel cartoon. Output is in Figure 7-12.

```
// Program to display a 4-panel comic strip with stick figures.
//          -- from _C++26 for Lazy Programmers_

#include "SSDL.h"

// Function declarations
void drawFrame     (const char* leftDialog, const char* rightDialog);[6]
void drawCharacter(int x, int y);
void drawDialog   (int x, int y, const char* dialog);
void hitEnterToContinue (); //wait for user to hit Enter
```

[6] We've seen parameters of type `const char*` in SSDL function declarations related to text (e.g., `void SSDL_SetWindowTitle (const char* text)`). We'll get to the true meaning of `const char*` in Chapter 14. For now, just think of it as meaning "text."

```
int main(int argc, char** argv)
{
    // Set up:  window title and font
    SSDL_SetWindowTitle ("My own 4-panel comic");
    const SSDL_Font COMIC_FONT = SSDL_OpenSystemFont("comic.ttf",18);
    SSDL_SetFont (COMIC_FONT);

    // Now the four frames
    drawFrame  ("Somebody said something really nasty\nto me "
                "on Internet.\nSo I put him in his place.",[7]
                "Maybe it's not a him.\nMaybe it's a her.  "
                "You never know.");
    hitEnterToContinue();

    drawFrame  ("OK, her.  Whatever.  She kept saying\nall this "
                "stuff about how superior\nshe was.  I found "
                "a spelling error and\ntold her she can't even "
                "spell so she\nshould just shut up.",
                "If it's a her.  It *might* be a him.\nThe point "
                "is we just don't know.");
    hitEnterToContinue();

    drawFrame  ("The *point* is, he went on a rant about\nhow you "
                "can spell things like \"b4\"\nand so on in l33t, "
                "and I told him l33t\nis for lusers -- with a u, "
                "you know.\nThen he told me I misspelled \"loser.\"",
                "If it's a him.  It could be both.\nSometimes "
                "married people\nshare accounts.");
    hitEnterToContinue();

    drawFrame  ("You're making me crazy!",
                "Can I have the link for that thread?\nI'm not "
                "done yet.");
    hitEnterToContinue ();
```

[7] It's called "string literal concatenation": if you jam "`quoted`" "`things`" together with only whitespace between, C++ will interpret them as one "`quoted thing`". This helps us break lines neatly wherever we like. Nice!
This has no effect on how lines break when *printed*; for that we use \n.

```
    return 0;
}

// draw a cartoon's frame, given dialog for each of two characters
void drawFrame (const char* leftDialog, const char* rightDialog)
{
    constexpr int LEFT_X  =   0, LEFT_Y  = 20;
    constexpr int RIGHT_X = 320, RIGHT_Y = 40;
    // right character is drawn a little lower
    // it doesn't look so much like a mirror image

    SSDL_RenderClear ();    // clear background to black
    drawCharacter    (LEFT_X,  LEFT_Y);
    drawDialog       (LEFT_X,  LEFT_Y,  leftDialog);
    drawCharacter    (RIGHT_X, RIGHT_Y);
    drawDialog       (RIGHT_X, RIGHT_Y, rightDialog);
}

// draw a stick-figure character, with its dialog at the top.
//   The upper-left corner of it all is x, y
void drawCharacter (int x, int y)
{
    constexpr int HEAD_RADIUS = 45;

    SSDL_RenderDrawCircle(x+140, y+195, HEAD_RADIUS);  // draw head

    SSDL_RenderDrawLine  (x+142, y+240, x+140, y+340); // draw body,
                                                       // slightly angled

    SSDL_RenderDrawLine  (x+142, y+260, x+115, y+340); // draw arms
    SSDL_RenderDrawLine  (x+142, y+260, x+165, y+342);

    SSDL_RenderDrawLine  (x+140, y+340, x+100, y+420); // draw legs
    SSDL_RenderDrawLine  (x+140, y+340, x+157, y+420);
}

// Draw the dialog for a character, with a line connecting
//   it to the character.  x, y is the upper-left corner of
//   the whole set (dialog plus character)
```

```
void drawDialog (int x, int y, const char* dialog)
{
    // line linking character to dialog
    SSDL_RenderDrawLine (x+90, y+100, x+112, y+130);
    // dialog itself
    SSDL_RenderText    (dialog, x+20, y);
}

void hitEnterToContinue()
{
    // How far up to put the "Hit a key" message
    constexpr int BOTTOM_LINE_HEIGHT = 25;

    // More succinct than "Hit any key to continue but not
    //  Escape because that ends the program"
    SSDL_RenderTextCentered("Hit Enter to continue",
                SSDL_GetWindowWidth() / 2,
                SSDL_GetWindowHeight() - BOTTOM_LINE_HEIGHT);

    SSDL_WaitKey();
}
```

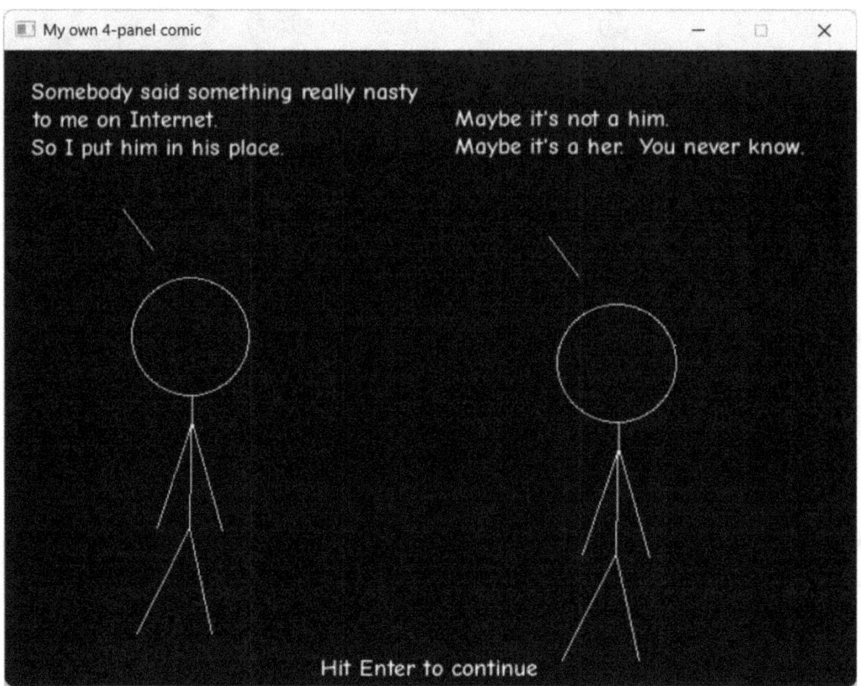

Figure 7-12. *Frame 1 of the four-panel cartoon program. The other frames are similar except way funnier*

Recap

Functions are an essential way to organize your code, so you and those reading your programs don't get lost in them. They also are essential for code reuse.

For both purposes, it's essential that function names be clear and that information is passed in the right way (through the parameter list, between the `()`'s). Return values go out through the `return` statement.

For each function you write, in the next chapter and until you're comfortable, please use the steps found in this chapter – they are crucial to the effective use of this powerful language feature.

EXERCISES

For each function, use the "four easy steps" found in this chapter.

1. Write your own multi-panel cartoon: first the algorithm (you'll need it fer sure!) and then the functions.

2. Write an algorithm for, then write, a program to display the flag of Greece. You'll at least want these two functions: `drawCanton` (the upper left) and `drawStripes`.

3. Write an algorithm for a function to draw the Australian flag (Figure 7-13), as in the last exercise in Chapter 6. Then, using functions appropriately, write that program. You'll want a function `drawStar` to draw any of the stars you see on the flag, which means it should be able to handle either five- or seven-pointed stars. You won't fill in the stars, but just do a rough outline, unless you can think of a trick.

***Figure 7-13.** The Australian flag, simplified for Exercise 5*

Wikipedia is a good source for flag specifications.

CHAPTER 8

Functions, continued

More things about functions: random number functions, Boolean functions, parameters that change, and "scope" – that is, where a variable can be seen and used depending on where it's declared.

Random Numbers

> *Anyone who considers arithmetical methods of producing random numbers is, of course, in a state of sin.*
>
> —John von Neumann, inventor of FORTRAN (Goldstine, 1972)

Random numbers aren't just useful for games. They're useful for simulations – predicting the average behavior of some system – and for scientific computing. You can tell people that why you're studying them. It isn't for games. Honest.

But computers are orderly machines. They can't really make random numbers, as von Neumann knew. I suppose you could drop one and see how it lands, but then how will you play solitaire on it?

Making a Random Number Generator

So what we'll do is make a sequence of numbers that *look* random to a human observer – but they'll actually be perfectly predictable, if you know how the computer is doing it.

Recall from Chapter 3 that the `%` operator, called "modulus," means "divide and take the remainder." So `36%10`, for example, gives us 6, because if you divide 36 by 10, the remainder is 6.

W. Briggs, *C++26 for Lazy Programmers*, https://doi.org/10.1007/979-8-8688-1859-2_8

Remember also that A += B means A = A+B; *= and %= are defined similarly:

```
int rand ()     // Return a pseudo-random integer
{
    static unsigned int seed                  =    76;
    static constexpr unsigned int INCREMENT = 51138;
    static constexpr unsigned int MULTIPLIER= 21503;
    static constexpr unsigned int MODULUS   = 32767;

    seed += INCREMENT;
    seed *= MULTIPLIER;
    seed %= MODULUS;

    return seed;
}
```

The static keyword here means that these variables will be created once, the first time the function is called, and will remain as long as the program is running. Ordinarily variables in a function are recreated each time the function is called. But we want seed remembered time to time, so we can get a different answer for each call, based on what happened previously. We'll also make the constexprs static so they won't have to be reinitialized each time we call the function.

Suppose seed starts at, oh, 76. Add that INCREMENT; multiply it by MULTIPLIER; then divide by MODULUS and take the remainder. What's the new value? You can't do that in your head?

Neither can anyone else. If you call this again and again, you'll get a sequence of large numbers that you can't predict without doing the math. It looks random; it isn't: 21306 20152 10309 31100 ...

Usually we don't want such big numbers. No problem: we can easily get them down to a manageable range, like so:

```
int numberLessThanTen = rand()% 10;
```

That gives us a number in the range 0–9 – since the maximum remainder after you divide by 10 is 9.

```
int oneThroughTen = rand()%10 + 1;
```

Now we have 1–10: 7 3 10 1 6 ...

That's how it's done.

There's one other thing we need. Do we always want to start with the same number, 76? If we do, we'll get an apparently random sequence of numbers ...but it'll always be the *same* sequence! If we're making a card game, those cards we pick will always be the same ones in the same order.

You may have seen a game that *asks* for a seed. If one of the options is "Select game" and you give it a number, what you're doing is initializing the seed for the random number generator. Example 8-1 amends the code to support this.

Example 8-1. A complete random number generator

```
unsigned long int seed;          // Current random number seed

void srand (unsigned int what)  // Start the random number generator
{
    seed = what;
}

int rand ()                      // Return a pseudo-random integer
{
    static constexpr unsigned int INCREMENT = 51138;
    static constexpr unsigned int MULTIPLIER= 21503;
    static constexpr unsigned int MODULUS   = 32767;

    seed += INCREMENT;
    seed *= MULTIPLIER;
    seed %= MODULUS;

    return seed;
}
```

You call srand ("s" for "seed"? For "start"? Either works for me) to start your sequence. Subsequent calls to rand get the next number in the sequence and the next and so on.

Now, this has a serious drawback: the variable seed is declared outside any function. That means any function in the entire program can mess it up. We avoid using global variables whenever we can – but in this unusual case, there's no other good way to do it: srand and rand both need access.

I'm on the naughty list now for sure. Sorry, Santa.

Using the Built-In Random Number Generator

Good news: other programmers besides us have wanted pseudo-random numbers! So the functions shown in Example 8-1 come with your compiler. Here's how to use them:

```
#include <cstdlib>     // for srand, rand

int main(int argc, char** argv)
{
      srand (someNumber);       // start random number generator
      int num = rand()%10 + 1; // pick a random # 0..9
      ...
```

cstdlib stands for "C standard library." cstdlib gives us rand, srand, and other functions.

I'm not too happy with that someNumber thing. Where does it come from? We can always make the user select the game by typing in a seed, but that's more work on the user.

Better: get the number from the computer. But how can we be sure it gives us a different one each time?

Consult the clock.

Every time you restart the program, it's a different time. If we can give srand a number based on the time, we'll get a different sequence each time.

Here's how:

```
#include <cstdlib> // for srand, rand
#include <ctime>    // for time

int main(int argc, char** argv)
{
     srand (static_cast<unsigned int> (time (nullptr)));
     ...
```

ctime contains a function time that returns the number of seconds since midnight January 1, 1970, Greenwich Mean Time. We don't care about the starting point, but we do care that the answer will be different each second – so we'll get different games.

It returns the time as a time_t, which is some kind of int. srand wants unsigned int; we convert it so the compiler won't give us a warning.

Don't worry what `nullptr` means; we'll get to that later.

Golden Rule of srand

Call it *once*, thus: `srand (time (nullptr));`

If you call it multiple times, you'll reset the "random" number sequence multiple times - and the first several "random" numbers you get (until the second changes) will be identical. I tried this (see Example 8-2) and got this result:

```
8 8 8 8 8 8 8 8 8 8 8 8 8 8 8 8 8 8 8 8 8 8 8 8 8 8...
```

Example 8-2. Repeating `srand` and what it gets you

```
for (int i = 0; i < 100; ++i)     // Print a bunch of random #'s
{
    srand (static_cast<unsigned int> (time (nullptr))); // WRONG!
    sout << rand() % 10 << ' ';
}
```

Call `srand` once; that's all you need.

As an example of doing things right, let's try a program that rolls a couple of dice, as in a craps game, and tells how you did. On the first try, if you get 2, 3, or 12, you lose. 7 or 11 wins. Any other number is your "point" for more betting.

Algorithm:

```
main:
    start things up with srand
    roll 2 dice
    print what you rolled
    print what happens to your bet
    wait for user to hit a key
```

How do we roll a die? A reasonable question:

```
roll die:
    pick a random number 1 to 6.
```

How do I do that? As earlier, divide by the range and take the remainder and then add 1:

```
roll die:
    return rand () % 6 + 1
```

The program is in Example 8-3.

Example 8-3. A program to do a craps roll, illustrating `srand` and `rand`

```
// One step in a game of craps
//          -- from _C++20 for Lazy Programmers_

#include <ctime>     // for time function
#include <cstdlib>  // for srand, rand
#include "SSDL.h"

constexpr int SIDES_PER_DIE = 6;

int rollDie ();                    // roll a 6-sided die

int main(int argc, char** argv)
{
    srand (static_cast<unsigned int> (time (nullptr)));
                                   // This starts the random # generator
                                   // It gets called once per program

    SSDL_SetWindowTitle("Craps roll");

    sout << "Ready to roll?  Hit a key to continue.\n";
    SSDL_WaitKey();

    int roll1 = rollDie(), roll2 = rollDie();
    sout << "You rolled a " << roll1 << " and a " << roll2;

    switch (roll1 + roll2)
    {
    case  2:
    case  3:
    case 12: sout << " -- craps. You lose the pass line bet.\n";
             break;
```

```
    case  7:
    case 11: sout << " -- natural. You win the pass line bet.\n";
             break;
    default: sout <<", so " << roll1 + roll2 << " is your point.\n";
    }

    sout << "Hit a key to end.\n";
    SSDL_WaitKey();

    return 0;
}

int rollDie() { return rand() % SIDES_PER_DIE + 1; }
```

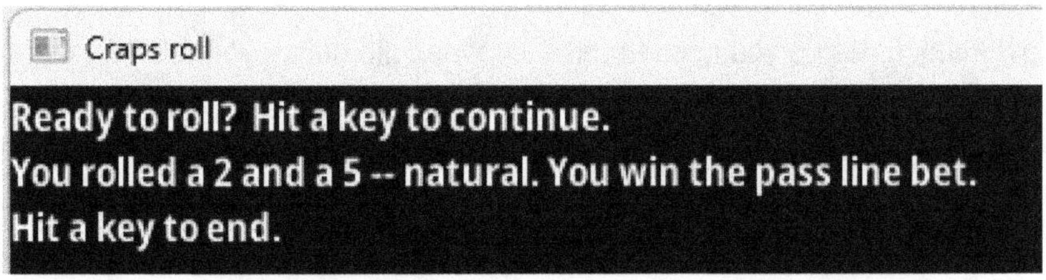

Craps roll

Ready to roll? Hit a key to continue.
You rolled a 2 and a 5 -- natural. You win the pass line bet.
Hit a key to end.

Figure 8-1. *Possible output of the craps program, Example 8-3*

Antibugging

When debugging, **you may want the same sequence of pseudo-random numbers every time**: if something goes wrong you want it to go wrong the same way each time so you can fix it. To make that happen replace `srand (time (nullptr))` with `srand (someInteger)` until it's debugged.

Now, something that can go wrong:

- **You get the same random number over and over.** See the Golden Rule of `srand`, above.

EXERCISES

For these exercises, please use the steps from "How to Write a Function in Four Easy Steps" in Chapter 7.

1. On paper, write what you think a sequence of 20 coin flips might be. Then write a program that flips coins and tells the user what the results are. Output might look like this:

   ```
   How many coins do you want to flip? 20
   Here are the results: HTTHTHHHTTHHTTTTTHHT
   That's 9 heads and 11 tails.
   ```

   Did the sequence look the way you expected?

2. How many times do you need to roll a six-sided die before you roll a 6? Write an algorithm for, then write and test, a program to roll until it does, and report the number of times it needed.

   Now do that a thousand times, and report the average.

3. Play against the computer, or against another player, with a dreidel, until someone is out of gelt. You can find the rules on Wikipedia or elsewhere.

4. Welcome to *The Price Is Right*, and come on down! Our task this time is to find the correct answer to the classic "Monty Hall" problem.

   You have a choice between doors 1, 2, and 3. Behind one is a Porsche and clear title to a South Pacific island; behind the other two are week-old pizza, a goat, and box mac and cheese. Hard as it is to pass up mac and cheese, you have your heart set on the Porsche and the island.

   You pick a door. The host then opens one of the other doors, one with no prize behind it. (If you picked wrong, he opens the only other door without a prize. If you picked right, he selects a prize-less door at random.) He offers you the chance to switch.

Should you?

Write a program that will simulate the entire process, and do it a large number of times. (What's a reasonable large number? You decide.) Be sure to do each part, all the way down to identifying the door the player switches to and comparing that to the door with the prize behind it. (Simplifying the problem may be valid, but simplifications can trip you up. Also, it's interesting to find a way to identify the door switched to.)

What percentage of the time do you win if you switch? If it's 50% or close, it must not matter.

So did it matter?

Extra The Monty Hall problem is a classic probability problem popularized at one point by Marilyn vos Savant, the high-IQ author of the "Ask Marilyn" column in *Parade* magazine. She gave the correct answer … and then wrote more columns as people kept writing in. A grade-school class tried running the scenario several times (without a computer, presumably) to find the answer. Several mathematics professors, giving their names and affiliations, wrote to ask her to recant, with such comments as "You blew it!" and "You are the goat!" How embarrassing – for them.

Boolean Functions

We've had functions to return true-or-false values before: `isupper`, for example, in Chapter 5. Here's how I'd write it (Example 8-4).

Example 8-4. My own `isupper`, a Boolean function

```
bool isupper (char ch) // returns whether ch is an upper-case letter
{
    bool result;

    if (ch >= 'A' && ch <= 'Z')
        result = true;
```

```
    else
        result = false;

    return result;
}
```

So if ch is in the uppercase range, it returns true; otherwise, false. On the other hand, in the next version ...if ch is in the uppercase range, it returns true; otherwise, false. They do exactly the same thing:

```
bool isupper (char ch) // returns whether ch is an upper-case letter
{
    return ch >= 'A' && ch <= 'Z';
}
```

I like the short one. Pick the one you find clearer.

EXERCISES

1. Write a function inRange that, given a number and a lower and an upper bound, tells if the number is between the bounds. As is usually the case, it won't print anything, but will return its answer. main can do the printing.
2. Write an algorithm for, then write, a function that puts boxes on the screen for "YES" and "NO" and another that waits for a mouse click and returns true if the YES box was clicked, and false if NO was clicked and continues to wait if the click is outside both boxes. Then make a program that demonstrates these functions' use.
3. Add the function from the previous exercise to the magical creature classifier program from Exercise 1 in Chapter 5's "chars and cctype" section, so the user can click, rather than type, their responses.

& Parameters

What if you want your function to give new values to variables? You can only return one thing from a function.[1]

In the analogy of the candy-making machine, you can only spit out one product. We need a different kind of machine: one that takes in one or more confections and changes them (bakes them, frosts them, whatever).

The function I want is one that can swap values: `swap (x, y)` should make `x` be what `y` was and `y` be what `x` was. Here's my first attempt:

```
void swap (int arg1, int arg2)
{
    arg1 = arg2; arg2 = arg1;
}
```

Trace this through. Here are states of these variables as we go through this process (Figure 8-2). Assume the values are initially 5 and 10.

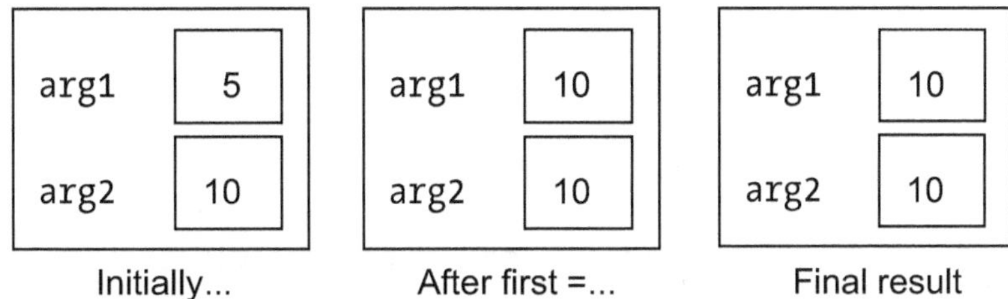

Figure 8-2. *What happens with `swap`: first attempt*

A variable is like a box that contains a value, but only one. If you wanted to swap what was in your hands, how would you do it? You'd find a place to put one of the objects – a temporary holding area. If the computer's going to swap, it'll need a third place too: a temporary variable. This should work (see Figure 8-3):

[1] Until Chapter 19.

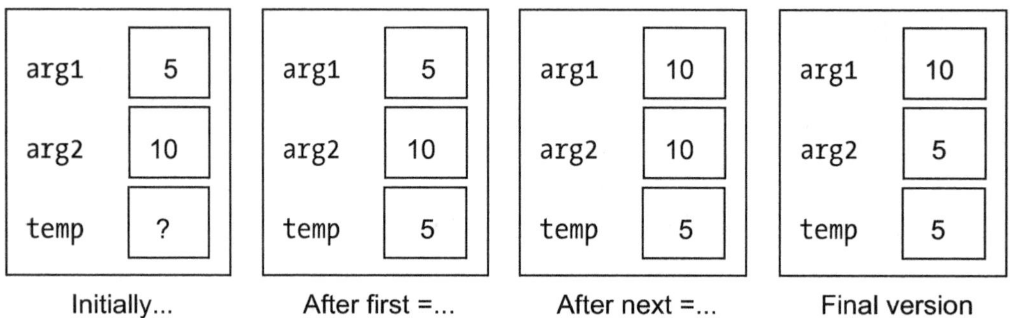

Figure 8-3. *swap: second attempt*

Now let's see what happens when we call it:

```
int main(int argc, char** argv)
{
    int x=5, y=10;

    swap (x, y);

    ...
}
```

We begin with main (Figure 8-4).

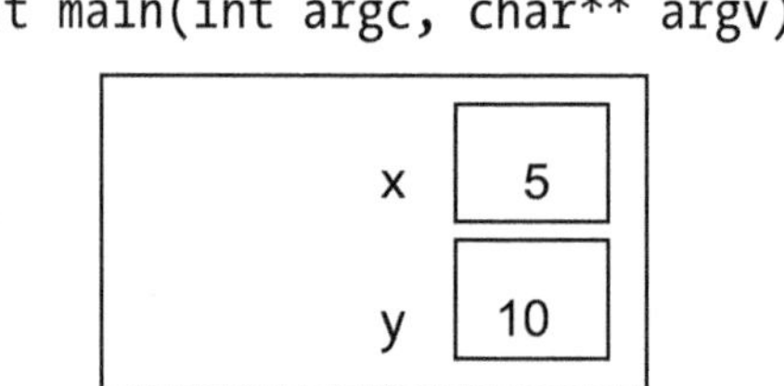

Figure 8-4. *main before calling swap*

Then we call swap. The compiler creates an instance of the swap function – the variables it contains and anything else it needs to know, copying arguments from main into the parameters (Figure 8-5).

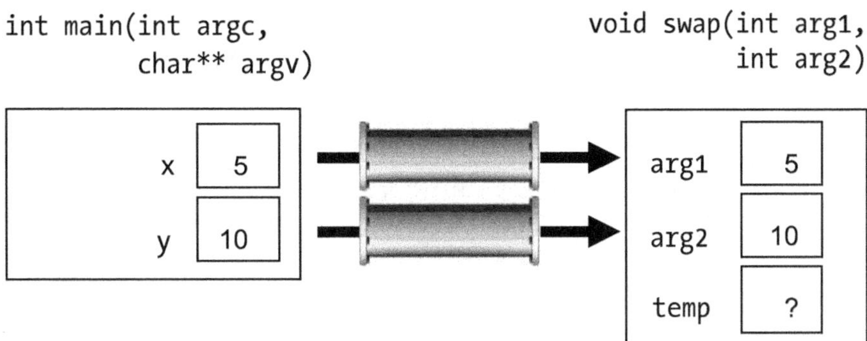

Figure 8-5. *swap begins*

We go through the same process as before, successfully swapping arg1 and arg2 (Figure 8-6).

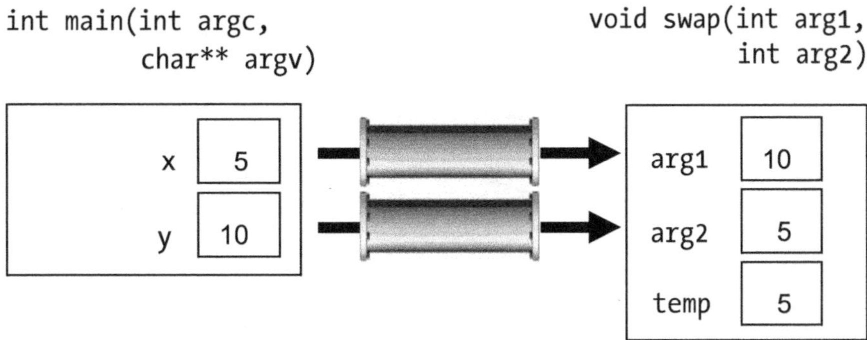

Figure 8-6. *swap completes*

Now we're done with swap, so it can go away (Figure 8-7).

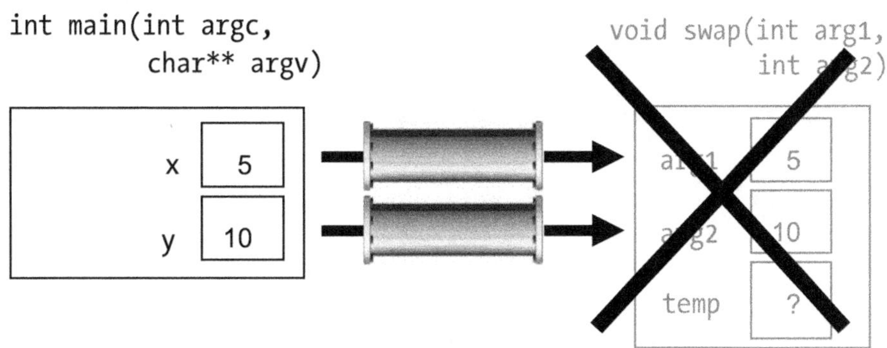

Figure 8-7. *swap goes away*

I suppose that was fun and all, but ...weren't we supposed to be changing x and y in main?

Instead, we altered swap's local variables arg1 and arg2. When swap went away, so did they.

The solution is to **put & after the type in the parameter**. This makes arg1 and arg2 not copies of what's passed in, but temporary aliases: arg1 *is* x, as long as we're in the call to swap. A for ampersand, A for alias:

```
void swap(int& arg1, int& arg2)
{

    int temp = arg1; arg1 = arg2; arg2 = temp;

}
```

Here's another walkthrough, starting with Figure 8-8.

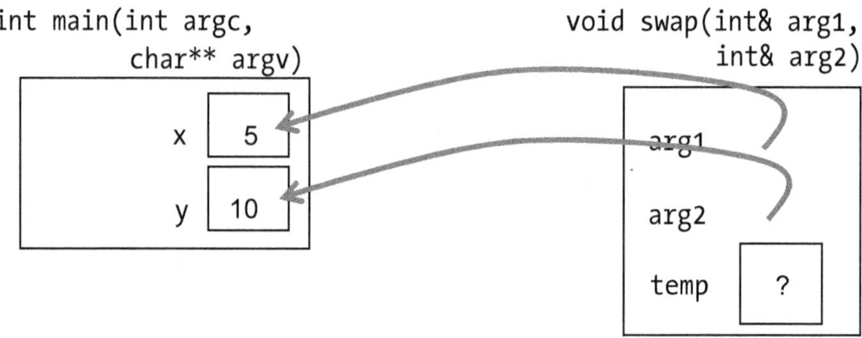

***Figure 8-8.** Calling swap, with & parameters*

Since `arg1` *is* `x` and `arg2` *is* `y`, what we do to `arg1` and `arg2` we really do to `x` and `y`. So `x` and `y` really get changed (Figure 8-9).

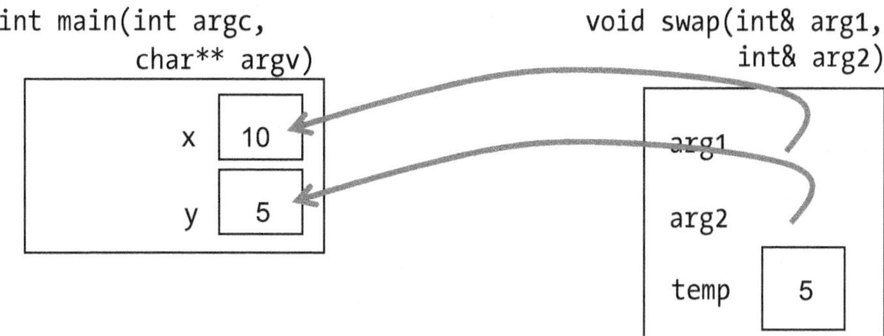

Figure 8-9. *`swap` actually swaps now!*

The function is finished and goes away (Figure 8-10), with `x` and `y` swapped.

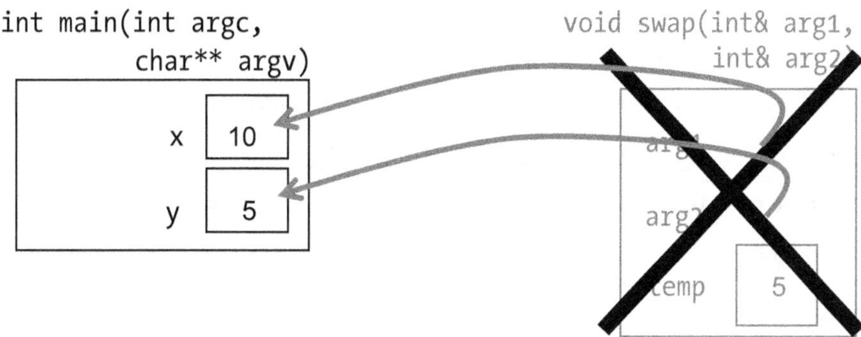

Figure 8-10. *`swap` completes (and correct)*

Generally, when should you get a value from a function with &, and when do you use a `return` statement? For now, if you have exactly one value to return, use `return`. If you have multiple values, you need a parameter list with &'s.

Golden Rule of Function Parameters and `return` (Version 1)

If the function provides no information to the calling function, its return type is `void`.

If it provides one piece of information, its return type is the type of that piece.

If it provides multiple pieces, its return type is `void`, and those pieces are provided through the parameter list using &.

Antibugging

- **The function seems to change its parameters; but when you leave the function, they're unchanged.** This came from forgetting the &. A common, and maddening, mistake.

EXERCISES

1. Write the algorithm for, and write, a function to generate a random location on the screen and provide it to the function that calls it.
2. ...then use that random-point function to fill the window with stars (dots) at random locations. Run it a few times to make sure you don't always get the same pattern.
3. Write a function to make a color darker. Here's how: cut the red, the green, and the blue each in half. This means you'll have to do it to the red, green, and blue `int` values, not to the `SSDL_Color` provided by `SSDL_CreateColor`. Then use this function to make a sequence of dots of progressively darker value. Ask the user the initial values.
4. Write a function to solve the quadratic formula. The solutions are $\left(-b+\sqrt{b^2-4ac}\right)/2a$ and $\left(-b-\sqrt{b^2-4ac}\right)/2a$ (the sign before the square root is the difference). This amounts to either two solutions or one solution (if both solutions are the same) or zero solutions (if the thing we take the square root of, $b^2 - 4ac$, is negative). So provide the main program with the solutions *and* a parameter saying how many solutions there are. (If there are 0, the contents of the solutions won't matter.)
5. Write a function to solve for π the "Monte Carlo" way. Here's how: make a square of some side length 2R. Randomly pick points in that square and draw them ...but if they're within R of the center – use the distance formula from earlier – draw them red; else, draw them blue. Count the red ones as you go, and return 4 times that number divided by the total dots drawn. (Why 4? It will become apparent!)[2] Pass in the number of dots to draw to your Monte Carlo function, and see if for large numbers your approximation of π gets better.

[2] OK, I'll tell you. The number of red dots divided by the total dots is the area of a circle of radius R divided by the area of a square of side 2R. That is, reds/total = $\pi R^2/(4R^2)$. Solve for π and you get 4 * reds/total.

Identifier Scope

The **scope** of an identifier (a variable name, a function name, or some other defined name) is the area in which it has meaning.

Consider the swap example. In the diagrams, we saw x and y as inside main (since they were); we saw arg1, arg2, and temp as inside swap (since they were). Variables inside functions can't be seen – or interfered with – by other functions. That means outside code *can't* mess them up. That's modularity: keeping separate things separate, mostly for security.

To look further at scope, consider again Example 8-3: a program to do a craps roll. It has two functions, main and rollDie. Here's a recap:

```
// One step in a game of craps
//         -- from _C++26 for Lazy Programmers_

...

constexpr int SIDES_PER_DIE = 6;

int rollDie ();                    // roll a 6-sided die

int main(int argc, char** argv)
{
    ...
    int roll1 = rollDie (), roll2 = rollDie ();
    sout << "You rolled a " << roll1 << " and a " << roll2;

    ...

    return 0;
}

int rollDie()
{
    int result = rand() % SIDES_PER_DIE + 1;

    return result;
}
```

Definitions can go into the pairs of curly braces, but they can't come out (see Figure 8-11). It's like a duck blind: if you're in the blind, you can see things outside, but they can't see you. Everybody can see SIDES_PER_DIE, since it's outside everything and definitions can always go in: rollDie can use it, and so can main. Nobody can see result except its owner rollDie, because it can't leave the {}'s in which it's declared. Similarly, nobody can see roll1 and roll2 except main.

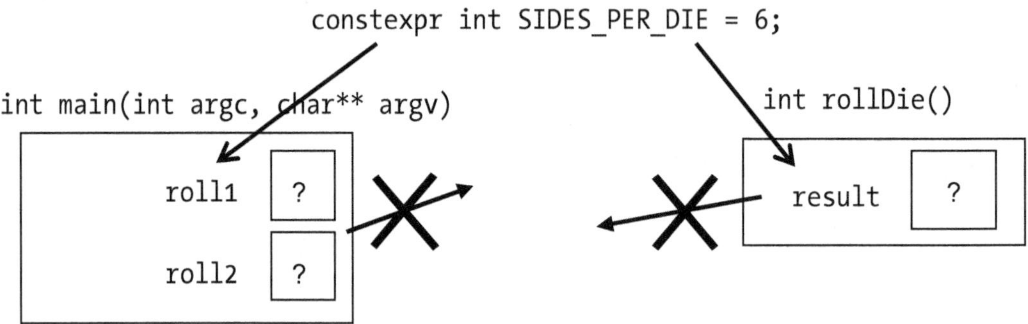

Figure 8-11. *Identifier scope. Definitions outside {}'s can be seen inside them; definitions inside can't be seen outside. Attempts to reference them get something like "identifier not found" or "not declared"*

This makes sense: SIDES_PER_DIE is everybody's business. roll1 and roll2 are main's business and no one else's. result, while rollDie is constructing it, is rollDie's business (though it will report to main when it ends).

So how do functions share information? Through parameter lists and return statements.

Golden Rule of Identifier Scope

Identifiers can't be seen outside of the {}'s where they were declared.

A Final Note on Algorithms

Through our exercises, we've continued to write algorithms for whatever we do as suggested in Chapter 6. I won't keep putting the reminder in, but I'll make a blanket statement now: it's best to get in the habit. It feels lazy to skip the step, but it's more work overall, so the lazy thing is: solve the problem of how to do it in the algorithm-writing step. Then coding can be relatively easy.

CHAPTER 9

Using the Debugger

The debugger lets you step through the program, line by line or function by function, seeing the values of variables so you can tell what's wrong. Good idea, right?

I think so. To cover useful debugger commands, let's use the debugger to repair the flawed program in Example 9-1. It's intended to draw a US flag: a sort of a groovy handmade-looking version with hollow stars as shown. (To do a better job, we'd use an image from a file – but for now I want to debug a star-writing function.) The design of the flag is illustrated in Figure 9-1.

Example 9-1. A buggy program to draw the US flag. Output is in Figure 9-2.

```
// Program to draw Old Glory on the screen
//       -- from _C++26 for Lazy Programmers_

#include <cmath> // for sin, cos
#include "SSDL.h"

constexpr double PI = 3.14159;


// Dimensions1
constexpr int HOIST                   = 390; //My pick for flag width
                                             //Called "A" in Fig. 9-1
constexpr int FLY                     = static_cast<int>(HOIST*1.9),   //B
              UNION_HOIST             = static_cast<int>(HOIST*0.5385),//C
              UNION_FLY               = static_cast<int>(HOIST*0.76);  //D
```

[1] Dimensions from en.wikipedia.org/wiki/Flag_of_the_United_States.

W. Briggs, *C++26 for Lazy Programmers*, https://doi.org/10.1007/979-8-8688-1859-2_9

```
constexpr int UNION_VERTICAL_MARGIN  = static_cast<int>(HOIST*0.0538),//E&F
              UNION_HORIZONTAL_MARGIN= static_cast<int>(HOIST*0.0633);//G&H

constexpr int STAR_DIAMETER          = static_cast<int>(HOIST*0.0616);//K

constexpr int STRIPE_WIDTH           = HOIST/13;                      //L
```

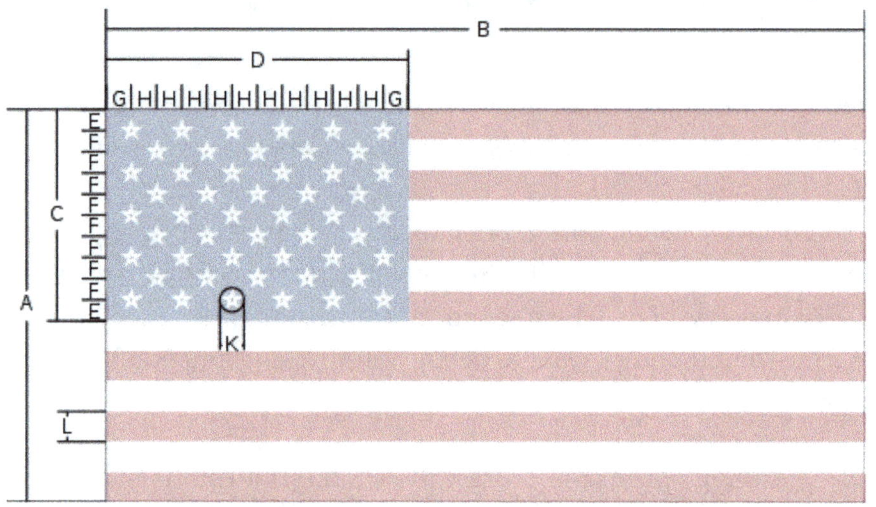

Figure 9-1. *Designing the US flag*

```
// Colors
const SSDL_Color RED_FOR_US_FLAG   = SSDL_CreateColor(179, 25, 66);
const SSDL_Color BLUE_FOR_US_FLAG  = SSDL_CreateColor( 10, 49, 97);

void drawStripes();             // the white and red stripes
void drawUnion  ();             // the blue square
void drawStar   (int x, int y); // draw a star centered at x, y

// draw a row of howMany stars, starting with the x, y position,
//  using UNION_HORIZONTAL_MARGIN to go to the right as you draw
void drawRowOfStars(int howMany, int x, int y);

int main(int argc, char** argv)
{
    SSDL_SetWindowTitle("Old Glory");
    SSDL_SetWindowSize (FLY, HOIST);
```

```
    drawStripes ();
    drawUnion   (); // draw the union (blue square)

    SSDL_WaitKey();

    return 0;
}

void drawStripes()
{
    SSDL_SetRenderDrawColor(RED_FOR_US_FLAG);
    SSDL_RenderFillRect(0, 0, FLY, HOIST); // first, a big red square

    // Starting with stripe 1, draw every other stripe WHITE
    SSDL_SetRenderDrawColor(WHITE);
    for (int stripe = 1; stripe < 13; stripe += 2)
        SSDL_RenderFillRect(0, stripe*STRIPE_WIDTH,
                            FLY, STRIPE_WIDTH);
}

// draw a row of howMany stars, starting with the x, y position,
//  using UNION_HORIZONTAL_MARGIN to go to the right as you draw
void drawRowOfStars (int howMany, int x, int y)
{
    for (int i = 0; i < howMany; ++i)
    {
        drawStar(x, y); x += 2*UNION_HORIZONTAL_MARGIN;
    }
}

void drawUnion()
{
    SSDL_SetRenderDrawColor(BLUE_FOR_US_FLAG);
    SSDL_RenderFillRect(0, 0, UNION_FLY, UNION_HOIST);
    // draw the blue box

    SSDL_SetRenderDrawColor(WHITE);
    int row = 1;  // What's the y position of the current row of stars?
    for (int i = 0; i < 4; ++i) // Need 4 pairs of 6- and 7-star rows
```

```
    {
        drawRowOfStars(6,
                       UNION_HORIZONTAL_MARGIN,
                       row*UNION_VERTICAL_MARGIN);

        ++row;

        // The 2nd row is staggered right slightly
        drawRowOfStars(5,
                       2*UNION_HORIZONTAL_MARGIN,
                       row*UNION_VERTICAL_MARGIN);

        ++row;
    }
    // ...and one final 6-star row
    drawRowOfStars(6, UNION_HORIZONTAL_MARGIN,
                   row*UNION_VERTICAL_MARGIN);
}

void drawStar(int centerX, int centerY)
{
    constexpr int RADIUS         = STAR_DIAMETER/2,
                  POINTS_ON_STAR = 5;

    int x1, y1, x2, y2;
    double angle = PI/2;     // 90 degrees: straight up vertically
                             // 90 degrees is PI/2 radians

    // Find x, y point at current angle relative to center
    x1 = static_cast<int>(RADIUS * cos(angle));
    y1 = static_cast<int>(RADIUS * sin(angle));

    for (int i = 0; i < POINTS_ON_STAR; ++i)
    {
       angle += (2 * PI / 360) / POINTS_ON_STAR;
                                         // go to next point on star

        // Find x, y point at new angle relative to center
       x2 = static_cast<int>(RADIUS * cos(angle));
       y2 = static_cast<int>(RADIUS * sin(angle));
```

```
        SSDL_RenderDrawLine(centerX+x1, centerY+y1,
                            centerX+x2, centerY+y2);

        x1 = x2;                        // Remember the new point
        y1 = y2;                        //   for the next line
    }
}
```

***Figure 9-2.** A buggy US flag*

That could have gone better. The stars are almost-invisible, or invisible, dots. Even the stripes are off: note how the blue union square doesn't line up with that middle red stripe; and the bottom stripe is too big.

What debugger will you use? If you're using Microsoft Visual Studio, it's built-in. For Unix (Ubuntu and Fedora), I recommend ddd, a friendly, free graphical interface to the gdb debugger.[2] MSys2 and other Unix distributions don't support ddd at this point, so I recommend gdb itself: text-based but standard and freely available.

As you go through upcoming sections ...it's easiest to remember things if you do them yourself, so I strongly recommend you copy this program from the book's sample code (ch9/1-flag) and follow along, doing the same things as in the book.

[2] When you run it, ddd may complain about missing fonts. You can ignore those complaints. There are definitely other graphical debuggers you may choose. I recommend this one because (a) it exposes you to the underlying gdb commands, which are unlikely to change and work even if your terminal's graphics are going wonky, and (b) its newest popular competitor, gdbgui, can be tricky to install.

Breakpoints and Watched Variables

Let's start by examining dimensions to see why the stripes don't line up. What dimensions? `STRIPE_WIDTH` seems relevant! So does `UNION_HOIST`, which is the height of the blue square, and `HOIST`, the height of the whole thing.

ddd

To debug the program `a.out` with ddd in Unix, go to its folder and type `./dddx`. If there is no `dddx`, copy it from the `basicSSDLProject` folder you've been using.[3]

Highlight `main`. (If you don't see any code, check the "Antibugging" section below.) Toward the right on the top row of controls, find the stop-sign icon labeled "Break"; click that. A stop sign appears on the line, meaning the program stops here when it runs. You should see something like Figure 9-3.

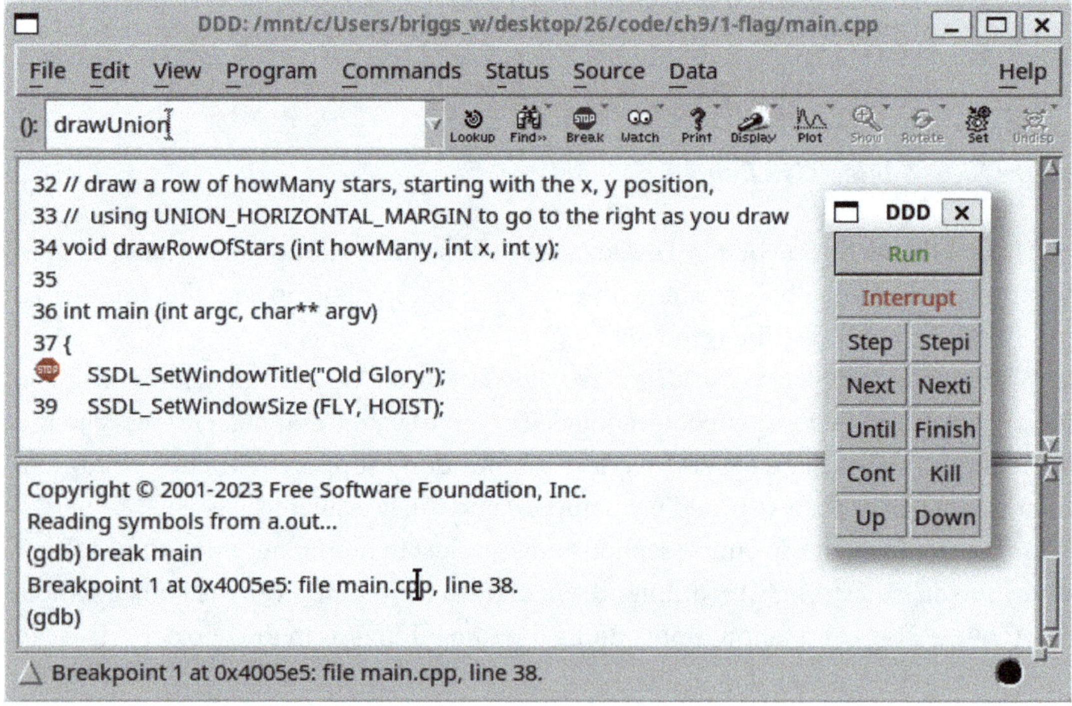

Figure 9-3. *The ddd interface to the gdb debugger*

[3] If you get warnings in the terminal about fonts, ignore them.

In the bottom window with the (gdb) prompt, the command `break main` should appear. ddd is a training-wheels interface, always telling you what gdb command you just chose. This way you learn gdb as you go.

To run, click Run on the menu on the right, or type `run` at the (gdb) prompt. `print STRIPE_WIDTH` and others at the prompt to get the values of `STRIPE_WIDTH`, `HOIST`, and `UNION_HOIST`.

Clicking the breakpoint may delete it. If not, `delete <breakpoint number>`. See the gdb window for the breakpoint number. To quit, type `quit`.

gdb

Go to the program's folder and type `./gdbx`.

To make the program stop on that first line, I type `break main` (Unix) or `break SDL_main` (MSys2). When I run the program, it'll break there and I can examine the values.

To start the program, type `run`. To see the values, type `print`: `print STRIPE_WIDTH`, `print HOIST`, `print UNION_HOIST`.

To end gdb, type `quit`.

Visual Studio

Be sure you compiled in Debug mode. You should see Debug, not Release, near the top under the menu bar (see Figure 9-4). If not, debugger commands won't work.

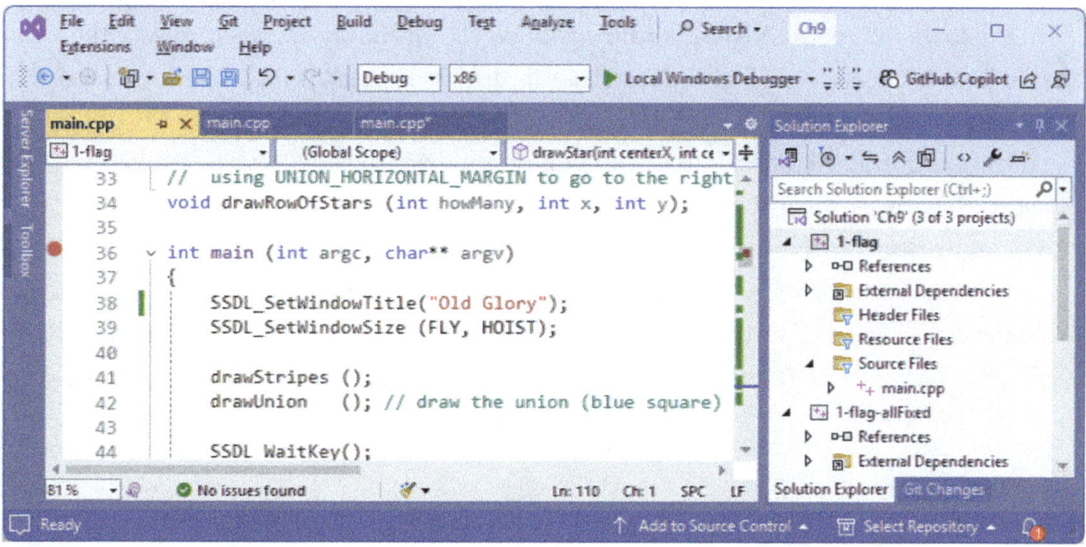

***Figure 9-4.** Setting a breakpoint in Microsoft Visual Studio*

Click the off-white bar left of `main`; a sort of red stop sign appears, as in Figure 9-4. (OK, it's a red dot. But "stop sign" is easier to remember.)

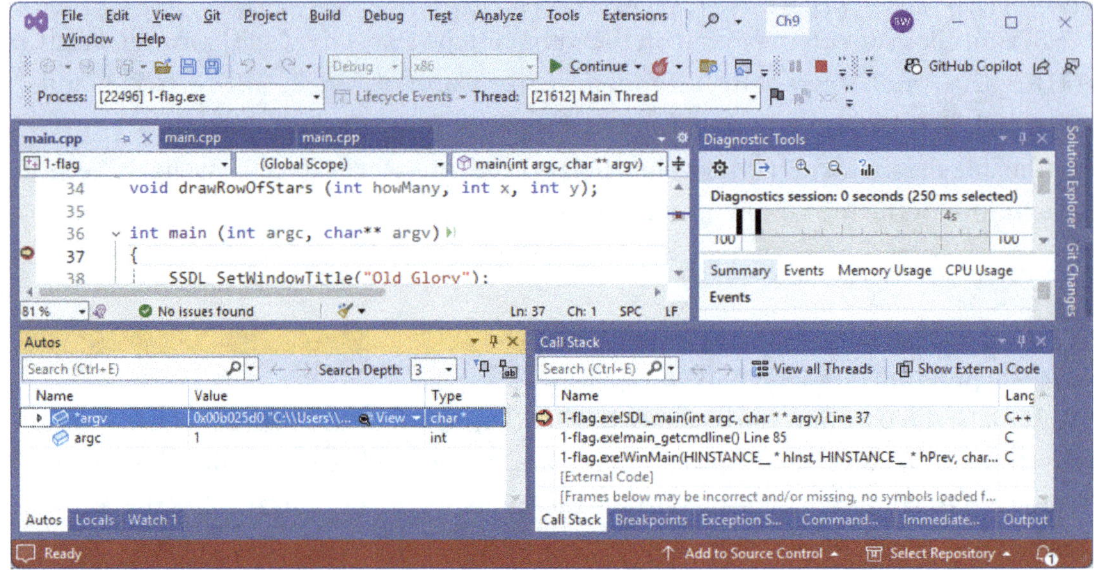

***Figure 9-5.** Starting a debugger session in Microsoft Visual Studio*

Start the program, same as always.

Visual Studio didn't like where my breakpoint was, so it moved it down a line (Figure 9-5). No problem. The yellow arrow means "This line is next." It's about to start `main`, so it's already done the initial constant declarations. Let's see what it made.

At the lower left of the Visual Studio window, you probably see a window with tabs for Autos, Locals, etc. (If you don't, try Window ➤ Reset Window Layout on the menu bar.)

Autos are things Visual Studio thinks you might want to see. It's wrong this time: I'm not worried about `argv` and `argc`.

Locals are local variables; we don't have any.

Watch 1 is a place where we can watch the values of variables. Click that tab. You can now click under "Name" and give the name of something you want to see. Try `STRIPE_WIDTH`, then `UNION_HOIST`, and `HOIST`.

These are the numbers we need. Click the breakpoint again to delete it if you like, and we'll continue.

Fixing the Stripes

Now we have the numbers; let's make sense of them.

A stripe should be 1/13 of the HOIST, which is 400. 400/13 is 30.76 something; STRIPE_WIDTH, being an int, is only 30. There should be seven stripes covered by that UNION_HOIST: the stripes cover 7*30 = 210 pixels, but the UNION_HOIST is HOIST*7/13 = 215.

The problem is we're doing integer division and losing decimal places.

Let's make HOIST not 400 but something divisible by 13. STRIPE_WIDTH was 30; 13*30 = 390. We'll change the initialization of HOIST accordingly

```
constexpr int HOIST                    = 390;  // My pick for flag width
```

and run again. The stripe problem is fixed!

Going Into Functions

The star problem requires further digging. So restore your breakpoint at main and start the debugger again.

ddd

In the "DDD" menu on the right in Figure 9-3, Next takes you to the next line, and Step steps into a function. The arrow on the left shows what line you're about to execute. Use Next to go to drawUnion. When there, Step into that function.

Using Next and Step, go into drawRowOfStars and then drawStar, until you get to the for loop.

At this point it makes sense to find out what the variables are. Under the Data menu, select Display Local Variables. You may need to make the Data area visible: View ➤ View Data Window. Figure 9-6 shows the result.

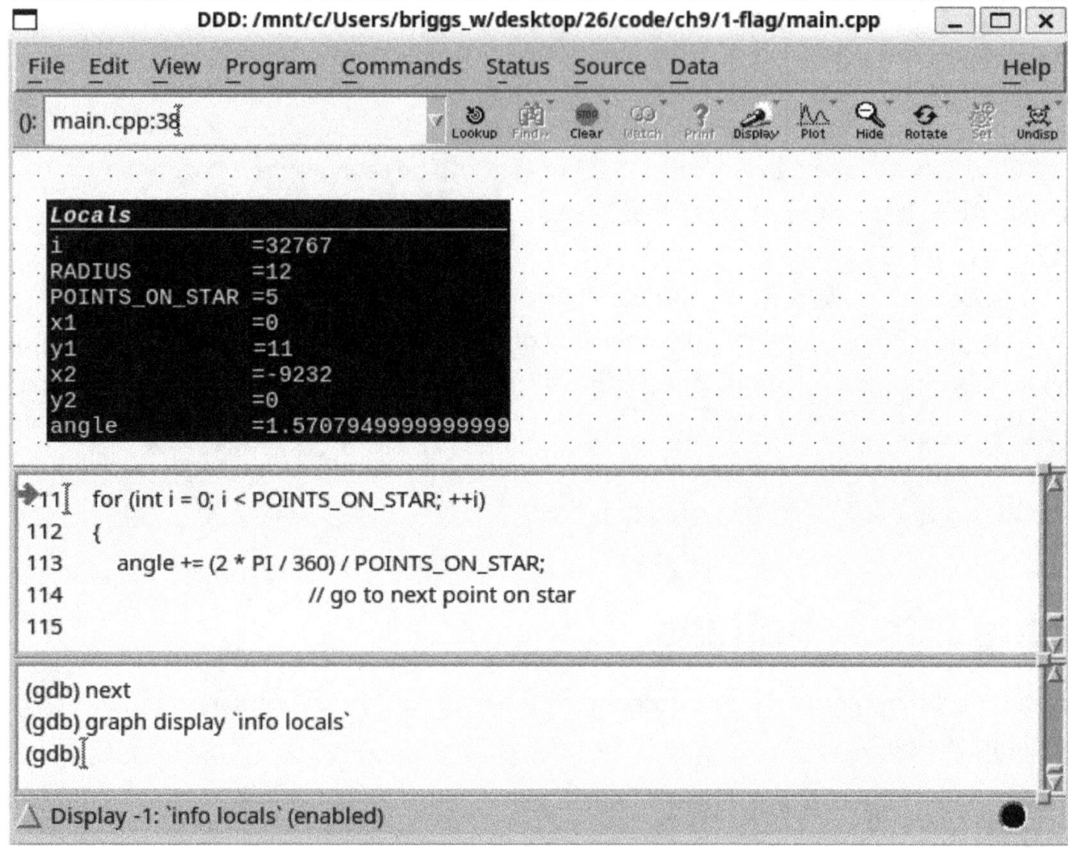

Figure 9-6. *Displaying local variables in ddd*

Nothing looks obviously wrong. Let's go on to `SSDL_RenderDrawLine`. Wasn't `angle` supposed to change more than that? `print (2 * PI/360)/POINTS_ON_STAR` at the gdb prompt and see what you get.

gdb

To go further in the program, you can type `next` (or `n`) to go to the next line and `step` (or `s`) to step into a function. (Enter repeats the last command.) As you progress, it will print the current line, so you know where you are. Use these commands to go into `drawUnion` and then through `drawStar`, until you get to the for loop.

You may want to put a breakpoint in case you need to come back to this line. `break` will put one on the current line. `break drawStar` will break at the start of the function. Just for grins, try that now, and type `run`. Then `continue`, or `cont`, or `c`, to get back to the breakpoint.

`delete <number of breakpoint>` deletes the breakpoint; `delete` deletes them all.

To print local variables, enter `info locals`.

Nothing looks obviously wrong. Let's go on to `SSDL_RenderDrawLine`. Wasn't `angle` supposed to change more than that? `print (2 * PI/360)/POINTS_ON_STAR` and see what you get.

Visual Studio

Looking at the Debug menu, you can Step Over (execute) a line by selecting Step Over or hitting F10 - Function F10 on some keyboards. When you do the yellow arrow goes down a line, executing the line as it goes.

When you're down to `drawUnion`, you want to Step *Into* (F11/Function F-11) that function.

Using F10 and F11, go into `drawRowOfStars` and then `drawStar`, until you get to the for loop, as in Figure 9-7. The Call Stack, lower right, shows what function you're in (its top line) and how you got there (lines beneath).

If you don't see the Locals window, click the Locals tab.

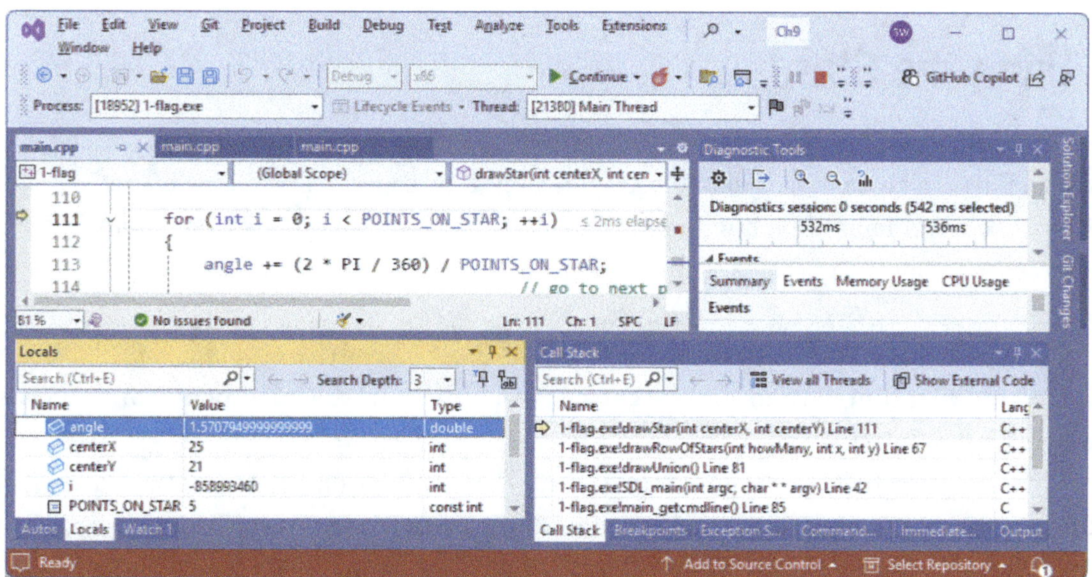

Figure 9-7. *The Locals window in Microsoft Visual Studio*

Nothing looks obviously wrong. Let's go on to `SSDL_RenderDrawLine`. Wasn't angle supposed to change more than that? In the Watch 1 window (see Figure 9-8), type or paste `(2 * PI/360)/POINTS_ON_STAR`. The debugger will calculate it for you.

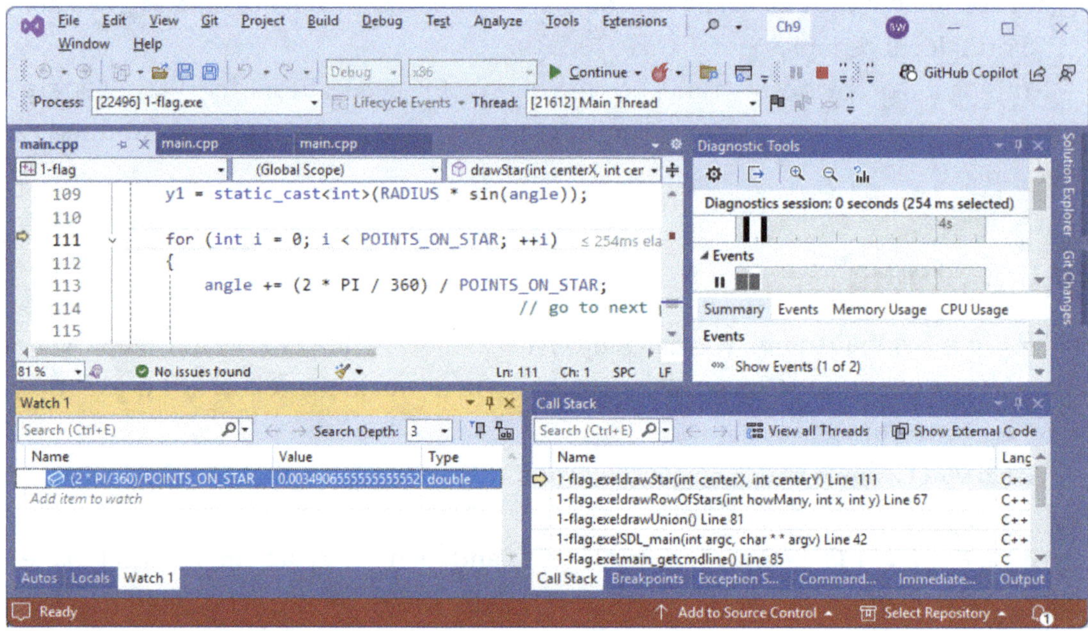

***Figure 9-8.** The Watch1 window in Microsoft Visual Studio*

Fixing the Stars

`(2 * PI/360)/POINTS_ON_STAR` was supposed to take us to the next point on the star. Isn't a fifth of a circle bigger than 0.00349? It should be a circle divided by 5. That's 360°/5, or, in radians, 2π/5, but that's not what the formula says. Looks like I mangled degrees together with radians. There's our problem, so here's our fix:

```
angle += (2 * PI)/POINTS_ON_STAR;      // go to next point on star
```

When we recompile and run, we get a flag with the stars drawn as pentagons. At least they have five sides!

The program tells the computer to go 5 steps around the circle, each time drawing a line covering 1/5 of that distance. Isn't that what a pentagon, not a star, does?

To draw a star, don't go 1/5 of the way around the circle. Go 2/5 of the way. Let's try that:

```
angle += 2*(2 * PI)/POINTS_ON_STAR; // go to next point on star,
                                    //    2/5 way around circle
```

Now the stars are there, but upside down. I think of 90 degrees as straight up, but with SDL we have increasing Y going *down* the screen. Is that the problem? I'll try starting at -90 degrees and see what happens:

```
float angle = -PI/2;          // -90 degrees -- straight up vertically
```

The result is in Figure 9-9. Much better.

Figure 9-9. *The flag with actual stars*

Wrap-Up

For a summary of common debugger commands, see Appendix G.

Antibugging

- **(ddd/gdb) There's no file. Maybe you forgot to** `make` **it?**
- **It just sits there, giving no prompt.** It may be waiting for input. Click the program's window and give it what it needs.

- **(ddd) It won't let you type in the command window.** Try killing the little command tool window and typing. You can restore the tool window under the View menu.
- **You're looking at some file you didn't write.** It's the compiler's code or a library's.

  Visual Studio: Step Out (Shift-F11) of the function(s) you're in to get back to your own code. Or set a breakpoint in your code and Continue (F5).

  `ddd/gdb`: `up` will take you up the "call stack" (the list of called functions, from the current one up to `main`); do this enough to see what part of your code you were in. Then set a breakpoint where you like, and `continue`.

Extra The GNU ("guh-NOO") Free Software Foundation (`www.gnu.org`) was formed in 1984 to provide free software for the Unix operating system. It's since expanded its mission, and people may use GNU Public License as a licensing agreement when they want to freely share their work.

This is how we get not only `ddd` and `gdb` but also `g++`, `emacs`, and other cool stuff.

GNU often applies funny names to things, and GNU itself is no exception. GNU is an acronym: it stands for "GNU's Not Unix."

Bottom-Up Testing

We looked at top-down design in Chapter 7: start with `main`, and then write the functions it calls and then the functions *they* call, until done.

Bottom-up testing is a natural corollary. It's sometimes too hard to test the whole program at once. Suppose you're doing economic forecasting with a program of many functions as illustrated in Figure 9-10, with `main` calling `getRevenue`, `getBorrowing`, and `getSpending` and those functions calling others, on down to `wildGuess`, `crossFingers`, and others.

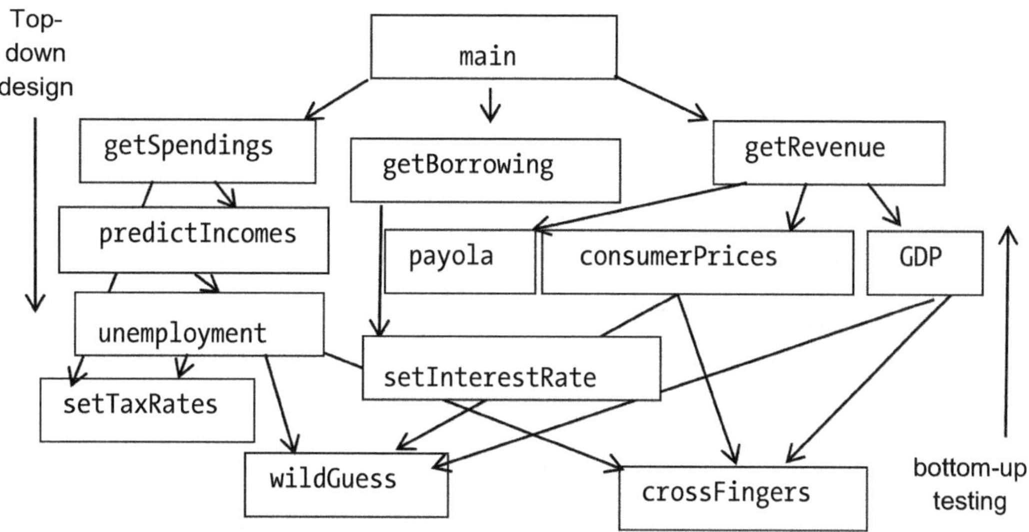

Figure 9-10. *A complicated mess to debug.* `main` *calls three functions* `getRevenue`*,* `getBorrowing`*, and* `getSpending`*, and they call lots of others*

You run the program, and it tells you

```
The nation will be bankrupt in -2 years.
```

That can't be right. But which function has a problem? `main`? `consumerPrices`? `wildGuess`? You can't get that information from a bare "–2"!

You need to know that you can trust every function. So you take the ones at the bottom (`wildGuess` and `crossFingers`), the ones that don't call the others but are called, and test them until you're confident.

Then test the ones that call them and the ones that call them ...all the way up to `main`.

More on Antibugging

Here are more hints on getting working programs:

- **Make plenty of backups.** If it's a large or difficult project, make a trail of them, so you can backtrack if something screws up.
- **Keep functions modular (no global variables).**

- **Display the information you need.** In the above example, the answer "-2" for the years until an event was clearly wrong, but otherwise wasn't informative.

  The biggest problem in testing often is you just don't know what values are in your variables. Here are two common fixes:

  - **Use the debugger**.
  - **Use lots of print statements.** If a variable has a value, then just while debugging, print it - clearly labeled: not

    ```
    sout << growthRate; // so 0.9 gets printed. What does it mean?
    ```

    but

    ```
    sout << "growthRate is " << growthRate << ".\n";
    ```

  That's longer, but it's better than struggling to remember what the numbers mean. Working blindly to fix an error you can't identify is too much work. Better to *see* the problem so you can fix it.

- **Don't let it get your gumption.** In *Zen and the Art of Motorcycle Maintenance*, author Robert Pirsig warns of things that suck out your "gumption," your ability to solve or even focus on problems with your bike. Or your essay. Or whatever.

  In programming, too, you can lose gumption. You just found a bug you thought you'd resolved, and the program's useless till you fix it, so now you're too frustrated to do anything but mope. I've been there. Recently.

  I once spent two working days tracking down what turned out to be misplaced parentheses. That's *it*? Tiny parentheses? They *are* tiny, but they were a big problem, because I couldn't go on till they were fixed.

  I just said "Whew!" and went on to the next issue.

  If you can suspend self-evaluation when there's an error and get back to the problem, you're on your way.

- **If you make stupid errors** ... See "gumption" above. Stupid errors are the *best* kind, because they're easy to fix. The hard ones are the subtle ones. Everyone makes stupid errors.
- **If you're just no good at this** ... Everyone feels that way in the beginning. I did. You wouldn't expect to be fluent in a new language after a few weeks of study, and C++ is way cooler than any mere spoken language.
- **Do it quick.** If you want to do something right, you probably have to do it wrong first. So go ahead and do it wrong. It's quicker to fix a broken program than stare at a screen till enlightenment strikes.

EXERCISES

No exercises yet – just be sure and use your debugger of choice in subsequent chapters!

CHAPTER 10

Arrays, Spans, and enum

In this chapter we'll cover sequences (arrays) of values, enumeration types, weather data, and board games.

Arrays

"If you don't like the weather in these parts," the old-timer said with a twinkle in his eye, "wait a few minutes."

Let's find out if he's right: we'll take ten temperatures at one-minute intervals and see the variation. I'll start like this:

```
double temp1; sout << "Enter a temperature: "; sin >> temp1;
double temp2; sout << "Enter a temperature: "; sin >> temp2;
double temp3; sout << "Enter a temperature: "; sin >> temp3;
```

That's getting old fast. Maybe there's a better way to store ten numbers. Here it is:

```
constexpr size_t[1] MAX_NUMBERS = 10;

double temperatures[MAX_NUMBERS]; //an array of 10 doubles
```

The BNF syntax for an array is *<base type> <name of array>* `[`*<array size>*`];` where *<base type>* is what you want an array of and *<array size>* is how many you want. Array size should be a constant integer.

Now we have an array of `temperatures`, starting with the 0th and ending with the 9th. (C++ starts counting at 0.)

To use one of the array's elements, just say which:

```
temperatures[3] = 33.6;
sout << temperatures[3];
```

[1] `size_t` is something often used for sizes of arrays and other things. It's essentially `unsigned int`.

W. Briggs, *C++26 for Lazy Programmers*, https://doi.org/10.1007/979-8-8688-1859-2_10

temperatures is an array of double, so you can use temperatures[3] anywhere you can use a double - since that's exactly what it is.

Note that here, the number in the [ ]'s is not the array size - that's in the declaration only! - but which element you want. This "index" should be some countable type like int, and we usually use ints:

```
//Get the numbers
for (int i = 0; i < MAX_NUMBERS; ++i)
{
       sout << "Enter a temperature: ");
       ssin >> temperatures[i];
}
```

For loops are a natural way to process arrays because they can easily go through each element. This loop starts at 0 and keeps going as long as i is less than 10 (MAX_NUMBERS), so we'll be seeing temperatures[0], temperatures[1], etc., up through temperatures[9] - all 10.

You get used to counting this way: an array of N elements starts with the 0th and ends with the N-1th. Maybe you'll soon be starting your to-do lists with 0.

Here is a complete program for reading in and spitting back out temperatures.

Example 10-1. Reading/writing a list of numbers using an array

```
// Program to read in and print back out numbers
//                -- from _C++26 for Lazy Programmers_

#include <cstddef> //for size_t, often included anyway
#include "SSDL.h"

int main(int argc, char** argv)
{
    constexpr size_t MAX_NUMBERS = 10;

    sout << "Enter " << MAX_NUMBERS
         << " temperatures to make your report.\n\n";

    double temperatures [MAX_NUMBERS];
```

```
    // Get the numbers
    for (int i = 0; i < MAX_NUMBERS; ++i)
    {
        sout << "Enter the next temperature: ";
        ssin >> temperatures[i];
    }

    // Print the numbers
    sout << "You entered ";
    for (int i = 0; i < MAX_NUMBERS; ++i)
        sout << temperatures[i] << ' ';

    sout << "\nHit any key to end.\n";

    SSDL_WaitKey();
}
```

We usually initialize variables. Here's how to do that with an array:

```
//where MAX_NUMS = 4...
double Numbers[MAX_NUMS] = {0.1, 2.2, 0.5, 0.75};
```
[2]

Unfortunately, the bracketed list only works at initialization time: we can't later set `Numbers` to a bracketed set of values. We'll have to do that one element at a time, possibly using a for loop, as in Example 10-1.

I needn't put `MAX_NUMS` in the `[]`'s, because C++ can count the values and deduce the size:

```
double temperatures[] = {32.6, 32.6, 32.7, 32.7, 32.7,
                         32.7, 32.7, 32.7, 32.7, 32.7};
    //I think the old guy was messing with us
```

If you give too few values, it fills in the rest with 0's:[3]

```
double temperatures[MAX_NUMS] = {};//If it's really 0's,
                                   //I hope we're using Centigrade
```

[2] Omit the = if you like: `double Numbers[] {0.1, 2.2, 0.5, 0.75};`.

[3] "Zero initialization." If the members of your array are of a type that has 0 (or 0.0!), they'll be set to that.

Arrays' Dirty Little Secret: Using Memory Addresses

Arrays aren't stored in memory the same way other variables are.

An array variable is actually an address: the address of a chunk of memory that contains the elements. When you declare an array, this makes the computer do these things: allocate the array variable (left in Figure 10-1); allocate a chunk of memory to store the elements (right in Figure 10-1); and put the address of the 0th element, that is, the start of that chunk, in your new array variable.

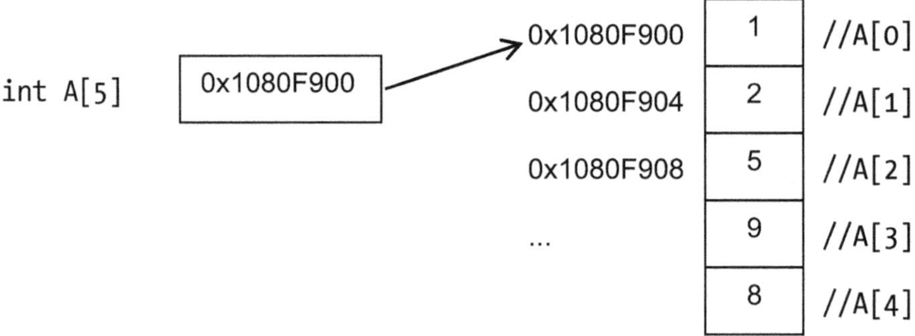

Figure 10-1. *How arrays are stored in memory*[4]

This scheme is why C++ starts with array index 0. To calculate the address of the `i`th element, it adds `i*sizeof(int)`, that is, `i` times the size of an `int`, whatever that is, to the location of the address. If you started at 1, it would have to add `(i-1)*sizeof(int)`. C++, and even more so its ancestor C, prefers to do things as efficiently as possible even if it sacrifices some clarity in the process.

One downside is that it doesn't check if the index you give it is reasonable. If you declare an array of five elements and try to access the fifth element (which, since C++ uses 0-based counting, doesn't exist), *it lets you*. This means you are reading a chunk of memory that's used for something else. It's even worse if you write to that chunk of memory, as in `A[5] = 0`. If you do you may overwrite data that makes up some other variable.

Going past array bounds is a big source of errors in C++. We'll get ways to make it less likely, some in this chapter (spans and ranges).

[4] In this illustration, I write the addresses in **hexadecimal** (base 16), which is conventional. The reason it goes up by 4 each row is I'm assuming `int` takes up 4 memory locations, that is 4 **bytes**. None of this matters here, but I don't want the C++ gods to laugh at my diagram.

Antibugging

- **Your loop goes one element too far in the array. I'd bet the less-than operator is to blame.** Change

  ```
  for (int i = 0; i <= N; ++i)
  ```

  to

  ```
  for (int i = 0; i <  N; ++i)
  ```

- **A variable's value changes, but you didn't tell it to.** You may have used an index too big for an array and thereby overwritten a *different* variable.

- **Your program crashes (stops running).** In Unix, you get `Segmentation fault: core dumped`. In other venues, you may get a window that says "<your program> has stopped working" or (in Visual Studio) "Exception thrown."

  A likely cause at this point is ...using an index too big for the array.

EXERCISES

In the following, be sure to use the debugger if something goes wrong.

1. Write a program that gets from the user all seven daily high temperatures and daily lows for the week and tells the user which days had the lowest low and the highest high.
2. Make the same program, but don't ask the user: initialize the array using {}'s.
3. Given an array of `char`s (use {}'s to initialize), report if the characters are in alphabetical order.
4. Read in a list of integers, and print them out in reverse.

Arrays as Function Parameters, Spans, and Range-Based For

When we want to pass a variable to a function, we essentially lift the declaration (without the semicolon) and use that to define the parameter: that is, we'd declare x with `int x;`, so if we want to send x into function f, we write `void f(int x);`.

We do the same with arrays:

```
void f (int myArray[ARRAY_SIZE]);
```

To understand how the parameter works, think back to the previous section – how an array really is a memory address pointing to the elements it stores – and consider this function:

```
void convertToKelvin(float temps [MAX_NUMS])
{
    for (int i = 0; i < MAX_NUMS; ++i)
        temps[i] += KELVIN_FREEZING_POINT;
                    // Looks like those were Centigrade temps
                    // This will convert them to Kelvin, or Absolute
}
```

Call it like so: `convertToKelvin(temperatures);`. (No `[]` – just the variable name, like with other variables.)

You might be thinking: *Wait a minute – there's no &. You can't alter a parameter without an &!*

And you'd be right: you can't alter the array. Which is a memory address. The *elements* of the array aren't in that parameter list, so you *can* alter them. The function works fine.

What if you don't want to alter the elements? C++ has that covered too (Example 10-2).

Example 10-2. `lowestTemp`, taking an array and returning its smallest element

```
double lowestTemp(const double temperatures[MAX_NUMS])
//returns lowest entry in temperatures
{
    double result = temperatures[0];
```

```
    for (int i = 0; i < MAX_NUMS; ++i)
        if (temperatures[i] < result)
            result = temperatures[i];

    return result;
}
```

Declaring the array as `const` ensures `lowestTemp` can't change its elements. Using `const` where possible can prevent errors, which is a Good Thing.

Making Your Functions Work for Different Array Sizes with Spans (Plus: Easier For Loops)

When you pass an array to a function, C++ totally ignores the size given between the [ ]'s. Put it in or leave it out; C++ doesn't care. *This means the same function can be used for any array of the same base type, regardless of size.*

Here's a version of `convertToKelvin` that doesn't restrict you to a particular size (Example 10-3).

Example 10-3. `convertToKelvin`, a function that can be used for any `double` array, any size. Too bad it doesn't work.

```
void convertToKelvin(double elements[])
{
    for (int i = 0; i < ??; ++i)
        elements[i] += KELVIN_FREEZING_POINT;
}

...

convertToKelvin3(temperatures);
```

The for loop clearly definitely needs to know the array size! But where's it stored? As Figure 10-1 shows, it's not anywhere in the array. It's in `main`, where the array was declared; let's try using that (Example 10-4).[5]

[5] Having C++ forget the size of an array outside the function where it was declared is called **array-to-pointer decay**. This section shows the fix.

Example 10-4. A version of convertToKelvin that works. The various versions of convertToKelvin and minimum here are in the source code under project Ch10/3-thru-6-temps

```
void convertToKelvin1(double elements[], size_t arraySize)
{
    for (int i = 0; i < arraySize; ++i)
        elements[i] += KELVIN_FREEZING_POINT;
}

...

convertToKelvin1(temperatures, MAX_NUMS);
```

Passing in the size worked for decades with this language, and it's still absolutely fine if you can remember that extra parameter! But this looks easier (see Example 10-5).

Example 10-5. A nicer version of convertToKelvin

```
#include <span>
void convertToKelvin2(std::span<double> elements)
{
    for (int i = 0; i < elements.size(); ++i)
        elements[i] += KELVIN_FREEZING_POINT;
}

...

convertToKelvin3(temperatures);
                    //Back to just passing in temperatures. Nice!
```

A **span** is, essentially, the array and its size. C++ stuffs in the array and its size into it automatically when you pass in the array. After that, you can use [] as you did before, but now you can also put .size(), a function that returns the size, at the end to find how big it is.

Between the <> in the parameter list is what you've got an array of: double.

You'll need to put #include <span> at the beginning so the compiler will know what it is (just like you put #include "SSDL.h" at the beginning so it'll know what SSDL_WaitKey, etc., are).

The `std::` at the start says "this is part of the C++ library's standard (std) equipment." If you leave it out, the compiler will yell at you.

Here's another nice tweak modern C++ gives us: a simpler version of the for loop.

Example 10-6. Using span and a range-based for loop, with an array parameter

```
double minimum (std::span<const double> myArray)
// returns lowest entry in elements
// I'm renaming it "minimum" because it'll be generally useful
//    -- we don't have to use it only on temperatures
{
    double result = myArray[0];

    for (double element : myArray)
        if (element < result)
            result = element;

    return result;
}
```

No counting. No index `i`. Just the `element` itself, which ranges from the first to the last.

We put `const double` in the span to ensure that minimum can't change its array (nor should it).

If we *do* want to change the array, we'll need to take that `const` out and put an `&` in the range-based for – like in function parameter lists – else, the loop will alter copies, not the actual elements (see Example 10-7).

Example 10-7. A version of `convertToKelvin` using a "range-based" for loop

```
void convertToKelvin3(std::span<double> elements)
{
    for (double& e : elements)
        e += KELVIN_FREEZING_POINT;
}
```

Range-based for loops work on arrays – not just spans – except when they don't.[6] To keep it simple, let's loop on arrays the old way: with an index.

Antibugging

- **The compiler complains about "invalid conversion from int to int*" or "int to int[]" on a function call.** It's saying it expected an array but got a single value. Didn't we give it an array? In this example

  ```
  double m = minimum(temperatures[MAX_NUMBERS]);
  ```

  I didn't. I gave it the `MAX_NUMBERS`th temperature, whatever that is.

  This problem is a confusion over two uses of `[]`. When declaring, what goes between the `[]`'s is array size. At all other times, it's which element we want to access.

  Since the array's name is `temperatures`, not `temperatures[MAX_NUMBERS]`, I'll pass that in: `minimum(temperatures);`.

Golden Rule of [ ] What goes between the `[]`'s in an array reference is which element you want (except at the time of declaration – then it's the array size).

EXERCISES

In these exercises, use spans to pass in arrays; use range-based for loops if you like; and remember to use your favorite debugger if something goes wrong.

1. Write a `maximum` function to correspond to `minimum` in Example 10-6, and use these to find the range in a given array of temperatures – thus answering the question the chapter started with: how quickly the weather is changing. If the range is more than half a degree, print "You're right; the weather really does change quickly here!"

2. For a month of temperatures, report the highest high, the lowest low, and the day with the biggest gap between, using functions as needed.

[6] It doesn't work if you've experienced array-to-pointer decay or if your array is dynamically allocated (see Chapter 14). Otherwise, it's fine.

3. Write a program that will graph the high and low temperatures for a given month (you'll want to initialize the array using {}'s; it'll be too much work to type them each time), displaying X and Y axes for day and temperature and putting dots to mark the data points. Use functions as needed. You'll definitely want to write the algorithm first.

Enumeration Types, and `switch`

In preparation for using playing cards or colored pieces in a board game or months of the year ...let's look over a way of making several constant symbols quickly: `enum`.

```
enum class Suit {CLUBS, DIAMONDS, HEARTS, SPADES}; //Playing card suit
```

is much like

```
constexpr int CLUBS    = 0, // we start at 0
              DIAMONDS = 1, // and go up by one for each new symbol
              HEARTS   = 2,
              SPADES   = 3;
```

but is quicker to write and also creates a new type `Suit` so you can declare variables of that type:

```
Suit firstCardSuit = Suit::HEARTS, secondCardSuit = Suit::SPADES;
                    //Yes, we have to put Suit:: first
```

What *is* `firstCardSuit`, really? It's really a `Suit`! But, yes, it is very much like an `int`. Why not just make it an `int`? Clarity: When you declare an `int`, it's not clear if you really meant it as a suit for cards. If you declare it as a `Suit`, it's obvious.

In BNF, the `enum` declaration is `enum class` *<typename>* `{`*<list of values>*`}`.

With the naming convention used in this book, new types we create are Capitalized (like `Suit`, but unlike `int`: types built into the standard are lowercase).

We can also specify what integer our symbols correspond to:

```
enum class Rank {ACE=1, JACK=11, QUEEN, KING}; //Playing card rank
```

We didn't specify a value for `QUEEN`, so it keeps counting from `JACK`: `QUEEN` is 12, and `KING` is 13.

enum values are meant as labels than numbers, so though you can assign to enum variables (=) and compare them (==, <, <=, etc.), the C++ standard fights you hard to stop you from doing real math with them: you can't use ++, --, +, -, *, /, or %. You can't print them with sout or read them with ssin. You can't assign ints into them (myRank = 8 won't compile). So what good are they?

Sometimes you don't need to do those things.

If you must do math, there's a workaround, but it's not fun. (We'll find a nicer way in Chapter 20.) Need to get the integral version of your card rank? Either of these will do:

```
#include <utility> //for std::to_underlying
...
int k = static_cast<int>  (Rank::KING);
int q = std::to_underlying(Rank::QUEEN);
```
[7]

Want to go the other way and convert an int to a Rank? Use casting:

```
Rank myRank = static_cast<Rank>(8);
```

OK, enough trying to make enums do what they're not designed for. What if you want to print one? There's no way the compiler would know how we want a Suit printed, so we'll tell it:

```
void print(Suit suit)
{
    if      (suit == Suit::CLUBS)    sout << 'C';
    else if (suit == Suit::DIAMONDS) sout << 'D';
    else if (suit == Suit::HEARTS)   sout << 'D';
    else if (suit == Suit::SPADES)   sout << 'D';
    else                             sout << '?';
}
```

That's a lot of if's. C++ has a control structure tailor-made for enum: switch. It lists the different values suit might take and what to do in each case:

[7] Technically std::to_underlying converts to int, short int, unsigned int, or who_knows_what_kinda int, and we don't know which. To use the true underlying version, we can use auto – a keyword that means "figure out the type of this variable from the initializer":

```
auto q = std::to_underlying(Rank::QUEEN); //q becomes the right underlying type
```

But int will be fine. (We'll find more uses for auto in Chapter 23.)

```
void print (Suit suit)
{
    switch (suit)
    {
    case Suit::CLUBS:    sout << 'C'; break;
    case Suit::DIAMONDS: sout << 'D'; break;
    case Suit::HEARTS:   sout << 'H'; break;
    case Suit::SPADES:   sout << 'S'; break;
    default:             sout << '?'; break;
    }
}
```

In BNF, a switch statement is

```
switch (<expression>)
{
case <value>: <action>*
    ...
[default: <action>*]
}
```

The * means "as many copies as you want, maybe zero."

What this does is the expression in the parentheses is evaluated. (It has to be something you can count by – integers or characters. No floats, no doubles.) If it matches a particular value, the computer goes to that `case` and executes whatever actions come after. If you specify a default action – which you should – that's what happens if the expression doesn't match anything.

`switch` works on characters and integers – any countable type. (No floats.) This illustrates using it with characters and explains why we have all those `break`s:

```
// Print classification of letters as vowel, semivowel, consonant
switch (toupper (letter))
{
case 'A':                  // if it's A, start here
case 'E':                  // if it's E, start here
case 'I':                  // ...
case 'O':
```

```
case 'U': sout << "vowel"; //  ...and print "vowel" for all those cases
          break;
case 'Y':
case 'W': sout << "semivowel";
          break;
default:  sout << "consonant";
}
```

Say you gave it an 'A'. The program goes to case 'A' and does whatever commands we have for it – ignoring the other cases – until we get to the end of the switch or a break. In this case, it keeps going till it hits sout << "vowel", does that, and then hits the break and it's done.

(Though some disapprove of breaking in a loop, nobody will gripe at you for using it here; switch can't function without it.)

Tip If you get tired of typing enum Suit:: all the time, tell C++ to look in Suit for your symbols without you having to specify:

```
void print(Suit suit)
{
    using enum Suit;

    switch (suit)
    {
    case CLUBS:    sout << 'C'; break; //No "Suit::" needed
    case DIAMONDS: sout << 'D'; break;
    case HEARTS:   sout << 'H'; break;
    case SPADES:   sout << 'S'; break;
    default:       sout << '?'; break;
    }
}
```

Antibugging

- **switch does what you wanted for that value ... then it does the options that follow as well.** This is the most common error with `switch`: forgetting the `break`. Solution: Go back and put `break`s between the different options you wanted.
- **The compiler complains something about case labels and variables.** This code has that problem:

```
switch (myChar)
{
case 'P':
      int turns = MAXTURNS;
      playGame (turns);
      break;
...
}
```

It doesn't like initializing a variable as part of a `switch`. No problem: we'll just put {}'s around the area that needs the variable:

```
switch (myChar)
{
case 'P':
      {
            int turns = MAXTURNS;
            playGame (turns);
            break;
      }
...
}
```

EXERCISES

1. Declare an enumeration type for chess pieces: king, queen, bishop, knight, rook, pawn.
2. Declare an enumeration type for the planets in the Solar System. Earth is the third planet, so adjust your numbering so that `EARTH` is 3 and all other planets are also correctly numbered. You decide what to do about Pluto.
3. Write and test a program that asks for a number and prints the associated ordinal: that is, for 1, print 1st; for 2, print 2nd; for 3, print 3rd; for everything else, print the number plus "th." (Doesn't use `enum`; does use `switch`.)
4. Write a function `printRank` that, given a `Rank`, prints it appropriately – as `A, 2, 3, 4, 5, 6, 7 8, 9, 10, J, Q, or K`. This and the next exercise will be useful in Chapter 20's card game examples. I'd use `default` for the ones that show up as integers.
5. Write a function `readRank` that returns the `Rank` it reads in using the same format as in Exercise 3. Yes, it's an issue that some input is numbers and some is letters – so what type variable will you need to handle both?
6. Have the user enter two single-digit numbers and return the sum. Here's the twist: the numbers entered are in base 16 ("hexadecimal"). In base 16, we use "A" to represent 10, "B" for 11, "C" for 12, and so on to "F" for 15. You can give the result in base 10. (Uses `switch`, but not `enum`.)
7. Menus are a time-honored (old-fashioned) way of getting user input. Make a menu offering to draw for the user a circle or a line or maybe some other shape, and then draw the selected shape. (Uses `switch`, but not `enum`.)

Multidimensional Arrays (optional)

Not all arrays are simple lists. You can have an array in two or more dimensions.

Here's an array for a Tic-Tac-Toe (noughts and crosses) board: a 3 × 3 grid. Each square can contain an X, an O, or nothing.

```
constexpr size_t MAX_COLS = 3, MAX_ROWS = 3;
enum class Square { EMPTY, X, O };
Square board[MAX_ROWS][MAX_COLS];
```

To set the square in row 1, column 2, to X, we say

```
board[1][2] = Square::X;
```

and to check the rowth, colth square, we say

```
if (board[row][col] == Square::X) ...
```

Figure 10-2 shows how C++ arranges the array in memory. First, we have the 0th row, from 0 to the last column, then the 1st row, and then the 2nd.

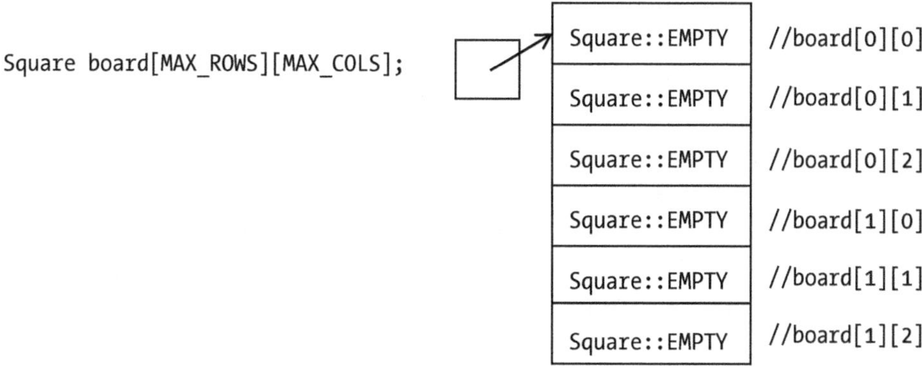

Figure 10-2. *How 2D arrays are arranged in memory (I omit actual addresses this time to emphasize that we don't have to know them)*

Each row has MAX_COLS squares, so to get to board[1][2], C++ calculates that it's 1*MAX_COLS+2 = 5 squares down. Counting 5 down from the initial element in Figure 10-2 takes us to board[1][2], which is what we wanted.

Displaying the Board

What are the two basic steps of drawing a board?

```
draw the board itself (the grid)
draw the X's and O's on the board
```

Drawing the grid is just making some lines, so I won't spend time on it here. We can break down drawing the Xs and Os piecemeal as we're used to doing:

```
for every row
    draw the row
```

How do we draw the row? Let's refine that:

```
for every row
    for every col
        draw the square
```

And how do we draw the squares? Last refinement:

```
for every row
    for every col
        if board[row][col] contains X draw an X
        else if it has an O draw an O
```

Example 10-8 shows the resulting program.

In it, to write the parameter list for `display`, we copy the definition of `ticTacToeBoard` between the `()`'s.[8] But unlike with one-dimensional arrays, you can't leave out the numbers between the `[]`'s willy-nilly. As we saw in Figure 10-2, `MAX_COLS` is used by C++ to determine memory locations of the elements. You could leave out the *first* dimension, but that doesn't make it clearer, so I don't.

Output is in Figure 10-3.

Example 10-8. Initializing and displaying a Tic-Tac-Toe (noughts and crosses) board

```
//Program to do a few things with a Tic-Tac-Toe board
//                -- from _C++26 for Lazy Programmers_

#include "SSDL.h"
```

[8] Why not use a span? `std::mdspan` (multidimensional span) exists, but it's not as easy as `std::span` and at time of writing your compiler doesn't support it.

```
//Dimensions of board and text notes
constexpr size_t MAX_ROWS     =   3, MAX_COLS    =   3,
                 ROW_WIDTH    = 100, COL_WIDTH   = 100,
                 BOARD_HEIGHT = 300, BOARD_WIDTH = 300;
                 //enough room for 3x3 grid, given these widths

constexpr int TEXT_LINE_HEIGHT = 20;

//A Square is a place in the TicTacToe board
enum class Square { EMPTY, X, O };

//Displaying the board
void display(const Square board[MAX_ROWS][MAX_COLS]);

int main(int argc, char** argv)
{
    using enum Square;

    //Shrink the display to fit our board
    // allowing room for 2 lines of text at the bottom;
    // set title
    SSDL_SetWindowSize (BOARD_WIDTH,
                        BOARD_HEIGHT + TEXT_LINE_HEIGHT * 2);
    SSDL_SetWindowTitle("Hit any key to end.");

    //Colors
    SSDL_RenderClear       (SSDL_CreateColor(30, 30, 30)); //charcoal
    SSDL_SetRenderDrawColor(SSDL_CreateColor(245, 245, 220)); //beige

    //The board, initialized to give X 3 in a row
    Square board[MAX_ROWS][MAX_COLS] =
        { {EMPTY, EMPTY,     X},
          {EMPTY,     X, EMPTY},
          {    X,     O,     O} };

    display(board);            //display it

    //Be sure the user knows what he's seeing is the right result
    SSDL_RenderText("You should see 3 X's diagonally, ",
                    0, MAX_ROWS * ROW_WIDTH);
```

```
    SSDL_RenderText("and two O's in the bottom row.",
                    0, MAX_ROWS * ROW_WIDTH + TEXT_LINE_HEIGHT);

    SSDL_WaitKey();

    return 0;
}

void display(const Square board[MAX_ROWS][MAX_COLS])
{
    //Make 'em static: loaded once, and local to the only function
    // that needs 'em. What's not to like?
    static const SSDL_Image X_IMAGE = SSDL_LoadImage("media/X.png");
    static const SSDL_Image O_IMAGE = SSDL_LoadImage("media/O.png");

    //draw the X's and O's
    for (int row = 0; row < MAX_ROWS; ++row)
        for (int col = 0; col < MAX_COLS; ++col)
            switch (board[row][col])
            {
            case Square::X: SSDL_RenderImage(X_IMAGE,
                                      col*COL_WIDTH, row*ROW_WIDTH);
                            break;
            case Square::O: SSDL_RenderImage(O_IMAGE,
                                      col*COL_WIDTH, row*ROW_WIDTH);
            }

    //draw the lines for the board:  first vertical, then horizontal
    //doing this last stops X and O bitmaps from covering the lines
    constexpr int LINE_THICKNESS = 5;

    SSDL_RenderFillRect(COL_WIDTH     - LINE_THICKNESS / 2, 0,
                        LINE_THICKNESS, BOARD_HEIGHT);
    SSDL_RenderFillRect(COL_WIDTH * 2 - LINE_THICKNESS / 2, 0,
                        LINE_THICKNESS, BOARD_HEIGHT);
    SSDL_RenderFillRect(0, ROW_WIDTH  - LINE_THICKNESS / 2,
                        BOARD_WIDTH, LINE_THICKNESS);
```

```
    SSDL_RenderFillRect(0, ROW_WIDTH*2- LINE_THICKNESS / 2,
                           BOARD_WIDTH, LINE_THICKNESS);
}
```

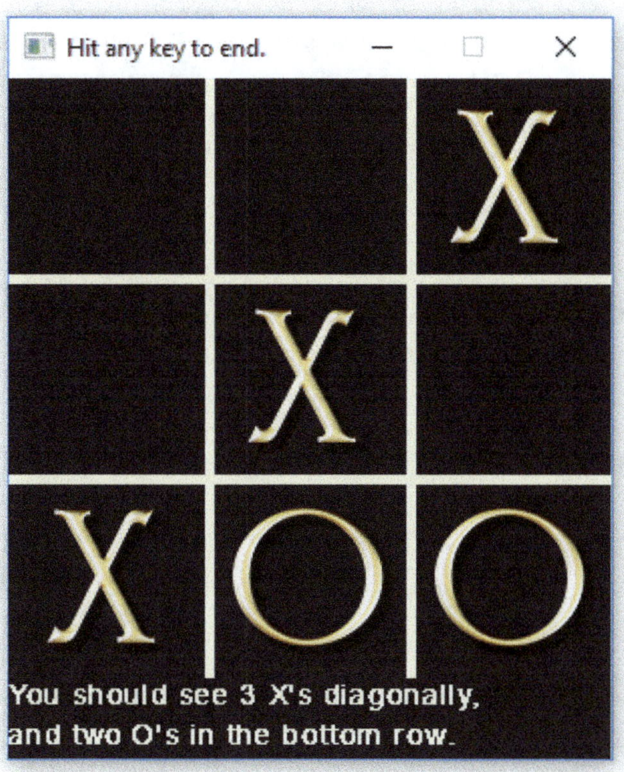

Figure 10-3. *A Tic-Tac-Toe board*

Note Example 10-8 doesn't just show the appropriate output; it prints what the output should be. Is this overkill?

I don't think so. It's a lot easier to see what the outcome should be on the screen than to search code for it. Later we'll see even lazier ways of testing.

Arrays of More Than Two Dimensions

In the previous example, our array was two-dimensional. Can we have 3D arrays? 4D? You can have as many dimensions as you're likely to want.

To initialize a 3D array, use another set of nested {}'s.

But the only uses I've found for 3D arrays are the 1971 text-based *Star Trek* game (going between "quadrants" fighting Klingon ships) and 3D Tic-Tac-Toe. I've never found a use for 4D arrays. If you find one, don't tell me. There are things I don't want to know.

Antibugging

- **Things in your 2D array are going into the wrong places.** That could result from using `row` when you mean `col` or `col` when you mean `row`.

  The best prevention is to be consistent in what you call rows and columns: don't use `row`, `col` sometimes, `x`, `y` sometimes, and `i`, `j` sometimes. Always use `row`, `col`. You can also use `row1`, `col1` or `rowStart`, `colStart`, but always something with `row` or `col` in the name.

EXERCISES

In these and subsequent exercises, remember to use the debugger if something goes wrong.

1. Make a checkerboard: eight rows, eight columns, alternating light and dark squares.
2. Put the pieces on the checkerboard for the initial game configuration: alternating squares, as shown.

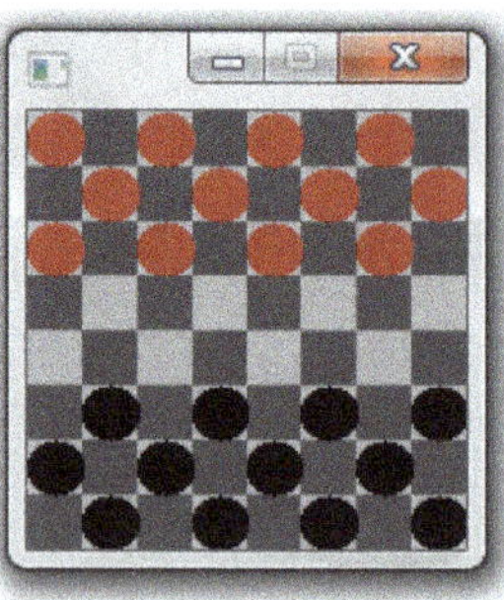

3. For the checkerboard, make a function that counts the checkers of a given color and returns the count.

4. ...and now a function that determines which side has more pieces. If neither has more, it can return `EMPTY`.

5. Write a function that takes a checkerboard, the location of a piece, and a direction `LEFT` or `RIGHT` (use `enum`) and returns whether that piece can move in that direction. A piece can move one square diagonally forward to an empty square or two squares diagonally forward, jumping an opponent's piece, to an empty square.

6. (Harder) In the game *Memory*, you have (say) eight pairs of cards, each pair showing an identical image. They're dealt face down in a 4 × 4 grid; the player picks two and turns them face up, and if they're identical, those two cards are taken away. You win by finding all matching pairs in relatively few turns.

   Make a program to play the game. (Definitely write the algorithm first.) Let the user click a pair of cards; show the cards by replacing the "card back" image with the "card front" images; wait for the user to see the card fronts (use `SSDL_Delay`); and then, if there's a match, replace the images with nothing and increment the player's score – else, replace them again with the "card back" image. Play different sounds depending on whether there was a match. Repeat till all cards are matched or the player has exceeded some maximum number of turns.

   You will need code for recognizing mouse clicks in a box area.

7. (Harder) Write a complete Tic-Tac-Toe game. For the computer moves, you could just pick a random location for the next move. Or you could go for something tougher and make the computer figure out what a good move would be.

8. (Hard) Play *Connect Four*. In this game, you have an initially empty grid, and players alternate putting tokens into the top row. A token automatically falls far as it can: it can't go past the bottom row and can't go into a square that's occupied. The winner is the one who gets four in a row in any direction.

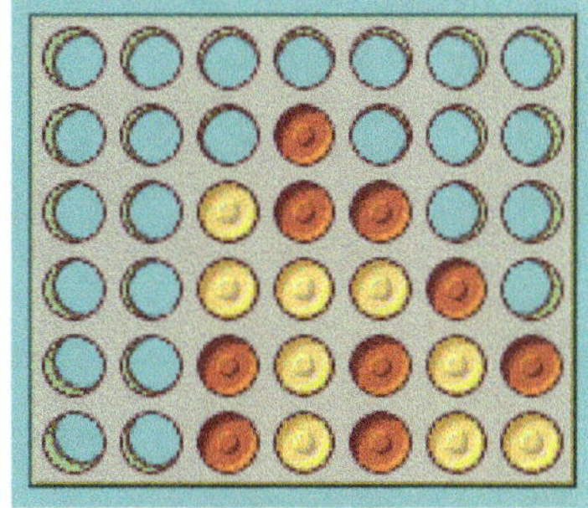

CHAPTER 11

Animation with structs and Sprites

Time to make some movies (and, soon after, arcade games). We'll need a few more features.

structs

A struct is a way of bundling information:

```
struct <name>
{
      <variable declaration>*
};
```

For example, here's a type we've needed for a while: a geometric point. It has two parts, x and y:

```
struct Point2D
{
      int x_, y_;
};
```

(The trailing _'s are a convention meaning "member of something else." We'll see why that's worth bothering with in Chapter 16.)

This version's even better: we'll build default values right into the struct. 0 is a good default:

W. Briggs, *C++26 for Lazy Programmers*, https://doi.org/10.1007/979-8-8688-1859-2_11

```
struct Point2D
{
      int x_= 0, y_= 0;
};
```

Now we can declare points using our new type:

```
Point2D p0; // The x_and y_ members are both 0
            //    since we made that the default
```

You can initialize a struct the same way you would an array – with a braced list:[1]

```
Point2D p1 = {0, 5};                // x is 0, y is 5
```

...but unlike with arrays, you can use {} to make a new value after initialization:

```
p1          = {1, 5};                // now x is 1
functionThatExpectsAPoint({2,6}); // make a Point2D on the fly
```

To get at the parts of a Point2D, use .:

```
p1.x_  += AMOUNT_TO_MOVE_X;
p1.y_  += AMOUNT_TO_MOVE_Y;
SSDL_RenderDrawCircle (p1.x_, p1.y_, RADIUS);
```

That should do it.

Why have structs?

[1] structs are way too flexible in their initializers. You can omit the =:

```
Point2D p1 {0, 5};
```

You can omit some initializers, and it'll use your defaults (or 0 if you didn't make any):

```
Point2D p2 {3}; //x_ becomes 3, y_ stays at 0
```

If your compiler is current, you can put in member labels:

```
Point2D p3 = { .x_= 0, .y_=5 };
Point2D p4 = { .y_ = 5 }; //leave x_ to its default
```

I usually go with the plain-vanilla version: `Point2D p5 = {0, 5};`.

- **Clarity**: It's easier to think of a point as, well, a point, than as an X and a Y.
- **Shorter parameter lists**: Your function to detect whether a mouse click is within a box need no longer have six parameters, as in

  ```
  bool containsClick (int x, int y,
                      int xLeft, int xRight,
                      int yTop,  int yBottom);
  ```

  but three, as in

  ```
  bool containsClick (Point2D p,
                      Point2D upperLeft,
                      Point2D lowerRight);
  ```

- **Arrays of `struct`s**: Suppose you want multiple objects in your universe (seems likely!). Each has an X, Y location. How can you make an array of these? Bundle X and Y into a `Point2D`, and have an array of that:

  ```
  Point2D myObjects[MAX_OBJECTS];
  ```

  To initialize them, you can use the {} initializer lists:

  ```
  Point2D myObjects[MAX_OBJECTS] = {{1, 5}, {2, 3}};
  ```

Example 11-1 shows use of this new type. Output is in Figure 11-1.

Example 11-1. Staircase program, illustrating `struct Point2D`

```
// Program to draw a staircase
//              -- from _C++26 for Lazy Programmers_

#include "SSDL.h"

struct Point2D  // A struct to hold a 2-D point
{
    int x_, y_;
};
```

```
int main(int argc, char** argv)
{
    SSDL_SetWindowSize(400, 200);
    SSDL_SetWindowTitle
                 ("Stairway example:  Hit a key to end");

    constexpr size_t MAX_POINTS        = 25;
    constexpr int    STAIR_STEP_LENGTH = 15;

    Point2D myPoints [MAX_POINTS];

    int x = 0;                     // Start at lower left corner
    int y = SSDL_GetWindowHeight()-1;   //  of screen

    for (int i = 0; i < MAX_POINTS; ++i)
                                   // Fill an array with points
    {
        myPoints[i] = { x, y };

        // On iteration 0, go up (change Y)
        // On iteration 1, go right
        //  then up, then right, then up...

        if (i%2 == 0)                   // If i is even...
            y -= STAIR_STEP_LENGTH;
        else
            x += STAIR_STEP_LENGTH;
    }

    for (int i = 0; i < MAX_POINTS-1; ++i) //Display staircase
        // The last iteration draws a line from point
        //  i to point i+1... which is why we stop a
        //  little short.  We don't want to refer to
        //  the (nonexistent) point # MAX_POINTS.
        SSDL_RenderDrawLine
                       (myPoints[i  ].x_, myPoints[i  ].y_,
                        myPoints[i+1].x_, myPoints[i+1].y_);
```

```
    SSDL_WaitKey();

    return 0;
}
```

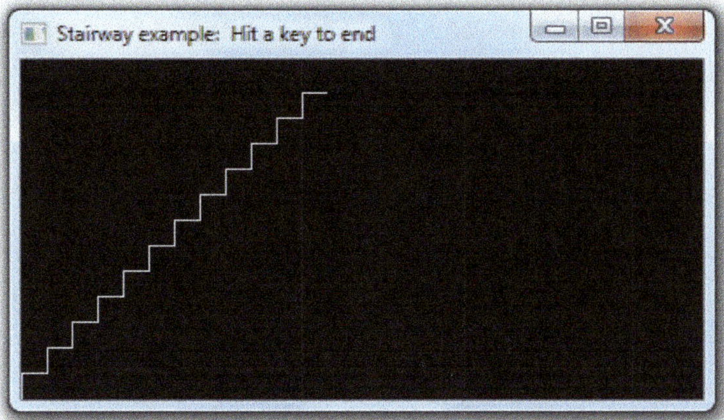

***Figure 11-1.** Staircase program*

EXERCISES

1. Write and test the `containsClick` function given above (the one taking a click and box information).

2. Make an array of `Point2D`s, and set the value of each with this function:

```
Point2D pickRandomPoint (int range)
{
   Point2D where;

   where.x_ =
     rand()%range+rand()%range+rand()%range;
   where.y_ =
     rand()%range+rand()%range+rand()%range;

   return where;
}
```

   Display them, and notice: are they evenly distributed? This shows something about what happens when you sum random numbers.

Making a Movie with `struct` and `while`

Think how movies are made. You see one still frame after another, but they come so quickly they look like one continuous, moving image.

We'll do the same thing. A real movie has a specific speed – frames per second – so the rate of movement is always the same. We'll tell C++ to keep a constant frame rate too.

Here's a rough version:

```
SSDL_SetFramesPerSecond(70);// Can change this,
                            //  or leave at the default of 60

while (SSDL_IsNextFrame())
{
      SSDL_DefaultEventHandler();

      // get input, if relevant...

      SSDL_RenderClear();      // erase previous frame

      // display things (draw images, print text, etc.)

      // update variables if needed
}
```

`SSDL_IsNextFrame` waits for enough time to pass to get to the next frame in our movie. It also refreshes the screen. It will do 60 frames per second unless we change that with `SSDL_SetFramesPerSecond`. If the user tries to quit by killing the window or hitting Escape, `SSDL_IsNextFrame` returns `false` and the loop ends.

But something's going to have to check for those quit messages. Before, we used `SSDL_WaitKey`, `SSDL_WaitMouse`, and `SSDL_Delay`. Since we aren't using them now, something else must check for quit messages.

That something is `SSDL_DefaultEventHandler`, which processes **events** – messages from the operating system telling the program, "Something happened that you may care about," like quit requests:

```
void SSDL_DefaultEventHandler()
{
    SDL_Event event;

    while (SSDL_PollEvent(event))
```

```
        switch (event.type)
        {
        case SDL_QUIT:
                // clicked the X on the window? Let's quit
            SSDL_DeclareQuit();
            break;
        case SDL_KEYDOWN:      // User hit Escape? Let's quit
            if (SSDL_IsKeyPressed(SDLK_ESCAPE))
                SSDL_DeclareQuit();
        }
}
```

`SDL_Event` is a `struct` that stores information on any kind of event SDL recognizes. `SSDL_PollEvent` gets the next available event, if any, failing if there is none; but if one is found, it stores the information in `event`, and the `switch` statement decides how to process it.

Let's use it in a program (Example 11-2) to make a ball move back and forth across the screen - whoo-hoo! Output is in Figure 11-2.

Example 11-2. A ball moving back and forth across the screen

```
// Program to make a circle go back & forth across the screen
//          -- from _C++26 for Lazy Programmers_

#include "SSDL.h"

constexpr int RADIUS = 20; //Ball radius & speed
constexpr int SPEED  =  5; //Move 5 pixels for every frame

enum class Direction { LEFT, RIGHT };

struct Point2D
{
    int x_=0, y_=0;
};
```

```
struct Ball             // A ball is an X, Y location,
{                       // and a direction, left or right
    Point2D   location_;
    Direction direction_;
};

int main(int argc, char** argv)
{
    SSDL_SetWindowTitle ("Back-and-forth ball example.  "
                         "Hit Esc to exit.");

    // initialize ball position; size; direction of movement
    Ball ball;
    ball.location_  = { SSDL_GetWindowWidth () / 2,
                        SSDL_GetWindowHeight() / 2 };
    ball.direction_ = Direction::RIGHT;

    constexpr int FRAMES_PER_SECOND = 70;
    SSDL_SetFramesPerSecond (FRAMES_PER_SECOND);

    while (SSDL_IsNextFrame())
    {
        SSDL_DefaultEventHandler();

        // *** DISPLAY THINGS ***
        SSDL_RenderClear();    // first, erase previous frame

        // then draw the ball
        SSDL_RenderDrawCircle(ball.location_.x_,
                              ball.location_.y_,
                              RADIUS);

        // *** UPDATE THINGS ***
        // update ball's x position based on speed
        //  and current direction
        if (ball.direction_ == Direction::LEFT)
            ball.location_.x_ -= SPEED;
        else
            ball.location_.x_ += SPEED;
```

```
        // if ball moves off screen, reverse its direction
        if      (ball.location_.x_ >= SSDL_GetWindowWidth())
            ball.direction_ = Direction::LEFT;
        else if (ball.location_.x_ <                      0)
            ball.direction_ = Direction::RIGHT;
    }

    return 0;
}
```

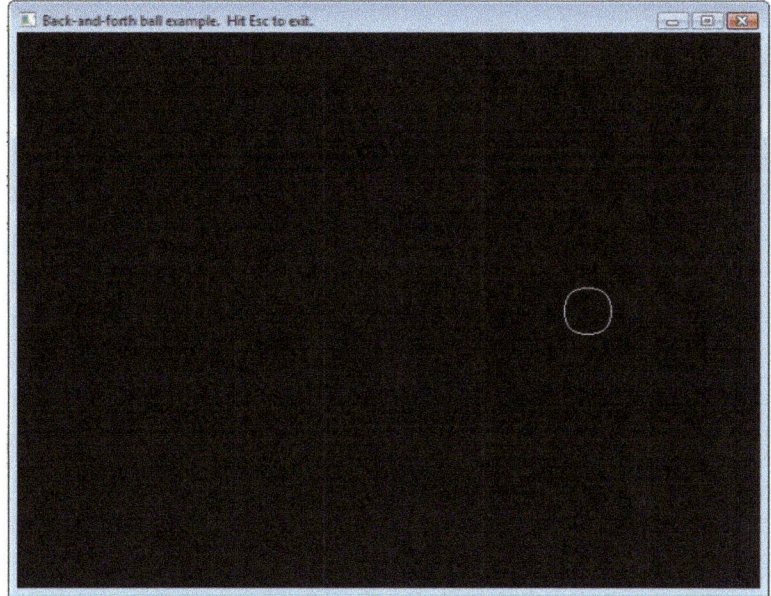

***Figure 11-2.** A ball moving back and forth across the screen*

What if we want more than one object moving? We can have an array of Balls and use for loops to initialize them, display them, etc.

main's getting a little long and less clear, so I'll put several tasks in their own functions (Example 11-3). Output is in Figure 11-3.

Example 11-3. An example with multiple moving balls

```
// Program to make circles move back & forth across the screen
//        -- from _C++26 for Lazy Programmers_

#include <span>
```

```
#include "SSDL.h"

constexpr int RADIUS = 20; //Ball radius & speed
constexpr int SPEED  =  5; // ...move 5 pixels for every frame

enum class Direction { LEFT, RIGHT };

struct Point2D
{
    int x_=0, y_=0;
};

struct Ball                 // A ball is an X, Y location,
{                           // and a direction, left or right
    Point2D   location_;
    Direction direction_;
};

// Ball functions
void initializeBalls(std::span<Ball> balls);
void drawBalls      (std::span<const Ball> balls);
void moveBalls      (std::span<Ball> balls);
void bounceBalls    (std::span<Ball> balls);

int main(int argc, char** argv)
{
    SSDL_SetWindowTitle ("Back-and-forth balls example.  "
                         "Hit Esc to exit.");

    // initialize balls' position, size, rate and direction
    constexpr size_t MAX_BALLS = 3;
    Ball balls [MAX_BALLS];
    initializeBalls (balls);

    constexpr int FRAMES_PER_SECOND = 70;
    SSDL_SetFramesPerSecond(FRAMES_PER_SECOND);
```

```
    while (SSDL_IsNextFrame())
    {
        // *** HANDLE EVENTS AND INPUT (if any) ***
        SSDL_DefaultEventHandler();

        // *** DISPLAY THINGS ***
        SSDL_RenderClear();   // first, erase previous frame
        drawBalls(balls);

        // *** UPDATE  THINGS ***
        moveBalls(balls);
        bounceBalls(balls);   // if ball moves offscreen,
                              //  reverse its direction
    }

    return 0;
}

// Ball functions

void initializeBalls(std::span<Ball> balls)
{
    // Where to put the next ball
    int x = 0, y = SSDL_GetWindowHeight() / 6;

    for (Ball& b : balls)
    {
        b.location_ = { x, y };
        b.direction_ = Direction::RIGHT;

        x += SSDL_GetWindowWidth() / 3;
        y += SSDL_GetWindowHeight() / 3;
    }
}
```

```
void drawBalls(std::span<const Ball> balls)
{
    for (Ball b: balls)[2]
        SSDL_RenderDrawCircle(b.location_.x_,
                              b.location_.y_, RADIUS);
}

// update balls' x positions based on speed & current dir
void moveBalls(std::span<Ball> balls)
{
    for (Ball& b: balls)
        if (b.direction_ == Direction::LEFT)
            b.location_.x_ -= SPEED;
        else
            b.location_.x_ += SPEED;
}

void bounceBalls(std::span<Ball> balls)
{
    // if any ball moves off screen, reverse its direction
    for (Ball& b: balls)
        if (b.location_.x_ >= SSDL_GetWindowWidth())
            b.direction_ = Direction::LEFT;
        else if (b.location_.x_ <  0)
            b.direction_ = Direction::RIGHT;
}
```

[2] If you get a warning of a "potentially expensive copy" or some such in a range for loop, ignore it. We'll get to that in Chapter 15.

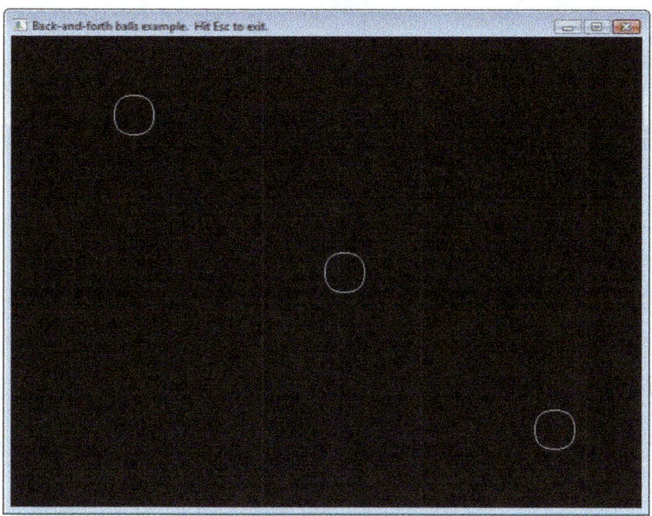

Figure 11-3. *An example with multiple moving balls*

EXERCISES

1. Make the balls capable of moving in other directions. A ball is no longer just an X, Y location and a direction; it's an X, Y location and an X, Y velocity. Each time you go through the main loop, you'll update the location based on the velocity:

```
for (Ball& b : balls)
{
   b.location_.x_ +=
                balls[i].velocity_.x_;
   b.location_.y_ +=
                balls[i].velocity_.y_;
}
```

   The velocity's X component is always reversed when it hits a left or right wall; same for the velocity's Y if it hits the floor or ceiling. It's OK to use `Point2D` for `velocity_`, or you can create a new `struct` for it.

   Add sound effects whenever a ball hits a wall.

2. Now let's add gravity. Velocity doesn't just change each time you hit a wall; it changes in each iteration of the loop, like so:

```
for (Ball& b : balls)
      b.velocity_.y_+= GRAVITY;
            // adjust velocity for gravity
```

   Now the balls should move more realistically.

3. Now add friction. Whenever a ball hits a wall, its velocity is not exactly reversed; instead, it's reversed, but it's a little smaller than it was. This will make the balls slower after each collision.

Sprites

Enough circles - let's move images.

We already have images, but they just sit there. Sprites are mobile images: they can move, rotate, flip, and other things. Here are the basics.

You create a sprite much as you do an image:

```
SSDL_Sprite mySprite = SSDL_LoadImage ("filename.png");
```

You can now set its location with `SSDL_SetSpriteLocation` and its size with `SSDL_SetSpriteSize`.

Here I use sprites to put a fish in the middle of the screen - maybe I'm going to make a video aquarium - and print some information about it using other sprite functions (Example 11-4). The sprite-related code is highlighted. Output is in Figure 11-4.

Example 11-4. Program to draw a fish, using a sprite

```
// Program to place a fish sprite on the screen
//              -- from _C++26 for Lazy Programmers_

#include "SSDL.h"

using namespace std;
```

```
int main(int argc, char** argv)
{
    // Set up window characteristics
    constexpr int WINDOW_WIDTH = 600, WINDOW_HEIGHT = 300;
    SSDL_SetWindowSize(WINDOW_WIDTH, WINDOW_HEIGHT);
    SSDL_SetWindowTitle
                ("Sprite example 1.  Hit Esc to exit.");

    // initialize colors
    const SSDL_Color AQUAMARINE(100, 255, 150); // the water

    // initialize the sprite's image and location
    SSDL_Sprite fishSprite
              = SSDL_LoadImage("media/discus-fish.png");
    SSDL_SetSpriteLocation(fishSprite,
                      SSDL_GetWindowWidth ()/2,
                      SSDL_GetWindowHeight()/2);

    // *** Main loop ***
    while (SSDL_IsNextFrame())
    {
        // *** HANDLE EVENTS AND INPUT (if any) ***
        SSDL_DefaultEventHandler();

        // Clear the screen for a new frame in our "movie"
        SSDL_RenderClear(AQUAMARINE);

        // Draw crosshairs in the center
        SSDL_SetRenderDrawColor(BLACK);
        SSDL_RenderDrawLine(0, SSDL_GetWindowHeight()/2,
                            SSDL_GetWindowWidth (),
                            SSDL_GetWindowHeight()/2);
        SSDL_RenderDrawLine(SSDL_GetWindowWidth ()/2,  0,
                            SSDL_GetWindowWidth ()/2,
                            SSDL_GetWindowHeight());
```

```
        // and print the statistics on the fish
        SSDL_SetCursor(0, 0);  // reset cursor each time or
                               //   the messages will run off
                               //   the screen!
        sout << "Sprite info\n";
        sout << "X:\t"
            << SSDL_GetSpriteX      (fishSprite) << endl;
        sout << "Y:\t"
            << SSDL_GetSpriteY      (fishSprite) << endl;
        sout << "Width:\t"
            << SSDL_GetSpriteWidth (fishSprite) << endl;
        sout << "Height:\t"
            << SSDL_GetSpriteHeight(fishSprite) << endl;

        // Show that fish
        SSDL_RenderSprite (fishSprite);
    }

    return 0;
}
```

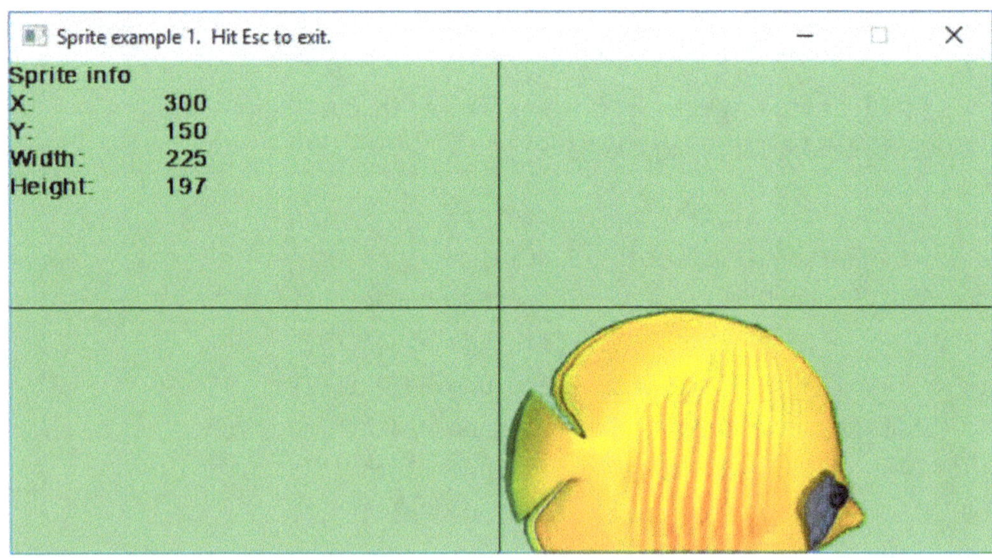

Figure 11-4. *A sprite and some of its current specs*

I think the fish is too big. According to the program its width is 225 and its height 197. We can put SSDL_SetSpriteSize before the main loop, to resize it, as in Figure 11-5:[3]

```
constexpr int FISH_WIDTH = 170, FISH_HEIGHT = 150;
SSDL_SetSpriteSize(fishSprite, FISH_WIDTH, FISH_HEIGHT);
```

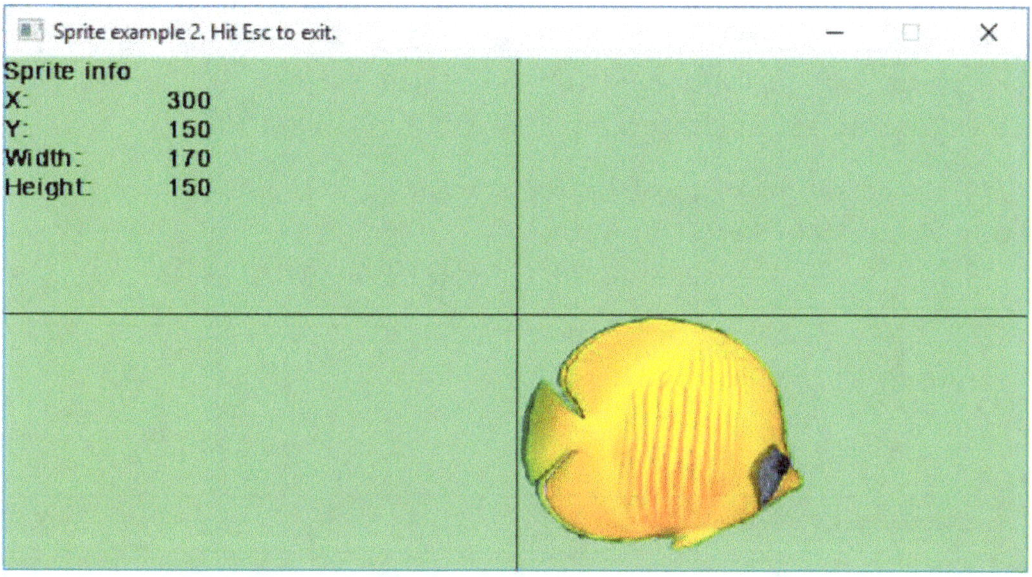

Figure 11-5. *A sprite, resized*

Now I want it centered. The X, Y location I gave it *is* in the center ...but that's the upper-left corner of the image.

Here is the call to offset the sprite so it's centered on the point we gave as its location:

```
SSDL_SetSpriteOffset(fishSprite,FISH_WIDTH/2,FISH_HEIGHT/2);
```

If it still looks off-center, I can play with the numbers to get a different offset.

I won't repeat the entire program, but here are the lines that changed to resize and center the sprite (Example 11-5). The result is in Figure 11-6.

[3] It's more efficient to set this in your graphics editor. If you must do it in the program, do it immediately after you load the image, so it's always the new desired size.

Example 11-5. Code to resize and center a sprite

```
int main(int argc, char** argv)
{
    ...

    // Init size & offset.
    // Image is offset so fish looks centered.
    constexpr int FISH_WIDTH = 170, FISH_HEIGHT = 150;
    SSDL_SetSpriteSize(fishSprite, FISH_WIDTH, FISH_HEIGHT);

    // This offset looks right on the screen, so I'll use it:
    SSDL_SetSpriteOffset(fishSprite,
                         FISH_WIDTH/2, int(FISH_HEIGHT*0.55));

    ...

    return 0;
}
```

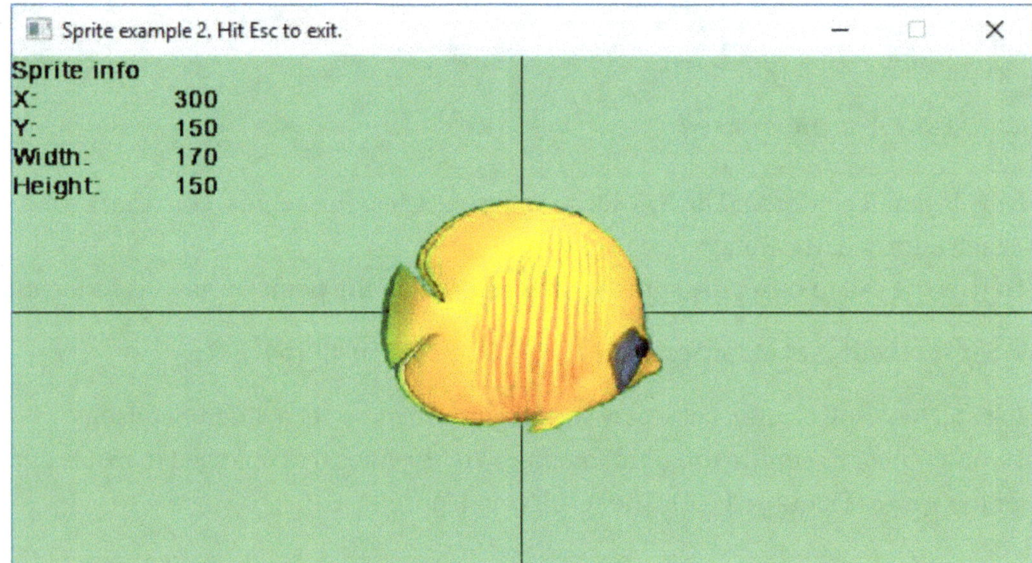

Figure 11-6. *A sprite, resized and centered*

You can do other things with sprites: rotate, flip horizontally or vertically, or use only part of your original image. You can also do anything to them you can do with an image – for example, `SSDL_RenderImage(mySprite, 0, 0)`. This will ignore the sprite's other characteristics (position, size, etc.) and only use the image aspects.

And now that you have this, you can (almost) make your own arcade games.

Table 11-1. *Common sprite commands. For a complete list, see Appendix G*

`SSDL_Sprite mySprite = SSDL_LoadImage("image.png");`	This is how to create one.
`void SSDL_SetSpriteLocation (SSDL_Sprite& s, int x, int y);`	Set the sprite's location on screen.
`void SSDL_SetSpriteSize (SSDL_Sprite& s, int w, int h);`	...and its size.
`void SSDL_SetSpriteOffset (SSDL_Sprite& s, int x, int y);`	...its offset.
`void SSDL_SetSpriteRotation (SSDL_Sprite& s, double angle);`	...its angle of rotation, in degrees.
`void SSDL_RenderSprite (SSDL_Sprite s);`	Draw the sprite at its current location.
`int SSDL_GetSpriteX (SSDL_Sprite s);`	Return the sprite's x position on screen.
`int SSDL_GetSpriteY (SSDL_Sprite s);`	...and its y.

Antibugging

- **The sprite doesn't show up.** Here are likely reasons:
  - The image didn't load: you're looking in the wrong folder, made a typo in the filename, or are using a bad or incompatible image.
  - It showed up, but it's off screen. What numbers do you get from `SSDL_GetSpriteX` and `SSDL_GetSpriteY`? Be sure they're in range.

- **The rotation isn't at all what you expected.** Be aware that unlike C++'s built-in `sin` and `cos`, `SSDL_Sprite` expects angles in degrees. Go figure.

EXERCISES

1. Make a video aquarium: a background and fish that move back and forth (facing whatever direction they go, so you'll need `SSDL_SpriteFlipHorizontal`).
2. Do Exercise 2 or 3 from the previous section (bouncing balls), but instead of drawing circles, use an image of a basketball. Let the basketballs spin as they go (see Table 11-1 for the function you need).

CHAPTER 12

Making an Arcade Game: Input, Collisions, and Putting It All Together

In this chapter we'll make our own 2D arcade games, putting together what we've got so far for a time-wasting experience to make others goof off so we can shine. Or something like that. The new things we need are better mouse and keyboard interaction, and collisions of objects.

Determining Input States

Mouse

We already can wait on a mouse click and get its coordinates ...but arcade games wait for no man.

Suppose we want our weapon to fire continuously if a mouse button is down. We need a way to detect that the button is depressed, without stopping to wait. This'll do it:

`int SSDL_GetMouseClick();`	Return 0 if no button is depressed; SDL_BUTTON_LMASK (left button depressed), SDL_BUTTON_MMASK (middle), or SDL_BUTTON_RMASK (right).

W. Briggs, *C++26 for Lazy Programmers*, https://doi.org/10.1007/979-8-8688-1859-2_12

As in:

```
if (SSDL_GetMouseClick() != 0) // mouse button is down
{
       x = SSDL_GetMouseX(); y = SSDL_GetMouseY();

       // do whatever you wanted to do if mouse button is down
}
```

Before getting to an example, let's see how to check the state of the keyboard.

Keyboard

`ssin` waits for you to hit Enter. That won't work for arcade games: we want to know whether a key is pressed as soon as it's hit. The function `SSDL_IsKeyPressed` tells if a given key is down – any key, including the ones not associated with letters, like Shift and Control.

`bool SSDL_IsKeyPressed (SDL_Keycode key);`	Returns whether key is currently pressed.

Though many key values this function accepts match what you'd expect ("0" for the 0 key, "a" for the A key – but not "A" for the A key!), it's not always obvious, so it's best to go with their official names. At time of writing a complete list is at `wiki.libsdl.org/SDL2/SDL_Keycode`; a few are listed in Table 12-1. Example 12-1 shows how you might use them.

Table 12-1. *Selected key codes for SDL*

SDLK_1	SDLK_F1	SDLK_ESCAPE	SDLK_LEFT	SDLK_LSHIFT
SDLK_2	SDLK_F2	SDLK_BACKSPACE	SDLK_RIGHT	SDLK_RSHIFT
...	...	SDLK_RETURN	SDLK_UP	SDLK_LCTRL
SDLK_a		SDLK_SPACE	SDLK_DOWN	SDLK_RCTRL
SDLK_b				
...				

Example 12-1. A program to detect Control keys, Shift, Caps Lock, space bar, and F1

```
// Program to identify some keys, and mouse buttons, being pressed
//        -- from _C++26 for Lazy Programmers_

#include "SSDL.h"

int main(int argc, char** argv)
{
    // Pressing many keys at once may confuse the keyboard.
    // Also, on some keyboards, hold down Fn key to
    //   use a Function key

    while (SSDL_IsNextFrame())
    {
        SSDL_DefaultEventHandler();

        // Display
        SSDL_RenderClear ();     // Clear the screen
        SSDL_SetCursor (0, 0);  // And start printing at the top

        sout << "What key are you pressing? ";
        sout << "Control, Shift, Caps lock, space, F1?\n";

        if (SSDL_IsKeyPressed(SDLK_LCTRL))   sout << "Left ctrl ";
        if (SSDL_IsKeyPressed(SDLK_RCTRL))   sout << "Right ctrl ";
        if (SSDL_IsKeyPressed(SDLK_LSHIFT))  sout << "Left shift ";
        if (SSDL_IsKeyPressed(SDLK_RSHIFT))  sout << "Right shift ";
        if (SSDL_IsKeyPressed(SDLK_CAPSLOCK))sout << "Caps lock ";
        if (SSDL_IsKeyPressed(SDLK_SPACE))   sout << "Space bar ";
        if (SSDL_IsKeyPressed(SDLK_F1))      sout << "F1 ";
        if (SSDL_IsKeyPressed(SDLK_ESCAPE))  break;
        sout << "\n";

        if (SSDL_GetMouseClick() == SDL_BUTTON_LMASK)
            sout << "Left mouse button down\n";
```

```
        if (SSDL_GetMouseClick() == SDL_BUTTON_RMASK)
            sout << "Right mouse button down\n";

        sout << "(Hit Esc to exit.)";
    }

    return 0;
}
```

Antibugging

- **You're hitting a function key, but nothing happens.** On some keyboards you have to hold down the Fn key as well.
- **You're hitting multiple keys at once but only some show up;** or **you're hitting a key and it won't register mouse buttons.** Keyboard "ghosting" is losing keypresses because the keyboard can only handle so many at once. It may also lose mouse clicks. At time of writing, if you care, you can test your keyboard and mouse at `https://keyboardtester.co/`.

  You're probably safe using Control, Shift, and Alt with other keys – that's expected.

Events

Sometimes we don't care if a mouse button is currently up or down, just that it's been clicked. Maybe you get one shot from your BFG per click. Or your program uses the mouse to turn sound on or off as the code below does (or at least tries to):

```
while (SSDL_IsNextFrame())
{
    SSDL_DefaultEventHandler();

    if (SSDL_GetMouseClick()) toggleSound (); // not gonna work

    ...
}
```

Thing is, computers are fast. Suppose your mouse click takes a tenth of a second. At 60 frames per second, sound will turn on and off *six times* before you release the button, and it's only good luck if it ends up the way you wanted.

What we need is to detect the click itself as a mouse click *event*, like the quit event handled in Chapter 11. We'll have a replacement for SSDL_DefaultEventHandler to detect that event and report it to main so main can toggle the music (Example 12-2); output is in Figure 12-1.

Example 12-2. Making your own event handler. For the complete program (of course), see the source code, ch12 folder; the project is 2-aliensBuzzOurWorld.

```
                                //replaces SSDL_DefaultEventHandler
void myEventHandler(bool& mouseClicked)
{
    SDL_Event event;
    mouseClicked = false;    // We'll soon know if mouse was clicked

    while (SSDL_PollEvent(event))
        switch (event.type)
        {
        case SDL_QUIT:     SSDL_DeclareQuit();
            break;
        case SDL_KEYDOWN: if (SSDL_IsKeyPressed(SDLK_ESCAPE))
                              SSDL_DeclareQuit();
            break;
        case SDL_MOUSEBUTTONDOWN: mouseClicked = true; // It was!
            break;
        }
}

// and the following in main:

while (SSDL_IsNextFrame())
{
    bool mouseWasClicked;
    myEventHandler(mouseWasClicked);          // handle events

    if (mouseWasClicked) toggleSound();
    ...
```

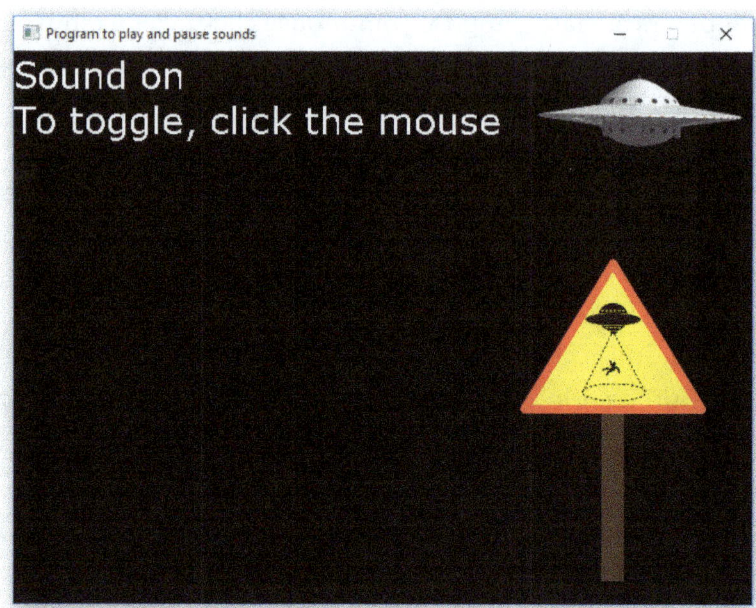

Figure 12-1. *A program that uses mouse clicks to toggle sound*

This way of thinking - **event-driven** - is at the core of programming such important operating systems as Windows, iOS, and Android.

Cooldowns and Lifetimes

Suppose we want an effect to linger a moment after something happens. Maybe there's a visual effect that should be there for only a second (its "lifetime") after a mouse click creates it. Or your BFG has to wait a while before you can fire again, however madly you click - a "cooldown" period.

We'll have an integer `framesLeftTillItsOver` that, when the mouse is clicked, gets set to the number of frames you want to delay.

This reasoning won't do:

```
framesLeftTillItsOver = 0       //effect is currently inactive
while SSDL_IsNextFrame()
    handle events

    SSDL_RenderClear()
    draw things
```

```
    if framesLeftTillItsOver == 0 && mouseWasClicked
        framesLeftTillItsOver = HOWEVER MANY FRAMES WE WANT IT TO LAST
        draw the visual effect

    --framesLeftTillItsOver // 1 frame closer to disappearance
```

The counting down is OK, but when you draw the effect, SSDL_RenderClear erases it on the very next iteration!

We must distinguish *changing the state* of the visual effect (from off to on) from *drawing* it; they're separate actions. This will work:

```
framesLeftTillItsOver = 0       //effect is currently inactive
while SSDL_IsNextFrame()
    handle events

    SSDL_RenderClear()
    draw things including, if it's on, the visual effect
      (consider it to be on if framesLeftTillItsOver > 0)

    if effect is on (that is, framesLeftTillItsOver > 0)
        -- framesLeftTillItsOver; // 1 frame closer to disappearance
    else if mouseWasClicked
        framesLeftTillItsOver = HOWEVER MANY FRAMES WE WANT IT TO LAST
```

Tip As a rule of thumb, inside that main animation loop, have three separate sections: handling events, drawing things, updating variables. The order doesn't matter, as they'll all get done eventually; what does matter is that you don't draw in the update section or check events in the draw section and so on.

In Example 12-3, when you click the mouse, the program puts a splatter image wherever you click. One second later it drops the image and lets you click again.

Example 12-3. Using a visual effect with specified duration: splatter on the screen

```
// Program that makes a splat wherever you click
//        -- from _C++26 for Lazy Programmers_

#include "SSDL.h"

void myEventHandler(bool& mouseClicked);

int main(int argc, char** argv)
{
    SSDL_SetWindowTitle("Click the mouse to see and hear a splat; "
                        "hit Esc to end.");

    const SSDL_Sound SPLAT_SOUND =
        SSDL_LoadWAV("media/445117__breviceps__cartoon-splat.wav");

    // Set up sprite with image and a size, and offset its reference
    //  point so it'll be centered on our mouse clicks
    SSDL_Sprite splatSprite = SSDL_LoadImage("media/splat.png");

    constexpr int SPLAT_WIDTH=50, SPLAT_HEIGHT=50;
    SSDL_SetSpriteSize  (splatSprite, SPLAT_WIDTH,   SPLAT_HEIGHT);
    SSDL_SetSpriteOffset(splatSprite, SPLAT_WIDTH/2, SPLAT_HEIGHT/2);

    while (SSDL_IsNextFrame ())
    {
        static int framesLeftTillSplatDisappears =  0;
        static constexpr int SPLAT_LIFETIME      = 60; //Lasts 1 sec

        // HANDLE EVENTS
        bool isMouseClick;
        myEventHandler(isMouseClick);

        // DISPLAY THINGS
        SSDL_RenderClear();
        if (framesLeftTillSplatDisappears > 0)
            SSDL_RenderSprite(splatSprite);
```

```
        // UPDATE THINGS (process clicks and framesLeft)
        if (framesLeftTillSplatDisappears > 0) // if splat is active
            --framesLeftTillSplatDisappears;   //  keep counting down

        else if (isMouseClick)      // if not, and we have a click...
        {
                                    // Reset that waiting time
            framesLeftTillSplatDisappears = SPLAT_LIFETIME;

                                    // Play splat sound
            SSDL_PlaySound(SPLAT_SOUND);

            SSDL_SetSpriteLocation  // move splat sprite to
                (splatSprite,       //  location of mouse click
                 SSDL_GetMouseX(),
                 SSDL_GetMouseY());
        }
    }

    return 0;
}

void myEventHandler(bool& mouseClicked)
{
     // exactly the same as in Example 12-2
}
```

EXERCISES

1. Adapt the program in Example 12-3 to allow multiple splatters to exist at once: you can fire every second, but each splatter lasts five seconds.
2. A *particle fountain* is a set of particles continually generated, going in various directions. This is how flames can be generated in computer games and rainstorms. You can also make a bubble fountain or a sparkler.

Let each particle start at the same location, with an initial random velocity. Each iteration of the main loop, draw the particle with `SSDL_RenderDrawPoint`. Also update its position, and if you want it to look more flame-like, use gravity, but in reverse: flame particles tend to fly upward rather than downward. Finally, when a particle has existed for some number of frames, reset it to its starting point and let it go again.

Collisions

There's one more thing we need before making our own games: collisions.

Detecting collisions is easy with SSDL sprites

`int SSDL_SpriteHasIntersection (const SSDL_Sprite& a, const SSDL_Sprite& b);`	Return whether sprites a and b overlap.

as in

```
if (SSDL_SpriteHasIntersection(robotSprite, playerSprite))
      playerDead = true;
```

Collisions *are* easy with sprites, but not always accurate. Since your sprite probably has a big chunk of itself transparent, you may find that SDL thinks two sprites are colliding even if the visible parts aren't touching. No reasonable person would consider the candy and the Halloween basket in Figure 12-2 (a) to be in collision - but SSDL would.

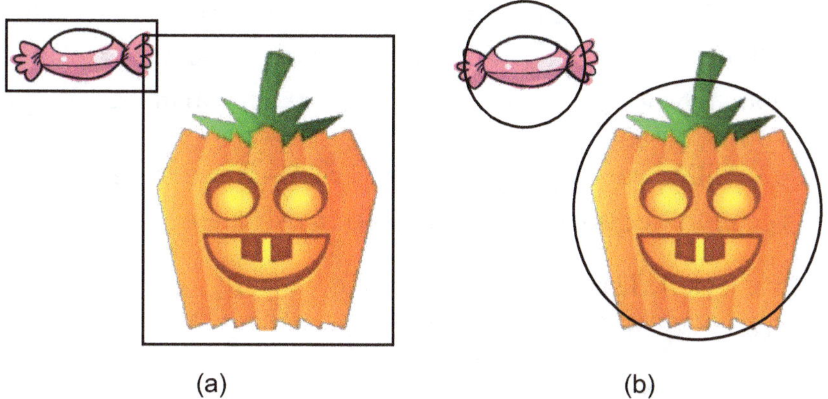

Figure 12-2. *Collisions between sprites, as evaluated by `SSDL_SpriteHasIntersection` (a) and by the circle-based method of the function `inCollision` (b)*

Here's an easy fix: find the distance between two points (which will probably be the centers of the sprites), and consider a collision to have happened if that distance is less than the sum of the radii `aSize` and `bSize` we give to our objects - that is, if bounding circles intersect (Figure 12-2 (b)):

```
bool inCollision(Point2D A, Point2D B, int aSize, int bSize)
{
      float aToBDistance = distance(A.x_, A.y_, B.x_, B.y_);
                           // see Chapter 7's first set of exercises --
                           //    or Example 12-7 below --
                           //    for the distance function
      return (aToBDistance < aSize + bSize);
}
```

Use whichever method fits your sprites best.

The Big Game

The rest of this chapter is about creating arcade games: first mine, then yours.

Examples 12-4 through 12-8 together show a game for catching Halloween candy in the basket. If you catch enough, you win; miss too many and you die. It has sounds, a background, silly graphics, and keyboard interaction (uses arrow keys), and to show use of the mouse, I allow the user to toggle a heads-up display showing stats on misses and catches. To illustrate specifying the lifetime of an effect, a floating "Yum!" message appears for a moment when you catch candy. Output is shown in Figure 12-3.

Example 12-4. Falling candy program, part 1 of 5. The complete program in the source code's ch12 folder is 4-thru-8-bigGame

```
// Program to catch falling Hallowe'en candy
//        -- from _C++26 for Lazy Programmers_

#include <cmath> // for sqrt
#include "SSDL.h"

// dimensions of screen and screen locations
constexpr int SCREEN_WIDTH=675, SCREEN_HEIGHT=522; // dimensions of bkgd

constexpr int CANDY_START_HEIGHT =  15; // where candy falls from

constexpr int MARGIN             =  25; //As close to the L/R edges
                                        // of screen as moving objects
                                        // are allowed to get
constexpr int BOTTOM_LINE        = 480; // Where last line of text goes
                                        // on instr & splash screens

// dimensions of important objects
constexpr int CANDY_WIDTH  = 60, CANDY_HEIGHT  = 20;
constexpr int BASKET_WIDTH = 70, BASKET_HEIGHT = 90;

// how many candies you can catch or miss before winning/losing
constexpr int MAX_CAUGHT   = 10, MAX_MISSED    = 10;
                                 // If you change this, change
                                 //  printInstructions too
                                 //  because it specifies this

// fonts for splash screens and catch/miss statistics
constexpr int SMALL_FONT_SIZE  = 12,
              MEDIUM_FONT_SIZE = 24,
              LARGE_FONT_SIZE  = 36;
```

```
const SSDL_Font SMALL_FONT = SSDL_OpenFont(
             "media/Sinister-Fonts_Werewolf-Moon/Werewolf Moon.ttf",
             SMALL_FONT_SIZE);
const SSDL_Font MEDIUM_FONT = SSDL_OpenFont(
             "media/Sinister-Fonts_Werewolf-Moon/Werewolf Moon.ttf",
             MEDIUM_FONT_SIZE);
const SSDL_Font LARGE_FONT = SSDL_OpenFont(
             "media/Sinister-Fonts_Werewolf-Moon/Werewolf Moon.ttf",
             LARGE_FONT_SIZE);

// how far our victory/defeat messages are from left side of screen
constexpr int FINAL_SCREEN_MESSAGE_OFFSET_X = 40;

// background
const SSDL_Image BKGD_IMAGE
     = SSDL_LoadImage("media/haunted-house.jpg");

// sounds and music
const SSDL_Music BKGD_MUSIC
     = SSDL_LoadMUS(
             "media/159509__mistersherlock__halloween-graveyd-short.mp3");
const SSDL_Sound THUNK_SOUND
     = SSDL_LoadWAV("media/457741__osiruswaltz__wall-bump-1.wav");
const SSDL_Sound DROP_SOUND
     = SSDL_LoadWAV("media/388284__matypresidente__water-drop-short.wav");

// structs
struct Point2D { int x_ = 0, y_ = 0; };

using Vector2D = Point2D;

struct Object
{
    Point2D     loc_;
    int         rotation_      = 0;
```

```
    Vector2D     velocity_;
    int          rotationSpeed_ = 0;

    SSDL_Sprite sprite_;
};

// major functions called by the main program
bool playGame            ();

// startup/ending screens to communicate with user
void printInstructions   ();
void displayVictoryScreen();
void displayDefeatScreen ();

int main(int argc, char** argv)
{
    // set up window and font
    SSDL_SetWindowTitle("Catch the falling candy");
    SSDL_SetWindowSize (SCREEN_WIDTH, SCREEN_HEIGHT);

    // prepare music
    SSDL_VolumeMusic(int (MIX_MAX_VOLUME * 0.1));
    SSDL_PlayMusic  (BKGD_MUSIC);

    // initial splash screen
    printInstructions();

    // The game itself
    bool isVictory = playGame();

    // final screen:  victory or defeat
    SSDL_RenderClear(BLACK);
    SSDL_HaltMusic  ();

    if (isVictory) displayVictoryScreen();
    else           displayDefeatScreen ();

    SSDL_RenderTextCentered("Click mouse to end",
                            SCREEN_WIDTH/2, BOTTOM_LINE, SMALL_FONT);
    SSDL_WaitMouse();  // because if we wait for a key, we're likely
```

```
                    //  to have left or right arrow depressed
                    //  when we reach this line... and we'll never
                    //  get to read the final message

    return 0;
}

//// Startup/ending screens to communicate with user ////

void printInstructions()
{
    constexpr int LINE_HEIGHT = 40;

    SSDL_SetRenderDrawColor(WHITE);
    SSDL_RenderTextCentered("Catch 10 treats in ",
            SCREEN_WIDTH/2,              0, MEDIUM_FONT);
    SSDL_RenderTextCentered("your basket to win",
            SCREEN_WIDTH/2, LINE_HEIGHT   , MEDIUM_FONT);
    SSDL_RenderTextCentered("Miss 10 treats and",
            SCREEN_WIDTH/2, LINE_HEIGHT*3 , MEDIUM_FONT);
    SSDL_RenderTextCentered("the next treat is YOU",
            SCREEN_WIDTH/2, LINE_HEIGHT*4 , MEDIUM_FONT);

    SSDL_RenderTextCentered("Use arrow keys to move",
            SCREEN_WIDTH/2, LINE_HEIGHT*6 , MEDIUM_FONT);
    SSDL_RenderTextCentered("left and right",
            SCREEN_WIDTH/2, LINE_HEIGHT*7 , MEDIUM_FONT);

    SSDL_RenderTextCentered("Click mouse to",
            SCREEN_WIDTH/2, LINE_HEIGHT*9 , MEDIUM_FONT);
    SSDL_RenderTextCentered("toggle stats display",
            SCREEN_WIDTH/2, LINE_HEIGHT*10, MEDIUM_FONT);

    SSDL_RenderTextCentered("Hit any key to continue",
            SCREEN_WIDTH/2, BOTTOM_LINE,    SMALL_FONT);

    SSDL_WaitKey();
}
```

```
void displayVictoryScreen()
{
    // sound and picture
    static const SSDL_Sound VICTORY_SOUND = SSDL_LoadWAV(
            "media/342153__robcro6010__circus-theme-short.wav");
    SSDL_PlaySound(VICTORY_SOUND);

    static const SSDL_Image GOOD_PUMPKIN = SSDL_LoadImage(
            "media/goodPumpkin.png");
    SSDL_RenderImage(GOOD_PUMPKIN, SCREEN_WIDTH / 4, 0);

    // victory message
    SSDL_SetRenderDrawColor (WHITE);
    SSDL_RenderText("Hooah!",
                    FINAL_SCREEN_MESSAGE_OFFSET_X,
                    SCREEN_HEIGHT/4,
                    LARGE_FONT);
    constexpr int LINE_DISTANCE_Y = 96; //arbitrarily chosen number...
    SSDL_RenderText("You won!",
                    FINAL_SCREEN_MESSAGE_OFFSET_X,
                    SCREEN_HEIGHT/4+LINE_DISTANCE_Y,
                    LARGE_FONT);
}

void displayDefeatScreen()
{
    // sound and picture
    static const SSDL_Sound DEFEAT_SOUND = SSDL_LoadWAV(
             "media/326813__mrose6__echoed-screams-short.wav");
    SSDL_PlaySound(DEFEAT_SOUND);

    static const SSDL_Image SAD_PUMPKIN  = SSDL_LoadImage(
             "media/sadPumpkin.png");
    SSDL_RenderImage(SAD_PUMPKIN, SCREEN_WIDTH / 4, 0);

    // defeat message
    SSDL_SetRenderDrawColor(WHITE);
```

```
    SSDL_RenderText("Oh, no!", FINAL_SCREEN_MESSAGE_OFFSET_X,
                    SCREEN_HEIGHT/4, LARGE_FONT);
}
```

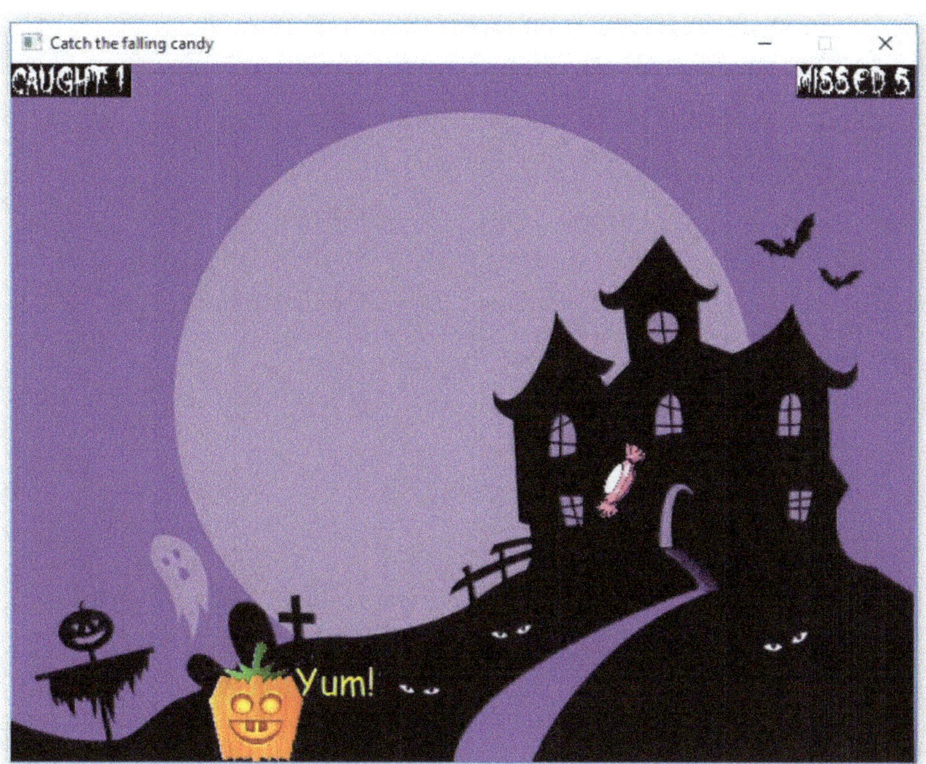

Figure 12-3. *The Halloween candy game in action*

So far we have the general outline of the program. I put a lot of information into the `Object struct`: position, velocity, sprite information, and rotation. Some isn't always needed – only candy rotates, for example – but having only one type of `Object` keeps things simpler.

Example 12-5. Falling candy program, part 2 of 5

```
///////////////////// Initializing /////////////////////////

void resetCandyPosition(Object& candy);

void initializeObjects(Object& basket, Object& candy,
                       Object& yumMessage)
```

```
{
    // load those images
    SSDL_SetSpriteImage(candy.sprite_,
        SSDL_LoadImage ("media/candy.png"));
    SSDL_SetSpriteImage(basket.sprite_,
        SSDL_LoadImage ("media/jack-o-lantern.png"));
    SSDL_SetSpriteImage(yumMessage.sprite_,
        SSDL_LoadImage ("media/yum.png"));

    // two images are the wrong size; we resize them.
    SSDL_SetSpriteSize(candy.sprite_, CANDY_WIDTH, CANDY_HEIGHT);
    SSDL_SetSpriteSize(basket.sprite_, BASKET_WIDTH, BASKET_HEIGHT);

    // move 'em so they're centered on the coords we set for them
    SSDL_SetSpriteOffset(candy.sprite_,
        CANDY_WIDTH / 2, CANDY_HEIGHT / 2);
    SSDL_SetSpriteOffset(basket.sprite_,
        BASKET_WIDTH / 2, BASKET_HEIGHT / 2);

    // put the objects in their starting positions
    basket.loc_.x_ = SCREEN_WIDTH / 2;
    basket.loc_.y_ = SCREEN_HEIGHT - BASKET_HEIGHT / 2;
    SSDL_SetSpriteLocation(basket.sprite_,
        basket.loc_.x_, basket.loc_.y_);
    resetCandyPosition(candy);

    // (We don't care about yumMessage position till we make one)

    // And set velocities
    // basket's can't be specified till we check inputs

    constexpr int CANDY_SPEED = 11;//11 pixels per frame straight down
    candy.velocity_.y_ = CANDY_SPEED;//11 per frame straight down
                                     //Increase speeds for faster game
    yumMessage.velocity_ = { 1, -1 };//Up and to the right

    // And rotational speeds
    candy.rotationSpeed_ = 1;         // Candy spins slightly
}
```

```
////////////////////////// / Drawing /////////////////////////////

// Display all 3 objects (2 if yumMessage is currently not visible)
void renderObjects(Object basket,    Object candy,
                   Object yumMessage,bool showYumMessage)
{
    SSDL_RenderSprite(basket.sprite_);
    SSDL_RenderSprite(candy.sprite_);
    if (showYumMessage) SSDL_RenderSprite(yumMessage.sprite_);
}

void renderStats(int Caught, int Missed)
{
    // Stats boxes, for reporting how many candies caught and missed
    SSDL_SetRenderDrawColor(BLACK);
    constexpr int BOX_WIDTH = 90, BOX_HEIGHT = 25;
    SSDL_RenderFillRect(0, 0,                         // Left box
        BOX_WIDTH, BOX_HEIGHT);
    SSDL_RenderFillRect(SCREEN_WIDTH - BOX_WIDTH, 0, // Right box
        SCREEN_WIDTH - 1, BOX_HEIGHT);

    // Statistics themselves
    SSDL_SetRenderDrawColor(WHITE);
    SSDL_SetFont           (SMALL_FONT);

    SSDL_SetCursor(0, 0);                             // Left box
    sout << "Caught: " << Caught;

    SSDL_SetCursor(SCREEN_WIDTH - BOX_WIDTH, 0);     // Right box
    sout << "Missed: " << Missed;
}
```

resetCandyPosition, called in initializeObjects, starts the candy at the top of the screen with a random X location. It's called again in handleCatchingCandy and handleMissingCandy.

renderStats prints how many pieces you've caught or missed, on two black boxes used to make those stats easier to read.

Example 12-6. Falling candy program, part 3 of 5

```
//////////////// Moving objects in the world ////////////////// /

void resetCandyPosition (Object& candy)  // When it's time to drop
                                         //  another candy...
{
                                         // Put it at a random X location
    candy.loc_.x_ = MARGIN + rand() % (SCREEN_WIDTH - MARGIN);
    candy.loc_.y_ = CANDY_START_HEIGHT;    // at the top of the screen

    SSDL_SetSpriteLocation (candy.sprite_,
                            candy.loc_.x_, candy.loc_.y_);
}

void moveObject(Object& object)
{
    object.loc_.x_ += object.velocity_.x_; // Every frame, move object
    object.loc_.y_ += object.velocity_.y_; //   as specified
    SSDL_SetSpriteLocation(object.sprite_,
                           object.loc_.x_, object.loc_.y_);

                                           // ...and spin as specified
    object.rotation_ += object.rotationSpeed_;
    object.rotation_ %= 360;  // angle shouldn't go over 360
                              // (unlike sin and cos, SDL/SSDL
                              //    functions use angles in degrees)

    SSDL_SetSpriteRotation(object.sprite_, object.rotation_);
}

void moveBasket(Object& basket, int basketSpeed)
{
    // Let user move basket with left and right arrows
    if (SSDL_IsKeyPressed(SDLK_LEFT )) basket.loc_.x_ -= basketSpeed;
    if (SSDL_IsKeyPressed(SDLK_RIGHT)) basket.loc_.x_ += basketSpeed;

    // ..but don't let the user touch the sides of the screen
    if (basket.loc_.x_ < MARGIN)
```

```
        basket.loc_.x_ = MARGIN;
    if (basket.loc_.x_ > SCREEN_WIDTH - MARGIN)
        basket.loc_.x_ = SCREEN_WIDTH - MARGIN;

    // Tell the sprite about our changes on X
    SSDL_SetSpriteLocation (basket.sprite_,
                            basket.loc_.x_, basket.loc_.y_);
}
}
```

moveObject is called on both the candy and the Yum! message. The player controls the basket, so that needs its own moveBasket function. moveBasket checks the state of the left and right arrows with SSDL_IsKeyPressed and moves the basket accordingly, ensuring with MARGIN that it doesn't go off screen.

Example 12-7. Falling candy program, part 4 of 5

```
////////What happens when a candy is caught or missed ////////

// Some math functions we need a lot...
int sqr (int num) { return num * num; }

double distance (Point2D a, Point2D b)
{
    return sqrt(sqr(b.x_ - a.x_) + sqr(b.y_ - a.y_));
}

// Circular collision detection, better for round-ish objects
bool inCollision (Point2D a, Point2D b, int aSize, int bSize)
{
    return (distance(a, b) < aSize/2 + bSize/2);
}

// Detect and handle collisions between basket and candy,
//  and update numberCaught
bool handleCatchingCandy (Object basket, Object& candy,
                          Object& yumMessage, int& numberCaught)
```

```
{
    if (inCollision(basket.loc_, candy.loc_,
                    CANDY_WIDTH, BASKET_WIDTH))
    {
        SSDL_PlaySound(THUNK_SOUND);

        ++numberCaught;

        resetCandyPosition(candy);

        yumMessage.loc_.x_    = basket.loc_.x_;
        yumMessage.loc_.y_    = basket.loc_.y_;

        return true;
    }
    else return false;
}

// Detect and handle when candy goes off bottom of screen,
//  and update numberMissed
void handleMissingCandy (Object& candy, int& numberMissed)
{
                                    // you missed it: it went off screen
    if (candy.loc_.y_ >= SCREEN_HEIGHT)
    {
        SSDL_PlaySound(DROP_SOUND);

        ++numberMissed;


        resetCandyPosition(candy);
    }
}
```

If the basket and candy collide, `handleCatchingCandy` resets the candy to the top of the screen; positions the Yum! message wherever the basket is; and returns true so `main` will know to start the countdown `framesLeftTillYumDisappears`, keeping the Yum! visible for a second.

If the candy falls to the bottom of the screen – if it's missed – it also resets the candy to top of the screen. Either way, the statistics are appropriately updated.

Example 12-8. Falling candy program, part 5 of 5

```
///////////////////// Events /////////////////////

void myEventHandler(bool& mouseClicked)
{
    SSDL_Event event;

    while (SSDL_PollEvent(event))
        switch (event.type)
        {
        case SDL_QUIT:            SSDL_DeclareQuit(); break;
        case SDL_KEYDOWN:         if (SSDL_IsKeyPressed(SDLK_ESCAPE))
                                      SSDL_DeclareQuit();
                                  break;
        case SDL_MOUSEBUTTONDOWN: mouseClicked = true;
        }
}

///// ** The game itself ** ////

bool playGame ()
{
    bool isVictory          = false; // Did we win?  Not yet
    bool isDefeat           = false; // Did we lose? Not yet
    bool letsDisplayStats   = true;  // Do we show stats on screen?
                                     //   Yes, for now

    int numberCaught = 0,            // So far no candies
        numberMissed = 0;            //   caught or missed

     // Initialize sprites
    Object basket, candy, yumMessage;
    initializeObjects (basket, candy, yumMessage);
```

```
    // Main game loop
    while (SSDL_IsNextFrame() && ! isVictory && ! isDefeat)
    {
        constexpr int FRAMES_FOR_YUM_MESSAGE = 60;
        static int framesLeftTillYumDisappears = 0;

        // HANDLE EVENTS
        bool mouseClick = false; myEventHandler (mouseClick);
        if (mouseClick) letsDisplayStats = ! letsDisplayStats;

        // DRAW THINGS
        SSDL_RenderImage(BKGD_IMAGE, 0, 0);
        renderObjects   (basket, candy, yumMessage,
                         framesLeftTillYumDisappears>0);
        if (letsDisplayStats) renderStats(numberCaught, numberMissed);

        // UPDATE THINGS

        // Move objects in the scene
        constexpr int BASKET_SPEED = 7;//7 pixels per frame, L or R
        moveBasket(basket, BASKET_SPEED);
        moveObject(candy); moveObject(yumMessage);

                                        // Did you catch a candy?
        if (handleCatchingCandy(basket, candy,
                                yumMessage, numberCaught))
            framesLeftTillYumDisappears = FRAMES_FOR_YUM_MESSAGE;

        if (numberCaught >= MAX_CAUGHT)
            isVictory = true;
        else                            // ...or did it go off screen?
        {
            handleMissingCandy (candy, numberMissed);
            if (numberMissed >= MAX_MISSED)
                isDefeat = true;        // You just lost!
        }
```

```
        // Update yum message
        if (framesLeftTillYumDisappears > 0)// if yumMessage is active
            --framesLeftTillYumDisappears;  //   keep counting down
    }

    return isVictory;
}
```

The main loop stops when we get victory or defeat. It's divided into the events section, the display section, and the update-things section. In the events section, this statement

```
if (mouseClick) letsDisplayStats = ! letsDisplayStats;
```

toggles whether the stats are shown.

Handling the Yum! message is distributed appropriately: it's displayed just like the other objects, but its lifetime is continually counted down in the update-things section.

For an easier or harder game, call `SSDL_SetFramesPerSecond` before the main game loop, or adjust `BASKET_SPEED`.

Antibugging

- ***SSDL_SpriteHasIntersection reports a collision, but the sprites are nowhere near each other.*** *Maybe a sprite is in a too-large image with a lot of empty space, as in Figure 12-4.*

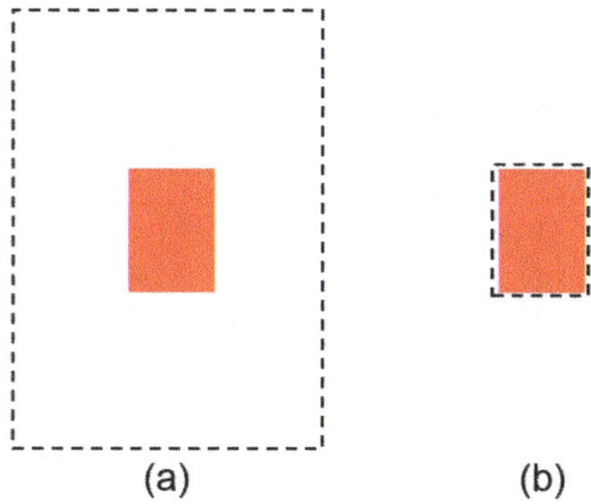

Figure 12-4. *An image with way too much transparent empty space (a) and the same image trimmed to reasonable size (b)*

Solution: Trim the image in GIMP or some other editor.

- **You've got a feature that's supposed to display for a while but never shows up. Something like the splat from earlier in this chapter. Maybe your code looks like this:**

```
while (SSDL_IsNextFrame())
{
    ...
    if (mouseClick)
    {
        framesLeftTillSplatDisappears = SPLAT_LIFETIME;
        while (framesLeftTillSplatDisappears > 0)
        {
            // display the splat
            --framesLeftTillSplatDisappears;
        }
    }
     ...
}
```

It displayed, all right - again and again, till `framesLeftTillSplatDisappears` reached 0 - all in 1/60 of a second! It displayed so quickly you never got to see it.

The problem is adapting to this new event-driven way of thinking. We don't want the program to do all the displaying of the splat and then go on to the next 1/60 of a second; we want it to set up the display and then let the frames pass while other things happen (including the user getting to see the splat).

A good rule of thumb is **avoid looping an action that's supposed to take time inside the main animation loop**. Just set it up, and let the main loop update it with successive frames.

Another good rule is the Tip from designing the splat program - **keep parts of the main loop separate**: handle events (say), then display, and then do updates.

So a way to fix this program is

```
while (SSDL_IsNextFrame())
{
   // HANDLE EVENTS
   ...
   if (mouseClick)
       framesLeftTillSplatDisappears = SPLAT_LIFETIME;
   ...

   // DRAW THINGS
   //   display the splat
   ...

    // UPDATE THINGS
    if (framesLeftTillSplatDisappears > 0)
        --framesLeftTillSplatDisappears;
    ...
}
```

- **You can't get a new feature to work.** Try a program that *does* work (a sample program from the text or the Internet or something you did earlier or even a program with empty `main`) and make gradual changes until it's the new program.
- **You just added a new feature, and now nothing works.** Here are a few suggestions.
    - As in Chapter 1, **keep a trail of backups**, copies of your entire folder, as you make changes, so if something goes wrong you can go back to an earlier version. It's more fun than pulling your hair out.
    - **Cut out all the code from a function that's misbehaving.** Then put half of it back. If the bad behavior returns, only put a quarter of it back; if not, add more code back in. Keep going till you've figured out what line is the problem

- **Test to destruction.** If I absolutely can't figure what's wrong, I'll make a copy of the folder (maybe named "`ttd`"), make a backup copy of that, and then remove code, especially code I think is irrelevant to the error. Is the error still there? If not, I've found the problem! But if so, repeat, still making backups, until the program's so short there's nothing left but the error.
- **Identify differences between versions**. Maybe one has a feature you want but a bug you don't. A precise report of differences can help you narrow down what you're interested in. In Unix, `diff file1 file2` lists the lines that differ. In Windows, **WinDiff** is a wonderful program from Microsoft you can find online that does the same. Both work for individual files or entire folders.
- **Talk about the problem to someone who can really listen: a duck.** Maybe if you explain your problem to an expert, it'll become clear. Sure, but what if there's no expert handy? Talk to a rubber duck instead - seriously. Explain the problem in detail. As you do, you may find your solution. **Rubber duck debugging** is a thing and at present even has its own website (rubberduckdebugging.com).

For more tips, review the "Antibugging" section at the end of Chapter 9.

EXERCISES

In these and subsequent exercises, plan in advance, and use the debugger if anything goes wrong.

1. Make those balls bounce, as in Chapter 11 ...and have your mouse control a little player on the screen. Avoid the bouncing balls.
2. Make a space game: a UFO flies overhead, dropping missiles while you shoot back. You'll need an array of missiles.
3. Make a version of a fairgrounds duck shoot game. To make it interesting, you could have slow missiles (going straight from your crosshairs to the duck, but taking a second to get there).
4. Make a gun that can rotate, put it in the middle of the screen, and shoot bad guys coming from random directions.
5. Make your own game, either a copy of an existing arcade game or your own idea.

CHAPTER 13

Standard I/O and File Operations

We've had too much fun. It's time to get serious.

Or maybe it's time to learn how to program when you *aren't* using a graphics-and-games library. After all, you usually aren't. Even if you are, you may need to access files (for loading a game level, say), and in C++ we handle files much as we do text-based user interaction – what we've done till now with `sin` and `sout`.

Standard I/O Programs

Example 13-1 is a program that uses standard I/O. It may look familiar.

Example 13-1. "Hello, world!" using C++ standard I/O

```
// Hello, world! program
//      -- from _C++26 for Lazy Programmers_

// It prints "Hello, world!" on the screen.
//   Quite an accomplishment, huh?

#include <iostream>

using namespace std;

int main()
{
    cout << "Hello, world!" << endl;

    return 0;
}
```


W. Briggs, *C++26 for Lazy Programmers*, https://doi.org/10.1007/979-8-8688-1859-2_13

Here are the changes from SSDL's Hello, world!, starting at the bottom and working backward:

- It's time to come clean: ssin and sout are cheap knockoffs of the built-in cin (pronounced "C-in") and cout ("C-out") that come with the compiler. cin and cout don't work with the SDL window, so we needed a substitute. cin and cout are like ssin and sout, but (a) you can't set the cursor - you can only go down the screen - and (b) you can't set the font or color.
- We needed main to have arguments (int argc, char** argv) for compatibility with SDL; now they can be omitted.
- using namespace std;: cout is part of the "standard" namespace, and you have to tell the compiler to use it, or it'll complain it doesn't know what cout is.
- Instead of "SSDL.h", we load <iostream>, which like <cmath> and <cstdlib> comes with the compiler. It defines cin, cout, endl (outputs '\n'),[1] and other things.

Extra International Output

We're still not there yet in international output for console programs, but we're getting there. Unix distributions including Ubuntu, Debian, and Fedora support it with no extra operating-system tweaks. You do have to make one change inside your programs (see the unicode-example folder in the book's source code):

```
cout << reinterpret_cast<const char*>
                          (u8"Ελλάδα 中国 ኢትዮጵያ\n");
```

cout, unlike sout, doesn't know how to print sequences of char8_t (which is what the above string is), so we have to cast. reinterpret_cast is for casting when C++ thinks the types aren't similar enough and we're saying, "Trust me, it'll be fine."

---

[1] It also tells C++ to send the output to the screen right now - to "flush" it. We usually don't care as long as it gets there eventually, so I tend to use '\n'.

Microsoft Windows programs may or may not require `#include <windows.h>`, and at the start of the main program, `SetConsoleOutputCP(CP_UTF8);`. This tells the console window to use UTF-8.

UTF-8 output is not currently recommended on MSys2.

Compiling Standard I/O Programs

You can compile them using folders from `newWork` in the book's sample code just as before, but now copy not `basicSSDLProject` but `basicStandardProject`.

g++ users, execute not with `./runx` but with `./a.out`. (We'll see how to get a name more indicative of what your program actually does in the next section.)

Building a Project from Scratch … (optional)

…with g++

To make your own program, make a folder for it, create `main.cpp` in that folder, and compile with this command:

```
g++ -std=c++2c -g main.cpp -o myProgram
```

That's it. `-std=c++2c` means "use the C++26 standard as much as g++ supports it"; the `-g` means "support debugging with gdb or ddd"; `-o myProgram` means "name the executable `myProgram`." If you leave off the `-o` option, the executable will be `a.out`.

To run, enter `./myProgram`.

To debug, use `ddd myProgram &`[2] or `gdb myProgram`. In MSys2, we used to `break SDL_main`; since SDL's gone, `break main` instead.

If your compiler doesn't like `-std=c++2c`, either upgrade your compiler or roll back to `-std=c++23` (C++23, not C++26).

[2] The `&` means "give me a command prompt again immediately; don't wait for `ddd` to finish." A good practice.

Extra Why do we put ./ before the program name in Unix?

When you type a command, Unix looks through a list of directories called the PATH: directories it thinks executable programs should be in. If the current directory (known in Unix as `.`, a single period) isn't in the PATH, it won't look there, so if you type the name of a program that's in your current directory, Unix won't find it.

I don't like that, so let's put `.` ("dot") in the PATH.

Suppose it's the first directory it checks. Then if a bad guy can get a malicious program into your directory and name it a common command like `ls`, he can get you to do awful things: you type `ls`, and it deletes the operating system or something.

OK, so we'll make it the *last* directory checked. Now, if you type `ls`, Unix will look in `/bin` (or wherever), find the right `ls`, and run it.

But if the bad guy guesses what typos people make and names his evil program `sl` and your fingers miss ...he's got you.

I don't know how likely that last scenario is, but it's a reason to leave `.` out of the PATH if you're concerned.

Antibugging

- **(gdb/ddd) The debugger says no debugging symbols are found.** In ddd it also gives a blank window. Compile again with the `-g` option or use `basicStandardProject` and type `make`.

...in Microsoft Visual Studio

To make your own project without reference to `basicStandardProject`, on starting Visual Studio, tell it to Create a new project (Figure 13-1), and then select Console App (Figure 13-2). In the next window (Figure 13-3), Visual Studio would prefer to put your project in a folder called "repos" that'll be hard to find; I use the Desktop. I also urge you to check "Place solution and project in the same directory" – otherwise, you get multiple Debug folders and cleaning up files is harder.

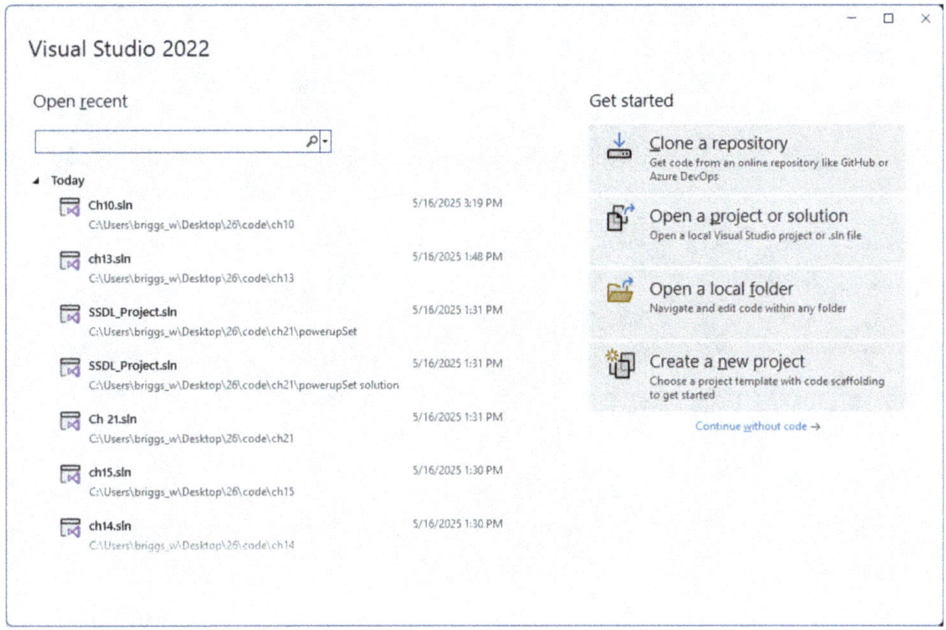

Figure 13-1. *Starting Visual Studio*

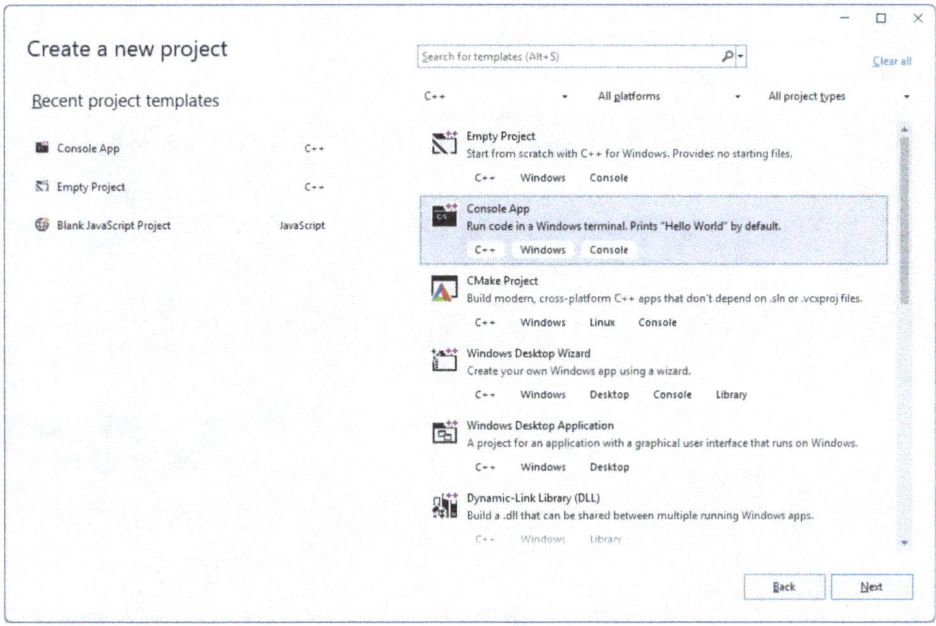

Figure 13-2. *Creating a new project in Visual Studio*

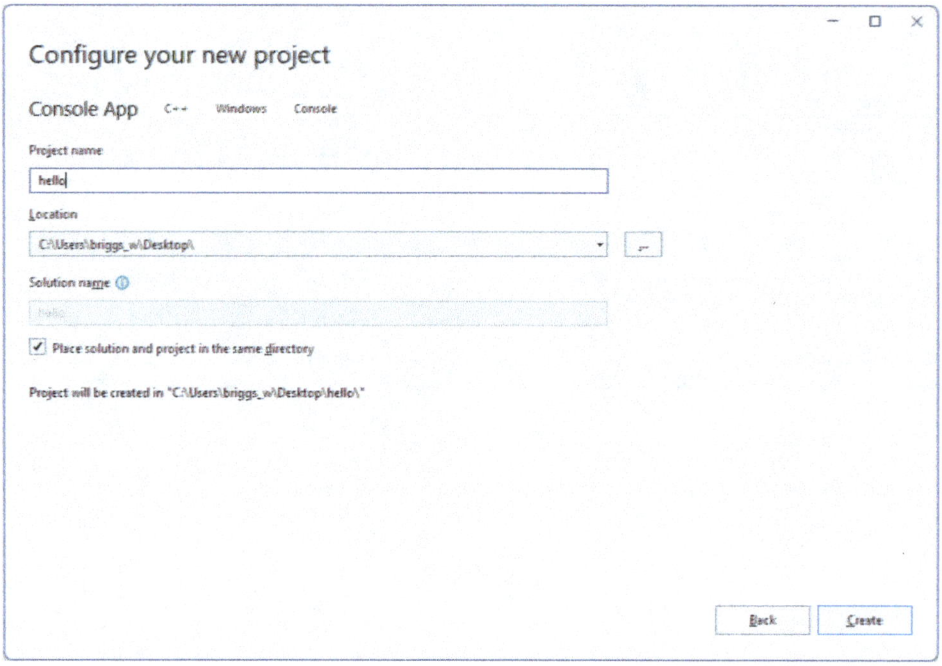

Configure your new project

Console App C++ Windows Console

Project name

hello

Location

C:\Users\briggs_w\Desktop\

Solution name

☑ Place solution and project in the same directory

Project will be created in "C:\Users\briggs_w\Desktop\hello\"

Back Create

Figure 13-3. *Configuring a new project in Visual Studio*

The default console project is Microsoft's take on Hello, world! (Figure 13-4). You can erase it and type in your own code.

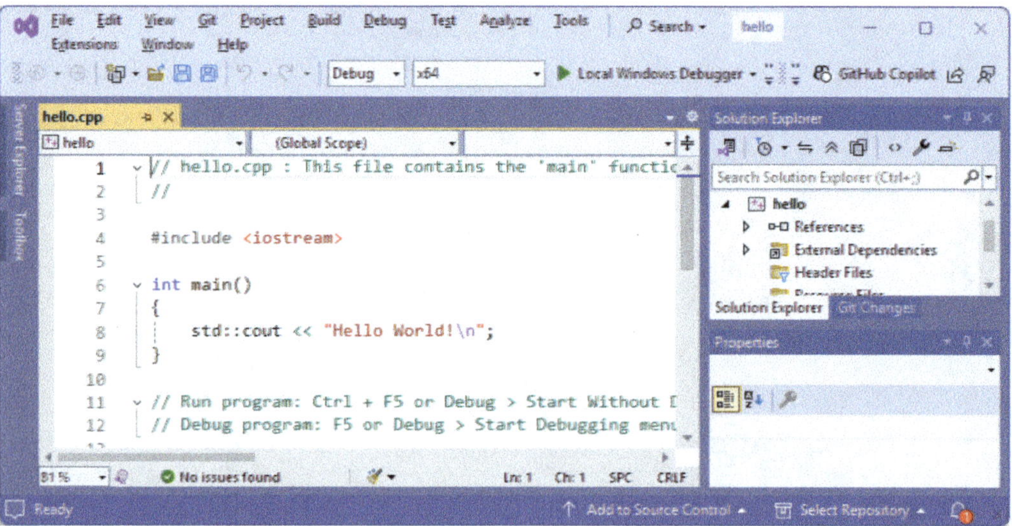

Figure 13-4. *The new project*

If you want to use the latest features from C++26 (and who wouldn't?), right-click your project (not the solution), be sure you're set for All Configurations and All Platforms, and change the standard to **Preview – Features from the Latest C++ Working Draft (/std:c++-latest)** (Figure 13-5).

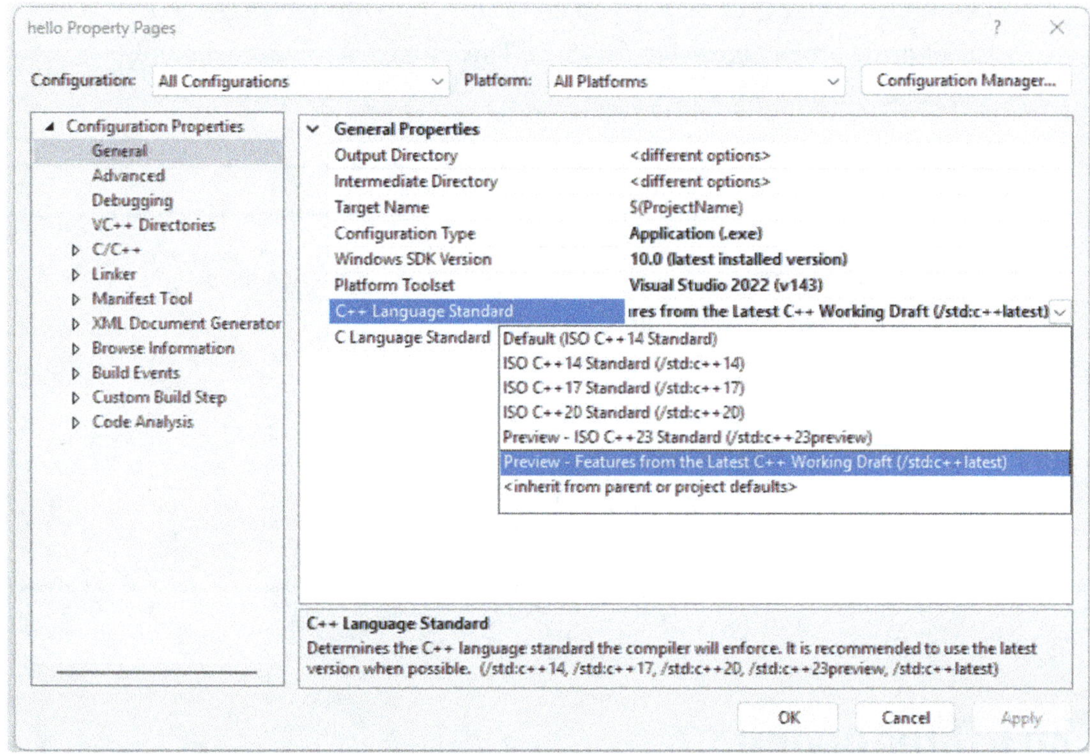

***Figure 13-5.** Changing Microsoft Visual Studio to use the latest standard*

Now you're ready to type your program, but before running it, I suggest reading the "Antibugging" section.

Antibugging

Here are some issues you may find moving to standard I/O with Microsoft Visual Studio:

- **The program closes before you have a chance to see anything.** Solution: Under Tools ➤ Options ➤ Debugging, uncheck Automatically close the console when debugging stops. This will apply to all console projects till you change it.

After that, if you're running it and then try to run another copy, that subsequent copy may automatically close before you can see. Just run one copy at a time.

- **The compiler can't find _WinMain@16, precompiled headers, or something else that makes you go "Huh?"** You probably selected the wrong project type (Figure 13-2). The easy fix is to start over and select Console App.

EXERCISES

1. Write a program that prints all 99 verses of "99 bottles of beer on the wall." In case you missed this cultural treasure, it goes like this:

```
99 bottles of beer on the wall
99 bottles of beer;
Take one down, pass it around,
98 bottles of beer on the wall!
```

The last verse is the one ending with 0 bottles.

File I/O (optional)

Programs useful for more than just homework generally need to access files. So let's see how to do this: first the easy way (using `cin` and `cout`) and then in a more generally applicable way.

`cin` and `cout` as Files

In a sense, we've been using files already – at least, two things that C++ considers to be files: `cin` and `cout`.

`cin` is an input file. It just happens to be an input file that gets its information from the keyboard as you type. `cout` is an output file: the output file that is your computer screen. A stretch of the definitions? Perhaps – but soon we'll use `cin` and `cout` as *actual* files.

To do this we must know how to use the command prompt. Unix and MSys2 users can skip the next section: you already know this.

Setting Up the Command Prompt in Windows

Open the Windows command prompt (click the Start Menu and type `cmd`) and go the folder for the project you're using. Here's an easy way: in the window for that folder, click the folder icon left of the address bar, the part that shows something of a form like `... > Desktop > 1-hello`. When you do it'll be replaced by a highlighted path like the one in Figure 13-6.

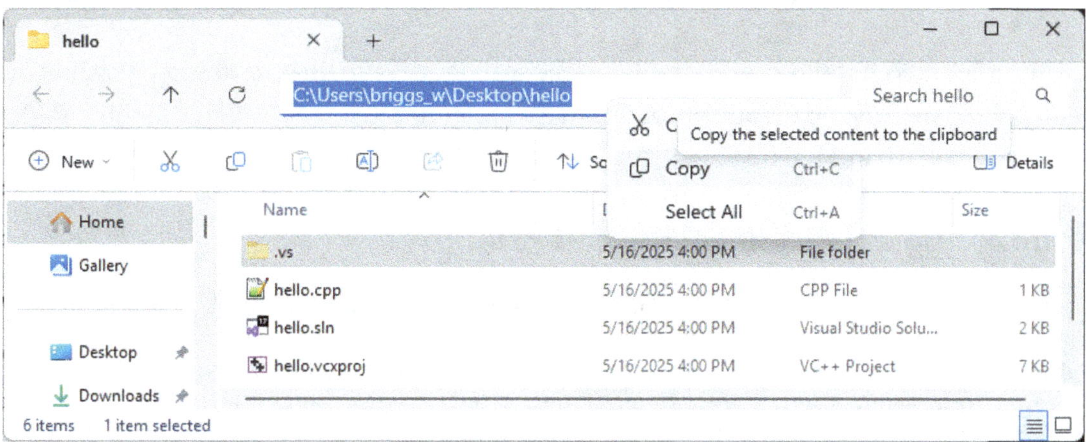

Figure 13-6. *Getting a path to use with the command prompt, in Windows*

If the drive you see in the command window prompt differs from what's at the left in the address you just copied (in my case, `C:`), enter the drive from the address, as in Figure 13-7.

Now, in the command window, type `cd` and paste in that path you copied, and hit Enter.

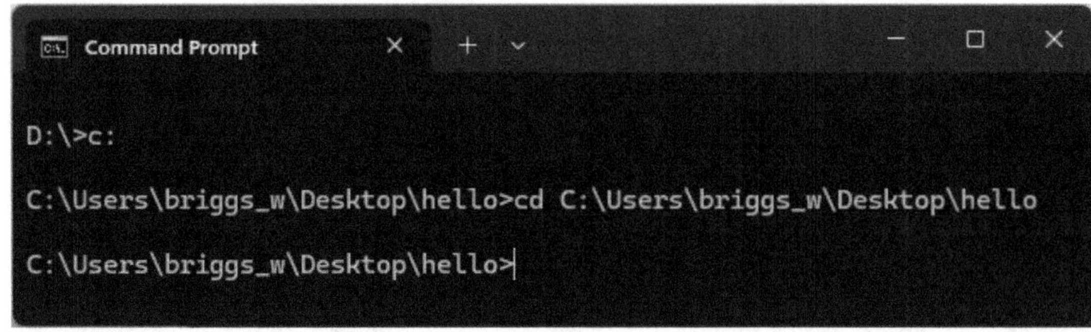

***Figure 13-7.** Changing to your project's drive and directory in* `cmd`*. Here, we change from the* `D:` *drive to* `C:`*, and then* `cd` *to the* `hello` *directory on the desktop*

Visual Studio puts your executable, `<your project>.exe`, in a subfolder, possibly `Debug.`, `Release`, `x64`, or some combination thereof. Find it and copy it to the same folder as your `.vcxproj` and it'll be able to find whatever files you put there.

Redirecting I/O at the Command Prompt

To make your program get input from `in.txt`, not the keyboard, type

```
myProgram < in.txt #[3]The < goes from file to program; makes sense
```

To make it also send its output to `out.txt`, not the screen, type

```
myProgram < in.txt > out.txt
```

Try sending the Hello program's output to a file and see what happens.

Online Extra "Save yourself and your users some time with I/O redirection": find it in the YouTube channel "Programming the Lazy Way," or at `https://www.youtube.com/watch?v=zQ3TY6oSAcQ`.

---

[3] #: the Unix comment marker. In Windows, use REM.

while (cin)

I've heard the letters that appear most frequently in English text are, starting with the super-frequent E, ETAOINSHRDLU. Let's see if that's true by giving the program some huge text, maybe off `gutenberg.org`, and counting the frequencies:

```
make an array of frequencies for letters, all initially zero

while there are characters left
    read in a character // we won't prompt the user; it's all coming
                        // from a file
    if it's a letter add 1 to frequency for that letter

print all those frequencies
```

I know how to create arrays, add 1 to `int`s, and read in characters. But how do I know there are characters left?

`while (cin) ...` will do it. If you put `cin` someplace you'd expect a `bool`, it's evaluated to something like "if nothing has gone wrong with `cin`." The usual thing that goes wrong with `cin` is reaching the end of the input file. Example 13-2 shows the program.

Example 13-2. Counting frequencies of letters in a text file

```
// Program to get the frequencies of letters
//      -- from _C++26 for Lazy Programmers_

#include <iostream>

using namespace std;

int main()
{
    // make an array of frequencies for letters, all initially zero
    constexpr int LETTERS_IN_ALPHABET = 26;
    int frequenciesOfLetters[LETTERS_IN_ALPHABET] = {}; // all zeroes

    // read in the letters
    while (cin)                 // while there are letters left
    {
        char ch; cin >> ch;     // read one in
        ch = toupper(ch);       // capitalize it
```

```
        if (cin)                 // Still no problems with cin, right?
            if (isalpha(ch)) //   and this is an alphabetic letter?
                ++frequenciesOfLetters[ch - 'A'];
                                 // A's go in slot 0, B's in slot 1...
    }

    // print all those frequencies
    cout << "Frequencies are:\n";
    cout << "Letter\tFrequency\n";
    for (char ch = 'A'; ch <= 'Z'; ++ch) // for each letter A to Z...
        cout << ch << '\t' << frequenciesOfLetters[ch - 'A'] << '\n';

    return 0;
}
```

Try this with `a.out < in.txt > out.txt` (g++) or `2-frequencies < in.txt > out.txt` (Visual Studio), and you'll get an `out.txt` file like

```
Frequencies are:
Letter  Frequency
A       40
B       5
C       9
D       20
E       63
...
```

If the letters are coming from a file, `while (cin)` stops when we reach the end of file. But actual keyboard input has no end of file. You can simulate it by hitting Ctrl-Z and Enter (Windows) or Ctrl-D (Unix). *It must be the first character on the line, or it may not work.*

Reading in Characters, Including Whitespace

New task: read in a file, every character, and capitalize everything. Here's our input file.

This looks like it should work, but doesn't:

```
while (cin)              // for each char in file
{
    char ch;  cin >> ch; //    read in char
    ch = toupper (ch);   //    capitalize
    if (cin) cout << ch; //    cin still OK? Then print
}
```

With this input

```
Twinkle, twinkle, little bat!
How I wonder what you're at!
```

we get this output:

```
TWINKLE,TWINKLE,LITTLEBAT!HOWIWONDERWHATYOU'REAT!
```

`cin >>` skips whitespace. Fine for user interaction and the ETAOIN SHRDLU program, but here we *need* the whitespace.

Solution: `ch = cin.get();`. `cin.get()` returns the next character, even if it's space, tab (`\t`), or end of line (`\n`).

Example 13-3 reads in a file and produces an ALL CAPS version. To execute, type `a.out < in.txt > out.txt` (g++) or `3-capitalizeFile < in.txt > out.txt` (Visual Studio).

Example 13-3. Capitalizing a file, character by character

```
// Program to produce an ALL CAPS version of a file
//      -- from _C++26 for Lazy Programmers_

#include <iostream>
#include <cctype>                // for toupper

using namespace std;

int main()
{
    while (cin)                  // for each char in file
    {
        char ch = cin.get();     //   read in char
        ch = toupper (ch);       //   capitalize
```

```
        if (cin) cout << ch; //   cin still OK? Then print
    }

    return 0;
}
```

Antibugging

- **You told it to stop at the end of file, but it goes too far.**

  ```
  /////////// get an average -- buggy version //////////////
  double total = 0.0;              // initialize total and howMany
  int  howMany = 0;
  while (cin)                 // while there are numbers in file
  {
      int num; cin >> num; //   read one in
      total += num;        //   keep running total
      ++howMany;
  }
  ```

  Your input file is

  ```
  1
  2
  ```

  and your average is ...1.6667. Huh?

  Trace it with the debugger. It reads in 1, adds it, and increments howMany. It reads in 2, adds it, and increments howMany again. Test for end of file with `while (cin)`; it keeps going.

  But aren't we at the end of the file? Maybe not: there may be another \n or space or something.

  So the program keeps going. It reads in the next number, and there isn't one, so it leaves num as 2, adds it again (!), and increments again. An error is born.

  It couldn't know there wasn't going to be another number till it tried to read it. So the solution is to **test the input file after every attempt to read, to ensure it didn't run out of input while reading**:

```
int num; cin >> num; // read one in
if (cin)             // still no problems with cin, right?
{
    total += num;    // keep running total
    ++howMany;
}
```

See the source code, ch13 folder/solution, for average, which is a complete and correct version of this program.

EXERCISES

In all these exercises, use standard I/O.

1. Read in a sequence of numbers from a file and print it in reverse order. You don't know how many, but you do know it's no more than, say, 100. (This way you can declare an array that's big enough.)
2. Count the characters in a file.
3. ...not including whitespace or punctuation.

Using Filenames

It's too much work to redirect I/O all the time. Maybe I have multiple input files – they can't all be cin. Or maybe I just want the program to remember the filename and not expect me to type it at a command prompt.

Say I have a game with angry robots wandering around trying to collide with my player. The player starts on the left side of the screen, and it's my job to get it to the right without any collisions.

It might make the game more interesting if I placed the robots in specific locations, designing each level successively tougher than the last. We'll start level 1 with three robots, so that's three locations.

If I got this from cin (way too annoying, but we'll change that in a minute), the code might look like Example 13-4. To run this example, type in six integers and it will spit them back out to you. Exciting, yes, I know.

Example 13-4. Code to read in several points from `cin`

```
// A (partial) game with killer robots
//    meant to demonstrate use of file I/O
// This loads 3 points and prints a report
//       -- from _C++26 for Lazy Programmers_

#include <iostream>

using namespace std;

struct Point2D { int x_=0, y_=0; };

int main()
{
                    // an array of robot positions
    constexpr int MAX_ROBOTS = 3;
    Point2D robots[MAX_ROBOTS];

    int whichRobot = 0;

    // while there's input and array's not full...
    while (cin && whichRobot < MAX_ROBOTS)
    {
        int x, y;
        cin >> x >> y;          // read in an x, y pair

        if (cin)                // if we got valid input (not at end of file)
        {
            robots[whichRobot] = {x, y}; // store what we read
            ++whichRobot;                // and remember there's 1
                                         // more robot
        }
    }

    for (int i = 0; i < MAX_ROBOTS; ++i)
        cout        << robots[i].x_ << ' '
                    << robots[i].y_ << endl;

    return 0;
}
```

Now let's make the program get the file without redirecting I/O. Here's what I must do to use a named input file:

1. `#include <fstream>`, which has definitions I need.
2. `ifstream inFile;`: This declares my input file. `ofstream` is for output files.
3. `inFile.open ("level1.txt");`: Opening a file associates it with a filename and ensures there's no problem.
4. Verify the file opened without error. If it's an input file, the error may be that the file doesn't exist or isn't in the folder you thought it was. If it's an output file, you may have a disk problem or a read-only file. Here's how to verify:

   ```
   if (! inFile) // handle error
   ```

5. Change `cin` to `inFile` wherever you want to use the new file. If it's an output file, change `cout` to `outFile`.
6. When done, close the file: `inFile.close ();`. This tells the operating system to forget the association between `inFile` and "`input.txt`" and thereby lets other programs that might need it use it again. Admittedly, when your program ends, all files it referenced will be closed – but it's wise to get in the habit of putting away your toys, I mean files, when you're done with them. Your mother would be proud.

Example 13-5 is the updated version of the program.

Example 13-5. Program that reads an input file and prints to an output file

```
// A (partial) game with killer robots
//    meant to demonstrate use of file I/O
// This loads 3 points and prints a report
//       -- from _C++26 for Lazy Programmers_

#include <iostream>
#include <fstream>  // 1. include <fstream>
```

```
using namespace std;

struct Point2D { int x_=0, y_=0; };

int main()
{
                    // an array of robot positions
    constexpr int MAX_ROBOTS = 3;
    Point2D robots[MAX_ROBOTS];

                    // 2. Declare file variables.
                    // 3. Open the files.
                    //  Here's two ways to do both; either's fine
    ifstream inFile; inFile.open("RobotGameLevel1.txt");
    ofstream outFile ("RobotSavedGame1.txt");

                    // 4. Verify the files opened without error
    if (!inFile)
    {
        cout << "Can't open RobotGameLevel1.txt!\n"; return 1;
                    // 1 is a conventional return value for error
    }
    if (! outFile)
    {
        cout << "Can't create file RobotSavedGame1.txt!"; return 1;
    }

    int whichRobot = 0;

                   // 5. Change cin to inFile, cout to outFile

    // while there's input and array's not full...
    while (inFile && whichRobot < MAX_ROBOTS)
    {
        int x, y;
        inFile >> x >> y;      //  read in an x, y pair

        if (inFile)            // if we got valid input (not at end of file)
```

```
        {
            robots[whichRobot] = {x, y}; // store what we read
            ++whichRobot;                // and remember there's 1
                                         // more robot
        }
    }

    for (int i = 0; i < MAX_ROBOTS; ++i)
        outFile     << robots[i].x_ << ' '
                    << robots[i].y_ << endl;

                    // 6. When done, close the files
    inFile.close(); outFile.close();

                    // can still use cout for other things
    cout << "Just saved RobotSavedGame1.txt.\n";

    return 0;
}
```

That worked: it saved `RobotSavedGame1.txt` in the same folder as the `.vcxproj` file.

The program erases whatever contents `RobotSavedGame1.txt` has when it starts and replaces them with new contents.

You can have multiple input and output files in your programs. You can also pass files into functions:

```
void readFile (ifstream& in,  double numbers[], int& howManyWeGot);
void writeFile(ofstream& out, double numbers[], int  howMany);
```

EXERCISES

1. Write a program to determine if two files are identical.
2. Write and test functions to read from, and print to, a file of `Point2Ds`.
3. Roll two dice 100 times, and store the resulting sums in a file …

4. ...then load that file and print a histogram: a bar showing how many times you got 2, another showing how many times 3, etc. Do this in SSDL (use `basicSSDLProject`; go ahead and use file variables; just don't expect `cin` and `cout` to work); or print Xs across the screen showing how many times each value showed up (Figure 13-8).

```
2       : X
3       : XXXXXXX
4       : XXXXXXXX
...
```

Figure 13-8. *A histogram printed with Xs*

5. Make your own cryptogram: a letter scheme, as in, A means R, B means D, etc. Then encode a message using your encryption scheme. Also write a decryption program and verify everything works.

6. (Hard) Is the earth getting warmer?

   There's a file `temperature.txt`[4] in the sample code for this chapter, which contains, for given years, year and estimated average global temperature. (The temperature given is degrees Centigrade relative to estimated average temperature for 1910–2000.)

   So what can we learn from it?

   The degrees increase per year: this is

$$m = \frac{N\sum xy - \sum x \sum y}{N\sum x^2 - \left(\sum x\right)^2}$$

   x is year and y is temperature. Σ x, read as "the sum of x," means "the sum of all the x's." m is the slope of the line y = mx + b that most closely matches the data.

   How closely the yearly temperatures actually match this line: this is

$$R = \frac{N\sum xy - \sum x \sum y}{\sqrt{\left[N\sum x^2 - \left(\sum x\right)^2\right]\left[N\sum y^2 - \left(\sum y\right)^2\right]}}$$

[4] Source: www.ncdc.noaa.gov/cag/global/time-series.

If R is –1 or 1, then the correlation is strong. If R is near 0, it's very weak. Negative R means that the temperature is decreasing with time (but we'd know this already from m).

Write a program that reads the file and provides the user with degrees increase per year and R. What functions will you need? Test them enough to be sure you trust them before giving your answer.

Of course, correlation does not prove causality. For example, people who drink coffee ski more (let's say). Does this mean coffee causes skiing? Maybe it's that ski lodges give free coffee. Or maybe people who like to have fun are more likely to ski and drink coffee. For causality we need a bit more (human) thinking.

CHAPTER 14

Character Arrays and Dynamic Memory

Character arrays – a.k.a. "character strings," or text – are important for many tasks. This chapter shows how to handle them and how to create those or other arrays when you don't know the size in advance. Along the way we'll learn the standard library's character array functions the most effective way we can: by building them.

Character Arrays

We've been using `char` arrays from the beginning. Our `"Hello, world!"` quote from Chapters 1 and 13 is a character array, with contents as shown in Figure 14-1.

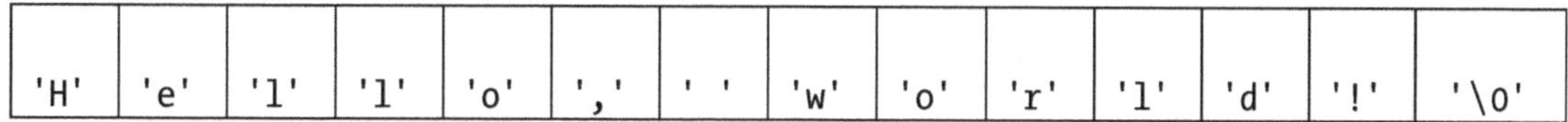

'H'	'e'	'l'	'l'	'o'	','	' '	'w'	'o'	'r'	'l'	'd'	'!'	'\0'

Figure 14-1. *The contents of the "Hello, world!" character array literal*

`'\0'`, the "null character," is a marker to tell C++ this is where our character string ends. `cout` stops printing not when it reaches the end of allocated space – it doesn't know or care how much space was allocated – but when it reaches `'\0'`.

Let's see what we can do with `char` arrays besides printing.

Here are two ways to **initialize a character array**:

```
char A[] = {'d','o','g','\0'}; // they both mean the same thing
char A[] = "dog";              // but this one's easier to read,
                               //   don't you think?
```


W. Briggs, *C++26 for Lazy Programmers*, https://doi.org/10.1007/979-8-8688-1859-2_14

You can also **read a word into a character array** from cin or an input file. We'll need to be sure the array we declare has enough room for what's typed in. We do this by allocating way more characters than we're likely to need:

```
constexpr int MAX_STRING_SIZE = 250;
char        name[MAX_STRING_SIZE];
cout << "What's your name? "; cin >> name;
```

That code reads in one word. If you want to **read the entire line** (maybe you want to let the user enter both first and last names), you'll want `cin.getline(name, MAX_STRING_SIZE);`.

We can **pass the array into a function**. In Example 14-1 we have a function that prints a question and gets a valid yes-or-no answer. We don't plan to change the array, so we pass it as const.

Example 14-1. A function that takes a char array as a parameter. Since it's short, it and Example 14-2 are together in the source code folder ch14, in project/folder 1-and-2-charArrays

```
bool getYorNAnswer(const char question[])
{
      char answer;

      do
      {
        cout << question;          // print a question
        cin  >> answer;            //   ...and get an answer
        answer = toupper(answer);//  capitalized so we can compare to Y, N
      }
      while (answer != 'Y' && answer != 'N');
                                   // keep asking till we get Y or N
      return answer == 'Y';        //   "true" means "user said Y"
}
```

If we call getYorNAnswer thus

```
getYorNAnswer("Ready to rumble (Y/N)? "); // same question, and reasoning,
                                          // as in Chapter 5's
                                          // section on while and do-while
```

our interaction might look like this:

```
Ready to rumble (Y/N)? x
Ready to rumble (Y/N)? 7
Ready to rumble (Y/N)? y
```

...at which point `getYorNAnswer` will return `true`.

Let's now find how long a character string is – not the allocated memory, but the part being used, up until the null character:

```
where = 0
while the whereth char isn't the null character (not at end of string)
  add 1 to where
```

Example 14-2 shows a complete version.

Example 14-2. The `myStrlen` function. Find it and Example 14-1 in the source code folder `ch14`, in project/folder `1-and-2-charArrays`

```
unsigned int myStrlen(const char str[]) // "strlen" is the conventional
                                        //    name for this function
{
    int where = 0;

    while (str[where] != '\0')    // count the chars
        ++where;

    return where;                 // length is final "where"
}
```

This and other functions are already provided in include file `cstring`. Table 14-1 lists the most commonly used.

Table 14-1. *Some* `cstring` *functions, simplified for clarity*

`unsigned size_t strlen(const char myArray[]);`	Return length of the character string in `myArray` (how many characters till the null character).
`void strcpy(char destination[], const char source[]);`	Copy contents of `source` into `destination`.
`void strcat(char destination[], const char source[]);`	Copy contents of `source` to the end of `destination`. If you call `strcat` on arguments containing "Mr." and "Goodbar", the resulting destination will be "Mr.Goodbar".
`int strcmp(const char a[], const char b[]);`	Return –1 if a comes before b in alphabetical order, as in `strcmp ("alpha", "beta")`; 0 if they are identical; 1 if a comes after `b`, as in `strcmp ("beta", "alpha")`;.

Note Microsoft Visual Studio may give a warning if it sees `strcpy`, `strcat`, etc.:

```
warning C4996: 'strcpy': This function or variable may
be unsafe. Consider using strcpy_s instead. To disable
deprecation, use _CRT_SECURE_NO_WARNINGS. See online help for
details.
```

`strcpy_s` and `strcat_s` are versions of `strcpy` and `strcat` that try to stop you from writing past the bounds of the array. Sounds wise, but this never caught on generally. I don't use them because I want code to be portable between compilers. Or maybe I just like living on the edge.

To suppress the warning, put this line at the top of any file referencing `strcpy` and others:

```
#pragma warning (disable:4996)
                          // disable warning about strcpy, etc.
```

Antibugging

- **In the debugger, you see your `char` array looking reasonable, but toward the end it's full of random characters.** That's OK: whatever's past the `'\0'` isn't printed or used anyway. You can ignore it.
- **You see reasonable characters in your char array being printed, then followed by extra garbage**. The string is missing its final `'\0'`. Solution: Insert the `'\0'`.
- **It acts like it's gotten some of your input before you had a chance to type it.** (If using file I/O, it skips part of the file.) Here's an example:

```
do
{
    cout << "Enter a line and I'll tell you how long it is.\n";
    cout << "Enter: "; cin.getline(line, MAX_LINE_LENGTH);

    cout << "That's " << strlen(line) << " characters.\n";

    letsRepeat = getYOrNAnswer("Continue (Y/N)? ");
}
while (letsRepeat);
```

First time through, you're good. Every time after that, when you say you want to do it again, it says your line length is 0 and asks if you want to continue.

Think of `cin` as providing a sequence of characters sent from keyboard to program, as in Figure 14-2.

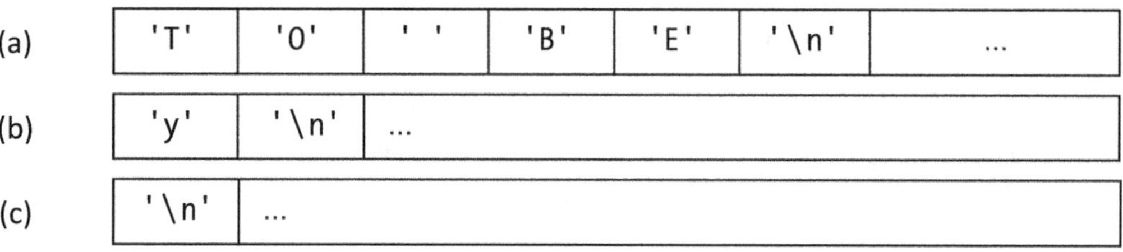

***Figure 14-2.** The `cin` buffer[1], with whatever the user typed as its contents*

[1] Buffer: temporary storage, especially for I/O.

In (a), you've entered your first line, `TO BE`. `cin.getline` takes all that, up through the '\n'.

In (b), you've entered your response to the "Continue (Y/N)?" question.

In (c), `getYOrNAnswer` has done *its* input: `cin>>answer`. `answer` becomes `'y'`, and `getYOrNAnswer` is done.

We're ready to start the loop again and get more input ...but look what was left in the `cin` buffer: a string for `cin.getline` to read. It's an empty string, same as if you typed nothing and hit Enter, but it's still a string. So `cin.getline` won't wait for you to type; it goes right on and reads that empty string ...and we're back in `getYOrNAnswer` being asked if we want to continue.

We need to dump the `'\n'` that `getYOrNAnswer` left, before `cin.getline` can be fooled. Here are two ways:

- `cin.getline` again, just to get rid of the `'\n'`
- `cin.ignore (MAX_LINE_LENGTH, '\n');`: This ignores all `chars` up through `MAX_LINE_LENGTH` or the first \n, whichever comes first.

I think let's put it in `getYOrNAnswer`: it's the function that asked the question that gave us trouble, so it should clean up after itself:

```
bool getYOrNAnswer (const char question[])
{
    ...
    cin.ignore (MAX_LINE_LENGTH, '\n'); // dump rest of this line
    return answer == 'Y';
}
```

- **`cin` won't read into an array passed in as a parameter.** See the last entry in the next "Antibugging" section.

Online Extra "That moment when you find garbage at the end of your string of characters": in the YouTube channel "Programming the Lazy Way," or `https://www.youtube.com/watch?v=57jkYKwN9hg`.

EXERCISES

1. Write and test `myStrcpy`, your own version of the `strcpy` function described in Table 14-1. (There is an answer later in this chapter.) To test whether it really is putting the `'\0'` at the end, fill the destination array with Xs (say) before you do the copy.
2. Write and test your version of `strcat`.
3. ...and `strcmp`.
4. Ask the user to enter the user's name, and repeat it back. If the first letter is lowercase, capitalize it.
5. (Uses file I/O) Determine the number of lines in a given file.
6. (Uses file I/O) ...and their average length.
7. (Uses file I/O) Write a program that finds and prints words in common between two given files. Assume each word appears at most once in a file.

Dynamic Allocation of Arrays

Sometimes you don't know till the program runs how big an array should be. But this won't work:

```
int size;
// calculate size somehow
int A[size];// compiler should complain: size must be a constant value
```

Here's what to do instead.

First, declare the array without allocating memory for its elements:

```
int* A;
```

A is not a set of `int`s but the address of – "pointer to" – some `int`s. It's like when we declared it with `[]`'s, but without storage for those `int`s yet.

Next, give it the memory it needs:

```
A = new int [size];
```

This asks part of C++, the "heap manager," to give us a chunk of that many `int`s. There's a whole heap o' memory available just for this, and the heap manager can give you chunks of it whenever you need. This is called "dynamic allocation" because it happens while the program is running. The way we've been doing it so far, with allocation at compile time, is "static allocation." (Memory allocated in these ways is called "dynamic" or "static.")

We use the array just as before. When done we tell the heap manager it can have it back, thus:

```
delete [] myArray;
```

`[]` is a reminder to the heap manager that what you're throwing back is an array. If you forget the `[]`, alas, the compiler won't tell you – you have to remember yourself.

In summation, to "dynamically allocate" an array of any `<type>`

1. `<type>* myArray = new <type> [size];`
2. Use the array as you normally would.
3. `delete [] myArray;` when you're done.

It's easy to forget to `delete []`. Does it matter? Sure: if you keep allocating memory and never handing it back – if you keep doing a "**memory leak**" – the memory eventually runs out and the program crashes. Later we'll have a way of making deleting easier to remember.

Example 14-3 shows how to use dynamic allocation.

Example 14-3. A program that dynamically allocates, uses, and deletes an array of `int`s

```
// Program to generate a random passcode of digits
//        -- from _C++26 for Lazy Programmers_

#include <iostream>
#include <cstdlib> // for srand, rand
```

```
#include <ctime>    // for time

using namespace std;

int main()
{
    srand (static_cast<int>(time (nullptr));// start random # generator

    int codeLength;                        // get code length
    cout<< "I'll make your secret passcode. How long should it be? ";
    cin >> codeLength;

    int* passcode = new int[codeLength]; // allocate array

    for (int i = 0; i <codeLength; ++i)  // generate passcode
        passcode[i] = rand() % 10;       // each entry is a digit

    cout << "Here it is:\n";             // print passcode
    for (int i = 0; i < codeLength; ++i)
        cout << passcode[i];
    cout << '\n';
    cout << "But I guess it's not secret any more!\n";

    delete [] passcode;                  // deallocate array

    return 0;
}
```

Here is a sample session:

```
I'll make your secret passcode. How long should it be? 5
Here it is:
14524
But I guess it's not secret any more!
```

Extra In 1992 Edmund Durfee, an artificial intelligence researcher, gave an invited talk to the National Conference on Artificial Intelligence (AAAI-92): "What Your Computer Needs to Know, You Learned in Kindergarten" – referencing the popular book *All I Really Need to Know I Learned in Kindergarten* by Robert Fulghum. Here's what Durfee said your computer needs from your early childhood education:

- Share everything.
- Play fair.
- Don't hit people.
- Put things back where you found them.
- Clean up your own mess.
- Don't take things that aren't yours.
- Say you're sorry when you hurt someone.
- Flush.
- When you go out into the world, watch for traffic, hold hands, and stick together.
- Eventually, everything dies.

Many of these are useful in operating systems. Maybe you have a program that hogs memory and CPU time, so that if you want to interact with a different program, you can't. (Share everything.) Or maybe it can only run if it takes up the whole screen. (Play fair.)

In the case of memory, we need "Put things back where you found them." Just like with crayons and toys, it'll be easier to find what we need if we always put it back.

Antibugging

The most common problem with dynamic memory is a program crash. What might cause it?

- **Forgetting to initialize:** If you haven't initialized myArray, its address points to some random location. It will almost certainly crash. Which is better than getting wrong output and not knowing it.

  There are two ways to prevent this:

  ```
  int* A = new int [size];
                               // initialize as soon as you declare
  ```

  or

  ```
  int* A = nullptr;
                      // we'll initialize to something sensible later
  ```

  By convention, nullptr means "pointing nowhere, so don't even think about looking at any elements." In older programs it's not nullptr but NULL.

- **Forgetting to delete:** Do this long enough and the program will run out of memory and crash.

- **Forgetting to use the [] in delete []:** This causes "undefined behavior," which means it might crash, behave perfectly, or start World War III. I wouldn't risk it.

Here are other problems:

- **Incorrectly declaring multiple pointers on one line:** It's strange, but

  ```
  int* myArray1, myArray2;
  ```

  doesn't create two pointers. It creates an int pointer myArray1 and another (single) int myArray2. Why so confusing? This is something left over from the C standard. Solution:

  ```
  int* myArray1;
  int* myArray2;
  ```

- **Using dynamic memory when you don't have to:** This isn't an error, but it leads to errors. Dynamic memory has more that can go wrong: you must remember to allocate with `new []` and deallocate with `delete []`. If you don't gain anything (say, if you know at compile time how big your array is), save yourself some work: allocate the old way.
- **You try to send your dynamically allocated array into a function that uses a span, and the compiler says no:** Spans have to get the array bound from what you pass in, and your dynamically allocated array doesn't know. You'll have to bundle the array with its size and send that in:

  ```
  myFunctionThatTakesSpan({dynArray, arraySize});
  ```

- **`cin` won't read into your dynamically allocated array or your array passed in as function parameter:**

  ```
  void read(char str [])
  {
      cin >> str;                             // compile-time error
  }
  int main()
  {
      char  s1 [FIXED_SIZE];          cin >> s1; // No problem
      char* s2 = new char[someSize]; cin >> s2;
      // compile-time error
      ...
  }
  ```

  `cin` won't read into a char array except a static one, inside the same function where it's declared. (C++ is trying to ensure there's enough room in the array, and it's not very good at it.)

  My fix is to always read into a locally declared fixed-size array and copy from that into the place where I do want it:

  ```
  static char buffer [REALLY_BIG_NUMBER];
  if there is room in str to store what we get, then
      strcpy (str, buffer);
  else
      complain
  ```

EXERCISES

1. Ask the user to enter the user's name. You'll need a buffer long enough to store any reasonable name. Then store it in an array that's exactly long enough.
2. Extend the previous exercise thus: read in a sequence of names, each stored in an array of exactly the right size. Calculate how much room it takes; compare that to if you used static arrays of some predetermined size, and see how much memory you saved.
3. Make a copy of a string that's widened by spaces. For example, "dog" becomes "d o g."
4. Make a reversed copy of a string, at the right size.
5. ...and use that to make a copy of an ASCII art image, flipped left to right. The image will be an array of character arrays, written like so: `const char* image[ROWS]` – leave off the `const` for the new image, of course. You can use one of these images or make your own.

Cow Cow after a Jolt Cola Cow after a Jolt 12-pack

6. (Uses SSDL) Ask the user how many stars to draw; generate an array of random stars; draw them. Use functions as needed.
7. (Uses file I/O) Write a program that counts lines in a file (see Exercise 5 in the previous section), dynamically allocates an array to store those lines, and reads them all in. Hint: You can open the file, count the lines, close it, and then open again.
8. (Harder) Dynamically allocate a game board, like a chessboard but of variable size. I can't just allocate a 2D array, so we'll have to make do with a 1D array. Decide on its size and how to access the rowth, columnth location.

9. (Uses SSDL, hard) Write your own bitmap: a dynamically allocated array, each of which contains the color of a pixel in the image. As in the previous exercise, we'll need to use a 1D array.

   Provide a render function: given the bitmap, a starting location on the screen, and the bitmap's width and height, display the bitmap at that location. To draw a pixel use `SSDL_SetRenderDrawColor` and `SSDL_RenderDrawPoint`.

   Would it be a good idea for the bitmap to be a `struct`, containing the array plus width and height?

Using the * Notation

We already use * to declare dynamically allocated arrays:

```
double* myArray = new double[sizeOfArray];
```

We can also use it to refer to individual elements. `*A` means `A[0]`, because `*A` means "what `A` points to," and `A` points to the 0th element.

`*(A+1)` means `A[1]`. The compiler is smart enough to know that `A+1` means the address of the next element. (Adding something to a pointer like this is called "pointer arithmetic.")

`A[1]` is easier to read than `*(A+1)` – so why do this new notation? One reason is to get you ready for what we'll be doing later with *.

Another is this interesting new way to traverse an array. Consider the `myStrcpy` function from Exercise 1 in the first section of this chapter. (The following code snippets are collected and compilable in `ch14/strcpyVersions`.)

```
void myStrcpy(char destination [], const char source[])
{
    int i = 0;

    while (source[i] != '\0')
    {
        destination[i] = source[i];
        ++i;
    }

    destination[i] = '\0'; // put that null character at the end
}
```

Here's a version that doesn't use []'s:

```
void myStrcpy(char* destination, const char* source)
{
    int i = 0;

    while (*(source + i) != '\0')
    {
        *(destination + i) = *(source+i);
        ++i;
    }

    *(destination + i) = '\0'; //  put null character at the end
}
```

Not clearly better, but it will work. Next, we eliminate the use of `i` and just update `source` and `destination` directly:

```
void myStrcpy(char* destination, const char* source)
{
    while (*source != '\0')
    {
        *destination = *source;
        ++source; ++destination;
    }

    *destination = '\0'; //  put null character at the end
}
```

Will it work? Yes. Now we're adding 1 to `source` each time we go through the loop – so each time, it points to its next element. (Same for `destination`.) When `source` reaches the null character, the loop stops.

Remember that when testing conditions, 0 means `false` and everything else means `true` (Chapter 4). So

```
while (*source != '\0')
```

can be written as

```
while (*source) // if *source is nonzero -- "true" -- we continue
```

We can therefore write the function as

```
void myStrcpy(char* destination, const char* source)
{
    while (*source)
    {
        *destination = *source;
        ++source; ++destination;
    }

    *destination = '\0'; // put null character at the end
}
```

This is where I really should stop. It's readable when you get used to it; it's short; and it gives us practice with * notation, which we'll use regularly in Chapter 21 and beyond. But this is too much fun to quit now.

Recall the post-increment operator (as in `X++`) from Chapter 5. `Y=X++;` really means `Y=X; X=X+1;`. Get the value, and then increment.

We can use it here for both destination and source – because we use their values to do assignment, then increment:

```
void myStrcpy(char* destination, const char* source)
{
    while (*source)
        *destination++ = *source++;

    *destination = '\0'; // put null character at the end
}
```

Also recall that the value of `X=Y` is whatever value was assigned – which in the case of `*destination++ = *source++` is simply `*source`. We want to continue as long as this is nonzero:

```
void myStrcpy(char* destination, const char* source)
{
    while (*destination++ = *source++); *destination = '\0';
}
```

This borders on evil and rude. I wouldn't want to write my code like this, but it *does* show the flexibility we get by using *.

Note * is called the "dereference" operator – since it takes a reference (address) of a thing and gives you the thing itself.

& is its opposite: the "reference" operator. It takes an object and gives you the address:

```
int  x;
int* addressOfX = &x;
```

I don't often use it in C++; it's more useful in C, which lacks our reference parameters. Which use the symbol & as well. Which makes life more confusing. Ah, well. If * can mean dereference (`*addressOfX`) *and* multiply (x*y), I'd suppose & can mean more than one thing too.

Antibugging

- **The compiler gripes that you're initializing a char* with a string constant**, as in `char* str = "some string";`.

  Say `const char* str = "some string";` or `char str[] = "some string";` instead.

EXERCISES

In all these exercises, use * notation – no [ ]'s.

1. Write `strcmp`.
2. ...and do the same for our other basic character array functions.
3. Count the words in a string. (Hint: Count the spaces. But not double spaces. How?)

4. (Harder) Write and test a function `contains` that tells if one character string contains another. For example

```
contains ("'Twas brillig, and the slithy toves"
          " did gyre and gimble in the wabe",
          "slithy")
```

would return true.

5. (Harder) Write a function `myStrtok` that, like the `strtok` in `cstring`, gets the next word ("token") in a character array. It might be called thus:

```
char myString[] = "Mary Mary\nQuite contrary";
const char* nextWord = myStrtok(myString, " \t\n\r");
                       // I use space, tab, return, and
                       // the less-used carriage return \r
                       // as "delimiters": separators
                       // between words
while (nextWord)
{
    cout << "Token:\t" << nextWord << '\n';
    nextWord = myStrtok(nullptr, " \t\n\r");
}
```

Here's expected output:

```
Token: Mary
Token: Mary
Token: Quite
Token: contrary
```

When you call it the first time for a given string, it should return a pointer to the first word. (If there isn't one, it returns `nullptr`.) Then, every time you pass in `nullptr`, it gives you the next word in the string you used earlier – returning `nullptr` when it runs out.

You'll want the `contains` function from the previous exercise. You'll also need a `static` local variable.

Just as with the compiler's `strtok`, you get to mangle the input string as you like. The usual way is to put `'\0'`, overwriting a whitespace character, wherever you want the currently returned token to end.

6. Write and test a function to convert a word – and another to convert a sentence – to Pig Latin. To make a word Pig Latin, take off any initial consonant, append to the end, and then add "ay" – so "pig" becomes "igpay." If there's no initial consonant, just append "ay."

7. (Requires SSDL) On the Japanese holiday of Tanabata, people celebrate by writing wishes on vertical strips of paper (*tanzaku*) and tying them to bamboo. Write a program to make several *tanzaku* on the screen, writing text vertically as in Figure 14-3. What functions will you write? What will you do if the string is too long to fit on the screen?

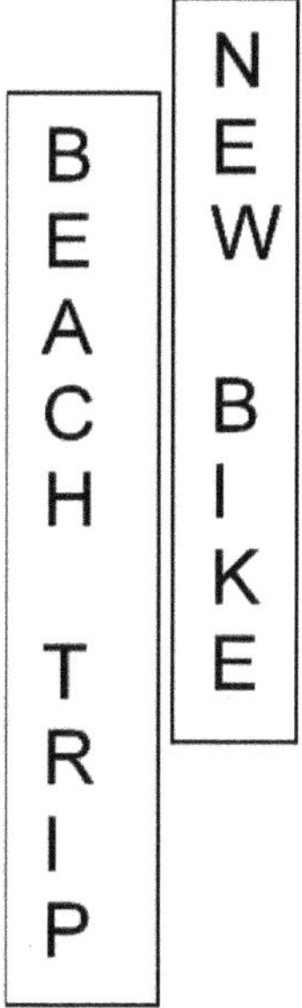

Figure 14-3. *Tanzaku for Exercise 7*

CHAPTER 15

Classes

Till now what we've covered has been essentially C with a few tweaks, notably `cin` and `cout`. Now it's time to add the thing that puts the + in C++: classes. They won't give us new abilities like `cin`/`cout`, SSDL functions, or control structures like loops. What they *will* do is help us keep things organized so we don't get confused, minimize errors, and make expressing things simpler – so we can trust the code we write and use it for bigger and better projects.

As an example, here's a class type to store a calendar date:

```
class Date
{
    int day_;
    int month_;
    int year_;
};
...
Date appointment; // Variables of a class type are called "objects"
                  // Using the term makes you sound smart at job interviews
```

We could have done that with a `struct`. As with `struct`s, we can declare variables of this type, pass them as parameters, get at the parts with ".", etc. – it looks much the same. But we're about to get new ways to reuse code and avoid errors.

The first way: I don't want `day_`, `month_`, and `year_` available to just any part of the program; they might get messed up. I'll have certain functions allowed to access them, called **member functions**.

This security measure comes from a metaphor that may make it easier to remember. Consider objects in the physical world. An object – say, a rubber ball – has characteristics: maybe it's red, bouncy, and has a certain mass and composition. You can't just set those characteristics to whatever you want when you want – can you set the color field on a real ball to be blue? Tell it to be light as a feather? Instead, the object itself

W. Briggs, *C++26 for Lazy Programmers*, https://doi.org/10.1007/979-8-8688-1859-2_15

affords ways you can interact with it. You can't set the color field, but you can paint it. You can't change its mass directly, but you can do things that would alter the mass, like chopping it or burning it. You can't set its position to 90 kilometers straight up, but you can throw it and see how far it goes.

We'll make our classes the same way: with characteristics (member variables) and methods (member functions) for interacting with those characteristics.

So what's something appropriate to do with a Date? For one thing, you can print it:

```
class Date
{
public:
      void print(ostream&);[1]

private:
      int day_;
      int month_;
      int year_;
};

...

Date appointment;

...

appointment.print(cout);
                  // or we could pass in a file variable -- see Chapter 13
```

The public section is for things the outside world (such as main) can access: that is, main can tell a Date to print itself. The private section is for parts that only Date can access directly. (If you don't specify, it's all private.)[2]

[1] It's ostream&, not ostream, because the designers of iostream disabled copying of ostreams, presumably on the grounds that it makes no sense. If you forget the compiler will remind you.

[2] And that's the only difference between a struct and a class: if you don't specify (which we always do, for classes), class members are private and struct members are public. We usually use struct for small, simple groupings without member functions and with everything public. That's because structs existed in C before classes were invented, and that's how C uses them.

BNF for a class is roughly

```
class <name>
{
public:
  <function declarations, variables, and types;
  usually declarations, almost never variables>
private:
  <function declarations, variables, types; usually variables>
};
```

Look at the `print` call above. Why aren't we telling `appointment` about day, month, and year? It already knows – it contains them! It doesn't know whether we want to print to `cout` or a file, so we do have to tell it that.

I didn't say *how* to print yet. Here's how:

```
void Date::print(std::ostream& out)
{
      out << day_ << '-' << month_ << '-' << year_;
}
```

The "`Date::`" tells the compiler, "This isn't just any function named `print` – it's the one belonging to `Date`."

When you call it

```
appointment.print (cout);
```

...whose `day_` will it print? `appointment`'s.

If you're using a friendly editor like Microsoft Visual Studio's, when you type in `appointment` and a period (see Figure 15-1), the editor will list available member functions – so far, just `print`, but we'll soon have more. You can click one and it'll paste it in for you. Add the opening parenthesis and it'll remind you what kind of arguments it expects.

Same for `Date::`. It'll list available members.

If it doesn't, don't worry: sometimes the editor gets confused.

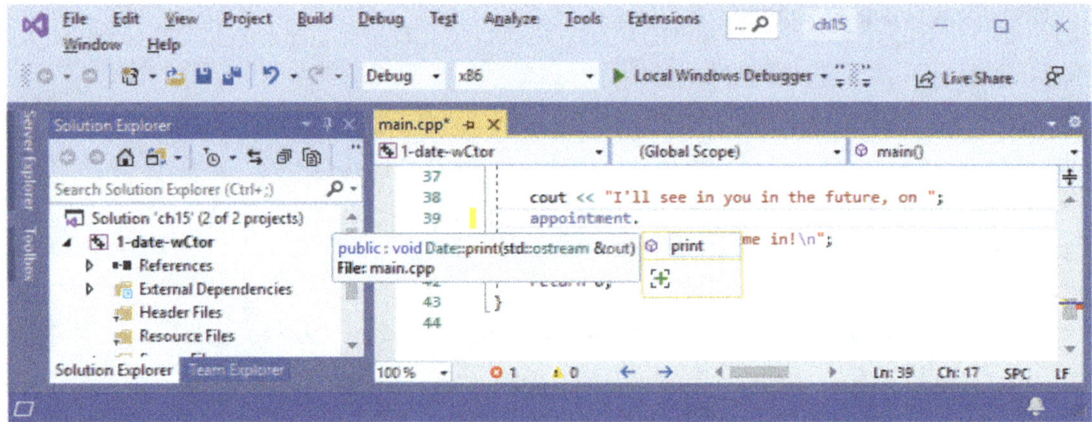

Figure 15-1. *Microsoft Visual Studio prompting with function declaration information*

Constructors

We already know it's wise to initialize variables. In classes, we have a special type of function called a **constructor** ("ctor," in a common abbreviation) to do this (see the highlighted parts of Example 15-1).

Example 15-1. The `Date` class, with a constructor, and a program to use it

```
// A program to print an appointment time, and demo the Date class
//   ...doesn't do that much (yet)
//        -- from _C++26 for Lazy Programmers_

#include <iostream>

using namespace std;


class Date
{
public:
    Date(int theDay, int theMonth, int theYear); // constructor declaration

    void print(std::ostream& out);
```

```
private:
    int day_;
    int month_;
    int year_;
};

Date::Date(int theDay, int theMonth, int theYear) :
// ...constructor body
    day_(theDay), month_(theMonth), year_(theYear)
    // theDay is the parameter passed into the Date constructor
    //   function.  day_ is the member that it will initialize.
{
}

void Date::print(std::ostream& out)
{
    out << day_ << '-' << month_ << '-' << year_;
}

int main()
{
    Date appointment(31, 1, 2595);[3]

    cout << "I'll see in you in the future, on ";
    appointment.print(cout);
    cout << " . . . pencil me in!\n";

    return 0;
}
```

The constructor's name is always the same as its class. When you declare a variable of class Date, it calls this function to initialize member variables. (There is no return type; essentially a constructor "returns" the object itself.)

The second line of the function definition

```
day_(theDay), month_(theMonth), year_(theYear)
```

[3] You can also use the {} notation: Date appointment {2595, 1, 31};. It calls the same constructor.

...tells it to initialize day_ to be equal to theDay and so on. By the time we reach the {}'s, there's nothing left to do, so the {}'s are empty this time.

You could instead initialize in the body of the function, using =:

```
Date::Date(int theDay, int theMonth, int theYear)
{
    day_ = theDay; month_ = theMonth; year_ = theYear;
}
```

But the member initialization syntax with the ()'s is more common, less error-prone (see the "Antibugging" section), and necessary in some situations, so it's lazier to get in the habit now.

To visualize how member functions interact with data members, consider this diagram of what happens in Example 15-1. main's first action is to allocate space for appointment and call its constructor (Figure 15-2), passing in arguments. I draw the constructor outside main, because it *is* a separate function ...but it's part of appointment, so I'll unify it and the data members with the dashed line.

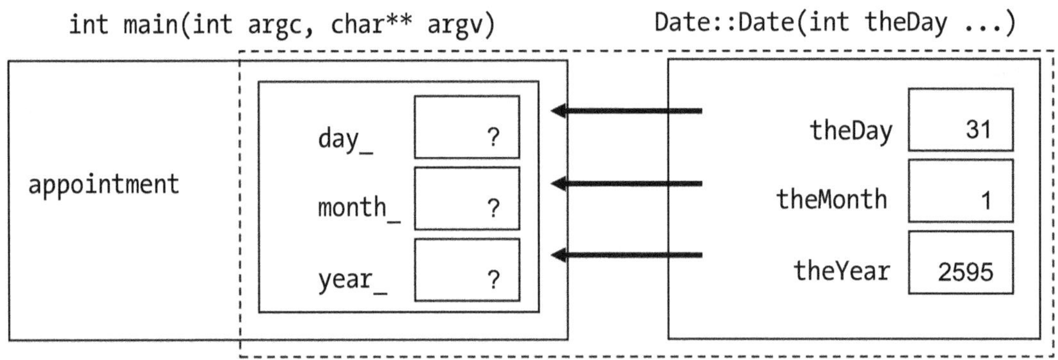

***Figure 15-2.** Calling the Date constructor*

The constructor copies theDay into day_, theMonth into month_, and theYear into year_ (Figure 15-3).

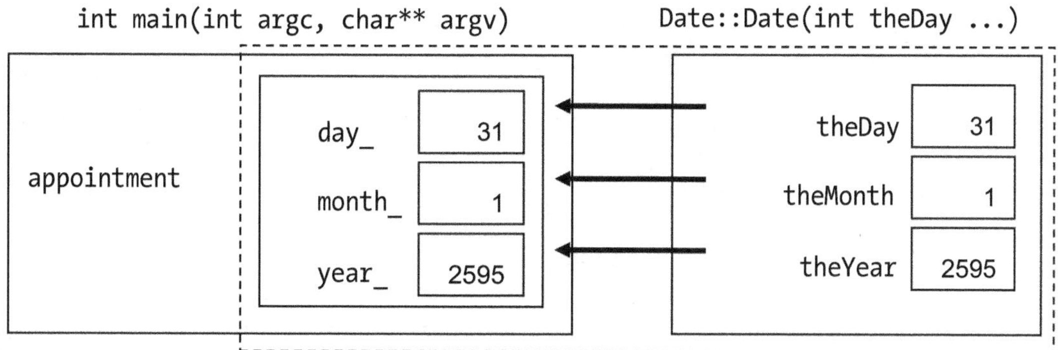

Figure 15-3. *The `Date` constructor initializes `appointment`'s data members*

When done, the constructor goes away (Figure 15-4).

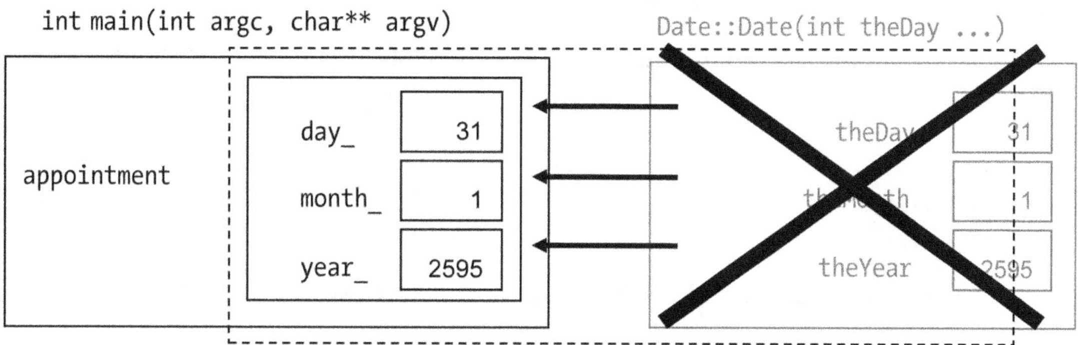

Figure 15-4. *The `Date` constructor is finished*

This shows the different roles of (for example) member `day_` and constructor parameter `theDay`: `day_` is persistent and remembers the day component of your appointment; `theDay` is a parameter `Date::Date` uses to channel information from `main` into `day_` and goes away when constructor `Date::Date` is done.

After this, `main` continues, printing `"I'll be getting up at "`, then enters `appointment`'s `print` function, which knows all about `day_`, `month_`, and `year_` (Figure 15-5).

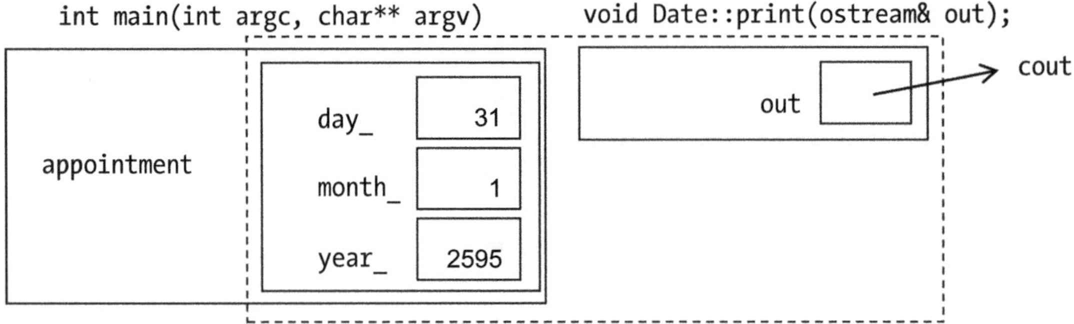

***Figure 15-5.** Calling `appointment`'s `print` function*

Golden Rule of Member Function Parameters

Don't pass in the object's data members. The function already knows them.

Antibugging

- **The constructor is called, but data members never get initialized.** If we use this constructor

  ```
  Date::Date(int theDay, int theMonth, int theYear)
  {
      theDay      = day_;
      theMonth    = month_;
      theYear     = year_;
  }
  ```

  we'll get bizarre output, maybe

  ```
  I'll see in you in the future, on -858993460--858993460-
  -858993460...pencil me in!
  ```

  I have `day_` and `theDay` swapped, so I'm copying *from* the data member I wanted initialized (which apparently had –858993460 in it – with uninitialized variables, you never know) *to* the parameter that had the value I wanted (Figure 15-6).

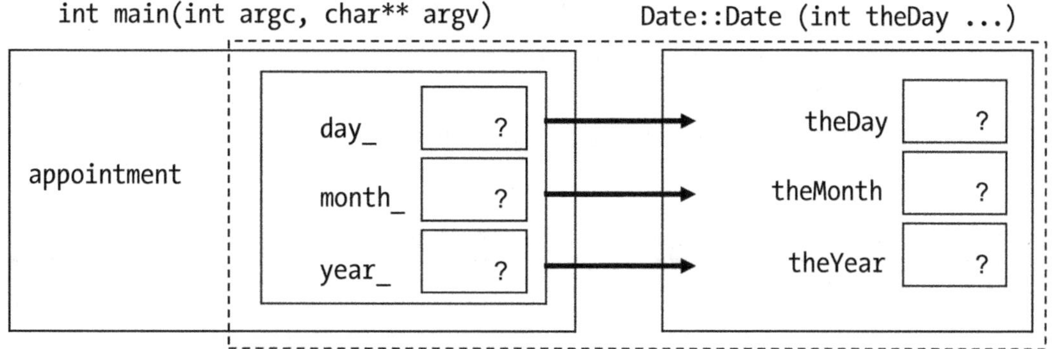

***Figure 15-6.** A constructor that has it all backward*

This can't happen if you use the initialization method with ()'s before the {, as in Example 15-1. It will report an error if you try to initialize the wrong thing.

EXERCISES

1. Write a `Time` class for remembering when to get up in the morning, when to nap, etc. Include relevant data members, a print function, and an appropriate constructor.

2. Write and test a function `Time currentTime()`. It will call `time` (just as we do when initializing the random number generator), getting the number of seconds since January 1, 1970. We only care about the number of seconds since midnight. Convert that to seconds, minutes, and hours and return the current `Time`. It is *not* a member of `Time`.

3. Augment the `Date` program with a function `Date currentDate()` that calls `time`, as in the previous problem, and gets the current `Date`. The function is *not* a member of `Date`. Is my earlier assumption that time starts at January 1, 1970, correct on your machine?

4. (Harder) Add a function `Date::totalDays()` that returns the number of days in the date since December 31, 1 B.C. You'll need to handle leap years. A solution is in the book's sample code in project `2-date-bestSoFar`.

5. (Harder) Add a function `Date::normalize()` that corrects if the `Date` has one or more fields out of range: for example, `Date tooFar(32, 12, 1999);` would make `tooFar` be the date 1-1-2000. It should be called by the constructor. A solution is in the book's sample code in project `2-date-bestSoFar`.

Is there an easier way to write `normalize` and `totalDays`?

const Objects, const Member Functions ...

Consider this code:

```
const Date PEARL_HARBOR_DAY(7, 12, 1941);

cout << "A date which will shall live in infamy is ";
PEARL_HARBOR_DAY.print(cout);
cout << ".\n";
```

It's reasonable to consider PEARL_HARBOR_DAY a constant, since it can never change. (Unless you have a working time machine.) However, if we make it `const`, the code will no longer compile. Why not?

C++ distinguishes member functions that can alter the object from those that can't. This is a way of preventing errors. If `print` is the sort of thing that can alter a `Date`, we shouldn't allow it to be called on a constant `Date`.

Since `print` *is* safe for `const` objects, we'll tell C++ thus:

```
class Date
{
    ...

    void print(std::ostream&) const;

    ...
};

void Date::print(std::ostream& out) const
{
    out << day_ << '-' << month_ << '-' << year_;
}
```

The word const after the ()'s tells the compiler: this function is OK for constant objects. It also tells the compiler, when compiling print, to generate an error if any changes are made to data members.

It's sometimes tempting if you get a lot of errors to strip out the word const from your program entirely. Resist that temptation. This feature does protect us from genuine errors.

Antibugging

- **You get errors about converting something from const.** Often this means you forgot a const at the end of a member function declaration (and the top line of its function body too).
- **It says your member function body doesn't match the declaration, but they sure look the same.** Check that they're both const or neither is.

...and const Parameters

Suppose we want to pass a Date to a function fancyDisplay, which prints the time in some cute way:

```
void fancyDisplay(Date myDate, ostream& out)
{
      cout << "*************\n";
      cout << "* "; myDate.print (out); cout << " *\n";
      cout << "*************\n";
}
```

I didn't use & for myDate, so myDate itself isn't passed in, but a copy.

In a way, this is fine, because we don't want to alter myDate. But copying costs more than it did for a mere int – three times more, as it has three ints. As we create bigger classes, we may find it slows down our programs.

Here's a partial fix:

```
void fancyDisplay (Date& myDate, ostream& out);
```

This isn't perfect, because now we allow `fancyDisplay` to alter `myDate`! This is better:

```
void fancyDisplay (const Date& myDate, ostream& out);
```

Now `fancyDisplay` won't take the time to copy `myDate` *and* can't alter it.

Golden Rule of Objects as Function Parameters

If you want to change an object passed in as a parameter, and it's large (containing more than, say, a couple of `ints` or `doubles`), pass it as `TheClass& object`.

If you don't, pass it as `const TheClass& object`.[4]

Small things like `std::span`, which is a pointer and a size, can be passed without &.

The same applies to range-based for loops. In Chapter 11 we had this loop:

```
for (Ball b: balls)
        SSDL_RenderDrawCircle(b.location_.x_,
                              b.location_.y_, RADIUS);
```

Since `Ball` is a class (OK, a `struct`, but close enough), it might be expensive to make a copy every time you go through the loop. Just like with parameters, we'll change the variable to use `const &` to prevent that copy *and* preserve `const`ness. (If you do want to allow changes, use & without `const`, as before.)

Multiple Constructors

There's no need to limit ourselves to one constructor. We may want other ways to create `Date`s:

```
Date d(21, 12, 2000);          // using our old constructor...
Date e(d);                     // e is now exactly the same as d
Date f;                        // now one with no arguments
```

[4] This isn't needed for spans, because a span is a pointer and a size – it's guaranteed to be a cheap copy. We'll find a few other classes that are too small to worry about later.

```
Date dateArray [MAX_DATES];   // still no arguments
Date g(22000);                // 22,000 days -- nearly a lifetime
```

Let's take them one by one.

Copy Constructors

Date's copy constructor is the one that has as its sole argument another Date. We call it this because it makes a copy (duh):

```
Date::Date(const Date& other) :                      // "copy" constructor
    day_(other.day_), month_(other.month_), year_(other.year_)
{
}
```

This declaration uses it

```
Date e(d);
```

as does this

```
Date e{d};
```

and this:

```
Date e = d; // Looks like =, but it's really calling the copy ctor
```

The = form is called "syntactic sugar": something not really necessary that makes code more readable.

There's something else special about the copy constructor. If ever C++ needs to make a copy of a Date, it will call it **implicitly**, that is, without you telling it to. Here are two examples:

```
void doSomethingWithDate(Date willBeCopied);
                             // I'd rarely do this, but if I did...
Date currentDate();          // No &, so it returns a copy
```

What if you don't write a copy constructor? C++ will make its best guess of how to copy, and that guess is sometimes dangerously wrong. A good rule: *Always specify the copy constructor.*

Default Constructors

```
Date::Date() :                              // "default" ctor
      day_(1), month_(1), year_(1)          // default is Jan 1, 1 AD
{
}

...

Date f; // or: Date f{};
Date dateArray[MAX_DATES];
```

If you don't know how to initialize your Date, you tell it nothing, and it uses its **default constructor**: the one that takes no arguments. It also needs this to initialize elements of an array of Date.[5] So we always write the default constructor.

Conversion Constructors

This constructor call

```
Date g(22000); // or Dateg{22000}; -- or Date g = 22000;
```

needs Date to convert these way too many days to a more conventional day, month, year arrangement. I'll use function normalize from Exercise 5 earlier: if we give it 22,000 days, it'll convert that to 26 days, 3 months, and 61 years:

```
Date::Date(int totalDays) :             // conversion ctor from int
      day_(totalDays), month_(1), year_(1)
{
      normalize();
}
```

The normalize function, called by this and any constructor that needs it, should go in the private section. Date functions will call it when needed, so nobody else has to.[6]

[5] Unless you use {}'s, as in Date myDates[] = {{31,1,2595},{1,2,2595}};.

[6] Functions in the private section are called "utility" functions since they perform tasks useful to the other, public functions. We don't really need the term, but using it makes me sound smart, so of course I use it.

A constructor with exactly one argument (not a `Date`) is called a **conversion constructor**, because it converts from some other type (like `int`) to the class we're writing.

Like with the copy constructor, if ever C++ needs a `Date` but you gave it an `int`, it will call this implicitly. Suppose you call `void fancyDisplay(const Date& myDate, ostream& out);` but pass in an `int`: `fancyDisplay(22000, cout);`. C++ will convert 22000 to a `Date` and `fancyDisplay` that `Date`. Nice!

Summary

It is the responsibility of each constructor to make sure the data members are in some acceptable state. Unfortunately, C++'s basic types let you declare *them* without initialization. But we can construct our classes so C++ initializes all data members.

Because of the issues mentioned earlier, I recommend this guideline:

Golden Rule of Constructors

Always specify **default** and **copy** constructors.

Extra There's a difference between using `{}`'s to initialize a variable and the older-style `()`'s and =:

```
Date g(22000.5);   // No problem: casts from int to double
Date g{22000.5};   // WRONG: "narrowing" conversion loses data
                   //    -- compile-time error
```

That might prevent us from doing some dumb things by accident.

Also, if you use `{}`'s, you can't confuse calling a constructor using `()`'s (as in `Date d(21, 12, 2000);`) with a function declaration, which also uses `()`'s – see the following "Antibugging" section.

To make things more complicated, there are `initializer_lists`, which support use of `{}` for another type of constructor (see Chapter 26).

I tend to use `{}` as we've already done – for `struct` and array initialization – partly for clarity's sake. But others including C++ founder Bjarne Stroustrup himself suggest using `{}` for all initializations, for the reasons above.

Antibugging

- **You declared an object, using the default constructor, but it doesn't recognize it.**

  ```
  Date z ();
  z.print(); // Error message says z is a Date() (?)
             // or at least isn't of a class type
  ```

  Using the ()'s made the compiler think you were writing a declaration for a function `z` that returns `Date`. I mean, how could it tell that's not what was meant?

  The solution is to ditch the parentheses or replace them with `{}`'s:

  ```
  Date z1;
  Date z2 {};
  ```

- **"Illegal copy constructor" or "invalid constructor"** with this copy constructor declaration:

  ```
  Date (Date other);.
  ```

  Suppose the compiler lets you call this function. Since there's no `&`, the first thing it would do is make a copy of `other`. How? By calling the copy constructor. Which means it has to make a copy of `other`. Which means it calls the copy constructor. And so on till you're out of memory.

  This is **accidental recursion**, that is, a function calling itself when you didn't intend it to. Good thing the compiler (Visual Studio or g++) catches the problem. Solution: `const &`.

Default Parameters for Code Reuse

We can save more work by telling C++ that if we don't give arguments to some of our functions, it should appropriately fill them in.

For example, I'm tired of specifying the `cout` in `myDate.print (cout);`. Isn't it usually `cout`? But I don't want to hard-code `cout` into the function, because I may later want to print to a file.

So I change the declaration:

```
void print(ostream& out = cout) const;
```

Now I can just say `myDate.print();`, and the compiler will think, *He didn't say, so he must want* `cout`.

I have a constructor that takes three `int`s, one that takes one, and one that takes nothing. If I use defaults, I can combine these into one function:

```
class Date
{
public:
      Date(int theDay=1, int theMonth=1, int theYear=1);
            // Defaults go in the declaration
      ...
};

...

Date::Date(int theDay, int theMonth, int theYear) :
      day_(theDay), month_(theMonth), year_(theYear)
{
      normalize();
}
```

Now I can call it with zero to three arguments:

```
Date Jan1_1AD;
Date convertedFromDays  (22000);
const Date CINCO_DE_MAYO(5, 5); //Got a new one free that takes day & month
Date doomsday            (21, 12, 2012);
                                        //Doomsday? Well, that didn't happen
```

Default arguments work for non-member functions too:

```
void fancyDisplay (const Date& myDate, ostream& out = cout);
                                        //if not specified, print with cout
```

If some parameters have defaults and some don't, those with defaults go last. The compiler doesn't want to be confused about which arguments you intend to omit.

Date Program (So Far)

Here's what we have (Example 15-2).

I also added an enumeration type `Month` and declarations for `isLeapYear` and two other functions. They relate to dates, but they're not members of `Date`.

I could make `Month` a member. But to refer to (say) `JUNE` I'd have to write `Date::Month::JUNE` ...that's getting ridiculously long.

It doesn't make sense for `isLeapYear` to be a member of `Date`: it's not something you do to a `Date`, but something you do to a year (an `int`). It doesn't need access to `Date`'s data members `day_`, `month_`, and `year_`. It belongs *with* `Date`, but I wouldn't make it a member.

Tip If a function can't reasonably be thought of as doing something *to* an object, it probably shouldn't be a member.

`main`'s purpose is to test the class and associated functions. This is an essential practice when designing a new class (shown again in Chapter 17, and in Chapter 20, in which we test new classes before using them to create something fun).

Example 15-2. A program using the `Date` class

```
// A program to test the Date class
//          -- from _C++26 for Lazy Programmers_

#include <iostream>

using namespace std;
```

```
enum class Month {JANUARY=1, FEBRUARY, MARCH, APRIL, MAY, JUNE,
                  JULY, AUGUST, SEPTEMBER, OCTOBER, DECEMBER};

bool isLeapYear  (int year);
int  daysPerYear (int year);
int  daysPerMonth(int month, int year);
                              // We have to specify year in case month
                              //   is FEBRUARY and it's a leap year
class Date
{
public:
    Date(int theDay=1, int theMonth=1, int theYear=1);
                             // Because of default parameters,
                             //   this serves as constructor taking 3 ints;
                             //   a new one taking days and months;
                             //   the conversion from int constructor;
                             //   and the default constructor

    Date(const Date&);       // copy constructor

    void print(std::ostream& out = std::cout) const;

    int totalDays() const; // total days since Dec 31, 1 B.C.
private:
    int day_;
    int month_;
    int year_;

    void normalize();
};

Date::Date(int theDay, int theMonth, int theYear) :
    day_(theDay), month_(theMonth), year_(theYear)
{
    normalize();
}
```

```
Date::Date(const Date& other) :
     day_(other.day_), month_(other.month_), year_(other.year_)
{
}

void Date::print(std::ostream& out) const
{
    out << day_ << '-' << month_ << '-' << year_;
}

// Date::totalDays and Date::normalize from earlier exercises
//   as well as isLeapYear, daysPerYear, and daysPerMonth
//   are omitted here, but they're in the book's sample code

void fancyDisplay(const Date& myDate, ostream& out = std::cout)
{
    cout << "*************\n";
    cout << "* "; myDate.print (); cout << " *\n";
    cout << "*************\n";
}

int main()
{
    constexpr int MAX_DATES = 10;

    Date d(21, 12, 2000);           // using our old constructor...
    Date e = d;                     // e is now exactly the same as d
    Date f;                         // now one with no arguments
    Date dateArray [MAX_DATES];     // still no arguments
    Date g(22000);                  // 22,000 days, nearly a lifetime

    cout << "This should print 26-3-61 with lots of *'s:\n";
    fancyDisplay(22000);            // tests conversion-from-int constructor

    return 0;
}
```

EXERCISES

1. Update the `Time` class to use what you learned in the rest of this chapter.

CHAPTER 16

Classes, continued

More things to make your classes work, and work well, especially putting parts of your programs in multiple files.

inline Functions for Efficiency

Consider the diagrams of what happens in function calls from Chapters 8 and 15. They show what the computer does. It creates a new copy of the function, an "activation record," containing everything the instance of the function needs, especially local variables. It copies parameters into a part of memory the function can access. It stores what it needs to know about the function it was in (the state of the registers in the CPU – if you don't know what that is, don't worry about it). Finally, it transfers control to the new function.

When done, it reverses the process: throws away the copy of the function with its variables and restores the state of the old function.

That's a lot of work on the computer at runtime. So what are we supposed to do? Stop using functions?

The solution is **inline** functions. An inline function is *written* as a function, behaves as a function as far as the programmer's concerned, and seems to compile as a function, but the compiler does something sneaky: it replaces the function call with a piece of code to do the same thing. Here's one way to make a function inline – just precede it with `inline`:

```
inline
void Date::print (std::ostream& out) const
{
      out << day_ << '-' << month_ << '-' << year_;
}
```

When you write this

```
d.print(cout);
```


W. Briggs, *C++26 for Lazy Programmers*, https://doi.org/10.1007/979-8-8688-1859-2_16

the compiler treats it as though you'd said

```
cout << d.day_ << '-' << d.month_ << '-' << d.year_;
      // but there's no problem with these members being private
```

thus saving the overhead of the function call.

If a function is big enough, the time overhead for the call isn't significant compared with time spent in the function itself, so it doesn't help much. And inline introduces a new overhead: multiple copies of a big function expanded inline would take up a lot of memory. Here's how to know whether you should make a function inline.

Golden Rule of inline Functions

A function should be inline if it

- Fits on a single line
- Contains no loops (for, while, or do-while)

---

inline expansion is merely a *suggestion* to the compiler, not a command. The compiler will overrule you if it thinks the function shouldn't be expanded. Fine by me: in this case, the compiler knows best.

Here's a quick, easy way to make a *member* function inline – put the whole thing inside the class definition:

```
class Date
{
    ...

      void print(ostream& out) const
            // inline, because it's inside the class definition
      {
            out << day_ << '-' << month_ << '-' << year_;
      }

      ...
};
```

Access Functions

Sometimes we want the rest of the world to be able to *see* our data members but not alter them. It's like with a clock: you have to set it through appropriate controls (member functions), but you can *see* the time whenever you like.

This is how it's done:

```
class Date
{
public:
      ...

      //Access functions -- all const as they don't change data,
      //just access it
      int day  () const { return day_;   }
      int month() const { return month_; }
      int year () const { return year_;  }

      ....
};
```

The way to call them is the same as with `print` – use a **.**:

```
cout << myBirthday.year() << " is the year of the lion. Fear me.\n";
```

It's often a good idea to use access functions, *even inside member functions.* Suppose I decide to dump `day_`, `month_`, and `year_` and have just one data member `totalDays_` from which member functions can calculate day, month, and year as needed. A function referring to `day_` will no longer compile! But if it refers instead to `days()`, which will still exist, it'll be fine.

And this is why we use underbars after data member names: `day_` and others. It's why I used the funny names `theDay`, `theMonth`, etc. as parameters to the first constructor I wrote. If I did this

```
class Date
{
public:
    Date(int day, int month, int year) :
        day(day),month(month),year(year)
```

```
    {
    }
    int day() const { return day; }
    ....
private:
    int day, months, years;
};
```

I'd have so many things named day I'd never sort them out![1] Nor would the compiler. The names must be distinct.

Separate Compilation and Include Files

By now our programs are long enough we should break them into multiple files. Here are general guidelines so you'll know where to find things:

- We usually give every class its own file.
- ...and let every set of clearly related functions share a file. For example, if you were writing the trigonometric functions sine, cosine, tangent, etc., you could put them together.
- We give `main` its own file, possibly shared with functions called by `main` that would not be useful to other programs. If you're writing a program for poker, say, functions related to bidding might go in the file with `main` (since only poker does poker-style bidding), but functions related to shuffling and dealing a deck would go elsewhere (since many games involve decks).

In terms of getting it all to work, though, there's a problem. This new file will need to know certain things (such as the class definition!) – and so will `main`. This information must be shared.

Fortunately, we already know how to do this: include files.

[1] Or I could have a data member days and an access function `getDays ()`; some use that convention. I find `myDate.getDays()` too hard to read – you be the judge.

What Happens in Separate Compilation

Suppose I create these files: `my_class.h` ("h" as in "header"), containing the class definition; `myclass.cpp`, containing the member functions; and `main.cpp`, containing the main program. (I give the `.h` and `.cpp` files the same name as the class. I use lowercase like `my_class` – conventions vary, so be consistent.) I include it like so:

```
#include "my_class.h" // <-- Use "" not <>; and let the file end in .h
```

Here are the stages the compiler goes through to build a program:

First, it **compiles** the C++ "source" files (your `.cpp` files; see Figure 16-1). When it encounters an `#include` directive, it stops reading the source file, reads the `.h` file you included, and then goes back to the source file.

The compiler produces for each source file an "object" file in machine language.

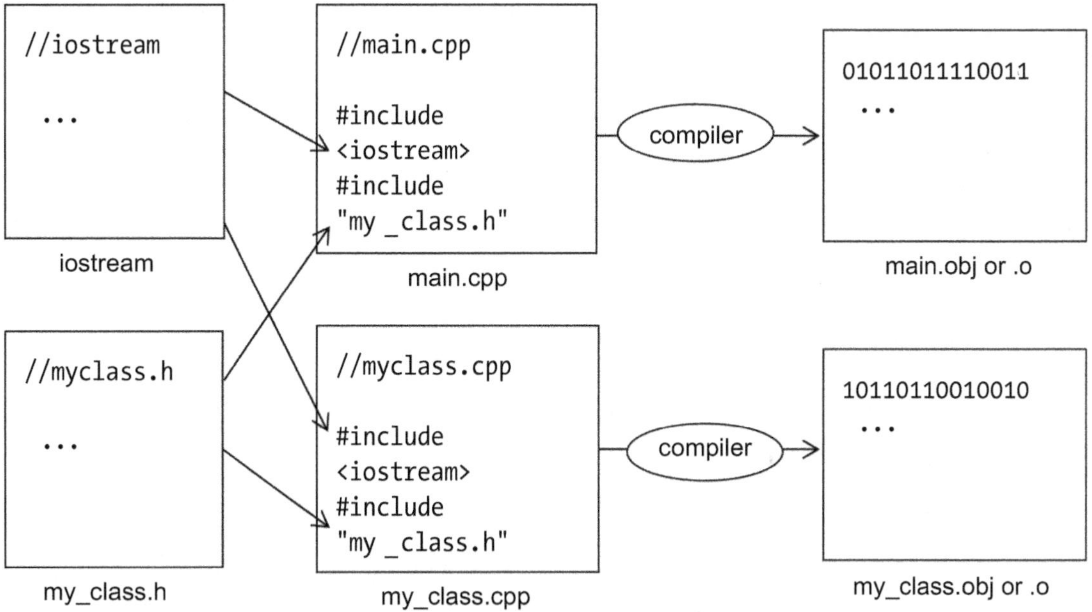

***Figure 16-1.** The compile stage of building a program*

If there are no errors, the compiler is ready to **link** (Figure 16-2). The object files know how to do what they do, but they don't know where to find function references, either from each other or from system libraries. The link stage "links" these files together by resolving the references and produces an executable file. The executable will end in `.exe` if you're using Visual Studio; g++ is flexible.

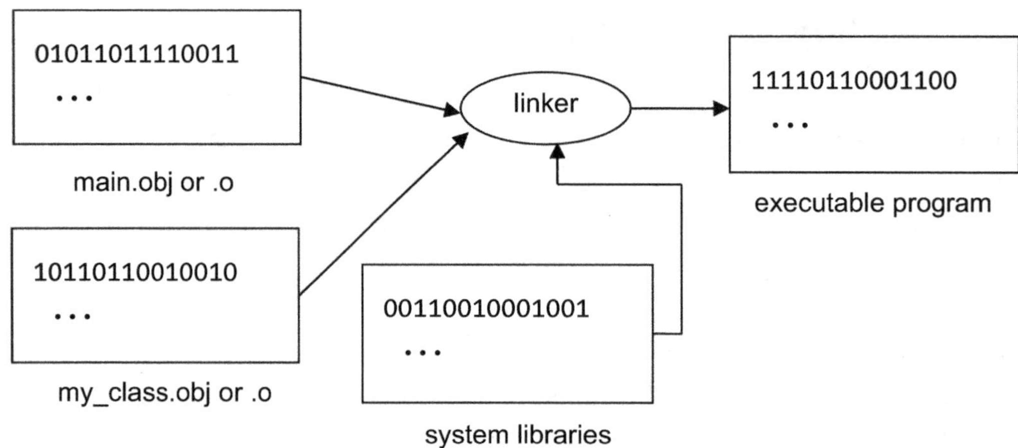

Figure 16-2. *The link stage in building a program*

Seeing this process enables us to understand precisely what should and shouldn't go into an include file.

Writing Your .h File

Here are what can go in an include file (so far):

- Types, including class definitions and enumeration types
- Function declarations
- Anything `inline`

Here are what shouldn't:

- Functions
- Constant or variable declarations (except `inline` – see below)

Here's why. If you put a function (or a variable declaration) in an include file, it will be included into different `.cpp` files. When you compile those files, you therefore get multiple copies of the same function. When you call the function, then, the compiler won't know which copy to use, and it's not smart enough to realize they're identical. You'll get an error saying it has **duplicate definitions**.

If you want your function in the include file ...make it `inline`.

If you want variables, consts, or constexprs in the include file ...make them inline too:

```
inline constexpr int DAY_PER_WEEK = 7;
inline const SSDL_Color  BABY_BLUE = SSDL_CreateColor(137, 207, 240);
```

inline isn't just for making function calls more efficient – it also prevents the duplicate definition problem. Not the clearest keyword, perhaps, but allowInIncludeFilesWithoutDuplicateDefinitionError would have been too much to type.

Including a .h File Only Once

Suppose that time.h (from exercises in Chapter 15; it defines class Time) is needed for a new class Stopwatch. We'll need to #include "time.h" so we can declare start_ and stop_:

```
// stopwatch.h: defines class Stopwatch
//        -- from _C++26 for Lazy Programmers_

#include "time.h"                    // trouble ahead...

class Stopwatch
{
public:
    Stopwatch() {}
private:
    Time start_, stop_;
};
```

Then we get to main.cpp (Example 16-1).

Example 16-1. A program that includes time.h and stopwatch.h. Since this and Example 16-2 work together, they're in the same project in the source code's ch16 folder; it's named 1-2-stopwatch.

```
// Program that uses Stopwatches and Times
//        -- from _C++26 for Lazy Programmers_
```

```
#include "time.h"
#include "stopwatch.h"

int main (int argc, char** argv)
{
    Time duration;
    Stopwatch myStopwatch;

    // ...

    return 0;
}
```

When compiling `main.cpp`:

First, the compiler includes `time.h`, which defines class `Time`.

Then it includes `stopwatch.h`. First thing *that* does is `#include "time.h"`, which defines class `Time`. *Again.* The compiler complains: duplicate definition for class `Time`!

The solution is to tell the compiler to read a `.h` file only if it hasn't already been read. There's a commonly used trick: define something in the `.h` file and then put something around the whole file saying only read this if you've never heard of it.

Example 16-2. `time.h`, written so it will only be processed once. Part of the `1-2-stopwatch` project in the source code's `ch16`

```
// time.h: defines class Time
//        -- from _C++26 for Lazy Programmers_

#ifndef TIME_H // If TIME_H is not defined...
#define TIME_H

class Time
{
    // ...
};

#endif //TIME_H
```

The first time through, it's never heard of `TIME_H`, so it reads the `.h` file. This defines class `Time` and also `TIME_H`.

Next time, it's heard of `TIME_H`, so it skips to the `#endif`. Class `Time` doesn't get redefined. Mission accomplished.

To prevent this issue I do this for *all* include files. Using the same form for the constant (`MYFILE_H`) means I always remember how I spelled it and prevents name conflicts.[2]

Avoid `using namespace std;` in Include Files

`using namespace std;` shouldn't be in your include file. What if someone includes your file, but didn't want to use the `std` namespace? To avoid forcing it on them, skip the `using` declaration. So that C++ will still recognize `cin` and `cout` and other things in the `std` namespace, preface them with `std::`, as in `std::cin >> x;`.

Backing Up a Multi-file Project

In Unix, to back up the directory `myproject`, enter this command: `cp -R myproject myprojectBackup1`.

In Windows, copy and paste the entire folder, ignoring anything that won't copy.

Antibugging

Circular includes make a strange error. Let's alter `time.h` so it needs `Stopwatch`:

```
#include "stopwatch.h"

class Time
{
    void doSomethingWithStopwatch(const Stopwatch&);
};
```

Let's say some `.cpp` file includes `time.h`. This defines `TIME_H` and then includes `stopwatch.h` (Figure 16-3, left).

[2] Microsoft Visual Studio has an alternative to this whole `#ifndef`...`#endif` scheme: put `#pragma once` at the top of the `.h` fie and forget it. I don't use it because then my code won't compile with other compilers.

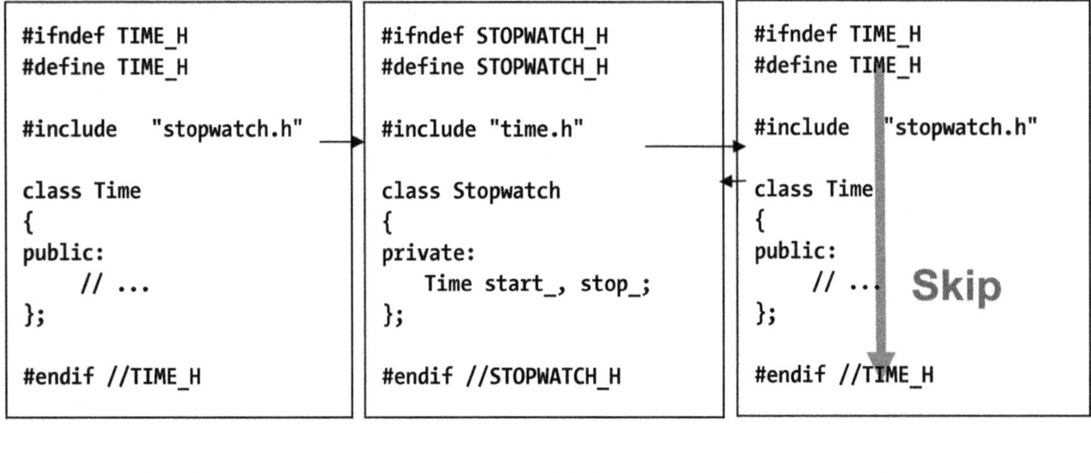

Figure 16-3. *`time.h` includes `stopwatch.h` includes `time.h` – there's gonna be trouble*

So it stops reading `time.h` for now and reads `stopwatch.h` (Figure 16-3, middle). That defines `STOPWATCH_H` and then includes `time.h` again (Figure 16-3, right).

Since `TIME_H` was already defined, the `#ifndef` makes us skip the contents. We go back to `stopwatch.h`, and when it reaches the line `Time start_, stop_;` it yells at us that it never read a definition for `Time`, which is true. So the program won't compile.

An include file can include another – but they can't include *each other.*

Here are some fixes:

- Rethink whether that function should be in `Time` at all. Should `Time` really depend on `Stopwatch`? Shouldn't it be the other way around? (That's the best answer for this code.)

- If that doesn't work ...you can refer to `Stopwatch` in `Time` without knowing what it is as long as the code doesn't need details. Tell `time.h` only that `Stopwatch` is a class:

```
class Stopwatch;
class Time
{
        void doSomethingWithStopwatch(const Stopwatch&);
};
```

  Problem solved.

Next problem: **What if you have lots of files and can't remember where you put one of your functions?**

- **Visual Studio:** Right-click the function name. "Go to Declaration" will take you to the declaration; "Go to Definition" will take you to the function itself if it's available.
- **Unix:** Though there are packages to help with this (ggtags for emacs is one), there's no guarantee they're on your system. This command is a quick-and-dirty[3] way to find the function and all references to it: `grep functionIWant *`.

Multiple-File Projects in Microsoft Visual Studio

To add new files, go to the Project menu and select Add New Item. You can add any `.h` or `.cpp` files you need this way; it'll put them in the right place.

Then build and run your project as usual.

Extra Now that you've got multiple source files, you may want an easier way to clean up the extra files Visual Studio creates.[4]

In the folder with your project, use Notepad or some other editor to create a file `clean.txt`. **Put it in a folder that only contains your work (and maybe mine) and nothing irreplaceable.** Here's what should be in it:

```
REM Erase folders you don't want -- here's my picks
for /r . %%d in (Debug,x64,.vs) do @if exist "%%d" rd /s/q "%%d"

REM Erase other files -- here's my picks.
REM /s means "in subfolders too"
del /s *.obj    REM Not needed, but now you know how to
                REM   erase all files with a particular extension
```

[3] Easy, not elegant.

[4] There's also an option in Visual Studio: Build ➤ Clean Solution. It won't hurt, but on my machine it leaves a file `Browse.VC.db`, which can exceed 5 MB. So I don't rely on it.

Save your text file and change its name from `clean.txt` to `clean.bat`. (Can't see the `.txt`? Uncheck Hide extensions for known file types – see Chapter 1.) Click Yes on the warning dialog box in Figure 16-4.

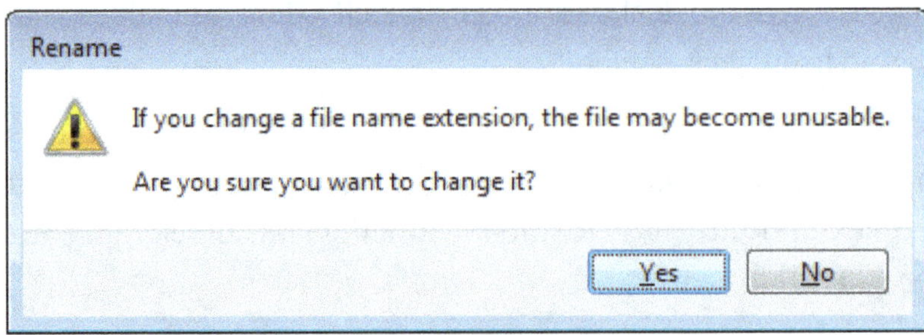

Figure 16-4. *Microsoft Windows' warning about changing a file extension*

...and get your new `clean.bat` file.

You can double-click this "batch" file – that is, a file of commands – whenever you want to erase the extra files. Be warned: `del` erases things permanently.[5]

Multiple-File Projects in g++

To use multiple files in your g++ project, just add them to the project folder copied from `basicStandardProject` (or `basicSSDLProject`). `make` will build everything as usual.

To do it yourself, with or without your own Makefiles, keep reading.

Command Line: More Typing, Less Thinking

You can build the program with this command:

```
g++ -g -std=c++2c -o myprogram myprogram.cpp myclass.cpp
```

[5] If you use the `clean.bat` that comes from the textbook source code, Windows may give a warning that "Running this app may put your PC at risk" and a recommendation that you don't do it. Windows is right: `clean.bat` in the wrong place might erase the wrong thing. *I* know it's OK, but ...make your own.

You can separate the compile and link stages:

```
g++ -g -std=c++2c -c myprogram.cpp
                                          #-c means "compile only -- don't link
g++ -g -std=c++2c -c myclass.cpp
g++ -g -std=c++2c[6] -o myprogram myprogram.o myclass.o #now link
```

Makefiles: More Thinking, Less Typing (optional)

Makefiles keep track of what files in your project have changed. When you make, it'll only rebuild the parts it needs to. This cuts compile time. It's also nicer to type make than g++ -g -o myprogram file1.cpp file2.cpp ...

Makefiles are far from easy, but they're essential for big projects or those using lots of libraries.

A Simple Version

Example 16-3. A simple Makefile. It's in the source code, ch16/3-4-5-makefiles, as Makefile.Ex-16.3. To use it, copy it to Makefile and type make

```
#This is a basic Makefile, producing one program from 2 source files

myprogram:  myclass.o main.o        #link object files to get myprogram
            g++ -std=c++2c -g -o myprogram myclass.o main.o

main.o:     main.cpp myclass.h      #create main.o
            g++ -std=c++2c -g -c main.cpp

myclass.o:  myclass.cpp myclass.h  #create myclass.o
            g++ -std=c++2c -g -c myclass.cpp

clean:
            rm -f myprogram
            rm -f *.o
```

[6] It isn't needed to put -std=c++2c in this "link" command – but I'll do it in every g++ command so I don't have to remember when to.

The first line in Example 16-3 is a comment, because it starts with a #.

I'll take things out of order for simplicity. The line

```
main.o:  main.cpp myclass.h
```

says that to compile the .o (object) file for main, you need main.cpp and myclass.h. If either changes, make will rebuild main.o. (make detects changes based on modification times of the files.)

The next line, g++ -std=c++2c -g -c main.cpp, is the command to compile it. If it fails, make stops so you can correct errors.

The lines for myclass.o are understood the same way.

Back to the top:

```
myprogram:  myclass.o main.o
            g++ -std=c++2c -g -o myprogram myclass.o main.o
```

establishes that myprogram depends on myclass.o and main.o and tells how to create it.

Since it's the first thing in the Makefile, this is what the computer tries to build when you type make.

clean is nice: if you say make clean, it'll erase the executable and all .o files. The -f option is so it won't report an error if there aren't any, because that's not a problem.

A Better Version

The Makefile above was too much work: we had to specify each .cpp file and which .h files it depends on. We'll now create a Makefile that should work on most projects you'll encounter in the rest of this text and elsewhere (Example 16-4).

Example 16-4. A Makefile for any project of .cpp source files – first attempt. It's in the source code, ch16/3-4-5-makefiles. To test, name it Makefile and type make

```
# Makefile for a program with multiple .cpp files

PROG        = myprogram             # What program am I building?
SRCS        = $(wildcard *.cpp)     # What .cpp files do I have?
OBJS        = ${SRCS:.cpp=.o}       # What .o   files do I build?

$(PROG):    $(OBJS)                 # Build the program
            g++ -std=c++2c -g -o $@ $^
```

```
%.o:        %.cpp                  # Make the .o files
            g++ -std=c++2c -g -o $@ -c $<

clean:                             # Clean up files
            rm -f $(PROG)
            rm -f *.o
```

First, we define some variables.

After that, we see that our program depends on the object files (as before). Note that variables take `$()` around them. Then the first g++ command tells how to create that program from the object files.

`$@` means "whatever's to the left of the `:` above" and `$^` means "everything right of the `:`" – that is, all the object files.

The section producing `.o` files makes one for each `.cpp` file. `$<` means "what's the *next* thing to the right," in this case, the next `.cpp` file.

(If you want to know everything about how to use these weird-looking constructions, the Internet is yours. If you just want to find something that works ...the Internet is still yours. That's what I do: look up tutorials and see what solves my problem.)

To see how these variables are translated into actual commands, type `make` – it'll print the commands as it executes them.

A Complete Version

The Makefile still has one big thing wrong (besides looking like it's written in Egyptian hieroglyphics). It doesn't refer to any `.h` files. If you change a `.h` file, `make` won't know to recompile on that basis – and it should.

So we add a magical incantation to the end of the Makefile:

```
%.dep:      %.cpp                        # Make the .dep files
            g++ -MM -MT "$*.o $@" $< > $@

ifneq ($(MAKECMDGOALS),clean)            # If not cleaning up...
-include $(DEPS)                         #  bring in the .dep files
endif
```

The first section says: for every `.cpp` file we have, we need a `.dep` file, which will contain information on dependencies. The `g++ -MM` line generates it. The `main.dep` file might look like this:

```
main.o main.dep:  main.cpp myclass.h
```

This means "Remake `main.o` and `main.dep` whenever `main.cpp` or `myclass.h` changes."

The `-MT "$*.o $@"` option specifies what goes left of that `:` – it should contain the relevant `.o` file `main.o`, plus `main.dep`, specified here as `$@`. The reason we put `main.dep` there is so if anything changes in either `main.cpp` or `myclass.h` (say, we add another `#include`), `main.dep` gets updated too.

`$<` is the relevant `.cpp` file.

`>` says store the output in a file, specifically, `$@`, which is the `.dep` file we're creating.

`include $(DEPS)` says include these rules into the Makefile. The initial `-` says don't report if there's an error, like the file not existing, as will happen the first time you run `make` after a `clean`. And the `ifneq ...` thing says don't bother about `.dep` files if you're just about to `clean` them up anyway.

Yes, it's complicated, but them's the breaks.

Example 16-5 shows our result. It should work unaltered for new projects; change `myprogram` if you want a different executable name.

Example 16-5. A complete Makefile. It's in the source code, `ch16/3-4-5-makefiles`. Run by typing `make`

```
# Makefile for a program with multiple .cpp files

PROG        = myprogram              #What program am I building?
SRCS        = $(wildcard *.cpp)      #What .cpp files do I have?
OBJS        = ${SRCS:.cpp=.o}        #What .o   files do I build?
DEPS        = $(OBJS:.o=.dep)        #What .dep files do I make?

###########################################################

all:        $(PROG)

$(PROG):    $(OBJS)                        # Build the program
            g++ -std=c++2c -o $@ -g $^
```

```
clean:                                          # Clean up files
            rm -f $(PROG)
            rm -f *.o
            rm -f *.dep

%.o:        %.cpp                               # Make the .o files
            g++ -std=c++2c -g -o $@ -c $<

%.dep:      %.cpp                               # Make the .dep files
            g++ -MM -MT "$*.o $@" $< > $@

ifneq ($(MAKECMDGOALS),clean)                  # If not cleaning up...
-include $(DEPS)                               #  bring in the .dep files
endif
```

Antibugging

- **Makefile:16: *** Missing separator. Stop.**

  No joke, this is because on the specified line you indented with spaces instead of tabs. Solution: Snort, roll your eyes, whatever, and use tabs.

Final Date Program

Examples 16-6 through 16-8 constitute is the finished program for `Date`, broken into files as discussed earlier. `main` is a driver, that is, a program designed to test the class.

Example 16-6. `date.h`. It's in the source code, `ch16`, as part of the `6-7-8-date` project/folder

```
// class Date
//       -- from _C++26 for Lazy Programmers_

#ifndef DATE_H
#define DATE_H

#include <iostream>
```

```
enum class Month { JANUARY=1, FEBRUARY, MARCH, APRIL, MAY, JUNE,
                   JULY, AUGUST, SEPTEMBER, OCTOBER, DECEMBER};

bool isLeapYear  (int year);
int  daysPerYear (int year);
int  daysPerMonth(int month, int year);// Have to specify year,
                                       // in case month is FEBRUARY
                                       //  and we're in a leap year
class Date
{
public:
    Date(int theDay=1, int theMonth=1, int theYear=1) :
       day_(theDay), month_(theMonth), year_(theYear)
    {
        normalize();
    }
    // Because of its default parameters, this 3-param
    //  ctor also serves as a conversion ctor
    //  (when you give it one int)
    //  and the default ctor (when you give it nothing)

    // Default is chosen so that the default day
    //  is Jan 1, 1 A.D.

    Date(const Date& otherDate) : // copy ctor
          day_  (otherDate.day_  ),
          month_(otherDate.month_),
          year_ (otherDate.year_ )
    {
    }

    // Access functions
    int days  () const { return day_;   }
    int months() const { return month_; }
    int years () const { return year_;  }

    int totalDays() const; // convert to total days since Dec 31, 1 BC
```

```
    void print(std::ostream& out = std::cout) const
    {
        out << day_ << '-' << month_ << '-' << year_;
    }

private:
    int day_;
    int month_;
    int year_;

    void normalize();
};
#endif //DATE_H
```

Example 16-7. `date.cpp`, abbreviated for brevity. A complete version is in the source code, `ch16` folder, as part of the `6-7-8-date` project/folder

```
// class Date -- functions
//          -- from _C++26 for Lazy Programmers_

#include "date.h"

bool isLeapYear(int year)
{
    //...
}

int daysPerYear(int year)
{
    //...
}

int daysPerMonth(int month, int year)
{
    //...
}
```

```
void Date::normalize()
{
    //...
}

int Date::totalDays() const
{
    //...
}
```

Example 16-8. A driver program for class `Date`. It's in the source code, `ch16`, as part of the `6-7-8-date` project/folder

```
// A "driver" program to test the Date class
//        -- from _C++26 for Lazy Programmers_

#include <iostream>
#include "date.h"

using namespace std;

int main()
{
    Date t(5,11,1955); // Test the 3-int constructor

    // ... and print
    cout << "This should print 5-11-1995:\t";
    t.print(cout);
    cout << endl;

    // Test access functions
    if (t.day() != 5 || t.month() != 11 || t.year() != 1955)
    {
        cout << "Date t should have been 5-11-1955, but was ";
        t.print();
        cout << endl;
    }
```

```
Date u = t;          // ...the copy constructor
if (u.day() != 5 || u.month() != 11 || u.year() != 1955)
{
    cout << "Date u should have been 5-11-1955, but was ";
    u.print();
    cout << endl;
}

const Date DEFAULT; // ...and the default constructor
                    // I do consts to test const functions
if (DEFAULT.day () != 1 || DEFAULT.month() != 1 ||
    DEFAULT.year() != 1)
{
    cout << "Date v should have been 1-1-1, but was ";
    DEFAULT.print();
    cout << endl;
}

// ...and total days
constexpr int DAYS_FOR_JAN1_5AD = 1462; // I found this number myself
                                        //   with a calculator
Date Jan1_5AD (1, 1, 5);
if (Jan1_5AD.totalDays () != DAYS_FOR_JAN1_5AD)
    cout << "Date Jan1_5AD should have had 1462 days, but had "
         << DAYS_FOR_JAN1_5AD << endl;

// Test normalization
const Date JAN1_2000 (32, 12, 1999);
if (JAN1_2000.day () != 1 || JAN1_2000.month() != 1 ||
    JAN1_2000.year() != 2000)
{
    cout << "Date JAN1_2000 should have been 1-1-2000, but was ";
    JAN1_2000.print();
    cout << endl;
}
```

```
    cout << "If no errors were reported, "
         << " it looks like class Date works!\n";

    return 0;
}
```

The output is

```
This should print 5-11-1995:  5-11-1955
If no errors were reported, looks like class Date works!
```

To be user-friendly, the driver gives as little output as possible if everything works. Less output to wade through when testing.

EXERCISES

In these exercises, use separate compilation; provide your classes with appropriate constructors, using default arguments where helpful; and write access functions and inline functions where relevant.

If it turns out that nothing goes in the `.cpp` file (could happen!), you don't need to write one.

1. Update the `Time` class to use what was covered in this chapter.

   Add a constant `Time MIDNIGHT` and make it available to `main.cpp`.

2. Add `Time` functions `sum` and `difference`, which return the sum/difference of this `Time` with another `Time`. Its return value is also a `Time`.

3. Write a member function for `Date` that returns the weekday. Hint: January 1, 1 A.D., was a Saturday.

   Now write a function to print the calendar for a particular month, one row per week. What parameter does it need?

4. What do you want engraved on your tombstone? Make a `Tombstone` class, which contains a birthdate, a death date, a name, and an epitaph. In addition to a member function `print`, give it a `lifespan` function, which returns the duration of the person's life as a `Date`.

5. Flesh out `Stopwatch` from Examples 16-1 and 16-2 to use what was covered in this chapter. Also add functions `start` and `stop`, which start and stop the `Stopwatch` (you'll want to have done Exercise 2 from the first set of exercises in Chapter 15: setting a `Time` to the current system time), and `duration`, which returns the difference. Then use the `Stopwatch` to time how quickly the user hits Enter.

6. Using SSDL, create one or more of these:

   - An on-screen stopwatch, based on the previous exercise, that you can start and stop with the space bar. You may want to change `Time` so that `seconds_` is a double, for more precision.
   - An on-screen clock that continually updates itself – either a digital clock or an analog one based on exercises from earlier in the book.
   - A timer, which sounds an alarm when it reaches 0.

7. Make a class `Track`, which contains title, artist, and duration (a `Time`) of a piece of music.

   Now make a class `Album`, which contains a title and an array of `Tracks`. Include, among the other functions you know you'll need, a function `duration()` that is the sum of all the `Tracks`' durations. This exercise is used again in Chapter 18's section on move semantics.

CHAPTER 17

Strings, and Operators

You may have seen this error:

```
char string1[] = "Hello", string2[] = "Hello";
if (string1 == string2) ...
```

This condition fails because == for arrays compares memory addresses not contents, and the addresses differ.

This also causes problems:

```
string2 = string1;
```

It copies not string2's contents but its address to string1. string1's contents are lost. This is wasteful and also error-prone:

```
string2[1] = 'a';       // string1 becomes "Hallo", though it
                        // wasn't even mentioned here!
```

So let's make our own string class, forcing the operators to do what *we* want, and never worry about this again.

Appendix B lists operators C++ lets us overload. Short version: Almost any, but you can't make up your own.

The Basic String Class

```
class String
{
public:
    String(const char* other=""); // conversion from char* constructor;
                                  //   default constructor
    String(const String &other);
```


W. Briggs, *C++26 for Lazy Programmers*, https://doi.org/10.1007/979-8-8688-1859-2_17

```
private:
    char* contents_;
};
```

I want my String class to handle strings of any length, so I'll use dynamic memory, as in Chapter 14.

Here are two ways to set the default:

- As nullptr. nullptr is by convention nothing, so this makes sense. But I'd need every function to check for nullptr before accessing contents_. Too much work.
- As a character array of length 1 containing only '\0', that is, as "" (the empty string). I'll use this.

I'll now write the constructors:[1]

```
String::String[2](const char* other = "")
                                             // conversion from char* constructor;
                                             //   default constructor
{
    contents_ = new char[strlen(other) + 1];
              // The +1 is room for final '\0'
    strcpy(contents_, other);
}

String::String(const String &other)
{
    contents_ = new char[strlen(other.contents_) + 1];
    strcpy(contents_, other.contents_);
}
```

[1] If I don't, C++ will, like so:

```
String::String() { };
String::String(const String& other) { contents_ = other.contents_; }
```

So the default constructor isn't useful, and the copy constructor will share memory between Strings so altering one alters the other. Avoiding these **implicit** constructors is a perfect justification for the Golden Rule of Constructors.

[2] When discussing a member function, I'll usually start it with String:: to clarify that it's a member. We omit String:: when inside the class definition.

That's too much redundant code. Maybe I could get one constructor to farm out its work to another? Sure. This "delegated constructor" lets the other do all the work. Code reuse, less typing, yay:

```
String(const String &other) : String(other.c_str())     {}
```

Now I'll make some useful functions. These go inside the class definition:

```
const char* c_str() const { return contents_;             }
void        print(std::ostream& out) const { out << contents_; }
                         //familiar?
std::size_t size () const { return strlen(c_str());     }
                         // Inefficient! Is there a better way?
```

Destructors

When using dynamically allocated arrays, we need `delete []` to throw back memory when we're done. But `contents_` is a private member of `String`, so `main` can't do it. Nor should it: it's `String`'s job. It needs a function to be called when we're done with the `String`.

Enter the destructor (or, per common abbreviation, "dtor"):

```
String::~String() { if (contents_) delete [] contents_; }
                          //Why "if (contents_)?" Paranoia. Deleting nullptr
                          // gives a crash. Which is better than wrong output.
```

This function, named "~" plus the class name, is called automatically whenever the `String` goes away (e.g., when the `String` is declared inside a function and the function ends).

This is

- Less work: write it once and you're done.
- Automatic, so you won't forget.

Memory management just got a lot easier, as long as you remember the Golden Rule:

Golden Rule of Destructors

If you're using dynamic memory in a class, always write the destructor.

I'll add another Golden Rule. You can violate it, but it *does* reduce errors:

Golden Rule of Dynamic Memory

If you can get what you want without it, don't use it. If you must, try to hide it inside a class and clean up with a destructor.

Destructors could be used for other things at the end of a variable's lifetime ...but I never do.

Comparison Operators

```
bool operator==(const String& a, const String &b) const
{
    return strcmp(a.c_str(), b.c_str()) == 0;
}
```

Using the == operator looks like this:

```
if (stringA == stringB)...
```

Here's something nice: != is the opposite of ==, right? So you don't have to write both: write == and C++ will implicitly write != as its negation.

We could now write operators < (meaning "precedes in alphabetical order"), <=, >, and >=, in a very similar way.

But if I'm too lazy for that, which I am, I'll just write one operator and let C++ make the rest. The one I have to write is a special operator <=> (called the "spaceship" operator because if you squint really hard it looks like a UFO). It's defined so that `String1 <=> String2` should return a negative number if `String1 < String2`, a positive number if `String1 > String2`, and 0 if they are equal.

...just like strcmp, the <cstring> function which, given two character arrays, returns exactly that. Here is our three-way comparison ("spaceship") operator:

```
int3 operator<=>(const String& a, const String& b)
                    // automagically generates <, <=, >, and >=
{
    return strcmp(a.c_str(), b.c_str());
}
```

EXERCISES

1. Make a Fraction class. You should be able to create fractions (specifying numerator and denominator or defaulting to 0/1), print them, and compare them with all available comparison operators.
2. Make a Point2D class. You should be able to create points (specifying the coordinates or defaulting to (0,0)), print them, and compare them. Two Point2Ds are equal if their Xs and Ys are identical, but one is greater than the other if its magnitude – its distance from (0,0) – is greater than the other's.

Assignment Operators and *this

How can we assign one String to another?

```
operator=(other)
    delete the old memory
    allocate the new memory, enough to hold other's contents
    copy the contents over
```

This is going to change contents_ - obviously! - so let's make = a member function:

```
String::operator=(const String& other);
```

I didn't specify the return type - and I must. What will it be?

[3] Purists may complain that <=> returns an int-like type (like std::size_t), not exactly int. They're right, but let's keep things simple.

We usually just call = like this – `A=B;` – but this is also legal:

```
A=B=C;
```

Since = is processed right to left, this means

```
A=(B=C);
```

which really means: when doing B=C, assign the value of C to B, return the value you get, and send it across the = to A. So B=C must return whatever B becomes.

```
operator=(other)
    delete the old memory
    allocate the new memory, enough to hold other's contents
    copy the contents over
    return "this"
```

or

```
String& String::operator=(const String& other)⁴
{
    if (contents_) delete[] contents_;                   // delete old memory
    contents_ = new char[strlen(other.c_str()) + 1]; // get new memory
              //The +1 is room for final '\0'
    strcpy(contents_, other.c_str());                 // copy contents over
    return *this;
}
```

When the computer gets to `stringA = stringB`, it goes into the function `String::operator=`.[5] There are two `String`s used. The one on the left, `stringA`, is "this" one: the one that owns this `operator=` function. The one on the right, `stringB`, is the "other" one, the one passed in as a parameter.

When you refer to a member specifying the owner, as in `other.c_str()`, that's the `c_str()` that belongs to `other`. If you don't say who it belongs to, it belongs to "this" one – the one on the left.

[4] See Exercise 3 for an interesting and necessary tweak on this function.

[5] This whole operator business is syntactic sugar. You *can* call = this ugly way:
`stringA = stringB;`

this is defined whenever you're in a member function, as the memory address of "this" object. Since this is a pointer to the object, *this is the object itself. (We rarely use this without the *, though we can.) We wanted = to return what "this" object has become; now it does.

*this is *always* the thing to return from =. Since operators for +=, -=, etc. also return the newly altered object, they also return *this.

I think I'll rewrite the conversion constructor and operator= to extract the code they have in common and put it in a new function copy. Code reuse:

```
String::String(const char* other="") { copy(other); }

String& String::operator=(const String& other)
{
    if (contents_) delete[] contents_; copy(other.c_str());
    return *this;
}

void String::copy(const char* str)
{
    contents_ = new char[strlen(str) + 1]; // get new memory
                                           // the +1 is room for final '\0'
    strcpy(contents_, str);                // copy contents over
}
```

The other thing that most needs explanation is ='s return type.

Suppose it were written thus:

```
String String::operator=(const String& other);
```

Since there's no &, it will call the copy constructor to make a copy of what it returns. This takes time since it has to copy the array character by character. We can save time if we return not a copy but the thing (*this) itself:

```
String& String::operator=(const String& other);
```

Golden Rule of Assignment Operators

Every assignment operator (=, +=, etc.) should return *this.

...by reference (e.g., String&).

And here's another rule:

Golden Rule of =

Always specify =.

The reason is the same as for copy constructors: *if you don't, the compiler will do it for you,* and it may do it in a stupid way. For `String` it will define it to copy the memory address. We were trying to get *away* from that.

Unary Operators

Operators we've seen so far are **binary**: each needs two `Strings`. A **unary** operator has only one argument, like the - ("unary minus") in `(-myInt)+2` or the ! in `if (! isReady)`. As an example I'll write ! for the `String` class. `! myString` will mean `myString` is empty:

```
bool String::operator! () const { return ! size(); }
```

Golden Rule of Operators as Class Members

If an operator has one argument, "this" object – the one whose members we can refer to without specifying whose they are – is the only object mentioned in the call of the operator.

If an operator has two arguments, "this" object is the one on the left of the operator in the call. The one passed as a parameter is the one on the right.

Operators don't have three arguments.[6]

---

[6] There's an exception: the `?:` operator. Here is an example of its use:

```
cout << (x>=0 ? "positive" : "negative");
```

This means `if (x>=0) cout << "positive"; else cout << "negative";`.

I don't use it much. C++ won't let you overload it anyway.

Antibugging

A common mistake is putting TheClassName:: in front of the wrong thing:

```
String::const char* c_str() const; //const is a member of String?!
```

The error messages may be confusing or clear depending on the compiler. Either way the solution is to stick TheClassName:: on the left end of the function name. const char* is the return type; String::c_str is the function.

EXERCISES

1. Add = and - to the Fraction class from the previous exercises, so we could say (for example) frac1 = -frac2;.
2. Add = and - to the Point2D class, so we could say point1 = -point2;.
3. What happens in String::operator= if you say this: myStr = myStr;? Fix it to avoid the problem. My answer is in Example 17-2.

Arithmetic Operators

Now we'll do the "arithmetic"-looking operator +. I think it's reasonable to define + to mean concatenation. If word is "cat" and addon is "fish", then word+addon should be "catfish".

We'll write += and +. Programmers using String may want either and have reason to be annoyed if they have to guess which we provided.

```
operator+=(other String)
    remember the old contents
    allocate new contents, big enough that we can add other.contents
    copy the old contents into the new
    append other contents
    delete the old contents
    return *this
```

Order matters. If we delete the old contents before we use them, we'll lose what's in them.

Here it is in valid C++:

```
String& String::operator+=(const String& other)
{
    char* oldContents = contents_;

    contents_ = new char [size() + other.size() + 1];
                                       // 1 extra space at end for the null char

    strcpy(contents_, oldContents);  // copy old into new
    strcat(contents_, other.c_str());// append other contents

    delete [] oldContents;

    return *this;
}
```

Good enough. Now I can do `operator+` (outside the class definition, following common convention). Should it return `String&` too?

```
String& operator+(const String& a, const String& b)
                                        // There's something wrong here...
{
    String result = a; result += b; return result;
}
```

Let's trace what happens when we call it.

Suppose, in `main`, we say `copied = word+addon`. First, we call `operator+`. It makes its `result` (Figure 17-1).

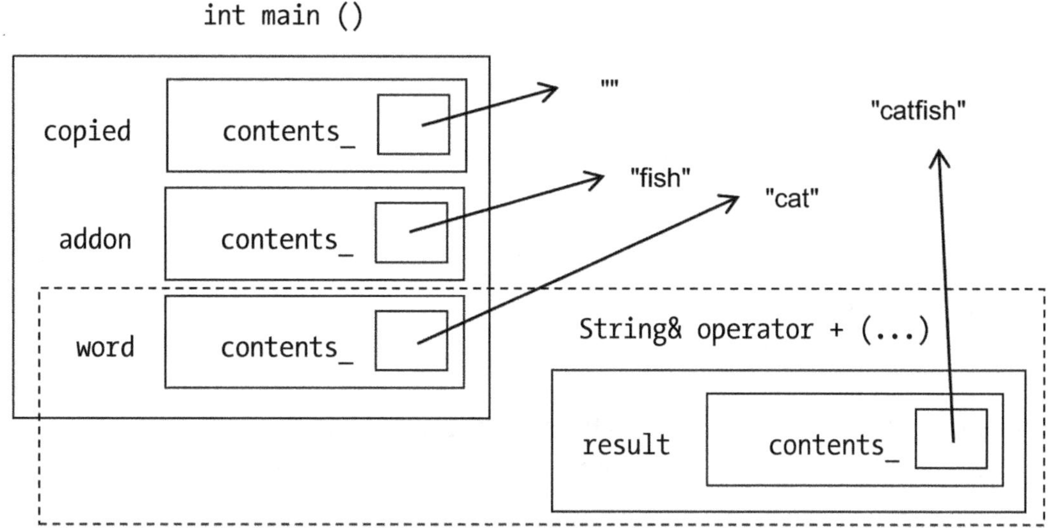

Figure 17-1. *operator+ (flawed version) at work*

Then it returns its `result` and goes away (Figure 17-2). But `result`, being +'s local variable, is destructed when + completes, so what `main` gets no longer exists by the time it gets it. Using it would be a Bad Idea.

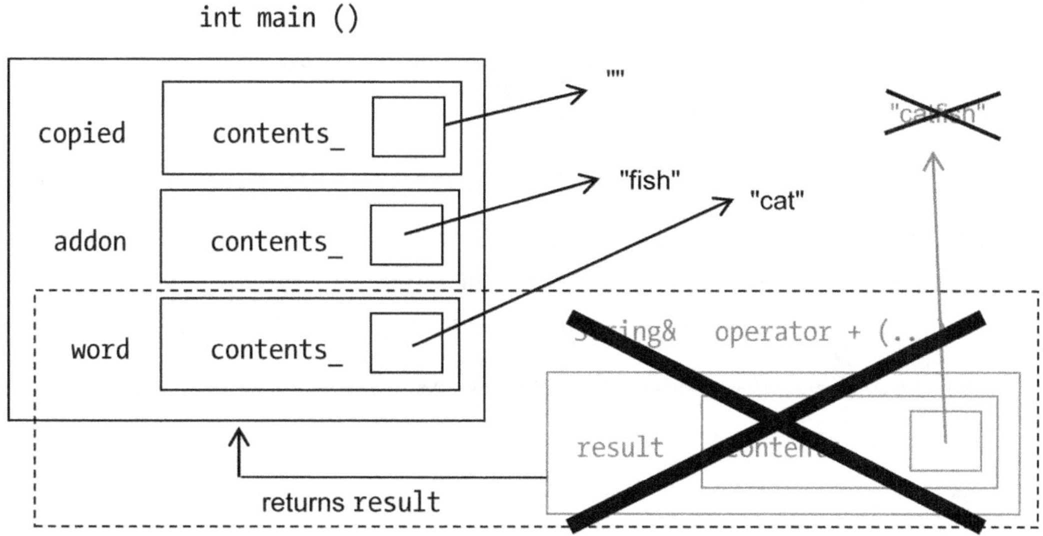

Figure 17-2. *operator+ (flawed version) returns its value*

The solution is to return a copy. It will persist till it's no longer needed:[7]

```
String operator+(const String& a, const String& b) const //That's better
{
    String result = a; result += b; return result;
}
```

Golden Rule of Returning `const &`

Local variables should not be returned with &.

Things that will persist after the function returns, including `*this` and data members, may be. If they're of class types and not trivially small like `std::span`, they should be.

Why make + call +=, rather than the reverse? + makes two copies: local variable `result` and the copy made when we return. += has no locals and returns `String&`, so it's pretty efficient. If we made it call + it would have to do extra copying.

+ can always be written as it is here, no matter if we're adding `String`s, numbers, or heffalumps (whatever they are) – just change `String` to whatever new type you want.

EXERCISES

1. Add +, -, *, /, and +=, -=, *=, and /= to `Fraction`.
2. Add +, +=, -, and -= to `Point2D`. Also add *, *=, /, and /=. It may not make sense to refer to `point1/point2`, but it *would* make sense to refer to `point1/2` – you'd divide both coordinates by 2 to get a new `Point2D`. So the "other" argument of *, *=, /, and /= would be a number.

++ and --

It wouldn't make much sense to say `myString++`, so I'll shift to the `Fraction` example from exercises.

[7] Inefficient? C++, compulsive for efficiency as usual, has a fix (see Chapter 18).

myFraction++ should add 1 to myFraction. Recall there are two versions of ++: ++myFraction, meaning add 1 and return what you get, and myFraction++, meaning add 1 and return what you had before adding.

This is the pre-increment version:

```
Fraction& Fraction::operator++() // used for ++myFraction
{
    *this += 1;                  // add 1 to this Fraction
                                 // (Surely Fraction can convert from int?)
    return *this;
}
```

How can we distinguish the post-increment version? Not by name or number of arguments ...so C++ has a hack[8] just for this:

```
Fraction Fraction::operator++(int junk) //used for myFraction++
{
      Fraction result = *this;
      ++(*this);                  //code reuse again
      return result;
}
```

The int argument here really *is* junk: it's just a placeholder, meant to distinguish this ++ operator from the other.

EXERCISES

1. Add both versions of ++ and -- to Fraction, and test.
2. Add both versions of ++ and -- to Point2D, and test. myPoint++ would add 1 to the x_ component.

[8] An inelegant solution.

operator[]

Now we'll support the use of [ ]'s to access individual characters:

```
char  String::operator[] (int i) const { return contents_[i]; }
```

We're only partly done, because though we can say

```
char ch = myString[0];
```

if we say

```
myString[0] = 'a';
```

the compiler will complain "l-value required."

This means (*very* roughly – I'm keeping it simple) that the thing left of the = (L for left) is not the sort of thing that *can* be left of =: it's not modifiable. If you want to alter `myString`, you need not a *copy* of the element but the element itself:

```
char& String::operator[] (int i)       { return contents_[i]; }
```

Won't the compiler get confused, having two functions identical but for return type? But they're *not* identical: one is `const`. So C++ will apply the `const` one to things that can't change and the non-`const` to things that can:

```
const String S ("hello");
cout << S[0] << '\n'; // OK; uses the const version of []

String T ("goodbye");
T[0] = 'G';             // Also OK; uses the non-const version, which
                        // returns something that can be changed
```

Golden Rule of []

If you define [ ], you need two versions:

```
<type>  operator[] (int index) const { ... }
<type>& operator[] (int index)       { ... }
```

The code between the { }'s will almost certainly be identical.

EXERCISES

1. Add `[]` (`const` and non-`const` versions) to `Point2D`. `point1[0]` is the x coordinate, and `point1[1]` is the y coordinate.
2. ...and to `Fraction`. `myFraction[0]` is the numerator and `myFraction[1]` is the denominator.

>> and <<

I also want to print `String`s using >> and << with `cin` and `cout` or other files.

We can't write these operators as members: the thing on the left of an operator is always "this" object. But in `cout << myString`, the left operand is `cout`. If we wrote `operator<<` as a member of `String`, `cout` would have to be a `String`.

So like == and +, it'll be a non-member:

```
                               // this must go outside the class definition
ostream& operator<<(ostream& out, const String& foo)[9]
{
      ...
      return out;
}
```

I have it return `ostream&` because of when I chain <<'s together (as in `cout << X << Y`). The order of operations is `(cout << X) << Y`; that is, `cout << X` does its work and then returns its "value" of `cout`, so the next << has `cout` as its left operand and can be used to print.

This is my first attempt:

```
inline                                                 // in string.h
std::ostream& operator<<(std::ostream& out, const String& foo)
{
    out << foo.contents_; return out;
}
```

[9] In the programming language LISP and elsewhere, foo is used to name a variable when it's obvious what foo is. If two such "placeholder" names are needed, it's often foo and bar. It's a good bet this is from the military acronym "FUBAR," meaning roughly "Fouled Up Beyond All Recognition."

Some programmers consider foo and bar evil because they aren't descriptive, but I think I'd rather read foo than theString or rightHandSide.

This won't compile. `foo.contents_` is private.

We could return `contents_` via an access function, but we already have a more versatile solution - use `String::print`:

```
inline std::ostream& operator<<(std::ostream& out, const String& foo)
{
    foo.print(out); return out;
}
```

We just fixed the privacy violation in a way that will work for any class we ever write - a Good Thing. Let's handle `cin >>` similarly:

```
void String::read(std::istream& in);

inline
std::istream& operator>>(std::istream& in, String& foo)
                                                     // foo is not const!
{
    foo.read(in); return in;
}
```

`String::read` is trickier than `String::print`. Here's my first try.

```
void String::read(istream& in)      { in >> contents_; }
```

Problem is, we don't know if `contents_` has enough space to store what's typed in.

Solution:

```
class String
{
public:
    static constexpr int BIGGEST_READABLE_STRING_PLUS_ONE    = 257;
       // biggest string we can read, incl '\0' What's this "static" thing?
      //  We'll get to it in the next section
    ...
};
```

```
void String::read(std::istream& in)
{
    static char buffer [BIGGEST_READABLE_STRING_PLUS_ONE];
              //Why reallocate each time? Save time by keeping just one!
    in >> buffer;
    *this = buffer;
}
```

EXERCISES

1. Add `ostream <<` and `istream >>` operators for the `Fraction` class.
2. ...and the `Point2D` class.

`static` Members

C++ loves to reuse - overuse - keywords, so there are three meanings of `static`.

One you know: **a local variable that doesn't go away when the function closes**, but remains for the next call. We've seen this multiple times, most recently here:

```
void String::read(std::istream& in)
{
    static char buffer [BIGGEST_READABLE_STRING_PLUS_ONE];
    in >> buffer;
    *this = buffer;
}
```

Another we won't think about much: **a global constant, variable, or function that we only want visible in the .cpp file it's written in.**

The third is, a member of a class that applies to the entire class, not to a particular instance of it:

```
class String
{
public:
    static constexpr int BIGGEST_READABLE_STRING_PLUS_ONE    = 257;
```

```
                        //biggest string we can read, incl '\0'
    ...
};
```

This isn't a characteristic of a *particular* String, but something that's true for *all* Strings.

You could also have a static member function, to report something that's true for all Strings:

```
class String
{
public:
    ...
    static10 int biggestReadableString()
    {
        return BIGGEST_READABLE_STRING_PLUS_ONE - 1;
    }
    ...
};
```

Temporary Object Creation

C++ can create temporary Strings as needed with an **explicit call to the constructor**:

```
String s;
s = String("moo") + String("cow");
```

On the second line, C++ generated two temporary String objects, initialized them with "moo" and "cow", and passed them to operator+. This is less typing than

```
String s;
String m("moo");
String c("cow");
s = m + c;
```

[10] static functions can't be const. Don't worry, the compiler will remind you.

I often use this for objects that are to be created, used immediately, and never referenced again. It's especially nice with Point2D:

```
myPoints[0] = Point2D(2, 5);
myPoints[1] = Point2D(3, 7);
```

I can get even lazier and have C++ call a class's constructor implicitly:

```
s = String("moo") + "cow"; //Implicitly converts "cow" to a String
s = "moo" + String("cow"); //Implicitly converts "moo" to a String
s = "moo" + "cow";           //ERROR
```

The last one won't work – at least one has to be a String or C++ won't know you want String involved.

Similarly

```
s += "cow";
```

is fine, but

```
"cow" += s;
```

would fail, partly because const char*, "cow"'s type, doesn't define +=, but mostly a const char* isn't the sort of thing you can add to.

EXERCISES

1. Write a program that declares five Fractions and multiplies them, without naming them as variables, by using an explicit call to the constructor.
2. Write a program that declares five Point2Ds and prints them, without naming them as variables, by using an explicit call to the constructor.

Final String Program

Our complete program is in Examples 17-1 through 17-3.

Example 17-1. `string.h`. The source code project containing this and Examples 17-2 and 17-3 is `1-2-3-string`.

```
// String class
//        -- from _C++26 for Lazy Programmers_

#ifndef STRING_H
#define STRING_H

#include <cstring> // uses cstring functions all over
#include <iostream>

#ifdef _MSC_VER
#pragma warning (disable:4996) // Disable a warning about strcpy, etc.,
#endif                         //  in Visual Studio

class String
{
public:
    static constexpr std::size_t BIGGEST_READABLE_STRING_PLUS_ONE   = 257;
                    // biggest string we can read, incl '\0'
    static int biggestReadableString()
    {
        return BIGGEST_READABLE_STRING_PLUS_ONE - 1;
    }

    String(const char* other="") { copy(other);             }
    String(const String &other) : String(other.c_str())   {}
                    // a "delegated" constructor
    ~String()       { if (contents_) delete [] contents_;  }

    // access function
    const char* c_str() const { return contents_;        }
```

```
    // functions related to size
    std::size_t size () const { return strlen(c_str()); }
                        // Inefficient! Is there a better way?
    bool operator!   () const { return ! size();         }

    // assignment
    String& operator= (const String& other);
    String& operator+=(const String& other);

    //I/O
    void  read (std::istream& in );
    void  print(std::ostream& out) const        { out << c_str();        }
private:
    char* contents_;
    void  copy(const char* str);
};

//I/O
inline
std::istream& operator>>(std::istream& in, String& foo)
{
    foo.read(in); return in;
}

inline
std::ostream& operator<<(std::ostream& out, const String& foo)
{
    foo.print(out); return out;
}

// comparisons
inline
bool operator==(const String& a, const String& b)
{
    return strcmp(a.c_str(), b.c_str()) == 0;
}
```

```
inline
int operator<=>(const String& a, const String& b)
                    // automagically generates <, <=, >, and >=
{
    return strcmp(a.c_str(), b.c_str());
}

//arithmetic ops
inline
String operator+(const String& a, const String& b)
{
    String result = a; result += b; return result;
}
#endif //STRING_H
```

Example 17-2. string.cpp

```
// class String, for char arrays
//        -- from _C++26 for Lazy Programmers_

#include <cstring>
#include "string.h"

using namespace std;

String& String::operator=(const String& other)
{
    if (this == &other) return *this;      // never assign *this to itself
                   // see Exercise 3 after the Assignment operators section
    if (contents_) delete[] contents_;
    copy(other.c_str());
    return *this;
}

void String::copy(const char* str)
{
    if (!str) str = ""; //Probably shouldn't let them send in nullptr
                          //  If they do, treat it as ""
```

```
    contents_ = new char[strlen(str) + 1]; // get new memory
                                           // The +1 is room for final '\0'
    strcpy(contents_, str);                // copy contents over
}

String& String::operator+=(const String& other)
{
    char* oldContents = contents_;

    contents_ = new char [size() + other.size() + 1];
                                         // 1 extra space at end for the
                                            null char

    strcpy(contents_, oldContents);  // copy old into new
    strcat(contents_, other.c_str());// append other contents

    delete [] oldContents;

    return *this;
}

void String::read(std::istream& in)
{
    static char buffer [BIGGEST_READABLE_STRING_PLUS_ONE];
    in >> buffer;
    *this = buffer;
}
```

The driver uses the function void assert(bool condition) that verifies condition is true – and if not, crashes the program. Good: if something's wrong, we'll know it. This is a quick easy way to test your functions.

Example 17-3. A driver for String

```
// Driver program to test the String class
//        -- from _C++26 for Lazy Programmers_

#include <iostream>
#include <cassert>  // for assert, a function which crashes
                    //   if the condition you give is false
                    // used for debugging
```

```
#include "string.h"

using namespace std;

int main()
{
                    // using consts to ensure const functions are right
    const String EMPTY;
    const String ABC("abc");

    // Testing default ctor, conversion ctor from char*, ==, !=, !
    assert(EMPTY == ""); assert(! EMPTY); assert(! (EMPTY != ""));
    assert(ABC != "");                    assert(! (ABC == ""));
    assert(String(nullptr) == EMPTY);

    // Testing c_str, size ...
    assert(strcmp(ABC.c_str(), "abc") == 0);
    assert(ABC.size() == 3);

    // Test >, >=, <, <=, !=,
    // We're doing lots of automatic calls to conversion ctor
    //   from const char*, so that's tested too
    assert(ABC <  "abd");  assert(! (ABC >= "abd"));
    assert(ABC <= "abd");  assert(! (ABC >  "abd"));
    assert(ABC >  "abb");  assert(! (ABC <= "abb"));
    assert(ABC >= "abb");  assert(! (ABC <  "abb"));
    assert(ABC <= ABC);    assert(ABC >= ABC);

    // Test []
    String xyz = "xyz";
    assert(xyz[1] == 'y'); xyz[1] = 'Y';
    assert(xyz[1] == 'Y'); xyz[1] = 'y';
    assert(ABC[1] == 'b'); //const version

    // Test =, ()
    xyz = "xYz"; assert(xyz == "xYz");
```

```
    // Test copy ctor
    assert(ABC == String(ABC));

    // Test + (and thereby +=)
    String ABCDEF = ABC+"def";
    assert(ABCDEF == "abcdef");

    // Test << and >>
    String input;
    cout << "Enter a string:\t"; cin >> input;
    cout << "You entered:\t" << input << '\n';

    cout << "If no errors were reported, "
         << "class String seems to be working!\n";

    return 0;
}
```

std::string

Here's what I've been hiding: C++ already has a string class, and you now know how to use it. You'll need `#include <string>`. The type is `std::string`, not `String`. Use it – it's very convenient!

I didn't show it, but variables of type `string` can be `constexpr`. (The most reliable way to see what can and can't be `constexpr` is try it and see what your compiler doesn't like.)

EXERCISES

1. Using `assert` and an explicit call to the constructor, test your `Fraction` class.
2. ...or your `Point2D` class.
3. Write a musical note class. Notes can be A, A#, B, etc. You should be able to go up to the next half-note or down to the previous.
4. Write a Roman numeral class, so that you can (say) add IX to IV and get XIII.

CHAPTER 18

String Views, Exceptions, Move Semantics, and O Notation

In this chapter we'll find a nicer way to pass in strings into functions, a better way of handling its error conditions, a way to do less copying, and see how to measure the efficiency of functions.

std::string_view (optional)

When we pass text into a function, it would be flexible if we could pass in either a `std::string` or a character array. What should the parameter be? `std::string`, like this?

```
bool hasDoubleLetters(const std::string& str);
      //returns true if there are doubled letters -- like "noon", not "neon"
...
if (hasDoubleLetters("bookkeeper")) ...
```

If we send in a character array as shown, C++ will create a `std::string` to hold it and proceed with the function call. This is fine, but it does take a little time. Suppose we use a `const char*` parameter instead and sometimes want to pass in a `std::string`:

```
bool hasDoubleLetters(const char* str);
...
const std::string word = "bookkeeper";
```


W. Briggs, *C++26 for Lazy Programmers*, https://doi.org/10.1007/979-8-8688-1859-2_18

```
if (hasDoubleLetters(word.c_str()) ...
```

No extra time required, but we did have to remember to add `.c_str()`.

A **string_view** enables us to write the function so that either type of argument works with no overhead and no extra typing. How to use it is shown in Example 18-1: you use it as the parameter, and then you can use `size` and the `[]` operators just like with `std::span`.

Example 18-1. Using `std::string_view`

```
// Program that uses string_view
//       -- from _C++26 for Lazy Programmers_

#include <iostream>
#include <string>
#include <string_view>

bool hasDoubleLetters(std::string_view str);

int main()
{
    const std::string word = "bookkeeper";

    if (! hasDoubleLetters(word))
        std::cout << "hasDoubleLetters isn't working!\n";
    if (! hasDoubleLetters("bookkeeper"))
        std::cout << "hasDoubleLetters isn't working!\n";
    return 0;
}

bool hasDoubleLetters(std::string_view str)
{
    for (int i = 0; i < str.size()-1; ++i)
        if (str[i] == str[i+1]) // Two in a row! Return true
            return true;

    return false;                // No doubles found
}
```

A `string_view` is just a *view*, so you can't alter the string inside `hasDoubleLetters`. It's trivially quick to copy, so we needn't bother with `const &`.

string_view is a little quicker than creating a std::string and a little more convenient than adding .c_str(). Use it if you like it. Often you can't, because your function with a text argument needs to pass to someone else's (fstream::open, SDL's IMG_Load) that needs a null-terminated char*, which string_view doesn't guarantee to provide.

EXERCISES

1. Write class StringView, your own version of string_view. Support conversions from char* and from std::string, =, ==, <=>, [], size(), empty(), and data() (returns the contents), printing with << and anything else you find useful – but no reading, because string_view can't make changes! Hint: Declare string_view's contents_ to be const.
2. Write contains for String, to return whether your string contains another given string or character. How many overloads should you have?
3. ...and the same for your own version of string_view.
4. Write operator + so you can add a String to a StringView or a StringView to a String (supported for std::string and std::string_view in C++26).

Exceptions

Suppose I ask a String to give me its 100th character, when the content is, say, "cat". That seems like a bad idea! I'll write a new function at(size_t index), which does the same thing as [] but detects the problem rather than letting me access the character and maybe crash the program. (I'll leave [] as it is for programmers who don't want the overhead of my error checking.)[1]

```
char String::at(int index) const
{
    if (index >= size()) ?? //out of range! do something!
    else return contents_[index];
}
```

[1] In C++26 this new **at** function is also featured in **string_view**, **span**, and others.

But if we find the error, how is it resolved?

Whatever we do, it won't be done in that function. Maybe `main` wants to print an error message and quit. Maybe it wants to just ignore that attempt and go on to whatever comes next. How could the `at` function know? So C++ separates the tasks of *reporting* an exceptional condition and *handling* it. Here's what we'll need to report a problem (see Example 18-2 for the code):

- A type to carry the message "out of range access attempted!" You could use an `int` variable, `char*`, whatever, but I'll make one that specifically identifies the type of error we have: `class OutOfRangeException {};`.

  The fact that this class has no members is fine – we just want to know it's an `OutOfRange` error, nothing more.[2]

- When we detect the error, report ("throw") it with the word `throw`. All other work stops: the program skips the rest of whatever function it's in, deallocates any variables (calling destructors if any), returns, and keeps returning from functions, until it gets to code that can handle the exception (if there is any).

Example 18-2. Updates to the `String` class, to use exceptions with the new `at` function. Code is in the repository, `Ch18`, under `2-thru-5-string`

```
// String class
//          -- from _C++26 for Lazy Programmers_

#ifndef STRING_H
#define STRING_H

//...

class OutOfRangeException {}; //exception class

class String
{
public:
    //...
```

[2] We *could* give it public and private sections, constructors, data members, etc., but I rarely do.

```
    char  at(int index) const
    {
        if (index >= size()) throw OutOfRangeException();
        else return contents_[index];
    }
    char& at(int index)
    {
        if (index >= size()) throw OutOfRangeException();
        else return contents_[index];
    }
    //...
};

//...
#endif //STRING_H
```

main or some other function may have a way of handling this type of error. The code that might have the error is in the {}'s after the word try; if an exception is thrown, it skips the rest of the code in the try block and transfers control to the catch block, which has code to handle the problem.

Example 18-3. A main program that can catch the exception

```
// Driver program to test the String class
//        -- from _C++26 for Lazy Programmers_

#include <iostream>
#include "String.h"

using namespace std;

int main()
{
    // Test at
    String xyz = "xyz";
    try
```

```
    {
        xyz.at(3) = 'a'; //no, that's out of range...
        cout << "This line will never be reached.\n";
    }
    catch (OutOfRangeException& err)
    {
        cout << "Out of range error caught!\n";
    }
}
```

What if there is no try–catch block? The program crashes. We've seen this already, when we were trying to load an image with a misspelled filename, say, or mishandled dynamic memory, and the program's libraries threw an exception. Which was fine: it let us know so we could debug. There's no rule you have to catch your exceptions.

So what *is* an `OutOfRangeException`? It's just what you see: an object of type `OutOfRangeException`, with no data members and no member functions. Is this stupid? Not at all. `throw`ing it tells `main` that an out-of-range error occurred. That's the information I think it's likely to care about.

Think of the exception as a hot potato. The `if` statement throws it. If the function it's in knows how to catch it, fine. If not, it relays the hot potato, I mean, the `OutOfRangeException`, to whatever function called *it*, then the one that called that one, and so on. Each time, the function stops what it's doing and returns immediately, delaying only enough to throw away its local variables, destructing as necessary. This continues until we return to a function that can catch the error, or we exit the program with an error.

The structure of throw is

```
throw <exception>
```

and that of a `try-catch` block is

```
try { <do stuff> }
catch (<parameter>) { <error handling code> }
[and possibly more catches]
```

If you're in an exception's `catch` block and want to throw it again, say `throw` without any arguments.

And if you want to forbid a function to throw an exception at all, append `noexcept` to the top line: `void mustNotThrowExceptions() noexcept;`. The next section shows one use.[3]

Should you use exceptions?

Yes! They're ideal for letting the error handling be done wherever it should be, with minimal extra coding. I use them regularly. (I'll admit I rarely catch them. Maybe that's because I'm more into writing libraries than user apps.)

EXERCISES

1. Add `at` (`const` and non-`const` versions) to `Point2D`, throwing an exception if you get a bad index.
2. ...and to `Fraction`.
3. ...and to `string_view` (`const` version only, of course).
4. Adapt the `istream operator>>` for `Point2D` or `Fraction`, from the previous chapter, so if something goes wrong with the `istream` (like typing in a `char` when it expected an `int`), it throws an exception. You can detect the problem like so: `if (! myIstream) ....`

Move Constructors and Move =

`String` is doing more copying than it should, and that may slow us down. (OK, *I've* never noticed, but the C++ community is persnickety about efficiency.) Consider this code:

```
newString = str1 + str2;
```

[3] By conventional wisdom (and C++ Core Guidelines, q.v.), destructors, move constructors, and move = - see the next section - should be `noexcept`, because they manipulate memory and it would be a shame if we left that memory in an inconsistent state (see the next section). Comparison operators and swap shouldn't because the standard library's sort operations use them, and if we prevent exceptions, the sort operations don't have to check for them. Default constructors shouldn't because, well, I'm sure there was some good reason. I'll make an effort to model this in subsequent code. But if you remember it on destructors and move functions, I think you'll be fine.

There is a temporary copy made in operator+, repeated below. It's when we return the `result`. This calls the copy constructor, which contains a call to `strcpy`. The bigger the string, the longer `strcpy` takes.

```
String String::operator+(const String& other) const
{
    String result = *this; result += other; return result;
}
```

Modern C++ has a mechanism whereby something can give up its memory to something else that needs it, avoiding the need for copying. Example 18-4 shows it.

Example 18-4. A move constructor for `String`. In the source code as part of project/folder `3-4-string`

```
String(String&& other) noexcept    // The "move" constructor.
    // I'll explain "noexcept" in a moment
{
    contents_ = other.contents_;  // 2 statements; no loops,
    other.contents_ = nullptr;    //    no strcpy. Cheap!
}
```

The && means "apply this function if the parameter is something that can give up its value and that's OK." That's surely true of `operator+`'s `result`! So we take the contents from `result` (temporarily called `other` in the move constructor). We give it `nullptr` so when it hits its own destructor it won't `delete[]` the `contents_` it gave us.

The other extra work comes after we leave +, when the temporary copy it provides is copied by `operator=`, which also does a `strcpy`. We can save time if we just move that copy's contents into `newString`. Example 18-5 presents the new = operator.

Moving like this, not copying, is called **move semantics** – a term we'll be seeing again.

Example 18-5. A move assignment operator for `String`. Also part of `2-thru-5-string` in the source code

```
String& String::operator=(String&& other) noexcept //move =
{
    if (contents_) delete[] contents_;
```

```
    contents_       = other.contents_; //no loops! no strcpy! efficient!
    other.contents_ = nullptr;

    return *this;
}
```

If move = or the move constructor threw an exception, weird things could happen, so the compiler may warn me if I don't put noexcept at the end. I like to keep it happy, so I do.

Another important thing to note is that things work differently if your class's data members are themselves classes and use move semantics themselves. But we'll cross that bridge when we come to it (in Chapter 21).

Because we have more options now, I want to supersede the old Golden Rule of Constructors and of = with this:

Golden Rule of Constructors and =

Either have

- No constructors and no = specified (old-style structs, essentially)
- Default constructor, copy constructor, and = specified
- Default constructor, copy constructor, and =, plus move constructor and move =

EXERCISES

1. Adapt Exercise 7 from the end of Chapter 16, with its Tracks and Albums, to use dynamic memory. Then write a move constructor and move = for Album. Test with the debugger to be sure you're really using move functions when you should. How? Put a breakpoint on any code that copies arrays element by element, and see if it gets called when you think it should be using move functions instead.

If you can't set a breakpoint in the copy constructor, the compiler may have optimized it away in something called "return value optimization" (RVO). Which means it's already efficient and you're good. We still write move constructors for situations in which RVO can't or may not happen.

Efficiency and O Notation

Suppose we want to sort a list of names. I know! Let's generate all possible orderings of names and stop when we get one that's perfectly ordered! Computers are fast, right?

```
do
   generate a new permutation of the elements
while we haven't found an ordered sequence
```

That's not much detail, but I predict a problem. Suppose there are four elements. There four possibilities for the first element. That leaves three possibilities for the next, which leaves two possibilities for the next, and one for the last: there are 4*3*2*1 possibilities – 4 factorial, it's called. So for N elements we'll have N factorial orderings to consider. With N=100 that's 10^{158}. Computers are fast, but they aren't *that* fast.

Sometimes the algorithm is obviously a bad idea. Sometimes you don't realize how bad it is till you run it – unless you use **O notation**, so you can know what program *not* to bring to management and *not* to spend your time writing.

Consider this code:

```
for (int i = 0; i < N; ++i)
    sum += array[i];
```

The initialization is done once; the comparison, array reference, assignment, and increment are each done N times. We could say there are 1+4N things being executed.

What about some other snippet with a loop? Maybe it's a little different and we get, oh, 5+3N. Which one's faster, or are they the same? Hm. We need a way to compare.

O notation greatly simplifies how we describe these time requirements and so helps us compare and evaluate them. Here are the simplifying rules for O notation:

- If one addend is clearly smaller than another when the data set is large, discard the smaller one. So if we have 1+3N, we discard the 1 and get 3N.
- Discard constant multipliers. 3N becomes N.

The result is written as O(N). The for loop above is O(N), or "is of order N."

The simplification is justified. What we care about is what happens when the data set is large (small data sets are always quick). When N is large, 3N+1 is approximately 3N: the difference in 3,000,001 and 3,000,000 is negligible. We also don't care about constant multipliers. Whether N doubles from 3,000 to 6,000 or 3N doubles from 9,000 to 18,000, it's still doubling, and we want to know how increasing N degrades performance. This tells us.

A few more examples. Consider this algorithm:

```
read in N         1
read in M         1
read in P         1
add them          1
divide by 3       1
print the average 1
```

Each line is one action. Add 'em up and we have six. We can discard constant multipliers; 6=6*1, so O(6)=O(1). This algorithm is of order 1: it'll require the same time regardless of what values we give it.

`strlen` is another. If N is string length, we have

```
while not at end of null-terminated char array     N x
    add 1 to length                                  1
```

Many string functions are O(N), because they look at each of N characters in the array once.

Here's another:

```
do
    for each successive pair of elements in an array
        if they are in the wrong order
            swap them
while our last iteration of the do-while loop had a swap in it
```

This algorithm is a way to sort an array. Here's how it works. Consider an array of *Sesame Street* characters:

Kermit	Grover	Bert	Oscar	Piggy	Elmo

The first iteration of the do-while loop above does swaps, as needed, for each successive pair. Kermit should be swapped with Grover

Grover	Kermit	Bert	Oscar	Piggy	Elmo

and Bert:

Grover	Bert	Kermit	Oscar	Piggy	Elmo

We keep moving through the array till we get to the end, swapping any wrongly ordered pairs.

Grover	Bert	Kermit	Oscar	Elmo	Piggy

It's still not in order, but we made progress. Here's what we get after another pass through the array:

Bert	Grover	Kermit	Elmo	Oscar	Piggy

Another:

Bert	Grover	Elmo	Kermit	Oscar	Piggy

And another:

Bert	Elmo	Grover	Kermit	Oscar	Piggy

This algorithm is called "bubble sort" because elements gradually "bubble" their way to correct positions. (And "bogo-sort" by people who say it's evil because it's too slow. I don't know what they'd call the permutation method I had earlier, but it wouldn't be nice.)

How long will it take, in O notation? "If they are in the wrong order swap them" is O(1). We go through the entire array, making N-1 comparisons; so a pass through the array is O(N-1)=O(N). How many passes do we make? If the array is very disordered – say, if Bert's in the last slot – we'll need N-1 passes, since each pass moves Bert left at most one slot. $O(N(N-1)) = O(N^2-N) = O(N^2)$.

$O(N^2)$ is called "quadratic time"; O(N) is predictably called "linear time." O(1) is "constant time." We try to avoid $O(2^N)$, "exponential time."

Online Extra To measure *actual* times ..."Measuring your code to the millisecond": find it in the YouTube channel "Programming the Lazy Way," or `https://www.youtube.com/watch?v=u_zyO7LgXog`.

or

Timing things in C++ at the Apress blog: `https://www.apress.com/us/blog/all-blog-posts/timing-things-in-c-plus-plus/17405398`.

EXERCISES

1. What is the time in O notation for the function in Example 10-6, which returns the smallest number in an array?
2. ...for a function to determine if a word is a palindrome?
3. ...for a function to print all the elements in an N × N grid?
4. Write a function `intersection` that, given two arrays, finds all those elements in common and puts them in a new array. What is the time requirement, in O notation?
5. Write bubble sort and verify that it works.

6. Write a program that finds all primes up to some limit using the Sieve of Eratosthenes: You go thru and eliminate numbers divisible by 2 except 2. Then by all divisible by 3 except 3. And so on.

   What is the time requirement, in O notation?

7. Time bubble sort above, on different (large) sizes of array, using the method from the Online Extra links above. Does it match what the O notation predicted? Expect a lot of random variation in the times you measure.

CHAPTER 19

Templates, Including vector

Would I write a function or class that takes ints and another just like it except it takes strings and another except it takes doubles? That doesn't sound lazy! This chapter enables us to write it *once*, using templates.

Function Templates

Recall this function for swapping ints, renamed here for convenience, from Chapter 8:

```
void mySwap(int& arg1, int& arg2) noexcept[1]
{
      int temp = arg2; arg2 = arg1; arg1 = temp;
}
```

That's fine for int, but what if I want doubles? Heffalumps? Or a mix? Here's the fix so I can swap int with int, int with double, heffalumps with snarks, anything, as long as C++ knows how to use = with them:

```
template<typename SomeType, typename AnotherType>
void mySwap(SomeType& arg1, AnotherType& arg2) noexcept
{
      SomeType temp = arg2; arg2 = arg1; arg1 = temp;
}
```

[1] Throwing an exception in the middle of all these ='s could leave arg1 and arg2 in an inconsistent state, so ...I won't throw.

W. Briggs, *C++26 for Lazy Programmers*, https://doi.org/10.1007/979-8-8688-1859-2_19

This is a **function template**: not a function in itself, but instructions on how to *make* a function once it knows what type we want.

The top line tells the compiler this will be a template and that we're calling the types of things to swap, SomeType and AnotherType. SomeType and AnotherType are each a sort of blank, to be filled in with an actual type when we decide on it. Example 19-1 illustrates its use.

Example 19-1. Using the mySwap function template

```
// Utterly useless program that uses a function template
//       -- from _C++26 for Lazy Programmers_

template<typename T, typename U> // T and U are shorter and less clunky than
                                 //   SomeType and AnotherType, so we'll
                                 //   follow convention and use them
void mySwap(T& arg1, U& arg2) noexcept
{
    T temp = arg2; arg2 = arg1; arg1 = temp;
}

int main()
{
    int    i = 10  , j = 20  ;
    double m =  0.5, n =  1.5;

    mySwap(i, j);
    mySwap(m, n);
    mySwap(i, n); // You'll get a warning abt loss of data
                  //   from mixing ints and doubles, but it'll work

    return 0;
}
```

The compiler doesn't create *any* version of mySwap until it gets to the line mySwap(i, j);. Then it notes that i and j are ints, so it substitutes int for T and U in the template and creates a mySwap function that takes two ints.

On the next line it generates a mySwap for double; after that, one that takes an int and a double.

I put the function template *above* main. If the compiler can't see it before it's used, it won't know *how* to create the function – it won't have read the instructions yet. So the function template goes at the beginning of the program or in a `.h` file.

To summarize how to convert a function into a function template:

1. **Put** `template<typename` *this*, `typename` *that*...`>` **in front.**
2. **Change the type to be replaced to T or const T& (or U/const U& or what have you).** If it's in a place where C++ would implicitly call something's copy constructor – a return type or parameter without an `&` – `const T&` will prevent needless copying.
3. **Put the new function template where you had its declaration.**

Exercises are after the next section, "Concepts (optional)."

Antibugging

- **Linking, the compiler says it can't find the function, but you can see it later in the program or in another `.cpp` file.** See step 3 above.

Here are other possible problems:

- **Converting int to `T/const T&` when you shouldn't.** Say I have this code for searching an `int` array

```
void repeatPrint(int thing, int howMany)
{
    for (int i = 0; i < howMany; ++i)
        std::cout << thing << ' ';
}
```

and convert it to

```
template<typename T>
void repeatPrint(const T& thing, const T& howMany)//bad idea!
{
    for (int i = 0; i < howMany; ++i)
        std::cout << thing << ' ';
}
```

If it's an array of strings, it doesn't make sense for howMany to be const string&! It should remain an int.

- **Using an operator that doesn't work correctly for type T.** Maybe you send to mySwap something that doesn't have = defined; or = doesn't do what you wanted (say T is a pointer, and you wanted to copy contents rather than do pointer assignment). The usual fix is to use templates only with things that make sense. The next section can help.
- **Sometimes the compiler just can't figure out what template arguments you wanted.** If that happens, specify:

```
mySwap<int>(i, j);
```

Concepts (optional)

Consider this function to tell if a number is even:

```
bool isEven(int n) { return n % 2 == 0; }
```

Fine, but maybe I want to do this on any-size int type, from unsigned char (which is really an int too) to long long int. No problem – I'll use a template:

```
template<typename T> bool isEven(T n) { return n % 2 == 0; }
```

Thing is, now we can use it on any type! At least it won't compile if I give it something crazy like std::string or SSDL_Image. It *will* compile if we give it a float, though it makes no sense to ask if a float is even. So I would like to restrict it to work only with integer-like types. For anything else, it'll say no:

```
#include <concepts>
...
template<std::integral T> bool isEven(T n) { return n % 2 == 0; }
```

std::integral is a **concept** we use to constrain what T can be. If it's not something C++'s creators think should be able to do integer-like things, the compiler will say something like "the associated constraints are not satisfied."

Now let's try something similar with mySwap. We don't know how to specify between the <>'s the relationship T and U have to have – swappability – so the code gets a little more wordy (Example 19-2).

Example 19-2. Converting mySwap to use concepts

```
#include <concepts>
...
template<typename T, typename U>
    requires std::swappable_with<T&,U&>
void mySwap(T& t, U& u)
{
    T temp = t; t = u; u = temp;
}
```

The &'s between the <>'s are because we want to swap the things themselves, not copies, as the parameter list shows.

Table 19-1 lists some concepts you might use. For more see (at time of writing) en.cppreference.com/w/cpp/concepts.

Table 19-1. *Common <concepts> for use with templates. All are in the std:: namespace*

default_initializable<T>	T can be constructed without arguments.
movable<T>	T can be moved (as with &&) and swapped.
copyable<T>	...and has a copy constructor and a non-move = operator.
destructible<T>	T can be destructed. If the creator of T didn't do something to stop it (~Mytype()=delete would do it), T is destructible.
assignable_from<T,U>	T=U is defined.
swappable_with<T,U> / swappable<T>	T can be swapped with U / with itself.
equality_comparable_with<T,U> / equality_comparable<T>	== and != are defined for T and U / for T.
totally_ordered<T>	...<, >, <=, and >= are defined too.
integral<T>	T is integral (bool, char, int, or variants; no enums).
floating_point<T>	T is some floating-point type.

One more example before going on – the minimum function from Chapter 10:

```
double minimum(std::span<const double> sp);
```

Recall that it returns `double`, so it must make a copy; it uses = to assign things to its result; and it uses < to compare elements. So when I turn it into a template, if I want to use concepts, I should use those that relate to copying and comparing. Example 19-3 shows my result.

Example 19-3. A very versatile `minimum` function, using concepts

```
template<typename T>
    requires std::copyable<T> && std::totally_ordered<T>
T minimum(std::span<const T> sp)
{
    if (sp.empty()) throw std::out_of_range("Empty span in minimum");

    T result = sp[0];
    for (const T& e : sp)
        if (e < result)
            result = e;

    return result;
}
```

Antibugging

You can print whether a concept applies to types, which is handy when you're having a hard time figuring why code with concepts isn't working (Example 19-4).

Example 19-4. Printing concepts as they relate to various types

```
cout << "Is int same as double?   " << same_as<int, double>
     << "\nIs B derived from A?   " << derived_from<B, A>
     << "\nIs char8_t integral?   " << integral<char8_t>
     << "\nIs double floating-pt? " << floating_point<double>
     << '\n';
```

That will print 0's for the concepts that don't apply and 1's for those that do.

Here is a potential problem using concepts:

- **What if you forget to put & on the type parameters?** You know full well your type parameters should work, but the compiler says no.

```
template<typename T, typename U>
    requires std::swappable_with<T, U>
void mySwap(T& t, U& u) noexcept ...
```

  It's right: T and U aren't swappable here ...but T& and U& are. Solution: use the &'s:

```
template<typename T, typename U>
    requires std::swappable_with<T&, U&>
void mySwap(T& t, U& u) noexcept ...
```

EXERCISES

These are exercises for function templates; use concepts if you chose to cover them.

1. Write your own version of `std::min`, which returns the lesser of two arguments.
2. Write a function template that'll take any floating-point number and return its most significant (leftmost) digit. For example, give it 678.9 and it'll return 6. You may want the `log10` function.
3. Make a function `sqr` to work for both integral and floating-point types. If you're doing concepts, here's a hint: you can use ||, not just &&, in the `requires` clause.

The Vector Class

Arrays are trouble. You can give an array an index of –2000 and it'll happily give you something dumb. If you declared an array to hold 50 elements but decide you want 51, too bad.

We can fix that by making a better-behaved array-like class called `Vector` (Example 19-5).

Example 19-5. vector.h, for a vector of ints

```
// Vector class:  a variable-length array
//       -- from _C++26 for Lazy Programmers_

#ifndef VECTOR_H
#define VECTOR_H

#include <iostream>

class Vector
{
public:
    Vector ()          { contents_ = new int[0]; howMany_ = 0; }
    Vector (const Vector& other)          { copy (other);      }
    Vector (Vector&& other) noexcept;                  // move ctor
    ~Vector() noexcept { if (contents_) delete [] contents_;   }

    Vector& operator=(const Vector& other);
    Vector& operator= (Vector&&      other) noexcept; // move =

    std::size_t size () const { return howMany_;     }
    const int*  data () const { return contents_;    }

    int  operator[](int index) const { return contents_[index]; }
    int& operator[](int index)       { return contents_[index]; }

    int  at(int index) const;
    int& at(int index);

    void push_back(int newElement);   // add newElement at the back
    void pop_back ();                 // left as an exercise
    int  back() const;                // left as an exercise

    void print(std::ostream&) const;  // left as an exercise
private:
    int*        contents_;
    std::size_t howMany_;

    void copy(const Vector& other);
};
```

```
bool operator==(const Vector& a, const Vector& b) noexcept;

inline
std::ostream& operator<<(std::ostream& out, const Vector& foo)
{
    foo.print(out); return out;
}
#endif //VECTOR_H
```

It's a lot like String, only of course I can't use strcpy and others. Pay special attention to push_back in Example 19-6.

Example 19-6. vector.cpp

```
// Vector class:  a variable-length array of ints
//       -- from _C++26 for Lazy Programmers_

#include <stdexcept>     // for std::out_of_range (below)
#include "vector.h"

Vector::Vector(Vector&& other) noexcept // move ctor
{
    contents_ = other.contents_; howMany_ = other.howMany_;
    other.contents_ = nullptr;
}

Vector& Vector::operator=(Vector&& other) noexcept // move =
{
    if (contents_) delete[] contents_;
    contents_ = other.contents_; howMany_ = other.howMany_;
    other.contents_ = nullptr;
    return *this;
}

Vector& Vector::operator=(const Vector& other)
{
    if (this == &other) return *this;
                           // don't assign to self -- you'll trash contents
```

```
    if (contents_) delete[] contents_; copy(other);
    return *this;
}

//...

int  Vector::at(int index) const
{
    if (index >= size())
        throw std::out_of_range("Out of range in Vector::operator[]");²
    else return contents_[index];
}

int& Vector::at(int index)
{
    if (index >= size())
        throw std::out_of_range("Out of range in Vector::operator[]");
    else return contents_[index];
}

// add newElement at the back
void Vector::push_back(int newElement)
{
    int* newContents = new int[howMany_ + 1]; //make room for 1 more...

    for (unsigned int i = 0; i < size(); ++i)
                                    //copy old elements to new array...
        newContents[i] = contents_[i];

    newContents[howMany_] = newElement;       // add the new element...

    ++howMany_;                               // remember we have 1 more...

    delete[] contents_;                       // throw out old contents_
    contents_ = newContents;                  //  and keep new version
}
```

[2] In Chapter 18, I declared my own OutOfRange exception. But since the standard library provides one, it's OK to use theirs. Here's how.

```
// Sort of like String::copy from Chapter 17, but without strcpy
void Vector::copy(const Vector& other)
{
    // set howMany to other's size; allocate that much memory
    contents_ = new int[howMany_ = other.size()];

    // then copy the elements over
    for (unsigned int i = 0; i < size(); ++i)
        contents_[i] = other[i];
}
```

Example 19-7 shows how you might use it.

Example 19-7. Using Vector

```
// Example with a Vector of int
//        -- from _C++26 for Lazy Programmers_

#include <iostream>
#include <cassert>
#include "vector.h"

using namespace std;

int main()
{
    Vector V;

    for (int i = 1; i < 11; ++i) V.push_back(i);

    cout << "Can you count to 10?  The Count will be so proud!\n";

    try
    {
        for (unsigned int i = 0; i < V.size(); ++i) cout << V.at(i) << ' ';
        cout << '\n';
    }
    catch (const std::out_of_range& e)
```

```
    {
        cout << "This shouldn't happen: " << e.what() << ".\n";
        //what() returns whatever message we gave the constructor
        //   when we created the out_of_range exception
    }

    return 0;
}
```

So it's safe, throwing an exception if we give a bad index, and we can add as many elements as we want.

Efficiency and O Notation

In Chapter 22 we'll have another container for elements, the "linked list." So that we can decide which container we want for this or that task - and for practice with O notation - let's consider the efficiency (time requirements) of `Vector`'s member functions.

You might take time to decide for yourself what these functions will be in O notation.

OK, you're back. `Vector::copy`, used by `operator=` and the copy constructor, has a loop in it that iterates `size()` times. `push_back` also has such a loop. Others just have some `if` statements. Table 19-2 shows the efficiencies of some functions, given N as the current size.

Table 19-2. *Time required for some* `Vector` *functions*

Function	Efficiency (Time Requirement)
`size`	O(1)
`operator[]`	O(1)
`operator=`	O(N)
copy constructor	O(N)
`push_back`	O(N)

The bottom line: If you want to do something to the whole vector, the time required is O(N) – no big surprise. If you're just doing something with one element, the time required is O(1) – *except* `push_back`. That takes O(N) time, because you have to copy the old `contents_` into a new chunk of memory.

Oh, well. It's better than not having the flexibility. And there may be ways to make it quicker (see Exercise 3).

EXERCISES

In the following, if you didn't do the "Efficiency and O Notation" subsection of the previous chapter, just skip the O notation question in each.

1. Write `back`, which returns the last element added. What is its time requirement, in O notation?
2. Write `pop_back`. What is its time requirement, in O notation? If it's not O(1), you're doing too much work!
3. (Harder) Rewrite `push_back` so that instead of reallocating every time you add a new element, it allocates enough for *ten* new elements – and only has to do this every tenth time. Does it change the time cost, in O notation? Do you think it's worth doing? Can you think of a better way?
4. (Uses move semantics) Write the move constructor and move = for `Vector`, checking against my solution in the book source code if you like. How long do they take in O notation?
5. Write a class `Queue`. It's like `Vector` except that you take items off the *opposite* end from where you add them. So they come out in the same order they go in.

   So we'll want a pop_*front* (not `pop_back`) and a `front` function to return what's next.

   What is the time for `front` and `pop_front` in O notation?
6. (Uses move semantics) Write the move constructor and move = for `Queue`, above. How long do they take in O notation?

Making Vector a Template

Am I going to write a brand-new class depending on whether I want a vector of integers, strings, or 1960s rock musicians? I'm a lazy programmer. There's no *way* I'll do that.

Enter the **class template**: essentially a set of instructions for making a class, just as a function template is instructions for making a function.

There's a short list of changes needed to convert `Vector` to be one and thus store different types:

1. **Change any** `Vector` **declaration to say what it's a** `Vector` **of.** In Example 19-8, `Vector` becomes `Vector<int>`. This is the *only* change we make in that file to use the new template class.

Example 19-8. Using a class template for `Vector`

```
// Example with a Vector of int
//        -- from _C++26 for Lazy Programmers_

#include <iostream>
#include <cassert>
#include "vector.h"

using namespace std;

int main()
{
    Vector<int> V;
    // Step #1: change declaration to say what it's a Vector of

    for (int i = 1; i < 11; ++i) V.push_back(i);

    cout << "Can you count to 10?  The Count will be so proud!\n";

    for (unsigned int i = 0; i < V.size(); ++i) cout << V[i] << ' ';
    cout << '\n';

    return 0;
}
```

2. **Put the contents of** `vector.cpp` **into** `vector.h`**; erase** `vector.cpp`. It's the same as in the "Function Templates" section: until you *call* `push_back`, the version of `push_back` that works with `ints` doesn't exist. On that line, the compiler needs to know how to create the function, which means it needs the body of the function template. So the body has to be in the `.h` file.

3. **Put** `template<typename T>` **in front of**

   a. **The class definition**

   b. **Each function body** that's outside the class definition

4. **Replace** `int` **with** `T` **or** `const T&` **where appropriate**, as with function templates.

5. **Replace** `Vector` **with** `Vector<T>`

   a. **When it's part of** `Vector::`,

   b. **In return types**, as in

   ```
   Vector<T>&   Vector<T>::operator=(const Vector& other);
   ```

   c. **Any time you're not in the class**, as in

   ```
   Vector<T> operator==(const Vector<T>& a,
                        const Vector<T>& b) noexcept;
                   // not a member. Operator << isn't either
   ```

   If you put `Vector<T>` in too many places, no one will shoot you. But it doesn't work for constructor names.

Let's see what that gives us (Example 19-9).

Example 19-9. Changing `Vector` to a class template. With Example 19-7, it's in the source code as `07-08-vectorTemplate`.

```
// Vector class:  a variable-length array
//      -- from _C++26 for Lazy Programmers_

#ifndef VECTOR_H
#define VECTOR_H
```

```
template<typename T>            // Step #3 (a): add template<typename T>
class Vector
{
public:
    class OutOfRange {};    // exception, for [] operators

    Vector ()   { contents_ = new T[0]; howMany_ = 0; }// #4: int -> T
    Vector (const Vector& other) { copy (other);        }
    Vector (Vector&& other) noexcept;  // move ctor
    ~Vector()   { if (contents_) delete [] contents_; }

    Vector& operator=(const Vector& other);
    Vector& operator=(Vector&& other) noexcept; // move =

    std::size_t size() const { return howMany_;  }
    const T* data() const { return contents_; } // #4: int -> const T&

    const T& operator[](int index) const;       // #4: int -> const T&
          T& operator[](int index);             // #4: int& -> T&

    const T& at(int index) const;               // #4: int -> const T&
          T& at(int index);                     // #4: int -> T&

    void push_back(const T& newElement);        // #4: int -> const T&
    void pop_back();
    const T& back() const;                      // #4: int -> const T&

    void print(std::ostream&) const;
private:
    T*          contents_;                      // #4: int -> T
    std::size_t howMany_;

    void copy(const Vector& other);
};

// #2: move contents of vector.cpp into vector.h
//    (still contained in #ifndef)
```

```
template<typename T>                        // #3b: add template<typename T>
Vector<T>& Vector<T>::operator=(const Vector& other)
                                            // #5a: Vector:: -> Vector<T>::
                                            // #5b: Vector&  -> Vector<T>&
{
    if (this == &other) return *this;
                            // don't assign to self -- you'll trash contents
    if (contents_) delete[] contents_; copy(other);
    return *this;
}

template<typename T>                         // #3b: add template<typename T>
bool operator==(const Vector<T>& a, const Vector<T>& b) noexcept ...
                          // #5c: Vector -> Vector<T> when not in the class

...

#endif //VECTOR_H
```

Now you can use that Vector with base types of your choosing. In Example 19-10 we use it with strings and more.

Example 19-10. Using the new Vector template from Example 19-9 with strings and more. In the source code as 10-vectorTemplate

```
// Example with a Vector of strings and more
//      -- from _C++26 for Lazy Programmers_

#include <iostream>
#include <cassert>
#include <string>
#include "vector.h"

using namespace std;

int main()
{
    // Setting up the band...
    Vector<string> FabFour;
    string names[] = { "John","Paul","George","Ringo" };
```

```
    constexpr int NUM_BEATLES = 4;

    for (int i = 0; i < NUM_BEATLES; ++i) FabFour.push_back(names[i]);

    // Printing them out...
    cout << "The Fab Four: ";
    for (int i = 0; i < NUM_BEATLES; ++i) cout << FabFour[i] << ' ';
    cout << endl;

    // Ensuring other base types compile...
    Vector<int> V; for (int i = 0; i < 10; ++i) V.push_back(i);
    Vector<Vector<double>> G1, G2; assert(G1 == G2);

    return 0;
}
```

pair

Here's another useful template class (struct, technically):

```
template<typename T, typename U> struct pair { T first; U second; };
```

It's used in exercises below and in later chapters and is generally too useful to ignore. It also has member functions you'd expect like constructors, =, ==, etc.

Antibugging

- **The compiler says you didn't write some member function of your class template, and you know you did.** Is everything moved into the .h file?
- **The compiler says, at your variable declaration, that the class template isn't a type.** Maybe you left off <yourBaseType>.

EXERCISES

There are further relevant exercises at the end of the chapter; they can be used with or without concepts. Please see that section to try them, especially the one involving queues.

1. Convert `Vector`'s `push_back`, `copy`, and `operator=` (also move functions if you know those) to work with `Vector` as a template. My solutions are in the book's source code.
2. Create your own version of `pair`.
3. Adapt the `Point2D` class from Chapter 17's exercises to be a class template. You can now have `Point2D`s made from `double`s or `int`s or `float`s or any other reasonable type.

Making Your Own Concepts (optional)

Let's now try applying concepts to `Vector`. `Vector`'s base type T uses = (in `push_back`). So T will need to be `assignable_from`. And since copy creates an array of T, T needs a default constructor, that is, it must be `default_initializable`. Finally, we call `delete []` on the array, so T must be `destructible`.

We can combine concepts in the `requires` clause using &&, ||, or `!`, in any combination. In our case we just need &&:

```
template<typename T>
    requires std::assignable_from<T&, T> && std::destructible<T> &&
             std::default_initializable<T>
class Vector ...
```

Typing all that is going to get old fast. Maybe we could name it and refer to it as needed (Example 19-11).

Example 19-11. Creating your own concept from existing ones

```
template<typename T>
    concept VectorElement = std::assignable_from<T&, T> &&
                            std::destructible<T> &&
                            std::default_initializable<T>;

template<VectorElement T>
class Vector ...

template<VectorElement T>
void Vector<T>::pop_back();
...
```

If the concept you want doesn't exist, you can make your own. Suppose you want to ensure the type is printable. Put the things you want doable in {}'s after `requires` – in this case, `{ out << t; }`, where `out` is of type `ostream` – after a parameter list that defines whatever you refer to.

Example 19-12. Creating your own concept from scratch, using it in conjunction with others

```
template<typename T>
concept Printable = requires(std::ostream& out, const T& t)
{
    out << t; //So "Printable" now means "you can send it to ostream with <<"
};

template<VectorElement T>
class Vector
{
public:
    ...
    void print(std::ostream&) const requires Printable<T>;³
    ...
};
```

[3] I could give a detailed explanation of when the requires clause comes after the function top line and when before, but the simplest answer is "do what the compiler lets you."

```
...

template<VectorElement T>
void Vector<T>::print(std::ostream& out) const requires Printable<T>...
```

Now the compiler will check, when you create a Vector, that T has the functions (like =) that Vector's functions need.

Is it worth the trouble? The C++ community seems excited about this. You can decide for yourself.

Non-type Template Arguments

You can make a template argument be a value as well.

Example 19-13. A class template that allows you to specify an integer

```
template<typename T, std::size_t N>
class Array
{
public:
    Array() {}
    Array(const Array& a)
    {
        for (int i = 0; i < N; ++i) contents_[i] = a[i];
    }

    std::size_t size() const { return N; }
    ...
private:
    T contents_[N];
};
#endif
```

```
int main ()
{
    Array<std::string, 4> fourNames;
    //...
    return 0;
}
```

The `std::array` template from `#include<array>` this approximates is recommended when you don't want dynamic allocation, over the C-style arrays we got in Chapter 10. But I almost always use a vector instead.

EXERCISES

In the exercises, use concepts if you covered them – it's good either way.

1. Convert class `Queue`, from the previous exercises, to be a template.
2. Using the `Queue` class template from the previous section, make a subclass `PriorityQueue`, in which each item has an associated priority. When you enqueue a new item, it goes ahead of all those in the `Queue` that have lower priority. You'll want `pair`.
3. (For concepts) Update operator== for Vector to use appropriate concepts.
4. Make a game for training bomb disposal techs. Each Bomb contains the number of turns before it goes off, randomly initialized. You start with a Table full of Bombs. (Table and Bomb should be classes; use templates appropriately.) Each turn you dispose of a Bomb, and a new one takes its place. If any Bomb gets down to 0, everything goes blooey. If you get to some number of turns before that happens, you win, and you get another game with a bigger Table.
5. Write a class `ModularInt` that is an integer, but loops around if it reaches its limit with addition. If the limit is 5, then 3+3 = 2 (i.e., 6 % 5). The limit, or modulus, is a template parameter.
6. Write a function template that takes an array and gets from the user each element of that array. Here's the cool part: it asks for exactly the right number of elements. Here's how:

```
template<typename T, int SIZE>
...
void inputArray(T (&myArray)[SIZE])
```

This way, the function knows not just the type of the array, but its size. (The & is there to preserve the size information of the array till the function template is made.)[4]

It'll only work on static arrays – not dynamic arrays or those passed in as parameters.

(This is how `istream& operator>>` can guarantee it won't read more input than the `char` array it's given can store.)

7. (Hard) Make a class template `BigInteger` that acts as an integer of arbitrary size. Let the template parameter be the number of bytes (`unsigned chars`) or digits you want in your `BigInteger`. Support all reasonable arithmetic operators and stream I/O.

#include <vector>

As you may have figured out, C++ already has a `std::vector` class template in `#include <vector>`. It isn't as cool as ours, because it lacks the `print` function given it in Exercise 2 above, but we can't have everything.[5]

Unlike `Vector`, `std::vector` can be automatically converted to a `std::span` for parameter passing, like Chapter 10's C-style arrays. So can `std::array`. So `span`s are still useful even with these new containers.

`std::swap` and `std::pair` are also built-in, in `#include <utility>`.

[4] Remember how when you pass an array to a function, it pays no attention to its size? Even if you write it thus - `void f (int a[SIZE])` - it means the same as `void f (int* a)`.

Using the & here means I'm not copying it to a pointer; I'm really bringing in an array of that size, as is, into the function. This enables the template mechanism to determine how to match this template to the array argument, thus identifying `SIZE` so we can use it in the function.

[5] Actually STL has good reason for not having a `print` function: how do you want it delimited? Commas? Spaces? Do you want []'s around it, <>'s, ()'s? STL's creators could work around it, and they have; we'll see how in Chapter 23.

CHAPTER 20

Inheritance

The purpose of this chapter is to enable us to reuse code between similar classes.

The Basics of Inheritance

Consider the class in Example 20-1: a Shape, which can be drawn, can calculate its area, things like that. (It would have made sense to have that in Chapter 1, but we didn't know classes yet.)

Example 20-1. A Shape class. Find it in the source code in Ch20, as 1-2-Shapes

```
// Shape class, for use with the SSDL library
//      -- from _C++26 for Lazy Programmers_

#ifndef SHAPE_H
#define SHAPE_H

#include <string>
#include "SSDL.h"
#include "point2d.h"

class Shape
{
public:
    Shape(const Point2D& p = {}, const SSDL_Color& c = WHITE)
       : location_(p), color_(c)
    {
    }
    Shape(const Shape& other) : Shape(other.location_, other.color_) {}

    Shape& operator=(const Shape& other);
```


W. Briggs, *C++26 for Lazy Programmers*, https://doi.org/10.1007/979-8-8688-1859-2_20

```
    // Color
    void  setColor(const SSDL_Color& c) { color_ = c;     }
    const SSDL_Color& color() const     { return color_; }

    // Access functions
    const Point2D&     location()    const { return location_;     }

    // Drawing
    void   draw() const;

    // Moving
    void moveTo(const Point2D& p) { location_ = p; }
    void moveBy(int deltaX, int deltaY)
    {
       moveTo({ location_.x_ + deltaX, location_.y_ + deltaY });
    }
private:
    Point2D     location_;
    SSDL_Color  color_;
};
#endif //SHAPE_H
```

Since I'm using the Point2D class, I need to copy `point2d.h` and `point2d.cpp` from the earlier chapter into my new project's folder. With g++ I'm done at that point; in Visual Studio, I right-click the project, say Add ➤ Existing Item, and add both.

Here is a sample declaration of a Shape:

```
Shape favoriteShape ({0, 0}, RED);
```

But of course it's no fun until we have particular *types* of shapes: `Circles`, `Rectangles`, whatever.

It would be redundant to write a whole new class for `Circle`, repeating those things also in Shape such as `location_`, `color_`, and `moveTo`. So instead we'll make `Circle` a **subclass** (or **derived class**, or **child class**) of Shape, as shown in Example 20-2. This is **inheritance**.

We call Shape now a **superclass**, **base class**, or **parent class** of `Circle`.

Example 20-2. Class `Circle`

```
// Circle class, for use with the SSDL library
//    -- from _C++26 for Lazy Programmers_

#ifndef CIRCLE_H
#define CIRCLE_H

#include "shape.h"

class Circle : public Shape
{
public:
    Circle(const Point2D& p={}, int theRadius=0, const SSDL_Color& c=WHITE);
    Circle(const Circle& other);
    Circle& operator=(const Circle& other);

    int radius() const { return radius_; }

    void draw()  const
    {
        SSDL_SetRenderDrawColor(color());
        SSDL_RenderDrawCircle(location().x_, location().y_, radius());
    }
private:
    int radius_;
};
#endif //CIRCLE_H
```

`class Circle: public Shape` – don't worry about the word `public` yet – means `Circle` is a subclass of `Shape` and thus has everything a `Shape` does (Figure 20-1). I don't have to (and shouldn't) write in the class definition that `Circle` has a `location_`, `color_`, or the various `Shape` functions: it does, because it's a `Shape`, and `Shape`s have those things. So this code will work:

```
Circle myCircle({ 50, 50 }, 25, RED);

                              // setColor(), color() are inherited from Shape
myCircle.setColor (BLUE);  // make it BLUE
                              // recall sout is SSDL's equivalent of std::cout
sout << "The circle's color is now " << myCircle.color() << ".\n";
```

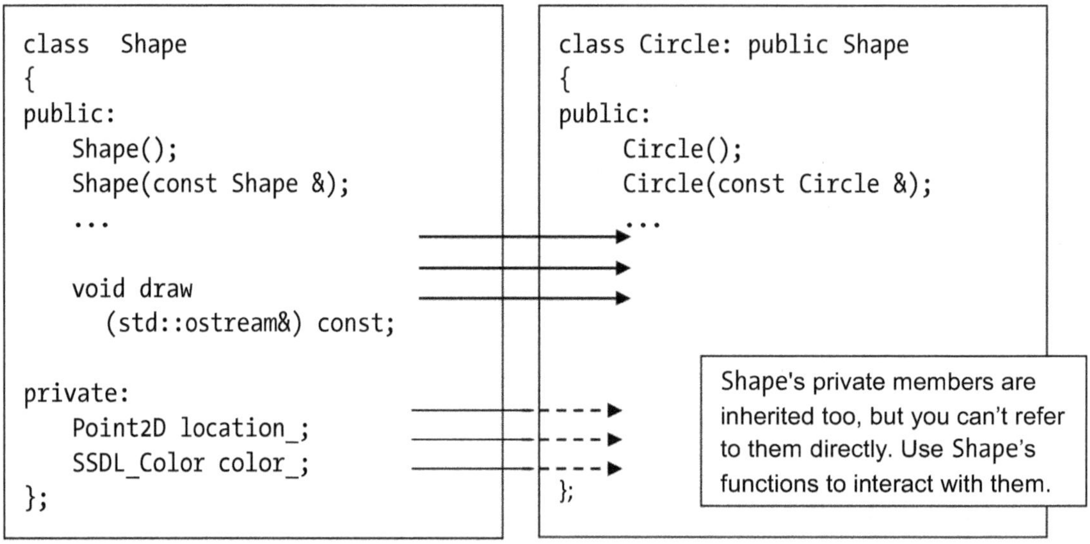

```
class  Shape                          class Circle: public Shape
{                                     {
public:                               public:
   Shape();                               Circle();
   Shape(const Shape &);                  Circle(const Circle &);
   ...                          ------>   ...
                                ------>
   void draw                    ------>
     (std::ostream&) const;

private:                        - - - >
   Point2D location_;           - - - >
   SSDL_Color color_;           - - - >
};                                    };
```

Shape's private members are inherited too, but you can't refer to them directly. Use Shape's functions to interact with them.

Figure 20-1. *How inheritance works*

Circle doesn't rewrite those functions – it just uses them. What you can do with a Shape you can do with a Circle – because a Circle *is* a Shape.

The same will also be true of other subclasses of Shape we may choose to make: Triangles, Rectangles, Text chunks, whatever (Figure 20-2). We'll save time by not rewriting location_, moveBy, moveAt, etc., in all of them. (There turn out to be other advantages, which we'll get to.)

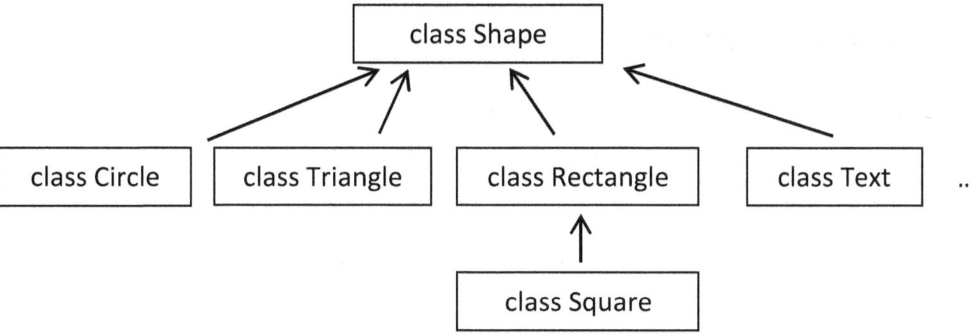

Figure 20-2. *Shape and some subclasses we may give it*

Constructors and Destructors, for Inheritance and Member Variables

We'll surely want to call Shape's constructor when we write `Circle`'s. No problem - we'll use the same syntax we use to initialize data members:

```
Circle (const Point2D& p, int theRadius, const SSDL_Color& c)
    : Shape (p, c), radius_ (theRadius)
{
}
```

The constructor does things in this order:

- The constructors after the ":" are called, parent class constructor first (even if you put it later) and then data members, in the order they're declared in the class.
- Whatever's between the {}'s gets done (in this case, nothing).

If you don't say what parent constructor to call, it will call the default.

When a `Circle` goes out of scope, its destructor (if any) is called first and then its parent's. (And then its grandparent's and so on.) You won't need to think about this - it's automatic.

If you don't write a destructor, you get the default destructor, which tells the parent class and all data members to call their destructors if they have them. Again, it's automatic - you won't have to remember.

Extra: Defaulted and Deleted Member Functions

If I'd written Shape::operator= above, it might look like this:

```
Shape& operator=(const Shape& other)
{
    location_ = other.location_; color_ = other.color_;
    return *this;
}
```

C++ can save us some work by writing that for us. As long as all it has to do is apply = to all the members, it'll build a default operator= for me if I say this:

```
Shape& operator=(const Shape& other) = default;
```

If I say `Circle& operator=(const Circle& other) = default`, Circle's = will call Shape::operator= and then copy its member radius_, which is exactly what I'd want.

= default also can replace the body for these member functions:

- **Copy constructors**: It calls the copy constructor for any parent class and all members that have copy constructors, or = for basic types like int.
- **Default constructors**: It calls all available default constructors for parents and parts. Basic types don't have default constructors and won't get initialized, so be wary of that.[1]
- **Move constructors and move assignment**: Everything gets moved as you'd expect.
- ==: Returns true if all the parts, and parent if any, are equal.
- <=>: Compares parent, then all the parts, in order. I never use this.

[1] Or assign to them in the class definition where they're declared, as in Chapter 11:
`struct Point2D { int x_= 0, y_= 0; }`

It *won't* work for `String`, because it wouldn't `copy()` over the `char*` `contents_` but use `=`, which we wrote `String` to get away from.

We can also tell C++ "I'm not writing this function and don't you do it either," by adding `=delete` or `=delete("Reason to delete")`,[2] as in

```
EntireGameOfMinecraft&
  EntireGameOfMinecraft::operator=(const EntireGameOfMinecraft&)
           = delete("We only need to run one game at a time!");
```

We'll see more examples of both deleting and defaulting functions throughout this chapter.

EXERCISES

For these exercises, be sure that **data members are private** (of course!), and just for now, **there are no access functions**. This is to ensure that the subclass only accesses its own data, not its parent's. For example, to print, the subclass should call its parent's print function and then print its own data members.

1. An Employee has a name and a salary; a Manager has these things, plus a function `micromanage (const Employee&)` that prints a message `"<employee name>, you're doing it wrong!"`. Write and test them.

	OD	OS
Sphere	-3.00	-2.00
Additional	2.50	2.50
Cylinder	+0.25	+0.50
Axis	150°	70°

Figure 20-3. *An eyeglasses prescription*

[2] Leave out the reason to delete if you don't want one or if your compiler isn't that C++26 compliant yet.

2. An eyeglasses prescription lists (as in Figure 20-3): **sphere** or power, **additional** correction for bifocals, and stuff for astigmatism (**cylinder**, **axis**). The two eyes are called "OD" and "OS" not "left" and "right," because what's cooler than calling your eyeballs weird Latin abbreviations?

   Write and test a class to contain, and neatly print, this information.

   And write and test a subclass for contact lenses to contain and print that plus a little more: **back curvature** and **diameter**, numbers to ensure the lens comfortably fits the eyeball.

3. A child in special education may have an "IEP," an Individual Education Plan, to spell out what special needs exist and how the school will address them. Write and test a class for a student record (name, whatever else looks relevant) and a subclass for the record of a student with an IEP. You can let the IEP be a single string.

Inheritance as a Concept

Subclasses are part of how we think outside the computer too. In biology, *animal* is a subclass of *organism*; *mammal* is a subclass of *animal*; *human* is a subclass of *mammal*; and *ubergeek* is a subclass of *human* (Figure 20-4). In each case the subclass has every characteristic of the superclass (or parent class, or base class), plus extra characteristics. An animal is an organism that can move; an ubergeek is a human who programs so well the gods themselves are impressed.

You aren't a *subclass* of human, because you aren't a class. You're an *instance* of human. (Apologies to my extraterrestrial readers.)

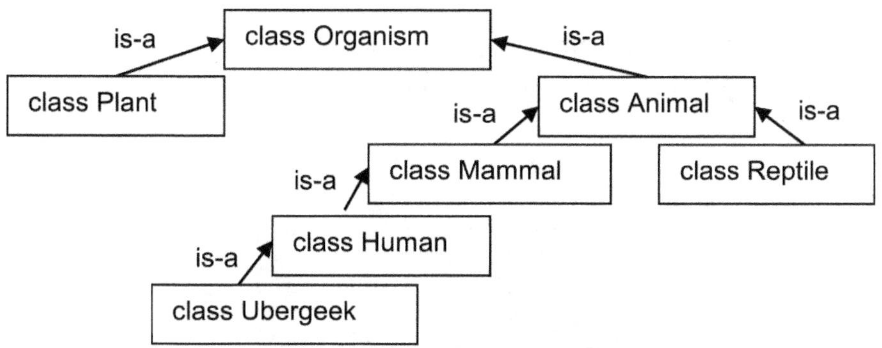

Figure 20-4. *A class hierarchy. An Ubergeek is a Human, which is a Mammal, and so on*

This is as good a point as any to mention a distinction commonly used in object-oriented thinking, between *is a* and *has a*. An Ubergeek *is a* Human (and a Mammal, and so on). An Ubergeek *has a* computer. So when God created the Ubergeek, His code must have looked something like this:

```
class Ubergeek: public Human // an Ubergeek is-a human
{
      ...
private:
      Computer myComputer_;  // an Ubergeek has-a computer
};
```

Things an Ubergeek *has* go in the private section. What an Ubergeek *is* goes on that first line.

Extra Your local philosophy professor will probably want to shoot me for saying this, but object-oriented programming is so very ...Platonic.

Figure 20-5. *Plato and Aristotle, the first two ever to have an argument about object-oriented programming. Sort of*

Plato, shown pointing up in Figure 20-5, considered classes ("ideals") to be what was ultimately real and the particular instances – the objects or variables in our vocabulary – to be imperfect examples of that ultimate reality. So `Human` is the real thing; you and I are just instances.

In radical materialism – as far from Plato as you can get – classes aren't real; only material objects are. Of course, since radical materialism isn't a material object, that might be a problem, but lazy philosophy, unlike lazy programming, is beyond the scope of this book.

Aristotle (pointing down in the picture) considered things themselves to be real and the classes to be their inherent natures. You're real, and Human is what you really are. He splits the difference.

However it works out in reality, C++ is Platonic: the class comes first. (You have to have the class definition before you can create a variable of that type.)

Classes for Card Games

People like to play cards on the computer, so let's make classes to help us build a variety of card games. Code reuse.

I'll provide class `Card` (Example 20-3) and give it things any class should have: default and copy constructors, `operator=`, access functions, and I/O. I also soup up the `Rank` and `Suit` enums from Chapter 10.

Example 20-3. The Card class (card.h). card.cpp and all subsequent examples through this chapter are in Ch20/3-thru-9-cardGames; Visual Studio users use appropriate projects in VS's Solution Manager; g++ users, go to the folder and type make

```
// Card class
//        -- from _C++26 for Lazy Programmers_

#ifndef CARD_H
#define CARD_H

#include <iostream>
#include <utility> //for std::to_underlying

// Rank and Suit:  integral parts of Card

enum class Rank  { ACE=1,  JACK=11, QUEEN, KING    }; // Card rank
enum class Suit  { HEARTS, DIAMONDS, CLUBS, SPADES }; // Card suit
enum class Color { BLACK,  RED                     }; // Card color

inline
Color toColor(Suit s)
{
    using enum Suit;
    using enum Color;

    if (s == HEARTS || s == DIAMONDS) return RED; else return BLACK;
}

// I/O on Rank and Suit
std::ostream& operator<<(std::ostream& out, Rank r);
std::ostream& operator<<(std::ostream& out, Suit s);
std::istream& operator>>(std::istream& in, Rank& r);
std::istream& operator>>(std::istream& in, Suit& s);

// Told you we'd find a way to do arithmetic with enums...
inline Rank operator+ (Rank  r, int t)
{
    return static_cast<Rank>(std::to_underlying(r) + t);
}
```

```
inline Rank operator+=(Rank& r, int t) { return r = r + t;         }
inline Rank operator++(Rank& r)        { r += 1; return r;         }
inline Rank operator++(Rank& r, int)
{
    Rank result = r; ++r; return result;
}

inline Suit operator++(Suit& s) { s = Suit(int(s) + 1); return s; }
inline Suit operator++(Suit& s, int)
{
    Suit result = s; ++s; return result;
}

class BadRankException {};  // used if a Rank is out of range
class BadSuitException {};  // used if a Suit is out of range
                            // ... you could also use a standard exception
                            // from #include <stdexcept>

// ...and class Card.

class Card
{
public:
    Card(Rank r = Rank(0), Suit s = Suit(0)) : rank_ (r), suit_ (s) {}
    Card            (const Card& other)      = default;
    Card& operator=(const Card& other)       = default;

    Suit  suit () const { return suit_;             }
    Rank  rank () const { return rank_;             }
    Color color() const { return toColor (suit()); }

    void print(std::ostream &out) const { out << rank() << suit(); }
    void read (std::istream &in );
private:
    Suit suit_;
    Rank rank_;
};
```

```
inline std::ostream& operator<<(std::ostream& out, const Card& foo)
{
    foo.print (out); return out;
}

inline std::istream& operator>>(std::istream& in,       Card& foo)
{
    foo.read  (in);  return in;
}

inline bool operator==(const Card& a, const Card& b) noexcept
{
    return a.suit() == b.suit() && a.rank() == b.rank();
}
#endif // CARD_H
```

An Inheritance Hierarchy

A few games we might create:

Freecell (Figure 20-6, left): At upper left are cells, each of which can store a single card; the upper right is foundations, each of which takes an ace, then a 2, and so on, in the same suit; at the bottom are piles, randomly dealt. You can take a card from a pile or add a card to a pile if it's down in alternating color. For example, you can move a black 10 onto that jack of diamonds if you have one free.

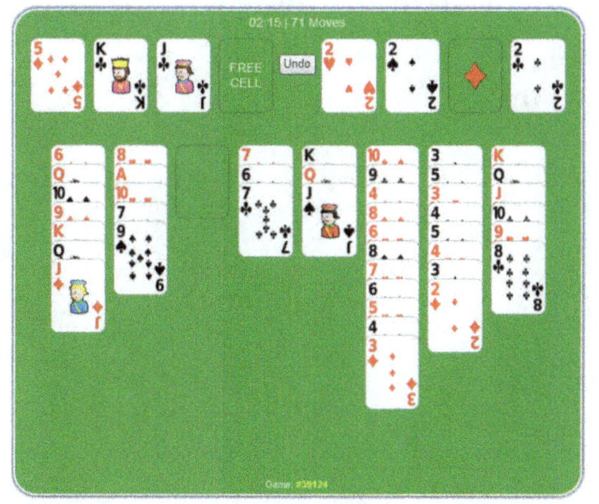

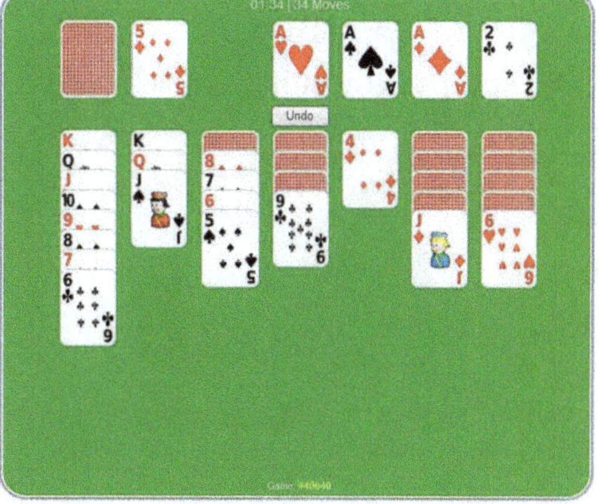

***Figure 20-6.** Two popular solitaire games: Freecell (left) and Klondike (right)*

Klondike (Figure 20-6, right): Like Freecell, it has foundations (top right); it also has a deck, a waste pile, and piles of its own type at the bottom.

Hearts, Spades, and other multiplayer games with a deck and hands.

Common card groupings include

- **Deck**: You can shuffle it and deal off the top.
- **Waste (discard pile)**: You can put a card on top or take one off.
- **Cell**: Like Waste, you can add to a cell or take from the top - but there can only be one card.
- **Foundation**: All one suit, starting with ace and going up.
- **Hand**: You can add to it and take out any card you want.
- **Freecell pile**: Add a card, down in alternating color; take a card off.
- **Klondike pile**: More complicated; left as an exercise.

These all have two things in common: contents and a size. Do any have more in common?

I'd say that a Cell *is a* Waste pile, because the way you interact with it is the same: add a card, and take one off the top. It just has a restriction on size.

Beyond that I'd say no. Foundation isn't a special case of Deck, nor is a Klondike pile a special case of a Waste pile. (Some of this may be a matter of opinion.) But they all have this in common: they're all groups of cards. So we can have a `CardGroup` class and inherit from it. What's a `CardGroup`? It would work to make it a vector of `Card`, so let's do that.

A `Hand` is a `CardGroup` with nothing added, so we'll make `Hand` an alias for `CardGroup`: `using Hand = CardGroup;`.

So I propose the inheritance hierarchy in Figure 20-7.

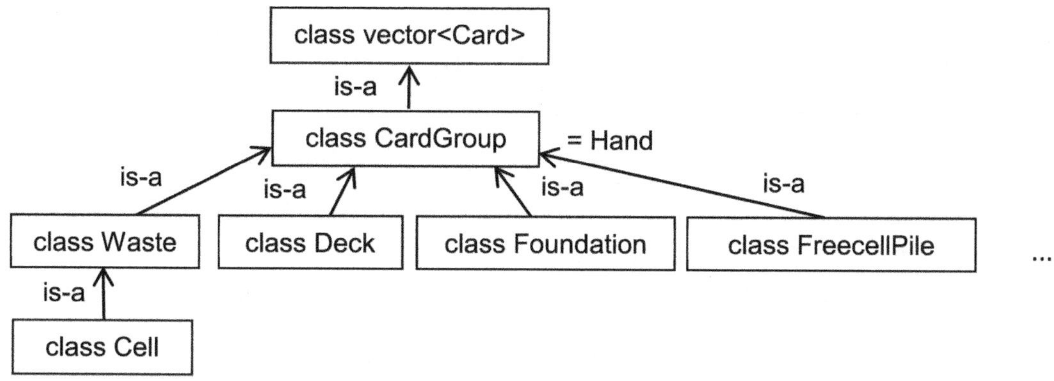

Figure 20-7. *A hierarchy of classes for groups of cards*

Example 20-4. `card_group.h`. Where are `empty` and the `[]` operators? Inherited from `vector<Card>`, so they needn't be written again here

```
// CardGroup class (for playing cards)
//        -- from _C++26 for Lazy Programmers_

#ifndef CARD_GROUP_H
#define CARD_GROUP_H

#include <vector>
#include "card.h"

class IllegalMove {};  // Exception class

class CardGroup: public std::vector<Card>
{
public:
    static constexpr int MAX_SIZE = 4 * 52;
                                     //4 decks should be enough for any game

    CardGroup()                          = default;
    CardGroup(const CardGroup& other) = default;

    CardGroup& operator=(const CardGroup& other)
```

```
    {
        std::vector<Card>::operator=(other); return *this;
        //Use vector<Card>'s version of =
    }

    Card remove   (int index);
    Card top() const { return vector<Card>::back(); }
    Card removeTop() { Card c = top(); vector<Card>::pop_back(); return c; }

    bool   full() const { return size() >= MAX_SIZE; }
                  //vectors don't get full -- but I decided CardGroups can

    bool   isLegalToAdd      (const Card& c) const { return !full (); }
    bool   isLegalToRemoveTop()              const { return !empty(); }

    // addCard does NOT check that it's legal to add a card.
    // We need it to create CardGroups during the deal.
    void addCard(const Card& c) { push_back(c); }

    // makes sure the addition of the card is legal, then adds it
    void addCardLegally(const Card& c)
    {
        if (isLegalToAdd(c)) addCard(c);   else throw IllegalMove();
    }
    Card removeTopLegally()
    {
        if (isLegalToRemoveTop()) return removeTop();
        else throw IllegalMove();
    }

    void print(std::ostream&) const;

private:
    //Nothing here -- it's all inherited from std::vector<Card>
};

inline
std::ostream& operator<<(std::ostream& out, const CardGroup& foo)
```

```
{
    foo.print(out); return out;
}

inline
bool operator== (const CardGroup& a, const CardGroup& b) noexcept
{
    //To use vector<Card>'s ==, cast a and b to be vector<Card>
    return static_cast<std::vector<Card>>(a) ==
                                 static_cast<std::vector<Card>>(b);
}

using Hand = CardGroup;
#endif // CARD_GROUP_H
```

`private` Inheritance

Consider the `Waste` class. We shouldn't allow random access of `Waste` through the `[]` operators; you can only look at the *top* card of a `Waste` pile.

To restrict access we change the type of inheritance:

```
class Waste: private CardGroup ...
```

This makes the `CardGroup`'s public members go in `Waste`'s private section (Figure 20-8).

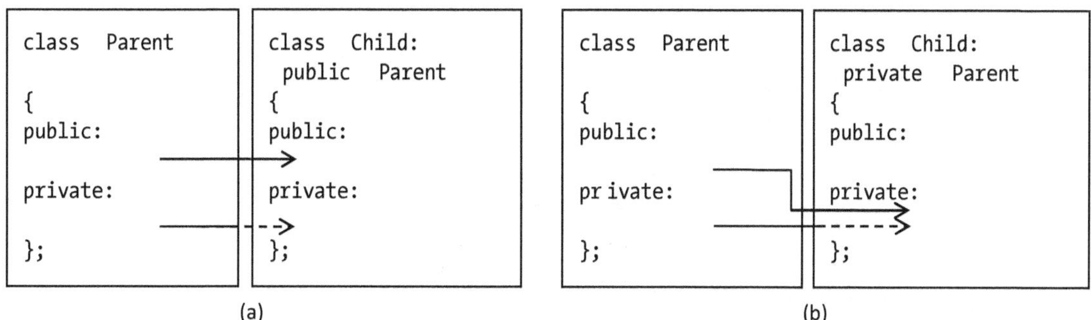

***Figure 20-8.** Public (a) and private (b) inheritance. Use private if there's any inherited public member that must be kept private in the child class*

operator[] is now private – good – but there are public members of CardGroup that we *want* Waste to make available to the outside: print, for example. We could make new public functions with the same names that just call the parent's functions, like this:

```
bool empty () const { return CardGroup::empty ();    }
```

But if I say

```
using CardGroup::empty;
```

in Waste's public section, it just drops that function there without me going into further detail, as in Example 20-5. A time saver.

When I say using CardGroup::CardGroup, it inherits *all* the constructors, unaltered. If that doesn't work for your inheriting class, you'll have to write your own, as we usually do.

Example 20-5. Class Waste, in waste.h, using private inheritance

```
// Waste class
//      -- from _C++26 for Lazy Programmers_

#ifndef WASTE_H
#define WASTE_H

#include "card_group.h"

class Waste: private CardGroup
{
public:
    using CardGroup::CardGroup;

    using CardGroup::operator=;

    using CardGroup::empty, CardGroup::full;
    using CardGroup::top;
    using CardGroup::removeTop;
    using CardGroup::addCardLegally;
    using CardGroup::print;
```

```
    bool isEqual(const Waste& other) const
    {
        return static_cast<CardGroup>(*this)
              == static_cast<CardGroup>(other);
    }
};

inline
std::ostream& operator<< (std::ostream& out, const Waste& foo)
{
    foo.print (out); return out;
}

inline
bool operator== (const Waste& a, const Waste& b) noexcept
{
    return a.isEqual(b);
}
#endif // WASTE_H
```

(Why have that function `isEqual`, called by `operator==` – why not just let `operator==` do the work? To get at `CardGroup`'s == requires casting to `CardGroup`, and as `Waste` inherits privately, its relationship to its parent is private and not visible to non-member functions. This is a hack to get around that problem.)

Hiding an Inherited Member Function

`Waste` has from `CardGroup` a member function `full`, true if the `Waste` has `MAX_SIZE` cards. A cell can only hold one card, so it needs to be full if there's even one. If you call `full` on a `Cell`, which will it use? The child's version "hides" the inherited version: if you call `full` on a `Cell`, you get `Cell`'s version.

But what if sometimes we still need the inherited version? In Example 20-6, `Cell`'s version of `addCardLegally` calls `Waste`'s version, specifying by preceding the call with `Waste::`.

Example 20-6. cell.h

```
// Cell class
//  -- from _C++26 for Lazy Programmers_

#ifndef CELL_H
#define CELL_H

#include "waste.h"

class Cell: public Waste
{
public:
  using Waste::Waste;
  Cell& operator=(const Cell& other) { Waste::operator=(other); return
  *this; }

  bool full() const { return !empty(); } //Can only have one card
in a Cell!

  // public inheritance, so all public members of Waste are here...

  void addCardLegally(const Card& card)
  {
     if (full()) throw IllegalMove(); // Cell must be empty
     else Waste::addCardLegally(card);
  }
};

inline
bool operator== (const Cell& a, const Cell& b) noexcept
{
   return static_cast<Waste>(a) == static_cast<Waste>(b);
}
#endif //CELL_H
```

A Game of Montana

Montana solitaire uses `Cell` and `Deck`, so it should be a good test of our hierarchy.

The rules: deal out all cards in a 4 × 13 grid of cells, remove the aces, and get a mess like in Figure 20-9.

Figure 20-9. *A game of Montana*

Your goal is to get four rows lined up from 2 to king, each with one suit.

The only valid move is to put a card into an empty cell. The card you put must follow whatever's on its left, in the same suit; for example, you can only follow 2♥ with 3♥. If it's in the leftmost column, you have to put a 2. A space following a king is unusable.

When you get stuck, redeal all the cards that aren't in sequences starting with 2 on the left and increasing in suit. You get four deals.

The code accompanying the text contains a working copy; the most important parts are shown in Examples 20-7 through 20-9.

Example 20-7. montana_main.cpp: a game of Montana

```
// A game of Montana solitaire
//     -- from _C++26 for Lazy Programmers_

#include <cstdio>        // for srand, rand
#include <ctime>         // for time
#include "io.h"          // for bool getAnswerYorN (const char[]);
#include "montana.h"

int main()
{
    srand(static_cast<unsigned int>(time(nullptr)));
                                                       // start rand# generator

    Montana montanaGame;

    do
        montanaGame.play();
    while (getYorNAnswer("Play again (Y/N)? "));

    return 0;
}
```

Example 20-8. montana.h

```
// class Montana, for a game of Montana solitaire
//  -- from _C++26 for Lazy Programmers_

#include <stdexcept> //for std::out_of_range
#include "grid_loc.h"
#include "cell.h"
#include "deck.h"

#ifndef MONTANA_H
#define MONTANA_H

class Montana
{
public:
    static constexpr int ROWS = 4, COLS  = 13;
```

```
    static constexpr int NUM_EMPTY_CELLS =  4;// 4 empty cells in grid
    static constexpr int MAX_TURNS       =  4;// 4 turns allowed

    Montana             ()                {}
    Montana             (const Montana&) = delete; //Nobody should ever
    Montana& operator=(const Montana&) = delete; //copy the whole game!

    void play();

private:
        // displaying
    void display            () const;

        // dealing and redealing
    void deal           (Deck& deck, Waste& waste);
    void cleanup        (Deck& deck, Waste& waste);
                                                // collect cards for redeal
    void resetGrid      ();                     // make it empty

        // playing a turn
    void makeLegalMove(bool& letsQuitOrEndTurn);
    void makeMove       (const GridLoc& oldLoc,
                         const GridLoc& newLoc);
    bool detectVictory() const;
    void congratulationsOrCondolences(bool isVictory) const;

        // working with empty cells

    // store in emptyCells_ the location of each empty cell
    void identifyEmptyCells();

    // which of the empty cells has this row and col? A B C or D?
    char whichEmptyCell     (int row, int col) const;

    // Is this a valid cell index? It must be 0-3.
    bool inRange(unsigned int emptyCellIndex) const
    {
        return (emptyCellIndex < NUM_EMPTY_CELLS);
    }
```

```
    // placing cards
    Cell&        cellAt(const GridLoc& loc)
    {
        if (inRange(loc)) return grid_[loc.row_][loc.col_];
        else throw std::out_of_range ("Bad grid location");
    }

    const Cell& cellAt(const GridLoc& loc) const
    {
        if (inRange(loc)) return grid_[loc.row_][loc.col_];
        else throw std::out_of_range("Bad grid location");
    }

    // Is this location within the grid?
    bool inRange(const GridLoc& loc) const
    {
        return(0<=loc.row_ && loc.row_<ROWS  &&
               0<=loc.col_ && loc.col_<COLS);
    }

    // Can Card c follow other card?
    bool canFollow(const Card& c, const Card& other) const
    {
        return c.suit() == other.suit() && c.rank() == other.rank() + 1;
    }

    // Can card c go at this location?
    bool canGoHere(const Card& c, const GridLoc& loc) const;

    // Is the cell at row, col ordered at its location? That is,
    //     could we put it here if it weren't already?
    bool cellIsCorrect(int row, int col) const
    {
        return ! grid_[row][col].empty() &&
               canGoHere(grid_[row][col].top(), GridLoc(row, col));
    }
```

```
    // data members
    Cell    grid_       [ROWS][COLS];      // where the cards are
    GridLoc emptyCells_ [NUM_EMPTY_CELLS];// where the empty cells are
};
#endif //MONTANA_H
```

Montana::play creates a new Deck and Waste every time it's called. You can see in it how they are used. Montana::makeMove shows how Cell can be used (cellAt returns the Cell at a given location).

Montana::makeLegalMove uses a try-catch block in case the input goes wonky.

Example 20-9. Part of montana.cpp (the rest is in the book's source code)

```
// class Montana, for a game of Montana solitaire
//      -- from _C++26 for Lazy Programmers_

#include <iostream>
#include "deck.h"
#include "io.h"         // for bool getAnswerYorN(const char[]);
#include "montana.h"

using namespace std;

void Montana::play()
{
    Deck  deck;
    Waste waste;
    bool  isVictory = false;

    resetGrid(); // prepare for deal by ensuring grid is empty

    for(int turn = 1; turn <= MAX_TURNS && ! isVictory; ++turn)
    {
        cout << "******************** New turn! "
                "*********************\n";

        // To easily test the detectVictory func: uncomment
        // setupForVictory, comment out deal, and see if
        // isVictory becomes true
        // setupForVictory(grid_, deck, waste);
```

```
        deck.shuffle();               // Shuffle deck
        deal(deck, waste);            // fill grid with cards
                                      //   and remove aces
        identifyEmptyCells();         // remember where the aces were
                                      //   in a list of 4 emptyCells_

        bool letsQuitOrEndTurn = false;
        isVictory = detectVictory();// already won? Unlikely, but...

        while (! isVictory && ! letsQuitOrEndTurn)
        {
            display();
            makeLegalMove(letsQuitOrEndTurn); // play a turn
            isVictory=detectVictory();        // did we win?
        }

        cleanup(deck, waste);         // collect cards for redeal

        // If user won, we go on and leave loop
        // If we're out of turns, we go on and leave loop
        // Otherwise give user a chance to quit
        if (!isVictory && turn < MAX_TURNS)
            if (getYorNAnswer("Quit game (Y/N)?"))
                break;
    }

    congratulationsOrCondolences(isVictory);
}

void Montana::makeLegalMove(bool& letsQuitOrEndTurn)
{
    bool isValidMove = false;

    do
    {
        cout << "Move (e.g. A 1 5 to fill cell A with "
             << "card at row 1, col 5; q to quit/end turn)? ";
```

```
        // Which empty space will we fill -- or are we quitting?
        char letter; cin >> letter;
        if (toupper(letter) == 'Q') letsQuitOrEndTurn = true;
        else
        {
            int emptyCellIndex = toupper(letter) - 'A';

            try
            {
                // Which cell are we moving from?
                GridLoc from;  cin >> from;
                // Which cell are we moving to?
                GridLoc to = emptyCells_[emptyCellIndex];

                // If the empty cell exists, and is really empty...
                if (inRange(emptyCellIndex) && cellAt(to).empty())
                    // if card to move exists, and move is legal...
                    if (!cellAt(from).empty() &&
                        canGoHere(cellAt(from).top(), to))
                    {
                        isValidMove = true;
                        makeMove (from, to);
                        emptyCells_[emptyCellIndex] = from;
                    }
            }
            catch (const BadInput&)         {}
            catch (const std::out_of_range&) {}
                            // reading GridLoc went bad -- just try again
        }
    } while (! isValidMove && ! letsQuitOrEndTurn);
}
```

Here is part of a sample game:

```
******************** New turn! *********************
      0    1    2    3    4    5    6    7    8    9    10   11   12
0:   JC   2H  >A<   7C  10S   5C   QS   KC   5S   KH   8D   7D   4D
1:  >B<   6C   JS   8C   8H  >C<   6H   KS   9C   JH   QD   2D   4C
2:   9S   6S   5H   KD   2S   3C   JD   6D  10C   3S   7S  10D   5D
3:  >D<   3H   8S   QH   3D   7H   4H   4S   2C   9H   9D  10H   QC
Move (e.g. A 1 5 to fill cell A with card at row 1, col 5; q to quit/end
turn)? a 3 1
      0    1    2    3    4    5    6    7    8    9    10   11   12
0:   JC   2H   3H   7C  10S   5C   QS   KC   5S   KH   8D   7D   4D
1:  >B<   6C   JS   8C   8H  >C<   6H   KS   9C   JH   QD   2D   4C
2:   9S   6S   5H   KD   2S   3C   JD   6D  10C   3S   7S  10D   5D
3:  >D<  >A<   8S   QH   3D   7H   4H   4S   2C   9H   9D  10H   QC
Move (e.g. A 1 5 to fill cell A with card at row 1, col 5; q to quit/end
turn)? d 2 4
      0    1    2    3    4    5    6    7    8    9    10   11   12
0:   JC   2H   3H   7C  10S   5C   QS   KC   5S   KH   8D   7D   4D
1:  >B<   6C   JS   8C   8H  >C<   6H   KS   9C   JH   QD   2D   4C
2:   9S   6S   5H   KD  >D<   3C   JD   6D  10C   3S   7S  10D   5D
3:   2S  >A<   8S   QH   3D   7H   4H   4S   2C   9H   9D  10H   QC
Move (e.g. A 1 5 to fill cell A with card at row 1, col 5; q to quit/end
turn)? a 2 9
```

EXERCISES

1. Write a subclass of class `Date` from earlier, adding a function `printInText`. It will print the `Date` not in numeric format (e.g., 12/12/2012), but in your favorite language: `12 de diciembre de 2012` (Spanish), `December 12, 2012` (English), whatever you like. What kind of inheritance will you use?

2. Write a subclass of `string` called `UnixFilename` that doesn't allow spaces – it immediately replaces them with _'s. And it won't let you interfere by changing the string's individual letters:

```
UnixFilename myFileName ("my file name");
                              // becomes "my_file_name"
myFileName[2] = ' ';         // forbidden
```

What kind of inheritance will you use?

3. Write a `Reserve` class. It's a group of cards; the only legal move is to take a card off the top. What should it inherit from?

   The next four exercises will be especially useful for the Freecell game exercise in Chapter 21.

4. Write the shuffle algorithm for `Deck`, quicker than the one in the source code.

5. (Requires O notation) …what's your shuffle's time requirement in O notation? Can you get it down to O(N)?

6. Write a `Foundation` class. A `Foundation`, remember, starts with `ACE` and goes up in suit, or it may be empty. Throw an exception if a call attempts to add an unsuitable card.

7. Write the `FreecellPile` class. Throw exceptions as appropriate.

8. Write the `KlondikePile` class. A Klondike pile is like a Freecell pile in that you can only add something going down by alternating color, but it's different in that you can add a *sequence* of such cards as long as the top card of the pile matches that criterion. For example, if the top of a Klondike pile is a black king, you can put a sequence on it if that sequence starts with a red queen. You can also remove a sequence of cards from a Klondike pile, as long as it's down in alternating color.

   So apparently you need to add and remove sequences. What class is a sequence? What class should your add-sequence and remove-sequence functions belong to?

   Also, a Klondike pile has 0 or more cards at the bottom, face-down. You can't move any sequence including a face-down card. If you remove all face-up cards, you can then expose the (face-down) top card.

   Throw exceptions as appropriate.

   The best way to be sure you understand the rules is to play the game, but I would never encourage anyone to find yet another way of wasting time at work.

9. (Involved, but not hard) Write a game of *Go Fish* (look online for rules).

10. Design a simple calculator class that can have two numbers and can do the four basic functions +, -, *, and /.

    Now write an engineer calculator class that does all those things, but also does some other fancy things (say, square root and exponentiation). What kind of inheritance will you use?

CHAPTER 21

Virtual Functions and Multiple Inheritance

Virtual Functions

As a lazy programmer, I'm all about not rewriting code in all those subclasses I made. Consider the function draw for the various Shapes. Every time I draw, I should be sure I'm using the Shape's color. I don't want Circle::draw, Rectangle::draw, etc. to all have to do this separately – if nothing else, I'll forget. So let's adapt Shape so it can remember:

```
class Shape   //Ready to draw -- but it won't work
{
    ...

    // Drawing
    void draw() const    //Sets the color appropriately, then calls drawAux
    {
        SSDL_SetRenderDrawColor(color()); drawAux();
    }
    void drawAux() const; //Does the actual drawing
    ...
};
```

Now when I tell my Circle to draw itself, it'll call draw, set the color, and then ...what? What does drawAux do? It'll be different depending on the type of Shape: SSDL_RenderDrawCircle, SSDL_RenderDrawRectangle, whatever. Looks like Circle needs its own version of drawAux:

W. Briggs, *C++26 for Lazy Programmers*, https://doi.org/10.1007/979-8-8688-1859-2_21

```
class Circle: public Shape //Buggy!
{
    ...
    void drawAux() const
    {
        SSDL_RenderDrawCircle(location().x_, location().y_, radius());
    }
    ...
};
...
myCircle.draw();
```

But this won't work. `myCircle.draw` calls `Shape::draw`, which then calls `Shape::drawAux`. It doesn't call `Circle::drawAux` because `Shape` has never heard of `Circle`; it has no way of knowing that function even exists.

Example 21-1 shows the fix.

Example 21-1. The `Shape` class, with a virtual function. This and all subsequent examples through this chapter are in `Ch21/1-thru-7-shapes`; Microsoft Visual Studio users use appropriate projects in its Solution Manager.

```
class Shape
{
    ...
    virtual void drawAux() const;
    ...
};
```

Here we tell the `Shape` class, "Whenever you call `drawAux`, use the child class's version, if there is one."

`Circle` needs to be told that its `drawAux` is overriding a virtual function, so we do that as well (Example 21-2).[1]

[1] `override` isn't required by the compiler, but it's a *very* good idea. It makes the compiler notice if you spelled the parent and child functions differently or gave slightly different parameter lists or `const` specifications.

Example 21-2. The `Circle` class, with the `override` specifier

```
class Circle: public Shape
{
    ...
    void drawAux() const override;
    ...
};
```

Behind the Scenes

Before, an object of a given class stored only data members (Figure 21-1). It didn't store member functions in memory with the object, as it would waste space.

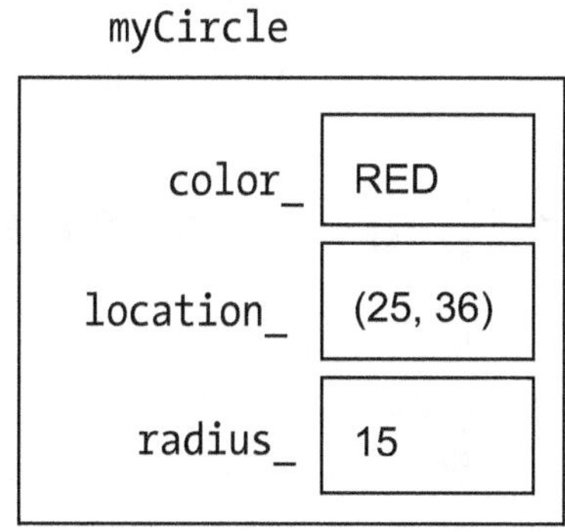

Figure 21-1. *A `Circle` object, before virtual functions*

But now the object also contains the address of any virtual function, so it remembers which version to call (Figure 21-2).

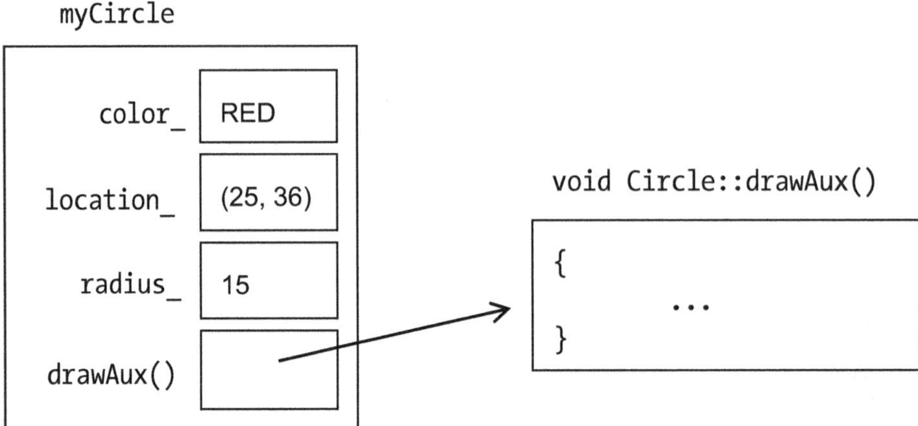

Figure 21-2. *A `Circle` object, using virtual functions*

We added some overhead: an extra pointer for the drawAux function in every Circle. But it's small overhead – nothing to be concerned about.

Pure Virtual Functions and Abstract Base Classes

Next question: how do we write Shape::draw(), anyway?

Unless we specify what *kind* of Shape it is – unless it's a Circle or another subclass – there's no answer to that question. So we'll take the easy way out: we won't write it for Shape, but will instead tell the compiler, "Don't expect me to write Shape::drawAux. Oh, and you can't have a Shape that's just a Shape, and the function in Example 21-3 is why."

Example 21-3. The Shape class, with a pure virtual function. This makes Shape an "abstract" class.

```
class Shape
{
public:
    ...
    virtual void drawAux()=0;
    ...
};
```

By adding =0, we make drawAux a **pure virtual** function and Shape into an **abstract class**, meaning one you can't use to declare variables:

```
Shape myShape;   // Nope, can't do this, the compiler will stop you
Circle myCircle; // No problem: it's a shape, but it's also a Circle,
                 //    and we can drawAux Circles
```

Why Virtual Functions Often Mean Using Pointers

Here's something we might want to do with Shapes: put them into a vector and do something (like draw()) to every Shape in the vector.

Example 21-4. A (buggy!) program to show, and move, the Olympics symbol

```
// This program uses Circle, and a subclass of Shape called Text,
//    to make the symbol
//         -- from _C++26 for Lazy Programmers_

#include <vector>
#include "circle.h"
#include "text.h"

int main(int argc, char** argv)
{
    SSDL_SetWindowSize(500, 300); // make smaller window

    // Create Olympics symbol
    std::vector<Shape> olympicSymbol; // No, this isn't going to work...
    constexpr int RADIUS = 50;

    // consisting of five circles
    olympicSymbol.push_back(Circle( 50,  50, RADIUS));
    olympicSymbol.push_back(Circle(150,  50, RADIUS));
    olympicSymbol.push_back(Circle(250,  50, RADIUS));
    olympicSymbol.push_back(Circle(100, 100, RADIUS));
    olympicSymbol.push_back(Circle(200, 100, RADIUS));
```

```
    // plus a label
    olympicSymbol.push_back(Text(150,150,"Games of the Olympiad"));

    // color those circles (and the label)
    SSDL_Color olympicColors[] = { BLUE,
                                   SSDL_CreateColor(0, 255, 255), // yellow
                                   BLACK, GREEN, RED, BLACK };
    for (unsigned int i = 0; i < olympicSymbol.size(); ++i)
        olympicSymbol[i].setColor(olympicColors [i]);

    // do a game loop
    while (SSDL_IsNextFrame())
    {
        SSDL_DefaultEventHandler();

        SSDL_RenderClear(WHITE);    // clear the screen

        // draw all those shapes
        for (unsigned int i = 0; i < olympicSymbol.size(); ++i)
            olympicSymbol[i].draw();

        // move all those shapes
        for (unsigned int i = 0; i < olympicSymbol.size(); ++i)
            olympicSymbol[i].moveBy(1, 1);
    }

    return 0;
}
```

This makes sense: create a sequence of Shapes, and then draw them. But it won't work. One reason is that Shape is now an abstract class; since you can't create something that's just a Shape, you certainly can't create a vector of them.

The other reason is that olympicSymbol[0], for example, has enough room to store a single Shape. That means it has room for a color_, a location_, and a pointer to drawAux. Where will you store the radius_ for a Circle? The contents ("Games of the Olympiad") of the Text object? There isn't room!

To fix this we need dynamic memory (Example 21-5). Yes, I know: lazy programmers avoid dynamic memory, as it's error-prone and harder to write. But sometimes you need it. In this case, when you create a `Circle` using `new`, it'll allocate the amount it needs.

It's different from how we used dynamic memory before. Then, we wanted an array, so we used `[]`, `char* str = new char [someSize]`, and `delete [] str` to clean up. This time, when we allocate a Shape, we allocate *one* Shape. So we omit the `[]`'s: `new Circle`, not `new Circle [...]`, and `delete`, not `delete []`. We'll get more practice allocating/deallocating single elements in the next chapter.

Example 21-5. A program that successfully uses a vector of Shapes to display and move a complex symbol. Output is in Figure 21-3.

```
// Program to show, and move, the Olympics symbol
// It uses Circle, and a subclass of Shape called Text
//        -- from _C++26 for Lazy Programmers_

#include <vector>
#include "circle.h"
#include "text.h"

int main(int argc, char** argv)
{
    SSDL_SetWindowSize(500, 300); // make smaller window

    // Create Olympics symbol
    std::vector<Shape*> olympicSymbol;
    constexpr int RADIUS = 50;

    // consisting of five circles
    olympicSymbol.push_back(new Circle( 50,  50, RADIUS));
    olympicSymbol.push_back(new Circle(150,  50, RADIUS));
    olympicSymbol.push_back(new Circle(250,  50, RADIUS));
    olympicSymbol.push_back(new Circle(100, 100, RADIUS));
    olympicSymbol.push_back(new Circle(200, 100, RADIUS));

    // plus a label
    olympicSymbol.push_back(new Text(150,150,"Games of the Olympiad"));

    // color those circles (and the label)
```

```
    SSDL_Color olympicColors[] = { BLUE,
                   SSDL_CreateColor(0, 255, 255), // yellow
                   BLACK, GREEN, RED, BLACK };
    for (unsigned int i = 0; i < olympicSymbol.size(); ++i)
        (*olympicSymbol[i]).setColor(olympicColors [i]);

    // do a game loop
    while (SSDL_IsNextFrame())
    {
        SSDL_DefaultEventHandler();

        SSDL_RenderClear(WHITE);    //clear the screen

        // draw all those shapes
        for (unsigned int i = 0; i < olympicSymbol.size(); ++i)
            (*olympicSymbol[i]).draw();

        // move all those shapes
        for (unsigned int i = 0; i < olympicSymbol.size(); ++i)
            (*olympicSymbol[i]).moveBy(1, 1);
    }

    // done with our dynamic memory -- throw it back!
    for (unsigned int i = 0; i < olympicSymbol.size(); ++i)
        delete olympicSymbol [i];

    return 0;
}
```

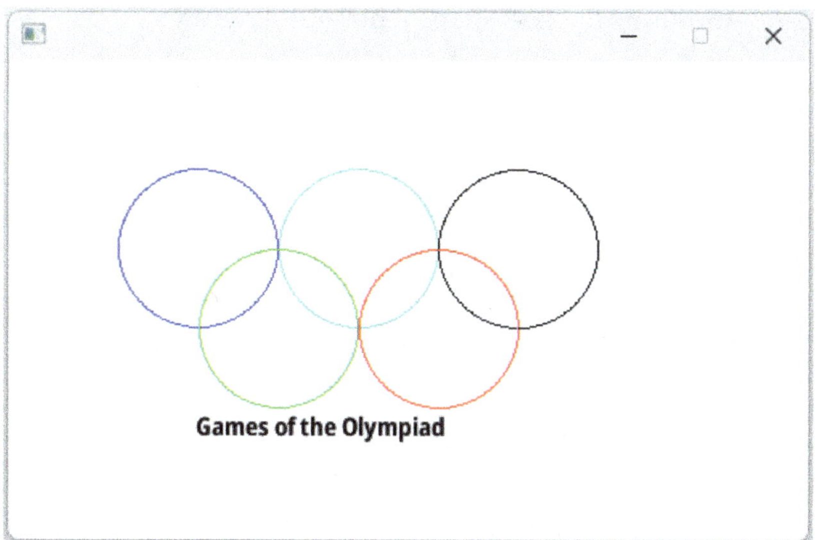

Figure 21-3. *Output of the Olympics symbol program in Example 21-5*

In this code we maintain a `vector` not of Shape but of Shape*. Then, when we use `new` to create a `Circle` or `Text`, it can get us a chunk of memory the right size for that subclass.

Since `olympicSymbol[i]` is a pointer, we say not `olympicSymbol[i].draw()` but `(*olympicSymbol[i]).draw()`.[2]

Finally, as always when using dynamic memory, we throw back the memory with `delete` when we're done.

To be sure it *all* gets thrown back, we need the next section.

Virtual Destructors

Suppose in addition to Shape's other characteristics, we give it a `char* description_` member so every Shape can have a name or note. (Ordinarily I'd use `std::string` because of course it's so easy! But I want to illustrate something about memory cleanup.)

Here's the new version of Shape.

[2] If all those parentheses make your pinkies tired, well, we get an easier way to write this in the next chapter.

Example 21-6. Additions to class Shape – not quite right yet

```
class Shape
{
public:
    Shape(const Point2D& p, const char* text = "",
          const SSDL_Color& c = WHITE);
    Shape(const Shape& other);
    ~Shape() { if (description_) delete[] description_; }

    Shape& operator=(const Shape& s);

    // ...

    const char* description() const { return description_; }
private:
    Point2D    location_;
    SSDL_Color color_;
    char* description_;  // Using char* not std::string helps illustrate
                         //   how Chapter 21 affects dynamic memory
    void copyDescription(const char*); //like String::copy in Chapter 17
};
```

Let's also have the Text object used in Example 21-5 that stores the phrase "Games of the Olympiad."

Example 21-7. The (buggy) Text class

```
class Text : public Shape
{
public:
    Text(const Text& other) : Shape(other) { copy(other.contents_); }
    Text(const Point2D& p, const char* txt="", const char* name = "",
          const SSDL_Color& c = WHITE)
    : Shape(p, name, c)
    {
        copy(txt);
    }
```

```
    ~Text() override { if (contents_) delete contents_; } //Not quite right...

    Text& operator=(const Text& other);

    void drawAux() const override
    {
        SSDL_RenderText(contents_, location().x_, location().y_);
    }

    const char* contents() const { return contents_; }
private:
    char* contents_;
    void copy(const char* txt);//used for copying contents
};
```

It uses dynamic memory to allocate its character array. Naturally when we're done we'll need to throw it back. But the statement in `main` that should do this

```
for (int i = 0; i < olympicSymbol.size(); ++i)
    delete olympicSymbol [i];
```

doesn't. `olympicSymbol [i]` is a pointer to a `Shape`, not a `Text`; so it will only delete things that belong to the `Shape`. It doesn't know about `Text`'s `contents_`.

The solution once again is to use the version of the function that *does* know: `Text`'s version. We do that by making `Shape`'s destructor `virtual` and `Text`'s an `override`:

```
virtual Shape::~Shape() { if (description_) delete[] description_; }

        Text::~Text  () override { if (contents_) delete contents_;        }
```

Now, when the destructor on a `Shape` is called, the `Shape` will know which version to call. If it's a `Text`, the destructor called will be `Text::~Text()` – which, when finished, then calls the destructor for parent class `Shape`, as destructors do whether they're virtual or not.

It's easy to forget, when you build an inheritance hierarchy, whether you used virtual functions in this or that class. And there's no way to know when you're writing the parent class that no descendant will ever use dynamic memory, like the Olympics symbol program. So if there is a possibility anyone will dynamically allocate an instance of some subclass – and how would you know? – it's safer to make the destructor virtual.

Golden Rule of Virtual Functions

(Usual version) If you're using virtual functions in a class hierarchy, make the destructors virtual.

(Stronger version) Since you don't know when you write a class what people using it will do ...make all destructors virtual. Period.

I used `char* contents_` in `Text` and `char* description_` in `Shape` to make it obvious we need destructors. But if they were `std::strings`, the same thing would have happened: when you deleted a pointer to `Shape` that was actually a pointer to a `Text`, `delete` wouldn't know that it was really a `Text`, so `Text`'s destructor – whether one we wrote or the compiler's default – wouldn't be called, and nothing could tell `Text`'s member `contents_` to delete its memory. So you still need to give `Shape` a virtual destructor:

```
virtual Shape::~Shape() { }
```

Antibugging

- **The compiler says your subclass's override function doesn't match any in the base class.** You may have left `const` off the function header or spelled the function name differently or given it a slightly different parameter list.

- **The compiler says your subclass is abstract, but it doesn't contain pure virtual functions.** For example

  ```
  Circle myCircle;
  ```

  might complain that `Circle` is abstract – but you didn't put any virtual functions in it at all!

You may have forgotten to override the parent's pure virtual functions. This makes the subclass abstract too.

Or you may have forgotten to make the corresponding child class function an `override`, and its header didn't perfectly match the parent's (see the previous entry in this "Antibugging" section). Solution: add `override`.

EXERCISES

1. In this simple shooting game, a *powerup* is a target you can hit with a mouse click. The types of powerup – FlashyPowerup, MegaPowerup, or Wormhole – give different points and show different animations when you hit one (see Figure 21-4).

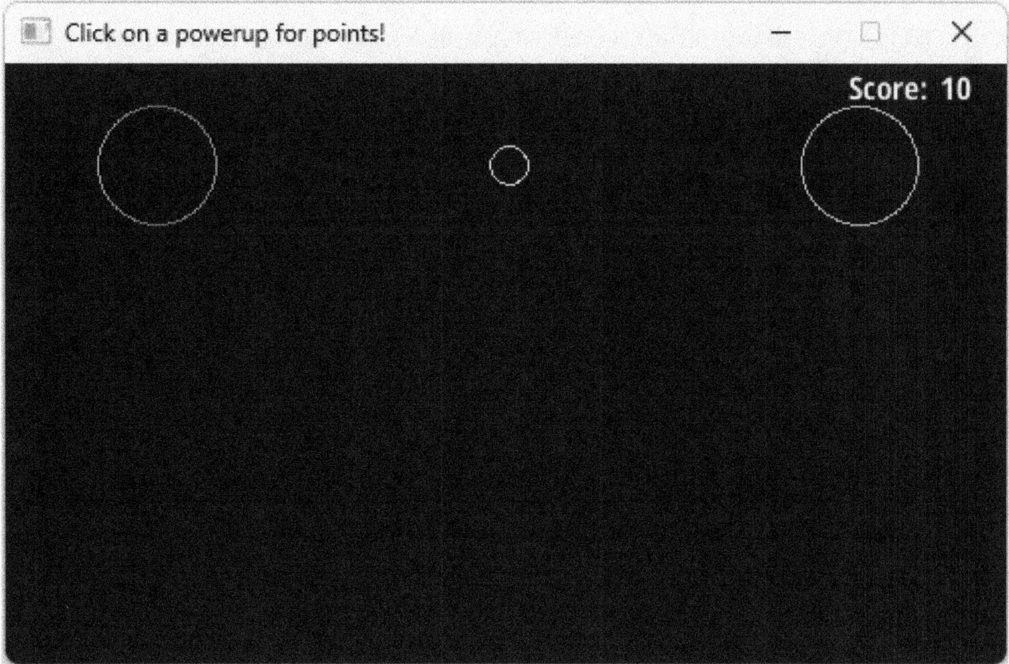

Figure 21-4. *The powerup exercise, showing the "Wormhole" animation*

In this chapter's section of the sample code, you'll find a partially written program for shooting powerups. It uses the `Shape` hierarchy above. To get it working, you'll need to alter `main.cpp` to use pointers and add `virtual` and `override` in the right places in the Powerup class hierarchy. Circle will also need a function contains to return whether a point is within its radius. I recommend making Powerup abstract, for the same reason as with Shape.

2. In the CardGroup class hierarchy from Chapter 20, add functions isLegalToAdd and isLegalToRemove to every subclass that might need them. (For example, Cell::isLegalToAdd returns true only if the cell is empty and Cell::isLegalToRemove only if it's not.)

   Let CardGroup's addCardLegally call isLegalToAdd, using virtual functions so it calls the appropriate subclass version. No other class should have its own addCardLegally.

   Test to be sure the right functions are actually called. You may want some try–catch blocks.

   Will your new virtual functions need to be pure virtual?

3. (Bigger project) Expanding on Exercise 2, write a nongraphical *Freecell* game. You should have an array or vector of CardGroup (CardGroup*, actually) including FreecellPiles, Cells, and Foundations. Let the user specify which CardGroup to move a card from or to ("F1" for foundation 1, "P2" for pile 2, say). The CardGroup chosen knows, based on what subclass it is, which version of isLegalToAdd or isLegalToRemove to use:

```
CardGroup* from = askUserToPickCardGroup();
if ((*from).isLegalToRemove()) // can we take card from top?
    ...
```

Inheritance, Class-Type Members, and Move Semantics

Suppose we have a class CaptionedImage: a subclass of SSDL_Image from Chapter 2, with a (string) caption added. You write the move constructor for it:

```
CaptionedImage(CaptionedImage&& other) noexcept
      : SSDL_Image(other), caption_(other.caption_) {}
```

...but it calls SSDL_Image's regular copy constructor, not its move constructor. Same for caption_: it ignores std::string's move constructor.

When you use CaptionedImage's move constructor, it's because C++ thinks the thing being copied is an "r-value," a thing that you can safely use up, mangle, etc., as it's not going to be used again, so we're perfectly safe stealing its memory.

But while it's in the constructor, we need to keep it around till we're done, not use it up immediately! So its r-value-ness is taken away. So when we call SSDL_Image(other) and caption_(other.caption_), it doesn't know to use the move constructors.

This wasn't a problem in Chapter 18 when writing the String class, because its only data member was char* contents_, and char*'s don't have move constructors. Simply copying it over was fine. That's not the case here with caption_ or with the parent class SSDL_Image.

C++'s fix is to force it back to an r-value for those calls. std::move turns things back into r-values, as in Example 21-8.

Example 21-8. The CaptionedImage class, using move semantics

```
//An image with a caption
//     -- from _C++26 for Lazy Programmers_

#ifndef CAPTIONED_IMAGE_H
#define CAPTIONED_IMAGE_H

#include <utility> //for std::move
#include <string>
#include "SSDL.h"

class CaptionedImage: public SSDL_Image
{
public:
    CaptionedImage() = default;
    CaptionedImage(const SSDL_Image& other, const char* c) :
        SSDL_Image(other), caption_(c)
    {
    }
```

```
    CaptionedImage(const CaptionedImage& other) :
        CaptionedImage(other, other.caption_.c_str())
    {
    }
    CaptionedImage(CaptionedImage&& other) noexcept :
        SSDL_Image(std::move(other)), caption_(std::move(other.caption_))
    {
    }

    CaptionedImage& operator=(const CaptionedImage& other)
    {
        SSDL_Image::operator=(other); caption_ = other.caption_;
        return *this;
    }
    CaptionedImage& operator=(CaptionedImage&& other) noexcept
    {
        SSDL_Image::operator=(std::move(other));
        caption_ = std::move(other.caption_);
        return *this;
    }
    void draw(int x, int y)
    {
        SSDL_RenderImage(*this, x, y);
        SSDL_RenderTextCentered(caption_.c_str(),
                                x + SSDL_GetImageWidth(*this) / 2,
                                y + SSDL_GetImageHeight(*this));
    }
private:
    std::string caption_;
};
#endif //CAPTIONED_IMAGE_H
```

It works the same for move =: before handing other off to Shape's move =, we need to turn it back into an r-value, as shown.

Bottom line: In any move function, if you hand it off to another move function (like `std::string`'s and `SSDL_Image`'s move constructor and move= above), wrap it in `std::move` first.

EXERCISES

1. Change the `char*`'s in the `Shape` hierarchy to `std::strings`, and adapt the hierarchy to use move semantics.

Multiple Inheritance (optional)

Consider these two classes for a 3D graphics program:

```
class Object
{
public:
  Object();
  Object(const Object&);
   ...
private:
  double velocity_;
  double acceleration_;
  Point3D position_;
};
```

```
class Model
{
public:
  Model();
  Model(const Model&);
  void load(const char* filename);
  void display() const;
  ...
private:
  vector<Triangle> contents_;
};
```

Class `Object` has position, velocity, and acceleration. It's for working with the laws of motion.

Class `Model` is something with a physical appearance. It's composed of triangles that fit together to make an apparently solid object.

Can you have `Objects` that aren't `Models`? Sure. You might have a model in some other format, not using triangles – a sphere, maybe.

Can you have `Models` that aren't `Objects`? Sure. You could be using CAD/CAM to design products for manufacturing.

So a `Model` isn't an `Object` and an `Object` isn't a `Model` ...but it makes sense to have something be both. I'll call that something `ModelObject` (Figure 21-5).

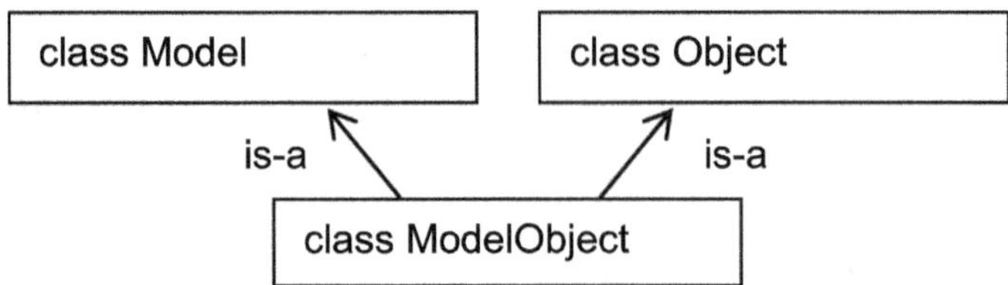

***Figure 21-5.** Inheriting `ModelObject` from `Model` and `Object`*

Since `ModelObject` is a `Model` and an `Object`, it inherits the characteristics of both: it will have position, velocity, and acceleration like an `Object` and a vector of `Triangles`, plus the `load` and `display` functions, from `Model`.

We can use public or private inheritance. `public` makes sense:

```
class ModelObject: public Model, public Object
{
public:
    ModelObject() {}
    ModelObject(const ModelObject& other) : Model(other), Object(other) { }
    ...
};
```

To call the parent constructors, use the ":" just as you do with ordinary inheritance; but this time, call both parent constructors (or use their defaults).

This isn't often needed, but when it is, it's convenient.

Antibugging

Suppose we make a role-playing game. In it we have class `Player`, with a `name_` and a number of `hitPoints_`. It also has a member function `takeAttack(int howMuch)` that reduces the hit points by a given amount.

We make two subclasses, `Fighter` and `Magician`. A `Fighter` has a member `attack`, which takes a `Player` and reduces its hit points. A `Magician` has a member `bespell`, which does a magic attack.

But some games let you make hybrid classes for your characters. We'll make FighterMagician a subclass of both Fighter and Magician. Now we have a class that can both attack and bespell. Cool.

But here's a problem. Fighter has members hitPoints_ and name_ (inherited from Player). Magician also has hitPoints_ and name_ (inherited from Player). So FighterMagician has two copies of hitPoints_ and two copies of name_!

This is called the "diamond problem," for some reason. Maybe Figure 21-6 will give us a clue?

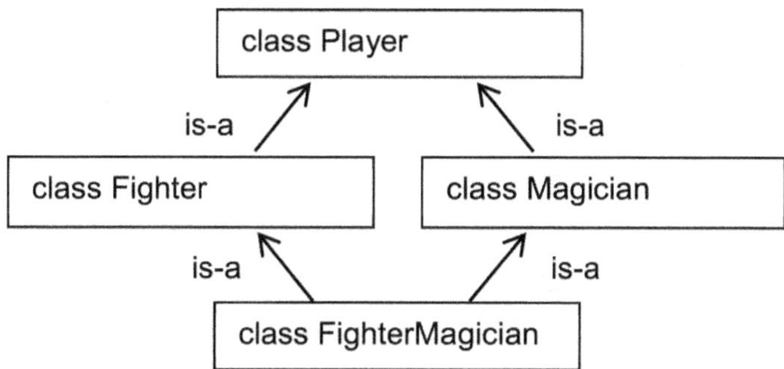

Figure 21-6. *The diamond problem in multiple inheritance*

We can't reason our way out of this one; C++ will have to help us. And it does: it lets us make Fighter and Magician "virtual" base classes, essentially saying, "Don't do that extra-copies-of-common-grandparent-members thing":

```
class Fighter:  virtual public Player ...
class Magician: virtual public Player ...
```

One more issue: since Fighter and Magician may call different Player constructors, which would lead to ambiguity, FighterMagician has to explicitly state what Player constructor it wants called, like so:

```
FighterMagician(const char* name) : Fighter (...some args...),
                                    Magician(...some args...),
                                    Player  (name)
{
}
```

If we don't specify, the compiler will use the default constructor.

EXERCISES

1. Write the classes from the "Antibugging" section above – Player, Fighter, Magician, and FighterMagician.

   Since you're not making a real game, to keep it simple, attack and bespell can both just pick random numbers to take from the opponent's hit points. It doesn't matter if the FighterMagician uses attack or bespell – just pick one in main for its method of fighting.

   Now let a Fighter (say) go up against a FighterMagician, and see who wins the match.

2. Using the Shape class, make a class Composite that is both a Shape (so it has a location, virtual drawAux, etc.) and a vector of Shape* (so it can be made of circles, texts, whatever). Be sure that your Composite can be created, moved, and displayed and is properly destructed. Also write the move constructor and move =.

   One tricky bit is that a Composite has two kinds of locations: the one inherited from Shape and the locations of all its subcomponents. Make your move functions update all locations.

3. If you did Exercise 1 in the section "Virtual Functions," above, you can extend it with a PowerupSet class, which is both a Shape and a vector of Powerup*. Be sure your PowerupSet can be created, drawn, and animated and is properly destructed. The functions in main.cpp that take `vector<Powerup>` (or some such) should be altered to take PowerupSet. If you covered move semantics, write the move constructor and move =.

   PowerupSet has two kinds of locations: the one inherited from Shape and the locations of its subcomponents. Make your move functions update all locations.

CHAPTER 22

Linked Lists

To add an element to a `Vector`, we must allocate new memory and copy over the existing elements. That's not quick! Here's a storage scheme that's faster to update.

What Lists Are and Why Have Them

All around the city a group of superheroes is waiting. They have a scheme for notifying each other if their powers are needed: each has the phone number of another, who has the number of another, until the last one on the list, who has none (see Figure 22-1).

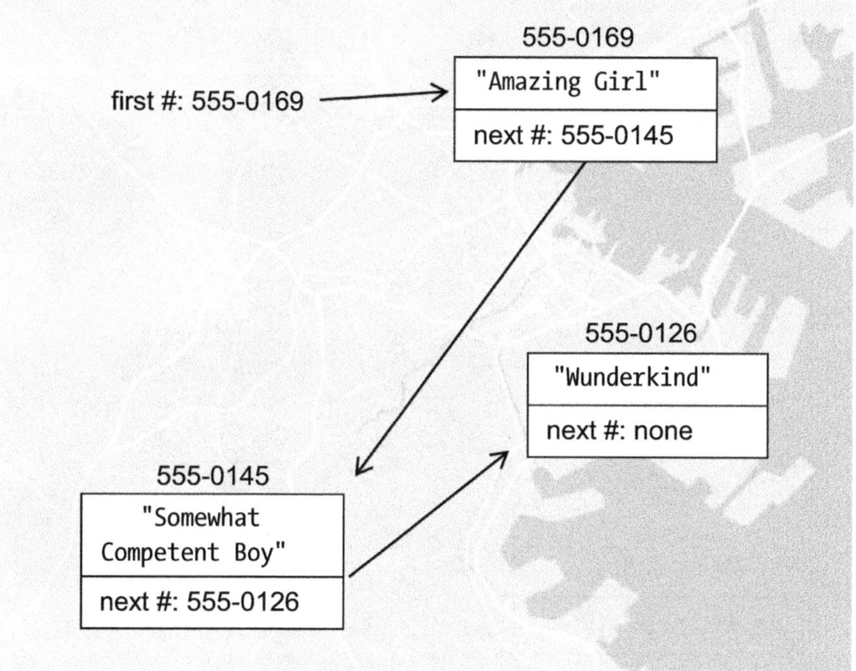

Figure 22-1. *Our city, with three superheroes in a linked list. Amazing Girl is first, at 555-0169; Somewhat Competent Boy is at 555-0145; Wunderkind is at 555-0126*

W. Briggs, *C++26 for Lazy Programmers*, https://doi.org/10.1007/979-8-8688-1859-2_22

In the computer, we don't use phone numbers, but memory addresses. This data structure holds the information each person has:

```
struct Superhero
{
    std::string name_;     // The Superhero's name
    Superhero*  next_;     // The address of the next Superhero
};
```

Remember, `Superhero*` means pointer to `Superhero` – where to find a `Superhero` in the computer's memory, just as in Chapter 21 `Shape*` meant where to find a `Shape`. Wunderkind comes last and has "none" as her next phone number, so we'll set her `next_` field to `nullptr`.

Suppose we want to add another hero, Bug Spray Man, to the list. It's quick and easy: give him the number of the current first in the list. He'll put it into his `next_` field. Then remember *his* contact information as the new first number (see Figure 22-2).

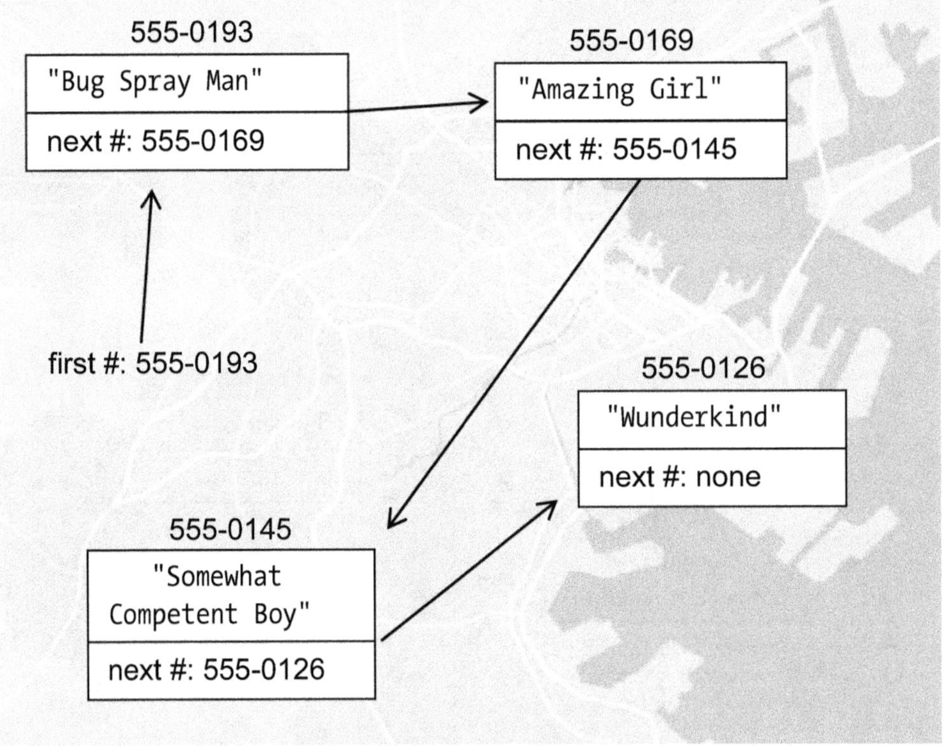

***Figure 22-2.** The same list after we add Bug Spray Man*

More formally, the algorithm is

```
create a new Superhero struct
put the name of the new person into the Superhero
put the pointer to the start of the list into the new Superhero, as "next"
set the start of the list to the address of the new Superhero
```

There's no loop here, so it's way quicker than `Vector::push_back`.

Efficiency and O Notation

There's no loop in that algorithm – it's O(1) – so `List`'s way of adding an element is a big improvement over `Vector`'s O(N).

But suppose we want to look at the indexth element (whatever index may be) – that is, use `operator[]`. How can we do this? With `Vector`, it was just `contents_[index]` – no loop, no repetition, and therefore O(1). Here, we have to go sequentially:

```
current position = start;

for j = 0; j< index; ++j
    current position = the address of the next Superhero
    if we go off the end of the list, throw an exception

return the name in the current position
```

This *does* have a loop – and its time requirement is O(index). On average, that'll be O(N/2), or O(N).

Table 22-1 shows how you'll know which is better for a given task, `Vector` or `List`. If you do a lot of lookup (`operator[]`), `Vector` is quicker. If you do a lot of adding elements, `List` is quicker.

Table 22-1. *Time required for some* `Vector` *and* `List` *functions*

Function	Efficiency (Vector)	Efficiency (List)
`operator[]`	O(1)	O(N)
`operator=`	O(N)	O(N)
copy constructor	O(N)	O(N)
`push_back`	O(N)	Not written
`push_front`	Not written	O(1)

I often use `Vector`, because I find that I look into a sequence more often than I build it. If the sequence is small, it won't matter much. If it's huge I pay more attention to picking the fastest.

Starting the Linked List Template

Let's move now to writing the `List`. We'll drop the superhero analogy and make `List` a template (Example 22-1).

Example 22-1. The `List` class, first version

```
// class List:  a linked list class
//      from _C++26 for Lazy Programmers_

#ifndef LIST_H
#define LIST_H

#include <iostream>

template<typename T>
class List
{
 public:
    class Underflow  {};                          // exception

    List() = default; //will use defaults given where members are declared
    List (const List& other);
    ~List() noexcept
```

```
    //move functions
    List            (List&& other) noexcept;
    List& operator= (List&& other) noexcept;

    List& operator= (const List& other);

    size_t size () const { return size_; }
    bool   empty() const { return size() == 0; }

    bool isEqualTo(const List& other) const;

    void push_front (const T& newElement); // add newElement at front
    void pop_front  ();                    // take one off the front
    const T& front  () const;

    void print(std::ostream&) const requires Printable<T>;
 private:
    struct Entry[1]
    {
        T      data_ = T();               // default for whatever T is
                                          //    even if it's a basic type
        Entry* next_ = nullptr;
    };

    Entry* start_    = nullptr;           // start_ points to first element
};
#endif //LIST_H
```

It's like Vector, except

- We use push_front, not push_back.
- The data members are different.

[1] One struct/class inside another? No problem. But the struct's data members are public (by default). Is this a security risk? Not at all. It's all in List's private section.

- I left out operator[]. It's so inefficient that after years of grousing that *I don't care if it's inefficient – just let me use it!* I've bowed to the community and left it out. We'll get a more appropriate way to access elements in the next chapter anyway.

Let's write some of those functions now, starting with the default constructor.

List<T>::List()

It makes sense to have the default List be empty. How do we specify that a list is empty? By convention, this is true when the pointer start_ is nullptr. You could say that it points to nothing – because there's nothing in the list.

One way to do this is to build it right into start_'s declaration. List() can now be defaulted (Example 22-2).

Example 22-2. List<T>'s default constructor

```
template<typename T>
class List
{
public:
    List() = default;
    ...
private:
    ...
    Entry start_ = nullptr;
};
```

void List<T>::push_front

When we begin push_front, we have the List as it was, containing start_, and a newElement. We need newElement added to the front, as shown in Figure 22-3.

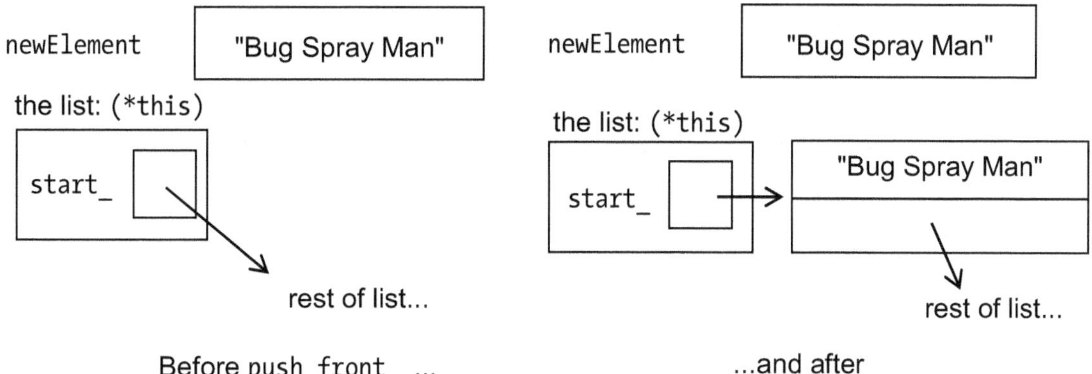

***Figure 22-3.** Before, and after, adding a new element to a `List`*

Here's how to make that happen:

```
create an Entry
put the newElement into its data field
put the old version of start into its next field
put the address of the new Entry into start
```

Seems straightforward. Example 22-3 shows it in code.

Example 22-3. `List<T>::push_front`

```
template<typename T>
void List<T>::push_front(const T& newElement)
{
    Entry* newEntry    = new Entry; // create an Entry
    (*newEntry).data_ = newElement;// put newElement in its data_ field
    (*newEntry).next_ = start_;    // put old version of start_
                                   //   in its next_ field

    start_            = newEntry;  // put address of new Entry
                                   //   into start_
}
```

Let's trace that line by line.

The first line, `Entry* newEntry = new Entry;`, uses dynamic memory to create the new `Entry`. Just as in Chapter 21 with new `Shape`s, we're only allocating one `Entry` at a time, not an array, so we don't need `[]`'s.

In the second line, newEntry is the address of the new Entry, so *newEntry is that Entry itself. (*newEntry).name_ therefore is its name_ field. The third line is similar.

The fourth line stores the address of newEntry in the start_ field of the List so we'll remember where to find it. Our new Entry now directs us to the rest of the List. If the List had elements, good; we'll see them. If the List was empty, then that pointer to the rest of the list is nullptr. Also good: we'll know that's the end.

void List<T>::pop_front

...a function to take off the first element. Here's my first attempt. (For brevity I just show the code, but of course I'd write the algorithm first.)

```
template<typename T>
void List<T>::pop_front()
{
    if (empty()) throw Underflow();

    delete start_;                 // delete the item
    start_ = (*start_).next_;      // let start_ go on to the next
}
```

(As in Chapter 21, we use delete, not delete [] – because we used new without the []'s, allocating not an array but a single Entry.)

So let's say we're taking Bug Spray Man off that list. Figure 22-4 shows what we start with.

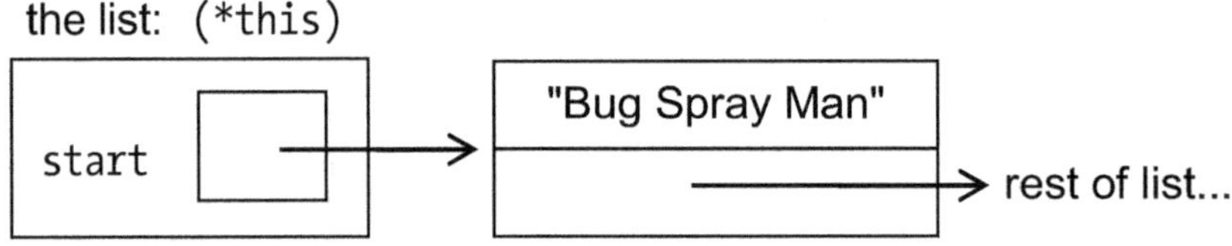

***Figure 22-4.** Getting ready to pop_front*

I'll trace through the steps. Is it empty? No problem there. Now we delete what start_ points to and get Figure 22-5.

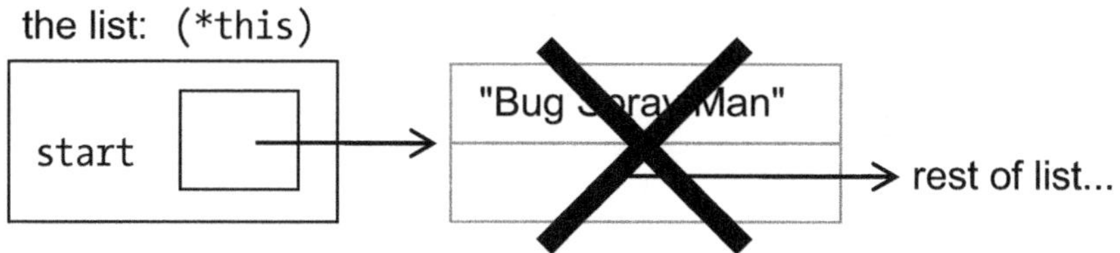

***Figure 22-5.** We deleted the element in pop_front. Nope, that's not right ...*

Then we access `(*start_).next_`. But what `start_` pointed to has been deleted and no longer exists. The address of the rest of the list is gone. Crash!

Maybe we could do this in a different order: delete things only after we're *sure* we're done with them (Example 22-4).

Example 22-4. `List<T>::pop_front()`, corrected version

```
template<typename T>
void List<T>::pop_front()
{
    if (empty()) throw Underflow();

    Entry* temp = start_;       // store location of thing to delete
    start_ = (*start_).next_;  // let start_ = next thing after start_

    delete temp;                // delete the item
}
```

Now let's see how it goes.

We check for the empty condition; no problem.

We set `temp` equal to `start_` (Figure 22-6) ...

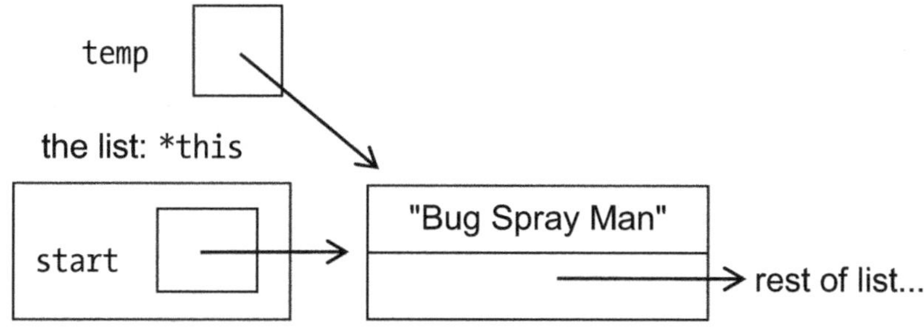

***Figure 22-6.** Starting pop_front (again)*

We move start_ to point to the rest of the list (Figure 22-7) ...

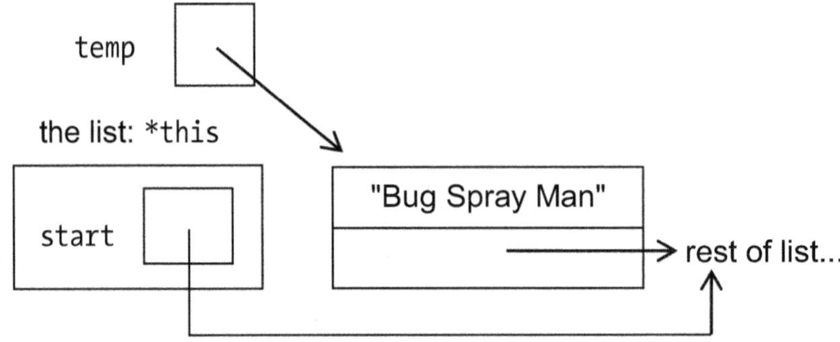

***Figure 22-7.** Setting start_ to where it should go ...*

...and we delete the Entry we no longer need (Figure 22-8).

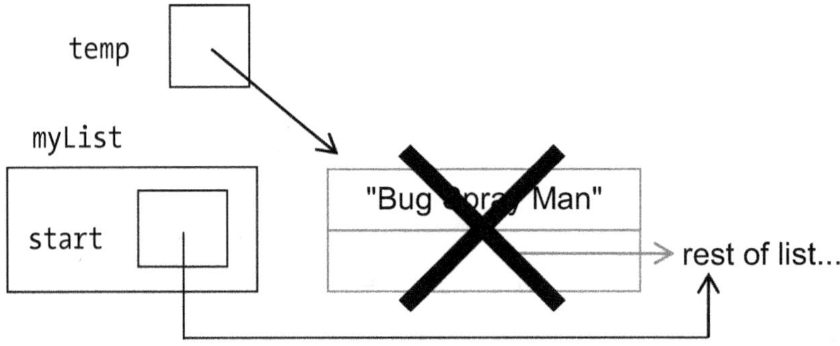

***Figure 22-8.** pop_front now works correctly*

When doing lists, I'm always drawing these boxes and arrows: without them, I'm bound to lose pointers, follow bad ones, etc. So I get this Golden Rule:

Golden Rule of Pointers

When changing or deleting pointers, draw diagrams of what you're doing.

List<T>::~List

Eventually we have to throw all those Entrys back.

I could write a while loop to delete them, making a diagram to make sure I don't lose any pointers, but I'm a lazy programmer. Do I already have something to throw back Entrys safely? Sure – pop_front:

```
template<typename T>
List<T>::~List() { while (!empty()) pop_front(); }
```

Done.

->: A Bit of Syntactic Sugar

Writing (*newEntry).next_ is wearing out my pinkies from using the Shift key. Fortunately C++ provides another way of writing exactly the same thing, easier to type and a little easier to read:

```
newEntry->next_; // means (*newEntry).next_;
```

So here's our new version of push_front:

```
template<typename T>
void List<T>::push_front(const T& newElement)
{
    Entry* newEntry = new Entry; // create an Entry
    newEntry->data_ = newElement;// put newElement in its data_ field
    newEntry->next_ = start_;    // put old version of start_ in
                                 //  its next_ field

    start_          = newEntry;  // put address of new Entry
                                 //   into start_
}
```

More Friendly Syntax: Pointers as Conditions

We often need code like this:

```
if (next_ != nullptr)...
```

or

```
while (next_ != nullptr) ...
```

Consider how conditions for if statements (and while loops and do-whiles) work. The expression between the ()'s is evaluated. If it evaluates to 0, that means false; anything else is true.

Well, nullptr is *kind of* like 0 – at least, it means "nothing." Nothing, false, 0, whatever. So you can write

```
if (next_ != nullptr)...
```

as

```
if (next_)...
```

"If next_ isn't nothing; if there is a next thing ..." is what this condition is saying. Use it if you find it convenient.

The Linked List Template

Example 22-5 contains completed versions of the functions above, plus a few others. Some are left as exercises.

There's another thing worth noting. Consider operator=. Before copying over the other list, we must throw away the old memory with delete. Weren't we doing that already in the destructor? Yes: so we make a function eraseAllElements that can be called by operator= *and* the destructor, for code reuse.

createEmptyList is another utility function for code reuse.

Example 22-5. list.h, containing the List class, some functions omitted. I invite the reader to do exercises below before examining the completed solution in ch23's project 1-2-lists.

```
// class List:  a linked list class
//      from _C++26 for Lazy Programmers_

#ifndef LIST_H
#define LIST_H

#include <iostream>

template<typename T>
class List
```

```
{
 public:
   class Underflow  {};                     // exception

   List () = default;
   List (const List& other) : List ()       { copy(other);         }
   ~List() noexcept                         { eraseAllElements(); }

   List& operator=(const List& other)
   {
       if (this == &other) return *this; //prevent self-assignment
       eraseAllElements (); createEmptyList(); copy(other);
       return *this;
   }

   bool isEqualTo(const List<T>& other) const;

   size_t size () const;
   bool   empty() const { return size() == 0; }

   void push_front(const T& newElement); // add newElement at front
   void pop_front ();                    // take one off the front
   const T& front () const
   {
       if (empty()) throw Underflow(); else return start_->data_;
   }

   void print(std::ostream&) const;
 private:
   struct Entry
   {
       T      data_ = T();                //default for whatever T is
                                          // even if it's a basic type
       Entry* next_ = nullptr;
   };

   Entry* start_= nullptr;                // points to first element

   void copy(const List& other);          // copies other's entries
                                          //   into this List
```

```
    void eraseAllElements();               // empties the list
    void createEmptyList ()
    {
        start_ = nullptr; size_ = 0;       // the list is...nothing
    }
};

//Comparisons

template<typename T>
bool operator==(const List<T>& a, const List<T>& b)
{
    return a.isEqual(b);
}

//...

// Adding and deleting

template<typename T>
void List<T>::eraseAllElements() { while (!empty()) pop_front();   }

template<typename T>
void List<T>::copy(const List& other)
{
    Entry* lastEntry = nullptr;    // last thing we added to this list,
                                   //   as we go thru other list
    Entry* otherP = other.start_; // where are we in the other list?

    // while not done with other list...
    //    copy its next item into this list
    while (otherP)
    {
        // make a new entry with current element from other;
        //  put it at end of our list (so far)
        Entry* newEntry = new Entry;
        newEntry->data_ = otherP->data_;
        newEntry->next_ = nullptr;
```

```
        // if list is empty, make it start_ with this new entry
        // if not, make its previous Entry recognize new entry
        //   as what comes next
        if (empty()) start_           = newEntry;
        else         lastEntry->next_ = newEntry;

        lastEntry = newEntry;  // keep pointer for lastEntry updated
        otherP = otherP->next_;// go on to next item in other list

        ++size_;
    }
}
#endif //LIST_H
```

Antibugging

When pointers go wrong, they *really* go wrong. You'll probably get a program crash.

Here are the worst and most common pointer-related errors:

- **Crash, from following a `nullptr`** – for example, saying `*myPointer` when `myPointer` is `nullptr`. The best preventative: Before you refer to what a pointer points to (by putting the * in front or `->` after), always check

  ```
  if (myPointer != nullptr) ...
  ```

  When pointers are involved, paranoia is a Good Thing.

- **Crash, from using a pointer that has not been initialized.** Solution: **Always initialize every pointer**. If you don't know what to initialize it to, use `nullptr`. Then `if (myPointer != nullptr) ...` (see previous paragraph) will prevent the error.

- **Crash, from following a pointer that points to something that's been deleted.** Tracing what the code does with diagrams, as I did in previous sections, is the best prevention I know. Once you have a few functions that you trust, you can be lazy, as I was with eraseAllEntries: let a trusted function like pop_front do the scary work.

- **The program gets stuck in a loop.**

```
Entry* p = start_;
while (p)
{
    ...
}
```

The problem here is I forgot to make the while **loop go on to the next entry:**

```
p = p->next_;
```

I am less likely to forget if I put it in the form of a for loop:

```
for (Entry* p = start_; p != nullptr; p = p->next)...
```

And here are two more thoughts on preventing errors:

- **Use smart pointers**, in Chapter 26.
- **If you decide to use a type** (like Entry) **declared in a template class, outside the class and its functions**, you may need to remind C++ that it's a type:

```
typename List<T>::Entry* myPointer …
```

The error message won't be clear – it'll just tell you myPointer is not defined.

EXERCISES

For these exercises, start with the project in ch22/listExercisesCode. Exercises 1–6 have answers in the chapter's source code (ch22/1-2-lists).

Throughout, you can use operator -> to save your fingers' typing.

1. Write List's member function front().
2. ...and size(). Can you make it work without a loop?
3. ...and print.

4. Clean up the code a bit by making `Entry` set the `next_` field to `nullptr` by default. This should help prevent the error of forgetting to initialize.
5. (Requires move constructors, move =) Give `List` a move constructor and move =.
6. (Requires concepts) Use concepts with your `List`. Make sure any `List` you try to print has printable elements.
7. Try making a new `Queue`, as in Chapter 19, but based on `List`, not `Vector`. Will it be more efficient?
8. (Harder) Add a data member `Entry::prev_`, so that you can traverse the list backward, and `List::rStart_`, so you'll know where to start. Also add `List` member functions `push_back`, `pop_back`, and `back`, and update all other functions (constructors, `push_front`, `copy`, etc.) as needed to keep the new data members `Entry::prev_` and `List::rStart_` correct.
9. (Harder) Rewrite *Montana* to add a new option: undo. To support it you'll need to keep a `List` of moves so you can undo your last move, the one before that, etc., until there are no moves left to undo. What information does a move contain? The `List` can be emptied when a new turn begins. (Why aren't we using `Vector`?)

#include <list>

Yes, the linked list class is also built-in. It's better than mine: it's got `push_back`, `pop_back` (see Exercise 8 above), and lots of other functions you can look up on your own.

So here's a problem: if you can't use `[]`, how *can* you get to the elements of a list? It's pretty useless if you can't! There is a way: it's called "iterators," and it's covered in the next chapter.

CHAPTER 23

The Standard Template Library and Functional-Style Programming

Should every programmer create and maintain a personal copy of vector, list, etc.? Oh, of course not. So some time back the Standard Template Library (STL) was put into the standard. In STL you'll find containers like `list` and `vector`, `string`s and `string_view`s, and commonly needed functions like `swap` and `find`.

And you'll find some easier ways to do things.

You'll also find an annoying emphasis on efficiency. I say "annoying" because STL promotes efficiency by *disabling* inefficient things. If you want to use `operator[]` with a `list`, you can forget it: it's too slow (O(N) time, if you do O notation). If you want `[]`, makers of STL reasoned you can use a `vector`. They're right. But I still get to be annoyed.

To get started, we've got to get at the elements of a list somehow. How? Let's deal with that now.

Iterators

`operator[]` for `list` doesn't exist. `Entry`s are private. What can we do?

STL's `list` class provides **iterators**: things that say where we are in the `list` and can traverse it. Here's what you can do with them:

```
// double each element of myList, from beginning to end
for (list<T>::iterator i = myList.begin(); i != myList.end(); ++i)
    *i *= 2;
```


W. Briggs, *C++26 for Lazy Programmers*, https://doi.org/10.1007/979-8-8688-1859-2_23

The `iterator` type is a member of `list<T>` like our `Entry` struct, but publicly available. As shown, it often starts at `begin()`, that is, the start of the list, and keeps going till it reaches the `end()` (Figure 23-1).

`end()` refers not to the last element, but to one *past* the last element. Think of the `list` as a train of cars, and this is its caboose. We check it to see if we're going too far, using `!=`, not `<`. (Whether one iterator is less than another is not defined, but whether they're equal is.)

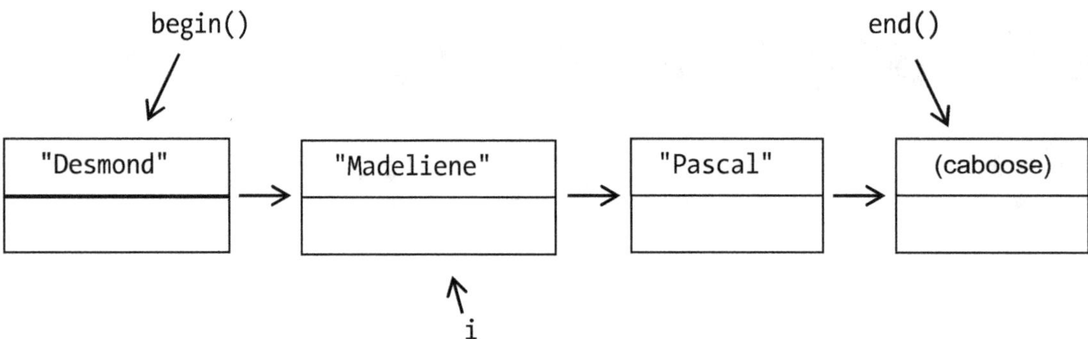

Figure 23-1. *A list, with its `begin()` and `end()` access functions, and an iterator `i` denoting the second element. `end()` is one step past the last element*

`++i` and `i++` work as expected: they take you to the next element.

To get not the iterator but the thing it's referring to, put the `*` in front, as in the loop above.

That's all there is to it!

Is your reaction something like "But what *is* an iterator?"

Formally, it's just as described: it's a thing that refers to an element in the list, and when you say `++`, it goes to the next element.

Informally ...it's not exactly a pointer, but it does point to something. You can use `*` with it, and `->`, just as you would with a pointer. But `++` means go to the next element in the list, *not* the next memory address, as it would with a pointer. Think of it as a finger you can put on an entry and can move to the next when you like – but what it really *is,* is a class, as in Example 23-1.

Example 23-1. An iterator class for `List`

```
template<typename T>
class List
{
    ...
```

```
private:
    ...

    Entry* start_;                          // points to first element
    Entry* end_;                            //  ...and the caboose

public:
    class iterator                          // an iterator for List
    {
    public:
        iterator(const iterator& other)  : where_(other.where_) {}
        iterator(Entry* where = nullptr) : where_(where)        {}

        const iterator& operator=(const iterator& other)
        {
            where_ = other.where_;
        }

        //Another way to do ==. The community mostly dislikes == as
                  //  a member, but this is simple to write & avoids
                  //  template-related complexities
        bool operator==(const iterator& other) const
        {
            return where_ == other.where_;
        }

        const iterator& operator++()     // pre-increment, as in ++i
        {
            if(where_->next_ == nullptr) throw BadPointer();
            else where_ = where_->next_;
            return *this;
        }
        iterator operator++(int)        // post-increment, as in i++
        {
            iterator result = *this; ++(*this); return result;
        }

        T& operator*()
```

```
        {
            if (where_->next_ == nullptr) throw BadPointer();
            return where_->data_;
        }

        T* operator->() // This really is how you do it.  It works!
        {
            if (where_->next_ == nullptr) throw BadPointer();
            return &(where_->data_);
        }
    private:
        Entry* where_;
    };

    iterator       begin() { return iterator(start_); }
    iterator       end  () { return iterator(end_   ); }
};
```

And now we can get to the List's data *outside* the List class.

...with vector Too

lists *need* iterators. But STL provides them for vector and other containers, and STL mavens recommend using them. Why?

- **Easy rewriting of code:** Consider these two versions of code with a vector:

  ```
  for (int i = 0; i < v.size(); ++i)
      v[i] *= 2;
  ```

  and

  ```
  for (vector<T>::iterator i = v.begin(); i != v.end(); ++i)
      *i *= 2;
  ```

  I write this and later think, *No, I see now* vector *isn't the way to go;* list *is better.*

If I used the first version, I've got major changes on both lines. If I used the second, all I have to do is change `vector` to `list`.

- **Generic programming:** Suppose there's something you want to do with different types of container:

```
myIterator = find(nums.begin(), halfwayIterator, 7);
                                         // Is 7 in the first half?
```

Since `find` for `list` must use iterators, `find` for `vector` uses iterators too. That way you can learn one way to call the function, and it'll work regardless of your choice of container. The section on ranges and views that follows introduces a few of many such functions STL provides.

But if you do use `int index` for `vectors` as before, the sky won't fall.

`const` and `reverse` Iterators

In this code, using an iterator gives a type conflict:

```
template<typename T>
double findAverageSize(const List<T>& myList)
{
      if (myList.empty()) throw EmptyList();

      double sum = 0;
      for (List<string>::iterator i = myList.begin();
           i != myList.end();
           ++i)
            sum += i->size();

      return sum / myList.size();
}
```

The compiler gives an error message that boils down to: `myList` is `const`, but you're using an `iterator` with it, and that's a type conflict.

This is how STL prevents you from using an iterator with a `const` container and doing something that alters the contents. The solution is to use a version of iterator that promises not to allow changes:

```
template<typename T>
double findAverageSize(const List<T>& myList)
{
      if (myList.empty()) throw EmptyList();

      double sum = 0;
      for (List<string>::const_iterator i = myList.begin();
           i != myList.end();
           ++i)
            sum += i->size();

      return sum / myList.size();
}
```

That's all it takes.

If you like you can go through the container backward (note the `rbegin` and `rend` – the same as `begin` and `end`, only in reverse):

```
for (List<string>::reverse_iterator i=myList.rbegin();
     i !=myList.rend();
     ++i)
        doSomethingTo(*i); // myList must be non-const
```

...or do backward *and* `const`:

```
for (List<string>::const_reverse_iterator i = myList.begin();
     i != myList.end();
     ++i)
        sum += i->size();
```

To know which to use

- If you don't plan to change the container, use `const_iterator`.
- If you do, use `iterator`.
- If you're going backward, stick `reverse_` in there somewhere.

Antibugging

- **You get an error message too long to read:**

  ```
  conversion from 'std::__cxx11::list<std::pair<std::__cxx11::basic_
  string<char>, std::__cxx11::basic_string<char> > >::const_
  iterator' {aka 'std::_List_const_iterator<std::pair<std::__
  cxx11::basic_string<char>, std::__cxx11::basic_string<char> >
  >'} to non-scalar type 'std::__cxx11::list<std::pair<std::__
  cxx11::basic_string<char>, int> >::const_iterator' {aka 'std::_
  List_const_iterator<std::pair<std::__cxx11::basic_string<char>,
  int> >'} requested
  ```

  Rip out things that don't look important. This gets us

  ```
  conversion from list<pair<string, string > >::const_iterator to
  list<pair<string, int> >::const_iterator requested
  ```

  My mistake is now clearer: I forgot what I wanted a pair of.

- **You get pages of error messages, reporting errors in system libraries.** Look for your own filename(s) in the messages and focus on those. If all else fails, comment out parts of your code until you find the offending bit.

- **You've declared a variable of some type declared in another type, like `List<T>::Entry`, but the compiler refuses to acknowledge it**. Try putting `typename` in front. Sometimes with templates the compiler gets confused as to what's a type.

Getting Really Lazy: Ranges and auto

If I type this much more

```
for (List<string>::reverse_iterator i=myList.rbegin();
     i !=myList.rend();
     ++i)
        doSomethingTo(*i);
```

I'll have to give up my lazy programmer license.

We've seen this keyword before, but it's especially useful now.

```
for (auto i=myList.rbegin(); i !=myList.rend(); ++i)
        doSomethingTo(*i);
```

auto means "let C++ figure out what type I meant from the variable's initialization." This is called **type inference,** and it's especially useful when the types are that long.

But there's a better way to be lazy. Now that List has begin() and end(), it is a **range**, and we can use the range-based for loop we're used to:

```
for (       char& s : myString) doSomethingTo(s); //& means "allow changes"
for (const string& s: myVector) useWithoutChanging(s);
for (          int i: intArray) useIntWithoutChanging(i);
```

Something is a range if it

- Has begin() and end() defined
- Is a C-style (Chapter 10) array, which has these defined implicitly

If you want auto, no problem, though it won't save your fingers much here:

```
for (auto& i: myVector) i *= 2;
```

EXERCISES

The first three exercises use the std::list we're emulating; the last exercises expand List.

1. Using iterators in a for loop, write a function reverse that returns a reversed copy of a std::list you give it.
2. Write a function find that takes a std::list and a value and returns an iterator pointing to the first instance of that value. If it's to found, it should return list's end().
3. Now write it so that it takes not a list, but a pair of iterators first and last (probably begin() and end()) from a list. It returns last if it can't find the value. You may need to write typename before the iterator type (as in typename std::list<T>::const_iterator) and/or specify T when you call the function (as in find<T>).

4. Add a `const_iterator` class to `List`.

   You'll need new `const` versions of `begin` and `end`, to return `const_iterator` instead of `iterator`.

5. Rewrite `List::operator==` so it doesn't need a helper function inside `List` – it can do it all itself. Here's how: use iterators, not `Entry*`. You'll need `const_iterator` from the previous exercise.

6. Exercise 8 in Chapter 22's last set of exercises dealt with equipping a `List` to be traversed backward. Using that, incorporate `reverse_iterator` and `const_reverse_iterator` into the `List` class.

std::tuple

Now that I have `auto`, I can use `std::tuple` – it's like `pair`, but can contain as many parts as you like – without my fingers writing out long, complicated typenames. Tuples are especially useful if you have several different things to return from a function, but they're also a super-fast way to write heterogeneous collections of data.

Example 23-2 shows a function to calculate and return the member of the Simpson family most likely to get the Nobel Prize.

Example 23-2. A function that uses tuples

```
#include <tuple>

...

auto smartestSimpson()
{
    //One way to initialize tuples: using {} initializer lists
    static std::tuple<std::string, int, int> Simpsons[] =
    {
        //each tuple is: name, age, IQ
        {"Homer",39,92}, {"Marge",36,105}, {"Bart",10,95}, {"Lisa",8,135},
        {"Maggie",1,100}
    };
```

```
    //Another way: std::make_tuple
    auto smartest = std::make_tuple(std::string(), 0, 0);
        //I didn't use "", because that's a constant literal
        //   and smartest must change (below)

    for (const auto& s : Simpsons)
        if (std::get<2>(smartest) < std::get<2>(s)) //get element 2: iq
            smartest = s;

    return smartest;
}
```

We see two ways to initialize – with {} and with the `std::make_tuple` function – and we also see a somewhat clunky way to get at the fields in the tuple, `std::get<whichField>`.

This will work for calling the function:

```
auto nobelWinner = smartestSimpson();
```

...but there's a way I like better that leads to less typing overall:

```
auto [name, age, iq] = smartestSimpson();
```

This declares three variables, `name`, `age`, and `id`, figuring out from the initialization what types they should have, and gives them their values. So we get the parts of the tuple without saying "`std::get<whichever>`" three times. This is called a **structured binding** as it binds the variables using this structure.

And if we don't care about `age` or `iq`, we don't even have to name them but can replace them with _'s, as placeholders for values we don't want. Example 23-3 shows the complete program.

```
auto [name, _, _] = smartestSimpson();[1]
```

[1] If your compiler isn't up to date on this, replace the second _ with something else that starts with _: `_iq`, `_____`, `_somethingElse`. Earlier versions of C++ wouldn't accept placeholders that were identical. Confusing, and fixed in C++26.

Example 23-3. A program to find out which Simpson might get the Nobel Prize. Its output, which will surprise no *The Simpsons* fan, is `The Simpson most likely to win the Nobel is Lisa.`

```
//Program to find out which Simpson is mostly likely to get the Nobel
//        -- from _C++26 for Lazy Programmers_

#include <string>
#include <tuple>
#include <iostream>

auto smartestSimpson()
{
    // ... no changes ...
}

int main()
{
    auto [name, _, _] = smartestSimpson(); //change 2nd _ to __
                                           // if compiler's not compliant

    std::cout << "The Simpson most likely to win the Nobel is "
              << name << ".\n";

    return 0;
}
```

In Chapters 7 and 8 I may have given the impression that a function can't return multiple things – but we just did! So I want to update that Golden Rule from Chapter 8:

Golden Rule of Function Parameters and `return` (New Version)

- If a function provides a value
  - If it's small, return it. **For multiples, return a tuple.**
  - If not, pass by &.

- If it takes a variable in and changes it, pass by &.
- If it takes it in and doesn't change it
  - If it's an object and might be large, pass as `const TheClass&` object.
  - Else, pass by value (no &).
- If it's a move constructor or move =, pass by &&.

...except arrays are passed in as parameters, with or without `const` depending on whether the contents are to change.

EXERCISES

In each exercise, let `main` use `auto [...]` to store the values returned.

1. Write and test a function `sortedTriple` that takes in a tuple of three elements, puts them in order, and returns the new version.
2. Write and test a function that searches a `std::span` for a given element and returns both the element found and the index it was found at.
3. Write and test a function that, given a string, returns the string, its length, and the number of vowels.

STL Functions Using Ranges and Views

Suppose I want to find all the numbers I have that are even. I can write a conventional for loop (`for (int i = 0; i < nums.size()...`), a range-based for loop (`for (int i: nums)...`), an iterator-based loop (`for (auto i = nums.begin(); ... )`...or I can reflect that people have done this for decades and a function to do this must already exist.

It does.

Example 23-4. Using `std::find_if` to find even numbers. You can find all the code in this section in project/folder `ch23/3-evens`.

```
bool isEven(int x) { return !(x % 2); }
...

auto where1 = std::find_if(nums.begin(), nums.end(), isEven);
if (where1 != nums.end())
      std::cout << "Found an even: " << *where1 << '\n';
```

This works for any container - `vector`, `list`, `array`, whatever - as long as it's a range, that is, as long as it has `begin()` and `end()`. What happens is `find_if` returns an iterator referencing the first even element of `nums`. If there is no such element, it returns `nums.end()`. (The type of the iterator was `std::whateverContainerIPicked<int>::const_iterator`, but I was too lazy so I used `auto`.)

I don't like specifying iterators all the time, so I'll let the compiler do it for me:

```
auto where2 = std::ranges::find_if(nums, isEven);
```

That's nicer. Now I want not just one even number (if any), but all of them:

```
auto[2] evens1 = std::views::filter(nums, isEven);
for (auto i : evens1) std::cout << i << ' ';
```

Just as a `string_view` lets you view a sequence of characters, without expensive copying, a **view** lets you view a sequence of elements, without expensive copying, and do some things with it like, well, filtering for evens.

There's another way to write this:

```
auto evens2 = nums | std::views::filter(isEven);[3] //"pipeline" syntax
```

We can use these "view" functions together. Assuming I have a function to give the square of a number, I can use them to take only the even numbers, square them, and give me the first three:

[2] The type returned here is `std::ranges::filter_view <std::ranges::ref_view<std::list <int>>, bool (*)(int)>`. I don't hate myself *nearly* enough to type that.

[3] `std::views::filter` takes 2 arguments, the range and the function. So C++ changes this to `std::views::filter(nums, isEven)`. The pipeline syntax is easier to read, so let's use that.

```
auto evenSquares2 = nums | std::views::filter(isEven) //"pipeline" syntax
                         | std::views::transform(square)
                         | std::views::take(3);
```

Maybe we want to erase all those evens from the original container? Here you go:

```
std::erase_if(nums, isEven);
```

There are more useful functions, too many to remember. Table 23-1 will give you a taste. If it's not enough, and it isn't, an Internet search will get you what you need.

I won't cover it here, but some STL functions can be parallelized, including `find_if` and `for_each`. The term to look for is "execution policy" or `execution::par`.

Table 23-1. *STL functions used in this chapter and Chapter 24. The ones belonging to* `std::views` *are written as they'd be used in pipeline format*

`std::views::take(int n);` / `std::views::drop(int n);` Found in `#include <ranges>`	Return a view taking only/dropping the first n elements of the input.
`std::erase(inputRange,valueType n);` / `std::erase_if(inputRange,booleanPredicate)` Found in the include file for your container type	Erase all instances of n/erase all entries for which `booleanPredicate` is true.
`std::ranges::find(inputRange,valueType n);` / `std::ranges::find_if(inputRange, booleanPredicate);` Found in `<algorithm>`	Return an iterator to the first element in `inputRange` which matches n/for which `booleanPredicate` is true. If none return `end()`.
`std::views::filter(booleanPredicate);` Found in `<ranges>`	Return a view keeping only elements for which `booleanPredicate` is true.
`std::ranges::fold_left (inputRange, int init, binaryFunction);` / `std::ranges::fold_right(...as above...);` Found in `<algorithm>`	Use `binaryfunction` to combine every element in `inputRange`, starting with `init`. `fold_left` starts with the first element and `fold_right` starts with the last.
`std::ranges::for_each(inputRange,func);` Found in `<algorithm>`	Apply `func` to every element of `inputRange`. Doesn't return a (useful) value.

(*continued*)

Table 23-1. *(continued)*

`std::views::iota(int start, int end= ∞);` Found in <numeric>	Return a view of integers from `start` to `end-1`. If end isn't specified, the range is infinite.
`std::ranges::sort(inputRange, [comparisonFunction]);`	Sort the input range. If no comparison function is specified, use `<`.
`std::ranges::to<RangeType>(inputRange)` Found in <ranges>	Return a `RangeType` (likely some container) based on `inputRange`, which could be a view.
`std::views::transform(func);` Found in <ranges>	Return a view in which each element is replaced by `func(element)`.

A New Kind of Lazy: Lazy Evaluation and Infinite Ranges

Recall that in the previous example code, evenSquares2 (for example) was of type "`std::ranges::filter_view`" something – not a `vector` or a `list` or any sort of container we know. It wasn't a sequence of numbers. Effectively it was a way of *making* such a sequence. The computer didn't bother making any actual results until we forced it to by doing something with it, like printing.

This is called lazy evaluation, and it can be a real help in avoiding extra storage and computation (Example 23-5).

Example 23-5. Lazy evaluation with STL functions

```
//Program to do some (more) processing of number sequences
//    -- from _C++26 for Lazy Programmers_

#include <iostream>
#include <ranges>
#include <vector>

int square(int x) { return x * x; }

int main()
```

```
{
    auto lotsaIntegers = std::views::iota(0, 1000000);
    auto firstFiftySquares = lotsaIntegers
            | std::views::transform(square)
            | std::views::take(50);
    std::vector<int> v = firstFiftySquares | std::ranges::to<std::vector>();
    for (int i: v) std::cout[4] << i << ' ';
    std::cout << '\n';

    return 0;
}
```

`std::iota` is a quick, easy way of generating our sequence of integers. It's lazy like `transform` and `take`, so it doesn't generate – or store – a million numbers. And a Good Thing!

But a vector *does* need to know what to store, so we have a function `std::ranges::to<std::vector>` that generates a container based on the view we gave it.

Actually, we didn't need to limit ourselves to a million. We can give it no upper bound at all, meaning all numbers up to infinity. It'll only `take` the ones we tell it to:

```
auto lotsaIntegers = std::views::iota(0); //from 0 to ∞!
```

Antibugging

I'm afraid we're leaving behind the days of helpful error messages. I'll just get something meaning "you can't do that here."

This is a good place to use artificial intelligence. You can give it the code and the error message, and it'll often know the problem (sometimes even without the error message). Be aware: it can also go off on wild tangents, seeking more and more irrelevant fixes when you really just (say) gave something the wrong type.

- **You construct your views, but the compiler won't let you do anything with the result.** Maybe you need to pass that result to `std::ranges::to<whateverContainerYouWant>`.

[4] The namespaces have gotten so confusing I'm giving up on using namespace std;. Some programmers think it's evil anyway.

- **The compiler says it's never heard of whatever function you're calling.** You may have the wrong namespace – `std::to` instead of `std::ranges::to`. Or maybe your compiler isn't completely up to date; find another way to do what you want or an updated compiler.
- **Your program compiles, but it gets stuck and never completes.** I can imagine two reasons:
    - You set up a range with `iota`, but only gave it a lower bound. It's chugging away to infinity. It'll take a while!
    - It may be not stuck but slow. I'm not getting clear opinions from the community, who don't like to talk about this, but I find that using views is not as quick as the old "`for (int i`..." sort of thing. Tip: If your code is slow, consider taking the part where you think it's doing most of its work and use more conventional code.
- **You add or remove elements in a loop and get a crash.** When you do anything to change the contents of your container, it may invalidate iterators already in the container. Consider this code (assume `nums` is a `list`):

```
for (auto i = nums.begin(); i != nums.end(); ++i)
    if (isEven(*i))
        erase(nums, *i);
```

After you erase whatever's at `i`, `i` points to a nonexistent element. The loop increments `i` and gets to another nonexistent element at who-knows-where, and the result is unpredictable.

Solution: Use the built-in `erase(myContainer, predicate)` function.

EXERCISES

In all these exercises, use STL functions from the previous sections to do the work.

1. In the string "SoxEr776asdCsdfR1234qqE..T12Ci-98j0apqwe0DweE" there is a secret code. Extract only the capital letters and read the code. Warning: You can't just use `isupper`; `filter` gets confused applying something that takes `int`s to a sequence of `char`s. You'll need to write your own version of `isupper` that takes `char`.
2. Print the first 100 primes. Don't worry about being efficient.
3. (Uses file I/O) First, make a file of strings. Then make two copies of it. In one, alter the order and the capitalization of some of the strings. In the other, replace some of the strings.

   Now write a program that can read two files into vectors or lists and tell how the files are different, ignoring order and capitalization. After changing each sequence to be all caps, you can find what's in one sequence but not the other thus:

   ```
   for each element in sequence 1 (using iterators)
      use the "find" function to see if it's also in sequence 2
   ```
4. Do the problem above, but instead of using `find` and a loop, use `set_difference` (also not covered above).

CHAPTER 24

Functional-Style Programming, continued

Functional-style programming – passing functions as arguments to other functions, pipelines, lazy evaluation – is all the rage in C++ right now.

It's not exactly **functional programming**, which attempts to reduce errors by emphasizing functions that don't alter their arguments and have no side effects. C++ isn't all-in on any one paradigm. It's more a set of tools you can use to do some things better.

Here is what it's good for:

- Clarity – sometimes
- Processing streams of data

Here is what it's not good for:

- Clarity – sometimes putting things in functional style is like solving a brainteaser.
- Computation-intensive work like graphics. It's hard to compete with the for loops we got in Chapter 5 and the arrays in Chapter 10 for speed.

Some of the examples involve file I/O, so if you skipped that part of Chapter 13 or need a refresher, you might want to go back over it. Or muddle through – it's not that difficult.

W. Briggs, *C++26 for Lazy Programmers*, https://doi.org/10.1007/979-8-8688-1859-2_24

Lambda Functions for One-Time Use

In the last chapter we filtered a container of numbers for being even, using function isEven.

This time I want to do things to a container of cities: maybe filter by name or population or how far they are from somewhere. That's a lot of criteria, and I don't want to write them all as functions. So I'll write them as temporary functions, called lambda functions, and pass them right into the filter function (Example 24-1).

Example 24-1. Sorting and filtering party spots using lambda functions. A complete program is in ch24/1-cities.

```
vector<City> cities =
{
    //city name, population, location ({latitude, longitude})
    {"London",  10'310'000, { 51,   -5}}, // The 's are like the commas
    {"Hamburg",  1'740'000, { 53,   10}}, //   in the more usual 10,310,000
    {"Paris",   10'840'000, { 49,    2}}, //   but commas were taken
    {"Rome",     3'720'000, { 42,   12}}, // Just there for easier reading
    ...
};

std::cout << "Cities with more than 10 million:\n";
auto bigCities = cities
    | std::views::filter([](const City& c) { return c.pop() > 10'000'000; });
```

The thing in filter starting with [] is a function. It doesn't have a name, but it does have a parameter list and a body. I could give it a return type like so – [](const City& c) -> **bool**[1] {...} – but it can figure that out from the return statement, so I almost never bother.

Now let's get those cities that are under 1,000 km from a particular location. Assume we have a distance function to give distance in kilometers between cities:

```
const City SHARD_END = ...;
std::cout << "Cities within 1000 km of Shard End:\n";
auto nearCities = cities
```

[1] A "trailing" return type.

```
    | std::views::filter([](const City& c)  //nope, not working...
        {
            return distance(c, SHARD_END) < 1000;
        });
```

If you have a local variable – a global's different, but we don't do globals – you can't just refer to it in a lambda; not allowed. We can't put it in the parameter list, either, because filter needs it to have exactly one parameter: the element of the range we're processing it.

So we send it in through the [ ]'s. This is called a **capture**.

```
auto nearCities = cities
    | std::views::filter([SHARD_END](const City& c)
        {
            return distance(c, SHARD_END) < 1000;
        });
```

SHARD_END is large enough maybe I should use & to prevent the copying, just as I would a function parameter. It won't let me do const&, but since SHARD_END is const that's not a problem:

```
auto nearCities = cities
    | std::views::filter([&SHARD_END](const City& c)
        {
            return distance(c, SHARD_END) < 1000;
        });
```

Table 24-1 shows what things we can put between the [ ]'s. Usually we don't need anything. But we can list specific variables, with or without &.

We can also say, using = or &, "let everything in." "Everything" here means variables that aren't global (ack!) and aren't static.[2] Globals and static locals can be referred to anyway without being listed in the [ ]'s.

[2] The correct term is "automatic variables."

Table 24-1. *Lambda captures. These go between the [ ]'s of a lambda function, to allow access to non-static local variables that are not the lambda function's parameters. They can be combined: [`arg1, &arg2, this`]*

`arg1`	Use arguments by value in the lambda function.
`&arg1`	Use arguments by reference (changing it in the lambda function changes it outside as well).
=	Use all available variables by value.
&	Use all available variables by reference.
`this`	Use members of current object. If in a non-const function, they can be modified.

I avoid bare & and = – it's safer to specify exactly what can go into the function.

EXERCISES

In all of these – of course – use lambda functions.

1. Sort the `Citys` in `ch24/1-cities` by latitude. You'll want `std::ranges::sort`.
2. Use the `for_each` function to print every element of a container, delimited by /'s. Maybe you'll use it to print the results for `Citys` in this section.
3. Use `transform` to capitalize every element of a container of strings.
4. In this game I just made up, there's one heart, one club, one diamond, and one spade in the kitty. Players trade cards trying to narrow down which cards are in that stash.

   Write code that can (a) generate all possible combos of the four suits – you'll want `std::views::cartesian_product`; look it up on Internet – and (b) filter out those combos contradicted by a vector of the cards you have seen. Print the remaining combos with `for_each`. Use lambda functions, structured bindings, and views.

fold_left, fold_right

Let's see if we can get functional programming to help us with some statistics. Don't worry, we'll make the computer do all the hard work.

First, let's do an average: Σ x / N, where x is the numbers and N is how many. The Σ means "sum them all up." So let's do that. Here's one way C++ does it:

```
double sum = std::ranges::fold_left(numbers, 0.0, std::plus{});
```

`fold_left` "folds" the numbers together using addition (`std::plus{}`, it's called here), starting with the initial value 0.0 and then adding the 0th number, the 1st one, the 2nd, and so on till they're all added. (`fold_right` goes backward through the numbers.) Yes, I think it's weird that they call addition "`std::plus{}`." No points for guessing what they call minus. If we didn't want plus, we could put our own (possibly lambda) function there, as long as it takes two numbers and returns one.

Let's go further and calculate standard deviation (σ), a number that tells us how closely clustered our values are - mostly close to the average or spread far and wide (see Figure 24-1). It's calculated like this:

$$\sigma = \sqrt{\frac{\Sigma(x - avg)^2}{N}}$$

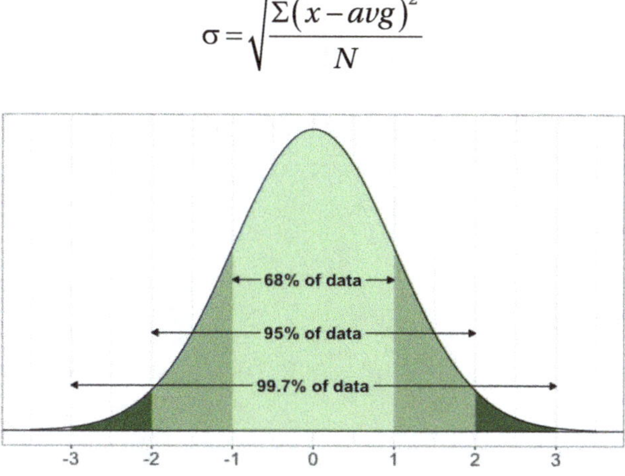

***Figure 24-1.** If the values are in what's called a "normal" distribution, about 68% of them will be within σ of the average*

What needs summing this time isn't x but $(x\text{-}avg)^2$. We can use `transform` to get what to sum

```
numbers | std::views::transform([avg](double x) {return sqr(x - avg); })
```

...and send *that* to `fold_left` to sum it.

The complete program is in Example 24-2.

Example 24-2. A program using `fold_left` to calculate standard deviation

```
// Program that uses calculates standard deviation
//      -- from _C++26 for Lazy Programmers_

#include <iostream>
#include <vector>
#include <ranges>
#include <algorithm> //for fold_left

double sqr(double x) { return x * x; }

int main()
{
    std::vector<double> numbers = { 2, 4, 4, 4, 5, 5, 7, 9 };

    double sum = std::ranges::fold_left(numbers, 0.0, std::plus{});
    double avg = sum / numbers.size();

    double innerSummation =
        std::ranges::fold_left
            (numbers
             | std::views::transform([avg](double x) {return sqr(x - avg); }),
            0.0,
            std::plus{});

    double standardDeviation = sqrt(innerSummation / numbers.size());

    std::cout << "Standard deviation should be 2 and is "
              << standardDeviation << ".\n";

    return 0;
}
```

Image Processing and Functional-Style Programming

After I went on about how functional-style programming might be too much for something already computation-intense like image processing ...here I am doing it. Because it's fun, the pictures are pretty, and we just won't do anything that'll break the processor. No comparing pixels to their neighbors, but we will alter their colors and change the image size.

To do this, I use an SSDL class not previously mentioned, `SSDL_ProcessibleImage`. It's like an `SSDL_Image`, but changeable. To use it

- Don't use `SSDL_LoadImage` but `SSDL_LoadProcessibleImage`.
- Use its members `width()`, `height()`, and `size()` to access that information if you like.
- To get at its pixels, use member `getPixels()`, which returns `std::span<SSDL_Color>`.
- To set its pixels, use member `setPixels(newPixels )`, which takes `std::span<SSDL_Color>` and possibly new image dimensions.
- You can save it to a BMP file with `save(const char* filename)`.

We're also using, from Chapter 7, a function to average three numbers (since we have it!) and have adapted a Chapter 7 function to make a color grayscale.

With these tools in hand, let's take a perfectly beautiful image and make it black-and-white (Example 24-3).

Example 24-3. Part of a program that does image processing. (`average` and `greyscale` are taken from Example 7-1.) The complete code is in `ch24/3-4-5-image-processing`. Output is in Figure 24-2.

```
// Program to make an image monochrome
//              -- from _C++26 for Lazy Programmers_

#include <ranges>
#include "SSDL.h"
```

```
int average(int, int, int);                 // Averages 3
SSDL_Color greyscale(const SSDL_Color& c);
       // Gets a greyscale color for a given r, g, b

int main(int argc, char** argv)
{
    SSDL_SetWindowSize(800, 450);
    SSDL_RenderClear(WHITE); SSDL_SetRenderDrawColor(BLACK);

    //The original
    SSDL_ProcessibleImage original =
                             SSDL_LoadProcessibleImage("media/fuji.bmp");

    //A monochrome version
    SSDL_ProcessibleImage monochrome = original;
    auto newPixelsView = monochrome.getPixels()
                          | std::views::transform(greyscale);
    auto newPixels = std::ranges::to<std::vector<SSDL_Color>>(newPixelsView);
    monochrome.setPixels(newPixels);

    SSDL_RenderImage(original,      0,   0);
    SSDL_RenderText ("original",    0, 150);
    SSDL_RenderImage(monochrome,  200,   0);
    SSDL_RenderText ("monochrome",200, 150);

    SSDL_WaitKey();

    return 0;
}
```

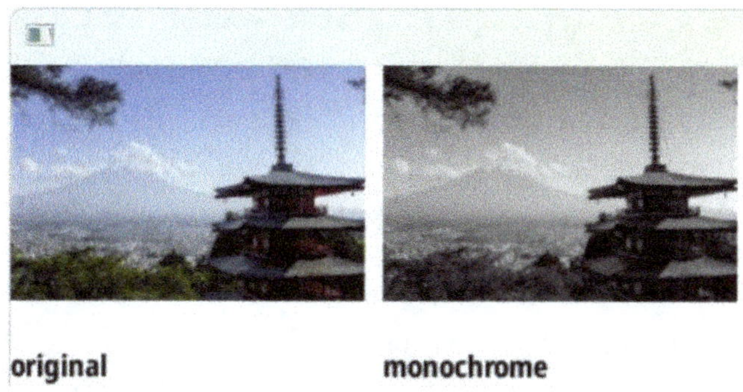

Figure 24-2. *An image and its grayscale version. If somehow your version of the book shows only black-and-white, trust me, the one on the left has blue skies and green trees*

Now let's try cropping an image.

Since getPixels returns a 1D array (a span, actually) to represent a 2D image, we need a way to get from an index i (in the 1D array) to an x, y pair (a coordinate in the image). The line calculating x and y in Example 24-4 does this.

Example 24-4. A function to crop an SSDL_ProcessibleImage

```
//Crops original starting at (imgX, imgY), to a size (w, h)
SSDL_ProcessibleImage crop(const SSDL_ProcessibleImage& original,
                           int imgX, int imgY, int w, int h)
{
    auto originalPixels = original.getPixels();
    int  originalWidth  = original.width();

    auto newPixelsView = std::views::iota(0, original.size())
        | std::views::filter([imgX, imgY, w, h, originalWidth](int i)
            {
                int x = i % originalWidth, y = i / originalWidth;
                return (imgX <= x && x < imgX + w &&
                        imgY <= y && y < imgY + h);
            })
        | std::views::transform([originalPixels](int i)
            {
                return originalPixels[i];
            });
```

```
    auto newPixels = std::ranges::to<std::vector<SSDL_Color>>
                                    (newPixelsView);
    SSDL_ProcessibleImage result;
    result.setPixels(newPixels, w, h);
    return result;
}
```

newPixels is calculated thus: All indices into that 1D array are generated by iota. There's a filter to throw out those whose (x,y) versions aren't in the range of the new cropped area. Then the surviving coordinates are to be transformed into the pixels at those coordinates. Finally, we tell the program (by calling std::ranges::to) it's time to do that filtering and transforming and store the result in a vector<SSDL_Color>.

The resulting image is setTo use those newPixels. The outcome is shown in Figure 24-3.

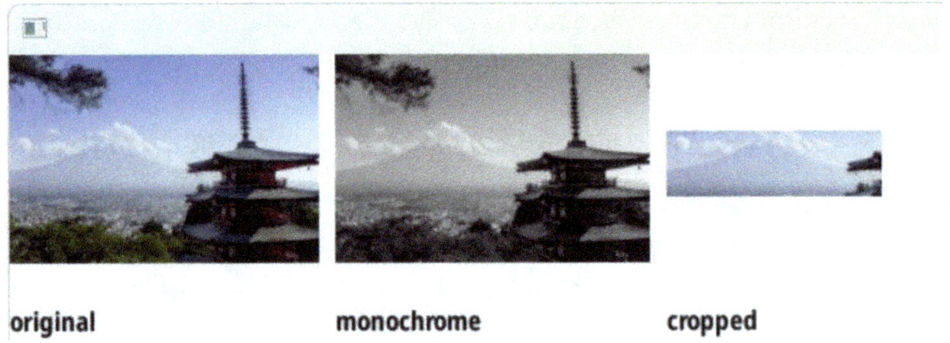

Figure 24-3. *The image processing program showing a cropped image*

Let's do one more thing: histogram equalization.

A histogram is an array with a count, for each pixel brightness, of how many pixels have that intensity. Define the intensity of a pixel to be its grayscale value, 0–255, and we'll have an array of 256 entries. This code

```
std::vector<int> histogram3(256, 0); //256 elements, each initialized to 0
std::ranges::for_each(cropped.getPixels(),
   [&histogram3](const SSDL_Color& c)
   {
    ++histogram3[average(c.r, c.g, c.b)];
   });
```

can fill it with the counts for each intensity. With the help of a function to display the histogram, ranging from 0 intensity at the top to 255 at the bottom, we can see what the distribution looks like (Figure 24-4).

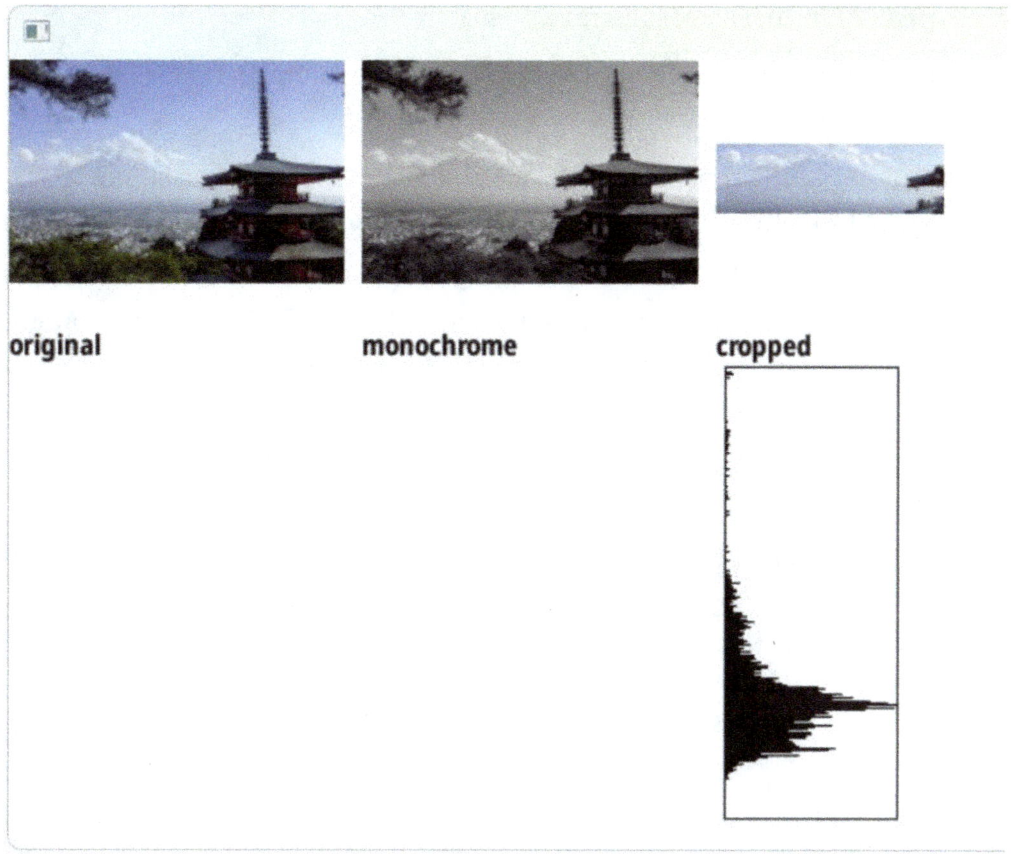

Figure 24-4. *The cropped image now has its associated histogram*

As we might expect from the sky colors dominating the image, it's mostly around the same, relatively high intensity. We could increase the contrast by moving pixels' brightness down if below the average, and up if above, so the histogram looks more flat. (It can't be perfectly distributed because we're dealing with integral, not continuous, values in a real-world image with gaps in the distribution, but it should look better.)

Let's now see how to do it. (If the method is confusing, don't stress - the purpose here isn't to become experts at image processing, but to see how the new C++ features do their work.) Here are the steps:

- Make the histogram (done).
- Divide the number for each intensity by the number of pixels, so that the sum for all intensities will be 1.0. The number for each is now the probability that a pixel has this intensity.
- Get a cumulative probability for each: the probability that a pixel has this or lesser intensity.
- Multiply each probability by the max intensity (255), so for each slot in the histogram, it's the new intensity that every pixel associated with this slot should have. This is the intensity map (see Example 24-5).

Now we need to convert that to colors. For each pixel, for each r, g, or b component, multiply that by the new intensity for that pixel divided by the old. The `std::clamp` is just in case one of those components gets too bright or too dark – keep it in range.

Finally, force all that work to actually be done and the result stored in a vector by calling `std::ranges::to`.

Example 24-5. The histogram equalization function

```
void histogramEqualize(       SSDL_ProcessibleImage& outImg,
                        const SSDL_ProcessibleImage& inImg,
                        const std::vector<int>& inHist)
{
   outImg = inImg;

   //Do histogram equalization
   int size = outImg.size();
   double sum = 0.0f;
   std::vector<double> intensityMap = std::ranges::to<std::vector<double>>(
      inHist
      | std::views::transform([size](int    x) { return double(x) / size; })
      | std::views::transform([&sum](double x) { return sum += x; })
      | std::views::transform([size](double x)
         {
            return static_cast<int>(255*x);
         })
      );
```

```
    auto newColors = std::ranges::to<std::vector<SSDL_Color>>(
       outImg.getPixels()
       | std::views::transform([intensityMap](const SSDL_Color& c)
           {
              int oldIntensity = average(c.r, c.g, c.b);
              if (oldIntensity == 0) oldIntensity = 1;
                                 //prevent divide by zero
              double scale = intensityMap[oldIntensity] / oldIntensity;
              SSDL_Color cNew;
              cNew.r = static_cast<int>(std::clamp(c.r * scale, 0.0, 255.0));
              cNew.g = static_cast<int>(std::clamp(c.g * scale, 0.0, 255.0));
              cNew.b = static_cast<int>(std::clamp(c.b * scale, 0.0, 255.0));
              cNew.a = 255;
              return cNew;
           }));

   outImg.setPixels(newColors);
}
```

The clouds are more distinct and Mt. Fuji really came into view (Figure 24-5). I'd call it a success.

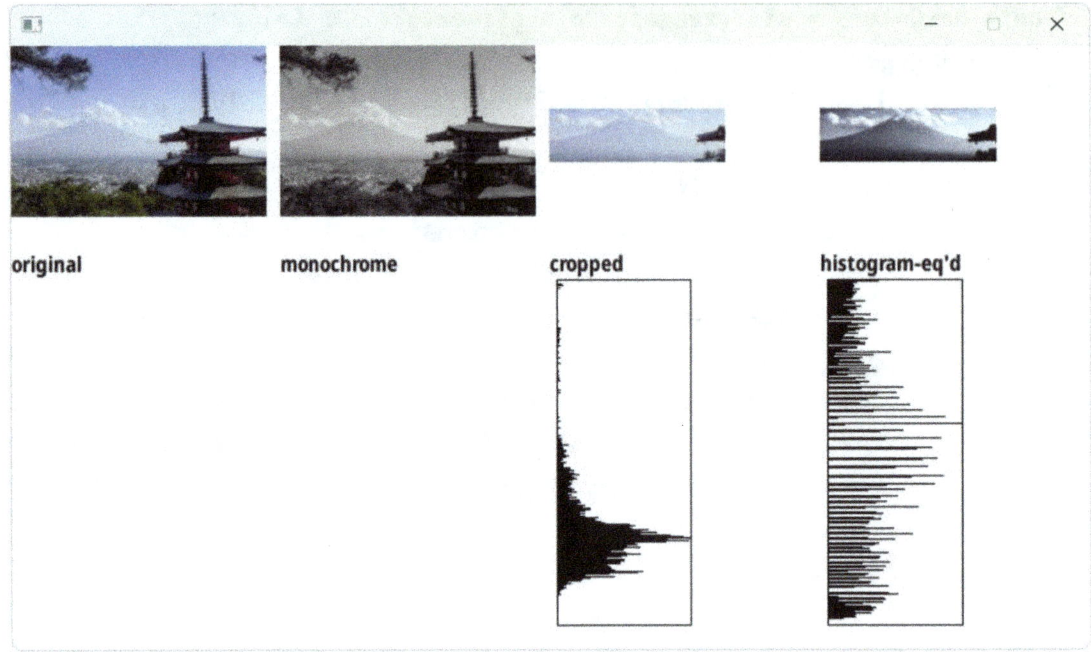

Figure 24-5. *The final program: original image, monochrome, cropped, and cropped with histogram equalization*

`std::expected` and `std::optional`

Let's go back to the standard deviation example. I want to read my data from a file.

I could throw an exception on a bad or missing file, but modern C++ has a new idea: a function that might fail can return either an error or a legit value. That was technically true before, but `std::expected` has a few new tricks up its sleeve (Example 24-6).

Example 24-6. A function to open a file

```
std::expected<std::ifstream, std::string> openFile(const char* filename)
{
    std::ifstream infile(filename);
    if (!infile) return std::unexpected("Can't open file");
    else return std::move(infile); //I'll explain in a moment
}
```

The return type now isn't the file we hope to return, but a `std::expected`, which is ready to contain either that (if all goes well) or an error message. If something goes wrong, we return `std::unexpected(SomeTypeOfErrorMessage)`. If not, we just return the correct value.

To handle it, we do something like this:

```
auto result=openFile("input.txt");
if (result)                    // if things worked...
   result.value() >> ...; //result.value() is what got returned
else
   std::cout << result.error();
```

(Now to explain the `std::move` at the end of `openFile`. It would be possibly expensive – and, worse, nonsensical – to copy the `ifstream` we're returning (as there's only one of it). We can't return it by reference, as it's a local variable. What we *can* do is return it with move semantics. `openFile`'s finished and doesn't need it anymore, and `ifstream` has a move constructor, so we can let it hand its memory off. Weird, but it works.)

One interesting aspect of `std::expected` is that just as we can chain views with `|`, we can chain functions returning `std::expected` in another way. Suppose I have this function for reading in the numbers (Example 24-7), and we're not going to be happy if there's no data in it.

Example 24-7. A function to read in a file of integers

```
std::expected<std::vector<int>, std::string> loadFile(std::ifstream in)
{
    std::vector<int> result;
    while (in)
    {
        int x=0; in >> x;
        if (!in) break; //reached end of file; discard failed read
        result.push_back(x);
    }
    if (result.empty()) return std::unexpected("Empty file");

    return result;
}
```

I can call both of them in main like this:

```
auto numbers = openFile("input.txt").and_then(loadFile);
if (!numbers)
    std::cout << numbersIn.error() << '\n';
else
{
    double sum = std::ranges::fold_left(numbers.value(), 0.0, std::plus{});
    double avg = sum / numbers.value().size();
    ...
}
```

openFile returns a std::expected. C++ then goes on to and_then. If the openFile returned an error, it just skips what comes next; it's done. If not, it peels off the std::expected wrapper, passes in the (successful) return value, and lets loadFile do its stuff.

std::expected is called a **monad**: a wrapper that can be passed to other functions that know how to go into the wrapper to what's inside, process it, and then return their own wrapped result. Useful for this very circumstance.

There is also std::optional, which works much the same way. By convention std::expected means "If you don't get a real result, something bad happened," and std::optional means "If you don't get a real result, there just wasn't one." We might return std::optional from a function that parses a string for its first number and returns either the number or a message saying there wasn't one.

Extra: Reference Variables

In the above code, it turned out we wanted numbers.value() a lot – four times – and I got tired of typing it.

I could have said std::vector<int> ns = numbers.value(); but that would have been a possibly expensive copy.

Just as we can make a reference or alias for a parameter, we can make one for a variable or (sometimes, like here) the result of a function call. It does no copying; it's just an alias:

```
std::vector<double>& ns = numbers.value();
double sum = std::ranges::fold_left(ns, 0.0, std::plus{});
double avg = sum / ns.size();
```

EXERCISES

In all exercises – of course! – use the language features in this chapter.

1. Sum the populations of the cities in Example 24-1.
2. Write a function that uses `fold_left` to get the factorial of N. factorial(0) is 1; factorial(N) for larger N is N * N-1 * N-2 ... 1.
3. Write a function to make an `SSDL_ProcessibleImage` darker.
4. ...or more red.
5. Make the crop function in `3-4-5-image-processing` return `std::expected`, and handle it appropriately in `main`. (What might go wrong is you might try to crop an area bigger than the original.)
6. Do Chapter 13's last exercise, on global temperatures, but this time do it using views.
7. (Hard) Write a program that reads in a file (or you can just give it a string) and converts emoticons (like `":)"` or ":o") to emoji (like u8"😊" or u8"😮"). Use `std::expected` for a function to read the file. To process the characters, keep a `std::string bank` of whatever emoticon you are currently working on: for example, if you get a `":"` (which means you may be headed for "😊" or "😮"), you store it in `bank`, and then if you get a `")"` you spit out the "😊" and empty the `bank`.

If you get a character that doesn't take you further toward any emoji, print and empty the `bank` and print that character.

Recall the note in Chapter 13 about how to print UTF-8 sequences.

You might use a vector of pairs to pair each emoticon with its emoji or, better yet, a `std::map` (look it up online), which does much the same thing.

You might also use `std::ranges::for_each` to loop over the characters and a view to filter which parts of your emoticon–emoji map are relevant to the current bank.

CHAPTER 25

Esoterica (Recommended)

You've now got the essentials of C++ and more. It's time to add bells and whistles.[1]

Before doing the next three chapters, it would make sense to go back and do any "optional" sections you may have skipped – specifically, file I/O (from Chapter 13).

The next three chapters are organized like this:

- **This chapter (Chapter 25)**: New capabilities – better formatted output, using command-line arguments (finally using the `argc` and `argv` in `int main(int argc, char** argv)`), "variadic" functions (functions with variable-length argument lists), bit manipulation
- **Chapter 26**: Useful things for organization and security
- **Chapter 27**: More organization help, useful in less ordinary situations

Let's get started.

Formatted Output

Suppose you want to print details of a game to your heads-up display (HUD), centered at the top:

```
Points: 32000  /  Time left: 30.2  /  Mood: Annoyed
```

You could calculate the width of each label and each value (good luck doing that with a variable-width font) and from those calculate the location to print each item …if you do, turn in your lazy programmer badge right now.

Or you could do a lot of conversions and string concatenations and send that to `SSDL_RenderTextCentered`, as below. Once more, turn in that badge:

[1] Nice-to-have extras.

W. Briggs, *C++26 for Lazy Programmers*, https://doi.org/10.1007/979-8-8688-1859-2_25

```
string finalString = string("Points: ")
          + std::to_string(points) // Standard way to convert 2 to "2"
          + "/ Time left: "
          + std::to_string(time)
          + " / Mood: " + mood;
SSDL_RenderTextCentered(finalString, SSDL_GetWindowWidth()/2, 10);
```

`std::format` can help. It's a way of constructing a string from different kinds of data. You put the text you want between the quotes, with a {} at every place you want to stick an argument, and put it in a `std::format` call with the things you want printed, like this:

```
std::format("arg1: {}, arg2: {}, arg3: {}.\n"; arg1, arg2, arg3);
```

Example 25-1 shows how to put several things in one string, which is then centered on the screen. Output is in Figure 25-1.

Example 25-1. A rudimentary heads-up display (HUD) using `format`

```
// Program to construct neat output for a HUD using std::format
//       -- from _C++26 for Lazy Programmers_

#include <format>
#include "SSDL.h"

using namespace std;

int main(int argc, char** argv)
{
    int points = 3200;        // Some arbitrary data to test
    double time = 30.2;       //  printing to HUD
    char mood[] = "Annoyed";

    SSDL_RenderTextCentered(
        std::format("Points: {}   /   Time left: {}   /   Mood: {}",
                    points, time, mood),
        SSDL_GetWindowWidth() / 2, 10);

    SSDL_WaitKey();          // Wait for user to hit a key
    return 0;
}
```

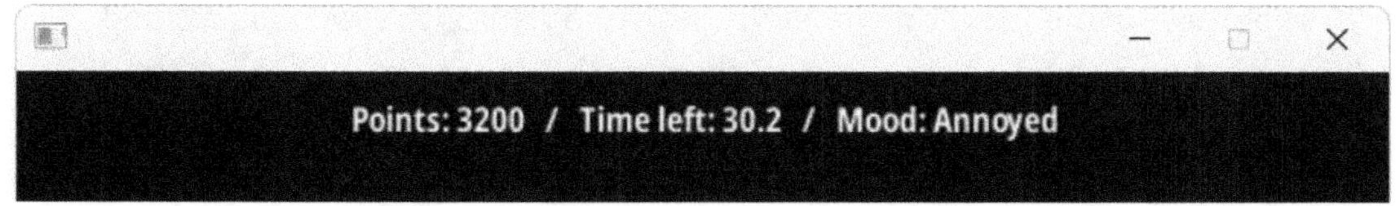

Figure 25-1. *Output of the `format` program*

If you want to do more special things with what's put into a blank – center it, change the width, set precision if it's floating-point, whatever – you can. `{:<10}` means "take 10 spaces for this, and put the contents on the left." `{:.2f}` means "print it as floating point, not scientific notation, and use 2 decimal places." This expression

```
std::format("{1} {0}", arg1, arg2)
```

means put the arguments in reverse order.

The {} construction has these parts:

- Opening { (required!)
- Argument number
- : (required if there are to be any formatting specifications)
- Alignment – <, ^, or >
- Width
- Precision – a decimal point followed by number of digits' precision desired
- Type – `f`, `g`, or `e` for floating point and `b`, `o`, `x`, or `d` (binary, octal, hexadecimal, decimal) for integers
- Closing } (required)

The other thing you might want is to format your own classes. `std::formatter<T>` is an existing template that you can extend to your own class. The `template<>` in Example 25-2 means this is a **template specialization**, that is, applying this template to a particular typename `T` (in this case, `Point2D`). (We use this when we want template functions to behave differently depending on what `T` is, which is certainly the case here.) It needs some member functions that it can inherit from the `std::string` version, so we inherit. `context` is, well, a thing we have to have.

The purpose of the format member function is to return what we want printed (wrapped appropriately), so we construct that and then return it.

Yes, I think it's an awful mess compared to the ostream& operators we've been making. Fortunately what we see in main is simple. Note how I throw an exception passing in a format string – one of the main things I use format for.

Example 25-2. Making your own std::formatter, to send your own classes to std::format

```
// Program to print some points with std::format
//       -- from _C++26 for Lazy Programmers_

#include <format>
#include <iostream>
#include <exception>

struct Point2D { int x_ = 0, y_ = 0; };

bool operator== (const Point2D& a, const Point2D& b)
{
    return a.x_ == b.x_ && a.y_ == b.y_;
}

template                                  //a template specialization
struct std::formatter<Point2D> : public std::formatter<std::string>
{
    auto format(const Point2D& point, std::format_context& context) const
    {
        std::string str = std::format("({}, {})", point.x_, point.y_);
        return std::formatter<std::string>::format(str, context);
    }
};

int main(int argc, char** argv)
{
    //Let's take a 2 step trip: {1,1} forward, same amount back
    Point2D step1 = { 1, 1 }, step2 = { -1, -1 };
    std::cout << std::format("Taking two steps: {} and {}.\n",
    step1, step2);
```

```
    Point2D whereWeWent = { step1.x_ + step2.x_, step1.y_ + step2.y_ };
    if (whereWeWent != Point2D())
        throw std::out_of_range(
            std::format("How can {} and {} not add to {}?",
            step1, step2, Point2D()));

    return 0;
}
```

EXERCISES

1. Use `format` to print a form – possibly an application taking in name, address, etc. – filled in with someone's answer.
2. Print some addition problems in binary, octal, hex, and decimal, like this:

```
 1111      17       f      15
+   1   +   1   +   1   +   1
-----   -----   -----   -----
10000      20      10      16
```

3. Print a table showing the number of times you fell down per year, starting at age two and ending at your current age. I hope it's dropped somewhat. Make it neat.
4. Print a table of the cost of various items at your surf shop: surfboard, surfboard bag, huaraches, whatever. The `.`'s in the dollar amounts should line up.
5. Print a table of the weights of the above items.
6. Using scientific notation, print the probability, in any given year, of these events: there is a major political scandal; life spontaneously forms on Mars; a comet hits the Yucatan Peninsula and makes us go the way of the dinosaurs; something more interesting than programming in C++ happens (the lowest probability, of course). Use scientific notation. Make the numbers up – that's what everyone else does.
7. Write your own `std::formatter` template specialization for Chapter 16's `Date` or `Time`, Chapter 17's `Fraction`, and Chapter 24's `City`.

Command-Line Arguments

It's sometimes necessary, especially in the Unix world, to give arguments to a program: `cd myFolder`, `gdb myProgram`, etc.

Suppose you want a program to check text files for differences. The command might look like

```
./mydiff file1.txt file2.txt
```

You'll need to write the first line of `main` like this:

```
int main(int argc, char** argv)
```
[2]

`argc` ("argument count") is the number of arguments, and `argv` ("argument vector," but it's an array, not a `vector`) is an array of character arrays, each containing one argument, starting with the program name.

So if your command is `./mydiff file1.txt file2.txt`, `argc` will be 3, and `argv` will contain the values shown in Figure 25-2.

argv[0]	"./mydiff"
argv[1]	"file1.txt"
argv[2]	"file2.txt"

Figure 25-2. *Some possible command-line arguments*

Example 25-3 shows code for the program.

First, it ensures we have the right number of arguments. If something goes wrong, it's conventional to tell the user what was expected. `argv[0]` is always the program name. (We don't hard-code it as " `./mydiff`" in case the program name is changed.)

`cerr` is like `cout`, but isn't redirected by `>`, so it's useful for error messages. But `cout`'s OK too.

[2] Or `int main (int argc, char* argv[])`, which more clearly shows that the second argument is an array of character arrays. The `char**` version seems the more common way to write this, alas.

Example 25-3. A program using command-line arguments. In the source code, the executable for g++ is named mydiff. Instructions on how to run and debug it are below.

```
// Program to find the difference between two files
//        -- from _C++26 for Lazy Programmers_

#include <iostream>
#include <fstream>
#include <cstdlib> // for EXIT_FAILURE, EXIT_SUCCESS
#include <string>

using namespace std;

int main(int argc, char** argv)
{
    // Did we get right # of arguments? If not, complain and quit
    if (argc != 3) // 3 args: 1 program name, plus 2 files
    {              // On failure, tell user what user should've entered:
        cerr << "Usage: " << argv[0] << " <file 1> <file 2>\n";
        return EXIT_FAILURE;
    }

    // Load the 2 files
    ifstream file1(argv[1]), file2(argv[2]); // open files
    if (! file1) // On failure, say file wouldn't load
    {
        cerr << "Error loading " << argv[1] << endl;
        return EXIT_FAILURE;
    }
    if (!file2) // On failure, say file wouldn't load
    {
        cerr << "Error loading " << argv[2] << endl;
        return EXIT_FAILURE;
    }

    string line1, line2;
```

```
while (file1 && file2)                  //While BOTH files are not
                                        finished
{
    getline(file1, line1);              //  read line from file1
    if (!file1) break;

    getline(file2, line2);              //  ...from file2
    if (!file2)                         //  if file2's done but
                                            file1 wasn't
    {
        cout << "<: " << line1 << endl;//    spit out last line
                                             from file1
        break;
    }

    if (line1 != line2)                 //  if lines differ print them
    {
        cout << "<: " << line1 << endl;//  < means "first file"
        cout << ">: " << line2 << endl;//  > means "second file"
                                        //  this is conventional
    }
}

// If either file has more lines than the other, print remainder
while (file1)
{
    getline(file1, line1);
    if (file1) cout << "<: " << line1 << endl;
}
while (file2)
{
    getline(file2, line2);
    if (file2) cout << ">: " << line2 << endl;
}
```

```
    // Clean up and return
    file1.close(); file2.close();

    return EXIT_SUCCESS;
}
```

To run this from the command line:

In Unix, type `./mydiff file1.txt file2.txt`.

Visual Studio users should first copy the executable from somewhere in `Debug/`, `Release/`, or `x64/` into the project folder, so it can find the text files. Its name is `4-cmdLineArgs.exe`, so type `4-cmdLineArgs file1.txt file2.txt`. Or rename it `mydiff` and use that command instead.

For a reminder on using the command prompt in Windows, see Chapter 13's subsection on that topic.

Debugging with Command-Line Arguments in Unix

Whether in `ddd` or `gdb`, at the prompt, type `set args file1.txt file2.txt` and you're ready to `run`.

Debugging with Command-Line Arguments in Visual Studio

If you start the program in Microsoft Visual Studio, it runs as if it has no arguments. Which it doesn't. To fix this, go into Project Menu ➤ Properties ➤ Configuration Properties ➤ Debugging, set Configuration to All Configurations and Platform to All Platforms, and add your arguments to Command Arguments (Figure 25-3).

The project's command-line arguments are stored in the `.user` file. If you delete it, you'll have to add them again.

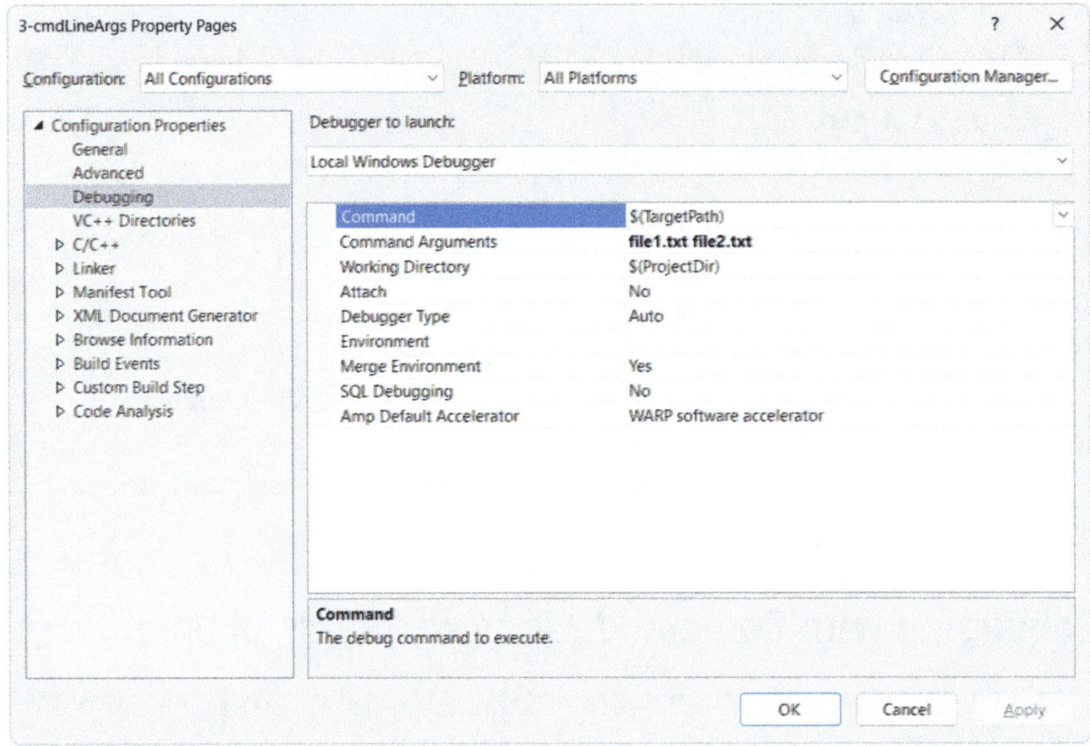

Figure 25-3. *Setting Command Arguments in Microsoft Visual Studio*

EXERCISES

1. Write a program `myGrep`, a simplified version of the Unix `grep` utility. It should repeat all lines from standard input that have a given word. So if you have a file `input.txt` with lines

```
alpha
beta
alphabet
```

then the command `myGrep` (or `./myGrep`) `alpha < input.txt` should print this on the screen:

```
alpha
alphabet
```

2. To the previous exercise, add an option `-n` that, if present, directs `grep` to print the line number of each line of output. (Options starting with - are common for Unix commands.) Given the above input, the command `myGrep -n alpha < input.txt` should print

   ```
   1: alpha
   3: alphabet
   ```

3. Write a program that, given input with numbers in columns, prints to standard output a version with only the columns specified. For example, if you give it arguments `0 3` and get input like this

   ```
   1900  -0.06  -0.05  -0.05  -0.08  -0.07  -0.07
   1901  -0.07  -0.21  -0.14  -0.06  -0.2   -0.13
   ...
   ```

   the output should show only columns 0 and 3:

   ```
   1900  -0.05
   1901  -0.14
   ...
   ```

Variadic Functions

Similar to command-line arguments is the variable-length argument list you can give to a function.

The easiest way to explain it is to show it, so here we go (Example 25-4).

Example 25-4. A function with variadic arguments

```
// Program to find max of a variable-length parameter list
//        -- from _C++26 for Lazy Programmers_

#include <cassert>

using namespace std;


template<typename T>
double myMax(T value) { return value;  } // single-argument version
```

```
template<typename T, typename... OtherArgs>
double myMax(T first, OtherArgs... otherArgs)
{
    double otherArgsMax = myMax(otherArgs...);
    if (first < otherArgsMax) return otherArgsMax; else return first;
}

int main()
{
    assert(myMax(32.0, 100, 0, 56.0) == 100.0);

    return 0;
}
```

Here's how it works. If you call `myMax` with a single argument, it just returns it.

If not, the first template doesn't apply, so it goes on to the next one. This matches when you have one argument of a type we'll call `T` and some other arguments of another sequence of types we'll call `OtherArgs`. To get its result, it calls `myMax` on the rest of the arguments and gets its answer. Then it returns the bigger of that and the first argument.

This practice of a function calling itself is **recursion** – not a C++ programmer's usual way of doing things, but here it's just the thing.

Unlike command-line arguments, I almost never use variadic arguments myself. But I do use some language features that take them, as we'll see in Chapters 26 (`unique_ptr`) and 29 (`printf`).

EXERCISES

1. Write a function to print any number of items in its argument list.
2. …and one to read in any number of items. Your parameter list may look like this: `(T& first, OtherArgs&... otherArgs)`.

Bit Manipulation: &, |, ~, and

All information in computer memory is in bits. A **bit** can be in a higher-voltage state (close to the voltage the chip can handle) or a lower-voltage state (close to 0). The lower voltage can be called "low," false, or 0; the higher "high," true, or 1.

Eight bits form a **byte**. The byte can be viewed as eight true-or-false answers or the 0's and 1's of a **binary** number (like 0b01000001) or thereby a decimal number or, by the convention described in the ASCII table, a letter, like "A." That decimal number can use the leftmost bit as a "sign" bit - 1 means negative - and range from –128 to 127; or it cannot and range from 0 to 255.

How a particular byte gets used depends on what we tell it. We can see this by casting:

```
char ch='A';
std::cout << ch << ' ' << static_cast<int>(ch); //prints: A 65
```

We might also group bytes into larger chunks. The size of an `int` is your compiler's choice, but `uint32_t` is 32 bits.

(If this is all new to you, you might take some time out to learn about binary numbers and arithmetic. We won't be using that here, but it's good to know.)

Or we might string together several in an array and get an ASCII string, like `"Hello"`. But not a string of international characters; that's going to take more work.

One Use of Bit Manipulation: Unicode

One of those `uint32_t` things would work for storing any character in any language. And it does: the Unicode standard contains even Chinese, which has more characters than all other languages combined. So maybe we could use strings made of that.

But if we're writing English, that's inefficient: each string will take up four times as much room as we're used to. When you're doing that with every character, the inefficiency builds up! So a different encoding was developed. UTF-8 uses 1 byte for Latin script (ASCII) and 2, 3, or 4 bytes, depending on the script, for other languages. It's used by Unix terminals, Microsoft Windows, and the web; I think it's fair to call it the default.

But how does (say) `cout` know whether the next byte it sees in a UTF-8 sequence is a standalone ASCII character or part of a 2–4-byte character?

It looks at the first bits.

If the byte starts with 0, if it's of form 0b0xxxxxxx (where x means "anything"), it's ASCII (1 byte).

C++, like C, provides operators we can use to get at those bits:

- **Bitwise or, as in** `x|y`: Each bit in `x|y` will be 1 if it's 1 in either `x` *or* `y` (Figure 25-4 (a)).

(a)	(b)	(c)	(d)
x: 010110011	x: 010110011		
y: 101010001	y: 101010001	x: 010110011	x: 00000011
x|y : 111110011	x&y : 000010001	~x : 101001100	x<<2 : 00001100

Figure 25-4. *Bitwise arithmetic*

- **Bitwise and, as in** `x&y`: A bit in `x&y` will be 1 if it's 1 in both `x` *and* `y` (Figure 25-4 (b)).
- **Bitwise not, as in** `~x`: All the bits are reversed (Figure 25-4 (c)).
- And we can move the bits left or right with shift operators `<<` and `>>` (now doing double duty for stream I/O and bit manipulation). `x << 2` has all the bits in `x` shifted left 2 bits (Figure 25-4 (d)).

(There's also xor, `x^y`, not covered here as it's less commonly used.)

So if I just want to see what a char has its leftmost bit set to, I can say `ch & 0b1000000`, and I'll get either 0b00000000 or 0b10000000:

```
if (ch & 0b10000000 == 0b0000000) ...//it's ASCII
```

The rules for UTF-8 sequences are as follows:

- If the first byte starts with 0, it's ASCII (1 byte).
- If it starts with 110, it's a 2-byte sequence; subsequent byte must start with 10.
- If it starts with 1110, it's 3-byte; subsequent bytes must start with 10.
- If it starts with 11110, it's 4-byte; subsequent bytes must start with 10.
- All other byte sequences are invalid.

Example 25-5 shows how we can use `&` to determine what's next in a character array.

Example 25-5. A function to determine the length of a UTF-8 sequence. Find it and the next example in the source code as `ch25/5-6-bits`

```
//How many bytes are in the next UTF-8 character in str?
int lengthOfUTF8Char(char* str)[3]
{
    if ((*str & 0b10000000) == 0b00000000) return 1;
                                        //If leftmost bit is 0,
                                        //   it's ASCII: 1 byte
    if ((*ptr & 0b11100000) == 0b11000000) return 2; //2 bytes long
    if ((*ptr & 0b11110000) == 0b11100000) return 3; //3 bytes
    if ((*ptr & 0b11111000) == 0b11110000) return 4; //4 bytes
    return 1;                //Not recognized! Just treat it as ASCII
}
```

Strictly speaking I needed to check the successive bytes to ensure they start with 0b10. That would be correct, but if those bytes are missing the 0b10, the sequence is invalid, so I'd just let `cout` print it best it can. (Throwing an exception seems like overkill for a bad character.)

With this, now, I can find the length of a UTF-8 string, find substrings, substitute characters, identify what the characters are, and many other things. Example 25-6 shows one use. Its output is

```
strlen thinks the length of αℵ字" is 9 but it's really 5.
```

Example 25-6. A function to determine the length of a UTF-8 sequence

```
// Program to get length of a UTF-8 string
//        -- from _C++26 for Lazy Programmers_

#include <iostream>

//How many bytes are in the next UTF-8 character in str?
int charLengthUTF8(const char* str);
int strlenUTF8    (const char* str);
```

[3] Or you could use `char8_t*`, often used with UTF-8, but let's keep it simple.

```
int main ( )
{
    const char* str = reinterpret_cast<const char*>(u8"α ℵ 字");
    std::cout << "strlen thinks the length of \"" << str
              << "\" is " << strlen(str)
              << " but it's really " << strlenUTF8(str) << ".\n";

    return 0;
}

int strlenUTF8(const char* str)
{
    int result = 0;
    while (*str)
    {
        ++result; //we'll add 1 for each UTF-8 char
        str += lengthOfUTF8Char(str);
                 //but move str ahead by each UTF-8 char's width
    }
    return result;
}

...
```

Another Use: Flags

Many libraries, SDL and its helpers, for example, require you to set some of their features with individual bits and report features the same way. Embedded systems, encryption, and file compression also benefit from manipulating individual bits.

To start the SDL_Image library, you call `IMG_Init`, which takes a single argument of type `int` telling it what image formats to support. How do we cram that into one `int`? `SDL_Image.h` provides **flags** (bits with assigned meaning): `IMG_INIT_JPG` is 0b00000001, `IMG_INIT_PNG` is 0b00000010, `IMG_INIT_TIF` is 0b0000100, etc. (These numbers are also known as 1, 2, and 4, but we're not doing arithmetic so it doesn't matter here.) We have to combine them into that one `int`, bit by bit, pun intended (see Figure 25-5).

...	0	0	0	1	0	1

***Figure 25-5.** How an `int` sent to `IMG_Init` is laid out. This one's set to support jpg's and tiff's*

Recalling the | operator from Figure 25-4 (a), we can see what `int flags = IMG_INIT_JPG | IMG_INIT_TIF` gives us

```
IMG_INIT_JPG: 000000001
IMG_INIT_TIF: 000000100
       flags: 000000101
```

...and we can pass it in it like this: `IMG_Init(flags);`.

So with | we can add flags together to send into such functions ...and if we write our own libraries, we can use & to get the bits back out of those flags.

Antibugging

- **You get the wrong answer to a bit manipulation expression, but you don't see how**. Maybe you used && for & or || for |. I do that. Or maybe you need some `()`'s.

EXERCISES

1. Write a function to determine if a number is odd or even by checking one of its bits.
2. Write a function that prints a number in binary by printing each individual bit. You may want `sizeof`.
3. Write a function that finds the $\log_2$ of an `int`, using `>>`, not `/`.
4. Write a function to tell if a sequence of bits in a number is symmetric (like 11000011 but not 11010011).
5. (Hard) Write a function to get a complete Unicode code point, that is, a `uint32_t`, from a UTF-8 sequence representing a character. Here's how it works: Figure out how many bytes you should use based on `lengthOfUTF8Char` above. For each byte, strip out the bits that were for

UTF-8 formatting. If it's 1 byte, just put those bits in your result. If it's more, do that with the first byte, then move it left with <<, and put the next byte's useful bits in the result; keep doing this till you're out of bytes.

So the Chinese character 字 (zì, "character") is the UTF-8 sequence

```
11100101 10101101 10010111
```

Stripping out the bits that are UTF-8 formatting gives us

```
    00101    101101    010111
```

and jamming them together gives us

```
0010110110101 0111
```

which is the UTF-32 version for the character.

You could test this by getting the UTF-32 version of a character and checking it against its binary representation online. If you need to convert to hexadecimal, `std::format` can help.

CHAPTER 26

Esoterica (Recommended), Continued

More extras to make your programs quicker, safer, and easier to write.

initializer_list

Going from C-style arrays to more sophisticated containers, I was sorry to give up the bracketed initializer list, as in `int array [] = {0, 1, 2, 3};`. Initializing element by element is more trouble.

But we can do this with our own classes too, and it's built-in for STL. Example 26-1 illustrates doing this with `Vector`.

Example 26-1. Adapting `Vector` to use an `initializer_list`

```
#include <initializer_list> // for std::initializer_list

template <typename T>
class Vector
{
public:
    Vector(const std::initializer_list<T>& other);
    // ...
};

template <typename T>
Vector<T>::Vector(const std::initializer_list<T>& other) : Vector()
{
    for (const T& i : other) push_back(i);
}
```


W. Briggs, *C++26 for Lazy Programmers*, https://doi.org/10.1007/979-8-8688-1859-2_26

Then we can initialize as we were used to with arrays:

```
Vector<int> V = { 1, 2, 3, 4, 5, 6, 7, 8, 9, 10 };
```

or, since the new constructor will be implicitly called as needed,

```
Vector<int> U;
// ...
U = { 1, 2, 3, 4, 5, 6, 7, 8, 9, 10 };
```

EXERCISES

1. If you go in order through an `initializer_list`, using `List::push_front` to add its elements to a `List`, the order will be reversed. (Work it out on paper if necessary, to confirm.) So go back and do Exercise 8 in Chapter 22 if you haven't – it provides `List::push_back` – and give `List` a constructor that takes an `initializer_list`.

Moving Work to Compile Time with `constexpr` and `static_assert`

C++ gurus now suggest you make as much `constexpr` as you can ("`constexpr` everything" is a thing): it's quicker at runtime (of course!); it takes up less memory; and it prevents "undefined behavior" (unpredictable results) because `constexpr` things with undefined behavior aren't supposed to compile. (If that works, can we do it to the rest of the language? Please?)

Despite its name, `constexpr` <variable> really means "do this at compile time," though it also makes things constant.

We can also mark *functions* with the word `constexpr` and use them to generate values at compile time provided the functions' inputs are known at compile time. (Otherwise, they work as usual functions. If you want your function to *only* work at compile time, mark the function not `constexpr` but `consteval`, to insist it be evaluated at compile time only. I never do this.)

Consider the Coordinate class, used by Citys in the Chapter 24 example: a class that contains latitude and longitude and is used to calculate distances. We go through it (see Example 26-2) and put constexpr in front of every function.

...almost. constexpr's great with calculations, but it doesn't do things that can only be done at runtime, which include I/O and dynamic memory. So we don't mark print or operator<<.

The other change we need: since a constexpr function must be able to do its work at compile time, the compiler has to know, as soon as it finds a call to it, how it does what it does. So it goes in the .h file, like templates and inlines, and is implicitly inline.

Example 26-2. A class with (almost) everything turned constexpr

```
// class Coordinate, latitude and longitude for global positioning
//        -- from _C++26 for Lazy Programmers_

#ifndef COORDINATE_H
#define COORDINATE_H

#include <iostream>
#include <numbers> //for pi
#include <cmath>   //for sqrt, sin, etc.

constexpr inline long double deg2Radians(long double deg)
{
    return deg * std::numbers::pi / 180;
}

class Coordinate
{
public:
    constexpr Coordinate() = default;
    constexpr Coordinate(int latIn, int longIn):latd_(latIn),longtd_
    (longIn){}

    constexpr Coordinate& operator=(const Coordinate&) = default;

    constexpr long double latdInDeg  () const { return latd_;        }
    constexpr long double longtdInDeg() const { return longtd_;      }
```

```
    constexpr long double latdInRad  () const { return
    deg2Radians(latd_);  }
    constexpr long double longtdInRad() const { return
    deg2Radians(longtd_);}

    void print(std::ostream& out) const //Not constexpr! Can't be: does I/O
    {
        out << latd_ << " deg " << longtd_ << " deg";
    }
private:
    long double latd_ = 0.0, longtd_ = 0.0;
};

                                                   //Also not constexpr!
inline std::ostream& operator<< (std::ostream& out, const Coordinate& foo)
{
    foo.print(out); return out;
}

// Function to square things should've been in cmath in my opinion
template <typename T> constexpr T sqr(const T& t) { return t * t; }

// Uses the "Haversine" formula to get distances between 2 Coordinates
// Trust me, it works
constexpr double distance(const Coordinate& x, const Coordinate& y)
{
    constexpr double EARTH_RADIUS = 6371; //km

    double a = sqr(sin((x.latdInRad() - y.latdInRad()) / 2.0))
                 + cos(x.latdInRad()) * cos(y.latdInRad()) *
                       sqr(sin((x.longtdInRad() - y.longtdInRad())
                       / 2.0));

    return EARTH_RADIUS * 2 * asin(sqrt(a));
}

constexpr inline Coordinate GREENWICH={51, 0};//inline constexpr in .h: cool
#endif //COORDINATE_H
```

The standard says we can put `std::vector`, `std::string`, and other things in a `constexpr` function as long as they're local and not returned. We can call other functions if they're `constexpr`. We can also have loops and call other `constexpr` member functions except when we can't.[1] My rule: keep functions simple, and if it won't let you, shrug.

We can now declare `constexpr Coordinates` (end of Example 26-2 and Example 26-3).

We can also move any `assert` we wanted to do to compile time, with `static_assert`.

Example 26-3. Declaring `constexpr Coordinates` and testing with `static_assert`

```
// Program that tests differences between Coordinates
//        -- from _C++26 for Lazy Programmers_

#include <iostream>
#include "coordinate.h"

int main()
{
    constexpr Coordinate QUITO    = {   0, -78 },
                         LIMA     = { -12, -77 },
                         SANTIAGO = { -33, -70 };

    static_assert(distance(LIMA, QUITO) < distance(LIMA, SANTIAGO),
        "Oops! Lima is closer to Quito than to Santiago");
    //Leave out the reason if you like, or if your compiler won't support it

    std::cout << "The distance from " << LIMA
              << " to " << QUITO << " is "
              << distance(LIMA, QUITO) << " km.\n";

    return 0;
}
```

[1] Which admittedly is likely something we did wrong. But if something that should be easy to do isn't, maybe don't spend a lot of time figuring it out.

If the assertion fails, then at compile time – or before, by waving your mouse pointer over it in your C++-friendly editor! – you'll get a message like this:

```
error: static assertion failed: Oops! Lima is closer to Quito than to
Santiago
```

EXERCISES

1. `constexpr` everything you can in `Fraction`, and calculate some `Fractions` (using +, *, whatever), all `constexpr`. Use `static_assert` where you can to verify your functions.
2. `constexpr` everything you can in `Point2D`, and declare some `constexpr` `Point2Ds` and use them in `constexpr` expressions. Use `static_assert` where you can to verify your functions.

Memory Safety with Smart Pointers

Preventing memory errors is a major focus at present. The Rust language exists essentially for this purpose (and does a better job than C++, but at a price of increased difficulty). Various US government agencies are looking into ways to encourage memory safety in their vendors; one is commissioning a way to automatically translate code from the notoriously lax C into Rust.[2]

We've already come a long way by stopping reading past array bounds: the `at` member function in standard `array`, `string_view`, `string`, and `vector` detects out-of-range references, and range-based loops prevent them. We still have the problem of ownership alluded to in Chapter 17, something like this:

```
char* a = new char[MAX];
char* b = a;
```

In this code, who gets to make changes in the array – `a` or `b`? (Both together will be a mess!) Who's responsible for `delete`-ing it?

[2] "Eliminating Memory Safety Vulnerabilities Once and For All," DARPA, July 31, 2024, `www.darpa.mil/news/2024/memory-safety-vulnerabilities`.

unique_ptr

C++'s unique_ptr is our main way of addressing this. As the name implies, a unique_ptr owns its memory and won't share ownership, so there's no question who's responsible for it. It'll be deleted exactly once (not zero times, not more), and one unique_ptr can't mess up another's memory.

unique_ptr's trick is that it has no copy constructor and no conventional operator =. Instead it uses move semantics. If you assign the value of your unique_ptr to a new one, the old one loses access to it:

```
#include <memory> //for unique_ptr, shared_ptr
...
unique_ptr<int> a = std::make_unique<int>(10);
                                    // a points to a new int,
                                    // initialized to 10
//unique_ptr<int> b = a;            // nope! no copy ctor, no copy assignment
unique_ptr<int> b = std::move(a); // std::move says: use move copy if
                                    // it exists
```

Since unique_ptr *does* have move copy, the last line of the above code calls it; it looks something like this:

```
unique_ptr::unique_ptr(UniquePtr&& other) noexcept
{
    contents_ = other.contents_; other.contents_ = nullptr;
}
```

So b gets a's contents_, and a gets nullptr. Ownership is transferred, and the pointer remains unique.

...and when the new owner goes out of scope, the destructor will be called and the memory deleted.

Here are some other ways to initialize unique_ptr:

```
unique_ptr<char[]>myArray = std::make_unique<char[]>(MAX_ELEMENTS);
unique_ptr<Date>  myDate  = std::make_unique<Date>(1,1,2026);
                             //Gave it Date's ctor's arguments here
Entry* pointerToEntry     = new Entry;
unique_ptr<Entry> myEntry = std::unique_ptr<Entry>(pointerToEntry);
```

(In the last case, you can't initialize using `std::make_unique`, because `make_unique` *makes* – allocates – but the allocation's already done. The constructor's the way to go.)

Operators are set up so you can use a `unique_ptr` as though it were just a pointer:

```
myArray[0] = '?';
std::cout << *myDate << " is in the year " << myDate->year() << "\n";
```

We can set it to new things by assigning to it (below). It will delete its old memory and take on the new:

```
myArray = std::make_unique<char[]>(SOME_ARRAY_SIZE);
myDate  = std::make_unique<Date>  (1,2,2026);
```

We usually don't pass it into functions. The idea is we'll just leave it wherever it is, and if some of that information is needed in a function, just pass in the raw pointer[3] it contains. The function gets to do things with the pointer's contents, but shouldn't change the pointer itself. You get the contents of `unique_ptr` with `get`:

```
int len = strlen(myArray.get());
```

So let's try it out, on the Olympic games symbol program. As Example 26-4 shows, it's a little simpler, but with `unique_ptr` taking responsibility for `delete`, definitely more secure.

Example 26-4. Example 21-5's Olympics symbol program, updated to use `unique_ptr`

```
// Program to show, and move, the Olympics symbol
// It uses Circle, and a subclass of Shape called Text
//      -- from _C++26 for Lazy Programmers_

#include <vector>
#include <memory> //for unique_ptr
#include "circle.h"
#include "text.h"
```

[3] "Raw" pointer: something like `int*`, not like `unique_ptr<int>`.

```
int main(int argc, char** argv)
{
   SSDL_SetWindowSize(500, 300); // make smaller window

   // Create Olympics symbol
   std::vector<std::unique_ptr<Shape>> olympicSymbol;
   constexpr int RADIUS = 50;

   // consisting of five circles
   olympicSymbol.push_back(std::make_unique<Circle>
                           (Point2D( 50, 50), RADIUS));
   olympicSymbol.push_back(std::make_unique<Circle>
                           (Point2D(150, 50), RADIUS));
   olympicSymbol.push_back(std::make_unique<Circle>
                           (Point2D(250, 50), RADIUS));
   olympicSymbol.push_back(std::make_unique<Circle>
                           (Point2D(100,100), RADIUS));
   olympicSymbol.push_back(std::make_unique<Circle>
                           (Point2D(200,100), RADIUS));

   // plus a label
   olympicSymbol.push_back(std::make_unique<Text>(Point2D(50,150),
                          "Games of the Olympiad",
                          "Title of figure"));

   // color those circles (and the label)
   SSDL_Color olympicColors[] = { BLUE,
                           SSDL_CreateColor(0, 255, 255), // yellow
                           BLACK, GREEN, RED, BLACK };
   for (unsigned int i = 0; i < olympicSymbol.size(); ++i)
      colorShape(olympicSymbol[i].get(), olympicColors[i]);
                                               //to pass in ptr, use get

   // do a game loop
   while (SSDL_IsNextFrame())
   {
      SSDL_DefaultEventHandler();

      SSDL_RenderClear(WHITE);    // clear the screen
```

```
        // draw all those shapes
        for (unsigned int i = 0; i < olympicSymbol.size(); ++i)
            olympicSymbol[i]->draw();

        // move all those shapes
        for (unsigned int i = 0; i < olympicSymbol.size(); ++i)
            olympicSymbol[i]->moveBy(1, 1);
    }

    //No need to delete -- unique_ptr's got that handled
    return 0;
}
```

shared_ptr

A unique_ptr owns its memory, and nobody else deallocates it.

A shared_ptr lets other shared_ptrs own the same memory. It maintains a record of how many shared_ptrs are using it (this is "reference counting"), and only when that number drops to 0 does the memory get deleted.

Here's a possible use: I have a 3D model I can load from a file. These things tend to be large. If I have 20 monsters of the same type in my game, I don't want 20 copies of all that graphics data!

So I put the graphics data in one object of type GraphicsData and create a Monster object for every instance of the monster. Let Monsters share their GraphicsData:

```
class GraphicsData
{
    ... lots of graphics info...
};

class Monster
{
    ...

    Point3D location_;
    shared_ptr<GraphicsData> _modelInfo;
};
```

Since everybody's depending on the shared data to not change unpredictably, it's a good idea to use shared_ptr for things that don't change – like GraphicsData on a 3D model.

I won't cover shared_ptr further, but I will note that you use it a lot like you do unique_ptr. shared_ptr, not unique_ptr, and make_shared, not make_unique, but otherwise it's quite similar.

Antibugging

The main problem I find with smart pointers is forgetting get():

```
strcpy (myChars, "totally unique"); // should be myChars.get()
```

The other problem is keeping track of what should be a unique_ptr and what should be raw. Suppose I change my List class so that start_ is a unique_ptr. Consider this code:

```
for(auto p = start_; p != end; p = p->next())
    doSomethingTo(p->data());     //  in real life I'd use iterators because
                                  //  why not
```

This looks like a simple loop to do something to each element of the list. But since start_ is a unique_ptr, it won't like that p = start_; no copy = allowed! Using std::move (for auto p = std::move(start_)...) is even worse, because it takes the memory from start_ and transfers it to p – trashing my List! The better solution is

```
for (auto p = start_.get(); p != end_; p = p->next_.get())
    doSomethingTo(p->data());
                              //end shd be a raw pointer too -- it owns nothing
```

The best principle here is: the unique_ptr owns the memory; use raw pointers for those that merely look at it.

Remember, as I have a hard time doing, that if you're passing in a pointer, don't use std::make_unique; use the constructor. make_unique expects to allocate, not take a pointer.

EXERCISES

1. Rewrite Chapter 14's example of a random passcode to use `unique_ptr`.
2. Rewrite the `String` class (use Chapter 18's so it'll have move copy and move =) to use `unique_ptr`.
3. ...and `Vector`.
4. ...and `List`. (Hard)

CHAPTER 27

Esoterica (Not So Recommended)

I rarely use these features. Part of the reason for this chapter is for those rare circumstances in which they *are* useful. Another is understanding why they're less popular.

protected Sections, protected Inheritance

Consider class Phone below. Phone has a member numCalls_ that keeps track of all calls made, ever, by any Phone. There's a function to change it, but it's private, because we really should only update numCalls_ when making a call():

```
class Phone
{
public:
    void call() { /*do some stuff, and then */ incNumCalls(); }
    static int numCalls() { return numCalls_; }

private:
    void incNumCalls   () { ++numCalls_;      }

    inline static int numCalls_ = 0;
};
```

But now we've reached the dawn of human civilization and there are MobilePhones. They make calls differently, using cell towers, but they need to increment that number too. They can't access Phone::incNumCalls(); it's private. And we decided for good reason not to make it public. What else can we do?

C++ provides another section: **protected** (see Example 27-1). The outside world can't see it (like private) but it's visible to child classes.

W. Briggs, *C++26 for Lazy Programmers*, https://doi.org/10.1007/979-8-8688-1859-2_27

Example 27-1. The Phone class, ready to share a family secret with its child classes

```
class Phone
{
public:
    void call() { /*do some stuff, and then */ incNumCalls(); }
    static int numCalls() { return numCalls_; }

protected:
    void incNumCalls    () { ++numCalls_;       }

private:
    inline static int numCalls_ = 0;
};
```

Now MobilePhone will be able to access incNumCalls():

```
class MobilePhone : public Phone
{
public:
    void call() { /* do stuff w cell towers, and */ incNumCalls(); }
};
```

Should we use public or private inheritance? Let's say when you do a mobile call, you need some extra security. So in MobilePhone I'll ditch the old call and add a new function secureCall:

```
class MobilePhone : public /*?*/ Phone
{
public:
    void secureCall()
    {
        makeSecure ();
        /* do cell tower stuff */
        incNumCalls();
    }

    void makeSecure (); // however that's done
};
```

With public inheritance (Figure 27-1), the inherited members are as public in the child class as they were in the parent. That's bad for `MobilePhone`: it lets the outside world use the insecure, inherited `call` function. Maybe private inheritance, as in Figure 27-2, would be better?

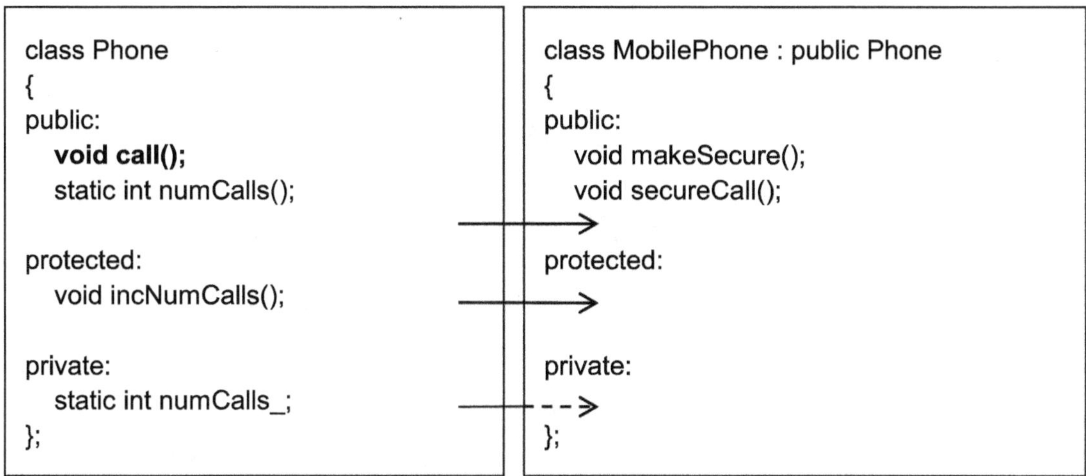

***Figure 27-1.** Public inheritance with a protected section*

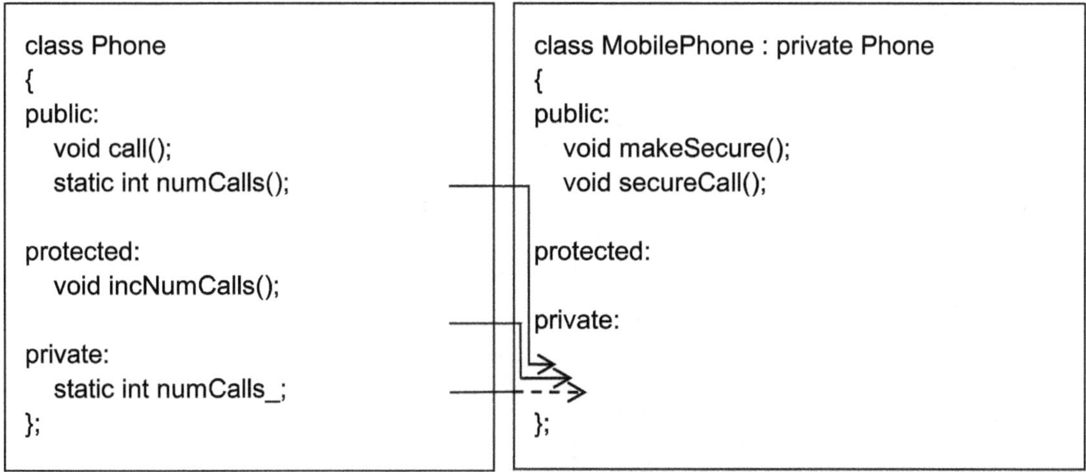

***Figure 27-2.** Private inheritance with a protected section*

Now I'll add a subclass of MobilePhone: a SatellitePhone. It does its calling differently:

```
class SatellitePhone : public MobilePhone
{
public:
    void secureCall()
    {
        makeSecure ();
        /* do satellite stuff */
        incNumCalls();
    }

    //  makeSecure is inherited from MobilePhone
};
```

Problem: SatellitePhone can't use incNumCalls. Private inheritance put it in MobilePhone's private section.

We can use **protected inheritance**, as in Figure 27-3. It's like public inheritance, except inherited public members become protected.

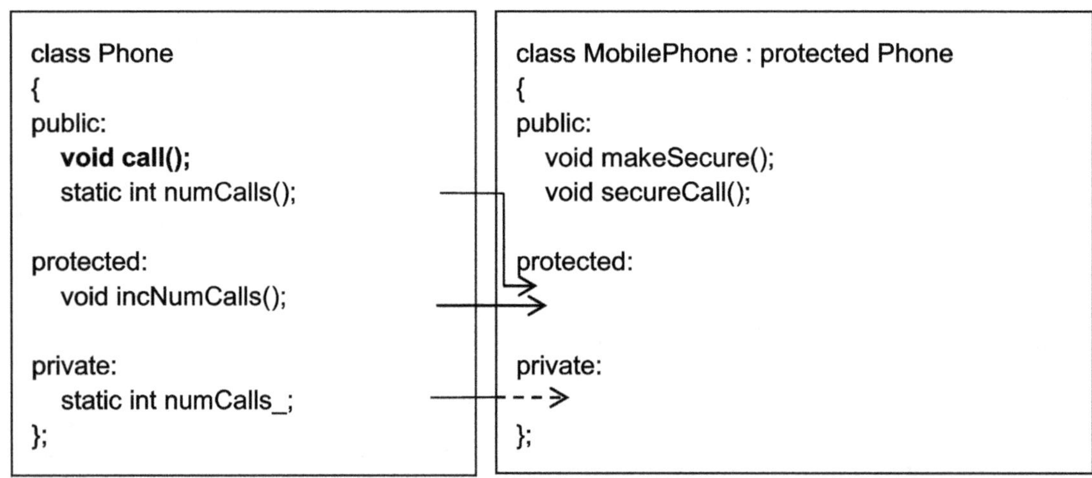

Figure 27-3. *protected inheritance: a solution to SatellitePhone's problem*

Now the subclasses are secure against use of the old call function, *and* all classes access incNumCalls() as needed.

Example 27-2. Verifying that no matter what kind of call we made, `Phone::numCalls_` got updated.

```
int main()
{
    Phone P;             P.call();
    MobilePhone MP;     MP.secureCall();
    SatellitePhone SP; SP.secureCall();

    assert(Phone::numCalls() == 3); // If this assertion succeeds,
                                    //  incNumCalls got called 3 times -- good!

    return 0;
}
```

It doesn't at all matter whether you use private or protected inheritance until you have a grandchild class. Even then it probably won't matter. I almost never need protected sections or protected inheritance.

`friend`s and Why You Shouldn't Have Any

Consider a program that uses maps. It reads in several `Area`s, as illustrated by Figure 27-4. Each `Area` has a name and bounding box (how far the `Area` extends north, south, west, and east). It then reports which `Area` is furthest north. Examples 27-3 and 27-4 show source code, with some code omitted for brevity.

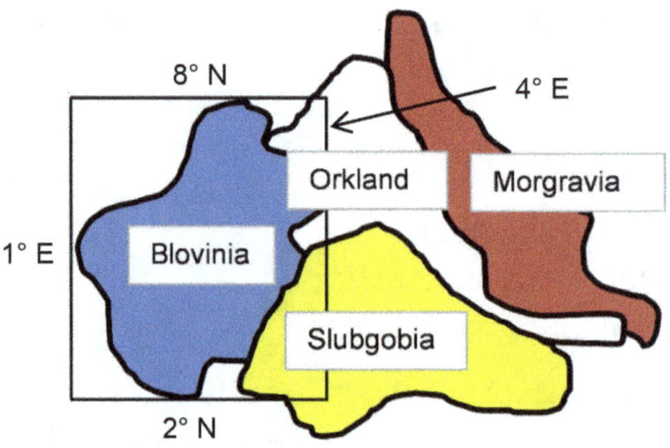

Figure 27-4. *A four-Area map, with a bounding box shown on one Area*

Example 27-3. `area.h`

```
// Class Area
// Each Area is read in as
//   <north bound> <south bound> <west bound> <east bound> <name>
//   as in
//   8 2 1 4 Blovinia
// ...and that's what an Area contains

//        -- from _C++26 for Lazy Programmers_

#ifndef AREA_H
#define AREA_H

#include <string>
#include <iostream>

class Area
{
public:
    static constexpr int NORTH = 0,
                         SOUTH = 1,
                         EAST  = 2,
                         WEST  = 3;
```

```
    static constexpr int DIRECTIONS = 4 ; // there are 4 directions

    Area() {}
    Area(const Area& other);

    Area& operator=(const Area& other);

    void read (std::istream& in );
    void print(std::ostream& out) const { out << name_; }

private:
    double boundingBox_[DIRECTIONS];
        // the northernmost, southernmost, etc., extent of our Area
        // bigger numbers are further north
        // bigger numbers are further east
    std::string name_;
};

inline
bool furtherNorthThan(const Area& a, const Area& b)
{
    return a.boundingBox_[Area::NORTH] > b.boundingBox_[Area::NORTH];
}
#endif //AREA_H
```

Example 27-4. The map program, which identifies the Area furthest north

```
// Program to read in regions from a file, and tell which
//   is furthest north.
//       -- from _C++26 for Lazy Programmers_

#include <iostream>
#include <fstream>
#include <vector>
#include "area.h"

using namespace std;
```

```
int main()
{
    vector<Area> myAreas;

    ifstream infile("regions.txt");
    if (!infile)
    {
        cerr << "Can't open file regions.txt.\n"; return 1;
    }

    while (infile)                  // read in Areas
    {
        Area area; infile >> area;
        if (infile) myAreas.push_back(area);
    }

    // find the northernmost Area
    int northernmostIndex = 0;
    for (unsigned int i = 1; i < myAreas.size(); ++i)
        if (furtherNorthThan(myAreas[i],myAreas[northernmostIndex]))
            northernmostIndex = i;

    // print it
    cout << "The northernmost area is "
         << myAreas [northernmostIndex]
         << endl;

    return 0;
}
```

I know I've written clear, well-commented code here (and I'm humble too), so I won't explain further. But when `furtherNorthThan` tries to access `boundingBox_`, the compiler complains of a privacy violation. It's right: `boundingBox_` *is* private.

C++ **friends** are a fix for this. If a function is so closely associated with a class that it may as well be a member – but it isn't convenient to make it one – you can give it access to all members, including the private ones, just as though it were. Here's how: somewhere in class `Area` (I put it at the top so it's always the same place), put a `friend` declaration for the function (Example 27-5).

Example 27-5. A `friend` for `Area`

```
class Area
{
    // "friend" keyword plus prototype of the trusted function
    friend bool furtherNorthThan(const Area& a, const Area& b);
    ...
```

Now the program should compile fine and report that Morgravia is furthest north.

You can also make a class a `friend`:

```
class Area
{
    friend class OtherClassITrust;[1]
    ...
```

Or make some other class's member function a friend:

```
class Area
{
    friend void OtherClassIPartlyTrust::functionIFullyTrust();
    ...
```

Is this a good idea?

According to Marshall Cline and the C++ Super-FAQ[2], yes. He argues that a `friend` function is part of the public interface just as a public member function is. It doesn't violate security, but is just another part of it.

I see his point, but I can't think of an example that can't be done another way. In the example above, we could replace

```
bool furtherNorthThan(const Area& a, const Area& b);
```

with

```
bool Area::furtherNorthThan(const Area& b) const;
```

[1] If the other class has already been declared, you can leave out the word class here.

[2] At time of writing, `isocpp.org/wiki/faq/`.

I make stream I/O operators >> and << call member functions `print` and `read`, and `List`'s external `operator==` calls a helper function `List<T>::isEqual`. Using `friend` might be easier, but not by much.

What happens if I make `operator==` a friend of `List<T>`?

First try:

```
template<typename T>
class List
{
    friend bool operator==(const List<T>& a, const List<T>& b);
    ...
```

It doesn't like that – says "unresolved external symbol" or "declares a non-template function." The fix is

```
    friend bool operator==<>(const List& a, const List& b);
```
[3]

The `<>` means something like "do a template specialization based on what we know, which is T." But `<T>` doesn't work. My theory is we have to do it this particular way because someone on the standards committee thought that would be funny.

It works, but it's yet another complication I'd rather be too lazy to know.

If you want `friend`, use it as experts suggest: for things tightly connected to the class in question, so they can be considered part of the class's interface to the world. I'm betting it won't be often.

User-Defined Conversions (Cast Operators)

Should we add a way to implicitly cast from `String` to `const char*` as needed? Makes sense: many built-in functions expect a `char*`, and you might prefer `myInFile.open(filename);` to `myInFile.open(filename.c_str())`, especially around the 100th time you type it. So we'll add this operator to `String`:

```
operator const char*() const { return c_str();}
                                              // called implicitly as needed
```

[3] `cppreference.com` thinks you should first declare, globally, `template<typename T> class List;` and then a function declaration for `operator==`. Your mileage may vary.

Works fine for that call to myInFile.open. Then we try a simple string comparison:

```
if (str1 == "END")
    cout << "Looks like we've reached the END.\n";
```

It no longer compiles – gives complaints about ambiguity or too many overloads.

It's right. There are now *two* ways to match the arguments of operator ==: implicitly convert "END" to another String and compare with String's == and implicitly convert str1 to a char* with the new cast operator and use char*'s ==.

The solution is to put the word explicit in front of the function.[4]

Example 27-6. Giving String a user-defined cast operator

```
class String
{
public:
    ...

    explicit operator const char*() const { return c_str(); }
        // will cast from String to const char* if explicitly called
    ...
};
```

Now we can cast, but we have to *say* we want to cast:

```
myInputFile.open(static_cast<const char*>(filename));
```

That's not exactly saving typing relative to filename.c_str()!

When do I use my own cast operators? In the SDL library, there are many functions that take a pointer to something called an SDL_Window. I keep that in the private section of my SSDL_Display class. Rather than SDL_RenderDrawPoint (myDisplay.sdlWindow(), x, y), with an *implicit* operator SDL_Window() I can say SDL_RenderDrawPoint(myDisplay, x, y). After saving that typing a few dozen times, I'm glad of the convenience. And since not much gets done with SDL_Window – unlike with std::string – I never ended up with an unexpected ambiguity. Yet.

[4] You can also put explicit in front of other functions sometimes called implicitly, like copy and conversion constructors, to disable implicit calls – but I never do.

EXERCISES

In each exercise, use `explicit` to avoid ambiguity.

1. Add a cast-to-double operator to the `Fraction` class. The `double` version of 1/2, for example, is 0.5 (of course).
2. Add a cast-to-double operator to the `Point2D` class from earlier exercises. The `double` version of a `Point2D` is the magnitude: $\sqrt{x^2 + y^2}$.

Coroutines

Ordinarily a function, if you call it a second time, starts at the beginning again. A coroutine can pick up right where it left off.

Example 27-7 uses a coroutine to calculate the next factorial. (Recall that factorial(N) is N*(N-1)*...1, with factorial(0) defined as 1.) It's replacing the usual `return` with `co_yield` that makes C++ recognize it as a coroutine.[5] The `std::generator<int>` return type means "set this up so `factorial` can generate `int`s."

Example 27-7. A program using a coroutine to generate factorials

```
// Program to print several factorials using a coroutine
//       -- from _C++ for Lazy Programmers_

#include <iostream>
#include <generator>6

std::generator<int> factorial()
{
    int whichOne = 0;                   // start with 0!
    int result = 1;                     // 0! is 1

    while (true)
```

[5] The presence of two other keywords not covered here, `co_await` and `co_return`, also makes a function into a coroutine.

[6] In Microsoft Visual Studio, say `<experimental/generator>` here and `std::experimental::generator` on the next line.

```
    {
        co_yield result;
        ++whichOne;                   // go on to next one
        result *= whichOne;           // and calculate next result
    }
}

int main()
{
    std::cout << "The first 8 factorials:\n";
    for (int i : factorial())
    {
        static int whichOne = 0;

        std::cout << whichOne << ": " << i << '\n';

        ++whichOne;                   // go on to next
        if (whichOne > 8) break;      // stop at 8
    }

    std::cout << std::endl;

    return 0;
}
```

To trace factorial's action: the first time it's called, it sets whichOne – which factorial we're to return – to 0. The result for 0 is 1. (You might load the source code example in the ch26 folder and trace it in the debugger. That's what I did.)

It enters the loop. First thing it's to do is provide the caller main with that result, with co_yield, which means "give result to the caller, and when called again, resume execution here." So control returns to main, which prints that result.

When main calls it again, it continues from where it stopped: at the co_yield. It goes on and adds 1 to whichOne (changing whichOne to 1), multiplies result by whichOne (getting 1 again), goes to the next iteration of the loop and co_yields that result.

When called again, it'll increment whichOne again (getting 2), multiply result by whichOne (getting 2), and co_yield that result.

The next time, whichOne will become 3 and result will be 6. And so on.

main is set up to call this again and again in a range-based for loop, breaking at 8 (gotta stop somewhere).

One advantage of coroutines is efficiency. Each time we call factorial, all it does is an increment, a multiplication, and a return. It's O(1)! Ordinarily it would be O(N). Programmers also report that for some problems coroutines are more intuitive and easier to write.

EXERCISES

1. Adapt Example 27-7 so that factorial returns not just result, but result with whichOne in a structured binding – so main won't have to keep track of which one it's on independently. This isn't really practice with coroutines but with structured bindings, but still worth doing, I think.
2. Write another generator function that returns the next prime number, starting with 2, and a version of main that prints the first 100 primes.

CHAPTER 28

Building Bigger Projects

One day you may want to build a bigger project. This chapter introduces some useful tools: namespaces, conditional compilation, and the construction of libraries.

Namespaces

Suppose I write a library for geographical information, to be used for maps, making voting districts, whatever. I make some classes: `maps`, `vectors` (XY pairs used for graphics), `regions`, and more.

Then I notice that I can't compile because `map` and `vector` already mean something in C++. OK. Call 'em `GeoLib_map`, `GeoLib_vector`, etc., like with SDL and SSDL functions.

And I'm using a third-party library, which happens to define `region` as something else ...this is getting tedious. Is there a shortcut?

Sure. Make a **namespace** `GeoLib` and put your code in it, as in Figure 28-1.

```
//geolib_map.h

#ifndef GEOLIBMAP_H
#define GEOLIBMAP_H

namespace GeoLib
{
    class map {...};
}

#endif //GEOLIBMAP_H
```

```
//geolib_map.cpp

namespace GeoLib
{
    map::map ( )
    {
        ...
    }

    ...
}
```

```
//geolib_vector.h

#ifndef GEOLIBVECTOR_H
#define GEOLIBVECTOR_H

namespace GeoLib
{
    class vector {...};
}

#endif //GEOLIBVECTOR_H
```

Figure 28-1. *A namespace can contain code from different files*

Programmers can now type `GeoLib::map` or `std::map`, and the compiler will know which they mean.

W. Briggs, *C++26 for Lazy Programmers*, https://doi.org/10.1007/979-8-8688-1859-2_28

If they get tired of typing `GeoLib::` over and over, they can use `using`:

```
using GeoLib::region;
        // after this you can omit the GeoLib:: in GeoLib::region

using namespace GeoLib;
              // now *all* GeoLib members can have GeoLib:: omitted

using namespace std;
              // now all std:: members can have std:: omitted too
              // If the compiler gripes, you can still use GeoLib::
              //  or std:: to clarify which you want
```

You can also specify that something isn't declared in *any* namespace (and thus is in the "global" namespace) with a plain `::`, as in: `::myNonNamespaceFunction();`.

To illustrate construction of namespaces, Examples 28-3 and 28-4 show the creation of a namespace `Cards`; Example 28-5 uses it.

It's a matter of debate whether `using namespace <whatever>;` is evil, that is, indefensibly awful. I say use it as you like in the privacy of your own `.cpp` files but don't mess up others' by putting it in `.h`'s they may include.

Conditional Compilation

Now I'm using my `GeoLib` code, and I'm finding my calculations are wrong, wrong, wrong. It's hard to tell which functions are screwing up. I want to generate a report of those calculations so I can check them:

```
map::area(region) thinks area of block group 6709 is 672.4
dist to center is 356.2
map::area(region) thinks area of block group 6904 is 312.5
dist to center is 379.7
...
```

I don't want this printed *all* the time – just when debugging.

So I create a `#define` in a `.h` file that every other file includes (Example 28-1).

Example 28-1. A `.h` file containing `#define DEBUG_GEOLIB`, for conditional compilation

```
// debugSetup.h

#ifndef DEBUGSETUP_H
#define DEBUGSETUP_H

#define DEBUG_GEOLIB

#endif //DEBUGSETUP_H       // Yes, that's the whole thing
```

I use it wherever I have debugging information to print:

```
#ifdef DEBUG_GEOLIB
    cout << " map::area(region) thinks area of block group "
         << bg->id() << " is " << bg->area() << endl;
    cout << "dist to center is "
         << distance(region.loc(), bg->loc()) << endl;
#endif
```

And I comment or uncomment the `#define DEBUG_GEOLIB` depending on whether I want to see this.

Libraries

Libraries come in two flavors, **static** and **shared**. A static library's code is brought right into the executable at link time; the shared library is in another file, loaded at runtime. So the static library is said to be quicker to run (I've never noticed a difference), and you don't have to worry where your shared library got moved to as it's always right there in the executable. But shared saves space, as many programs can use the same code, and it's more easily updated.

I lean toward shared. It's common for Unix and seems to help with portability between compiler versions.

I'll try it both ways here, for both compilers. For my example I'll use the card games code from Chapter 20, with generally useful classes (`Card`, `Deck`, etc.) going into the library. The Montana game will use that library.

You might create some other library as you go. See Exercises at the chapter's end, or choose your own.

g++

Code demonstrating this is in the source code, ch28/g++. The library is in subdirectory cardLibg++, and a tester program is in subdirectory montana.

Static Libraries

To create a static library, compile the object files as usual:

```
g++ -g -c deck.cpp
...
```

Then link with

```
ar rcs libcards.a deck.o card.o cardgroup.o
                                    #ar for "archive"; rcs is needed program options
```

Shared Libraries

The shared library needs object files "relocatable" in memory, so compile them like this:

```
g++ -g -fPIC -c deck.cpp #PIC: "position independent code."
```

In Unix, shared libraries end in .so, so link like this:

```
g++ -shared -o libcards.so  deck.o card.o cardgroup.o
```

Windows uses the extension .dll, so for MSys2, type this:

```
g++ -shared -o libcards.dll deck.o card.o cardgroup.o
```

Linking

g++ needs to know where to find the include files, where to find the library files, and what libraries to use.

We tell it with these command-line options:

- -I<name of directory> to find include files.
- -L<name of directory> to find library files.

- `-l<library>` to say what libraries we want linked in. Library names have an initial `lib` and the extension `.a`, `.so`, or `.dll`, stripped off, as here:

```
g++ -o montana -g montana.o io.o montana_main.o \¹
    -I../cardLibg++ -L../cardLibg++ -lcards
                                    #uses libcards.<something>
```

If you have both versions (which you wouldn't), it'll link to the `.so` or `.dll` over the `.a`.

You can have as many copies as you want of these options.

Running

If you used a static library, you can just run the program now as usual.

If it's dynamic, the system needs to know where to find it. Here are solutions:

- Bribe the system administrator to put the `.dll` or `.so` file in the system path. This makes sense if multiple programs use it and your program's important enough.
- Copy the `.dll` or `.so` to the folder with the executable. Good for a single project; not so good if you have lots of folders and therefore lots of copies.
- Set the environment variables so the system can find it. There are scripts in the source code folder for Unix (`runx`, `gdbx`, `dddx`, just as with SSDL). MSys2 users, your scripts end in m for MSys2: `runm`, `gdbm`. The content is like this:

```
export LD_LIBRARY_PATH=../cardLibg++ #Unix
PATH="../cardLibg++:$PATH"           #MSys2
```

[1] \ means "continue on the next line."

Makefiles

These long commands get tedious to type repeatedly, so they're bundled into files in the chapter's source code: Makefiles for building the library in Unix, as with SSDL; another for building a program that uses the library (it works for both platforms); and in the latter's folder, scripts for running the program (see above).

To make your own, edit the library-building Makefile to pick the kind of library to create and then edit all the files for paths, executable names, whatever you like.

Microsoft Visual Studio

Code demonstrating this is in the source code, `ch28/VisualStudio`. `cardLib*` (there are different versions; read on) are the libraries, and `uses*` are projects that use these libraries.

Static Libraries: The Easy Option

To build a static library in Visual Studio, click Create New Project and select Static Library.

When it creates the project, it expects you to use "precompiled headers."[2] You can

- **Support this by putting this line at the start of each source file:**

  ```
  #include "pch.h"
  ```

  It must come before any other includes, or your code won't compile.

  Or fix it in one step:

- **Eliminate precompiled headers.** Under Project ➤ Properties, for All Configurations/All Platforms (top row), set Configuration Properties ➤ C/C++ ➤ Precompiled Headers ➤ Precompiled Header to Not Using Precompiled Headers. You can ignore the files the compiler gave you with the project.

[2] Microsoft Visual Studio and g++ both have this method of helping with compile times. The idea is that instead of recompiling a `.h` file anew for each source file you include it in, you can reduce compile time by compiling it once. I haven't felt the need, but with STL and recent language changes, header files do seem to keep growing ...

Then build the library. I do it for Debug *and* Release, x86 *and* x64, so I needn't wonder which I did.

Now create a project that uses the library. It'll need to know where to find the include files. Under Project Properties for All Configurations/All Platforms, set Configuration Properties ➤ C/C++ ➤ General ➤ Additional Include Directories appropriately (see Figure 28-2).

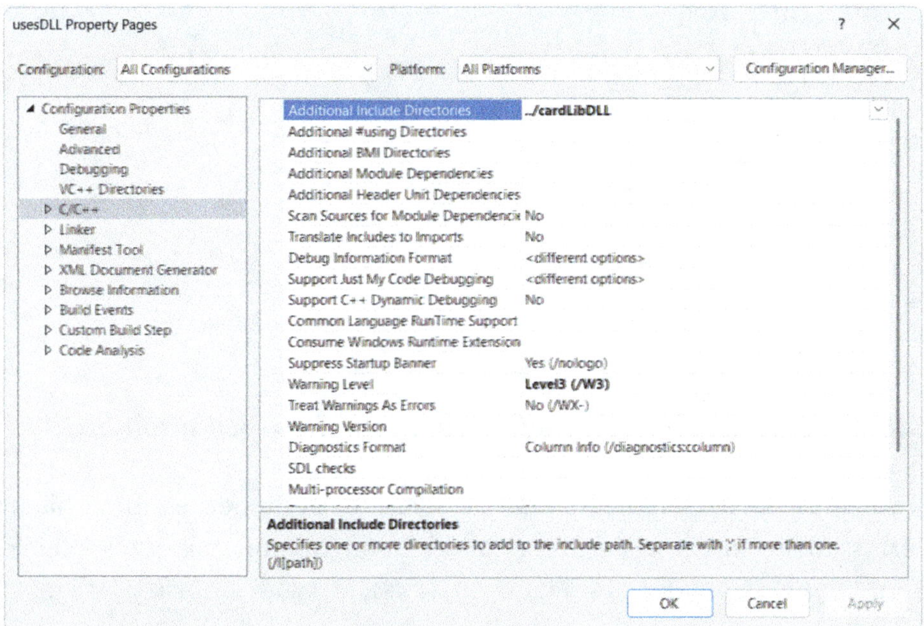

Figure 28-2. *Telling a project where to find library include files, in Visual Studio*

Add your library's path to Configuration Properties ➤ Linker ➤ General ➤ Additional Library Directories (Figure 28-3). Hard-code the location for each configuration and platform, or better yet, use variables as shown.

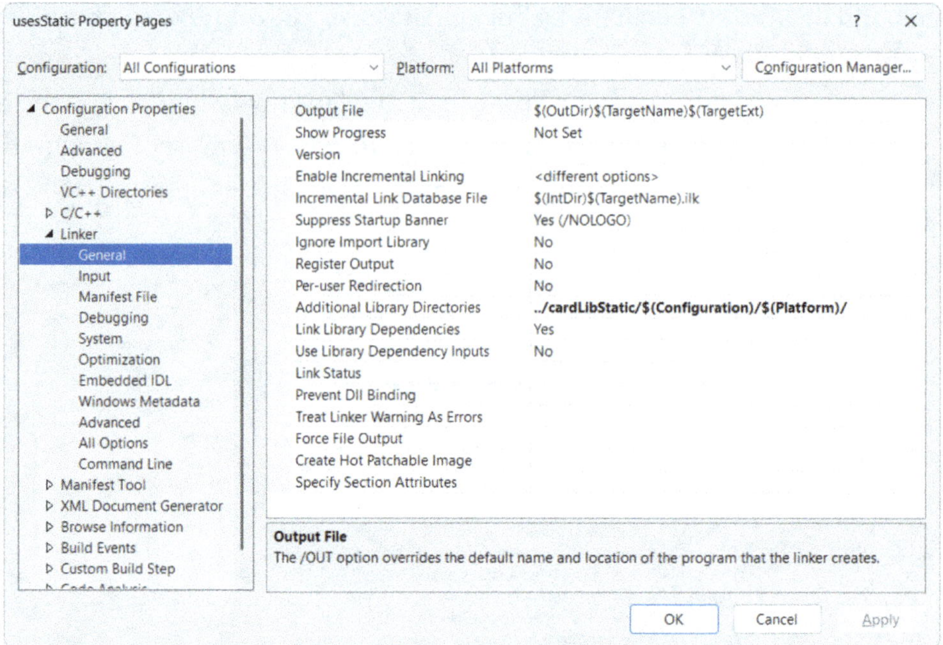

Figure 28-3. *Telling the project where to find your library in Visual Studio*

Now you must tell it *what* the library is. Under Project Properties, All Configurations/All Platforms, add the name of the library under Configuration Properties ➤ Linker ➤ Input ➤ Additional Dependencies (Figure 28-4). It'll be `<your library project>.lib`.

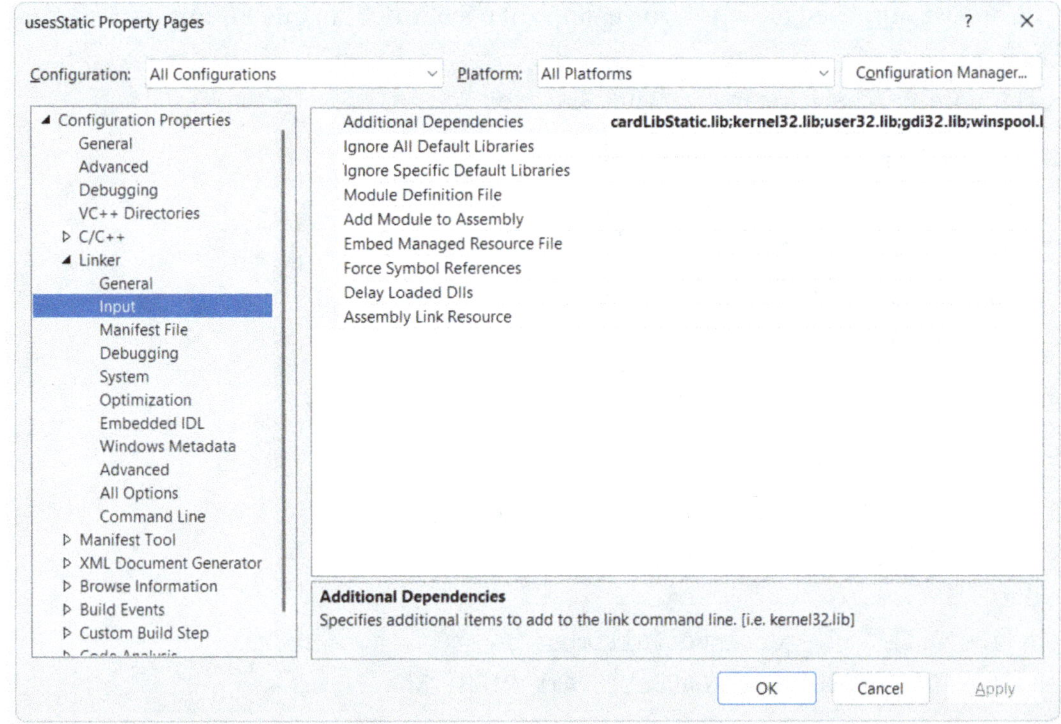

Figure 28-4. *Adding a library dependency in Visual Studio*

Dynamic Link Libraries (DLLs): The Not So Easy Way

To make your own DLL, go back through the previous section, but for project type select Dynamic Link Library (DLL). But don't build yet!

In directing new programs to use your library, when you tell Project Properties about the library (Figure 28-4), it'll still be `<your project>.lib`. I thought we were creating a DLL? Yes, but we're really creating two things: the `.dll`, which contains the runtime code, and a `.lib` file that tells the program at compile time, "You'll get to import these things from a DLL later."

This is where it gets weird. When the compiler sees a function declaration, it needs to know if it's going to be compiling and exporting it (because it's compiling the library) or importing it from a DLL (because it's compiling a program that uses the library). The way to say this is to prepend to the declaration either `__declspec(dllexport)` or `__declspec(dllimport)`. `__declspec` means "I'm about to tell you something about this function" and `dllexport`/`dllimport`, well, that's obvious.

So are we supposed to write two versions of each function, one for import and one for export?

This common hack means we won't have to:

1. Write a `.h` file like in Example 28-2.

Example 28-2. A `.h` file to help with DLL projects

```
// Header to make DLL functions import or export
//        -- from _C++26 for Lazy Programmers_

#ifndef CARDSSETUP_H
#define CARDSSETUP_H

# ifdef IM_COMPILING_MY_CARD_LIBRARY_RIGHT_NOW
#  define DECLSPEC __declspec(dllexport)
# else
#  define DECLSPEC __declspec(dllimport)
# endif //IM_COMPILING_MY_CARD_LIBRARY_RIGHT_NOW

#endif //CARDSSETUP_H
```

   Now `DECLSPEC` means "this is to be exported" *or* "this is to be imported" ...depending on whether we're compiling the library or using it. Just right.

2. In each `.cpp` file in the library, write this `#define`:

   ```
   #define IM_COMPILING_MY_CARD_LIBRARY_RIGHT_NOW
   ```

   That's how it'll know `DECLSPEC` should be the export version.

   This must be done before any `.h` files related to your project, so they can see it, but after `#include "pch.h"` if we're using that, because that always comes first.

3. Put `DECLSPEC` before everything being exported from the `.cpp` files.

4. ...and before the corresponding function declarations in the `.h` files too. They have to match.

5. Include the `.h` file from step 1 as needed to define `DECLSPEC` throughout. I put it in `cards.h`.

Library files will look like Examples 28-3 and 28-4. Example 28-5 shows how to use Cards members in montana.h; in montana.cpp, I just said using namespace Cards; and made no other changes.

Example 28-3. Parts of card.h, set up to make a DLL, and forming a namespace

```
// Card class
//        -- from _C++26 for Lazy Programmers__

#ifndef CARD_H
#define CARD_H

#include <iostream>
#include "cardsSetup.h" // defines DECLSPEC

namespace Cards
{
    enum class Rank  { ACE=1,  JACK=11, QUEEN, KING    }; // Card rank
    enum class Suit  { HEARTS, DIAMONDS, CLUBS, SPADES }; // Card suit
    enum class Color { BLACK,  RED                     }; // Card color

    inline
    Color toColor(Suit s)           // DECLSPEC isn't needed for inlines
    {
        if (s == HEARTS || s == DIAMONDS) return RED; else return BLACK;
    }

    // I/O on Rank and Suit
    DECLSPEC std::ostream& operator<<(std::ostream& out, Rank r);
    DECLSPEC std::ostream& operator<<(std::ostream& out, Suit s);
    DECLSPEC std::istream& operator>>(std::istream& in, Rank& r);
    DECLSPEC std::istream& operator>>(std::istream& in, Suit& s);

    ...

    class Card
    {
    public:
        Card(Rank r = Rank(0), Suit s = Suit(0)) :
            rank_(r), suit_(s)
```

```
        {
        }
        Card(const Card& other) : Card(other.rank_, other.suit_){}

        ...

        DECLSPEC void read (std::istream &in );
    private:
        Suit suit_;
        Rank rank_;
    };

    ...
} //namespace Cards
#endif //CARD_H
```

Example 28-4. Part of `card.cpp`, set up to make a DLL, and forming a namespace

```
// Card class
//        -- from _C++26 for Lazy Programmers_

#include "pch.h"
#define IM_COMPILING_MY_CARD_LIBRARY_RIGHT_NOW
                    // see cardsSetup.h. Must come before card
                    //  related includes, after "pch.h" if any
#include "card.h"

using namespace std;

namespace Cards
{
    DECLSPEC void Card::read(std::istream &in )
    {
        try {   in  >> rank_  >> suit_;  }
        catch (BadRankException&) // if reading rank_ throw an exception
```

```
        {
            in >> suit_;            //    consume the suit as well
            throw;                  //    and continue throwing the exception
        }
    }

    DECLSPEC istream& operator>>(istream& in, Suit& s)
    {
        ...
    }

    ...
} //namespace Cards
```

Example 28-5. Parts of `montana.h`, showing use of namespace Cards

```
// class Montana, for a game of Montana solitaire
//        -- from _C++26 for Lazy Programmers_

#include "gridLoc.h"
#include "cell.h"
#include "deck.h"

#ifndef MONTANA_H
#define MONTANA_H

class Montana
{
public:
    static constexpr int ROWS = 4, CLMS  = 13;
    static constexpr int NUM_EMPTY_CELLS =  4;// 4 empty cells in grid
    ...
private:
    ...

        // dealing and redealing
    void deal   (Cards::Deck& deck, Cards::Waste& waste);
    void cleanup(Cards::Deck& deck, Cards::Waste& waste);

...
```

```
    // data members
    Cards::Cell  grid_ [ROWS][CLMS];      // where the cards are
    GridLoc emptyCells_ [NUM_EMPTY_CELLS];// where the empty cells are
};
#endif //MONTANA_H
```

If that goes well, there's one more thing to set in the program that uses your library: it needs to find the DLL at runtime.

The easiest way is to copy the DLL into the project folder. Or put it in the system PATH (which may require administrator access).

If that's not what you want, go to Project Properties, and set Configuration Properties ➤ Debugging ➤ Environment. It needs an update to the PATH variable, without forgetting the old PATH ...if the location of the DLL is `..\cardLibDLL\Debug`, you can give it `PATH=..\cardLibDLL\Debug\;%PATH%`. Or use `$Configuration` and `$Platform` as in Figure 28-5.

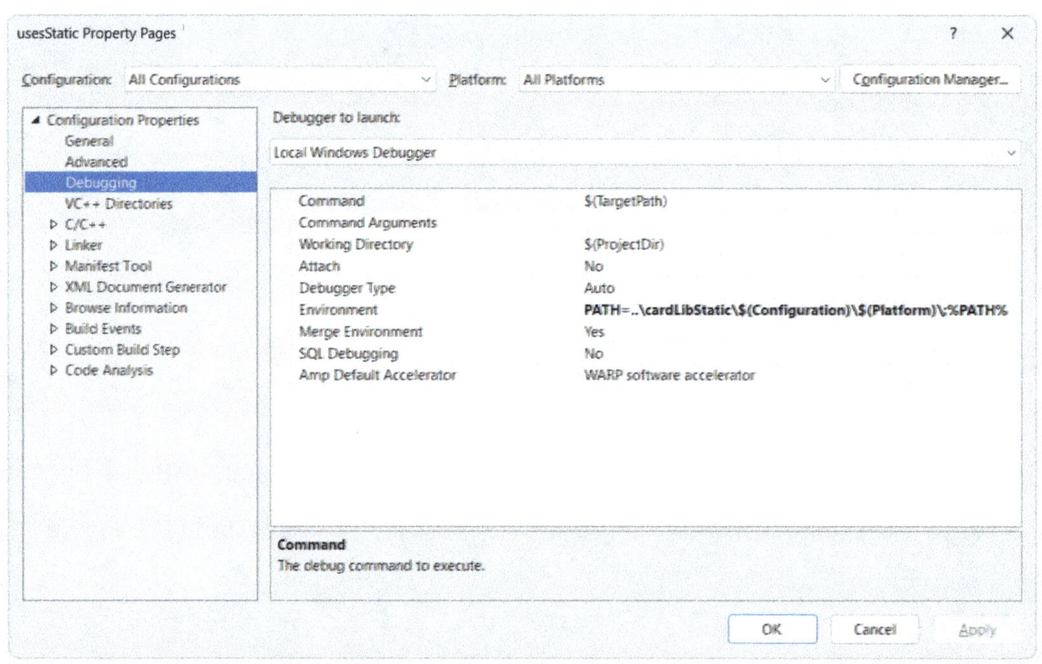

Figure 28-5. *Setting the PATH in Visual Studio*

Antibugging

- **You make changes to Project Properties, but they have no effect.** It's easy to overlook the top line of the Project Properties window (Figure 28-5). Sometimes you correct one configuration, but you're using another. I prefer to edit All Configurations, All Platforms, wherever possible.
- **The compiler complains that common things like `cout` don't exist.** Put `#include "pch.h"` *before* other includes or stop using precompiled headers; see the beginning of this section.
- **At runtime, the program can't find the DLL. But you set the PATH variable, as above.**

  If it's not a typo in the PATH, maybe you erased the `.user` file. This is what contains the environment information. Recreating it should solve the problem.
- **At runtime, the program can't start; the error message isn't clear.** Maybe your program's Platform (Win32 or x86 v. x64) doesn't match the DLL's.

EXERCISES

1. Put `PriorityQueue`, `List`, `Time`, `Fraction`, or some other class you did in previous exercises into its own library, and link it to something that uses it.
2. Make a library named `shapes` (in a namespace `Shapes`), using the `Shape` hierarchy from Chapter 21, extending it as you like; and link it into a program that uses the `Shapes`. You'll need to adapt the Makefile or .vcxproj.

CHAPTER 29

C

If you know C++ you almost know C. Experience with C gets you another brag – one character long, so it should fit on your resume! It's currently third on the TIOBE Index of popular programming languages, right after C++. (The list is volatile; it'll be different tomorrow.) It's useful for operating systems and embedded systems, and because of its relative simplicity, there are a lot of C libraries used in other languages including C++. SDL, which you've been using through SSDL, is one of them.

The C language is essentially what we covered before getting to classes, excluding

- SDL/SSDL
- `cin`, `cout`, and `fstream` variables
- `&` parameters
- `bool` (use `int` instead)
- `constexpr` (use `const` instead)

There are no classes, exceptions, overloaded operators, templates, spans, ranges, or namespaces. `struct`s exist but don't have member functions or public/private/protected sections (it's all public).

There are smaller differences, including the following:

- Casting looks like `(int*) myPtr`, not `static_cast<int*>(myPtr)`. (And if `myPtr` was a pointer to something else and this is a Bad Idea, then unlike C++, C won't stop you.)
- `struct S {...};` does declare a `struct` named S, but to declare a variable of that type requires an extra word:

```
struct S myStruct;
```

`cplusplus.com` and `cppreference.com`, despite the names, are good resources on C as well as C++.

W. Briggs, *C++26 for Lazy Programmers*, https://doi.org/10.1007/979-8-8688-1859-2_29

Compiling C

In **Visual Studio** you can't select "C file" as something to add to your project, but you can select "C++ file" and name yours `<something>.c`. The compiler will treat it as a C file. Compile and run as usual.

In **Unix** or **MSys2**, you can name your program `<something>.c` and compile with the `gcc` command, which works like g++ only for C files. The sample code has this built into its Makefiles.

Here in Example 29-1 is the obligatory "Hello, world!".

Example 29-1. "Hello, world!" in C

```
// Hello, world! -- again!  This time in C.¹
//    -- from _C++26 for Lazy Programmers_

#include <stdio.h>

int main()
{
    printf("Hello, world!\n");

    return 0;
}
```

Here are some things to note:

- Include files, belonging to the system or not, end in `.h`. Those C++ inherits from C have the initial `c` taken back off: `stdlib.h`, not `cstdlib`, and `math.h`, not `cmath`.
- We print with `printf`; more on that in the next section.

Extra If you want both C++ and C files in the same project, that'll work, but there are tricks required. You'll need to put `main` in a C++ file, and for any C include files to be used in a C++ file, wrap the include thus:

[1] If your compiler doesn't understand comments //like this – "C++-style comments" – comment /* C-style */ instead. Or get a newer compiler.

```
extern "C"
{
#include "mycheader.h"
}
```

If you're using gcc/g++, link with g++.

For more on this, at time of writing, see the C++ Super-FAQ at isocpp.org/wiki/faq/mixing-c-and-cpp.

I/O

All these I/O functions are in stdio.h.

printf

Instead of cout >>, C has the function printf ("print-f," meaning "print with formatting"):

```
printf("Ints like %d, strings like %s, and floats like %f -- oh, my!\n",
       12, "ROFL", 3.14159);                        // %d is for "decimal"
```

will print

```
Ints like 12, strings like ROFL, and floats like 3.141590 -- oh, my!
```

The % sequences are placeholders in the "format string" ("Ints like %d..."), showing where to put each successive argument. You can have as many arguments as you want, that is, printf is variadic. The most common % sequences are %d for decimal integer; %f for fixed floating point; and %s for string, that is, character array. %% means "just the % character."

There are modifiers you can put inside them; for example, %.2f puts two digits right of the decimal point.

scanf and the address-of (&) operator

scanf ("scan-f") replaces cin >> and looks like this:

```
scanf("%f %s", &myDouble, myCharArray);
```

& means "take the address of." C and C++ both have this operator, but C uses it all the time. scanf needs to know where myDouble is so it can alter it (more on that in the next section). It doesn't need the address of myCharArray because myCharArray *is* an address.

Visual Studio gives a warning, if you use scanf or some other functions in this chapter, that the function is unsafe, just as it does with some cstring functions (see Chapter 14). If you want to disable the warning, put this line before main:

```
#pragma warning (disable:4996)
```

Example 29-2 shows uses of printf and scanf.

Example 29-2. printf and scanf

```
// Program to test C's major standard I/O functions
//          -- from _C++26 for Lazy Programmers_

#include <stdio.h>

int main()
{
    float number;              // number we'll read in and print out
    int   age;                 // your age
    enum {MAXSTR = 80};[2]     // array size
    char  name [MAXSTR];       // your name

        // A printf showing float, and use of % sign
    printf("%3.2f%% of statistics are made up on the spot!\n\n",
            98.23567894);

        // printfs using decimal, hex, and char array
        // %02d means pad number to a width of 2 with leading 0's
    printf("%d is 0x%x in hexadecimal.\n\n", 16, 16);
    printf("\"%s\" is a $%d.%02d word.\n\n", "hexadecimal",
            5, 0);

        // scanf needs & for the variables it sets
    printf("Enter a floating-point number:  ");
```

[2] The enum hack is a way of declaring MAXSTR. It takes less typing (and memory, and runtime) than const int MAXSTR=80;.

```
    scanf("%f", &number);
    printf("%g is %f in fixed notation and %e in scientific.\n",
           number, number, number);
    printf("...in scientific with a precision of 2:  %.2e.\n\n",
           number);

        // ...except arrays, since they're already addresses
    printf("Enter your name and age:  ");
    scanf("%s %d", name, &age);
    printf("%s is %d years old!\n\n", name, age);

    return 0;
}
```

This is what the output might look like:

```
98.24% of statistics are made up on the spot!

16 is 0x10 in hexadecimal.

"hexadecimal" is a $5.00 word.

Enter a floating-point number: 2
2 is 2.000000 in fixed notation and 2.000000e+000 in scientific.
Here it is in scientific with a precision of 2: 2.00e+000.

Enter your name and age: Linus 7
Linus is 7 years old!
```

Table 29-1 is a partial list of format codes for `printf` and `scanf`. For more detail, go to `cplusplus.com` and search for `printf` and `scanf`.

Table 29-1. Format codes for printf and scanf

% sequence	meaning
%d	Integer in decimal format.
%o	Integer in unsigned octal (base 8).
%x/%X	Integer in unsigned hexadecimal (base 16). Hex 1f will show up as 0x1f/0X1F.
%c	Character.
%s	Character array.
%f	Fixed-point floating point.
%e/%E	Scientific notation floating point. The E will be uppercase if you say %E.
%g/%G	Default floating point. The E (if any) will be uppercase if you say %G.
%p	Pointer.
%%	The % character itself.

fprintf and fscanf; fopen and fclose

File I/O in C uses variants of printf and scanf. Consider this code:

```
FILE* file = fopen("newfile.txt", "w"); // open file
if (!file) { printf("Can't open newfile.txt!\n"); return 0; }
                                          // did it work? if not, quit main

fprintf(file, "Avagadro's number is %.4e.\n", 6.023e+023);
                                         // use it

fclose (file);                          // close it
```

To open the file for writing, we call fopen ("f-open"), give it the filename, and "w" meaning "write" (to an output file). The file information is stored in a pointer of type FILE*, which will be NULL – C's equivalent of C++'s nullptr – if fopen fails.

Closing the file is simply sending the file pointer to fclose, as above.

In between, adapt your printfs to fprintfs by adding the file as the first argument.

If you want to read instead or write, open the file with "r" for "read," and adapt scanf similarly:

```
file = fopen("newfile.txt", "r");
if (!file) { printf("Can't open newfile.txt!\n"); return 0; }
fscanf(file, "%s %s %s %e", word1, word2, word3, &number);
fclose(file);
```

If successful, fscanf and scanf return the number of arguments you gave. If the number is different, something went wrong. Probably you reached the end of file. Test for that like so:

```
while (1)                              // while true
{
    if (fscanf(file, "%d", number) != 1)
        /* it didn't work -- handle that */;
    //...
}
```

Example 29-3 shows some uses of these functions.

Example 29-3. fprintf, fscanf, fopen, and fclose

```
// Program to test C's major standard I/O functions
//        -- from _C++26 for Lazy Programmers_

#include <stdio.h>

int main()
{
    FILE* file;                // a file to write to or read from
    float number;              // number we'll read in and print out
    enum { MAXSTR = 80 };      // array size
    char junk [MAXSTR];        // a char array for reading in (and thus
                               //        discarding) a word

        // printing to file. The number gets 4 digits of precision
    file = fopen("newfile.txt", "w");
    if (!file)
    {
        printf("Can't open newfile.txt for writing!\n"); return 0;
    }
```

```
    printf (       "Avagadro's number is %.4e.\n", 6.023e+023);
    fprintf(file, "Avagadro's number is %.4e.\n", 6.023e+023);
    fclose (file);

        // reading from a file
    file = fopen("newfile.txt", "r");
    if (!file)
    {
        printf("Can't open newfile.txt for reading!\n"); return 0;
    }
    fscanf(file, "%s %s %s %e", junk, junk, junk, &number);
                          // Read in 3 words, then the number we want
    fclose(file);
    printf("Looks like Avagadro's number is still %.4e.\n", number);

    return 0;
}
```

The file will contain

```
Avagadro's number is 6.0230e+023.
```

and the output to the screen will be

```
Avagadro's number is 6.0230e+023.
Looks like Avagadro's number is still 6.0230e+023.
```

sprintf and sscanf; fgets, fputs, and puts

Here are a few more I/O functions:

- **sscanf ("s-scan-f")** reads from a character array. If myCharArray is "2.3 kg", we can say

  ```
  sscanf(myCharArray, "%f %s", &myDouble, myWord);
            // myDouble gets 2.3, myWord gets "kg"
  ```

- **sprintf** prints to a character array:

  ```
  sprintf(myCharArray, "%s %f", name, number);
  ```

- **fgets** reads a line of text, either from a file

  ```
  fgets(myCharArray, MAX_STRING, someFile);
                                  // read myCharArray,
                                     which should
                                  //   be no more than MAX_STRING
                                  //   long, from someFile
  ```

  or the keyboard:

  ```
  fgets(myCharArray, MAX_STRING, stdin);
  ```

- **fputs** prints a char array to a file:

  ```
  fputs(myCharArray, someFile);
  ```

  You could let that file be stdout, but usually we use a shorter version for that:

  ```
  puts(myCharArray); //sends to stdout
  ```

  We don't similarly abbreviate fgets to gets: gets exists but is considered insecure, doesn't behave like fgets, and is thus not used.

Example 29-4 illustrates these functions.

Example 29-4. A program using sprintf, sscanf, fgets, etc.

```
// Program to test sprintf, sscanf, fgets, fputs, puts
//        -- from _C++26 for Lazy Programmers_

#include <stdio.h>

int main()
{
    while (1)                   // forever, or until break...
    {
        enum {MAXLINE=256};     // array size for line
        char line [MAXLINE];    // a line of text
        enum {MAXSTR = 80};     // array size for word
        char word [MAXSTR];     // your word
        int  number;            // a number to read in
```

```
        // get an entire line with gets; on end of file quit
        printf("Enter a line with 1 word & 1 number, EOF to quit: ");
        if (! fgets(line, MAXLINE, stdin)) break;

        // repeat line with fputs
        printf("You entered:  ");
        fputs(line, stdout);
                        //You *can* use fputs w/ stdout; puts is more usual

        // Use char array as source for 2 arguments
        if (sscanf(line, "%s %i", word, &number) != 2)
            puts("That wasn't a word and a number!\n");
        else
        {
            // Print using sprintf and puts
            sprintf(line, "The name was %s and the number was %i.\n",
                    word, number);
            puts  (line);
            // If this weren't a demo of new functions, I'd say
            //    printf("The name was %s and the number was %f.\n",
            //          name, number);
        }
    }

    puts("\n\nBye!\n");

    return 0;
}
```

Here's sample output:

```
Enter a line with 1 word and 1 numbers, end of file to quit: Mila 18
You entered:  Mila 18
The name was Mila and the number was 18.

Enter a line with 1 word and 1 numbers, end of file to quit: Catch 22
You entered:  Catch 22
```

```
The name was Catch and the number was 22.

Enter a line with 1 word and 1 numbers, end of file (Ctrl-D or Ctrl-Z)
to quit:

Bye!
```

Summary of Commands

In Table 29-2, if I don't give the meaning of what's returned by a function, it's because with that one we rarely care. With `fopen`, `fgets`, and the `scanf` family, we do.

Table 29-2. *Common* `stdio` *functions in C*

printf and Variants	
`int printf(const char* formatString, ...);`	Print to screen arguments after `formatString`, as specified by `formatString`.
`int fprintf(FILE* file, const char* formatString, ...);`	Same as `printf` but prints to `file`.
`int sprintf(const char* str, const char* formatString, ...);`	Same as `printf` but prints to `str`.
scanf and Variants	
`int scanf(const char* formatString, ...);`	Read arguments after `formatString` as specified by `formatString`. Returns `EOF` (`end of file`) if it reaches `EOF` before reading any; else, # of arguments successfully read.
`int fscanf(FILE* file, const char* formatString, ...);`	Same as `scanf` but reads from `file`.
`int sscanf(const char* str, const char* formatString, ...);`	Same as `scanf` but reads from `str`.

(continued)

Table 29-2. (*continued*)

Opening/Closing Files	
`FILE* fopen(const char* filename, const char* fileMode);`	Open, and return pointer to, the file specified by `filename`. Common `fileModes` include `"r"` (read), `"w"` (write), and `"a"` (append).
`int fclose (FILE* file);`	Close the file.
Reading/Writing Strings	
`int puts (const char* str);` `int fputs (const char* str, FILE* file);`	Print `str`/print `str` to `file`.
`char* fgets(char* str, int max, FILE* file);`	Read `str` from `file` (which may be `stdin`), reading at most `max-1` characters (so `str`'s size should be `max` or greater). Returns `NULL` on failure.

Antibugging

- **`scanf` fails for lack of &:**

  ```
  scanf("%f %s",  myDouble, myCharArray);
  ```

  should have been

  ```
  scanf("%f %s", &myDouble, myCharArray);
  ```

  It's easy to forget the &'s, and the compiler may not warn you.

Parameter Passing with *

C doesn't have & parameters, but like C++, it considers other parameters to be unchanged by a function call. Uh-oh.

```
void swap(int arg1, int arg2)
{
    int temp = arg1; arg1 = arg2; arg2 = temp;
}

int main()
{
    int x, y;
    ...
    swap(x, y);  // x, y will not be changed
    ...
}
```

C expects you to send in the *address* of the argument:

```
int main()
{
    int x, y;
    ...
    swap(&x, &y); // x's and y's addresses are sent, not x and y
    ...
}
```

The function takes that address and uses * to refer to the thing it points to, which *can* be altered:

```
void swap(int* arg1, int* arg2)
{
    int temp = *arg1; *arg1 = *arg2; *arg2 = temp;
}
```

It works! But it's clunky and introduces a maddeningly common error: forgetting the *'s.

Example 29-5 shows a program that uses it (and doesn't forget the *'s).

Example 29-5. Program using parameter passing with *'s in C

```
// Program to do statistics on some strings
//        from _C++26 for Lazy Programmers_

#include <stdio.h>  // for printf, scanf
#include <string.h> // for strlen

void updateLineStats(char line[], unsigned int* length,
                     float* averageLineLength);

int main()
{
    printf("Type in a line and I'll reply. ");
    printf("Type the end-of-file character to end.\n");

    while (1)   // forever (or until a break) ...
    {
        enum { MAXSTRING = 256 };       // max line length
        char line [MAXSTRING];          // the line
        int  length;                    // its current length
        float averageLineLength;

        // get line of input
        if (!fgets(line, MAXSTRING, stdin)) break;

        // do the stats. We send addresses, not variables, using &
        updateLineStats(line, &length, &averageLineLength);

        // give the result
        printf("Length of that line, ");
        printf("and average so far: %d, %.2f.\n",
                length, averageLineLength);
    }

    return 0;
}
```

```
void updateLineStats(char line[], unsigned int* length,
                     float* averageLineLength)
{
    static int totalLinesLength = 0;    // have to remember these
    static int linesSoFar = 0;          //   for next time

    // length is a pointer, so *length is the length
    *length = (unsigned int) strlen(line);
                      // casting from size_t to unsigned int
    // fgets included the final \n, but I won't count that:
    --(*length);

    ++linesSoFar;
    totalLinesLength += *length;

    *averageLineLength = // and averageLineLength needs its *, too
        totalLinesLength / ((float) linesSoFar);
}
```

Here's a sample session:

```
Type in a line and I'll reply. Type the end-of-file character to end.
alpha
Length of that line, and average so far: 5, 5.00.
bet
Length of that line, and average so far: 3, 4.00.
soup
Length of that line, and average so far: 4, 4.00.
```

Antibugging

- **"<variable> differs in level of indirection" or "cannot convert from <type> to <type>*" or "makes pointer from integer without cast."** There are various ways to complain, but the bottom line is it's hard to remember to put the &'s in the function call and even harder to remember the *'s *every! time!* you use the variable passed in. I never found a fix. At least you know that's a likely culprit for what goes wrong.

Dynamic Memory

Forget new, new[], delete, and delete[], and *definitely* forget unique_ptr and shared_ptr – C's dynamic memory is simpler, if uglier:

```
#include <stdlib.h>                    // for malloc, free

...

someType* myArray = malloc(myArraySize * sizeof(someType));
              // allocate a myArraySize element array of some type

...use the array...

free(myArray);                         // throw it back
```

There are no destructors to help you remember to free things – you're on your own.

Example 14-3, an earlier program using a dynamic array, is adapted to C here in Example 29-6.

Example 29-6. A C program using dynamic memory

```
// Program to generate a random passcode of digits
//        -- from _C++26 for Lazy Programmers_

#include <stdio.h>
#include <stdlib.h> // for srand, rand, malloc, free
#include <time.h>   // for time

int main()
{
    srand((unsigned int) time(NULL));// start random # generator
                                     // NULL, not nullptr

    int codeLength;                  // get code length
    printf("I'll make your secret passcode. How long should it be? ");
    scanf("%d", &codeLength);

                                      // allocate array
    int* passcode = malloc(codeLength * sizeof(int));
```

```
    for (int i = 0; i < codeLength; ++i)// generate passcode
        passcode[i] = rand() % 10;     // each entry is a digit

    printf("Here it is:\n");           // print passcode
    for (int i = 0; i < codeLength; ++i)
        printf("%d", passcode[i]);
    printf("\n");
    printf("But I guess it's not secret any more!\n");

    free(passcode);                    // deallocate array

    return 0;
}
```

EXERCISES

Do the exercises from Chapters 13 and 14, excluding those that use SSDL, in C.

CHAPTER 30

Moving on with SDL

By using SSDL you've gone most of the way toward becoming an SDL programmer. To keep going, you can

- Dump SSDL and get a tutorial on SDL. You'll see a lot that you recognize. Many SSDL functions are SDL functions with an "S" stuck on the front (as in, `SDL_PollEvent` became `SSDL_PollEvent`). Usually SDL functions need one more initial argument, often of type `SDL_Window*` or `SDL_Renderer*`, two types you'll learn right away. You can usually guess what'll be needed (hint: functions with "Render" in the name probably need `SDL_Renderer*`). Or ...
- Keep SSDL, but extend with more SDL features – say, joystick support.

Either way it'll be useful to look behind SSDL to what it's been hiding from you. Let's start with initialization and cleanup code.

The typical SDL program has a version of `main` that looks like Example 30-1.

Example 30-1. A simple SDL program

```
// An SDL program that does nothing of interest (yet)
//      -- from _C++26 for Lazy Programmers_

#include <iostream>
#include "SDL.h"
#include "SDL_image.h"
#include "SDL_mixer.h"
#include "SDL_ttf.h"
```


W. Briggs, *C++26 for Lazy Programmers*, https://doi.org/10.1007/979-8-8688-1859-2_30

```
int main(int argc, char** argv)
{
    // initialization

    constexpr int DEFAULT_WIDTH = 640, DEFAULT_HEIGHT = 480;
    if (SDL_Init(SDL_INIT_EVERYTHING) < 0) return -1;

    SDL_Window* sdlWindow
        = SDL_CreateWindow("My SDL program!",
                           SDL_WINDOWPOS_UNDEFINED,
                           SDL_WINDOWPOS_UNDEFINED,
                           DEFAULT_WIDTH, DEFAULT_HEIGHT,
                           0);      // flags are 0 by default
    if (!sdlWindow) return -1;      // nope, it failed

    int rendererIndex = -1;         //pick first renderer that works
    SDL_Renderer* sdlRenderer
        = SDL_CreateRenderer(sdlWindow, rendererIndex,
                             0);    // flags are 0 by default

    if (!sdlRenderer) return -1;    // nope, it failed

    SDL_ClearError();               // Initially, no errors

    static constexpr int IMG_FLAGS  // all available types
        = IMG_INIT_PNG | IMG_INIT_JPG | IMG_INIT_TIF;
    if (! (IMG_Init(IMG_FLAGS) & IMG_FLAGS))  // start SDL_Image
        return -1;

    if (TTF_Init() == -1) return -1;          // ...and SDL_TTF

                                              // ...and SDL_Mixer
    int soundsSupported = Mix_Init
                 (MIX_INIT_FLAC|MIX_INIT_MOD|MIX_INIT_MP3|MIX_INIT_OGG);
    if (!soundsSupported) return -1;

    int soundInitialized = (Mix_OpenAudio(88020, MIX_DEFAULT_FORMAT,
                                          MIX_DEFAULT_CHANNELS,
                                          4096) != -1);
```

```
    if (!soundInitialized) SDL_ClearError();
            // if it failed, we can still do the program
            //   -- just forget the error

    // STUFF YOU ACTUALLY WANT TO DO GOES HERE

    // cleanup: we're about to end the program, but it's considered
    nice anyway

    if (soundInitialized) { Mix_AllocateChannels(0); Mix_CloseAudio(); }
    Mix_Quit();
    TTF_Quit();
    IMG_Quit();
    SDL_DestroyRenderer(sdlRenderer);
    SDL_DestroyWindow  (sdlWindow);
    SDL_Quit();

    return 0;
}
```

In SSDL, the initialization code in Example 30-1 is done by the constructors for `SSDL_Display` and `SSDL_SoundSystem`. Example 30-1 has simplifications. One biggie is: we can't throw an `SSDL_Exception` without SSDL (duh), so instead we deal with failure to launch with `return -1;`.

See what it does: initializes SDL (this must be done first); creates the window (good!); creates a "renderer," needed to draw or paste images; and initializes SDL_Image and SDL_TTF, needed for image and fonts. If anything goes wrong, we give up, because you can't really go on without these things.

It also supports sound by initializing SDL_Mixer if it can.

The cleanup code shuts down the helper libraries, kills the window and renderer, and finally shuts down SDL.

I obviously prefer my way, for organization, neatness, and not having to type all that code in every new program; but since we're looking at the messy guts of it all, I guess we'll leave it in `main` as game programmers often do. At least I'm not using global variables.

Writing Code

So can we get a program that will actually do something? Sure, but first let me talk about what else SSDL has been covering up.

- Many SSDL types represent SDL types, usually pointers.
- SSDL_Color is essentially an SDL_Color.
- SSDL_Display is essentially an SDL_Renderer* and an SDL_Window*. (If you care how these get passed into SDL functions that want them, see the SSDL_Display class definition, specifically two user-defined conversions or cast operators.)
- SSDL_Font is a TTF_Font*.
- SSDL_Image is an SDL_Texture*.
- SSDL_Music is a Mix_Music*.
- SSDL_Sound is a Mix_Chunk* and an int (for channel).
- SSDL_Sprite is an SDL_Texture* plus a lot of fields, to be sent to SDL_RenderCopyEx in a complicated call (see SSDL_RenderSprite).

  These classes exist mostly to protect beginners from pointers and everyone from having to do their own dynamic allocation and cleanup.
- Besides RGB, SDL_Color and SSDL_Color have an "alpha" member that also ranges from 0 to 255. 0 means completely transparent and 255 means completely opaque. To use it you'll need SDL functions with "blend" in the name.
- Forget ssin and sout; you'll use TTF_Render* (maybe TTF_RenderUTF8_Blended like I have or the more basic TTF_RenderTextSolid) - see SSDL_Display::RenderTextLine.
- SDL is always using dynamic memory, but you can't use new and delete: SDL and its helpers provide their own allocation and deallocation functions, for example, SDL_CreateTexture and SDL_DestroyTexture and TTF_OpenFont and TTF_CloseFont. You have to use them.

OK, so let's do something, cheating by seeing how SSDL did it. I'll put an image on the screen and wait for someone to hit a key. Hoo-ah!

I'll use code from `SSDL_LoadImage` and `SSDL_RenderImage` for the image (searching for these in the SSDL code – they've got to be there somewhere). If you're following along by searching yourself – please do! – you'll see I leave out calls to `SSDL_Display::Instance` (that's just there to ensure the initialization code gets called first, and we did that already). We won't stretch the image, so I'll omit references to `stretchWidth` and `stretchHeight` and use the image's actual size. I rename variables as needed. With a little more cleanup, I get the code in Example 30-2, which goes immediately after the initialization code in Example 30-1.

Example 30-2. Displaying an image in SDL

```
// Draw an image

SDL_Surface* sdlSurface = IMG_Load("media/pupdog.png");
if (!sdlSurface) return -1;

SDL_Texture* image      = SDL_CreateTextureFromSurface
                                  (sdlRenderer, sdlSurface);
if (!image) return -1;
SDL_FreeSurface(sdlSurface);

SDL_Rect dst;                  // dst is where it's going on screen
dst.x = 0; dst.y = 0;

SDL_QueryTexture(image, nullptr, nullptr, &dst.w, &dst.h);
                               // get width and height of image
SDL_RenderCopy(sdlRenderer, image, nullptr, &dst);
```

Waiting for a key ...I read `SSDL_WaitKey`, then the thing that it calls, and then the things *it* calls and eventually can construct the monstrosity in Example 30-3. It goes right after the image-display code in Example 30-2.

Example 30-3. Waiting for a keystroke in SDL

```
// Waiting for a response

SDL_Event sdlEvent;

SDL_RenderPresent(sdlRenderer);       // display everything

bool isTimeToQuit = false;
while (!isTimeToQuit)
{
    if (SDL_WaitEvent(&sdlEvent) == 0) return -1;

                                          // handle quit messages
    if (sdlEvent.type == SDL_QUIT) isTimeToQuit = true;
    if (sdlEvent.type == SDL_KEYDOWN
        && sdlEvent.key.keysym.scancode == SDL_SCANCODE_ESCAPE)
      isTimeToQuit = true;

    if (sdlEvent.type == SDL_KEYDOWN)// Got that key? quit
            isTimeToQuit = true;
}
```

Figure 30-1. *The SDL program from Examples 30-1, 30-2, and 30-3. Was it worth it?*

Well, what do you know, it works. And it only took me 100 lines!

Admittedly, I wrote some awful code there: everything's in `main`. But I already did my good coding (I hope) in building the SSDL library. If I were going to write *good* code, I'd have just said

```
int main(int argc, char** argv)
{
    const SSDL_Image PUPPY = SSDL_LoadImage("media/pupdog.png");
    SSDL_RenderImage(PUPPY, 0, 0);
    SSDL_WaitKey();

    return 0;
}
```

Game programs are notorious for bad practices: long functions like this one, global variables, pointers out the wazoo. As you start programming SDL, you can show everyone how to do it right.

Antibugging

Sometimes I get a crash at program's end: SDL or a helper library fails on part of its cleanup. I'm probably not supposed to, but I admit I comment out cleanup code. It won't matter after the program ends anyway.

Compiling

With g++, take an SSDL-capable `Makefile` and remove all references to SSDL.

In Microsoft Visual Studio, take an SSDL-capable project (`.vcxproj`, plus `.vcxproj.filters`, and `.vcxproj.user`), load it, and remove all references to SSDL – that is, under Project ➤ Properties, Configuration Properties:

- **C/C++ ➤ General ➤ Additional Include Directories**: Take out the path to SSDL includes.
- **Linker ➤ General ➤ Additional Library Directories**: Take out the path to SSDL libraries.
- **Linker ➤ Input ➤ Additional Dependencies**: Take out ssdl<whatever it is>.lib.

Then compile, and run, as you would an SSDL project.

Further Resources

I think the best reference is libsdl.org. Documentation on `SDL_Image` and others is there; you just have to find it (I do a web search for what I want and it'll take me there). And it's hard to beat Lazy Foo' (lazyfoo.net) for tutorials.

APPENDIX A

Help with Setup

Setup instructions for using SDL and SSDL are in Chapter 1. If something there doesn't work or if you're a Unix system administrator looking for hints on installing needed packages, read on. There's also a section here on sound issues and one on making your own Makefiles and Visual Studio projects.

...for Microsoft Visual Studio Users

If you've installed the parts specified in Chapter 1, Visual Studio should work. This section can help if it doesn't.

Antibugging

- **You can look at files, but it doesn't offer an option to compile.** Maybe you didn't install the C++ part of Visual Studio (see Chapter 1). Or maybe you opened something other than a solution file, which is what tells C++ what projects to compile. You can identify a solution file by its `.sln` extension (if extensions are visible) or wave your mouse pointer over the file so Windows will tell you what it is. It should be a Visual Studio solution.
- **You can't compile because of missing includes or library files.** See Chapter 1: source code examples should not be moved, and your project folders should stay in the source code's `newWork` folder.
- **You get a runtime error message about a dll file.** Maybe you erased the `.user` file, which tells Visual Studio where to look. If so, recopy it.

W. Briggs, *C++26 for Lazy Programmers*, https://doi.org/10.1007/979-8-8688-1859-2

...for MSys2 Users

As long as you've installed the parts specified in Chapter 1, MSys2 should work. This section can help if it doesn't.

Antibugging

- **You can't compile because of missing includes or library files.** See Chapter 1: source code examples should not be moved, and your project folders should stay in the source code's `newWork` folder.
- **It can't find SSDL2's library or doesn't like it.** Go to `<repository>/external/SSDL/MSys2` and type `make`.

...for Unix Users

Distributions differ, and there is no one answer guaranteed to work on all Unix boxes. But I'll share what worked for me on a few of the most popular distributions.

First, be sure you're running the latest version of your distribution - an outdated operating system causes problems. As a Unix pro, you knew that. If you're not a Unix pro, consider consulting one. Unix isn't for the fainthearted.

Debian/Ubuntu

```
sudo apt-get update && sudo apt-get upgrade && sudo apt-get autoremove
sudo apt-get install build-essential #installs g++, make, and more
sudo apt-get install ddd
sudo apt install xfonts-base xfonts-75dpi #fonts for ddd
sudo apt-get install emacs           #(if you want the emacs editor)
sudo apt-get install libsdl2-dev
sudo apt-get install libsdl2-image-dev libsdl2-mixer-dev libsdl2-ttf-dev
```

Ubuntu, at time of writing, wants you to do the next two lines to get the latest g++, which introduces C++26:

```
sudo apt-get install g++-14       #make sure we have latest version of g++
sudo update-alternatives --install /usr/bin/g++ g++ /usr/bin/g++-14 100
                                         # ...and use it
```

Debian doesn't support the latest g++ yet.

Red Hat/Fedora

```
sudo dnf update
sudo dnf group install development-tools
sudo dnf install gcc-g++
sudo dnf install ddd
sudo dnf install emacs                #(if you want the emacs editor)
sudo dnf install SDL2-devel
sudo dnf install SDL2_image-devel SDL2_mixer-devel SDL2_ttf-devel
```

openSUSE

openSUSE doesn't have SDL2 as standard in its repositories. I recommend you don't use this distribution unless you really know what you are doing.

Manjaro

```
sudo pacman -Syu
sudo pacman -S base-devel
sudo pacman -S emacs                  #(if you want the emacs editor)
sudo pacman -S sdl2 sdl2_image sdl2_mixer sdl2_ttf
```

SSDL

To build SSDL for each of these distributions, go into `external/SSDL/unix` and type `make`.

Antibugging

- **You get a message that says the system can't find an include file or library.**

  Maybe it's not there. See above for notes on installation. **Or maybe it's looking in the wrong place.** See Chapter 1: source code examples should not be moved, and your project folders should stay in the source code's `newWork` folder, so they can find SSDL. The `Makefiles` in the source code use the `sdl2_config` command, which knows path information for SDL2; if `sdl2-config --cflags --libs` can't find things you need, you may want to reinstall.

- **`./runx` won't run; the message is some variation of "Permission denied."** Maybe its permissions were set so it's no longer executable. If so, `chmod +x runx`.

Sound

First, the obvious. Is sound working for other programs? Pull up YouTube and play something. Is there a problem with source code programs using sound or just with a new project you're developing? If it's just the new thing, the problem may be with the sound file or the new program.

If sound isn't working at all for SDL2/SSDL programs, see one of the earlier sections in this appendix. But if quality is the problem, read on.

It may help to change the numbers used to initialize SDL_Mixer's `Mix_OpenAudio`. SSDL has two ways:

- Put this line in your file that has `main` in it, after the `#includes` but before anything else

  ```
  SSDL_SoundSystemInitializer
      initializer(88020, MIX_DEFAULT_FORMAT,
      MIX_DEFAULT_CHANNELS, 4096);
  ```

  and start fiddling with the numbers (see below). This method may change if SSDL goes into a new version.

- Edit those same numbers in SSDL itself and rebuild. You can find them as defaults in the `Instance` member function of `SSDL_SoundSystem`.

The first argument, `frequency`, usually seems to be a multiple of 22,005 Hz. Too small and it may cause static; too large and it may skip.

There's a list of possible values for the second argument, `format`, in the SDL_Mixer documentation online, currently at `wiki.libsdl.org`; play with them to see which sounds best. Look for documentation on SDL2, not SDL3. (SDL3 isn't in the default repositories for most Unix distributions at present, so I'm not using it.)

The third argument, `channels`, should be 1 (mono) or 2 (stereo).

The fourth is `chunksize`. I see multiples of 1,024 used.

Any sufficiently wrong number may cause the music not to play.

I found no benefit in changing the last two arguments, but could improve sound by stumbling onto the right format and having a high enough frequency.

Making Your Own Projects

...in g++

If you want to create your own projects, look into the `Makefile` of any SSDL project in the sample code and do something similar.

Unix SSDL programs need to know where to find the SDL libraries. Examine `runx` to see how to set the relevant path environment variable. MSys puts the SDL libraries in its global PATH – you won't need to do anything special for it.

...in Microsoft Visual Studio

There's a lot to be done to make your own Visual Studio project file work with SDL and SSDL ...and here it is. Create a Console Project, and under Project ➤ Properties, Configuration Properties

- Be sure you're editing either All Configurations (top left) or at least the one you want, probably Debug, and the All Platforms or your chosen platform (top middle).
- Under Configuration Properties ➤ General, set C++ Language Standard to **Preview - Features from the Latest C++ Working Draft (/std:c++latest).**
- C/C++ ➤ General: set Additional Include Directories to find SDL's and SSDL's includes. I did it like this: **..\..\external\SDL2\include;..\..\external\SSDL\include.**
- Linker ➤ Input ➤ Additional Dependencies should include needed libraries. Mine looks like this: **SSDL.lib;sdl2.lib;SDL2main.lib;SDL2_image.lib;SDL2_ttf.lib;SDL2_mixer.lib;$(CoreLibraryDependencies);%(AdditionalDependencies).**
- Linker ➤ System ➤ Subsystem should be **Windows**. If you leave it as **Console**, it'll give you a window for standard output - fine, if that's what you want.
- Under Debugging ➤ Environment, set the PATH to include wherever SDL's `dll`'s are stored. In the repository, that's **PATH=..\..\external\SDL2\lib\x86;%PATH%** for the x86/Win32 platform and **PATH=..\..\external\SDL2\lib\x64;%PATH%** for x64. If they're already installed somewhere in the PATH, you can omit this step. This is stored in `<your project>.vcxproj.user`, so erasing that file will erase this information.
- Linker ➤ General: set Additional Library Directories to find the libraries. I did it like **..\..\external\SDL2\lib\x86;..\..\external\SSDL\libvs\$(Platform)\$(Configuration)** for the 32-bit platform and like **..\..\external\SDL2\lib\x64;..\..\external\SSDL\libvs\$(Platform)\$(Configuration)** for 64.
- C/C++ ➤ Code Generation ➤ Runtime Library should show **/MDd** (for Debug) or **/MD** (for Release). This could change; see the `newWork` folder.
- Add whatever source files you want to the project - `main.cpp` sounds good - and go. `main` must start with this line - `int main(int argc, char** argv)` - and return an `int`.

APPENDIX B

Operators

Associativity

Unary operators (as in -a) are evaluated right side first (perhaps because there is no left side).

Assignment operators (as in A=B) are evaluated right side first and then left.

All other operators are evaluated left to right.

Precedence

Here are the groupings of C++ operators from highest precedence (evaluated first) to lowest.

::
. -> [] () ++ (post-increment) -- (post-decrement) C++-style cast (<type>())
++ (pre-increment) -- (pre-decrement) Unary operators: ~ ! & * - + new, new[] delete, delete [] sizeof co_await
.* ->*
* / %
+ -

(*continued*)

W. Briggs, *C++26 for Lazy Programmers*, https://doi.org/10.1007/979-8-8688-1859-2

`>> <<`

`<=>`

`< <= => >`

`== !=`

`&`

`^`

`|`

`&&`

`||`

`?:`
Assignment operators: `= += -= *= /= %= ^= &= |= <<= >>=`
`co_yield`
`throw`

`,` (comma)

Overloading

These are the operators available for overloading in C++:

- **Arithmetic**: `+ - * / % ++ --`
- **Assignment**: `= += -= *= /= %= ^= &= |= <<= >>=`
- **Logical and bitwise**: `& | ! && || ~ ^`
- `<< >>`
- **Comparison**: `<=> > >= < <= == !=`
- `[] ()`
- `-> ->* new new[] delete delete[]`
- `co_await`
- `,` (comma)

APPENDIX C

Fundamental Types

Type	Example Literal Values
bool	true, false
char, unsigned char, signed char	'A', '\0', '0', '\n', '\u41'
char8_t	u8'A' and others; u8'\u41'
char16_t	u'A', u'\u3053'
char32_t	U'A', U'\u3053', U'\U000096e8'
wchar_t	L'A', L'\xff00', L'0', L'\n'
float	2.71828F, 6.023E23F
double	2.71828, 6.023E23
long double	2.71828L, 6.023E23L
int, signed int, short int, signed short int	-42, 42
unsigned int, unsigned short int	42U
long int, signed long int	-42L, 42L
unsigned long int	42UL
long long int, signed long long int	-42LL, 42LL
unsigned long long int	42ULL
std::nullptr_t[1]	nullptr
void	No values

[1] Defined in #include <cstddef>.

W. Briggs, *C++26 for Lazy Programmers*, https://doi.org/10.1007/979-8-8688-1859-2

There are also fixed-width integer types like `int8_t` (signed 8-bit integer) and `uint32_t` (unsigned 32-bit), too many to list here. See cppreference.com for a full list.

APPENDIX D

Common Escape Sequences

Symbol	Meaning
\"	Quote (").
\'	Single quote (').
\\	Backslash (\).
\<up to 3 digits>	The digits form an octal (base 8) number; the escape sequence is the corresponding character. For example, "\101" is "A," ASCII 65. \0 is the commonly used "null" character (see Chapter 14).
\a	Alert (often a beep).
\n	New line.
\N{<name>}	Character corresponding to the given name, listed at www.unicode.org/Public/UCD/latest/ucd/NameAliases.txt.
\o{<digits>}, \x{<digits>}, \u{<digits>}	Character corresponding to the specified octal, hexadecimal, Unicode (also hexadecimal) digits.
\r	Carriage return (rarely used).
\t	Tab.
\u<4 digits>, \U<8 digits>	The Unicode character or characters corresponding to the hexadecimal digits used; not used in this book.
\x<digits>	The 1 or more digits form a hexadecimal number, and the value is the corresponding character. For example, "\x5A" is "Z," ASCII 90.

W. Briggs, *C++26 for Lazy Programmers*, https://doi.org/10.1007/979-8-8688-1859-2

APPENDIX E

Basic C Standard Library

Below are commonly used functions from standard libraries incorporated from C. For a complete listing, go online, possibly to `www.cplusplus.com`.

cmath

Trigonometric Functions	
`double sin (double angle);`	Sine
`double cos (double angle);`	Cosine
`double tan (double angle);`	Tangent
`double asin(double angle);`	Arcsine
`double acos(double angle);`	Arccosine
`double atan(double angle);`	Arctangent
`double atan(double x, double y);`	Arctangent (x/y)

Exponential Functions	
`double exp   (double num);`	e to the `num` power
`double log   (double num);`	Base e log of `num`
`double log10(double num);`	Base 10 log of `num`
`double pow   (double b, double p);`	b to the p power (bp)

W. Briggs, *C++26 for Lazy Programmers*, https://doi.org/10.1007/979-8-8688-1859-2

Other Functions	
`constexpr double abs(double num);`	Absolute value
`constexpr int abs(int num);`	Absolute value
`double sqrt(double num);`	Square root

cctype

Classifying Functions	
`int isdigit(int ch);`	Return whether ch is a digit ('0'...'9').
`int isalpha(int ch);`	Return whether ch is a letter ('A'...'Z' or 'a'...'z').
`int isalnum(int ch);`	Return whether ch is either of the above.
`int islower(int ch);`	Return whether ch is lowercase (false for non-letter characters).
`int isupper(int ch);`	Return whether ch is uppercase (false for non-letter characters).
`int isspace(int ch);`	Return whether ch is whitespace (' ', '\f', '\n', '\r', '\h', or '\v').
`int ispunct(int ch);`	Return whether ch is punctuation: not space, letter, or digit.

Conversion Functions	
`int tolower(int ch);`	Return the lowercase version of ch. If ch is not a letter, returns ch.
`int toupper(int ch);`	Return the uppercase version of ch. If ch is not a letter, returns ch.

cstdlib

`void srand (unsigned int seed);`	Starts pseudo-random number generation, starting the pseudo-random sequence with seed.
`int rand();`	Return the next pseudo-random number in a range 0...RAND_MAX.
RAND_MAX	Maximum number returned by `rand`.

APPENDIX F

Common Debugger Commands

Microsoft Visual Studio

- To set a breakpoint, or "stop sign," click just past the left margin on the line you want. To erase it, click the red circle that created.
- To start debugging, Start Debugging (F5) or otherwise run the program. Function keys require holding down "Function" or "Fn" on some keyboards.
- To stop debugging, stop the program.
- To go down one line, Step Over (F10).
- To go into a function, Step Into (F11).
- To step out of a function, Step Out (Shift-F11).
- To go to a particular line, right-click and choose Run To Cursor (Ctrl-F10).
- To see the value of a variable, look to the lower left, and select Autos tab, Locals tab, or select Watch 1 and type it in.
- You can do calculations of a formula by typing in the formula into Watch1.

W. Briggs, *C++26 for Lazy Programmers*, https://doi.org/10.1007/979-8-8688-1859-2

gdb/ddd

`break`	Set breakpoint on current line.
`break <line number>`	Set breakpoint on line in current file.
`break <function-name>`	Set breakpoint for function. For example, `break myFunc` or `break myFunc (int, int, int)`.
`clear <function-name>`	Clear breakpoint on function.
`continue`	Keep running to the next break (if any).
`delete/delete <number>`	Delete all breakpoints/delete breakpoint #<number>.
`down`	Go down the call stack (toward current line).
`finish`	Finish the current function.
`help`	Help. It really does help!
`info locals`	
`print <expression>`	
`quit`	
`run [<arg1> <arg2>...]`	Run the program in the debugger [with these arguments].
`set <variable>`	Change the value of a variable.
`set args <argument>*`	Set command-line arguments (`argv`).
`step`	Go to the next line in execution.
`up`	Go up the call stack (toward `main`).
`watch <variable>`	Set the debugger to break if the value of variable changes.
`where`	Show the current call stack.

Many of these commands can be abbreviated; for example, `c` means `continue`.

Commands can often be repeated simply by hitting return (`next` and `step` have this property).

To quit, type `quit`.

APPENDIX G

SSDL Reference

In the listings below, if you don't understand the explanation for an entry (say, if you don't know what "Mix_Music" means), that may be something you won't need unless moving from SSDL to SDL. Some descriptions are simplified for clarity.

Updating the Screen

`void SSDL_RenderPresent();`	Render whatever is presently drawn; that is, update the screen. Automatically called by `SSDL_Delay`, `SSDL_IsNextFrame`, `SSDL_WaitEvent`, `SSDL_WaitMouse`, and `SSDL_WaitKey`.

Added Types

`struct SSDL_Color { int r, g, b, a; };`	Same as `SDL_Color`, but with constructors. Fields mean red, green, blue, and alpha (opacity) and range 0–255.
`class SSDL_Exception;`	An exception thrown by SSDL functions.
`class SSDL_Font;`	A wrapper for `TTF_Font*`.
`class SSDL_Image;`	A wrapper for `SDL_Texture*`, as used by the `SDL_Image` library.
`class SSDL_Music;`	A wrapper for `Mix_Music*`.
`class SSDL_Sound;`	A wrapper for `Mix_Chunk*` and associated channels.
`class SSDL_Sprite;`	An `SSDL_Image` with added capabilities.

W. Briggs, *C++26 for Lazy Programmers*, https://doi.org/10.1007/979-8-8688-1859-2

Clearing the Screen

`void SSDL_RenderClear ();`	Clear the screen to current erasing color.
`void SSDL_RenderClear (const SSDL_Color& c);`	Clear screen to color `c`.

Colors

`const SSDL_Colors` include `BLACK`, `WHITE`, `RED`, `GREEN`, `BLUE`.

`SSDL_Color SSDL_CreateColor (int red, int green, int blue, int a=255);`	Create and return a color. Max value for each parameter is 255. `alpha` (transparency) defaults to 255 (completely opaque).
`void SSDL_SetRenderDrawColor (const SSDL_Color& c);`	Set drawing, including text, to use color `c`.
`void SSDL_SetRenderEraseColor (const SSDL_Color& c);`	Set erasing (backspacing, clearing of the screen) to use color `c`.
`SSDL_Color SSDL_GetRenderDrawColor();`	Return current drawing color.
`SSDL_Color SSDL_GetRenderEraseColor();`	Return current erasing color.

Drawing

`void SSDL_RenderDrawPoint (int x, int y);`	Draw a point.
`void SSDL_RenderDrawPoints (const SDL_Point* points, int count);`	Draw points.
`void SSDL_RenderDrawLine (int x1, int y1, int x2, int y2);`	Draw a line.
`void SSDL_RenderDrawLines (const SDL_Point* points, int count);`	Draw lines between `points`.

(*continued*)

`void SSDL_RenderDrawRect (int x, int y, int w, int h);`	Draw a `w` by `h` rectangle with its upper left at `(x, y)`.
`void SSDL_RenderDrawRect (const SDL_Rect& rect);`	Draw a rectangle.
`void SSDL_RenderDrawRects (const SDL_Rect* rects, int count);`	Draw `count` rectangles.
`void SSDL_RenderFillRect (int x, int y, int w, int h);`	Draw a filled rectangle.
`void SSDL_RenderFillRect (const SDL_Rect& rect);`	Draw a filled rectangle.
`void SSDL_RenderFillRects (const SDL_Rect* rects, int count);`	Draw `count` filled rectangles.
`void SSDL_RenderDrawCircle (int x, int y, int radius);`	Draw a circle.
`void SSDL_RenderFillCircle (int x, int y, int radius);`	Draw a filled circle.

Images

`SSDL_Image SSDL_LoadImage (const char* filename);`	Return an `SSDL_Image` loaded from `filename`.
`void SSDL_RenderImage (SDL_Image image, int x, int y, int stretchWidth=0, int stretchHeight=0);`	Display `image` positioned with its top-left corner at `x, y`. If `stretchWidth` and `stretchHeight` are specified, it makes the image fill a rectangle with that specified width and height.

(continued)

`void SSDL_RenderImageEx (SDL_Image image, const SDL_Rect& src, const SDL_Rect& dst, double angleInDegrees = 0.0, SDL_RendererFlip flipValue = SDL_FLIP_NONE);`	Display the portion of `image` bounded by `src` rectangle in the image, stretched or shrunk as needed to fill `dst` rectangle on the screen. Image will be rotated by `angleInDegrees` and flipped either not at all (`SDL_FLIP_NONE`), horizontally (`SDL_FLIP_HORIZONTAL`), vertically (`SDL_FLIP_VERTICAL`), or both (`SDL_FLIP_HORIZONTAL | SDL_FLIP_VERTICAL`). Called by `SSDL_RenderSprite`.
`int SSDL_GetImageWidth (SDL_Image image);`	Return `image`'s width.
`int SSDL_GetImageHeight (SDL_Image image);`	Return `image`'s height.

Mouse, Keyboard, and Events

`int SSDL_GetMouseX ();`	Provide current X of mouse.
`int SSDL_GetMouseY ();`	Provide current Y of mouse.
`int SSDL_GetMouseClick ();`	Return whether mouse is clicked and, if so, which button: `SDL_BUTTON_LEFT`, `SDL_BUTTON_MIDDLE`, `SDL_BUTTON_RIGHT`, and some others (see SDL documentation online).
`bool SSDL_IsKeyPressed (SDL_Keycode whichKey);`	Return whether a given key is currently pressed. Keys are `SDL_Keycode`s, not `char`s; see Chapter 12 or SDL documentation online.
`int SSDL_PollEvent (SDL_Event& event);`	Return true if there is an event in the event queue, and put its information into `event`. Called again, it goes on to next event.

(continued)

`void SSDL_WaitEvent (Uint32`[2] `eventType, SDL_Event& event);`	Refresh the screen and wait for an event of the given `eventType` (or a quit event).
`int SSDL_WaitMouse ();`	Refresh the screen and wait for mouse click; returns which button was clicked.
`SDL_Keycode SSDL_WaitKey ();`	Refresh the screen and wait for a key hit. Return value is the key hit but is usually ignored.
`void SSDL_DefaultEventHandler ();`	Read all events on queue, and process the quit events.

Music

In the following table, each function parameter or return type shown as `SSDL_Music` may actually be of type `Mix_Music*` – but you can ignore that and pass in `SSDL_Music`. See SDL_Mixer documentation online for more information.

If a function doesn't have music as an argument, it works on what's currently playing.

`void SSDL_FadeInMusic (SSDL_Music m, int repeats, int ms);`	Fade in music over `ms` milliseconds, and play for specified number of times. -1 means repeat forever.
`void SSDL_FadeInMusicPos (SSDL_Music m, int repeats, int ms, double pos);`	...do the same, starting at position `pos`. What `pos` means depends on file type.
`Mix_Fading SSDL_FadingMusic();`	Return whether music is fading in or out. Return values are `MIX_NO_FADING`, `MIX_FADING_OUT`, `MIX_FADING_IN`.
`void SSDL_FadeOutMusic (int ms);`	Start music fading out over `ms` milliseconds.
`Mix_MusicType SSDL_GetMusicType (const SSDL_Music music);`	Return file type of music. See SDL_Mixer documentation online for details.

(continued)

[2] A `Uint32` is an `int` of a particular size. It's used here for consistency with SDL. You can ignore that and just think of it as `int`.

`void SSDL_HaltMusic ();`	Halt music.
`SSDL_Music SSDL_LoadMUS (const char* filename);`	Load music from `filename`.
`void SSDL_PauseMusic ();`	Pause music.
`bool SSDL_PausedMusic ()`	Return whether music is paused.
`void SSDL_PlayMusic (SSDL_Music m, int loops=-1);`	Play music for specified number of times. –1 means repeat forever.
`bool SSDL_PlayingMusic ()`	Return whether music is playing.
`void SSDL_ResumeMusic();`	Resume (unpause) music.
`void SSDL_RewindMusic();`	Rewind music; works on some file types.
`void SSDL_SetMusicPosition (double position);`	Start music at given position. How (and whether!) it works depends on file type.
`int SSDL_VolumeMusic (int volume=-1);`	Set the volume, which should be 0 to `MIX_MAX_VOLUME` (128), and return the new volume. If volume is –1, it only returns the volume.

Quit Messages

`void SSDL_DeclareQuit ();`	Post a quit message. Rarely used as SSDL handles this itself. This tells `SSDL_WaitEvent`, `SSDL_WaitKey`, `SSDL_WaitMouse`, and `SSDL_IsNextFrame` not to wait.
`bool SSDL_IsQuit ();`	Check whether a quit message has been posted.
`void SSDL_ToggleEscapeIsQuit ();`	Turn on/off whether hitting the Escape key constitutes a quit message. Default is on.

Sounds

In the following table, each function parameter or return type shown as SSDL_Sound may actually be of type int (representing a sound channel) - but you can ignore that and pass in SSDL_Sound. See SDL_Mixer documentation online for more information.

`int SSDL_ExpireSound (SSDL_Sound snd, int ms);`	Cause the sound to halt after ms milliseconds.
`int SSDL_ExpireAllSounds (int ms);`	Cause all sounds to halt after ms milliseconds.
`void SSDL_FadeInSound (SSDL_Sound& sound, int repeats, int ms);`	Fade in sound over ms milliseconds, repeating the specified number of times. If repeats is –1, it repeats forever.
`void SSDL_FadeInSoundTimed (SSDL_Sound& sound, int repeats, int ms, int duration);`	Same as above, but play for at most duration milliseconds.
`int SSDL_FadeOutSound (SSDL_Sound snd, int ms);`	Fade out sound over ms milliseconds.
`int SSDL_FadeOutAllSounds (int ms);`	Fade out *all* sounds over ms milliseconds.
`Mix_Fading SSDL_FadingChannel (SSDL_Sound);`	Determine if the sound is fading. Return values may be MIX_NO_FADING, MIX_FADING_OUT, or MIX_FADING_IN.
`void SSDL_HaltSound (SSDL_Sound);`	Halt sound.
`void SSDL_HaltAllSounds ();`	Halt all sounds.
`SSDL_Sound SSDL_LoadWAV (const char* file);`	Load sound from file. Despite the name, some formats other than WAV are supported. See SDL_mixer documentation online.
`void SSDL_PauseSound (SSDL_Sound);`	Pause sound.

(*continued*)

`void SSDL_PauseAllSounds ();`	Pause all sounds.
`void SSDL_PlaySound (SSDL_Sound sound, int repeats=0);`	Play sound one time plus specified number of repeats. –1 means repeats forever.
`void SSDL_PlaySoundTimed (SSDL_Sound sound, int repeats, int duration);`	Same as above, but plays at most `duration` milliseconds.
`void SSDL_ResumeSound (SSDL_Sound);`	Resume sound if paused.
`void SSDL_ResumeAllSounds ();`	Resume all paused sounds.
`bool SSDL_SoundPlaying(SSDL_Sound);`	Return whether the sound is playing.
`bool SSDL_SoundPaused (SSDL_Sound);`	...or paused.
`int SSDL_VolumeSound (SSDL_Sound snd, int volume=MIX_MAX_VOLUME);`	Set volume of sound, from 0 to `MIX_MAX_VOLUME`, which is 128; return the volume. If volume argument is –1, it only returns the volume.
`int SSDL_VolumeAllSounds (int volume=MIX_MAX_VOLUME);`	...or do the same for all sounds.

Sprites

Miscellaneous	
`void SSDL_RenderSprite (const SSDL_Sprite&);`	Draw sprite at its current location.
`void SSDL_SpriteFlipHorizontal (SSDL_Sprite&);`	Flip sprite horizontally.
`void SSDL_SpriteFlipVertical (SSDL_Sprite&);`	...vertically.
`bool SSDL_SpriteHasIntersection (const SSDL_Sprite& a, const SSDL_Sprite& b);`	Return whether sprites a and b intersect.

Get	
`int SSDL_GetSpriteX (const SSDL_Sprite&);`	Return sprite's x position on screen.
`int SSDL_GetSpriteY (const SSDL_Sprite&);`	...and y.
`int SSDL_GetSpriteWidth (const SSDL_Sprite&);`	Return sprite's width as it will appear on screen.
`int SSDL_GetSpriteHeight (const SSDL_Sprite&);`	...and height.
`int SSDL_GetSpriteOffsetX (const SSDL_Sprite&);`	Return x part of sprite's offset (see Chapter 11).
`int SSDL_GetSpriteOffsetY (const SSDL_Sprite&);`	...and its y component.
`int SSDL_GetSpriteClipX (const SSDL_Sprite&);`	Return x component of the starting point of the sprite in its image file.
`int SSDL_GetSpriteClipY (const SSDL_Sprite&);`	...and its y component.
`int SSDL_GetSpriteClipWidth (const SSDL_Sprite&);`	...and its width.
`int SSDL_GetSpriteClipHeight(const SSDL_Sprite&);`	...and its height.
`bool SSDL_GetSpriteFlipHorizontal (const SSDL_Sprite&);`	Return whether sprite is flipped (mirrored) horizontally.
`bool SSDL_GetSpriteFlipVertical (const SSDL_Sprite&);`	...and vertically.
`double SSDL_GetSpriteRotation (const SSDL_Sprite&);`	Return sprite's rotation in degrees, not radians; default is 0.

Set	
`void SSDL_SetSpriteImage (SSDL_Sprite& s, const SSDL_Image& img);`	Set sprite's image.
`void SSDL_SetSpriteLocation (SSDL_Sprite& s, int x, int y);`	...and its location on the screen.
`void SSDL_SetSpriteSize (SSDL_Sprite& s, int w, int h);`	...and its size.
`void SSDL_SetSpriteOffset (SSDL_Sprite& s, int x, int y);`	...and its offset.
`void SSDL_SetSpriteClipLocation (SSDL_Sprite& s, int x, int y);`	...and where it starts in its image file.
`void SSDL_SetSpriteClipSize (SSDL_Sprite& s, int width, int height);`	...and the size of the part of the image file it uses (default is all).
`void SSDL_SetSpriteRotation (SSDL_Sprite& s, double angle);`	...and angle of rotation, in degrees, not radians.

Text

In the following table, each function parameter or return type shown as SSDL_Font may actually be of type TTF_Font* – but you can ignore that and pass in SSDL_Font.

`sout << thing;`	Print `thing` on the screen. `thing` must be printable.
`ssin >> thing;`	Read variable `thing` from the keyboard. `thing` must be readable.
`void SSDL_SetCursor (int x, int y);`	Position the cursor at x, y for the next use of `sout` or `ssin`.
`SSDL_Font SSDL_GetCurrentFont();`	Return current font.

(*continued*)

`SSDL_Font SSDL_OpenFont (const char* filename, int point);`	Create a TrueType font from `filename` and `point`.
`SSDL_Font SSDL_OpenSystemFont (const char* filename, int point);`	Same, but loads from the system fonts folder(s).
`void SSDL_SetFont (const SSDL_Font& f);`	Use `f` as the font for `sout`, `ssin`, and render functions (below) unless font is specified.
`void SSDL_RenderText (const T& thing, int x, int y, const SSDL_Font& font = currentFont);`	Print `thing` (which may be any printable type) at position x, y, using `font` if specified, otherwise using current font, which may be changed with `SSDL_SetFont`.
`void SSDL_RenderTextCentered (const T& thing, int x, int y, const SSDL_Font& font = currentFont);`	Like `SSDL_RenderText`, but centers the text on x, y.

Time and Synchronization

See also "Mouse, Keyboard, and Events."

`void SSDL_Delay (Uint32 milliseconds);`	Refresh the screen and wait this many milliseconds.
`void SSDL_SetFramesPerSecond (Uint32 FPS);`	Set the number of frames per second `SSDL_IsNextFrame` will wait. Default is 60.
`bool SSDL_IsNextFrame();`	Refresh the screen and wait for the duration of the current frame (since the last time `SSDL_IsNextFrame` was called) to pass.

Window

`void SSDL_GetWindowPosition (int& x, int& y);`	Get window's x, y position.
`void SSDL_GetWindowSize (int& width, int& height);`	...and size.
`const char* SSDL_GetWindowTitle ();`	...and title.
`int SSDL_GetWindowWidth ();`	...and width.
`int SSDL_GetWindowHeight();`	...and height.
`void SSDL_MaximizeWindow ();`	Expand window to maximum size.
`void SSDL_MinimizeWindow ();`	Minimize window to icon size.
`void SSDL_RestoreWindow ();`	Restore window that was maximized, or minimized, to normal size.
`void SSDL_SetWindowPosition (int x, int y);`	Put window at x, y on computer screen.
`void SSDL_SetWindowSize (int w, int h);`	Set window's width and height.
`void SSDL_SetWindowTitle (const char* t);`	Set window's title.

References

cplusplus.com. 2025.

cppreference.com. 2025.

Cline, Marshall, Bjarne Stroustrup, et al. 2025. C++ Super-FAQ. `https://isocpp.org/wiki/faq`.

DARPA. 2024. "Eliminating Memory Safety Vulnerabilities Once and For All." `www.darpa.mil/news/2024/memory-safety-vulnerabilities`.

Durfee, Edmund H. "What Your Computer Really Needs to Know, You Learned in Kindergarten." In *Proceedings of the Tenth National Conference on Artificial Intelligence,* pages 858–864, July 1992.

"Flag of the United States." 2025. Wikipedia. `https://en.wikipedia.org/wiki/Flag_of_the_United_States`.

Goldstine, Herman H. *The Computer from Pascal to von Neumann.* Princeton, NJ: Princeton Univ. Press, 1972.

"Hacker's Dictionary." 2001. `https://hackersdictionary.com/html/`.

Persig, Robert. *Zen and the Art of Motorcycle Maintenance.* Morrow Quill, pp. 278–280, 1974.

Simple Direct Media Layer (SDL). 2025. `https://www.libsdl.org/` and `https://wiki.libsdl.org/SDL2/FrontPage`.

Stonebank, Michael. 2001. UNIX Tutorial for Beginners. `http://www.ee.surrey.ac.uk/Teaching/Unix/`.

Stroustrup, Bjarne, and Herb Sutter. 2025. C++ Core Guidelines. `https://isocpp.github.io/CppCoreGuidelines/`.

Sung, Phil, and the Free Software Foundation. 2007. A Guided Tour of Emacs. `https://www.gnu.org/software/emacs/tour/`.

"Very Basic Emacs Tutorial." 2025. `http://ocean.stanford.edu/research/quick_emacs.html`.

W. Briggs, *C++26 for Lazy Programmers*, https://doi.org/10.1007/979-8-8688-1859-2

Index

Symbols and Numbers

W. Briggs, *C++26 for Lazy Programmers*, https://doi.org/10.1007/979-8-8688-1859-2

D

K

L

M

N

O

P

Q

R

S

T

U

V

W

X, Y

Z

www.ingramcontent.com/pod-product-compliance
Lightning Source LLC
LaVergne TN
LVHW081343060526
838201LV00050B/1700
9798868818585